Data Protection

for Virtual Data Centers

Data Protection
for Virtual Data Centers

Jason Buffington

WILEY
Wiley Publishing, Inc.

Acquisitions Editor: Agatha Kim
Development Editor: Dick Margulis
Technical Editor: Paul Robichaux
Production Editors: Angela Smith; Dassi Zeidel
Copy Editor: Liz Welch
Editorial Manager: Pete Gaughan
Production Manager: Tim Tate
Vice President and Executive Group Publisher: Richard Swadley
Vice President and Publisher: Neil Edde
Book Designer: Maureen Forys, Happenstance Type-O-Rama; Judy Fung
Compositor: James D. Kramer, Happenstance Type-O-Rama
Proofreader: Publication Services, Inc.
Indexer: Robert Swanson
Project Coordinator, Cover: Lynsey Stanford
Cover Designer: Ryan Sneed
Cover Image: © istockphoto/Pazhyna

Published simultaneously in Canada

ISBN: 978-0-470-57214-6

For general information on our other products and services or to obtain technical support, please contact our Customer Care Department within the U.S. at (877) 762-2974, outside the U.S. at (317) 572-3993 or fax (317) 572-4002.

Wiley also publishes its books in a variety of electronic formats. Some content that appears in print may not be available in electronic books.

Library of Congress Cataloging-in-Publication Data

Buffington, Jason, 1970–
Data protection for virtual data centers / Jason Buffington. — 1st ed.
p. cm.
ISBN: 978-0-470-57214-6 (pbk)
ISBN: 978-0-470-90823-5 (ebk)
ISBN: 978-0-470-90825-9 (ebk)
ISBN: 978-0-470-90824-2 (ebk)
1. Virtual computer systems. 2. Data protection—Management. 3. Microsoft Windows server. I. Title.
QA76.9.V5B94 2010
005.8—dc22
2010015508

10 9 8 7 6 5 4 3 2 1

Dear Reader,

Thank you for choosing *Data Protection for Virtual Data Centers*. This book is part of a family of premium-quality Sybex books, all of which are written by outstanding authors who combine practical experience with a gift for teaching.

Sybex was founded in 1976. More than 30 years later, we're still committed to producing consistently exceptional books. With each of our titles, we're working hard to set a new standard for the industry. From the paper we print on, to the authors we work with, our goal is to bring you the best books available.

I hope you see all that reflected in these pages. I'd be very interested to hear your comments and get your feedback on how we're doing. Feel free to let me know what you think about this or any other Sybex book by sending me an email at `nedde@wiley.com`. If you think you've found a technical error in this book, please visit `http://sybex.custhelp.com`. Customer feedback is critical to our efforts at Sybex.

Best regards,

Neil Edde
Vice President and Publisher
Sybex, an Imprint of Wiley

This book is dedicated to some of the people who have really shaped my life and defined who I am or want to be:

My mother, Mary Buffington, who exhibits more compassion for others and zeal for life than anyone else I've ever met. The sacrifices that she made while I was growing up helped shape what kind of heart I have today. She is an amazing grandma to my kids, who I am hopeful will be as affected by her legacy as I was.

My father-in-law, Buddy Bland, who is the epitome of what I believe a Christian patriarch should be. He has a standard of gentlemanly conduct and faith that I can only aspire to—and he is really good with power tools. He is the kind of man that I hope to be someday.

And of course my wife, Anita, who works harder in one day as the mom of our three kids then I do in a week in the "real world." I cannot imagine life without her and am thankful that I don't have to. Everything I do, I can only do because of her support—including this book, much of which she edited from my voice-recognition software into these hopefully coherent thoughts.

Beyond those three special people, my world revolves around my three children—Joshua, Jaden, and Jordan—and my savior Jesus Christ.

Acknowledgments

This is my first book, so without sounding like a long-winded Oscar winner speech, I do want to recognize some people who have had a direct impact on my career and thereby prepared me to write this book:

Technology (chronologically) Willis Marti at Texas A&M University; Brett Husselbaugh and Kim Trif from Network Engineering; Phill Miner at Symantec; Keat Chandler from Cheyenne Software; Don and Rob Beeler, Peter Laudenslager, and Dan Jones from Double-Take Software; as well as Ben Matheson, Claude Lorenson, and Karandeep Anand from Microsoft. I could name specific milestones in my career that each one of these gentlemen were uniquely responsible for and thereby equipped me to deliver this book.

Book I should also thank the nice folks at Wiley Press, particularly Agatha Kim who was so easy to work with and made the entire process seem easy, and Dick Margulis, who showed me how much the education system failed to teach me about grammar and constructing thoughts in the written form. Also, thanks to Paul Robichaux, whom I am honored to call a friend and who was gracious enough to be my technical editor. Paul challenged almost every technical concept and drove me to better clarity. There were hardly any paragraphs that didn't have red marks from either Dick or Paul. Both the book and I are better for it. Thank you, gentlemen.

I have a few other friends who have similar product manager roles to mine in Microsoft, but managing different technologies that I covered in this book. They were kind enough to offer feedback and make those chapters better: Drew McDaniel, Mahesh Unnikrishnan, Scott Schnoll, and John Kelbley. I must also put some blame on John, along with Allen Stewart and Mike Sterling. Those three graciously invited me to write the data protection chapter for their *Hyper-V Insiders* book (which started this whole adventure).

Collaborators One of the greatest privileges that I have in my current job is working alongside some of the most passionate and experienced technologists whom I have ever met. Three of them were kind enough to write most of Chapters 10 and 11 around Systems Management and Monitoring: Wally Mead, Edwin Yuen, and Sacha Dawes. Thank you so much for your valuable time and technical insight!

About the Author

Jason Buffington is a senior technical product manager in Microsoft System Center, focusing primarily on Data Protection Manager (DPM) as well as the System Center management solutions for midsized organizations.

Jason has been working in the networking industry since 1989, focusing mainly on data protection and storage technologies, including roles at Cheyenne/CA for ARCserve and NSI Double-Take. He is previously a Certified Business Continuity Planner, MCSE, and MCT, and he was recognized as a Microsoft Most Valuable Professional (MVP) in storage technology. Jason speaks around the world at numerous Microsoft and storage/data protection events, and his work has been published in several industry journals. Jason studied computer science at Texas A&M University.

When not writing or speaking about data protection, he can most often be found either working with Cub Scouts and Boy Scouts or playing video games with his family and writing about them at `www.XboxDad.com`.

Jason lives in Dallas Texas, telecommutes to Redmond, and blogs at `http://JasonBuffington.com`.

Contributing Authors

Wally Mead has been with Microsoft since 1992. He started in the training group at Microsoft, developing and delivering training on Microsoft's first release of Systems Management Server, SMS 1.0. From that time, he has worked on training for all subsequent releases of SMS. Wally now works in the Configuration Manager product group as a Senior Program Manager. He supports customers who test prerelease versions of Configuration Manager. Wally also speaks at many industry conferences on Configuration Manager, including conducting hands-on training on the product. He also conducts training on Configuration Manager for various Microsoft product teams.

Sacha Dawes has more than 15 years of experience in the technology field, having worked in many areas, including operations, security software engineering, product management, marketing, and consulting. Sacha is a currently a Senior Product Manager with the System Center team at Microsoft, where he focuses on educating Microsoft sales teams, partners, and customers on best practices in datacenter management across physical and virtualized environments. Prior to Microsoft, Sacha has held positions across the world with Attachmate, NetIQ, Cable & Wireless, and Schlumberger. He holds a master's degree in computer science, and is a Certified Information Systems Security Professional (CISSP).

Edwin Yuen is a Director for Virtualization at Microsoft. Edwin came to Microsoft with the July 2006 acquisition of Softricity. Prior to joining Microsoft, Edwin was one of the Services Engagement Managers of Softricity for six years, leading most of the initial Softricity implementations. Edwin has 15 years of technical consulting experience in both the commercial and federal space, and holds a bachelor's degree in electrical engineering from Johns Hopkins University.

Contents at a Glance

Contents

Introduction

When an operating system or an application is initially created (version 1), there are lots of features that cannot be included. After all, if the manufacturer waited until every feature was included, it would never ship. Instead, it is released as a hopefully high-quality product but with several missing features or use scenarios that are left for third-party partners to fill. Certainly, that was true for most aspects of data protection or resiliency in regard to Windows. For the first several years, from Windows NT 3.1 through Windows Server 2003, an ecosystem developed that offered richer backup solutions and more flexible data replication and failover solutions to meet the needs of Microsoft customers.

But around 2003, some of those needs started being met by the core products themselves. This included improving backups via Volume Shadow Copy Services (VSS) and distributed file systems. It continued with SQL database mirroring and Exchange replication technologies. With the release of Windows Server 2008, we saw failover clustering become infinitely more accessible, and the past few years have seen not only continued evolution within the products, but also new standalone products such as System Center with Data Protection Manager. And on top of everything, virtualization is quickly becoming a mainstream game changer.

These technologies and their implementations are no longer just for advanced data centers with expensive IT staffs and high-dollar budgets. This book is meant to be your better backup, higher-availability advisor, help you be more virtualized and well managed, and keep your business continuously operating and regulatory compliant.

Why Did I Write this Book

Why did I write this book? There are certainly times that my wife asked this question, repeatedly. It was not for the extra cash. With the number of hours put in, it likely equates to just under minimum wage, and it really put a cramp in my gamer score.

I am a backup guy. 2010 marks my twentieth year as an IT pro, and for almost all of it, I have been a backup and availability guy, because IT really is all about the data.

I am not a database administrator, but I know enough about SQL to deploy the servers, architect the storage, and create some databases. More importantly (to me), I know how Microsoft SQL Server's databases work well enough that I know how to back them up. It's the same story for Exchange, for SharePoint, and even for Windows file services.

When you are a backup guy, you tend to also be a storage guy. I confess that I do not have a fiber channel SAN in my house, but I do have an iSCSI solution. As a storage guy, you again get the opportunity to touch a great deal of Exchange, and SQL Server, and SharePoint, and Windows Server in general.

When you are a backup guy, you tend to also be a high-availability guy. The reason for this is because many folks start their availability efforts with a reliable backup plan and deploying resilient storage. And as a storage guy, you get to be close friends with the clustering guys (especially in the Windows Server 2000 and 2003 days). And even as some applications started doing their own availability, they still needed storage—so the storage guy gets to be pretty friendly with the application guys.

Over the last several years, I've become something of a disaster recovery guy. Again, the skill set requires enough understanding of all of the server offerings to understand what it would take to resume services from another facility or from bare metal, and more interestingly, understanding the business processes enough to help facilitate which IT mechanisms need to come up first or last, so that the rest of the business can resume operation.

Most recently, I have started becoming a systems management guy. In part, it is a similar skill set of understanding a little bit about how each of those Windows servers work, so that you can monitor their health or maintain their services. Also, more and more, we are seeing data protection be considered less of a tactical tax in the IT department and more of the overall systems management plan, especially when terms like business continuity and disaster recovery start getting more air time. That's why, when I joined Microsoft to manage Data Protection Manager (a backup product), I became part of the System Center family of management solutions.

In my heart, I am a "*What if this happens? Then we should plan to. . .*" backup and availability guy. But the information that I needed to be successful always seemed to be scattered across a variety of material that I didn't need. My bookshelf is full of books where I perhaps bought a book on SQL Server, but I really only needed the chapter on database mirroring or clustering. I've gone to a class on Windows Server, when I really just needed the lessons on File Services. If you were an Exchange administrator, then it was probably logical to spend 5 days in a class and there was one module on Thursday morning related to Exchange replication. But that doesn't work, if you are focused on the backups or storage of the data. So, I pulled as much of this kind of information together as I could, so that maybe your bookshelf won't have as many unread books on it—which is ironic as an author, I know.

What Does the Title Mean

The title of this book means different things to different people:

Data Protection We cover a range of data protection and availability technologies that are available today. In this case, ensuring access to near-current data (availability) is part of "protection," though we'll consider "identity access" and "malware/virus" to be outside of the conversation in this book. At its core, this is about backup, availability, and all the things that happen in between.

Virtual Datacenter This primarily means the modern Windows datacenter that is moving toward a virtualized infrastructure. This book is definitely for you! But for midsized organizations that are equally dependent on your data, regardless of actual size, your "virtual datacenter" might fit inside the closet of your small business or the back room of a branch office or remote site. It is still where your data resides and what your business is dependent on, so it is your datacenter (large or small).

Who Should Read This Book

This book is meant for a few different groups of people:

Backup Folks You are my peeps. If your career description or passions are similar to how I described myself, then you have probably been frustrated about how to gain the knowledge to do your tasks. This book was written as potentially one of the only books that you need (or at least get you started in all the right directions).

Midsized Organizations without Deep IT Staffs I started out working at a few resellers that service local or regional accounts. Later, I was a freelance consultant servicing small and medium-sized organizations. Eventually, I started working for software companies that sold through channel partners and finally landed at Microsoft. But for most of my career, I have had the opportunity to take datacenter, expert-level capabilities and try to apply them to the smaller-scale but just as pressing needs in midsized companies.

If you are in a midsized organization, you need high availability, arguably more than large companies, because when something breaks, you don't have deep IT staffs onsite and ready to fix it. High availability, reliable backups, and even systems management do not have to be hard, and they certainly are not only for large enterprises. That is one reason why this book's title includes the words *Virtual Datacenters*. The IT assets of a midsized organization may take up a small workroom, or perhaps is its own room with an extra air conditioner, and not the glamorous raised floor, rows of racks, and wire plants that some enterprises have. But to you, it is still all your data and your business is relying on it. It is your datacenter. This book was written to put a backup and availability expert on your IT team, or at least on your IT bookshelf.

Large Enterprise BC/DR Architects and Consultants There are usually two ways that someone gets into business continuity or disaster recovery. You either started out as a backup/availability/systems person or you started out as an operations person who understands the business practices. If you are the latter, then this book was written to help you understand the technologies that you will need as part of a holistic business continuity or disaster recovery plan.

Microsoft Windows Planners and Consultants It often surprises me when a company has a highly resilient Exchange solution but standalone file servers. They might have a great high availability architecture but unreliable backups. Many companies have an advanced corporate datacenter, with branch offices that are unreliable and unprotected. Often, this is because they have an expert managing one server workload, so that is the only workload that is well managed. It doesn't have to be that way. This book was written so that you could look across your organization and see the symmetry of data protection and availability solutions that can be applied across the entire organization.

In short, after working with folks like you in each of these areas for 20 years, I stopped saying "Someone needs to collect this information" and started saying "I need to collect this information."

How to Read This Book

You could read it cover to cover as a way to understand the bigger picture. The hands-on tasks are written in such a way that you can skip them when you are reading on an airplane without losing understanding, and then put them into practice when you are back in front of your servers.

You can also use it as a reference book, as you wrestle with different data protection challenges within your environment. If you do, please start by reading the first two chapters, but then you can bounce around a little more. Overall, the book was written in a good–better–best model:

- Chapters 1 and 2 give the bigger picture of why and what we need data protection and availability.
- Chapters 3 and 4 explore data resiliency and data protection with better backups.
- Chapters 5 through 8 discuss providing high availability on a per-workload basis.
- Chapter 9 looks at virtualization to show how it changes what we have learned so far. Sometimes it makes things easier, sometimes more of a challenge. Either way, virtualization is a game changer.
- Chapters 10 through 12 look across your Windows infrastructure at systems management, as well as business continuity and disaster recovery.

If you are working with a Microsoft account team or channel partner, you are likely familiar with the Microsoft Core Infrastructure Optimization Model, or Core IO. This book can help you move some aspects of your infrastructure from basic, through standardized, rationalized, and even dynamic.

What You Will Learn

In each chapter, we will first look at the basics of the technology. We will see what came before it (and what you might already have in your environment), as well as how the technology works and what it is intended to address. I include step-by-step guidance on most workflows, so that you can be successful with your own first experiences with it. This is not written like a formal how-to guide, because I am not a formal guy.

Instead, it is written in the same way that I would explain it if you and I were doing a weekend deployment and sitting side by side in front of the keyboard, or how I discuss it during my technical sessions at events like Microsoft Tech-Ed or the Microsoft Management Summit. By the end of a chapter, you will understand how it works, you will have some factors to consider for your own environment, and you will have had your own hands-on first experiences.

What You Need

My whole goal for this book is to help IT generalists become proficient in a range of high-availability and data protection technologies. So, you do not need to be an expert in SQL Server or Exchange, but you should have an administrator's understanding of Windows Server and TCP/IP networking and at least an awareness of Active Directory, as well as whichever applications are likely to be in your environment. All I ask is that you suspend any preconceptions that this stuff is hard, complicated, or expensive, so that you can learn with a fresh mindset.

Everything that I did in the hands-on exercises was done by downloading the evaluation software from the Microsoft TechNet website or using the TestDrive virtual machines that were preconfigured base operating systems, some with applications preinstalled. This was intentional so that you can build it yourself. If you have a well-powered Hyper-V virtualization host and an Internet connection, you can do almost everything that I did in the book.

How to Contact the Author

I welcome feedback from you about this book or about books you'd like to see from me in the future. Here are a few ways that you can connect with me:

- My primary blog is `http://JasonBuffington.com`.
- My gaming blog is `www.XboxDad.com`.
- Follow me on Twitter: `@jbuff`.

Sybex strives to keep you supplied with the latest tools and information you need for your work. Please check their website at `www.sybex.com`, where we'll post additional content and updates that supplement this book if the need arises. Enter the book's title on the Sybex website's Search box (or type the book's ISBN—**9780470572146**), and click Go to get to the book's update page.

In addition, I have set up a website for discussion and updates on the topics of this book at `www.DataProtectionBible.com`.

Chapter 1

What Kind of Protection Do You Need?

The term *data protection* means different things to different people. Rather than asking what *kind* of protection you need, you should ask what data protection *problem* you are trying to solve. Security people discuss data protection in terms of *access*, where authentication, physical access, and firewalls are the main areas of focus. Other folks talk about protecting the integrity of the data with antivirus or antimalware functions. This chapter discusses protecting your data as an assurance of its availability in its current or previous forms.

Said another way, this book splits data protection into two concepts. We'll define *data protection* as preserving your data and *data availability* as ensuring the data is always accessible.

So, what are you solving for — protection or availability? The short answer is that while you'd like to say both, there is a primary and a secondary priority. More importantly, as we go through this book, you'll learn that it is almost never one technology that delivers both capabilities.

In the Beginning, There Were Disk and Tape

Disk was where data lived — always, we hoped.

Tape was where data rested — forever, we presumed.

Both beliefs were incorrect.

Because this book is focused on Windows data protection, we won't go back to the earliest days of IT and computers. But to appreciate where data protection and availability are today, we will briefly explore the methods that came before. It's a good way for us to frame most of the technology approaches that are available today. Understanding where they came from will help us appreciate what each is best designed to address.

We don't have to go back to the beginning of time for this explanation or even back to when computers became popular as mainframes. Instead, we'll go back to when Windows was first becoming a viable server platform.

During the late 1980s, local area networks (LANs) and servers were usually Novell NetWare. More notably for the readers of this book, data protection typically equated to connecting a tape drive to the network administrator's workstation. When the administrator went home at night, the software would log on as the administrator, presumably with full access rights, and protect all the data on the server.

In 1994, Windows NT started to become a server operating system of choice, or at least a serious contender in networking, with the grandiose dream of displacing NetWare in most environments.

Even with the "revolutionary" ability to connect a tape drive directly to your server, your two choices for data protection were still either highly available disk or nightly tape. With those as your only two choices, you didn't need to identify the difference between data protection and data availability. Data protection in those days was (as it is now) about preventing data loss from happening, if possible. These two alternatives, highly available disk or nightly tape, provided two extremes where your data loss was measured at either zero or in numbers of days.

The concept of *data availability* was a misnomer. Your data either was available from disk or would hopefully be available if the restore completed, resulting in more a measure of restore reliability than an assurance of productive uptime. That being said, let's explore the two sides of today's alternatives: data availability and data protection.

Overview of Availability Mechanisms

Making something more highly available than whatever uptime is achievable by a standalone server with a default configuration sounds simple — and in some ways it is. It is certainly easier to engage resiliency mechanisms within and for server applications today than it was in the good ol' days. But we need to again ask the question "What are you solving for?" in terms of availability. If you are trying to make something more available, you must have a clear view of what might break so that something would be unavailable — and then mitigate against that kind of failure.

In application servers, there are several layers to the server — and any one of them can break (Figure 1.1).

FIGURE 1.1
Layers of a server

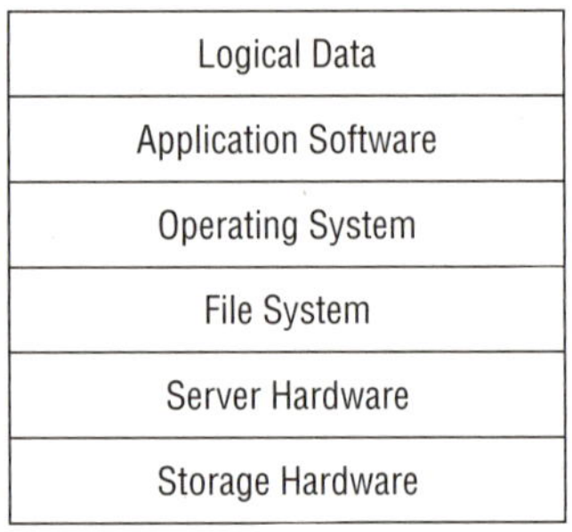

Figure 1.1 isn't a perfect picture of what can break within a server. It does not include the infrastructure — such as the network switches and routers between the server and the users' workstations. It doesn't include the users themselves. Both of these warrant large sections or books in their own right. In many IT organizations, there are server people, networking people, and desktop people. This book is for server people, so we will focus on the servers in the scenario and assume that our infrastructure is working and that our clients are well connected, patched, and knowledgeable, and are running applications compatible with our server.

For either data protection or data availability, we need to look at how it breaks — and then protect against it. Going from top to bottom:

- If the logical data breaks, it is no longer meaningful. This could be due to something as dire as a virus infection or an errant application writing zeros instead of ones. It could also be as innocent as the clicking of Save instead of Save As and overwriting your good data with an earlier draft. This is the domain of backup and restore — and I will cover that in the "Overview of Protection Mechanisms" section later in this chapter. So, for now, we'll take it off the list.

- In the software layers, if the application fails, then everything stops. The server has good data, but it isn't being served up to the users. Chapters 5 through 9 will look at a range of technologies that offer built-in availability. Similarly, if the application is running on an operating system (OS) that fails, you get the same result. But it will be different technologies that keep the OS running rather than the application — and we'll delve deeply into both of these availability methods in Chapters 5 through 9.

- The file system is technically a logical representation of the physical zeros and ones on the disk, now presented as files. Some files are relevant by themselves (a text file), whereas other files are interdependent and only useful if accessed by a server application — such as a database file and its related transaction log files that make up a logical database within an application like MicrosoftSQL Server. The files themselves are important and unique, but in most cases, you can't just open up the data files directly. The server application must open them up, make them logically relevant, and offer them to the client software. Again, the file system is a good place for things to go badly and also an area where lots of availability technologies are being deployed. We'll look at these starting in Chapter 5.
- In the hardware layers, we see server and storage listed separately, under the assumption that in some cases the storage resides within the server and in other cases it is an appliance of some type. But the components will fail for different reasons, and we can address each of the two failure types in different ways. When we think of all the hardware components in a server, most electrical items can be categorized as either moving or static (no pun intended). The moving parts include most notably the disk drives, as well as the fans and power supplies. Almost everything else in the computer is simply electrical pathways. Because motion and friction wear out items faster than simply passing an electrical current, the moving parts often wear out first. The power supply stops converting current, the fan stops cooling the components, or the disk stops moving. Even within these moving components, the disk is often statistically the most common component to fail.

Now that we have one way of looking at the server, let's ask the question again: what are you concerned will fail? The answer determines where we need to look at availability technologies.

The easiest place to start is at the bottom — with storage.

Storage arrays are essentially large metal boxes full of disk drives and power supplies, plus the connecting components and controllers. And as we discussed earlier, the two types of components on a computer most likely to fail are the disk drives and power supplies. So it always seems ironic to me that in order to mitigate server outages by deploying mirrored storage arrays, you are essentially investing in very expensive boxes that contain several of the two most common components of a server that are most prone to fail. But because of the relatively short life of those components in comparison to the rest of the server, using multiple disks in a RAID-style configuration is often considered a requirement for most storage solutions.

Storage Availability

In the earlier days of computing, it was considered common knowledge that servers most often failed due to hardware, caused by the moving parts of the computer such as the disks, power supplies, and fans. Because of this, the two earliest protection options were based on mitigating hardware failure (disk) and recovering complete servers (tape). But as PC-based servers matured and standardized and while operating systems evolved and expanded, we saw a shift from hardware-level failures to software-based outages often (and in many early cases, predominantly) related to hardware drivers within the OS. Throughout the shift that occurred in the early and mid-1990s, general-purpose server hardware became inherently more reliable. However, it forced us to change how we looked at mitigating server issues because no matter how much redundancy we included and how many dollars we spent on mitigating hardware type outages, we were addressing only a diminishing percentage of why servers failed. The growing majority of server outages were due to software — meaning not only the software-based hardware drivers, but also the applications and the OS itself. It is because of the shift in why servers were failing that data protection and availability had to evolve.

So, let's start by looking at what we can do to protect those hardware elements that can cause a server failure or data loss. In such cases, when a tier-one server vendor is respected in the datacenter space, I tend to dismiss the server hardware at first glance as the likely point of failure. So, storage is where we should look first.

Introducing RAID

No book on data protection would be complete in its first discussions on *disk* without summarizing what RAID is. Depending on when you first heard of RAID, it has been both:

- Redundant Array of *Inexpensive* Disks
- Redundant Array of *Independent* Disks

In Chapter 3, we will take an in-depth look at storage resiliency, including RAID models, but for now, the key idea is that statistically, the most common physical component of a computer to fail is a hard drive. Because of this, the concept of strapping multiple disks together in various ways (with the assumption that multiple hard drives will not all likely break at once) is now standard practice. RAID comes in multiple configurations, depending on how the redundancy is achieved or the disks are aligned:

Mirroring — RAID 1 The first thing we can do is to remove the single spindle (another term for a single physical disk, referring to the axis that all the physical platters within the disk spin on). In its simplest resolution, we mirror one disk or spindle with another. With this, the disk blocks are paired up so that when disk block number 234 is being written to the first disk, block number 234 on the second disk is receiving the same instruction at the same time. This completely removes a single spindle from being the single point of failure (SPOF), but it does so by consuming twice as much disk (which equates to at least twice the costs) power, cooling, and space within the server.

RAID 5, 1+0/10, and Others Chapter 3 will take us through all of the various RAID levels and their pros and cons, but, for now, the chief takeaway is that you are still solving a spindle-level failure. The difference between straight mirroring (RAID 1) and all other RAID variants is that you are not in a 1:1 ratio of production disk and redundant disk. Instead, in classic RAID 5, you might be spanning four disks where, for every N-1 (3 in this case) blocks being written, three of the disks get data and the fourth disk calculates parity for the other three. If any single spindle fails, the other three have the ability to reconstitute what was on the fourth, both in production on the fly (though performance is degraded) and in reconstituting a new fourth disk.

But it is all within the same array, storage cabinet, or shelf for the same server. What if your fancy RAID 5 disk array cabinet fails, due to two disks failing in a short timeframe, or the power failing, or whatever?

In principle, mirroring (also known as RAID-1) and most of the other RAID topologies are all attempts to keep a single hard drive failure from affecting the production server. Whether the strategy is applied at the hardware layer or within the OS, the result is that two or more disk drives act together to improve performance and/or mitigate outages. In large enterprises, synchronously mirrored storage arrays provide even higher performance as well as resiliency. In this case the entire storage cabinet, including low-level controllers, power supplies, and hard drives, are all duplicated, and the two arrays mirror each other, usually in a synchronous manner where both arrays receive the data at exactly the same time. The production servers are not aware of the duplicated arrays and can therefore equally access either autonomous storage solution.

So far, this sounds pretty good. But there are still some challenges, though far fewer challenges than there used to be. Back then, disk arrays were inordinately more expensive than local storage. Add to that the cost and complexity of storage area network (SAN) fabrics and the proprietary adapters for the server(s), and the entire solution became cost-prohibitive for most environments. In 2002, Gartner's "Study of IT Trends" suggested that only 0.4 percent of all IT environments could afford the purchase price of synchronously mirrored storage arrays. For the other 99.6 percent, the cost of the solution was higher than the cost of the problem (potential data loss). Of course, that study is now eight years old. The cost of synchronously mirrored storage has gone down and the dependence on data has gone up, so it is likely that 0.4 percent is now too low of a number, but it is still a slim minority of IT environments. We will discuss this statistic, including how to calculate its applicability to you, as well as many metrics and decision points in Chapter 2.

While you could argue that the parity bits in a RAID configuration are about preserving the integrity of data, the bigger picture says that mirroring/striping technologies are fundamentally about protecting against a component-level failure — namely the hard drive. The big picture is about ensuring that the storage layer continuously provides its bits to the server, OS, and application. At the disk layer, it is always one logical copy of the blocks — regardless of how it is stored on the various spindles.

This concept gets a little less clear when we look at asynchronous replication, where the data doesn't always exactly match. But in principle, disk (hardware or array)-based "data protection" is about "availability."

Decision Question: Is It Really Mission Critical?

The first decision point, when looking at what kinds of data protection and availability to use, is whether or not the particular platform you are considering protecting is mission critical (we're ignoring cost factors until Chapter 2). But in principle, if you absolutely cannot afford to lose even a single mail message, database transaction, or other granular item of data, then a particular server or platform really is mission critical and you'll want to first look at synchronous storage as part of your solution along with a complementary availability technology for the other layers of the server (for example, application or OS).

Note that crossing the line between synchronous and asynchronous should be looked at objectively on a per-server or per-platform basis — instead of just presuming that everything needs the same level of protection.

Even for key workloads, the idea that they are mission critical and therefore immediately require synchronously mirrored disks and other extraordinary measures may not be universally justified. Consider two of the most common application workloads — SQL Server and Microsoft Exchange.

- In a large corporation with multiple Exchange Servers, you might find that the Exchange Server and/or the storage group that services email for the shipping department might be considered noncritical. As such, it may be relegated two nightly or weekly tape backups only. In that same company, the executive management team might require that their email be assured 24/7 availability, including access on premises or from any Internet location. Even within one company, and for a single application, the protection method will differ. As an interesting twist, if the company we are discussing is Amazon.com, where their entire business is driven by shipping, that might be the most mission-critical department of all. Microsoft Exchange provides four different protection methods even within itself, not including array mirroring or disk- and tape-based backups (more on that in Chapter 7).

- Similarly, Microsoft SQL Server might be pervasive across the entire range of servers in the environment — but not every database may warrant mirroring, clustering, or replication at all.

If the data protection landscape was a graph, the horizontal X axis could be defined as a data loss, starting at 0 in the left corner and extending into seconds, minutes, hours, and days as we move across the graph. In short, what is your recovery point objective (RPO)?

We'll cover RPO and cost in Chapter 2. For now, know that RPO is one of the four universal metrics that we can use to compare the entire range of data protection solutions. Simply stated, RPO asks the question, "How much data can you afford to lose?"

In our rhetorical question, the key verb is *afford*. It is not *want* — nobody wants to lose any data. If cost was not a factor, it is likely that we would all unanimously choose zero data loss as our RPO. The point here is to recognize that even for your mission-critical, or let's just say most important, platforms, do you really need synchronous data protection — or would asynchronous be sufficient?

Should You Solve Your Availability Need with Synchronously Replicated Storage?

The answer is that "it depends." Here is what it depends on: If a particular server absolutely, positively cannot afford any loss of data, then an investment in synchronously mirrored storage arrays is a must. With redundancy within the spindles, along with two arrays mirroring each other, and redundant SAN fabric for the connectors, as well as duplicated host bus adapters (HBAs) within the server to the fabric, you can eliminate every SPOF in your storage solution. More importantly, it is the only choice that can potentially guarantee zero data loss.

This is our first decision question to identify what kinds of availability solutions we should consider:

- If we really need "zero data loss," we need synchronously mirrored storage (and additional layers of protection too).
- If we can tolerate anywhere from seconds to minutes of lost data, several additional technologies become choices for us — usually at a fraction of the cost.

Synchronous vs. Asynchronous

Synchronous versus asynchronous has been a point of debate ever since disk mirroring became available. In pragmatic terms, the choice to replicate synchronously or asynchronously is as simple as calculating the cost of the data compared with the cost of the solution. We will discuss this topic more in Chapter 2, as it relates to RPO and return on investment (ROI), but the short version is that if the asynchronous solution most appropriate for your workload protects data every 15 minutes, then what is 15 minutes' worth of data worth?

If the overall business impact of losing those 15 minutes' worth of data (including both lost information and lost productivity) is more expensive to the business than the cost of a mirrored and synchronous solution, then that particular server and its data should be synchronously mirrored at the storage level. As I mentioned earlier, the vast majority of corporate environments cannot justify the significantly increased cost of protecting those last (up to) 15 minutes of lost data — and therefore need an asynchronous protection model.

If your RPO truly and legitimately is zero, synchronously mirrored arrays are the only data protection option for you, or at least for that particular application, on that particular server, for that particular group within your company. To paraphrase a popular US television commercial tagline: "For everything else, there's asynchronous."

Asynchronous Replication

Even in environments where one platform demands truly zero data loss and therefore synchronous storage, the likelihood is that the remaining platforms in the same company do not. Again, the statistics will vary, but recall the extremes described in the previous sections: 0.4 percent of IT environments can cost-justify synchronously mirrored storage but only 1 percent of environments can rationalize half a business day of data loss with typically 1.5 days of downtime. If those statistics describe both ends of the data protection spectrum, then 98.6 percent of IT environments need a different type of data protection and/or availability that is somewhere in between the extremes. In short, while the percentages have likely changed and though your statistics may vary, most IT environments need better protection than nightly tape, which is less expensive than synchronous arrays.

In the Windows space, starting around 1997, the delivery of several asynchronous solutions spawned a new category of data protection and availability software, which delivered host-based (running from the server, not the array) replication that was asynchronous.

Asynchronous replication, by design, is a disk-to-disk replication solution between Windows servers. It can be done throughout the entire day, instead of nightly, which addresses the mainstream customer need of protecting data more frequently than each night. To reduce costs, asynchronous replication software reduces cost in two different dimensions:

Reduced Telecommunications Costs Synchronous mirroring assures zero data loss by writing to both arrays in parallel. The good news is that both of the arrays will have the same data. The bad news is that the servers and the applications could have a delay while both disk transactions are queued through the fabric and committed to each array. As distance increases, the amount of time for the remote disk to perform the write and then acknowledge it increases as well. Because a disk write operation is not considered complete until both halves of the mirror have acted on it, the higher-layer OS and application functions must wait for the disk operation to be completed on both halves of the mirror. This is inconsequential when the two arrays are side by side and next to the server. However, as the arrays are moved further from the server as well as from each other, the latency increases because the higher-layer functions of the server are waiting on the split disks. This latency can hinder the production application performance. Because of this, when arrays are geographically separated, companies must pay significant telecommunications costs to reduce latency between the arrays. In contrast to that, asynchronous replication allows for the primary disk on the production server to be written to at full speed, whereas the secondary disk has a replication target and is allowed to be delayed. As long as that latency is acceptable from a data loss perspective, one can be several minutes apart between the two disks and the result is appreciably reduced telecommunications costs.

Hardware Costs Typically, storage arrays that are capable of replication (synchronous or asynchronous) are appreciably more expensive than traditional disk chassis. Often, while the arrays are capable, they require separately licensed software to enable the mirroring or replication itself. As an alternative, replication can also be done within the server as an application-based capability, which is referred to as *host-based replication*. Host-based replication is done from server to server instead of array to array. As such, it is very typical to use less expensive hardware for the target server along with lower-performing drives for the redundant data. We will explore this topic later in Chapter 3.

Real World Scenario

THE PLATFORM AND THE ECOSYSTEM

Years before I joined Microsoft, I was listening to a Microsoft executive explain one aspect of a partner ecosystem for large software developers (Microsoft in this case, but equally applicable to any OS or large application vendor). He explained that for any given operating system or application, there's always a long list of features and capabilities that the development team and product planners would like to deliver. Inevitably, if any software company decided to wait until every feature that they wanted was included in the product and it was well tested, then no software product would ever ship.

Instead, one of the aspects of the ecosystem of software developers is that those companies typically identify holes in the product that have enough customer demand to be profitable if developed. Thus, while Windows Server was still initially delivering and perfecting clustering, and while applications like SQL Server and Microsoft Exchange learned to live within a cluster, there was a need for higher availability and data protection that could be filled by third-party software, as discussed earlier.

The Microsoft speaker went on to explain that the reality of which holes in a product would be filled by the next version was based on market demand. This creates an unusual cooperative environment between the original developer and its partner ecosystem. Depending on customer demand, that need might be solved by the third-party vendor for one to three OS/application releases. But eventually, the hole will be filled by the original manufacturer — either by acquiring one of the third parties providing a solution or developing the feature internally. Either way, it allows all mainstream users of the OS/application to gain the benefit of whatever hole or feature previously filled by the third-party offering, because it was now built-in to the OS or application itself.

The nature and the challenge within the partner ecosystem then becomes the ability to recognize when those needs are being adequately addressed within the original Microsoft product to identify new areas of innovation that customers are looking for and build those.

Adding my data protection and availability commentary on that person's perspective — for nearly ten years, third-party asynchronous replication technologies were uniquely meeting the needs of Microsoft customers for data protection and availability by filling the gap between the previous alternatives of synchronous disk and nightly tape.

But as the largest application servers (SQL and Exchange) and Windows Server itself have added protection and availability technologies to meet those same customer needs within the most common scenarios of file services, databases, and email, the need for third-party replication for those workloads has significantly diminished. The nature of the ecosystem therefore suggests that third parties should be looking for other applications to be protected and made highly available, or identify completely different business problems to solve.

Undeniably, asynchronous host-based replication solved a real problem for Windows administrators for nearly 10 years. In fact, it solved two problems:

- Data *protection* in the sense that data could be "protected" (replicated) out of the production server more often than nightly, which is where tape is limited
- Data *availability* in the sense that the secondary copy/server could be rapidly leveraged if the primary copy/server failed

Asynchronous replication addressed a wide majority of customers who wanted to better protect their data, rather than making nightly tape backups, but who could not afford to implement synchronous storage arrays. We will cover asynchronous replication later in this book. For now, note that as a file system–based mechanism, asynchronous replication on its own is a category of data protection that is arguably diminishing as the next two technologies begin to flourish: Clustering and Asynchronous Replication.

Clustering

Ignoring the third-party asynchronous replication technologies for a moment, if you were a Microsoft expert looking at data protection in the early days of Windows Server, your only choice for higher availability was redundancy in the hardware through network interface card (NIC) teaming, redundant power supplies and fans, and of course, synchronous storage arrays. When the synchronous arrays are used for availability purposes, we must remember that hardware resiliency only addresses a small percentage of why a server fails. For the majority of server and service outages that were software based, Microsoft originally addressed this with Microsoft Cluster Services (MSCS) and other technologies that we'll cover later in this book.

MSCS originally became available well after the initial release of Windows NT 4.0, almost like an add-on or more specifically as a premium release with additional functionality. During the early days of Windows clustering, it was not uncommon for an expert-level Microsoft MCSE or deployment engineer (who might be thought of as brilliant with Windows in general) to struggle with some of the complexities in failover clustering. These initial challenges with clustering were exacerbated by the first generation of Windows applications that were intended to run on clusters, including SQL Server 4.21 and Exchange Server 5.0. Unfortunately, clustering of the applications was even more daunting.

In response to these challenges with the first built-in high availability mechanisms, many of the replication software products released in the mid-1990s included not only data protection but also availability. Initially, and some still to this day, those third-party replication technologies are burdened by support challenges based on how they accomplish the availability. But in principle, they work by either extending the Microsoft clustering services across sites and appreciable distances but allowing the cluster application to handle the failover. Or they use a proprietary method of artificially adding the failed server's name, IP, shares, and even applications to the replication target and then resuming operation. The industry leader in asynchronous replication is Double-Take from Double-Take Software, formerly known as NSI Software. Another example of this technology is WANSync from Computer Associates, acquired from XOsoft. XOsoft provided the initial WANSync for Data Protection, and followed up with WANSync^{HA}, which included data availability. We will discuss these products in Chapter 3.

MSCS continued to evolve and improve through Windows 2000, Windows Server 2003, and Windows Server 2003 R2. That trend of continued improvement would continue through the more recent Windows Server 2008 and the newly released Windows Server 2008 R2. But that isn't the whole story. MSCS will be covered in Chapter 6.

More and more, we see MSCS used for those applications that cannot provide availability themselves, or as an internal component or plumbing for their own built-in availability solutions, as opposed to an availability platform in its own right. Examples include Exchange cluster continuous replication (CCR) and database availability groups (DAGs), both of which we cover in Chapter 7.

Application Built-in Availability

From 1997 to 2005, asynchronous replication was uniquely filling the void for both data protection and data availability within many Windows Server environments — and as we discussed, Windows Server was not yet becoming commonplace except in larger enterprises with high IT professional skill sets. But while the clustering was becoming easier for those applications that could be clustered, another evolution was also taking place within the applications themselves. Starting around 2005, Microsoft began filling those availability and protection holes by providing native replication and availability within the products themselves.

File Services' Distributed File Services (DFS)

As the most common role that Windows Server is deployed into today, it should come as no surprise that the simple file shares role that enables everything from user home directories to team collaboration areas is a crucial role that demands high availability and data protection. To this end, Windows Server 2003 R2 released a significantly improved Distributed File System (DFS). DFS replication (DFS-R) provides partial-file synchronization up to every 15 minutes, while DFS namespace (DFS-N) provides a logical and abstracted view of your servers. Used in parallel, DFS-N transparently redirects users from one copy of their data to another, which has been previously synchronized by DFS-R. DFS is covered in Chapter 5.

SQL Server Mirroring

SQL Server introduced database mirroring with SQL Server 2005 and enhanced it in SQL Server 2008. Prior to this, SQL Server offered log shipping as a way to replicate data from one SQL Server to another. Database mirroring provides not only near-continuous replication but failover as well. And unlike the third-party approaches, database mirroring is part of SQL Server, so there are no supportability issues; in fact, database mirroring has a significantly higher performance than most third-party replication technologies because of how it works directly with the SQL logs and database mechanisms. By using a mirror-aware client, end users can be transparently and automatically connected to the other mirrored data, often within only a few seconds. SQL Server database protection will be covered in Chapter 8.

Exchange Replication

Exchange Server delivered several protection and availability solutions in Exchange Server 2007 and later in its first service pack. These capabilities essentially replicate data changes similarly to how SQL performs database mirroring, but leverages MSCS to facilitate failover. Exchange 2010 changed the capabilities again. The versions of Exchange availability solutions are as follows:

SCC Single copy cluster, essentially MSCS of Exchange, sharing one disk

LCR Local continuous replication within one server, to protect against disk-level failure

CCR Cluster continuous replication, for high availability (HA)

SCR Standby continuous replication, for disaster recovery (DR)

DAG Database availability group, for HA and DR combined

Exchange Server protection options will be covered in Chapter 7.

Decision Question: How Asynchronous?

Because built-in availability solutions usually replicate (asynchronously), we need to ask ourselves, "How asynchronous can we go?"

Asynchronous Is Not Synonymous with "Near Real Time" — It Means Not Synchronous

Within the wide spectrum of the replication/mirroring/synchronization technologies of data protection, the key variance is RPO. Even within the high availability category, RPO will vary from potentially zero to perhaps up to 1 hour. This is due to different vendor offerings within the space, and also because of the nature of asynchronous protection.

Asynchronous replication can yield zero data loss, if nothing is changing at the moment of failure. For replication technologies that are reactive (meaning that every time production data is changed, the replication technology immediately or at best possible speed transmits a copy of those changes), the RPO can usually be measured within seconds. It is not assured to be zero, though it could be if nothing had changed during the few seconds prior to the production server failure. For the same class of replication technologies, the RPO could yield several minutes of data loss if a significant amount of new data had changed immediately prior to the outage. This scenario is surprisingly common for production application servers that may choke and fail during large data imports or other high-change-rate situations, such as data mining or month-end processing.

However, not all solutions that deliver asynchronous replication for the purpose of availability attempt to replicate data in near real time. One good example is the DFS included with Windows Server (covered in Chapter 5). By design, DFS-R replicates data changes every 15 minutes. This is because DFS does not reactively replicate. In the earlier example, replication is immediately triggered because of a data change. With DFS-R, replication is a scheduled event. And with the recognition that the difference in user files likely does not have the financial impact necessitating replication more often than every 15 minutes, this is a logical RPO based on this workload.

Even for the commonplace workload of file serving, one solution does not fit all. For example, if you were using DRS-R not for file serving but for distribution purposes, it might be more reasonable to configure replication to occur only after hours. This strategy would still take advantage of the data-moving function of DFS-R, but because the end goal is not availability, a less frequent replication schedule is perfectly reasonable. By understanding the business application of how often data is copied, replicated, or synchronized, we can assess what kinds of frequency, and therefore which technology options, should be considered. We will take a closer look at establishing those quantifiable goals and assessing the technology alternatives in Chapter 2.

AVAILABILITY VS. PROTECTION

No matter how frequently you are replicating, mirroring, or synchronizing your data from the disk, host, or application level, the real question comes down to this:

> *Do you need to be able to immediately leverage the redundant data from where it is being stored, in the case of a failed production server or site?*

- If you are planning on resuming production from the replicated data, you are solving for *availability* and you should first look at the technology types that we've already covered (and will explore in depth in Chapters 5–9).
- If you need to recover to previous points in time, you are solving for *protection* and should first look at the next technologies we explore, as well as check out the in-depth guidance in Chapters 3 and 4.

We will put the technologies back together for a holistic view of your datacenter in Chapters 10–12.

Overview of Protection Mechanisms

Availability is part of the process of keeping the current data accessible to the users through

- Redundant storage and hardware
- Resilient operating systems
- Replicated file systems and applications

But what about yesterday's data? Or even this morning's data? Or last year's data? Most IT folks will automatically consider the word *backup* as a synonym for *data protection*. And for this book, that is only partially true.

Backup Backup implies nightly protection of data to tape. Note that there is a media type and frequency that is specific to that term.

Data Protection Data protection, not including the availability mechanisms discussed in the last section, still covers much more, because tape is not implied, nor is the frequency of only once per night.

Let's Talk Tape

Regardless of whether the tape drive was attached to the administrators' workstation or to the server itself, tape backup has not fundamentally changed in the last 15 years. It runs every night after users go home and is hopefully done by morning. Because most environments have more data than can be protected during their nightly tape backup window, most administrators are forced to do a full backup every weekend along with incremental or differentials each evening in order to catch up.

For the record, most environments would likely do full backups every night if time and money were not factors. Full backups are more efficient when doing restores because you can use a single tape (or tapes if needed) to restore everything. Instead, most restore efforts must first begin with restoring the latest full backup and then layer on each nightly incremental or latest differential to get back to the last known good backup.

Full, Incremental, and Differential Backups

We will cover backup to tape in much more detail as a method in Chapter 3, and in practice within System Center Data Protection Manager in Chapter 4, as one example of a modern backup solution. But to keep our definitions straight:

Full Backup Copies every file from the production data set, whether or not it has been recently updated. Then, additional processes mark that data as backed up, such as resetting the archive bit for normal files, or perhaps checkpointing or other maintenance operations within a transactional database. Traditionally, a full backup might be done each weekend.

Incremental Backup Copies only those files that have been updated since the last full or incremental backup. Afterward, incremental backups do similar postbackup markups as done by full backups, so that the next incremental will pick up where the last one left off. Traditionally, an incremental backup might be done each evening to capture only those files that changed during that day.

Differential Backup Copies only those files that have been updated since the last full backup. Differential backups do not do any postbackup processes or markups, so all subsequent differentials will also include what was protected in previous differentials until a full backup resets the cycle. Traditionally, differential backup might be done each evening, capturing more and more data each day until the next weekend's full backup.

NOTE If your environment only relies on nightly tape backup, then your company is agreeing to half a day of data loss and typically at least one and a half days of downtime per data recovery effort.

Let's assume that you are successfully getting a good nightly backup every evening, and a server dies the next day. If the server failed at the beginning of the day, you have lost relatively little data. If a server fails at the end of the day, you've lost an entire business day's worth of data. Averaging this out, we should assume that a server will always fail at the midpoint of the day, and since your last backup was yesterday evening, your company should plan to lose half of a business day's worth of data.

That is the optimistic view. Anyone who deals in data protection and recovery should be able to channel their pessimistic side and will recall that tape media is not always considered reliable. Different analysts and industry experts may place tape recovery failure rates at anywhere between 10 percent and 40 percent. My personal experience is 30 percent tape failure rate during larger recoveries, particularly when a backup job spans multiple physical tapes.

Let's assume that it is Thursday afternoon, and your production server has a hard drive failure. After you have repaired the hardware, you begin to do a tape restore of the data and find that one of the tapes is bad. Now you have three possible outcomes:

- If the tape that failed is last night's *differential*, where a differential backup is everything that has been changed since the last full backup, then you've only lost one additional day's worth of data. Last night's tape is no good, and you'll be restoring from the evening prior.
- If the tape that failed is an *incremental*, then your restorable data loss is only valid up until the incremental before this one. Let's break that down:
  - If you are restoring up to Thursday afternoon, your plan is to first restore the weekend's full backup, then Monday's incremental, then Tuesday's incremental, and then finally Wednesday's incremental.

- If it is Wednesday's incremental that failed, you can reliably restore through Tuesday night, and will have only lost one additional day's worth of data.
- But if the bad tape is Tuesday's incremental that failed, you can only reliably recover back to Monday night. Though you do have a tape for Wednesday, it would be suspect. And if you are unlucky, the data that you need was on Tuesday night's tape.

- The worst-case scenario, though, is when the full backup tape has errors. Now all of your incremental and differentials throughout the week are essentially invalid, because their intent was to update you from the full backup — which is not restorable. At this point, you'll restore from the weekend *before* that full backup. You'll then layer on the incrementals or differentials through last Thursday evening. In our example, as you'll recall, we said it was Thursday afternoon. When this restore process is finished, you'll have data from Thursday evening a week ago. You'll have lost an entire week of data. But wait, it gets worse. Remember, incrementals or differentials tend to automatically overwrite each week. This means that Wednesday night's backup job will likely overwrite last Wednesday's tape. If that is your rotation scheme, then your Monday, Tuesday, and Wednesday tapes are invalid because its full backup had the error. But after you restore the full backup of the weekend before, the days since then may have been overwritten. Hopefully, the Thursday evening of last week was a differential, not an incremental, which means that it holds all the data since the weekend prior and you'll still have lost only one week of data. If they were incrementals, you'll have lost nearly two weeks of data.

YOUR RECOVERY GOALS SHOULD DICTATE YOUR BACKUP METHODS

The series of dire scenarios I just listed is not a sequence of events, nor is it a calamity of errors. They all result from *one bad tape* and how it might affect your recovery goal, based on what you chose for your tape rotation.

One of the foundational messages you should take away from this book is that you should be choosing your backup methods and evaluating the product offerings within that category, based on how or what you want to recover.

This is not how most people work today. Most people protect their data using the best way that they know about or can believe that they can afford, and their backup method dictates their recovery scenarios.

Disk vs. Tape

The decision to protect data using disk rather than tape is another of the quintessential debates that has been around for as long as both choices have been viable. But we should not start the discussion by asking whether you should use disk or tape. As in the previous examples, the decision should be based on the question, "What is your recovery goal?"

More specifically, ask some questions like these:

- Will I usually restore selected data objects or complete servers?
- How frequently will I need to restore data?
- How old is the data that I'm typically restoring?

Asking yourself these kinds of questions can help steer you toward whether your recovery goals are better met with disk-based or tape-based technologies. Disk is not always better. Tape is not dead. There is not an all-purpose and undeniably best choice for data protection any more than there is an all-purpose and undeniably best choice for which operating system you should run on your desktop. In the latter example, factors such as which applications you will run on it, what peripherals you will attach to it, and what your peers use might come into play. For our purposes, data granularity, maximum age, and size of restoration are equally valid determinants.

We will cover those considerations and other specifics related to disk versus tape versus cloud in Chapter 3, but for now the key takeaway is to *plan how you want to recover, not how you want to be protected.*

As an example, think about how you travel. When you decide to go on a trip, you likely decide where you want to go before you decide how to get there.

If how you will recover your data is based on how you back up, it is like deciding that you'll vacation based on where the road ends — literally, jumping in the car and seeing where the road takes you. Maybe that approach is fine for a free-spirited vacationer, but not for an IT strategy. For me, I am not extremely free spirited by nature, so this does not sound wise for a vacation — and it sounds even worse as a plan for recovering corporate data after crisis. In my family, we choose what kind of vacation we want and then we decide how to get there. That is how your data protection and availability should be determined.

Instead of planning what kinds of recoveries you will do because of how you back up to nightly tape, turn that thinking around. Plan what kinds of recoveries you want to do (activities) and how often you want to do them (scheduling). This strategy is kind of like planning a vacation. Once you know what you want to accomplish, it is much easier to do what you will *need* to do so that you can do what you *want* to do.

Recovery is the goal. Backup is just the tax in advance that you pay so that you can recover the way that you want to. Once you have that in mind, you will likely find that tape-based backup alone is not good enough. It's why disk-based protection often makes sense — and almost always should be considered in addition to tape, not instead of tape.

Microsoft Improvements for Windows Backups

When looking at traditional tape backup, it is fair to say that the need was typically filled by third-party backup software. We discussed the inherent need for this throughout the chapter, and Windows Server has always included some level of a built-in utility to provide single-server and often ad hoc backups. From the beginning of Windows NT through Windows Server 2003 R2, Microsoft was essentially operating under an unspoken mantra of "If we build it, someone else will back it up." But for reasons that we will discuss in Chapter 4, that wasn't good enough for many environments. Instead, another layer of protection was needed to fill the gap between asynchronous replication and nightly tape backup.

In 2007, Microsoft released System Center Data Protection Manager (DPM) 2007. Eighteen months earlier, DPM 2006 had been released to address centralized backup of branch office data in a disk-to-disk manner prior to third-party tape backup. DPM 2007 delivered disk-to-disk replication, as well as tape backup, for most of the core Windows applications, including Windows Server, SQL Server, Exchange Server, SharePoint, and Microsoft virtualization hosts. The third generation of Microsoft's backup solution (DPM 2010) was released at about the same time as the printing of this book. DPM will be covered in Chapter 4.

Similar to how built-in availability technologies address an appreciable part of what asynchronous replication and failover were providing, Microsoft's release of a full-fledged backup product (in addition to the overhauled backup utility that is included with Windows Server) changes the ecosystem dynamic regarding backup. Here are a few of the benefits that DPM delivers compared to traditional nightly tape backup vendors:

- A single and unified agent is installed on each production server, rather than requiring separate modules and licensing for each and every agent's type, such as a SQL Server agent, open file handler, or a tape library module.
- Disk and tape are integrated within one solution, instead of a disk-to-disk replication from one vendor or technology patch together with a nightly tape backup solution built from a different code base.
- DPM 2010 is designed and optimized exclusively for Windows workloads, instead of a broad set of applications and OSs to protect, using a generic architecture. This is aimed at delivering better backups and the most supportable and reliable restore scenarios available for those Microsoft applications and servers.

The delivery by Microsoft of its own backup product and its discussion in this book is not to suggest that DPM is absolutely and unequivocally the very best backup solution for every single Windows customer in any scenario. DPM certainly has its strengths (and weaknesses) when compared with alternative backup solutions for protecting Windows. But underlying DPM, within the Windows operating system itself, are some internal and crucial mechanisms called Volume Shadow Copy Services (VSS). VSS, which is also covered in Chapter 4, is genuine innovation by Microsoft that can enable any backup vendor, DPM included, to do better backups by integrating closer to the applications and workloads themselves. Putting this back within the context of our data protection landscape: while we see more choices of protection and availability through third-party replication and built-in availability solutions, we are also seeing a higher quality and flexibility of backups and more reliability for restores through new mechanisms like VSS and DPM, which we will cover in Chapters 3 and 4.

Summary

In this chapter, you saw the wide variety of data protection and availability choices, with synchronous disk and nightly tape as the extremes and a great deal of innovation happening in between. Moreover, what was once a void between synchronously mirrored disks and nightly tape has been filled first by a combination of availability and protection suites of third-party products, and is now being addressed within the applications and the OS platforms themselves. The spectrum or landscape of data protection and availability technologies can be broken down into a range of categories shown in Figure 1.2.

FIGURE 1.2
The landscape of data protection and availability

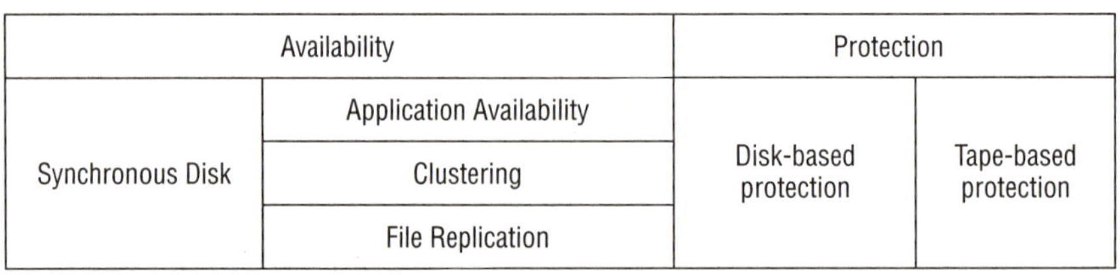

Each of these capabilities will be covered in future chapters — including in-depth discussions on how they work as well as practical, step-by-step instructions on getting started with each of those technologies.

Selecting a data protection plan from among the multiple choices and then reliably implementing your plan in a cohesive way is critical — no matter how large or small, physical or virtual, your particular "enterprise" happens to be. There are a few key points that I hope you take away from this chapter:

- Start with a vision of what you want to recover, and then choose your protection technologies (usually plural) — not the other way around.
- Tape is not evil and disk is not perfect — but use each according to what each medium is best suited for.
- Be clear among your stakeholders as to whether you are seeking better protection or better availability. It's not always both and rarely does one technology or product cover them equally.
- Deliver "availability" within the workload/server if possible and achieve "protection" from a unified solution.
- No single protection or availability technology will cover you. Each addresses certain scenarios and you will want to look at a "balanced diet" across your enterprise — protecting each according to their needs.

Now that you know what you want to accomplish, let's move on to Chapter 2, where you'll learn how to quantify your solution, compare choices, and cost-justify.

Chapter 2

Data Protection by the Numbers

Numbers make everything equal.

That applies to the wide range of data protection technologies, though it does not imply that synchronous storage arrays are equal to nightly tape backup. What we should think about is that comparative metrics like RPO allow us to look at that range of availability and protection alternatives objectively, without the bias of vendor preference, past experience, or preconceptions. We'll explore those kinds of comparative metrics in this chapter.

In this chapter, we will look at several metrics. We'll define each one and apply it to the discussion of what kinds of data protection and availability you need for different scenarios.

The Technical Metrics: RPO and RTO

When comparing the wide range of data protection technologies and methodologies, the two technical metrics that provide us with a standard for comparison are the recovery point objective (RPO) and the recovery time objective (RTO). As an introduction to these terms, consider a traditional tape backup scenario, where a full backup is done every weekend and an incremental backup is done every evening after the users go home.

Recovery Point Objective

In Chapter 1, we looked at the range of data protection solutions as categories that could be effectively delineated by the questions "How much data can you afford to lose?" and "How frequent is the data protection event?"

The proper term for this metric is recovery point objective (RPO). Where RPO really matters is as a method of objectively comparing the diverse range of data protection and availability technologies.

RPO is often thought of as the amount of data that could be lost. That's not the whole story, but we'll start there. If you are backing up every evening and we assume nothing goes wrong during the backups or the recovery, then the most you could lose is one business day's worth of data. If your data is made up solely of documents from Word or Excel, then you have lost only those documents that were updated during that day. If your data consists of transactions such as financial records, then the consequences could be worse. Imagine that you work in a bank and in one day, most if not all of your accounts have some kind of activity. If you lose a day's worth of those transactions, your entire data set is no longer valid. The key point here is that you must assess your potential for data loss in two ways: time spent re-creating lost data and the scope of data that will be lost or affected.

To expand on that, let's assume that a reliable backup takes place every evening and the restores will always work. I'll explain later why that doesn't usually apply; but for now, that supposition helps for the example. With that in mind, there are two extreme scenarios:

- If the server were to fail at the beginning of the business day, almost no data would be lost since the last backup. The actual data loss would be measured at near zero because nearly nothing would have changed since the last *recovery point* or backup event.
- If the server were to fail at the end of the business day, that entire day's worth of data would be lost, because no backups (recovery points) would have been created since the midnight before. We would measure the data loss as a full day's worth.

If we take the average of these two extremes, we can presume that the server will always fail at noon—halfway into the business day. Statistically speaking, this means that companies that use tape backup will lose half of a day's worth of data on average.

To learn the whole story when looking at RPO, it is the "O" that is most important. RPO is an objective (or goal). It specifies how much data you are willing to lose. In nightly tape backup, the statistical probability is that you will lose a half day of data. But if you establish your RPO at "half of a day" and then your server fails in the afternoon, you have actually lost more data than you planned, and you fall short of your goal or objective. So, most would set an RPO as "one day," meaning that it is an acceptable business loss to lose an entire day of data because of the recognition that backups are only occurring nightly and the server could fail in the afternoon.

In the case of tape backup, we measure RPO in days (for example, half day or full day) because we normally do backup operations on a daily, or more specifically, on a nightly basis. To have an RPO, or goal, for how much data we can afford to lose (which can be measured in less than days), we have to protect our data more often than nightly. That usually takes tape out of the equation. When we look at the wide range of disk-based protection, we can see that disk-based solutions often replicate hourly, or every few minutes or seconds, or real time. RPO essentially becomes the measurement of that data protection frequency.

DEFINING YOUR RPO

If your business goals say that you don't want to lose more than two hours of data, that is your RPO—your objective or goal for how frequently you need a reliable recovery point.

In the case of a two-hour RPO, you have to look at data protection technologies that operate at least every two hours. As we look at the sampling of protection technologies in this book, we'll consider how often they protect and relate that back as the respective RPO of each solution.

Recovery Time Objective

From a technology perspective, almost all data protection and availability solutions can be compared with one another by charting them on a graph, with RPO as one axis and RTO as the other. That's how we'll assess the technologies later in the book—by looking at them in part by how they compare in RTO and RPO. In real terms, RTO asks the question "How long can you afford to be without your data?" which could also be asked as "How long can your services be out of operation?"

Using the same scenario as the RPO discussion (where you are doing a nightly tape backup), the RTO is the goal (objective) for how long it takes to conduct a recovery. The question is, how long will the restore take?

In the example of nightly tape backup, RPO for tape backup is measured in days or partial days, because that is how often a data protection (backup) event is actually occurring—every night. But for this same example, RTO is measured in hours, because it is a performance measure of the components in your solution itself. If your backup software and tape hardware can restore up to 2 TB per hour and the server has 6 TB of data, time to recover the data is effectively 3 hours—or at least 3 hours from when the restore actually begins.

If your largest server holds 10 TB of data and your tape hardware can restore 2 TB per hour, and you are confident that you could immediately locate the right tapes and restoration could begin soon after, then you might specify an RTO of 5 hours—or 6 to be cautious. But because you may need to prepare for the restore and locate the tapes, you will likely round up and specify an RTO of one day.

Putting RPO and RTO Together

Let's combine the examples that we have used so far. We'll assume that the server we have been protecting in this chapter's scenario failed on Wednesday at 4:00 p.m.

It will take us most of the next day to recover the server. If we have IT personnel in the same office, we can optimistically identify what has failed and, if necessary, arrange for replacement parts (for example, new hard drives) to arrive early Thursday morning. On Thursday, we'll repair the server and restore the data. By Thursday evening, the server will be rebuilt and recovered. The recovery time will be one business day and that hopefully was within our RTO.

The unfortunate part of this scenario is twofold for the users:

- Thursday is a wasted day for the users, because they cannot get to their server or its data while things are being repaired, replaced, and restored.
- Wednesday's data is likely lost, because when the server is restored, it will be restored to the latest successful backup (Tuesday night). Everything that was created during Wednesday (after the Tuesday backup) will likely have been lost when the server storage failed. The recovery point was within one day of lost data (Tuesday midnight through Wednesday at point of failure), which again is hopefully within the set RPO.

NOTE To improve the RTO, we need a faster restore medium, which usually points us to disk instead of tape for routine restores.

To improve the RPO (frequency of backups), we need to perform data protection more often than nightly. For this we must turn to replication technologies, including the range from sub-hourly replication, to database mirroring within seconds, to synchronous disk.

But just doing the technical measurements of RPO and RTO isn't enough. We have to describe the RPO and RTO characteristics of our technology as something predictable that can be understood and agreed to by the business and operational stakeholders of the company. We have to set a service level agreement (SLA).

Making RPO and RTO Real with SLAs

When we recognize that the "O" in both RPO and RTO is *objective*, we run into one of the key problems in most data protection and availability plans. An objective is a goal, not a promise. The promise comes when we describe our capabilities to the stakeholders in the business, when we tell the management of the people who rely on the server that they will be "running again within one business day and will lose an average of half a day of data but potentially a full day of data." We might tell the management team that with nightly tape backup, we could have an RPO of half a day of lost data and that the RTO might be one business day to repair the server and restore the data. But those are goals based on ideal circumstances.

What happens when the circumstances are not ideal? In our scenario of tape backup of a failed server, we made a few assumptions:

- We assumed that we are able to react quickly to the server outage.
  - If we have IT staff on-site, they can identify the issue almost immediately.
  - If we don't have IT on site, our entire restore time window will be longer because nothing can happen until we get there (or remotely connect in).
- We assumed that the server is readily repairable. In our example, the server failed at 4 p.m. on Wednesday.
  - If parts are available, we can begin repairs immediately.
  - If we happen to be on the US East Coast, we can expedite parts from a West Coast provider, where they can overnight them and we can begin repairs the next morning.
  - If we happen to be on the US West Coast, we may not be able to get parts for another whole business day—and everything else will be prolonged accordingly.
- We assumed that every tape is readable.
  - If the latest Tuesday evening tape is unreadable, we will only be able to restore up through Monday's tape. We will have lost another day of data (RPO), and we will likely lose time trying to restore Tuesday's data before we can identify the failure (longer RTO).
  - If you are doing incrementals (only nightly changes) instead of differentials, then if Monday's tape is bad, Tuesday's tape is mostly irrelevant. Tuesday's incremental contains the differences between Monday and Tuesday, but without a successful restore of Monday's data, Tuesday's changes may not be substantive. This will vary by the production workload (as well as the backup software's tolerance for failed tapes in a recovery set).
  - If one of the weekend full tapes is bad, then Monday's and Tuesday's are irrelevant, because everything is in the context of the last full backup (which is unusable). Instead, we have two last-resort recovery scenarios:
    - If the daily incremental tapes are not overwritten each week (that is, Tuesday overwrites last Tuesday), we can restore the full backup from a week prior, and then the incrementals or differentials from the previous week. In short, when the server is repaired on Thursday afternoon (accessed Friday morning), the data will be as it was the Thursday of a week before—the last good tape.
    - If the daily tapes are overwritten, our data will only be back to the full backup from a week ago. All data for the previous week, as well as the beginning of this week, is lost (10 days of data in our example).

These aren't calamity-of-errors or niche cases. They are just examples of how easy it is for our reality to fail to match the ideal RPO and RTO that is defined by the hardware and software of our data protection solution. It is for these reasons (where reality doesn't match our ideal RPO and RTO) that our SLA—our commitment to the business units as to what our recovery capabilities are—needs to be broader than just stating the RPO and RTO of the technologies themselves. We need to consider the processes and potential pitfalls as well:

Time to React Sites without IT staff should have longer RTO SLAs than sites with IT staff, because it will take time to get there, depending on the arrangement. Perhaps IT staff can drive or fly from their primary location to the remote office. Perhaps a local integrator or channel reseller can be dispatched; in that case, a pre-negotiated contract may have to be put into place, including an SLA from them to you on their committed response rate to your issue.

Time to Repair the Server Should spare parts or even complete cold-standby servers be acquired? Where can parts or servers be expedited from? Does a pre-negotiated agreement need to be signed between you and a vendor or distributor?

Technical RPO and RTO This relates to issues involving the RPO and RTO, as well as the perceived failure rate of the media.

Notice that technology wasn't mentioned until the last item. The first aspects of a server recovery SLA relate to people and process, followed by materials and access. Once we get to the technology, we are likely more in the comfort zone of the IT professional, but there are still unknowns concerning the technology.

Recall from Chapter 1 that an estimated 12 percent of modern server failures are caused by hardware rather than software (at 88 percent). In that case, the hardware-failed scenario that we've been using may only affect you one out of eight times, and that doesn't sound like too much. But in a datacenter with 100 production servers, the statistical probably is that 12 of them will have hardware issues. This means that you will have to enact this recovery scenario once per month.

After the server is ready to be restored, RTO will still vary based on whether you are restoring from Monday or Friday:

- With *differentials*, you might need the weekend full plus the Thursday night differential. But that differential will have appreciably more data to restore than the Monday differential. Each tape will have everything (the *difference*) since the last full backup.
- With *incrementals*, we see a similarly linear increase in restore time, as each subsequent incremental is layered on top of the one before it. Unfortunately, in our imperfect world, if a tape fails, and depending on the kind of interdependence data that is being restored, you may have to wipe the production volume and repeat the recovery exercise only up through the previous day's tape.

All of these overly dire and pessimistic examples are designed simply to prompt you to compare your data protection technology's presumed RPO and RTO to what you as the backup administrator can assure your management of being able to deliver.

This is the secret to a successful SLA. Salespeople call this sandbagging, where what you forecast that you'll sell is less than what you believe is likely. Personal life coaches might call this underpromising and overdelivering. As a consultant and IT implementer, I call it planning for Murphy's law.

Real World Scenario

MAKING "SENIOR" PREDICTIONS

Several years ago, I was working for a systems integrator, and my team and I were on site doing a deployment. The company had recently gone through a formalized standardization of job titles, and mine at the time was senior systems engineer. One of the other folks on my team was a systems engineer. During a break, we were chatting and he asked, "What makes you 'senior'?"

At that time, I was younger than most of the other people working on my team. My response, though thoughtful, probably sounded arrogant. I replied, "I've done more things wrong and have the scars to prove it." In theory, that meant that I would not do those things again and could help others avoid them.

Perhaps they weren't all things that I actually did wrong, but I was there when the bad things did go wrong. That includes dealing with tapes that were unreadable, mirroring the clean drive over the copy with the data, doing something unsupported with an application and then not being able to get support, and more.

The lesson learned here is that SLAs can sometimes be more art than science, because to have good ones that both the IT staff and business management can be satisfied with takes creative planning, usually by folks who have suffered through the things that can go wrong. Balance must be achieved:

- If the IT team is overly conservative and cautious, they may set the SLA performance bar so low that the business management team believes that the IT staff is unknowledgeable or low-performing.
- If the IT team is overly optimistic or unrealistic, the SLA performance bar may be so high that even well-executed recoveries may fail to meet the measure established in the SLA.

When negotiating your IT SLA with the business leaders, consider first doing a brainstorming session with your senior IT folks to map out the recovery plans, identifying the likely failure points and your mitigating actions when the plan does break down. Once you have that workflow, only then should you talk to the business managers about SLAs.

When you are setting your own SLAs, don't believe the RPO and RTO on the outside of the box of whatever technology you are looking at. And certainly don't repeat the RPO and RTO to the business managers. Test it. Assume something will go wrong and think about how you would address such issues. Heck, you can even go to the extreme of thinking everything will go wrong and then negotiate with the business managers back to a point of reality.

Business Metrics: RA and BIA

Now that we have some metrics to assess what our alternative technologies are by understanding RPO and RTO and setting an SLA for how well we can act upon them, let's see how to apply them to the business, as well as how to pay for the technologies that we believe we need.

Risk Analysis (RA): The Science of Worrying

How likely is it that your particular tape solution will have a problem?

Perhaps more important, how likely is it that your production resource will suffer failure? Consider my house in Dallas, Texas. How likely is it that I will suffer a flood? Or a monsoon? Or an earthquake? Or a tornado?

Let's focus on this last question to take technology out of the process. As I mentioned, I live in Dallas, Texas, which is approximately 400 miles from the nearest large body of water, the Gulf of Mexico. Because of this, I have no fear of a monsoon. Statistically speaking, the likelihood of Dallas being hit by a monsoon is effectively zero. Speaking of water, my home is in a 100-year flood plain, meaning that, statistically, my land will be flooded once per century. I could buy flood insurance for my home, but the probability is low enough that I choose not to. If I lived in Houston, Texas, which is much closer to the coast, flooding is more likely and I might want flood insurance. But, because the probability is so much higher, I probably could not afford it, as the insurance actuaries will have already calculated it. Case in point: hail damage is frequent enough in Dallas that I can't afford to buy insurance for it.

This has meaning for our discussion. Insurance is an entire industry built upon a consumer's presumption that they pay a little every month to avoid a potentially significant and perhaps life-altering financial impact later. The amount of insurance that you pay is based predominantly on two factors:

- How likely is the crisis that you are anticipating?
- What is the financial impact that you are mitigating?

NOTE Concepts such as data protection and data availability are very similar to the idea to buying insurance. First, you assess what could go wrong and consider how much it will cost if it does, and then you purchase something that costs appreciably less than that to mitigate the crisis.

What Could Possibly Go Wrong?

The first step in planning your data protection and availability strategy is to look at each of the servers and applications in your environment and think about what could go wrong.

Go crazy. Think about *everything* that could possibly go wrong. The most important rule of this exercise is to simply list everything that could go wrong. Do not (yet) think about the probability of something occurring, but just the potential of its occurring. And let yourself think small and think big.

In the case of a core application, don't just consider the application itself. An end user does not care if the reason they can't get to their data is because the application crashed, the OS hung, the hard drive failed, the DNS server isn't resolving correctly, Active Directory won't let you log on, or your PC browser isn't reading the page correctly. They don't care, because their data and their productivity is impacted, regardless of the cause.

That's from the user's perspective. Now think about the big problems. Is your company in a flood zone? If you are in Southern California, are you near a forest that can catch on fire? If you are in Northern California, what would an earthquake do? If you're in the Midwest, are you in tornado country? In the North, what would a blizzard do? On the East Coast, how likely is a hurricane? If you live in Florida, hurricanes are a *when*, not an *if*.

NOTE Several years ago, I was conducting a disaster recovery seminar, in a town in Florida. My opening remark to them was, "According to the National Weather Service, this city is in the eye of a hurricane every 2.83 years. It has been 3 years since you have actually been hit. You are due."

How Likely Is It?

I am not suggesting that every IT professional should turn into an actuary, someone who lives with the statistics of risk all day long. What I *am* suggesting is that when you are first imagining the entire realm of bad things that could happen to your data, servers, infrastructure, and even people, first just list them. Having done that, put your practical hat back on and consider the reasonable probability of each one. The reason I don't buy flood insurance is because a flood, while possible, is not probable for me. I cannot buy hail insurance at a reasonable price, because it is almost certain it will happen to me.

In technology, there are some calamities that are certain to happen:

- You will lose a hard drive.
- The system board will fail.
- An application will crash.
- A database will become corrupted.
- A user will accidentally overwrite last month's file with this month's data and then regret it.

In business, there are some crises that are very likely:

- Someone may steal something, perhaps a laptop, from your company.
- Someone may maliciously delete data on their last day at work.
- Your server room may catch fire or might be flooded from the bathroom immediately above you.

In life, natural disasters could affect your company facilities.

So what is the likelihood of each thing that you listed? You may not have exact figures, but stack the kinds of things you're protecting against in relative probability to each other. This exercise is half of what you need to start planning your data protection and availability plan.

Business Impact Analysis (BIA): How Much Will It Cost?

Data protection and availability is not just about technology—it is about reducing financial impact. To do that, not only do we need to look at the technologies that we could use and the calamities that we fear, but we also need to turn all of them into financial ramifications.

Let's look at the potential technology and business crises listed in the previous section. They are ordered approximately from most likely to least likely, with the exception of the end user who accidentally overwrites precious data (it is guaranteed that a user will overwrite data). Let's look at the two extremes of the list. Everything else will fall in between from a likelihood perspective as well as a financial impact.

- If I were to lose one hard drive within a production server, the physical costs are likely a few hundred dollars or less. Whether it was for a data drive or the operating system will determine the level of lost productivity. And how long since my last backup will determine the amount of lost data that I may or may not have to re-create.
- On the other end of the list, if my production facility were to be flooded, the entire server room as well as many other production resources, desktops, infrastructure, even copy machines and coffee makers would be destroyed. My business could be down for days and in fact might never reopen.

The goal of a business impact analysis (BIA) is to financially quantify what the cost of any crisis might be. Say we calculate that the total cost of a hard drive failure, lost productivity, and replacement is $1,000. We believe that it is a highly likely event, so we need to aggressively seek a data protection or availability solution that mitigates that $1,000 of impact to our business by finding a mitigation solution that costs less than the $1,000—hopefully, a lot less. This may be RAID or backup or replication, all of which are discussed in this book. Similarly, while we may believe that a flood would cost $3 million, it is admittedly far less likely than a hard drive failure. That statistical probability factors into determining what we might spend to mitigate that risk.

Always Turn Technologies into Dollars

Most often, the person who writes the checks, particularly the checks for buying new assets like software and hardware, doesn't care about RPO and RTO, or DLT versus DAT, or disk versus tape. To move business-driven decision makers forward on data protection projects, we always want to quantify the risk or the reward in dollars, not gigabytes, minutes, or subjective assessments.

Data protection and availability projects are among the easiest in financial terms. Availability, or said another way productivity, can be calculated by looking at the cost of downtime. Protection and recoverability can be quantified based on the impact of lost data, as it relates not only to lost productivity but also to lack of compliance.

In short, if we can objectively state that 1 hour of downtime equates to $10,000 and the solution to resolve it cost $800, it is easy to justify new data protection or availability solutions.

Calculating the Cost of Downtime

The key idea that we need to take away from this chapter is how to turn technology problems in financial problems. If you can fiscally quantify the impact something has on the business, then you can have a different kind of discussion with business (and budget) leaders on why you need to fix it. To start that conversation, we need to understand the cost of downtime. In other words, when a server breaks, how much does it cost the company?

If a server fails, you actually have to look backward as well as forward. Figure 2.1 shows a server failing at 2 p.m. on Wednesday.

FIGURE 2.1
Downtime, forward and backward

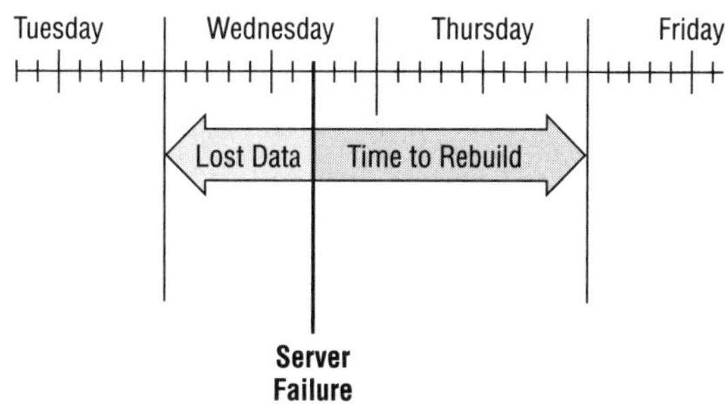

For this first example, we will make three assumptions:

- The business day is exactly 8 a.m. to 5 p.m.
- We have a successful backup from Tuesday night that is restorable.
- The server will be fixed by the end of the next business day (Thursday).

With this in mind, we can quantify two kinds of time:

Lost Data If a server fails, the new data since the last backup is potentially lost. Since our server failed at 2 p.m. on Wednesday and we are assuming a reliable restore from a successful backup on Tuesday night, we can presume that we could lose whatever data was changed between 8 a.m. to 2 p.m. on Wednesday.

In our diagram, this arrow starts at the time of the server failure and points backward to the left to whenever the last successful backup can be reliably restored from—in this case, the previous evening. If the last backup had failed or was not able to be restored, the arrow would point further to the left until a successful backup could be restored. But for now, data loss is quantified at 6 business hours.

T_d = Time of lost data, which in this case is 6 hours

We are quantifying lost data in a measurement of time because for our basic example, we are assuming that if the end users took 6 hours to originally create the data, then they will likely consume another 6 hours of business time to create the data again.

Outage Time Because the server failed in the afternoon, we are assuming that the end users may be idle for the remainder of the day and (in our example) idle for the whole next business day.

In our diagram, this arrow starts at the time of the server failure and points forward to the right until the server is completely back online, which in this case is the end of the next business day. If this is true, the outage time is the remaining 3 hours of Wednesday afternoon plus all 9 business hours of Thursday.

T_o = Time of outage or lost productivity, which is 12 hours in our example

Added together, we can say that $T_o + T_d = 12 + 6$. So the total time impact of the server failure is 18 hours. Now, we need to decide how much those 18 hours are worth in dollars. Again, there are two kinds of $/hour costs to consider:

Human Costs If we presume that an end user is completely idle while the IT resources are offline, then the company is essentially paying the salary or hourly wage of that person for no benefit.

H_r = Hourly cost of impacted personnel ($ per hour)

Consider the following:

> In a restaurant that is not able to do any business, you might reduce your losses by sending the waiters and cooks home for the day. But if 15 hourly staff who each costs the company $8 per hour (along with two salaried managers paid $40,000 annually or $20/hour) were to sit idle, then (15 × $8) + (2 × $20) = $160 per hour for idle time.
>
> In an office, perhaps there are other activities that the people can do, so they are not completely idle but simply impacted. In that case, you might choose to take the salaried costs and divide them in half to show that they are half-impacted as opposed to idle and nonproductive.

Every business is different, but you should be able to assess a $/hour number for some percentage of your hard costs of paying people who are unable to do their primary role due to an IT outage.

Profitability When a team that creates revenue is affected, revenue is affected. So, if you know what the weekly or monthly profitability of a team is, you can quantify how much profit that they are generating or not generating during an outage.

P_r = Hourly profitability or loss ($ per hour)

Consider the following:

A team may produce $9,000 per day in profit, so their hourly profitability between 8 a.m. and 5 p.m. is $1,000 per hour.

In a team that is subject to service contracts, you may be liable for fines or recouped losses if you are not offering your service.

A shipping department may not lose any money for a few hours of downtime, but if an entire day is lost, expedited shipping charges may be incurred in order to make timely deliveries the next day.

Every business is different, but you should be able to assess a $/hour for the business value that a team creates per day or per hour. Some of that productivity is lost or penalties incurred when the team is unable to do their primary role due to an IT outage.

Adding H_r and P_r together gives us the total dollars per hour impact that an IT outage has on our team. Using the first example from each description, a team may cost $160/hour by sitting idle (H_r) and also not create revenue (P_r) at $1,000/hour. Thus, every hour is worth $1,160 to the company.

This brings us to a basic formula for measuring systems availability in financial terms. We can take the total time for data loss plus outage time, and multiply that by how much an hour is worth to our business or team in consideration of human costs, as well as profitability or losses:

$$\text{Cost of Downtime} = (T_o + T_d) \times (H_r + P_r)$$

T_o = Time, length of outage

T_d = Time, length of data loss

H_r = Human cost $/hr (per person)

P_r = Profitability $/hr

In our examples, this would be:

T_o = 12 hour outage

T_d = 6 hours of lost data

H_r = $160/hour for the team to sit idle

P_r = $1,000/hour in lost revenue

Cost of Downtime = (12 hours + 6 hours) × ($160/hour + $1,000/hour)

Cost of Downtime = 18 hours × $1,160/hour

Cost of Downtime = $20,880

This particular company will lose nearly $21,000 if a server fails and is recoverable by the end of the next day.

Your Math May Vary from This, and That Is Okay

I guarantee that a good percentage of people who read that formula will find something that does not quite align with their business.

Perhaps team profitability should be reduced to half (½P_r).

Maybe data is never lost—in the sense that it does not have to be re-created—because of the nature of the business ($T_d = 0$).

The point is to take the formula as a starting place and adapt each of the four variables to correctly reflect your business:

- Hours of data loss or repeated work
- Hours of downtime or reduced-productivity
- Cost of sitting idle
- Lost profitability

So, although the basic formula works for me, it may not be your final formula. In fact, the best possible outcome for you taking this formula to your management would be the shreds of doubts that immediately follow, because then you can work together on adapting it to your business model. We will take a closer look at that throughout this chapter.

That is the formula, but it is still not the answer. The idea here is simply to help identify the variables that we'll need in order to quantify the cost of downtime.

The Cost of Downtime for Nightly Backup for a Small Office

We're still considering the same outage scenario of an environment that is using nightly tape backup that includes a full backup every weekend and incrementals each night. Consistent with the scenario we've used for this chapter, the production server fails at 2 p.m. on Wednesday. As we discussed earlier in the chapter, the users are affected for the rest of Wednesday and the recovery takes a good part of Thursday. By the end of Thursday, the server is running, the users are mostly happy, and business resumes. Two months from now, that incident will be thought of from long-term memory as a minor blip. Yes, the server went down, but everything resumed within a day. Pretty good, right?

$$\text{Cost of Downtime} = (T_o + T_d) \times (H_r + P_r)$$

T_o = Time, length of outage

T_d = Time, length of data loss

H_r = Human cost \$/hour (for team)

P_r = Profitability \$/hour

$$\text{Nightly Backup} = (1\text{d} + \tfrac{1}{2}\text{d}) \times (H_r + P_r) \times \text{hrs/day}$$

where

T_o = RTO = 1 day recovery, including parts, shipping, and installation

T_d = RPO = average ½ day (could fail early morning or late afternoon)

H_r = Human cost \$/hour (per person)

P_r = Profitability \$/hour

T_o (time of outage) or RTO will likely be one business day, which includes identifying why the server failed, repairing those components, and restoring the data. If everything goes well, this should typically be one business day. If things do not go well, this might measure two or three days of downtime. In a perfect world, additional parts are already standing by, technicians are ready to go, and perhaps the server is up in just a few hours.

T_d (time of data loss) or RPO is statistically probable as one half of a business day. As discussed earlier in the chapter, the server could fail at the beginning of a business day, resulting in near zero data loss since the last nightly backup, or could fail at the end of the business day, resulting in a complete day of data loss. Splitting the difference, we will assume data is lost from a half of the day.

If we take a closer look at this particular office, perhaps a retail store, we will assume a 10-hour workday (d = 10 hours).

Small Store Using Nightly Backup = (1d + ½d) × (H_r + P_r) @ 10hours/day

For this particular store, managerial costs (H_r) are \$24.00 per hour, while the five employees cost \$8.00 per hour. We will assume that the manager does not directly create profitability but will suffer from lost data:

Administrative Productivity Loss = (10hr + 5hr) × (\$24 + 0) = \$360

The five employees might not lose data, but they lose the ability to impact productivity and will have a hard cost of sitting idle:

Retail Employees = (10hr + 0) × (\$8 × 5 employees + \$\$\$/day) = \$400

And, in retail, of course, profitability is everything. Presume this small store generates \$100,000 in revenue over the course of one year. That would mean that within a six-day sales week, each business day generates \$320.

Resulting cost of a "minor" server outage:

Cost per Outage = \$360 (manager) + \$400 (employees) + \$320 (lost profit) = \$1080

Every time the server has an outage that must be recovered, the immediate cost to this small 6-person storefront is \$1,080, not including replacement parts/shipping, lost customer loyalty, and services from either headquarters or a local reseller to resolve the issue. This last penalty, of the additional expense for technology professional to be dispatched to the office and resolve the issue, exacerbates everything else. For a small business, while employees are down, the last thing that their budget can handle is an expensive emergency service call. They might spend \$250/hour for a technician to come out for a day to repair the process. At that point, they will have spent \$2,000 in labor to fix something that costs \$1,080. The total business impact is now \$3,080.

THE COST OF DOWNTIME FOR NIGHTLY BACKUP FOR A BIGGER OFFICE

We don't have to lay out the entire scenario again, but it is worth recognizing how quickly this scales. Assume that this takes place within a larger organization, perhaps one division within a good-sized company, such as the inside sales team of a medium-sized company. Various surveys presume that the average white-collar worker in the United States costs $36/hour. The reality of a statistic this broad is that it is guaranteed to be wrong for your workforce, but it serves as a placeholder for now. We will continue to presume a 10-hour workday, and that this team generates $10,000,000 in revenue annually.

Cost of Downtime = $(T_o + T_d) \times (H_r + P_r)$

T_o = Time, length of outage

T_d = Time, length of data loss

H_r = Human cost $/hour (for team)

P_r = Profitability $/hour

Inside Sales Team Relying on Nightly Backup = $(T_o + T_d) \times (H_r + P_r) \times$ hours/day

T_o = RTO = 1 day recovery, including parts, shipping, and install

T_d = RPO = average ½ day (could fail early a.m. vs. late p.m.)

H_r = Human cost = $36/hour/person × 50 employees = $1,800/hour

P_r = Profitability = $10M annually = $3,850/hour (10-hour workday, 5-day workweek)

Inside Sales Team relying on Nightly Backup = (1d + ½d) × (1800 + 3850) × 10 hrs/day

Business Impact per Server Outage = $874,000

This is not a typographical error. If the primary file server fails for an average group of 50 office employees that creates revenue (all of our earlier presumptions), then the business impact to that group is $874,000.

ADAPTING THE FORMULA TO YOUR BUSINESS

To be fair, this isn't the whole story. The likely outcome of first evaluating this formula is that management will disagree with its validity. And that is fine, because they are probably correct.

- If your users cannot get to their file server, they might catch up on e-mail or they might have some documents on their local workstation or laptop. In this case, let's assume that that the employees are not completely idle but are simply affected. If that were the case, we might add a multiplier to the formula to imply that the user base is operating at 2/3 efficiency. If so, a 1/3 multiplier against the formula results in a business impact of only $291,000. That is still over a quarter-million dollars per server incident.
- In today's information worker world, we might presume that the users have a variety of activities that they could do. Between e-mail, database applications including contact management, as well as traditional office applications from a file server, perhaps we could presume only a minor inconvenience to a percentage of the users. Perhaps this results in a 10% impact to 10% of the employees. Literally, this would mean only 5 of the 50 employees had any impact and therefore the cost would only be $8,710.

- But some departments don't have multiple functions that they can balance between. In the example of inside sales, what if all of the data was within a single SQL Server database, or the sales folks fundamentally could not operate without access to the database. In that case, they would suffer the whole (and what may have originally seemed extreme) business impact of $871,000.

The business impact may be even higher when we recognize that a server doesn't usually go down just once. While these minor inconveniences may fade in the memory of users, they typically don't fade from your system's event log. You might be surprised to find that a particular server fails twice per year, in which case we would double all the previous numbers (which still don't include hardware or services costs). But even at one failure per year, if we presume that a typical server asset is expected to have a 3-year lifespan, then we should multiply the per outage cost times the number of outages per year times the number of years the resource will be in service.

Total Cost per Server = $C_o \times O_{per\ year} \times LS$

C_o = Cost per Outage = the result of our earlier formula)

$O_{per\ year}$ = Number of Outages per year (let's presume only 1 per year)

LS = Expected Lifespan of Server (typically 3 years)

Total Cost per Server = $8,710 × 1/yr × 3 = $26,000

Here is the punch line: the file server that has been recently purchased and deployed to service the inside sales team of our company is considered reliable and well managed; so it is presumed to only suffer one outage per year. With that in mind, the company should plan to lose over $26,000 over its lifetime of service.

That is the BIA for this one server. It took a while in this chapter to break this down, but in real life, this goes quicker than you might expect. Essentially, as you are looking at what kind of protection or availability solutions that you might consider per server or application platform, you first need to understand what kind of risks you are protecting against as well as the financial impact if one were to occur.

Risk Mitigation: Fixing It in Advance

You might be thinking, This won't happen to me because I have <fill in the blank>.

You might be right. Risk mitigation (RM) is the set of steps you do to avoid the more common or anticipated types of crises. In data protection and availability terms, this might be as simple as mirroring your hard drives or as complex as deploying replication software with failover capabilities between multiple geographic sites.

Risk Mitigation Is a Core Goal for This Book

The technology chapters of this book are intended to make you successful in deploying the technologies and methods necessary to avoid productivity outages and data losses. To do that, Chapter 1 describes the landscape of what kinds of options are available, while this chapter focuses on the financial impact that we are trying to avoid. In this section of the chapter, we will discuss determining the appropriate level of protection or availability, based on the business impact, in order to mitigate our risks.

Protection or Productivity?

Usually, you cannot solve for both protection and productivity equally. There are exceptions, and most people desire both. But for most technology approaches, the solution is optimized for either addressing robust protection and recovery scenarios or ensuring higher availability. Certainly, it can be as fine a line as 60:40 or completely exclusive to one goal or the other.

One example is Microsoft Cluster Services (MSCS), as shown in Figure 2.2. MSCS is exclusively a high-availability solution and makes no pretenses about data protection. In fact, MSCS typically has a single point of failure in its shared storage architecture.

FIGURE 2.2
A Microsoft MSCS cluster for higher availability (productivity)

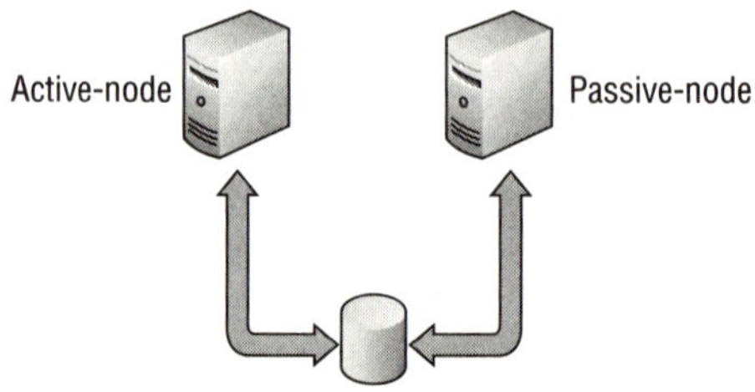

In Figure 2.2, we see two physical nodes, each running Windows Server and attached to a shared storage array. MSCS creates a logical layer between the independent operating systems and forges an identity as a single *cluster*. Applications requiring high availability are installed onto the cluster, whereby the application (as well as a virtualized identity of the server) may be running on either one clustered node or the other. If anything happens, whether at the application, OS, or node–hardware layer, the virtualized application server moves the entire instance to the surviving clustered node for assured uptime.

The single point of failure for a cluster, its shared storage solution, is made up almost entirely of disks, which we have previously discussed as the computer component most likely to fail. If the storage array fails, the cluster is left as two heads with no body. To mitigate this risk, clustered nodes often use mirrored storage arrays behind the scenes. We'll discuss this more in Chapter 6, but for now, consider it an example of a solution focused exclusively on productivity, whereas traditional backup focuses on protection.

Availability

Availability is best handled in the platform that you are trying to make highly available.

The original method of ensuring higher availability was deploying more reliable storage, in the form of synchronously mirrored disk arrays. In those early days of LAN servers, this approach made a great deal of sense, since the majority of server outages were due to hardware and storage often had the components most likely to fail. Times have changed. Today, only a minority of crises are due to hardware, and not all of those are related to storage. Because of this evolution, most availability goals are now met by software-based solutions instead of expensive, redundant hardware. Even in those cases where redundant hardware is leveraged, such as mirrored storage, it is usually done within the larger implementation of clustering or other application or OS availability configuration.

The next leap forward in higher availability was generic cluster services or application-agnostic failover. In the case of MSCS, the idea was to create a highly available and a virtualized server that could be run in any of the nodes of the physical cluster. The model then became to install your production server applications, such as SQL Server or Microsoft Exchange, within the clustered server instead of physical hardware. In those early clustering days, this approach was hindered by two key factors:

- Many production server applications were not originally designed to be "clusterable." This often meant additional engineering and complexity for implementing the application into the cluster. You might install the entire application from node one and then install part of the same application repeatedly on nodes two through *N*. In other cases, you might have to run a customized script to force the application into a cluster. The latter approach was especially common in third-party alternatives to MSCS such as Veritas Cluster Server (VCS).
- The original releases of MSCS also had some limitations and complexities that often made Windows Server experts feel like novices. This was especially true in Windows NT 4.0 and Windows 2000.

In Chapter 1, I shared the anecdote that an application or an OS vendor often looks externally to partner developers to fill feature holes that it cannot initially deliver, but if the feature is requested enough by customers, it will usually be filled by the original developer. In this case, we see that availability for today's applications is not relegated to hardware, nor is it delivered by changing the OS environments on which the application was originally intended. Instead, primary applications are now delivering higher availability within their own technology. Examples of this include SQL Server database mirroring, Exchange 2007 CCR and 2010 DAG, and Distributed File System (DFS) namespaces and replication. We will cover it each of these specific technologies in future chapters on availability, as well as the application-agnostic approaches to availability, including MSCS and third-party software.

NOTE Whenever possible, application availability is (usually) best achieved by the application itself.

Protection

Data protection and recovery is exactly the opposite of data availability with respect to where it should be delivered from. The reason that availability is best achieved through the application itself is because availability is still about the delivery of the original service. Similar to software debugging and error handling, availability mechanisms are part of ensuring the delivery of the application, whether that be servicing mailboxes, offering databases, or sharing files.

For example, consider Microsoft Exchange Server. In much the same way that the Exchange development team has made significant investments to improve the integrity of its own database within Exchange Server, their next development in Exchange 2007 was additional availability solutions such as LCR, CCR, and SCR, as well as DAG in Exchange 2010 (all of which are covered in Chapter 7). But in principle, these new technologies are all additional layers of availability, as they all are focused on providing you with current or near-current data. To achieve any other (previous) recovery point, you must stop looking at availability technologies and start looking toward protection mechanisms. But protection, in the sense of data backup and recovery, is not built into Exchange as availability solutions are. Exchange now enables its own high-availability scenarios but requires outside mechanisms to gain protection and recovery.

Similarly, SQL Server has replication for the purposes of availability but does not include the concept of built-in backup and recovery in the traditional sense. Instead, both of these applications have made an appreciable investment to facilitate data protection via external means.

The key point in this protection and availability section is to recognize that you may already have deployed some level of risk mitigation in the form of secondary availability or backup and recovery technology. That's what a good part of this book is about—identifying and successfully deploying those technologies that are appropriate for your environment.

NOTE In contrast to application availability, application protection and recovery is (usually) best achieved outside the platform itself.

Total Cost of Ownership

So far, in this chapter, we have discussed data protection and availability technologies in terms of cost, meaning the business cost of not doing something. There is, of course, the factor of price, which is different depending on to whom you are talking.

In this section, we want to recognize that the price is always more than the sticker or invoice. In fact, in many backup and recovery scenarios, the greatest contributing cost has nothing to do with the product at all but is labor. Let's consider a traditional nightly tape backup solution.

The initial acquisition costs might include:

Backup server (software)	$2,500	
Backup agents (software)	$995	per production server
Backup server (hardware)	$2,500	
Tape backup drive (hardware)	$2,000	

Assume a traditional mid-sized company network with 25 servers.

Collectively, then, to purchase a nightly tape backup solution for this environment, you might be requesting $37,000, not including deployment services.

That is our first mistake, because you will pay for deployment, even if you do it yourself. If you contract a local reseller or backup specialist, there is likely a fixed cost for the deployment, which hopefully also results in a fast and reliable solution, because presumably the reseller has previous experience and close ties with your backup software vendor. But as anyone who has ever done a significant home improvement project will tell you, while you might choose to save the additional labor, you will pay for it in time—literally. Your own IT staff, who would otherwise be doing other projects, will be deploying this instead. The project will likely take longer if your staff has not deployed this particular technology before, and their not following best practices may result in additional labor at a later date. But presuming that everything is equal, let's assume 8 hours for the server deployment plus 30 minutes per production server for agent installation and backup scripts configuration. Splitting the difference between an in-house IT professional at $75/hour and a local reseller, which might charge $250 per hour, this results in 20 hours, which we could equate at approximately $150/hour, or an additional $3,000 total labor.

But we aren't done yet. We should also calculate the cost of media. If we assume that each of the servers has 5 TB of storage, then we would have 125 TB of active storage across the environment. At an average 60 percent utilization rate, we would need approximately 75 TB of data to be protected. With an aggregate daily change rate of 5 percent (more for applications, less on file shares), you'll be writing about 4 TB of new data per day—but with most tape backup software, you'll use a different tape for each daily job, plus 4 weekly tapes and 12 annuals. Conservatively, this puts you at 20 tapes at $100 each for an additional $2,000 in tape media (not including additional costs like offsite storage or services, which we discuss in Chapter 12).

There will also be ongoing costs such as power, space, and cooling. Space would be associated with your facilities costs, but simply running the new backup server in standard form factor might use a 500 W platform (plus the tape drive's 200 W). The monthly power costs for this server alone is:

700 W × 24 hours per day = 16,800 WH or 16.8 KWH per day

16.8 KWH × 30 days in a month = 520.8 KWH per month

At $0.06 per KWH, this server will cost $31.20 per month or $375/year.

We also need to add in the ongoing labor costs for:

- Rotating the tapes on a daily basis, which isn't a lot, but perhaps 10 minutes per business day
- Checking the backup jobs, 10 minutes per business day, plus one one-hour error resolution every 2 weeks

Those aren't significant numbers when looked at that way, but when added up, we see 8,220 minutes, or 137 hours, or 3.4 working weeks per year, just managing backups (and assuming most things go right most of the time) and not including restores. The labor for managing backups in this environment will consume at least a month of every year with no productivity benefit and will cost $10,300.

This gives us the bigger picture, the total cost of ownership (TCO):

> The initial purchase price of our backup solution might be $37,000, plus $3,000 to install it.
>
> But the operational costs in the first year will be an additional $12,800.
>
> Assuming that most hardware and software assets have a presumed lifespan of three years, we can add software maintenance (15 percent), upgrade labor (half of deployment), and new annual plus daily tapes (5 annually) for years two and three. The ongoing costs for the second and third years are $6,100 annually.

Thus, the TCO for this backup solution would be $65,000, which is nearly double what the initial purchase price was and does not include any restores at all.

Return on Investment

If TCO is thought of as the bad number to consider in any financial assessment, then return on investment (ROI) would be the good one. Dig way back to the beginning of the chapter to BIA: how much does the problem cost?

If a problem costs $150,000, we can assume that that is lost money. But if you solve the problem, the company gets $150,000 back. Think of it like an ante in poker or a coin dropped into a slot machine; that money is gone. If you make any money from poker or slots, then that is positive—winnings. Of course, if you bet $5 and then later won $5, you haven't actually won, you've broken even. Similarly, if your technology problem or vulnerability costs $150,000 and you got it back by spending $150,000 on a protection solution, then you haven't actually solved the problem of losing the money for the business—you've just chosen to spend it in a different way. That may be okay to your CFO, based on tax rules, but that's outside the scope of this book.

If you spent $65,000 (TCO) to solve a problem that will cost the company $150,000 (BIA), then you have solved the problem. You literally added $85,000 to the company's bottom-line profitability because they otherwise would have lost those dollars due to the outages that you mitigated. This is where ROI comes into the picture: how much you saved or gained for the company, in comparison to what you had to spend to accomplish it.

Calculating ROI

There are different ways to quantify ROI. You might prefer to think about it as we discussed earlier, where you saved the company $85,000. Taking servers completely out of the discussion, if you could show your accounting manager that they are used to spending $150,000 per year on something but you could save them $85,000 by doing it a different way, that is usually an easy business decision.

Some measure it as the percentage of BIA/TCO. In this case, $150,000 divided by $65,000 yields 2.3—or a 230 percent yield. Others invert the percentage (TCO/BIA) as the percentage of the problem that you are spending to solve it. In this case, you can spend 43 percent of the problem to resolve it. That also means that we save 57 percent of our projected losses.

Alternatively, you might think in terms of payback windows. If a problem costs $150,000 over the three-year lifespan of the asset, then consider how long into that window before the solution pays for itself. In this case, with an average of $50,000 costs annually, the first-year cost of $52,800 is basically breaking even, but years two and three go from $50,000 to $6,000 annually, saving almost everything.

TIME TO VALUE

Somewhat related to the ROI of a solution is how quickly you will start to see the benefits of the solution you are deploying. When considering that you will see *x* dollars over the lifespan of the project; look also at when you will see those dollars.

Compare when the costs are to be incurred to when the savings will start to be realized. Will you just break even for the first year and then see gains in the second and third years (such as when you deploy a new component that will solve an ongoing problem)? Or will you see gains the first year but fewer gains in later years, as you postpone a problem or take on incremental costs throughout the project?

How else you might use (and grow) the earlier money can also affect the overall costs for the project.

The actual calculation for ROI is to take the net gain ($150,000 minus the costs of $65,000) of $85,000 and then divide it by the costs, after which you can multiply it by 100 to arrive at a percentage:

(Total Gain – Costs) ÷ Costs

($150,000 – $65,000) ÷ $65,000

$85,000 ÷ $65,000 = 1.31, which is 131 percent ROI

Any positive ROI is a relatively good decision and any negative ROI is a relatively poor decision. Consider a $10 problem:

- Spending $6 to solve a $10 dollar problem is good because ($10 – $6) ÷ $6 = $4 ÷ $6 = 0.66, or 66 percent ROI. Said another way, for every $1 that you spent in this way, you would get it back as well as an additional 66 cents.
- Spending $9 to solve a $10 dollar problem is not as good because ($10 – $9) ÷ $9 = $1 ÷ $9 = 0.11, or 11 percent ROI. Said another way, for every $1 that you spent in this way, you would only gain an additional 11 cents. There are likely other ways that the business could invest that dollar and gain more than 11 cents in return.
- Spending $12 to solve a $10 dollar problem is obviously not a good idea: ($10 – $12) ÷ $12 = a negative 12 percent ROI. Said another way, for every $1 that you spent, you lose 12 more cents than what the original problem was already costing. It would (obviously) be cheaper to live with the $10 problem than to solve it for $12.

The third example may have been overly obvious, but sometimes IT administrators do solve $10 backup or availability problems with $12 solutions because they do not understand the BIA or TCO well enough, or because they are not aware of the $6 alternative solutions.

Which ROI Method Is Most Accurate?

This chapter has been about converting technology issues into quantitative, and specifically financial, assessments. Once you have converted your protection or availability problem and potential solution(s) into this financial language, you can easily convert it from one denomination (ROI metric) to another, as easily as converting the denominator of a fraction by multiplying or dividing it by a common number.

But there is a rule of thumb worth noting:

> 25 percent ROI may be better than 60 percent ROI

One of the reasons that I prefer to deal in actual dollars is because CFOs and other accounting types can often crunch the numbers to their own liking, once you present two key numeric facts (though they must be defensible facts and not subjective opinions):

- The problem is currently costing the company $XX,XXX. (BIA)
- I can solve the problem by spending $YY,YYY. (TCO)

From there, some will subtract one from the other for savings, whereas others will find a ratio that helps them appreciate it. However, based on some anecdotal findings from surveys and the experience of many years in supporting sales efforts, there is a credibility concern to be aware of.

The Credibility Challenge of ROI

Notwithstanding the recognition that every technology vendor (or other sales organization) always preaches how wonderful their widget is and how amazing their ROI (often unfounded) could be, ROI does have a credibility challenge.

Using the percentage ROI method, let's assume that the ROI of a solution is 43 percent, meaning that we are spending $70 to solve a problem that costs $100. The challenge is that the solution is costing over half of what the problem costs. That means that if your assessment of the cost of the problem is perceived as too high (qualitatively, not necessarily quantitatively) or you may have underestimated something in your TCO, then your ROI goes down from 43 percent as your costs start getting closer to what the problem itself costs. If your CFO is willing to wager that a problem won't happen as often as you project, she might actually save money (or at least break even) by just allowing the problem to happen on a (hopefully) less frequent or less impactful nature than you have predicted. The project does not have enough ROI to warrant the initial expenditure.

On the other hand, what if you only needed to spend $5 to save $100—1,900 percent ROI? This has the opposite challenge: it sounds too good to be true. If you have a good amount of credibility with the financial decision maker, then you will be seen as a hero and your project will be approved (although with that much credibility between you and your CFO, you may not have calculate a specific ROI to begin with). For the rest of us in reality-land, if it sounds too good to be true, some financial decision makers will assume that it is not true (or viable as a "real" solution). There must be some significant cost factor that is either drastically inflated in the problem or underestimated in the solution. Either way, the solution is not perceived as credible. After all, how likely is it that you can purchase a mere toy to solve a real problem?

Based on anecdotes, experience, and a few old surveys, it appears that 20–25 percent ROI is the best way to justify a solution. The gain is enough that the solution is likely worth pursuing, though the investment is substantive enough that the solution can be considered reasonable for addressing the issue. Using this approach, we might consider the following ROI boundaries:

- Over 33 percent may lack credibility.
- Under 15 percent may not offer enough potential gain.

One the most interesting pieces of advice that I ever heard related to ROI was from someone at a Gartner CFO conference who attended a session on ROI. They heard that if a significant proposal was submitted for review and it had a TCO projection and ROI analysis on its first submission, it would be approved over 40 percent more often than those that did not have those calculations. If the same type of proposal was pushed back down to get the TCO/ROI analysis and it was resubmitted, it only had a 15 percent greater likelihood of approval over similar projects without one. The first ROI success tip: present the TCO and ROI assessment with the initial proposal, as it not only clarifies the legitimacy of the project to you, but also proactively clears a big hurdle for you with those who guard the dollars.

Real World Scenario

YOU SHOULD HOPE THEY ARGUE WITH YOUR FORMULA

This is my own advice, and I have never had someone challenge it. The best thing that can happen when you present your methodology and resulting BIA/TCO/ROI justifications for a project is that the business/operational/financial stakeholder challenges your formula (in a constructive way). When working with your business leaders and establishing the formula that you will use in your process, here are a few key ideas to frame the conversation:

- Working backward, ROI is just a comparison of BIA to TCO.
- TCO is simply a prospective invoice, along with some simple assumptions of fixed costs. Likely, challenges here will be minor tweaks to the fixed values, not wholesale changes to the math.

- BIA is where challenges occur—your business stakeholder doesn't agree with how you calculated the cost of downtime (one example from earlier in this chapter). This is great news because then you two get to decide why the formula doesn't apply to a particular business unit or technology resource.

If your discussion circle can collectively agree that when the database server is down for up to a day, employees can catch up on email, or vice versa (and thereby reduces some variable by half), then the collective team has turned your formula into their formula.

If the HR person can provide more specific hourly dollar values across a large department (though you are unlikely to get a list of individual salaries), your team now has much more accurate fixed values that both the IT management and the operational management will agree on.

In short, every pushback that can be discussed or refined brings buy-in and agreement by the other parties. When you have five variables to work with, the formula may seem academic. But if you get more accurate modifiers, and the dollar variables are filled in with real numbers, you are only left with the technology numbers, such as:

- How often does the server go down?
- What is the cost of replacement hardware?
- How much do tapes cost?

These numbers are usually easily accessible by IT management and complete the equation. From there, you now have a new BIA that is even more defensible and that now has credibility in the eyes of the other stakeholders. TCO comes from the invoice and projections. ROI is simply the mathematical comparison of the BIA and the TCO.

But now, because everyone has weighed in on the financial values and the relational impact of the formula, everyone believes the ROI, no matter how big or small. Going back to the concern we had around presumed credibility of the ROI formula:

- If the ROI is less appealing (for example, TCO is 50 percent of BIA), at least everyone was involved in understanding the legitimacy of the numbers, and you have a greater likelihood of them agreeing to the project.
- If the ROI is too appealing (not emotionally credible), you have the simpler problem of working with the vendor through side meetings to educate your stakeholding peers as to the legitimacy of the solution and the higher potential of being that hero by spending $10 to save $100.

Either way, having the initial formulas and variables challenged turns the project from yours to theirs and will help you pay for what you already know you want.

Turning IT Needs into Corporate Initiatives

High availability (HA) and backup and recovery (B&R) are technology terms. In many companies, they are considered similar to taxes to the budget. No one likes the time or money spent on backup until they need a restore. Most folks think availability solutions cost too much until they are in the middle of an outage. But as logical as these tactical initiatives are, they often are among the first to suffer during budgetary sacrifices.

Business continuity (BC) and disaster recovery (DR) are usually considered strategic, not tactical. More importantly, they are often funded by higher-level organizations and typically have VP-level or C-level executive sponsorship. Your company may even have a Chief Risk Management Officer (CRMO). Although these initiatives are often included in the early budget-chopping process, it is usually for different reasons. BC and DR initiatives are often unwieldy, especially in their first year or two of delivery. They are often considered too expensive or too complex to deploy and maintain. As such, they are often put off until "next year."

One key to success is to look at how your HA or B&R solution contributes to your company's BC and DR needs.

If your BC goal has a guaranteed system uptime requirement, shape your HA deployment within that context, even to the point of calling it Risk Management, which is definitely part of most BC technology plans.

If your DR goal requires data to be offsite, how are you going to get it there? Would it come from your backup tapes? Would implementing a disk-to-disk replication solution give you your offsite capability without courier services for the tapes?

The key is twofold:

- Frame your HA or B&R project within the company's BC and DR goals so that you get higher executive sponsorship, which will result in friendlier financial and operational stakeholders when you are calculating BIA, TCO, and ROI.
- You may be able to pay for your new backup solution from the company's DR budget (instead of your IT budget), if you can show that the solution facilitates a desired capability for disaster recovery.

Summary

That's it for this chapter; the big takeaways are to:

- Look at RPO and RTO as a way to distill different data protection and availability technologies into consistent and comparable performance metrics.
- Understand what kinds of crises that you are solving using RA and BIA.
- Most importantly, convert your technology issues into dollars (BIA), and get everyone on the same page for how much you need better availability or protection.

Then, you can create a fair assessment to decide what you need. From there, understand the real costs (TCO) including acquisition, and be proactive in communicating the benefit (ROI), not just the needs.

Assuming that you've done all that, the rest of this book is intended to help you be successful in selecting and deploying different technologies in protection and availability.

Chapter 3

The Layers of Data Protection

In this chapter, you'll learn some different perspectives for what the term "data" means, as well as how your data is stored in various logical and physical layers of the server so that you can better understand your options and their ramifications in various protection and availability scenarios. Then, we'll look at the media types used for data protection — from multiple storage arrays to disk-, tape-, and cloud-based repositories.

In short, we'll address the questions "How should I protect my data?" and "How should my data be stored in production as well as in redundancy?"

What Data Looks Like from the Server's Perspective

You can look at data essentially as layers within the server that holds them. As a simple example, this chapter was originally written as a single document (named `DP4VDC-ch03.docx`) in Microsoft Word that you can view four ways:

Logical View Logical view is what the data means to the user — in this case, strings of words that make up the paragraphs and pages of a chapter. That's what the word "data" means to you and me.

Format View In format view, the chapter is an XML document readable by Microsoft Word. This XML document has no other knowledge or context in relation to any other Word document unless you explicitly define one. Word doesn't know that this document is a chapter in a book.

File View File view is how the Windows operating system sees the single object with the filename `DP4VDC-ch03.docx`, with various permissions and date, time, and size attributes. Windows assumes that this is a Word document because the Windows Registry says that all DOC and DOCX files are Word documents, but the OS doesn't know anything else. And if the file extension wasn't recognized, Windows wouldn't even know that.

Disk View In disk view, this chapter is a series of eight blocks scattered around a partitioned disk drive on my home server. Each block is 64KB and has no linkage to anything except the blocks in front and behind it in the series.

If we were to consider a record in a SQL database, things are surprisingly similar:

Logical View In logical view, a record has rows and columns that organize related information in a table.

Format View In format view, the data is part of a logical table held within something that the SQL Server application considers a database.

File View In the file view, the two files that make up a logical SQL Server database are accessed by the application in very different manners. First, the data changes are appended to other file changes in a file ending in `.ldf` (the log). Later, the data changes are stored somewhere in the middle of a big file ending in `.mdf` (the database), and the data in the LDF file is modified slightly immediately after.

Disk View In disk view, numerous blocks appear on the logical disk. Some blocks make up the LDF file, and others make up the MDF. For performance reasons the blocks are residing on a logical disk within a storage array that is made up of a few physical disks; the blocks are physically spread out, with some on each of the disks in the array.

When seen through these lenses, looking at a database versus a single Word document is not really that different. Here is the punch line: you can protect your data at each of these layers, and each method has its own pros and cons.

Now let's look at things from the server perspective, which is more in line with this book:

Application Layer Where the data has logical meaning

File Layer Where the data is managed by the OS

Hardware Layer How the data is stored

Hardware-centric Protection

We briefly mentioned RAID in Chapter 1 as part of understanding disk-based protection, but that wasn't the whole story.

Let's begin with the single physical disk. It is an essential part of the bigger server solution and unfortunately is also the component most likely to fail. Of all the various computer components that could fail and thus cause a server outage, a spinning disk drive is the most common culprit. Because it has moving parts and variable electric current, the physical disk is more likely to fail than the circuit board, a memory chip, or video controller, not including electrical surges or other physical calamities.

FAILURE DEFINITIONS

Let's define a couple of terms:

Mean Time Between Failures (MTBF) Often, each component in an engineering-designed solution will be assessed by the manufacturer to determine the statistical probability of how long the component will last. This is the MTBF, also known as the predicted lifespan.

In our example, because a hard disk drive has more moving parts than the purely electrical components of the system board, for example, the disk has a lower MTBF than the system board and therefore will likely fail first.

Single Point of Failure (SPOF) When assessing an overall solution, we want to identify unique components that, if they were to fail, would compromise the entire solution.

The goal for availability solutions is to eliminate as many as possible, if not all, SPOFs from the overall solution so that any single component could fail and the solution not be compromised.

Storage Level 1: Protecting Against Spindle Failure

The irony is that a single hard disk is not only the component most likely to fail, but is also a single point of failure (SPOF) for the entire computer. But there are lots of alternatives for how we handle this.

RAID 0: Striping

Although not actually a configuration for protection, RAID 0 is related to performance: blocks are striped across multiple disks so that multiple spindles service every disk request. Here's an example: we have four disks in RAID 0, and a disk operation for seven consecutive blocks of data is requested. The requests might be serviced as block1 from disk1, block2 from disk2, block3 from disk3, block4 from disk4, and block5 from disk1 again (as you can see in Figure 3.1). The performance would be roughly four times as great because of the four independent disk spindles. Unfortunately for data protection folks like us, the likelihood of failure is also four times as great — because if any disk fails, the striped volume is completely compromised.

FIGURE 3.1
RAID 0, or striping for performance

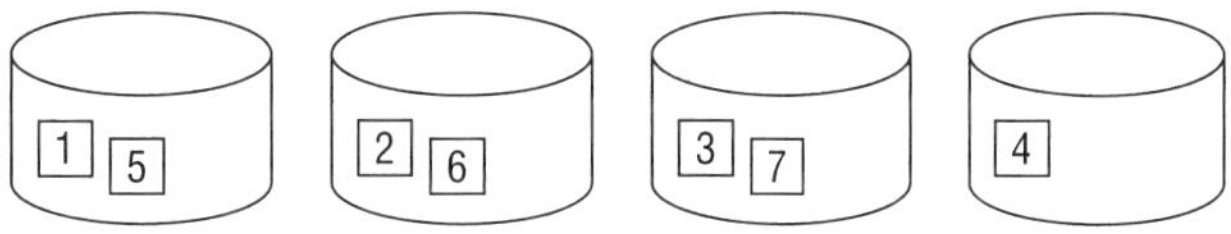

RAID 1: Mirroring or Duplexing

The first thing we can do is remove the single spindle (another term for a single physical disk, referring to the axis that all the physical platters within the disk spin on). In its simplest resolution, we mirror one disk or spindle with another. With this, the disk blocks are paired up so that when disk block number 234 is being written to the first disk, block number 234 on the second disk is receiving the same instruction at the same time. This completely removes a single spindle from being the SPOF, but it does so by consuming twice as much disk (which equates to at least twice the acquisition cost), power, cooling, and space within the server.

Today, most people refer to this process as *mirroring*, where two disks each maintain the same disk blocks and information. Every disk write is *mirrored* and executed at the same time to both disks. If either disk were to fail, the other could continue to operate with no interruption of service. In the early LAN server days (about 1990), the difference between *disk mirroring* and *disk duplexing* was whether the paired disks were using the same disk controller or separate controllers. Mirroring the spindle eliminates the disk as the SPOF, but an outage by the disk controller would cause the same outage. If the single controller failed, both mirrors of the disk would be unavailable.

Splitting the disks across controllers is a recommended best practice because a shared disk controller is the SPOF and performance benefits can be gained by splitting the input/output (I/O) between the mirrored spindles, as shown in Figure 3.2. While disk writes are done in parallel at regular speed, disk read performance is often increased in mirrors because both disks can service disk reads separately — particularly with separate controllers. Unfortunately, it does consume twice the capacity — so two 1TB drives will only yield 1TB of useful storage. In fact, many hardware systems provide what is called *N-way* mirroring, with two or more copies of each primary disk. So, for critical data, you might have three or more copies (which would require triple or more the number of raw storage devices).

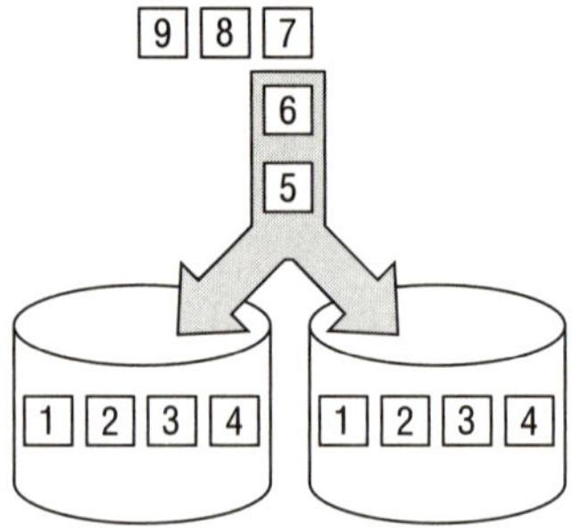

FIGURE 3.2
RAID 1 or mirroring for fault tolerance

RAID 2, 3, AND 4

RAID 2, 3, and 4 configurations are mostly academic configurations that are not often implemented, so I am choosing to leave these out of a book intended for pragmatic guidance. Each of these three RAID modes attempts to achieve some level of data redundancy without consuming twice the space of disk mirroring (RAID 1).

RAID 5

RAID 5 is what most folks call RAID. Remember that the danger of RAID 0 is that if one disk fails, the entire set is compromised. Instead, with RAID 5, data are striped across three or more disk spindles (similar to RAID 0) but with parity data interleaved. The parity information is a mathematical calculation whereby if one of the striped disks were to fail, the parity bits can determine what information was on the failed drive. While one disk has failed, the set will continue to operate, though in a degraded state because the parity information is constantly decoding what was lost so that the data is still accessible. But when the failed disk is replaced, it can be completely rebuilt by the striped data and parity information, as shown in Figure 3.3.

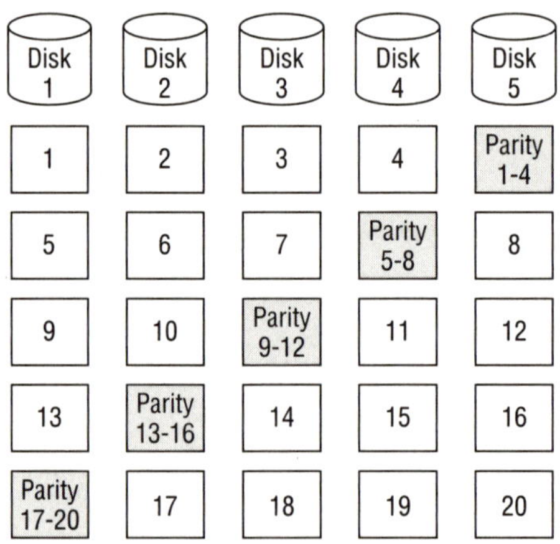

FIGURE 3.3
RAID 5

You typically see significant size increases since the disk set can contain three, five, or even ten or more disks and the overall usable size is N – 1. For example, 5 1TB drives will appear as N – 1 (5 – 1), or 4TB of usable storage. However, because a RAID 5 set can only survive a single drive failure (two will kill the array), you typically limit the total number of members.

Performance is a key determinant for or against RAID 5. Disk writes are very poor, especially when the writes are smaller than one complete stripe across the disk set. Random access writes, such as for file services, can be poor as well. However, read performance is nearly as good as RAID 0 due to the individual disk services to different read requests.

RAID 6

There is a RAID 6, which is based on RAID 5 but with two parity drives. However, there is no appreciable benefit compared to a RAID 5 set with a hot spare drive.

Hot Spare, or Hot Standby, Disk

Particularly in RAID 5 environments but elsewhere as well, many disk solutions allow for a hot (already installed and powered-up) standby. If the disk controller determines that a drive in the RAID set has failed, the standby disk is automatically logically inserted into the set as a replacement. Imagine having a flat tire, and your car could automatically take the spare out of the trunk and replace the failing tire — all while the car is still driving down the road. This is the beauty of a hot spare, or hot standby, disk.

RAID 0+1, 1+0, and 10

You've seen the benefits of spanning disks for performance (RAID 0), mirroring for protection (RAID 1), and some middle ground (RAID 5). To gain more of these protection benefits without sacrificing performance, you can "nest" multiple configurations. The overall solution size is the same either way and equal to half of the total aggregate storage capacity (because mirroring is involved). In these scenarios, it is usually preferable to have performance spans across the mirrored pairs (1+0 instead of 0+1) so that fewer disks need to be replaced. You can also mitigate more failures concurrently.

RAID 0+1 While less common, this scenario has two RAID 0 spanned disk sets that are then mirrored. In this configuration, we might start with six drives:

RAID 0 set A — with three disks A1, A2, and A3, striped for performance

RAID 0 set B — with three disks B1, B2, and B3, striped for performance

Then, set A and B are mirrored, as Figure 3.4 shows.

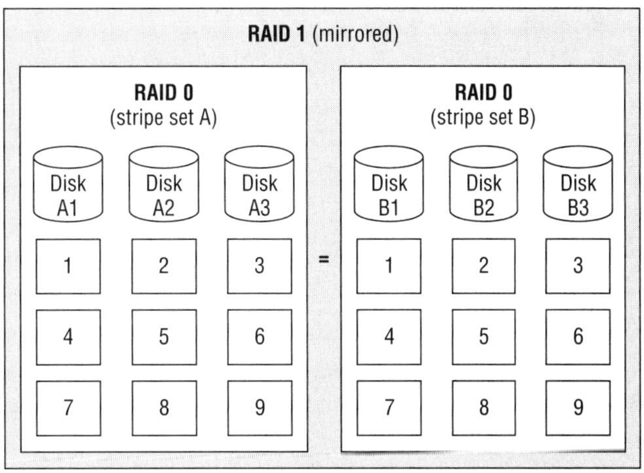

FIGURE 3.4
RAID 0+1, mirrored stripes

Although this solution offers performance, scale, and redundancy, it should still only be considered for protecting against a single drive failure. In our six-drive example, losing disk A2 fails the entire set A while set B continues to service all requests. But with everything running on set B, if any drive in set B were to fail, the entire solution would go offline.

RAID 1+0 (Also Called RAID 10) RAID 1+0 is much more common than RAID 0+1 and is becoming a best practice because it offers the same protection as mirroring but with the size, scale, and performance of RAID 0. In this configuration, we first have multiple mirrored pairs of disks:

RAID 1 pair A — with disks A1 and A2, mirrored for protection

RAID 1 pair B — with disks B1 and B2, mirrored for protection

RAID 1 pair C — with disks C1 and C2, mirrored for protection

Then, the three mirrored pairs (now acting logically as three disks that just happen to be very resilient) are striped in a RAID 0 set, as shown in Figure 3.5.

FIGURE 3.5
RAID 1+0, also called RAID 10

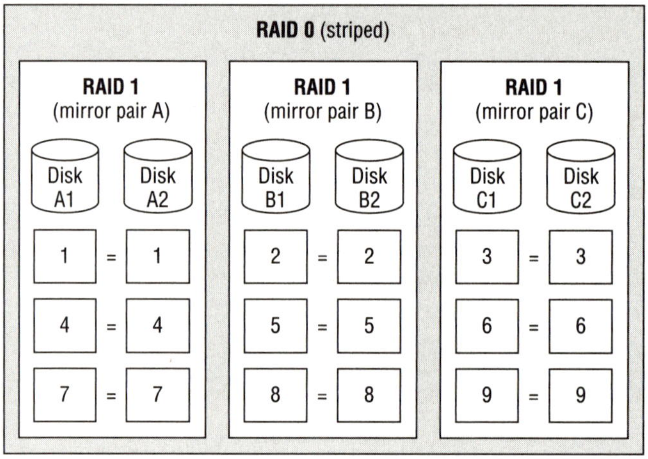

Like 0+1 or most RAID configurations, it can survive a single drive failure (such as A2 in the previous example). But it could also survive failures of drives in set B and set C concurrently. The solution would only fail if both drives of a pair (A1 and A2) were to fail at the same time. By using at least one hot spare within this same configuration, you can hopefully rebuild A2 before A1 were to have a failure — allowing this solution to continue to service disk requests indefinitely.

RAID 0+1 and 1+0 will both yield half the aggregate size of the disk storage, so six drives at 1TB each will deliver a 3TB solution (due to the mirroring).

RAID 50

Again for performance or space reasons, you can also stripe across RAID 5 sets, so a RAID 5+0 (called 50) would include multiple RAID 5 arrays that were striped. To understand this, we need to expand our scenario to nine drives, but we'll start with three-disk RAID 5 sets:

RAID 5 set A — with A1, A2, and A3 (2TB of capacity along with parity)

RAID 5 set B — with B1, B2, and B3 (2TB of capacity along with parity)

RAID 5 set C — with C1, C2, and C3 (2TB of capacity along with parity)

We then stripe them for greater performance and scale.

FIGURE 3.6
RAID 50, or RAID 5+0

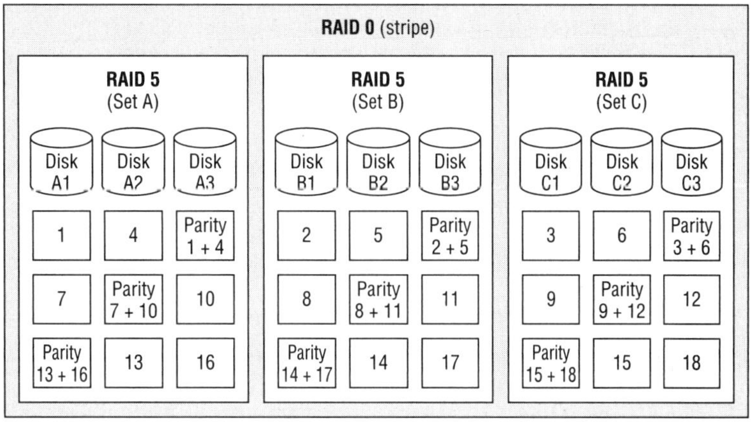

In Figure 3.6, we see a 6TB solution out of nine drives where again more than one drive can fail. A2 can fail and drive set A continues (as well as set B). A drive from set B or set C can also fail, and those RAID 5 arrays will continue as well. However, if any two drives in the same array (A, B, or C) were to be offline at the same time, then that array would be offline. Unfortunately, this will take down the entire RAID 0 striped set because one of its unique components is now offline.

CONCURRENT DRIVE FAILURES

Two drives likely won't fail simultaneously, just concurrently. When considering what might happen when more than one drive fails, don't build your plan based on the assumption that you will have two drives that fail simultaneously. Even with multiple drives with similar serial numbers and build dates, it is highly unlikely that they will fail at the same time. If two drives were to fail simultaneously, that would probably be due to a bigger problem related to the power, backplane, or controller level and not the drives. Only then is it likely that more than two disks will be affected, whether immediately or soon after.

What you are protecting against is concurrent failures, where the first disk fails on Monday and you are still waiting for its replacement when another disk fails on Thursday as a completely unrelated event. Even worse would be a scenario where one disk fails on Friday night and another one on Sunday afternoon. That will cause a real "Monday" for you! By keeping at least one, if not more, spare disks within our inventory, you can mitigate much of this. Having at least one hot spare in the system can help alleviate some of your troubles, and keeping a second or third spare on a nearby shelf can mitigate the rest. When disk 1 fails, the hot spare replaces it and the environment is self-healed. By exchanging your first failed drive with a cold standby from the shelf, it becomes your new hot standby if a second production drive fails in the future. And then, of course, when you take one off of the shelf, you'll want to order a new one — and the process continues (and the storage remains spinning).

Real World Scenario

Don't Sigh with Relief Until the RAID Rebuild Is Complete

Here is an unpleasant anecdote of mine that I hope you might learn from. It took place early in my career when RAID was not yet an assumed standard.

A disk within an array had failed, but the RAID set kept going. We put in a spare drive and started the rebuild. Everything was going fine, until a second drive failed too and, with it, the array.

As discussed, it is relatively unlikely that two drives will fail concurrently unless something else in the system caused the primary drive failure and affected the others, such as a firmware upgrade or electrical issue within the array cabinet. There is another potential contributing factor: inordinately high I/O.

One day, while I was overseeing a server farm, one of the servers did have a drive failure in its RAID array. We were relieved that RAID kept the array going and very soon after put in a replacement disk from our cold storage to start the rebuild. I was overly proud that my mitigation plan appeared to work perfectly, including not only the RAID solution but the cold standby drive to ensure things were perpetually protected.

But I was overly aggressive in my zealous preparedness, so to protect against an error happening during the rebuild of the storage, I kicked off a tape backup of the volume. A full backup is a horrible enemy to data volumes. Essentially, a backup job tells the data volume "Give me all of your stuff, as fast as you can, so I can write it to tape."

So now, in the middle of a business day, my disks were rebuilding a RAID set while servicing a full backup. And the array went down hard. Today's storage controllers are much more mature, so I likely would not kick users off the production volume while RAID is rebuilding. Storage subsystems do not have to be babied during rebuilds. But I also wouldn't add inordinate additional I/O, nor would I rest easy until my rebuild status showed complete.

Choosing a RAID Level

After going through all the various RAID levels and their pros and cons, the key takeaway for this topic is that you are still solving a spindle-level failure. The difference between straight mirroring (RAID 1) and all other RAID variants is that you are not in a 1:1 ratio of production disk and redundant disk. Instead, in classic RAID 5, you are spanning perhaps four disks where for every N – 1 (three in this case) blocks being written, three disks get data and the fourth disk calculates parity for the other three. If any single spindle fails, the other three have the ability to reconstitute what was on the fourth, both in production on the fly (though performance is degraded) and in reconstituting a new fourth disk.

But it is all within the same array or storage cabinet or shelf, for the same server. What if your fancy RAID 5 disk array cabinet fails, due to the failure of two disks within a short timeframe, the power, the backplane, or whatever?

Slicing Arrays into LUNs

Imagine that in an actual physical storage cabinet on the left are 16 physical disk drives. However, the storage cabinet has taken the first five drives and created a RAID volume called a logical unit (LUN). The term LUN is a holdover from storage area network (SAN) terminology where each volume was identified by its logical unit number. Today, the term LUN doesn't imply an identifying number, but simply the logical unit of storage itself.

A LUN is a portion of the storage array that is offered to the server as if it was a single disk. When LUNs are created within the disk cabinet, the individual drives are no longer visible from the server or OS perspective. All that the OS might see from within the Disk Administrator console of Windows would be the three logical disks.

As an example, Figure 3.7 shows the physical view (left) and logical view of a storage cabinet with 16 drives (with each drive having 1TB of capacity):

- A RAID 5 set from the first five drives would yield a 4TB LUN (N – 1 drives times the capacity).
- Another five disks make up a second LUN, also with 4TB of capacity.
- Four more disks make up a third LUN, this one with 3TB of capacity.
- The remaining two disks are hot spares, prepared to replace a failed drive in any of the three LUNs, labeled LUN 0, LUN 1, and LUN 2.

FIGURE 3.7
Physical and logical views of the storage array

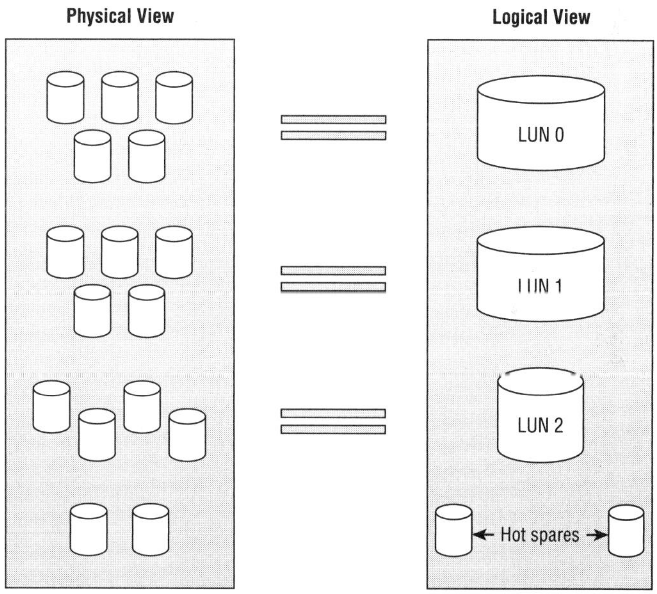

So, while the cabinet actually has sixteen 1TB drives in it, the usable storage capacity is the sum of the size of the LUNs, which would be 4TB + 4TB + 3TB, or 11TB of total storage, available to the server and OS.

Storage Level 2: Protecting Against Array Failure

At the storage level of a server, protection is all about real-time (synchronous) redundancy of components. In the previous example, we used RAID 1 or higher to provide redundancy of spindles so that a single disk drive failure does not become the SPOF for an entire server failing.

Now, we must think out of the box (pun intended). We need to think outside of the storage array cabinet and consider what would happen if the cabinet failed due to power, cooling, circuitry,

I/O bus, or multiple disk failures. In this case, we have two approaches: including redundant components in a high-end cabinet, or replicating the contents of the cabinet someplace else (such as another cabinet).

There are certainly storage array vendors who recognize that the array can be the SPOF within a server solution and have therefore gone to great lengths to mitigate the risk of failure of components within the array. For many of those vendors, redundant power supplies, redundant cooling, error-checking memory, and other resilient components eliminate many of the chances that the array will fail due to a component within it.

It is also not uncommon in such arrays to have provisions for hot spares within the drives, so that one or two spares may be identified and not actively spinning in production. At the first sign of a disk failure within the RAID configuration, the array may (automatically or manually) logically remove the failing or failed disk from the RAID set, power up the hot spare, and begin reconstituting the failed disk's data on the fly. I often think of this as changing a flat tire on your car with the spare in your trunk — while you are still speeding down the highway. Presumably, in the car example, you will stop at a convenient future time and have the flat tire replaced and put into your trunk. Similarly, one would presume that you would replace the failed disk with a new drive, and the new drive becomes the hot spare for the next failure. If you follow this pattern, your disk array may spin from the day that you power it up until the day you power it down for good, like driving a car on a never-ending highway. Where things don't look good for the car is when more than one tire has a problem, which is not impossible since most folks buy all four tires at the same time. The analogy works in the array too, but statistically not quite as precisely; when you first purchased the array, you probably got several hard drives from the same manufacturing batch. Interestingly, many arrays provide for multiple (usually just two) hot spares, which is analogous to two spare tires in the car. It's overkill to have two spare tires for a car that uses four, but it may not be overkill for a disk array with 16 slots to have two spares. The more disks in the array, the more likely that more than one will fail in a short period. Therefore, while this arrangement consumes a second parity disk, you might have two arrays at 7 disks each instead of one array with 14 disks. And either way, in a 16-slot chassis, those two hot spares start to look pretty reasonable.

Storage Level 3: Protecting Against Storage Node Failure

At some point, though, we can assume that the array or chassis will fail. There are two ways to protect against a failed chassis — either by redundancy and resiliency within the chassis, as described earlier, or by using two chassis or arrays.

In this case, you get two *intelligent* (they have their own controllers and microcode) storage arrays, almost always from the same vendor, and configure them to replicate with each other. Each vendor configures their arrays differently, so it isn't possible to cover the getting-started tasks here, but it is worth talking about *how* they replicate.

NOTE When you start adding descriptions to IT devices like *intelligent* or *managed*, you can usually replace those descriptors with words like *expensive*. This includes not only the appliances themselves, but also the replication and other management software.

The default configuration for two storage array chassis is synchronous replication, which behaves in a similar way as spindle-level mirroring or RAID 1. As disk blocks in chassis 1 are being written to, reciprocal blocks in chassis 2 are being written to at the same time. There are some differences, depending on what is controlling the replication.

Some folks will configure each chassis to appear as one or more logical disks, so in a chassis with 16 slots, you might have three RAID 5 arrays made up of five disks each, plus a single hot spare. The storage chassis then presents those three logical disks to the server as if they were three very fast, resilient disk drives, which is what would be seen in Windows Disk Administrator, for example. The individual disks, including the handling of the hot spare and the configuration of the RAID sets, is all handled through a controller within the storage cabinet. If you did this with two equally configured cabinets, you might choose to mirror logical disk 1 from chassis A with logical disk 1 from chassis B (see Figure 3.8):

Chassis A logical disk 1 ↔ first logical disk Chassis B

Chassis A logical disk 2 ↔ second logical disk Chassis B

Chassis A logical disk 3 ↔ third logical disk Chassis B

By doing the mirroring within Disk Administrator (as a software RAID-1 set within Windows), you can be assured that things are operating in a synchronous fashion and you likely won't pay for replication software from the array vendor. But, of course, nothing is free: you'll pay in CPU and I/O overhead in the server for having to handle the multiple writes and reads.

FIGURE 3.8
Array replication

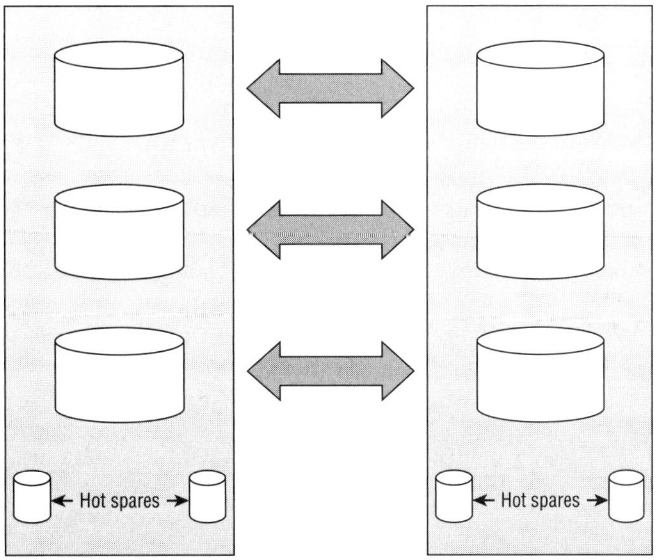

As seen in Figure 3.8, a 16 × 1TB storage chassis might present three 4TB LUNs plus have a hot spare, resulting in 12TB of usable storage.

To offload the disk handling where the server OS and hardware are managing the storage replication (as seen in Figure 3.8), we can introduce a SAN switch, which will connect the two storage arrays and the server together, as seen in Figure 3.9.

The fabric, which refers to all the cables and the SAN switch, connects the two arrays together and enables them to communicate with each other. Courtesy of the management and replication (if sold separately) software from the array vendor, the two storage chassis can handle the synchronizations and present themselves as unified storage. In Figure 3.9, the left diagram shows what it really is, while the right diagram shows what it looks like to the server hardware and operating system.

FIGURE 3.9
Array replication, within SAN fabric

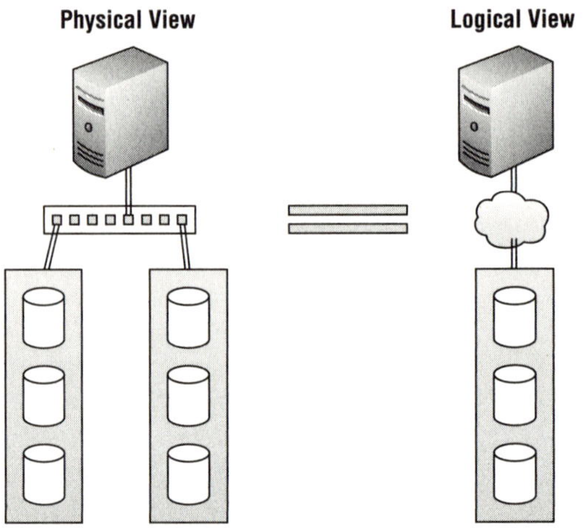

Storage Level 4: Protecting Against SAN Fabric Failure

We have a scenario where not only are spindles not a point of failure, but neither is any other single component of the storage chassis. But as we saw in Figure 3.8, there are still a few SPOFs in the storage solution related to the networking switch and the cables/interconnections to the storage chassis and the storage controller in the server (usually referred to within SAN terminology as a host bus adapter, or HBA).

As always, the answer to storage redundancy at any level is duplication. With most intelligent or managed storage solutions, such as SANs, we can do the following:

- Use redundant networking cables from the disk arrays in the fabric.
- Use two network switches to eliminate the SPOF.
- Use two HBAs (storage controllers within the server).

The ideal configuration is to have each of the two storage controllers within the server connect to a different SAN switch. Similarly, each disk array can be cabled into each of the two SAN switches. This type of configuration provides many combinations of paths from the server, through either HBA, through either network switch, to either storage array. The result is that if a component fails, there is still a pathway from the server to at least one array, which is resilient internally and has a complete copy of the data from its synchronous mirroring, as you can see in Figure 3.10.

This solution does not come cheap. In fact, it is not uncommon to pay inordinately more for the storage solution than for the rest of the server hardware, operating system, and server applications. But based on your RPO and RTO requirements (see Chapter 2), this may be what your environment needs: an assured "zero data loss" (RPO) and one part of a "zero downtime" (RTO) solution.

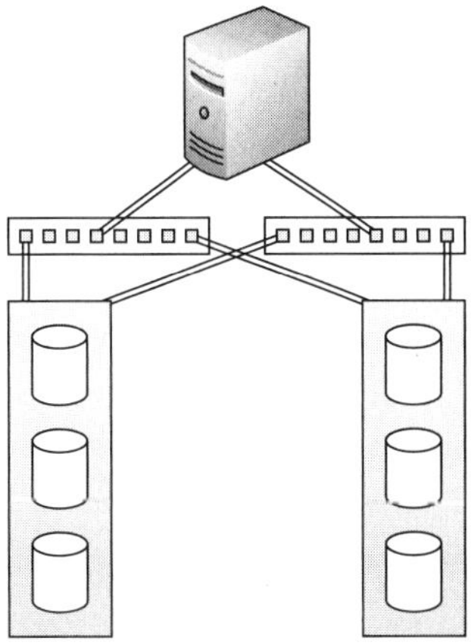

FIGURE 3.10
Completely resilient storage

How Disk-Based Communication Works

Before moving on to how the replication works, it is worth looking at how all of these components communicate with each other.

> **SMALL COMPUTER SYSTEMS INTERFACE (SCSI)**
>
> Early in PC networking, the language that became one of the standards for communication between disks and controllers was *SCSI* (pronounced "scuzzy"). As a standard, it means that any SCSI disk and any SCSI controller from various vendors ought to be able to interact with one another.
>
> Over the years, as technology advanced, new standards came about, such as SCSI 2 and SCSI 3. And while the cable types and connectors have changed, many of today's storage solutions for business are still based on the SCSI language between initiators (controllers) and targets (disks). SCSI, which uses parallel bit pathways within its circuitry, also has a variation, serial-attached SCSI (SAS), that sends the data serially.

The other main standard is advanced technology attachment (ATA), originally termed integrated drive electronics (IDE), which has also evolved from parallel ATA (PATA) into the serial ATA (SATA) disks that are in most desktops and laptops today. In traditional storage terms, namely from SCSI, the conversation between disks and controllers is termed as being between initiators (the host controllers) and the targets (the disks or array chassis presenting themselves as disks).

In the simplest of configurations, like a desktop computer, the solution has a disk controller (initiator) built into the system board and a single cable connects it to the one disk drive (target) in the PC chassis. That's all. Where things get more confusing is when storage arrays get involved, because storage is always about initiators controlling targets, whereas targets service I/O requests.

A storage chassis (array) is composed of disks, I/O interconnects, power supplies, and a storage controller, within the chassis. The storage controller serves two roles — upstream and downstream:

- Within the chassis, the controller is the initiator, which is serviced by the physical disks. The initiator manages the RAID configuration of the disks and communicates to the individual disks within the array.
- Outside of the chassis, the controller presents itself on behalf of the entire chassis as the disk (target) to the server's controller (initiator). In this way, the server and its operating system do not have visibility into the chassis. All that is seen by the OS is one or more SCSI LUN's, regardless of the layout of the physical disks within the chassis.

Using our earlier example of a 16-slot chassis, suppose you have a hot spare, along with three RAID 5 sets of five disks each. The controller inside the chassis will act as an initiator to all of the 16 disks in the chassis. But the chassis will be seen by the server hardware as simply offering up three target disks (secretly built from the three RAID sets), also referred to as three LUNs, as we saw in Figure 3.1.

This is not much different from a rigid company hierarchy, where your immediate manager is your initiator and sometimes you feel like a target. But to your director (the next manager up), the director is the initiator and your manager is seen as the target. All your director sees below is perhaps one team as a single resource or perhaps two–three functions within that team, like virtual disks presented from the arrays.

This same behavior is seen all the way up the chain as we look at the layers of storage protection that we just outlined. At each tier, there is an initiator talking to a target, and for the most part, what happens on the layers above or below is irrelevant to the conversation happening at that layer.

When we mirror two storage arrays from the server's perspective, as we did in Figure 3.8, we usually have either one or two initiators, depending on whether both arrays are plugged into the same disk controller in the server or separate channels. Those initiator(s) then connect to the two or more target LUNs. In Figure 3.1, we essentially mirrored the following:

Array A LUN 0 with Array B LUN 0

Array A LUN 1 with Array B LUN 1

Array A LUN 2 with Array B LUN 2

We did this through the operating system so the Windows Disk Administrator would see all six logical disks. But once the mirroring was configured, Windows Explorer and the other higher functions in the operating system would only see three disks (that are being transparently mirrored).

In contrast, when we mirror the same two storage arrays within the SAN fabric, as shown in Figure 3.10, the server's perception changes. Now, the arrays replicate between themselves, where the controllers inside the chassis are managing this. The reciprocal LUNs are being replicated between the arrays' controllers so the Windows Disk Administrator would only see the three LUNs (which are still transparently being mirrored). Figure 3.10 has the additional benefit of being resilient to a SAN switch or a server controller failing. Following the diagram, there are multiple paths from the server to the switches and from the switches to the storage. The technology that makes this seamlessly transparent to the server is called multipath I/O (MPIO).

Synchronous Replication in Storage

Each storage array vendor uses its own management interfaces, so it is not appropriate to give screenshots or commands in a book that is not devoted to SAN storage. But there are a few consistent operating methods that you should understand.

Replication can occur at multiple levels within the server stack:

Storage-Based Replication Occurs at a block level and is controlled by storage controllers and disk subsystems

Application-Based Replication Occurs between instances of the application, such as SQL Server database mirroring

Host-Based Replication Occurs between hosts (servers) or OS entities

Host-Based Storage Mirroring

When the host OS manages the storage mirroring, it means that the operating system is able to see both disks from the storage arrays, and the OS manages the writes and reads. Similar to how a server might see two internal disks and mirror them within the server chassis, the server could also see two external storage arrays and mirror them using the OS. The server OS sees them both and handles the mirroring by writing to both simultaneously and reading from either for better performance.

Array-Based Storage Mirroring

This scenario is a little more challenging because all the mirroring happens within the storage layers. This means that the server hardware and operating system see only one disk connected to the system, and the OS will read and write to that one disk like any other. Unbeknownst to the server operating system, a lot of extra moving parts are working within the storage system. While the array may behave like a disk from the OS's perspective, the array is not just a disk.

Data Movement Through a Server

Data moves through layers of the server, and each of these movements takes a relatively predictable, albeit asynchronous (not necessarily real-time), amount of time. Here are the fundamental steps that data takes as it moves through the layers of the server:

Applications talk to the OS. Applications request that I/O operation be done, and then receive the results of those I/O operations. As an example, while SQL Server sees a database and a log, the OS sees an MDF and an LDF file. The language between applications and the OS are APIs. As an example, the application might make an API call to `CreateFile` or write to a file that already exists.

The OS uses the file system to talk to the server hardware. In this step, SQL-transactional information is appended to the LDF file. Alternatively, sections of the MDF are written to by 4KB pages from the logical database. The language between the OS and the hardware is the driver. But specifically, the OS directs its instructions to the I/O Manager, as seen in Figure 3.11; these instructions are eventually received by the storage stack. (For more on the I/O Manager, see the section "How Application-Agnostic Replication Works" later in this chapter.)

FIGURE 3.11
The I/O Manager intersection

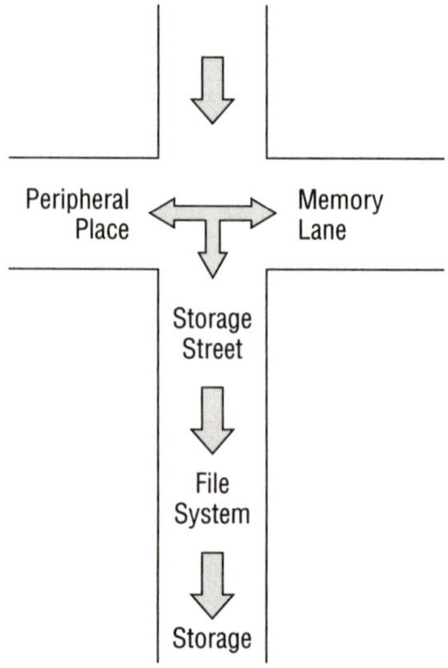

The server hardware talks to the storage. Next, every logical file within the file system is translated to a series of blocks. The server asks for operations to be done for particular disk blocks and then waits for the storage to confirm the write or service the read. The language between the hardware (controllers) and the storage is usually SCSI, which is facilitated by the hardware device drivers.

To the server, a mirrored array appears as and behaves like a single disk. But behind the scenes, there is some interesting work going on. Assume that an I/O operation goes the normal course with a single disk:

1. Data is created and moves from the application…
2. …to the operating system…
3. …to the hardware drivers for storage.

With a regular disk:

4. The write is sent from the disk controller to the disk.
5. The block is updated within the disk.
6. The disk acknowledges the write to the controller.

After that, everything is good as it bubbles back up:

7. The controller notifies the hardware drivers that the I/O was serviced.
8. The operating system (file system) notifies the app that the I/O was done.
9. The application continues with additional operations.

With mirrored storage, the first workflow (steps 1–3) and third workflow (steps 7–9) happen the same way. But the second workflow, where our single disk is actually a mirrored synchronous array, is more exciting. Steps 4–6 are replaced with the following:

- The write is sent from the disk controller in the server to the mirrored storage solution via the SAN fabric.
- Both arrays receive a copy of the I/O write request via either the controllers within the arrays or within the switches. This next step can vary by manufacturer, but most work off a similar method where the request is queued to confirm that both sides have it and it is staged to commit. In that case, once both have confirmed the IO instruction to be at the top of the queue, both arrays act on the disk write, they confirm with each other that both disk commits were successful, and the controlling logic is notified that both arrays have serviced the request.

How Arrays Communicate During Synchronous Mirroring

During the milliseconds where two synchronous arrays are servicing an I/O request, there is a dialogue between the array controllers in the chassis. It starts with Array A asking Array B, "I have it ready, do you?"

- With some vendors, Array B says, "Yes, I have it, too. Are you ready to write it?" Array A replies, "Yes, go ahead."
- With other vendors, Array B says, "Yes, I have it, too, and since you have already said that you have it, I am going to write it; you should too." And Array A replies, "OK."

Either way, now both arrays have serviced the request. Confirmations can also vary based on how the vendor controllers talk to each other.

With some vendors, both Array A and Array B independently report their confirmations of the disk I/O to whatever logic board (in the array, switch, or HBA) is driving the I/O upstream to the server. When the collection point receives both, it passes up the acknowledgment. This model is commonly in use when the solution components can also be used in an asynchronous manner.

What is more typical is where Array A knows that it has successfully serviced the I/O, but it doesn't tell anyone yet. Instead, because Array A knows that it was successful, it asks Array B, "Did it work for you?"

Array B acknowledges the I/O operation back to Array A by replying "Yes."

And Array A, now knowing that both sides were successful, acknowledges the I/O request to the higher-layer storage controllers on behalf of both arrays and reports that they both are ready to respond to the next I/O request.

This may seem a little overly simplistic, but the reality for our purposes is that the overhead in mirroring disks is not removed when the arrays perform it. Instead, the overhead is simply absorbed by the arrays, fabric, and controller logic.

What is more important for our topic is that because the two arrays must guarantee that every operation is serviced in tandem, the higher-order functions of the server, operating system, and application won't see a disk commit confirmation from either disk independently. Both sides have to act synchronously at all times, and they respond to service and confirmations as one.

Because of that, the reality is that most synchronous disk solutions have the two arrays in close proximity to each other in order to eliminate potential latency in communication between the arrays that would cause additional latency in the higher layers.

Because of the need to (a) separate the two arrays for site resilience purposes and (b) reduce costs from disk array–based solutions, asynchronous replication solutions have flourished. Although some storage arrays technically can do asynchronous replication, you can typically get the same performance using most of the same components (but often with a reduced cost) by simply choosing to replicate from the host's perspective and replicate *files* as opposed to letting the arrays mirror *blocks*.

File-centric Protection

With file-centric replication, the server transmits partial file updates from one server to another. For this discussion, we will ignore the file replication technology within Windows Server itself, namely DFS-R, as it is covered in Chapter 5. In this context, we are looking at host-based replication that is workload- or application-agnostic.

Application-Agnostic Replication

Application-agnostic implies that the data replication method is unaware of (or doesn't care) what kind of data is within the files that are being replicated. Literally, a huge file from Notepad is treated the same way as a SQL Server database MDF file, an Exchange Server database (EDB) file, or a virtual hard disk (VHD) file. They are all considered really big files with lots of zeroes and ones.

Application-agnostic replication (AAR) is both good and bad:

- The benefit of AAR is that for niche applications that do not have a replication capability of their own, AAR provides a viable way to replicate and protect those application files.
- The downside of AAR is that its behavior doesn't change based on the behavior or special needs of the application. Database files (MDF or EDB) and VHD files may all be big files, but they have different requirements for best protection.

Prior to SQL mirroring (covered in Chapter 6) and Exchange replication (covered in Chapter 7), these mission-critical workloads had no internal method for protecting their data other than expensive storage arrays with block-based replication. And although that was fine for large enterprises, it wasn't a cost-effective option for mid-sized businesses and mainstream companies. Host-based replication as a software solution solved that problem.

Common application workloads, such as SQL or Exchange, have developed internal mechanisms for replication and availability. The widespread applicability of AAR has diminished greatly. But because many applications do not yet have replication capabilities, AAR is worth discussing here.

How Application-Agnostic Replication Works

Software vendors will have their own variations on this, but in principle, most file-centric replication technology works in a similar way. One of the industry leaders, based on mindshare and longevity, is Double-Take from Double-Take Software. We will base our discussion on their method, although XOsoft WANSync or ARCserve Replication from Computer Associates, Replication Exec from Veritas, and others have similar mechanics.

Host-based file replication technology usually works by inserting a file system filter into what is called the intermediate file system stack. In the Windows Server operating system, there is a process called the I/O Manager. Think of the I/O Manager as a police officer who is directing traffic. For our analogy, all traffic comes from the top or north of the intersection (Figure 3.11). Depending on what kind of I/O it needs, the traffic cop will direct it to

- Accessory Avenue (west), for other peripherals
- Memory Lane (east), to the server's memory
- Storage Street (south), to the storage solution

Once the I/O is headed down Storage Street, the I/O requests are on their way to the file system (NTFS, in this case) and eventually to the storage controllers and finally the disk subsystems. What is important to understand is that Storage Street is an expressway with no additional exits, on-ramps, or off-ramps. What comes in the top of the file system stack will exit out the bottom and will still be intact and in order. However, the intermediate file system stack provides a way for other software to monitor what comes down the road, somewhat similar to toll gates on the expressway.

File System Filter Modes

The intermediate file system stack allows vendors to insert their filter technology like toll gates along this storage street. There are two kinds of filters or toll gates on our road:

- Some filters are *blocking filters*, like a toll booth with a gate, where you must stop and be inspected. With antivirus technologies, the filters stop I/O at the gate to verify that the files or partial-file updates are safe. If the file is safe, the gate opens and the file operations continue along the way to the storage drivers.
- Other filter drivers are *nonblocking filters*, like toll booths that scan you as you drive past without even asking you to slow down. Replication filters are nonblocking filters and allow file I/O to continue moving down the path with no interruptions at all. But they take a copy of the file operation as it passes through their gate.

Using our roads and gates example, most replication technologies deploy a file system filter that transparently monitors all file I/O as it traverses the file system stack. The filter (or agent) can immediately ignore all read type operations since they are querying what is already on the disk. Because no new data is coming down, there is no need to replicate reads. Interestingly:

- The behavior for a typical file server is 80 percent reads, 20 percent writes. So, the filter can immediately ignore 80 percent of the I/O of a file server.
- The behavior for a typical database server is 95 percent reads, 5 percent writes, with the filter again able to ignore the large percentage of reads.

Your performance will vary, but the key to remember is that the file system filter for replication technology is only interested in write or change type operations. For those, the filter makes a copy of the file I/O operation and allows the original I/O instruction to continue down the file system stack.

The captured transactions from the file system filter are then usually passed up from the filter, which operates in the OS kernel mode area, to a user-mode process, which is typically implemented as a system service. The service or user mode has additional intelligence to determine whether the file instruction is relevant and should be replicated. For example, most file-based replication technology allows the administrator to select only certain files or directories to be replicated. So, while the filter driver might capture every file write instruction, the intelligent process may only be interested in transmitting those operations related to specific files and directories.

Everything Goes Up, but Not Everything Goes Across

Consider what happens when software has a significant error while running within the operating system:

- Errors by applications running in *user mode* may in the worst-case scenario break that application, perhaps forcing the application or service to restart.
- Errors by applications running in *kernel mode* can cause the entire server to crash.

In addition, while user-mode memory is easy to allocate, many parts of kernel mode, including the intermediate file system stack, have a fixed-memory area, so it is important to keep kernel-mode modules as small as possible. For these reasons, most replication vendors that utilize a kernel-mode driver put as much of the operating intelligence into the user-mode part of their solution as possible. This ensures that your protection and/or availability solution doesn't crash the server.

The only downside is that the intelligence to discern whether or not a particular file write should be transmitted happens in the user-mode process. Thus, while every file read is ignored by the filter, every file write is sent up to the user-mode process. From there, only those file operations related to files that were selected for protection are then transmitted out of the source server to the target.

Network Queuing Modes

After the file I/O has been captured by the filter and passed up to the user-mode process/service that will transmit the I/O to the other server, the next step will vary by software offering.

- Some file-based replication technologies use an approach called *store and forward (S&F)*. In an S&F model, the file operations behave similarly to database operations, where each file instruction that is captured by the filter is first written to a journal or transactional file. Then, as the network is available, those operations are read from the journal and transmitted from the source server to the target server. After receiving a confirmation from the target server that the file instruction has been applied, the source server removes the instruction from the journal file. This behavior is somewhere between a to-do list with first in, first out (FIFO) characteristics and that of a perpetually applying log file or log shipping of micro transactions. Whatever metaphor you'd like to use, the reality is that for each write operation in the file system stack, the server will perform up to two additional writes, plus a read:

  1. Write to the journal.
  2. Read from the journal.
  3. Delete from the journal.

- Because of those I/O penalties, most replication technologies use a real-time replication model. In this model, as operations are captured from the file system filter, they are immediately queued for network transmission. As fast as the networking stack will allow, these I/O instructions are stored in memory as they are packaged and transmitted. Unlike the S&F model, this mode does not require any additional reads or writes. The I/O operations are transmitted as fast as the server process and network stack will allow. Something to note is how most real-time replication technologies will queue operations for a short time if the network is unavailable to send due to network congestion, other busy server processes, or an infrastructure failure separating the production server from the replica server. After a predetermined number of queued transactions, most real-time replication technologies will simply purge their queued transactions so that they do not continue to consume all of the server's memory. Unfortunately, without a journal or the queued transactions when the source and target servers are able to connect again, some kind of comparison must be done across the entire production data set in order to determine what has changed and resynchronize. This can be a I/O- and bandwidth-intensive process, so it is important that real-time solutions have predictably ample bandwidth and very few long-latency windows.

Applying the I/Os on the Target

Regardless of how the queuing happened, the rest of the process is fairly similar. The file I/O operations are encapsulated in networking packets and transmitted from the source server to the target server(s). On the target server, the service or application receiving the data is another legitimate user-mode process on the target server and simply submits its I/O requests like any other process (such as the production source server's applications) might. The result is the same file instruction (that was first applied to the primary copy of the file on the source server) is applied to a second copy of the file on the target server. The file instruction might appear something like "Go into file X and update bytes 1025–1096 with the following string". Because the target server has the same file already, it can apply the same file instruction to go into its copy of file X and update the same bytes with the same data string.

Protection and Availability

Like most near-real-time replication technologies, the typical-use scenario for file-centric, application-agnostic replication is availability, not protection. Because the replication occurs responsively and soon after the original file write occurs, it means that almost anything that occurs within the data of the primary server (source) will be replicated to the other servers (targets) shortly afterward. So, these technologies do not normally offer protection for the data other than the scenario of losing the primary server completely. In this case, the data will survive on the secondary server. But more often, the immediate response is that the secondary server fails over or somehow assumes the identity and functionality of the production server as an availability solution. This solution can be both elegant as well as dicey.

Identity Spoofing

As a result of either a manual decision or an automated threshold, the secondary server assumes the identity of the primary server. There are multiple methods for this, and the most common is to simply start responding to the Server Message Block (SMB) networking requests that are being sent across the network to the primary server's name, as well as the target server's original name. Similarly, the target server can adopt the IP address of the primary server if the two servers are on the same subnet.

Reverse ARP for Faster IP Spoofing

One clever trick that some of replication-with-failover solutions do with IP adoption is to "reverse-ARP" the primary IP address. In normal networking behavior, when a client tries to connect to a server using IP addressing, they look up the name of the server using Domain Name Service (DNS) or Windows Internet Naming Service (WINS) and are told of the server's IP address. After that, the client reaches out using TCP/IP and sends out an Address Resolution Protocol (ARP) request to any nodes on the same physical subnet that are using the server's IP address.

- If the client and server are on the same subnet, the server replies to the ARP request with its Media Access Control (MAC) address. The lower-layer networking functions in the client stack will cache the server's MAC address.
- If the client and server are not on the same subnet, the network interface card (NIC) within the router responds to the ARP request with its MAC address, since that is where the packets will need to be sent to eventually reach the server.

Either way, from that point on, the networking packets are sent to that MAC address within the client's cache.

When a server fails over for another, it can adopt the original server's IP address, but its MAC address will be different. The client machines will eventually figure this out by repeatedly trying to send packets to the old MAC address but eventually timing out. At that point, they send a new ARP request to make sure that nothing has changed. The new server responds with its MAC address, as if it had changed network cards — and everything continues normally.

The elegant trick that some replication technologies use is that when they adopt a new IP address, they proactively respond to the ARP request, as if it had just been sent. This updates all of the local caches with the new MAC address for the old IP address — which is kind of like sending out change-of-address notices when you move. Because the caches are updates as part of the failover, the clients immediately know where to connect, and the timeout lag is avoided.

File Share Resumption

Now that the target server is responding to the production server's name and IP address, it needs to resume doing what the primary server was doing. If the primary server is a file server, it simply shares the same directories. Because file-centric replication usually replicates the file attributes as well as the contents, everything is right there from permissions to access control lists (ACLs). And even if the directories are in a different physical location than they were on the production server, the shares can be created with the same names and no one will care. For example, a file share of `\\FS1\data` might physically be on FS1's `D:\data` directory, but on the target server it may be on `T:\fs1\d-drive\data`. But since the ACLs are preserved and the share name is the same, everything works fine.

This all sounds great — but why pay for replication of file shares and protection against failover when the Windows file system has built-in replication and availability for file shares? More on that in Chapter 5.

Application Service Resumption

If the production server was an application server, those application services need to be started on the target server and use the replicated data from the production server. This usually requires that the data files be replicated to identical locations (for example, `D:\sqldata` on the source should be replicated to `D:\sqldata` on the target), in case the application has internal pointers to where certain data is expected to reside. Often, this requires you to manually install the application(s) on the target in a configuration similar to how they were installed on the source so that the application will work the same way. The best application-agnostic replication solutions offer a wizard or other utilities to automate as much of this process as possible.

Regardless of how the preparation is done, if the primary server fails and the secondary server assumes the name of the IP and file shares, it will also start those pre-staged services and the application will resume.

If the application uses a transactional database, it may need to compare its databases and transaction logs, and potentially either roll forward or roll back transactions in order to get the data to a consistent state. This behavior is built in for those transactional applications because the same process will need to be done if a single application server (without replication) suffers a hard power outage and then is powered back up. The application is designed to be as resilient as possible, so this scenario validates the data and then brings the application and its data online.

Two points of consideration here:

- Large databases will take longer than small databases to bring online. And databases with suspect transaction logs or disparity will take longer than databases in a near fully committed state. The result is that your RTO (see Chapter 2) may vary by several minutes, but will assuredly not be near immediate.
- For applications that have built-in replication and availability solutions, there is little reason to pay for third-party software to do it — especially when the built-in mechanisms replicate data at a more granular level (less bandwidth is consumed) and fail over more quickly and in a more predictable fashion, often measured in seconds or less.

When to Use Application-Agnostic Availability

In the previous section, we asked the question, "If the production file and application services already have replication with availability features, why use application-agnostic replication and failover?"

Although it is true that DFS (Chapter 5); Exchange CCR, SCR, and DAG (Chapter 7); and SQL mirroring (Chapter 8) have usurped much of the need for third-party replication and failover technologies in regard to those particular workloads, there are still scenarios where the third-party solution makes sense:

- In the case of file services, DFS replicates changes every few minutes as files close, whereas third-party technologies may replicate data in near real time with the target only a few seconds behind even when the file remains open. If you have a business need where those few minutes of potentially lost data costs more than the $2,500–$7,500 (US) price of the third-party software, using a third-party continuous data replication product is a justifiable solution.
- There are certainly numerous applications, including many developed within your own environment, that use proprietary data sets and that do not have built-in replication and availability solutions. These application-agnostic solutions are perfectly suited for those types of proprietary applications because they do not have to be designed for that application. Be careful, though; many proprietary applications are built on a foundational platform like .NET and SQL Server. In that case, SQL mirroring may still be a better approach.
- Some of the application-agnostic, third-party vendors explain that their customers could use the built-in DFS, SQL, and Exchange protection and availability solutions, but because they also need the application-agnostic solution for their proprietary applications, they

prefer to deploy and manage only one replication and availability tool across their environment. Again, taking into account the significant price tag per server, you need to understand the ROI/TCO, weighing the management costs versus the software costs. Also, as most of the built-in technologies are now in at least their second generation, the management of the built-in availability solutions is usually seamlessly integrated into managing the application themselves.

As a comment on the industry overall (as mentioned in Chapter 2), often solutions that are demanded by customers are initially filled by third-party solutions like that of application-agnostic, host-based replication and availability solutions. As the platforms and applications mature, it is natural that those needs be fulfilled by the original vendor, as we've seen in SQL Server and Microsoft Exchange. It therefore becomes incumbent on the third-party vendors to continue to innovate and identify new customer needs that can be met by evolutions of their existing technology or new products.

The nimble vendors in the application-agnostic replication space have started to lessen their emphasis on protecting the applications that have native resiliency. They are now addressing needs like the following:

- Geographically distributed clusters, also known as geo-clustering, where all nodes need access to synchronized data
- Solutions that move servers from one hardware solution to another, or between physical servers to virtual servers, and vice versa (more on that in Chapter 9)

Application-centric Protection

So far in this chapter, we've looked at how storage can deliver data protection and availability because at that level, all data is essentially blocks. One principal challenge with storage-based data protection and availability is that it costs nearly the same to protect critical data as it does noncritical data, since everything is just blocks.

We've also looked at how file system–based data protection and availability has been delivered. By treating big Exchange storage groups as we would large SQL databases or super-large Microsoft Office documents, the replication software considers all of these data types as simply generic files. The good news is that everything is likely to be protected (or at least replicated). The challenge is how the application will deal with the replicated data during availability scenarios or whether the replication method is supported by the application at all. Because of this, we have seen a shift from maturing applications needing third-party file-based data protection and availability to features being delivered within the application or workload itself.

When your data is no longer generically protected as *blocks* or *bytes* or *files* but instead is treated the way that the application views it, data protection and availability is not quite as simple. In fact, that is one reason why this book was published. To answer the big questions, we've devoted four chapters to the major workloads that are now highly available within their own rights: file systems (Chapter 5), clustered OSs (Chapter 6), Exchange Server (Chapter 7), and SQL Server databases (Chapter 8). We'll also cover data protection in the traditional sense in Chapter 4. The latter half of the book then takes things to the next level.

To make a short story long, we couldn't have a chapter on layers of protection without acknowledging the application layer. Check out Chapters 4–9 for data protection and availability at an application level.

Where to Store Your Protected Data

Earlier this chapter, we discussed how your data can be protected and made more available within the primary server. Next, we'll look at another set of layers from a data protection perspective: what kind of media we should use to store our protected data.

Tape-Based Protection

Tape is not dead.

Tape as a protection medium is not going away. Tape gets a bum rap from most disk-based protection vendors. Somewhere in their zeal to convince you that tape was not enough and that disk-based protection was necessary, the industry got the message that tape was going away. I was a marketing guy for a disk-based backup solution in one of my past careers, so I was and am very much a proponent for disk-based backup. But before we go there, let's be clear that tape is not the enemy. Tape is not leaving the datacenter and will likely always be part of your data protection strategy. For the record, I am not a fan of most general claims like that one, especially in an industry where processing power and storage are nearly exceeding the laws of physics and industry expectation. There aren't many claims that you can always make in IT, but my guess is that using tape to back up is one of them.

Tape will always be part of an overall data protection plan because nothing does long-term retention better. What makes tape so suitable is the sheer simplicity by which you can take a tape out of a drive and put it on a shelf for an indeterminate amount of time usually measured in years.

I worry about measuring retention in double-digit years, not just because of the tape media, which has always had a reputation of failing after years, but because of the availability of tape drives that are suitable to read the media. But if you have a mandate to retain data for over 90 days, you will likely be using tape.

Aside from truly long-term retention, tape is also *king* when it comes to portability. Whether you need the data in your vault, in a courier's warehouse, or at your lawyers' desk, tape makes large amounts of information extremely portable. With no power requirements and a near universal ability to be read by any tape drive with the same form factor, there is no denying that tape has its place.

Disk-Based Protection

So, now that you know that I do not hate tape, let's talk about why disk is better for most scenarios except for those just discussed. Disk surpasses tape in two primary categories, which have driven every respectable backup solution to offer a disk-to-disk-to-tape (D2D2T) solution, or for those not using tape for retention, a disk-to-disk (D2D) solution. Those categories are

- Backup (protection) behavior
- Restore behavior

Real World Scenario

DOUBLE-DIGIT RETENTION (10+ YEARS) IS THE WORST KIND OF HARD

There are all kinds of policy makers out there. Some are politicians, statistical analysts, influencers of industry, or even just your own company's executives. And some of these folks have created mandates stating that you will keep your data for 10 years or 100 years. In principle, some of these concepts seem reasonable, such as keeping healthcare data for as long as the patient lives (plus some extended time after death for postmortems and estate affairs). It seems like a logical idea and I am sure that many pharmaceutical lawsuits influenced those policies — but how do you really do it?

If you check your storeroom or the back filing cabinets in the server room, you may find a computer catalog from at least five years ago, perhaps ten. But try finding a tape drive from today that will read tapes from ten years ago. Now imagine finding one of those tape drives ten years from now.

You could work out a plan to restore the key data every five years, and then back it up with current technology. But then you would wake up from your nap and realize how much procedural time that would take and that as an IT administrator, you don't have those cycles. Also, some of the mandates do not consider the copy to be defensibly valid because the data could have been altered, intentionally or erroneously, during the restore and backup processes.

Some institutions, when faced with the complexity and expense of keeping their data on nearline storage, have opted to implement a corporate policy of keeping no long-term backups at all. Data is kept on replicated disk for availability and server-rebuilding purposes (no more than seven days' worth), and nothing is kept for retention. As a standing policy, it got them out of their requirements.

Depending on what regulations your organization must comply with, this may not be an option for you. But at some point, it is better for IT to tell senior management that they can't do something instead of simply shrugging off a mandate that seems unachievable. That discussion either creates a new corporate policy or frees up budget so that IT can find a way to achieve the goal.

BACKUP BEHAVIOR

By design, tape backup solutions protect whole files. There is not a well-defined concept of storing byte- or block-level changes to tape media, with the exception of some database add-ons that can use tape in conjunction with transactional logging. Because of this, significantly more data is usually acted upon during backups to tape and therefore backup processes are relegated to nightly operations. Unfortunately, and as we've discussed in Chapters 1 and 2, most environments cannot justify the RPO that comes with nightly tape backup: losing up to half a day's worth of data. Because disk-based backups can usually act at a partial-file or data-object level, it is much simpler to capture less data in a shorter window of time. This results in an RPO that's far less than for daily backup. By having a media that enables more granular backups, secondary disk becomes an ideal first stage of data protection, whether for D2D2T in front of a tape solution or a D2D replication and/or availability scenario.

Recovery Behavior

Recovery behavior is actually the driving factor for adopting a D2D or D2D2T solution. Every analyst has his or her own stats whose specific numbers are different but whose conclusions are consistent:

- Most recoveries are of single files or objects. This is almost universal with the exception of *whole server* recoveries after a physical crisis.
- Most recoveries are for data less than 14 days old. Again, this statistic becomes even higher when *whole server* restorations are excluded, since they restore all the stagnant data as well.

With these two facts in mind, we can see that linearly accessed tape is not the optimal media to locate and restore single items that are only days old from a rapidly spinning strip of magnetically coated cellophane tape that is going between two spindles. In fact, tape drive manufacturers have an industry term, *shoe shining*, for when a tape must be rapidly and repeatedly forwarded and reversed in order to locate a particular location. Shoe shining is a leading cause of tape drive and tape media failure, as the drive seeks out the particular millimeter of tape that holds the requested data.

How Disk-Based Backup Works Today

Disk-based media is usually accessed as a random access device, whereby the file system can immediately identify the blocks required and provide them to the restore application. Using disk in this way has not always been consistently implemented. When tape backup software vendors were initially trying to figure out how to improve backup and restore speeds, some of them essentially turned disk into tape. What I mean by that is that the disk would store monstrously large BKF or other *virtual tape* files. Essentially, the tape backup software still thought it was managing a large capacity, linearly accessed tape medium, but the tapes were just files on the disk. Although this earlier method of treating disk like tape avoided shoe shining due to the better control of disk access, it still had some of the behaviors of treating a random access medium as a sequential medium by traversing the virtual tape (file).

There are good reasons to synthesize tape with disk, but deploying a D2D2T scenario where the data goes from production disk (the first D) to synthetic disk (the second D) to tape (T) is not one of them. The opposite approach is where you are in a D2D2T scenario (primary disk to secondary disk) but you want another layer of random access medium like a WORM (write once, read many) or removable disk medium. In this case, one of my favorite mechanisms is a product called Firestreamer by Cristalink, which creates a virtual tape device that uses disk storage. Firestreamer is covered in Chapter 4.

Today, most disk-based backup solutions use disk as disk, meaning that they do not try to utilize a random access medium like disk but treat it like a sequentially accessed medium-like tape. There are two different behaviors for how data is stored during disk-based protection based on the assumed percentage of data redundancy:

- If a majority of the data is presumed redundant, such as *bare metal recovery (BMR)* for large groups of Windows Servers, you can assume that the Windows OS is duplicated numerous times. Because of this, intelligent disk-based backup solutions will hold those files or file segments only once for duplication purposes. Each individual source that has those files or file segments just sees the files and segments that are relevant to that source. But by assuming a high degree of redundancy, storing the data on top of each other in a sort of consolidated file set can yield a significant amount of disk savings and efficiency.

- If a majority of the data is presumed to be unique, such as protecting application and perhaps file servers, the disk-based storage will often mimic the original file set, including directory trees and permissions or attributes. By storing the data in its native format, you can make restore actions as simple as copying the file from the replicated store back to the production server.

Once the data has been protected from production disk to secondary disk (D2D), additional layers of protection can be added, such as the following:

- Using snapshots for previous points in time
- Using tape (D2D2T) for longer-term retention
- Using a cloud (D2D2C) for offsite or outsourced retention

Cloud-Based Protection

In the previous two scenarios, the roles (and order) of tape and disk were fairly straightforward with three logical patterns, from disk (D):

- Protection to disk only = D2D
- Backup to tape only = D2T
- Disk to disk (for faster recovery) to tape (for retention) = D2D2T

Cloud-based, or service-based, protection changes the model and can be included in your data protection plan in various ways, based on the business model:

- Straight to the cloud = D2C
- Straight to the cloud, and then backed up to tape = D2C2T
- Replicated to on-premise disk first, then to the cloud = D2D2C
- Replicated to on-premise disk first, then to the cloud, and finally backed up to tape = D2D2C2T

The goal with software as a service (SaaS) offerings such as cloud-based backup is to determine whether that service will be implemented instead of or in addition to your on-site delivery. While it is too early to tell in mainstream environments, early adopters seem to be falling into two distinct camps:

D2D2C2T This approach is particularly interesting to larger companies that wish to deploy disk-based protection on-site with cloud-based retention off-site for a *subset* of the data. Many businesses are finding that strategy to be cost effective; they are choosing only a subset of the most critical data to be sent to the cloud facility. This gives the local administrators the ability to recover anything for perhaps 30 days but retain the business-critical information for up to a year or longer. For those kinds of long-term retention windows, the client may presume that the service provider is storing the data on tape, but as it is a service and not a burden to the client to maintain, do you really care how? You definitely care that they can restore the data in a way that satisfies your business needs as well as your compliance and retention directives. But whether the service provider stores your data on disk, tape, DVDs, or holographic film is mostly out of your realm, as long as the provider can deliver the restore in a usable way or agrees to financial penalties or perhaps even indemnification if the data is not restorable. As long as the data is assured to be restorable for up to whatever your retention requirements are, the service provider's media choice may be irrelevant (other than ensuring their reliability). We will cover this topic more when dealing with disaster recovery topics in Chapter 12.

Straight to Cloud (D2C) For small businesses, the idea of completely offloading tape backup, which is perceived as a burden, can be a compelling scenario. In these cases, the overworked IT administrator can simply install an agent on the production resources and pay a service fee every month. While not having as many restore scenarios and not having any restore capability within the company can be somewhat daunting at first, the relief of outsourcing your backup can be compelling.

Things to consider when choosing the cloud-based component of your data protection include the long-term credibility of the provider, your retention requirements and budget, and your anticipated recovery scenarios.

What Is Your Provider's Long-Term Credibility?

Regardless of contracts, service-level agreements, or customer service mandates, the reality is that no one outside of your organization cares as much about your data as you and your company do. And if you are reading this book, it is likely that no one within the company cares as much about recovering your data as you.

With that in mind, while it can certainly be liberating to offload your data protection (backup) management, here are two keys to your personal success:

- "Inspect what you expect" is an old saying that certainly applies for folks new to service provider engagements. Take some of the time that you have just reclaimed by not doing so many routine backups and restores and plan for ad hoc restore testing on a regular basis. Randomly identify a data source and try to restore it using whatever process or personnel as will be asked to do it for real. If it is a database, work with the DBA to verify that the restore was viable and successful. If it is a file server, randomly select a few users whom you know have recently created new material and verify that their items are successfully restorable.

- Choose a provider who understands data vaulting. Technically, this one should be the first of the two, but I didn't want the "inspect what you expect" to be dismissed by picking a supposedly reputable vendor. The key here is to pick a vendor who understands your business and/or data model (for example, a Health Insurance Portability and Accountability Act [HIPAA]–specific vaulting provider for healthcare clients) or one who understands the business and technical requirements of vaulting (not just backup), such as Iron Mountain. We will talk more about regulatory compliance, as well as vaulting solutions, in Chapter 12.

What Are Your Retention Requirements and Budget?

Your retention requirements may drive you to or from a service-based backup (cloud). For example, if you are mandated to keep data for seven years but the only cloud-based providers that are available to you (due to factors like locale and budget) cannot provide a seven-year retention window, then the cloud isn't a comprehensive solution for you. It may be that you still need to use tape to satisfy your seven-year window but choose a cloud-based vault for disaster recovery purposes. Or you might need to work out a nonstandard service contract with the provider of your choice to do tape backups for seven years, even if their normal service has a one-year window. But looking back to the last section regarding choosing the right vaulting vendor, if they can't do long-term tape backup and that is a requirement for you, they likely aren't the right vendor for your scenario.

On the other side of the discussion, you may have a mandate that your data be retained by a trusted guardian (a third party that does not have a vested interest in your data) rather than its protection and restoration features. This kind of mandate is usually found in some interpretations of industry compliance regulations. Notice I said *interpretations*. I have not seen a regulation that actually mandates it in clear language (although your senior executive and head lawyer may have read in between the lines with a bigger goal in mind). If that is the case, cloud-based protection is at least part of your solution.

Your budget can also impact this decision thread. If your financial executive would rather pay for a service rather than capital assets (hardware), depreciable assets (software), and labor (to manage everything), then cloud becomes a compelling scenario, even if the total annual costs are exactly the same or even slightly higher. In this case, tax advantages may be the trump card that sends your data to the cloud. On the other side of the discussion, while you might have originally wanted to send everything to the cloud, you may find that most providers bill their services against the amount of data protected. Based on your budget, it may not be practical to protect everything to the cloud. Instead, this may drive you back to a D2D2T/C model, where everything is protected using an on-premise disk and only a critical subset of the data is sent to the cloud.

What Are Your Anticipated Recovery Scenarios?

If you expect to regularly do lots of minor restores and need to do them from a centralized console, like a corporate help desk, a cloud-based solution will not be your primary recovery media — disk will. Similarly, if you routinely have issues with your hardware and expect to do whole-server recoveries, cloud should not be your primary recovery media — disk should. If either of these applies to you, you are looking for at least D2D2C.

- If you will be doing your own tape backup, you use D2D2CT.
- If the service provider is doing the tapes, you use D2D2C2T.

However, if you use reliable hardware and earnestly are looking for fewer recovery actions but want an outsourced model, cloud-based backup was built with you in mind!

Use Each Media Type for What It Does Best

If you are looking for a magic formula that will specifically dictate what kinds of media you need and why, I can't give it to you. What I hope that I've done is clearly lay out the key considerations and ramifications for each data protection layer so that you can start a meaningful conversation with the other key stakeholders in your recovery planning. Once you understand your recovery goals (and budget), the choices should start becoming more apparent. The key takeaway for data protection media is to use each media type for what it's best at while it is mapped against your recovery goals.

Don't pick your data protection solution (software/hardware) and then start determining and communicating what your recovery capabilities are. Turn that discussion around. Decide what your recovery goals are and let the media pick itself. Then, validate the media and tiers against the considerations that I offered earlier in this chapter:

- Disk is best suited for routine restores or restores where performance is especially important, and is the best way to improve the granularity and frequency of your protection activity.
- Tape is best suited for long-term retention or where recovery speed isn't as important as the incremental cost of storing ever-growing amounts of data.
- Cloud is best suited for predisaster recovery vaulting, as well as compliance-mandated backups and general outsourcing of the backup burden.

Summary

In considering the layers of protection, we need to look at layers within the production server(s) and the protection platform. In the production servers:

- Disk or storage-based solutions are designed predominantly around storage performance. As a secondary benefit, most architectures provide for protection of one or more physical spindles within the storage array. This does not *protect* the data from a backup definition, but it does *ensure* its accessibility to the higher-layer server hardware and OS/application functions.
- File-based replication can be a powerful way to provide near-real-time replication and availability. Its availability benefits are gradually being usurped as the primary applications deliver faster, cheaper, and arguably superior availability within the applications themselves. But for applications that cannot be made available by themselves, this always has had and likely will continue to be a great solution.
- Application-centric data protection and availability is where each application deals with things separately. This topic is covered in Chapters 5–8, and the advanced scenarios are explored in the latter part of the book.

As for the layers or choices of media within the data protection platform, the primary goal is to use each medium based on what it is best suited for and in alignment with your recovery goals:

- Disk for fast recovery, particularly of single items
- Tape for long-term retention where shelf life and portability are key
- Cloud for service-based delivery or when using a third-party provider has other benefits

Chapter 4

Better Backups

In the first three chapters, we talked about disk-to-disk backups, where tape is still a good solution, and discussed how cloud solutions are changing the game. In this chapter, we'll cover three key topics related to making better backups:

- Volume Shadow Copy Services (VSS), the internal plumbing within the Windows operating system that enables better backups across workloads and applications
- The built-in backup utilities within Windows Server 2008 and 2008 R2, which are worth a fresh look
- The Microsoft backup solution, System Center Data Protection Manager, an example of where the next generation of data protection is headed in the modern Windows datacenter

For our hands-on activities in this chapter, we will perform several tasks with DPM 2010:

- In Tasks 1–3, we will get started using DPM 2010.
- In Tasks 4–5, we will protect different kinds of data.
- In Tasks 6–12, we will look at how various applications and workloads require various restore capabilities.
- In Task 13, we will extend our backups across datacenters for disaster recovery capability.

Solving the Problem from the Inside Out

For the first 10 years that Microsoft was shipping a Windows server operating system, you could say that they had a mentality of "If we build it, someone else will back it up." It wasn't that Microsoft had abdicated responsibility for protecting your data. They had included a functional utility that was best used for ad hoc backups on a periodic basis. (The utility was a licensed subset of Backup Exec when it was still Seagate Software, before Veritas acquired it, which was also before Symantec acquired it.) Backup Exec is still a market-leading product for Windows-based backup—arguably, in part, due to the easy transition from the built-in utility (which could have been termed Backup Exec Lite) to the full product (which includes application protection, scheduling, and media-change management).

In fact, the lack of a full-featured backup solution in the Windows operating system created a complete partner ecosystem and industry around protecting Windows data. This model had worked for the last leader in PC networked servers (Novell NetWare), so Microsoft followed suit. And for nearly 10 years, that was sufficient.

But by the early 2000s, things were beginning to change (primarily within the applications) and in two different directions:

- Supportability
- Reliability

Real World Scenario

THE SUPPORTABILITY GAP DURING BACKUP AND RESTORE

To illustrate a common example of the disconnect that has hampered many Windows environments when it comes to protecting and recovering advanced applications like Microsoft Exchange Server, here is a customer anecdote with the names changed to protect the guilty.

Contoso Company was happily backing up their Exchange servers with Acme Backup v6.0. Everything was going great until their Exchange server failed and the restore from the backup failed.

1. The IT administrator called Acme Backup technical support, who then read through the event logs and confirmed that the backup logs showed that the backups were completed successfully.
2. Acme's support confirmed that the restore completed successfully, thus absolving Acme of any responsibility. They recommended that their customer call Microsoft customer support, assuring them that the failure was likely due to Microsoft Exchange, or possibly Microsoft Active Directory, which Exchange relies on.
3. The Contoso IT administrator then called Microsoft support, who (after their best effort) came to the conclusion that the customer likely did not have good data for Exchange to recover with.

The result was that the customer—and likely their reseller/integrator partner who originally installed Exchange and the backup application—were stuck in the middle without their data.

Both Microsoft and the backup software vendor gave their best effort to support, and both reasonably concluded that the other vendor was at fault. Unfortunately, in most cases the backup vendor can't or won't tell Microsoft about their particular method of backing up the data, and in some cases, Microsoft can't ask. No matter how the conversation takes place, the result is the same: a failed Exchange server recovery.

This issue was so prevalent that some application teams, including Microsoft Exchange, ended up publishing support advisories on what they could and could not support related to third-party backup solutions. See Microsoft Knowledge Base article 904845 (`http://support.microsoft.com/kb/904845`), "Microsoft support policy for third-party products that modify or extract Exchange database contents," which details the mandatory characteristics of backup and recovery solutions in order to receive Microsoft support for an Exchange deployment.

Supportability and Reliability in Legacy Backup Solutions

In the early days of Windows application backup, most backup vendors had to deduce their own methods of backing up each data source, such as Microsoft Exchange or SQL Server. This often led to reverse-engineering or other unsupported methods of backing up and restoring the data.

And the unfortunate result was that Microsoft's customers and partners were often stuck in supportability issues that fell into a gap between the original application vendor—Microsoft is one example—and the various tape backup software vendors.

Similarly, while your legacy backup solution might successfully protect a standalone Exchange 2003 server, it might have challenges with Exchange Server 2007 in a CCR or SCR environment, or DAG in Exchange 2010 (see Chapter 7 to learn about Exchange data protection capabilities). Or perhaps your legacy solution was reliable for protecting a standalone SQL Server platform but faces challenges when backing up the distributed components of a Microsoft SharePoint farm (much of which is built upon SQL Server). The specific applications are not the issue; the issue is recognizing that most general-purpose backup solutions are designed to be extensible and flexible in backing up a wide variety of data sources. That makes sense, as a third-party vendor is interested in backing up as many potential data sources as possible. But the general-purpose architecture between the agent and the back end may have difficulty in supporting more advanced workloads, particularly when the workload or application is distributed across multiple physical data sources.

How Microsoft Addressed the Issue

Microsoft recognized that not having a reliable or supportable backup solution for key applications like Exchange or SharePoint or its virtualization platforms was limiting some customers' willingness to fully deploy the new platforms. After all, if you are going to put all your eggs in one basket, it better be a good basket.

With that in mind, Microsoft had to find a way to enable more reliable backups and recoveries of their core applications and deliver those capabilities in a way that would help assure customers and partners of supportability. In this chapter, we will look at evolution of three Microsoft technologies that help deliver better backups:

1. Better backups begin with Volume Shadow Copy Services (VSS), which was delivered as part of Windows Server 2003. We will cover VSS in the next section, but to continue our story, Microsoft had to do more.

2. A better way to protect the whole machine, not just the data, was needed still with the mandate of assured reliability and supportability. The result was a new built-in backup utility that was different from what had shipped since the beginning of Windows. Out went NT Backup and in came what we will cover later in the section "The Windows Server Backup Utility."

3. However, some legacy backup products do not or cannot leverage VSS, in part due to their heterogeneous architecture. To ensure that Windows customers had a reliable and supported way to back up key workloads such as Exchange, SharePoint, and Hyper-V, Microsoft delivered its own full-featured backup solution for Windows environments, which we will cover later in the section "System Center Data Protection Manager."

Volume Shadow Copy Service (VSS)

Delivered initially in Windows Server 2003, and every Windows operating system afterward, the *Volume Shadow Copy Service* (*VSS*) provides a consistent set of mechanisms that backup vendors and application vendors (including Microsoft) can follow that assures a supportable and reliable backup and recovery. VSS is a software service within the Windows operating system that coordinates various components in order to create data-consistent shadow copies of one or more volumes.

A *shadow copy,* sometimes referred to by vendors as a *snapshot,* is a collection of blocks on the disk that are effectively frozen in a specific point in time. But instead of the shadow copy being invoked at random times and without regard to what state the data is in, VSS provides a coordinated way to invoke a shadow copy of data when the data is in an application-consistent state.

Instead of each backup vendor having to independently reverse-engineer or otherwise figure out how the backups should be done, VSS provides a set of APIs that any backup vendor can invoke. Similar APIs are available to any application vendor in order to define how their application should be backed up. These components are called VSS writers and requestors.

VSS Writer

A *VSS writer* is developed by the application or platform vendor as a component of that application or OS platform. The VSS writer defines how the application or platform should be backed up. This allows the application development team to define a supportable way for the application to be backed up. If the backup solution uses VSS, the application development and support teams do not have to be concerned about how the data is being backed up or how the restore will be accomplished. Not only is reliability increased, but the customer and partners will not be stuck in a supportability gap since the backups and restores will be done in a way that was defined in accordance with the application team's wishes and design.

VSS Requestor

A *VSS requestor* invokes the backup process on behalf of the backup software from any given backup vendor. An example might be the DPM Protection Agent (covered later in the section "How Does DPM Work") or the agent from any other traditional backup vendor. Instead of each backup vendor creating their own software that interacts directly with Exchange (or any other production application or platform), the backup vendor simply needs to architect its agent to communicate with VSS, which in turn will communicate with any VSS writers that are currently running in a production server.

VSS Provider

The third component of VSS is the *VSS provider,* which creates and maintains the shadow copies. VSS providers can be delivered in hardware storage arrays, as software-based providers, or included with the Windows operating system. These VSS components work together through the Volume Shadow Copy Service, as seen in Figure 4.1.

FIGURE 4.1
Volume Shadow Copy Services (VSS)

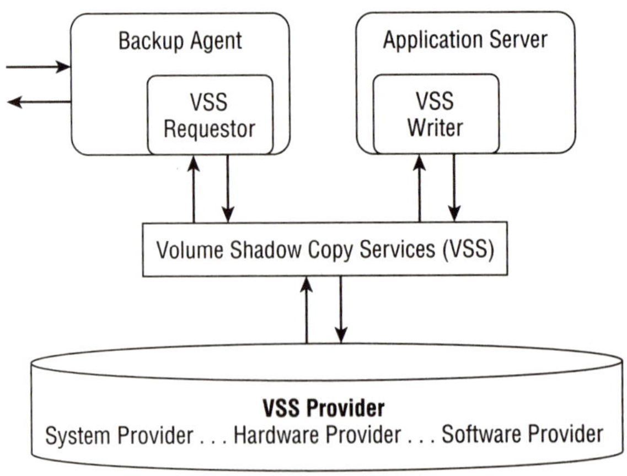

THE *VSSadmin.exe* COMMAND-LINE TOOL

From any administrator-level command prompt, you can run `VSSadmin.exe` with additional parameters to list which writers or providers have been registered with the operating system and the VSS service. Additionally, you can do maintenance on the resizing of the ShadowStorage volume or delete previous shadows. Typing `VSSadmin` without parameters will list the available commands, including these:

```
VSSadmin Delete Shadows
VSSadmin List Providers
VSSadmin List Volumes
VSSadmin List Writers
VSSadmin Resize ShadowStorage
```

How VSS Backups Work

Now that we have all the parts, we can look at their interaction in delivering a shadow copy that is useful and supportable for application backups. In this example, we can use Exchange 2007 running on Windows Server 2008 as the production server, with Data Protection Manager (DPM) as the backup software. For a complete understanding of data protection and data availability for Microsoft Exchange, read Chapter 7. For this discussion, we are simply backing up the Exchange data as an example of a VSS-enabled backup.

Before the Backup

Before the first backup ever happens, two things will have occurred:

- All of the VSS writer components of software running on the production server register themselves with VSS. We can see this by running `VSSadmin List Writers` from a command prompt on the production server, which in this example will include the Microsoft Exchange VSS writer.
- Later, when initially configuring the backup job, the backup agent (DPM in this case) will ask VSS for an inventory of all the registered VSS writers, and thereby identify what is able to be backed up. The agent may also look for non-VSS-capable backup sources in the same process. The system administrator would then configure the backup of Exchange for some schedule in the future.

With the backup software now configured to protect Microsoft Exchange on a regular schedule, everything waits for the backup to begin.

Phase 1: The VSS Requestor Requests a Backup

Here is the sequence of events during a VSS-enabled backup of a data source like Microsoft Exchange. It occurs in multiple phases, centered on the VSS requestor, the VSS writer, and the backup server itself.

1. The backup application, DPM in this case, determines when it should next do a backup. At that time the DPM server reaches out to the DPM agent running on the Exchange server.

2. The DPM agent includes a VSS requestor, which interacts with the Volume Shadow Copy Service running in the Windows Server OS on the production server. Specifically, the requestor asks VSS which VSS writers are available or whether a particular writer is available.
3. VSS will confirm to the VSS requestor (the DPM agent) that a VSS writer for Microsoft Exchange is available, and the VSS requester is instructed by VSS to wait until the data is in a consistent state.

Phase 2: The VSS Writer Ensures Data Consistency

With the backup agent and VSS requestor now standing by, an internal backup can now be done:

4. VSS instructs the VSS writer within the application to do its process to make the data consistent. Depending on the application or workload, this may involve applying transaction logs into the database or other preparation. As an example, in the case of Microsoft Exchange, the writer flushes any pending transactions and freezes write I/O to the databases and logs on the volume(s) to be backed up. When the writer has completed this operation, it signals VSS to continue. Different applications will perform different operations in order to prepare their data to be backed up, but the key takeaway is that VSS provides a common framework of interaction from the backup agent to the application, so that the application does whatever it needs to do, and then the process continues.
5. When the data is determined to be in a suitable state, the VSS writer notifies VSS that the data is ready to be backed up.
6. VSS uses a VSS provider (either hardware or software based) to create the shadow copy of the volumes where the data resides. This shadow copy effectively freezes the logical blocks that make up the data source on those volumes. This creates two perspectives of the disk blocks: a frozen instance for use by the backup software and the live instance the application continues to use in production. We will discuss this copy on write functionality in more detail later in the section "The Power of Copy on Write."
7. After a shadow copy has been successfully created by the VSS provider, VSS notifies the VSS requestor (agent) that the shadow copy is available. It also notifies the VSS writer that it has the data copy. The application can then return to its production state.

Phase 3: The Backup Itself

With the volume now providing a frozen set of blocks delivered in a shadow copy, the backup software can now do what it needs to do for streaming the data to the backup (DPM) server.

8. The backup software begins its process of identifying the files, bytes, or blocks that need to be sent from the production server to the backup server. This may take seconds or hours, depending on the kind of backup software, what type of backup is being done, and how much data is involved. More specifics on how DPM does this will be covered later in the section "How Does DPM Work."

When the backup is complete from the perspective of the backup software, the post-backup operations can occur.

9. Upon a successful backup, the application may wish to do its own maintenance processes. In the case of Microsoft DPM and Microsoft Exchange, DPM runs the `ESEUTIL.exe` process on its copy of the database (instead of the production instance), which validates the integrity of its disk-based backup. Upon notification of a successful integrity check, Exchange then updates its database and may truncate its logs to show that a backup has been successfully completed. Other backup software and other production applications may have other behaviors.

10. With the backup complete, the shadow copy on the production storage volume may no longer be desired. In that case, the backup agent using its VSS requestor will notify VSS that the backup has successfully completed, and VSS will delete the shadow copy from the VSS provider's storage pool. This ensures that no long-term disk space is consumed by the backup process.

The Power of Copy on Write

What makes the shadow copy so effective is that the blocks that make up the data source are frozen for the purposes of the backup software and its VSS requestor. The actual blocks on the disk that make up the data at the point in time that the backup was taken will not be overwritten, which allows the backup software to then do what it needs to do without being hindered by changing data within the application itself. However, the production application is not dormant during this time, and there is no perceived downtime by the system or the users. The challenge happens after the shadow copy is created and ready for the backup software to do its process: what happens if data is changing while the backup agent is streaming its information to the backup server?

To handle this, VSS uses a model called *copy on write* (COW) to ensure that data can be changed in real time by the production application but still remain frozen to the backup software.

- For any disk block in the data set that is not changed during the backup, there are no challenges. The backup agent simply reads those disk blocks and acts accordingly.
- But for any disk block in the data set that the production application attempts to write to, VSS uses COW to create two disk paths. Instead of the original block being overwritten, an alternative disk block receives the writes instead, hence the term *copy on write*.
    - The production application transparently sees the new disk block and its data, and is unaware that the anything is different.
    - The VSS requestor and the backup agent see the old disk block as part of the shadow copy creation.

In Figure 4.2, we see five blocks of data that are being protected by a VSS-enabled backup solution. Block 4 has been updated by the application, so the application sees the new block 4, whereas the backup agent continues to see the original block 4 that was provided by the shadow copy.

This separation is what enables the backup software to act in its own manner and perform its tasks without causing downtime to the production server. As discussed in Phase 3, after the backup is complete the VSS shadow copy is usually removed, so the old disk blocks that had been duplicated due to COW are simply deleted and the space is available again.

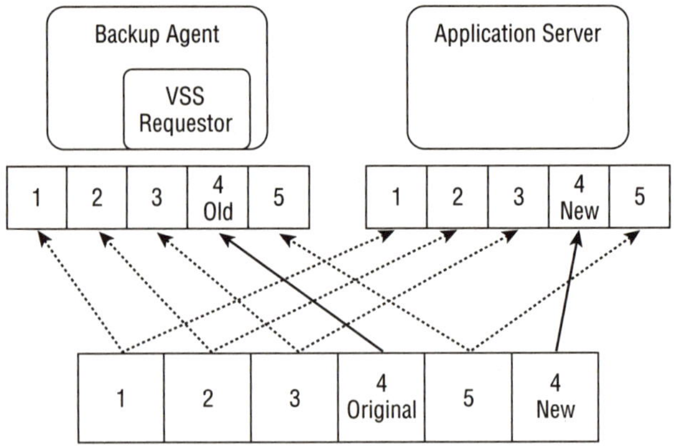

FIGURE 4.2
Copy on write, with block 4 changed

PLANNING FOR DISK CONSUMPTION DURING COPY ON WRITE

Copy on write can use a lot or a little disk space. How much is strictly dependent on the rate of change for the data during the backup itself:

- If little to no data is changing during the backup itself, then little to no space will be required.
- If a great deal of data is changing during the backup itself, then VSS will consume disk space equal to the size of blocks that are being duplicated.

Backup software like DPM only uses the shadow copy temporarily, so the disk blocks will be returned as free space after the backup has successfully completed. But you still need to plan for the potential disk consumption if you intend to do VSS-based backups during a busy period of the day.

The Windows Server Backup Utility

As discussed earlier, Microsoft's first significant step to improving the reliability and supportability of protecting data in its Windows environments was to create VSS to intermediate between backup software and production applications and data. The next step was to redesign the built-in backup utility that is provided with the Windows operating system.

From Windows NT 3.1 through Windows Server 2003 R2 (including most of the Windows client platforms), the built-in backup utility called *NTBackup* had not dramatically changed, even though the data and applications had. Windows Server 2008 introduced a new utility called *Windows Server Backup* (WSB).

WSB is an optional component in Windows Server 2008 and 2008 R2. You install it from Server Manager by using the Add Features Wizard; this includes the WSB itself as well as the command-line tools, as seen in Figure 4.3.

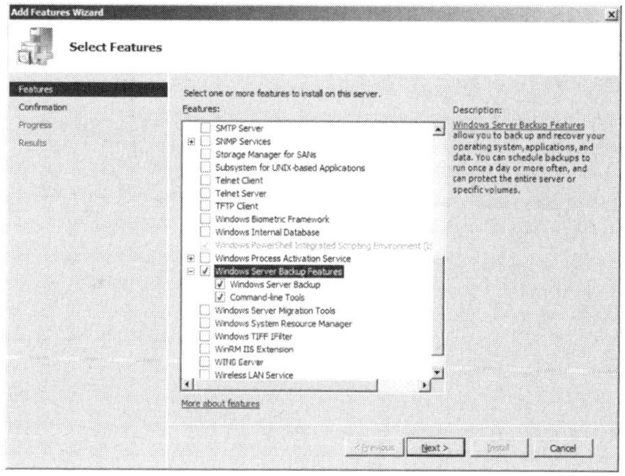

FIGURE 4.3
Installing the WSB feature

After installation, a link to WSB appears in the Administrative Tools menu.

Getting Started with WSB

To get started with WSB, perhaps to do an ad hoc backup prior to installing a new application, go to the Administrative Tools folder and open Windows Server Backup. Then follow these steps:

1. In the upper-right corner are the action tasks. For this simple exercise, click Backup Once. If you are looking to do a regular bare metal recovery (BMR) or system state (SS) backup, you could choose to create a backup schedule.
2. On the first screen, WSB offers to use settings from a previous backup. Of course, since we just installed WSB and haven't run a backup yet, that choice is grayed out. Click Next.
3. Choose whether to do a full or custom backup. If your server is of any appreciable size, it is impractical to do full backups with WSB except as an ad hoc that you won't be retaining long term. More typically, you will choose a custom backup.
4. On the next screen, choose which items to back up. This is a big change from the earlier generations of NT Backup, and also varies between Windows Server 2008 and 2008 R2.

   In Windows Server 2008, WSB protects and restores at a volume-level only. As seen in Figure 4.4, you can choose to protect any of the volumes. There's also a System Protection option, which will automatically select the C: drive (boot and system volumes) and other elements as required.

   In Windows Server 2008 R2, as seen in Figure 4.5, you can click Add Items to open a browser listing all volumes on the local machine, as well as BMR and SS backup choices. Notice that BMR and SS are at the top, since those are the key usage scenarios for WSB.
5. By selecting BMR, you ensure that the entire C: drive, along with any system or reserved volumes, is automatically chosen.

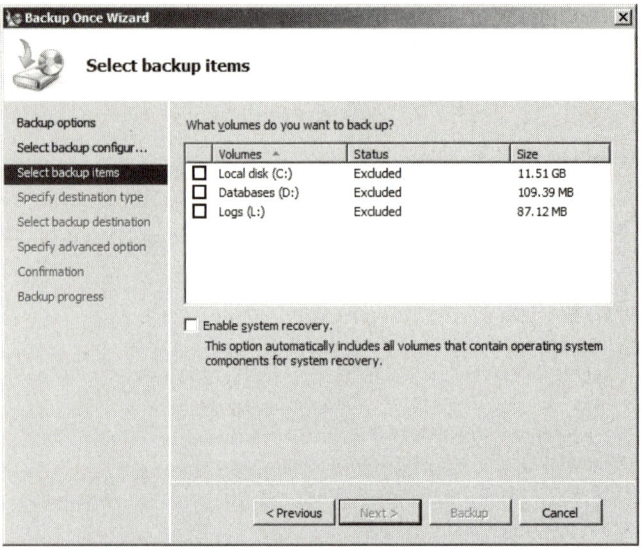

FIGURE 4.4
Windows Server 2008 WSB volume protection

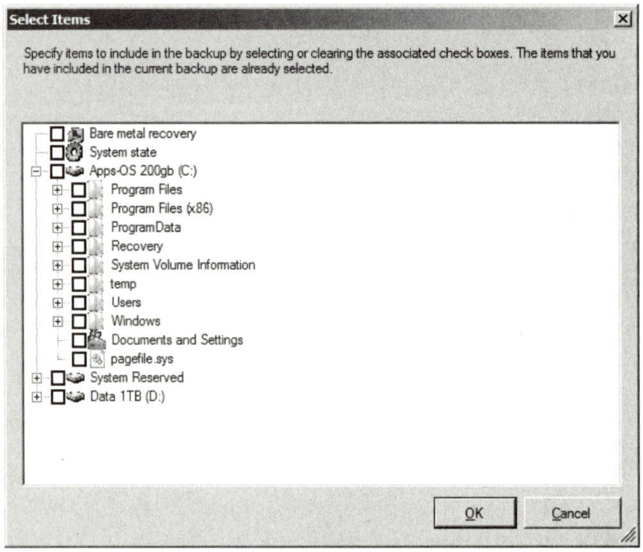

FIGURE 4.5
Windows Server 2008 R2 WSB protects files, folders, volumes, system state backup, and bare metal recovery.

6. The next screen asks whether you want to use local storage or remote storage for the backup media. Notice that tape is not a choice. WSB is designed as a disk-to-disk solution (only) for faster local server recovery and is intended to complement another backup solution that may do long-term retention—one example is DPM.

7. Clicking Backup on the last screen starts the backup, which by default will use the VSS processes that we discussed earlier in this chapter.

WSB creates a folder named `WindowsImageBackup` in the root of the volume you pointed it to. Under that folder, WSB creates a folder named after the computer name that ran the backup. WSB uses a process similar to a DPM Express Full (covered later in the section "How DPM Storage Works"). By using block-based protection, the performance and small data transfer resembles an incremental backup, but the blocks are stored on disk in such a way that the points in time are able to be restored in one pass without layering. The folder also includes the catalog file so that the backup can be restored by an instance of WSB other than the one that originally backed it up. This is common for when you have rebuilt a generic OS and wish to restore data from the original OS again.

NOTE One of the most noticeable changes from `NTbackup.exe` to WSB is the absence of tape media usage by the backup utility. The Windows operating system still provides device-level support for tape drives to be used with other backup software, including third parties and DPM. But the built-in WSB utility is primarily intended for ad hoc backups and quick, whole-server recoveries, long-term retention, and therefore tape as a media choice, is not available.

Restoring with WSB

Restoring with WSB is an intuitive process:

1. In the right pane, click Recover.
2. WSB first asks whether the backup media that it will be restoring from is local or remote.
3. A calendar then shows the dates that have recoverable points, with a pull-down time window on the right side to select one of multiple points in time per day, as seen in Figure 4.6.

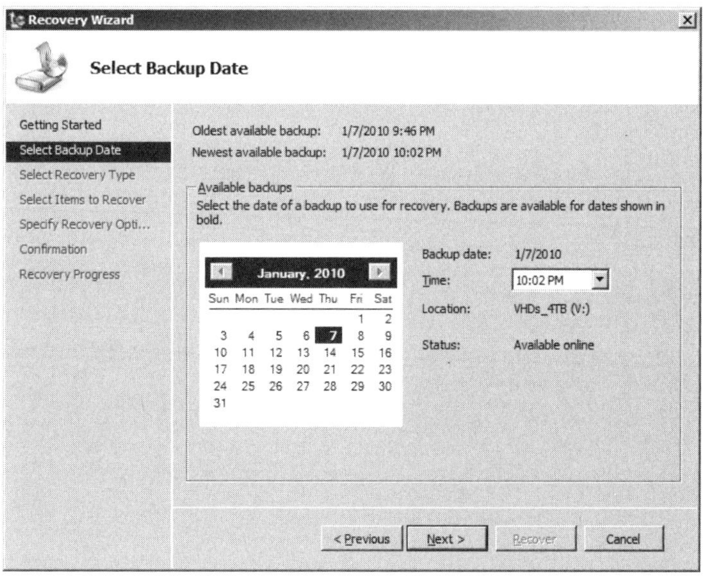

FIGURE 4.6
WSB date and time restore selection

NOTE If the WSB calendar or workflow look familiar to you, you may find it interesting to know that some of the same Microsoft people who developed the DPM console also contributed to the development of WSB.

4. The next screen, shown in Figure 4.7, allows you to select files or folders, volumes, or the system state for recovery.

FIGURE 4.7
WSB restoration options

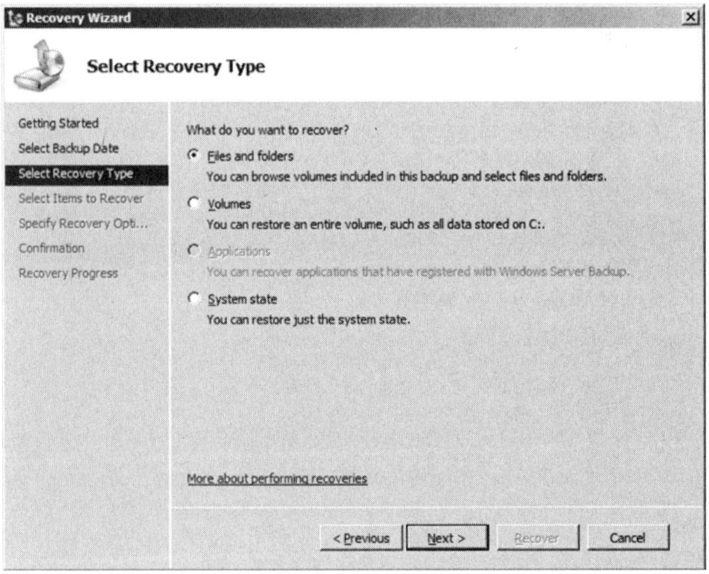

- Selecting Files Or Folders is new in Windows Server 2008 R2 and provides an Explorer-like view to select objects for restoration. WSB in Windows Server 2008 was at a volume level only.
- Selecting Volume provides a choice of restoring to another volume. This can be an interesting scenario for moving data during a storage migration
- Selecting System State enables you to roll back a configuration, perhaps to immediately before an errant patch or software installation failure.

5. Depending on what kind of restore you choose, you may see additional options for restoring to alternate locations and whether the original permissions or new location's permissions should be applied.
6. After a confirmation screen, the restore will commence. After a system state restore, you must reboot to complete the recovery.

WHERE DOES WSB FIT?

Depending on how you measure it, some would say that the built-in backup utility, including both the earlier NT Backup and the new WSB, are the most widely used backup products for Windows. And certainly for single-server, small businesses, that could be the case. There are a lot of single-server businesses out there, so this should not be discounted.

But in the bigger picture of mulit-server environments, the primary use cases for WSB are more typically related to server rollback after a bad software installation or incomplete patch, or as part of a preliminary, just-in-case procedure before doing something significant with the server.

In addition, the mechanisms that WSB uses for system state backup and bare metal recovery are often the only supported ways to do that in Windows Server 2008 and 2008 R2. For that reason, many fuller featured backup products will use the WSB features via either a script or API. The other backup product manages the backups and policies, and WSB performs some of the work in regard to system state or BMR.

System Center Data Protection Manager

In Windows Server 2003, Microsoft addressed supportability issues by delivering Volume Shadow Copy Services (VSS) within the operating system. In Windows Server 2008, Microsoft delivered a new backup utility that was designed for whole server protection and recovery scenarios.

But what was missing was a comprehensive backup solution that utilized VSS and the best practices guidance of the ever-more complex applications such as a distributed SharePoint farm or an Exchange 2010 DAG (see Chapter 7). To address those goals and other issues, Microsoft released its own backup product in 2005.

NOTE DPM is not the only disk-to-disk-to-tape (D2D2T) solution with the ability to replicate data to secondary locations as well as tape. If you want to use only a single agent on the production server, the list of alternatives goes down. And if you want to use VSS to protect your workloads, DPM becomes unique (as of this writing).

Based on those criteria as best practices, DPM is being referenced here as an example of a best practice data protection solution and to demonstrate where next generation data protection solution are headed.

Why Did Microsoft Build a Backup Product?

For over 10 years and four generations of Windows, backup was relegated to third parties to deliver—and then DPM was released. So what changed? Although other factors contributed, here are the three primary goals Microsoft had for releasing its own backup product:

- Supportability
- Protection of core applications and Windows Server
- Customer demand for using a single backup mechanism that utilized multiple media types, instead of having to deploy and manage multiple protection products on each production server

Supportability

As discussed earlier in the chapter, VSS enables a supportable protection and recovery capability that leverages the intended mechanisms for backup and restoration, as developed by each individual application via its VSS writer. The challenge is that many third-party backup products are unable or unwilling to create a VSS requestor within their backup agents.

Considering that some backup products developed for protecting Windows environments are currently shipping their fifth, eighth, or even twelfth release, it should not come as a surprise that the architecture of their agents and servers were not developed with VSS or any other original-vendor APIs in mind. In fact, for engineering efficiencies, many backup solutions have a generic architecture that may allow the same basic agent components to back up Macintosh, Linux, and Windows machines, including server applications such as SQL Server, Oracle, and Lotus Notes. But with such a variety of potential data sources, many backup agent architectures often can only accommodate a generic stream of data. It would be a significant undertaking for those backup agents and engines to utilize VSS. Subsequently, some vendors make the choice to use their own methods instead of VSS when backing up Windows workloads..

Also, consider that a VSS backup and recovery solution has positive and negative aspects for supportability:

- The positive aspects of VSS-based data protection are that the solution uses only supported backup and recovery mechanisms and will therefore be more supportable by Microsoft.
- The negative aspects of VSS-based data protection are that the only capabilities for protection and restore scenarios are those enabled through each application's VSS writer.

There are some desirable recovery scenarios that may not be enabled with a VSS-based backup solution. One example is the ability to restore a single mail item from Microsoft Exchange directly back into the active mailbox database. The Microsoft Exchange VSS writer and its backup implementation do not allow for granular item recovery, without first restoring the complete mailbox database to a recovery storage group (RSG) or recovery database (RDB)—Exchange 2007 and 2010, respectively. From the RSG or RDB, you can restore individual items. With some third-party backup solutions, their backup is not done using VSS, and they offer single-item or mailbox restores without the RSG or RDB. But those products also fall subject to Microsoft Knowledge Base article 904845, "Microsoft support policy for third-party products that modify or extract Exchange database contents" (`http://support.microsoft.com/kb/904845`).

Protection of New Applications and Servers

Similar to our previous discussion of whether a backup mechanism is supported by application servers is the question of whether the newest applications and server operating systems are protectable at all.

In looking at the legacy backup solutions that are on the market today—particularly the heterogeneous backup solutions whose platform can protect everything from a mainframe down to a PDA—it can be difficult to develop backup agent technology that can protect the newer application servers and operating systems. For example, your legacy backup solution may protect SQL Server 2008 databases adequately but not be able to protect even the SQL components of a SharePoint 2007 farm. Similarly, your backup solution may be able to protect a standalone Exchange 2003 server but not an Exchange 2010 DAG (see Chapter 7).

As discussed earlier, when Microsoft observed this dilemma, what sometimes happened was that customers became reluctant to upgrade or deploy the new platforms because their legacy backup solution couldn't maintain protection of the data. For this reason, if no other, it became important for Microsoft to not only continue working with the Microsoft partners who developed third-party backup software, but also to deliver its own comprehensive backup solution in order to ensure that customers had a reliable backup and recovery capability for the latest Microsoft server platforms and were unhindered in their deployments.

Heterogeneity in Backup Mechanisms

As discussed in Chapter 3, regarding the layers of data protection, there are logical reasons why you would simultaneously protect your data with multiple mechanisms that might include the following:

- Tape backup for long-term retention
- Disk-based replication for fast item-level or whole-server recovery
- Long-distance for disaster recovery

Unfortunately, this often resulted in running three different data protection products on each production server and invariably, this created supportability conflicts, resource constraints, and confusion due to overlaps in functionality.

Does Heterogeneity of Backup Media Imply Heterogeneity of Protected Servers?

No—Microsoft took a different approach to heterogeneous backups than most third-party vendors. Many third-party vendors have developed flexible agent architectures that enable the backup servers to protect a wide range of production platforms, often across multiple operating systems and platforms. The generic approach of the architecture makes it easier to protect a wider array of platforms, but usually makes it less capable of utilizing specific methods of data protection, such as Volume Shadow Copy Services (VSS).

Also, the multiplatform backup solutions often focus on one type of media, such as nightly tape backup or disk-to-disk replication, either exclusively or with a legacy bias.

Microsoft addressed heterogeneity of media by unifying all of the media types within DPM: disk, tape, and long-distance/cloud, but only for protecting Windows-based data sources. If DPM were to extend its architecture to non-Windows data sources, it would likely face many of the same application supportability challenges that the existing heterogeneous backup vendors face today.

Because all those woes reduced customer satisfaction and confidence in the primary platforms, such as Windows Server, Exchange, SQL or SharePoint, Microsoft's answer was to deliver a single data protection solution that provides tape-, disk-, and cloud/DR-based protection within a single product, and more importantly, the new product uses a single agent on each production server.

The resulting product was *System Center Data Protection Manager* (*DPM*):

- DPM 2006 was first released in September 2005 and focused on disk-based protection of Windows file servers only, as a method of centralized backup of branch offices.

- DPM 2007, also known as DPM v2, was released in September 2007 and provided the integrated disk- and tape-based protection of the Windows application and file servers that were discussed before. In reality, DPM 2007 was what a Microsoft data protection solution should look like.
- DPM 2010, also known as DPM v3, was released in April 2010. Shown in Figure 4.8, DPM 2010 is the basis for the rest of this chapter.

FIGURE 4.8
DPM 2010 solution diagram
Source: Microsoft Corporation

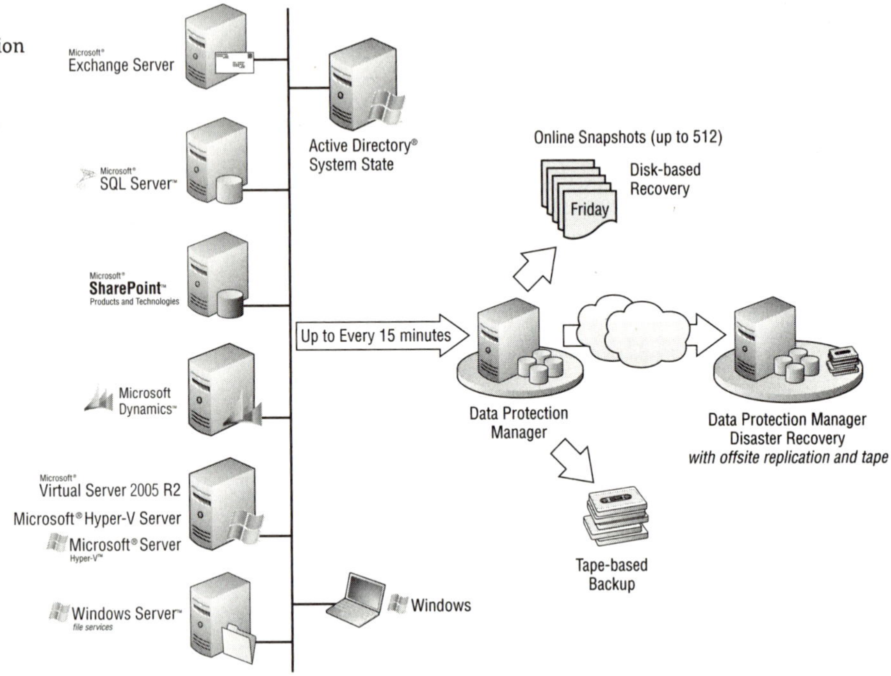

How Does DPM Work?

System Center Data Protection Manager (DPM) uses two concurrent methods for protecting Windows-based data:

- Block-based Express Full backups
- Transactional log replication

But before we explore these methods, you need to understand how the DPM agent operates on the production server.

How the DPM Agent Works

In the next sections of this chapter, we will go through several hands-on tasks to help you get experience with the technologies being discussed. Chapters 4–11 each have tasks for their hands-on exercises. In this chapter's Task 3, we will install the agent using either a push method from the DPM administrator console or a manual method used in larger enterprise deployments. In either case, the DPM agent initializes with a filter driver that monitors the file system on the production server.

When data protection is initially configured, the data sources to be protected are identified by the administrator, as we will do later in Task 4. At that time, you will identify which databases or farms or virtual machines that you wish to protect, and that information is sent to the DPM agent on that production server. The data sources are then converted from their logical representation to the disk blocks that store them, as follows:

1. The DPM administrator chooses to protect a Sales database within SQL.
2. DPM identifies that the Sales database is made up `Sales.mdf` and `Sales.ldf` on the SQL server.
3. DPM learns that the `Sales.mdf` file resides in the D: database directory on the SQL server.
4. The DPM agent's filter driver begins monitoring the 58 disk blocks that compose the MDF file.

At this point, the DPM agent is operational and monitoring the disk blocks that make up the files that in turn make up the data sources that DPM has been configured to protect. The DPM agent will perform different tasks for each of two kinds of data protection, which we will discuss next.

DPM AGENTS VS. DPM LICENSES

There is a single DPM agent for all workloads (with x86 and x64 variations), but there are three licenses of the agent, based on what is being protected.

- *S DPML*, or *Standard Data Protection Management License*, can be thought of as a file agent for protecting files, directories, and shares on Windows Server operating systems. It has a street price of about $175.
- *C-DPML*, or *Client Data Protection Management License*, can be thought of as a client license for Windows desktops and laptops. It has the same functionality (files only) as an S-DPML, but is priced less and will install only on client operating systems. The C-DPML is also planned for inclusion in the Microsoft Enterprise Client Access License (E-CAL) package in spring 2010. It has an individual street price of about $35.
- *E-DPML*, or *Enterprise Data Protection Management License*, protects all applications as well as files, including Exchange, SQL, SharePoint, and virtualization. It also enables disaster recovery. This means that unlike most other backup software—which sells separate licenses and agent binaries for each type of workload being protected—this license and the ubiquitous agent protects them all. The E-DPML has a street price of about $425.

Because DPM is part of System Center, the E-DPML can also be acquired as part of the System Center suites: the Systems Management Suite for Datacenters (SMSD) and the Systems Management Suite for Enterprises (SMSE). These suites are discounted bundles, which combine the E-DPML from DPM with the agent licenses of the other System Center products, including a CML from System Center Configuration Manager (Chapter 10), VMML from System Center Virtual Machine Manager (Chapter 10), and an OML System Center Operations Manager (Chapter 11). Midsized organizations can also purchase "Essentials Plus" suites which include not only a DPML but also the ML for System Center Essentials (Chapter 10).

As of June 2010, C-DPMLs are now part of Microsoft's E-CAL suite, as well.

You can install the agents on as many machines as you like, which we will do later in Task 2. Licensing does not take effect until data is selected for protection. At that time, based on what kind of data that DPM is protecting, it will add 1 to the reported number of C-DPMLs, S-DPMLs, or E-DPMLs in use within the UI. For example:

- **If you chose to protect information on a Windows client, a C-DPML will be counted.**
- **If you chose to protect files on a Windows server, an S-DPML will be counted.**
- **Or if you chose to protect application data on a Windows server or data on another DPM server, an E-DPML will be counted.**

How DPM Storage Works

The storage can be any disk that appears as locally mounted storage within the Windows Disk Administrator utility, including direct-attached storage (DAS), iSCSI, and Fibre Channel SANs. However, the disk does have to be locally mounted in order for DPM to manage it, so remote volumes, mount points, or proprietary appliances with their own file systems will not work with DPM. Once the storage is mounted, do not format the volumes. Instead, simply leave the disks in their raw state.

When you initially assign the storage to the DPM server (as we will do in Task 2 later in this chapter), the DPM server simply adds the raw capacity to its storage pool. For most protectable data sources, when you select an object for protection, the DPM server creates two NTFS volumes out of the storage pool per data source that you select. There are two exceptions:

- For SQL databases, you can optionally choose to co-locate multiple databases from the same SQL server and in the same protection group within a single pair of NTFS volumes. This enables DPM to handle larger numbers of small databases, particularly in cases where databases are dynamically spawned during operation.
- For file shares, the data is stored by volume, so that if you select multiple file shares whose data resides on the same production volume, only one pair of NTFS volumes is created in the DPM storage pool. This enables DPM to easily handle new shares and the dynamic nature of file serving. For example, if three shares on a production server each are built from directories on the `E:\` of the production volume, then the volume is protected once but only includes the directory trees specified by the shares (`E:\Acct`, `E:\Mgmt`, and `E:\Sales`). Those three parts of the volume are protected, whereas the rest of the volume is not protected, all completely transparent to the user and the DPM administrator.

But in principle, every data source or collocated data source being protected will have two NTFS volumes allocated for it within the DPM storage pool: the replica volume and the recovery point volume.

The *replica volume* holds the most recent complete set of data, as provided by the Express Full operation. As you'll learn in the next section, during each Express Full operation, the blocks that have changed on the production server are replicated and applied to the copy of the data within the DPM storage pool. Specifically, the changed blocks are applied to the copy of the data residing in the replica volume. Because the *replica* holds a complete copy of the data as of the latest Express Full, a complete server restoration can be done simply using the copy of the replica.

The *recovery point volume* (RPV) holds the displaced blocks from the replica. This means that if an Express Full operation were to overwrite five blocks within the replica, then those five blocks are not deleted from the DPM server, but are instead moved from the replica volume to the recovery point volume. DPM retains the blocks and the points in time with which they are associated. This results in a predictable recovery time objective (RTO) because all the previous points in time are equally accessible as disk blocks within the DPM storage pool.

If you wish to recover all of today's data, it resides on the replica. If you wish to recover yesterday's data, most of it resides in the replica and the remaining elements will be in the recovery point volume. This is unlike legacy backup solutions in which first the full backup is restored and then the differentials or incrementals are layered over the top. DPM's restore simply pulls the disk blocks that are relevant from the combined replica and recovery point areas. Some blocks come from each, but there is no layering during the restore from the volumes.

The blocks for the previous points in time are held within the recovery point volume until one of the following conditions is met:

When the Number of Days Retention Is Exceeded In Task 4, when configuring protection, we will determine the number of days of data to retain. So, for a 30-day retention window, the disk blocks representing the differences between the 30th day and the 31st day are discarded each night. This enables the DPM server to maintain the live copy of the data within the replica, and N–1 days of data within the recovery point volume.

When the Recovery Point Volume Is Full The RPV will retain as many days as configured, as long as all data for each day is held. Thus, if only 23.5 days of data can be stored due to the size of the RPV, the half day is also discarded so only 23 days are on disk. DPM will not store a partial recovery point. A report from DPM will tell you how many days are being stored, and the RPV can be resized by right-clicking on the protection group and selecting Modify Disk Allocation.

Sizing the Replica and Recovery Point Volumes

The replica volume needs to store the live data plus at least one day of transactional logs. This means that if your production server has a 1 TB volume with 500 GB of data, the replica volume should be at least 500 GB and likely around 550 GB. As the size of your data grows, the replica volume will also need to grow. New in DPM 2010 is Auto-Grow, the ability to "grow" volumes as the production data exceeds capacity.

The recovery point volume stores all the disk blocks that comprise the previous points in time that are recoverable. Here's a rough rule of thumb: size the RPV equal to *N* (number of days retained) times *Dc* (Data change rate). Hence, if the production server changed 5 percent of its data per day, then a 100 GB volume would generate 5 GB of changes per day. If you wish to retain the data for 30 days, the recovery point volume should be $30 \times 5 = 150$ GB. It is likely that this scenario would take appreciably less than 150 GB, because in most environments, much of the data that was changed today will be changed again tomorrow.

DPM Express Full Backups

DPM uses a process which Microsoft refers to as an *Express Full* for its VSS-based, block-level backups of the production data sources. As you know, the DPM agent and its filter driver monitor the disk blocks that make up the data source for changes. As changes occur (reads are ignored), the DPM bitmap is simply updated to mark that the block will need to be synchronized.

On a schedule defined within the DPM console, which we will do in Task 4, the Express Full process will occur typically between one and four times per day. When an Express Full is triggered:

1. The DPM server contacts the DPM agent on the production server and instructs it to invoke a VSS shadow copy using its VSS requester.
2. All of the data sources that are scheduled for the Express Full are then contacted through VSS, and their individual VSS writers put their data sets into consistent states, which are then snapped by the software-based VSS provider in the production server's operating system, as seen in Figure 4.1.

Now, the DPM agent has two key resources available:

- The list of blocks that have been changed since the last Express Full backup, as provided by the DPM agent's filter driver
- A frozen copy of all the blocks on the production volume, as provided by Volume Shadow Copy Services

Putting those together, the DPM agent simply copies the blocks that have changed from the snapshot and replicates them to the DPM server. The DPM server then applies those blocks into a replica of the data set within the DPM storage pool stored in its replica volume. This process is called an *Express Full.*

In traditional terms, the result is a Full Backup, meaning that the storage pool has a single set of data that includes everything necessary to restore the production data set in a single operation, without layering of any incremental or differential backup sets. However, unlike a traditional full backup, where everything is copied from the production server to the backup server (whether or not the data had been modified), only the changes are replicated with DPM.

It is worth noting that while an Express Full does not incur the I/O penalty of sending stagnant data to the backup service, it does in most other aspects behave like a full backup, such as causing the production application to perform its normal post-full-backup process.

This is why Microsoft uses the term *Express Full.* It is the same result, without the penalty of transmitting the unchanged data.

An Express Full vs. a Synthetic Full

Some backup technologies offer a capability known as a Synthetic Full backup, which has some of the same resulting characteristics as an Express Full, but the means of creating them are very different.

A Synthetic Full backup is usually derived within the backup software, after the incremental or differential backups are done. Normally, every legacy backup solution's restoration starts with a full backup and then layering either incrementals or differentials over it. The amount of layering therefore adds additional, and often unpredictable, time to the restore window, which affects the RTO of your overall solution (to learn more about RTO, see Chapter 2). To address this, some legacy backup software will compile the partial backups and the last full into a new Synthetic Full, which can be used as a full backup for restore purposes, without you having done an actual full backup of the production server.

An Express Full, as described earlier in this section, is done by identifying the changes (with similar granularity as a differential) and then applying them to the DPM replica. The result is a consistently updated full backup, which has a predictable RTO, without any additional efforts within the backup server.

To better understand how an Express Full works, consider the following scenario:

1. Day one: The original data object contains eight blocks on disk (ABCDEFGH).
2. Upon initially protecting the data source with DPM, two volumes within the DPM storage pool are allocated for the replica volume and the recovery point volume. Immediately after that, DPM does its initial baseline, which populates the replica volume with an exact copy of the production data (ABCDEFGH).
3. Day two: During the day, two blocks (*IJ*) are updated, resulting in AB*IJ*EFGH.
4. At the next scheduled synchronization or *Express Full*, the two changed blocks (*IJ*) that were identified by the DPM agent and filter are replicated from the production volume to the DPM replica, resulting in the replica also having AB*IJ*EFGH. The two displaced blocks (*CD*) are then moved from the replica into the recovery point volume.
5. Day three: After another day, three more blocks (*B*, *J*, G) are overwritten (with *K*,*L*,*M*) and synchronized during the next Express Full, resulting in A*KIL*EF*M*H. Again, DPM replicates just the three changed blocks within the data source to the DPM replica, and the displaced blocks are moved to the recovery point volume.

This process can occur up to 512 times, based on a limit of 512 snapshots via VSS. This may equal 512 daily points in time equaling nearly 1.5 years, or at 4 per day would result in 128 days (four months) of changes, or with a maximum of 8 per day would result in 64 days on disk, with recovery points every few hours.

DPM Transactional Log Replication

If you run an Express Full every evening, perhaps when your old backup window used to be, then there are still over 23 hours per day in between your backups. For transactional applications, including Microsoft Exchange (Chapter 7) and Microsoft SQL Server (Chapter 8), DPM can protect the transactional data up to every 15 minutes. We will see this in Task 4 when we define protection of application servers and again in Tasks 7 and 8 when we restore a database to any 15-minute point in time.

This is done by the DPM agent, which will replicate a copy of the transaction logs from the production server. The method varies, based on workload:

- In the case of Exchange, the Exchange server uses multiple log files that are 1 MB in size each for Exchange 2007 and 2010 (Exchange 2003 log files are 5 MB each). As each fills up, a new one is incrementally started. Thus, if in 15 minutes the Exchange server has used logA, logB, and logC (and is currently using logD), then the DPM agent replicates the A, B, and C logs. Fifteen minutes later, if the Exchange server is using log H, then the DPM agent replicates logs D, E, F, and G.
- In the case of SQL Server, there is only one log file for each database, the LDF file. Instead, the DPM agent invokes a transaction log backup within SQL, which packages up the log for

third-party backups. Because DPM knows what the last log looked like, the DPM agent can discern what is new within the log for the past 15 minutes and replicates those changes to the log file on the DPM server.

Either way, the DPM server is able to get copies of the transaction logs up to every 15 minutes, which it stores on a replica volume in the DPM storage pool.

NOTE It is important to note that the DPM server does ***not*** apply the replicated transaction logs to its copy of the database, similar to SQL log shipping or Exchange continuous replication. Those methods of replication and application are for high availability. Instead, DPM retains the logs as a differential backup, so that it can play the logs forward during the restore operation. We will look closer at SQL and Exchange replication mechanisms in Chapters 8 and 7, respectively.

Getting Started with DPM 2010

System Center Data Protection Manager 2010 was released to beta in September 2009, a release candidate appeared in January 2010, and the final release was announced in April 2010. It is the third generation of DPM and protects the following data sources:

- Windows XP, Vista, and 7
- Windows Server 2003, 2003 R2, 2008, and 2008 R2
- Microsoft Exchange 2003, 2007, and 2010
- SharePoint Products and Technologies 2003, 2007, and 2010
- SQL Server 2000, 2005, 2008, and 2008 R2
- Virtual Server 2005 R2, Hyper-V, and Hyper-V R2

Almost all of these data sources provide their own VSS writers, which is a prerequisite for protection directly by DPM 2010. To begin with, we will:

1. Build a DPM server.
2. Configure its tape and disk storage.
3. Deploy agents to the production servers to be protected.

Task 1: Installing the DPM Server

DPM 2010 must be installed on a 64-bit version of either Windows Server 2008 or 2008 R2. The DPM server does not necessarily need to have inordinately high amounts of CPU processing power or memory, but will need fast I/O for the storage and networking. As with most of the other tasks in this book, these exercises were done using the TechNet evaluation TestDrive VHDs and downloadable evaluation software, in this case Windows Server 2008 R2.

NOTE If you are installing DPM 2007, be sure to install it on a platform running 64-bit Windows Server 2008 or 2008 R2, because DPM 2010 does provide an in-place upgrade path (and because DPM 2007 runs much better on 64 bit).

From the server console, run the `SETUP.exe` file, which will check for the minimum hardware requirements as well as the necessary prerequisites, such as Windows PowerShell. If anything is cautionary or required, the lower window will give explanations and links to downloadable software prerequisites, as seen in Figure 4.9.

After confirming that the prerequisites are met, you will see the typical installation questions, such as where you want to install the program binaries. What is important here is in the middle of the screen. DPM 2010 uses SQL Server 2008 Standard edition or higher as its database, but includes it within the DPM installation media. You can also choose to use an external SQL server by selecting the Use An Existing Instance Of SQL Server 2008 radio button seen in Figure 4.10.

Which SQL server to use should be based on the scale requirements of the DPM servers, and how many data sources will be protected. If you will have multiple DPM servers within a given site, centralizing their databases onto an external and highly available SQL server (Chapter 8) may be advisable. This also provides the DPM server with additional I/O and memory since it will not be running the SQL services. If you are only intending to run one or two DPM servers within a location and they are not backing up inordinate amounts of production servers, running the included SQL Server 2008 standard license is perfectly acceptable.

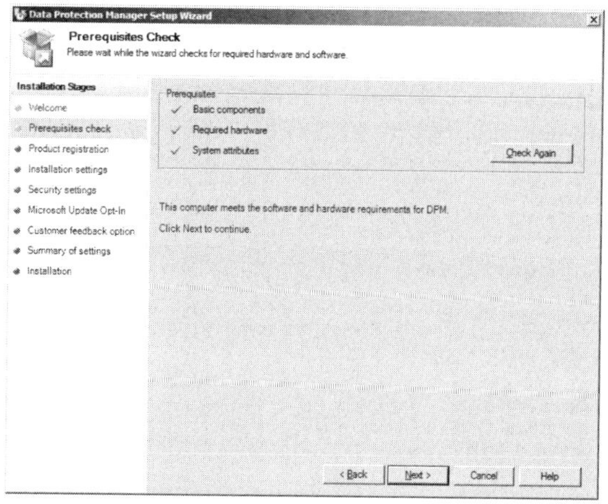

FIGURE 4.9
Prerequisite checking for DPM 2010

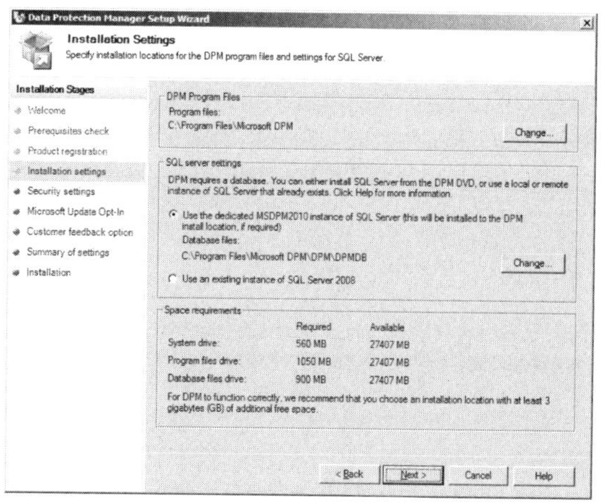

FIGURE 4.10
Installing DPM and SQL Server 2008

NOTE The SQL Server license included with DPM 2010 is Microsoft SQL Server 2008 Standard edition, and not Workgroup or otherwise. This is because DPM uses the Reporting Services of SQL Server. Be aware that DPM 2010 requires SQL Server 2008 and cannot use SQL Server 2005. Also notable is that the SQL Server license included with DPM is strictly for use by DPM, per the EULA, as well as within the installable software, meaning that you cannot use that instance of SQL for other databases other than DPM's.

The remainder of the installation is fairly mundane, as a scroll bar will go across the screen for approximately 40 minutes. With the exception of possibly having to acknowledge any Windows components that are installed first, the installation will continue without you and finish with a complete DPM 2010 server. Though not always required, it is recommended that you reboot the server after the installation is complete to confirm that the core services are functional and initialized in the proper sequence.

INTRODUCING THE DPM ADMINISTRATOR CONSOLE

If you are familiar with the administrator console of DPM 2007, you will be comfortable with the interface in DPM 2010, which is similar but enhanced. On the top of the interface is a ribbon that breaks down the operations and management of DPM into five areas, as seen in Figure 4.11.

FIGURE 4.11
The DPM Administrator Console

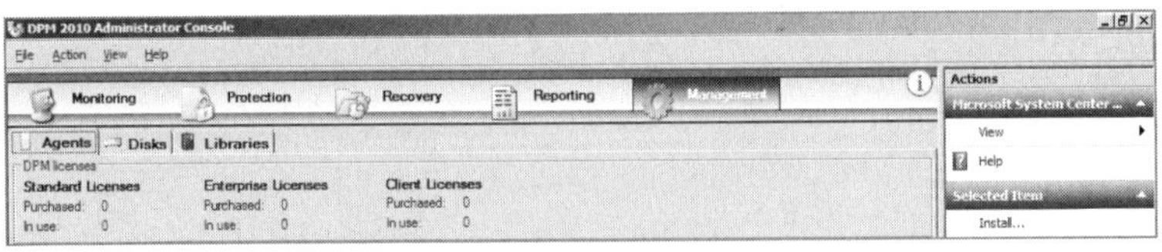

Monitoring Tab Provides troubleshooting insight for how DPM is performing by displaying the active jobs and the status of any previous jobs.

Protection Tab Allows us to configure data protection, which we will use in Tasks 4 and 5.

Recovery Tab Enables us to restore data, which we will use in Tasks 6 through10.

Reporting Tab Provides canned reports that pull from the SQL Server database and utilize the SQL Server 2008 Reporting Services. These reports can be automated and emailed to the administrators or data source stakeholders, including information on tape and disk usage, job status, protection compliance, and so on.

Management Tab Manages the DPM server itself with three subtabs for Agents, Disk, and (Tape) Libraries. We will use all of these functions in Tasks 2 and 3.

It is worth noting that unlike many Microsoft consoles, there is no left pane to select a server or right pane for the management tasks themselves. Instead, each console manages only the DPM server that it is running on.

RUNNING THE DPM CONSOLE ON YOUR DESKTOP

You can also use Windows Server 2008's RemoteApp functionality to enable the DPM console to be invoked by and appear to run on an administrator's local desktop.

My friend and Microsoft MVP David Allen wrote a great blog on exactly how to do that: `http://wmug.co.uk/blogs/aquilaweb/archive/2010/01/18/dpm-console-on-your-desktop.aspx`.

TASK 2: CONFIGURING THE DPM DISK AND TAPE

As seen in Figure 4.11, the Management tab of the DPM console includes three subtabs: Agents, Disk, and Tape. By clicking on the Disk subtab, we can see any disk that is already assigned to DPM; in a new installation, this will be blank and the Actions pane on the right will likely have most of its options grayed out except for Add Storage.

By clicking Add Storage, we see any locally attached disk with free space (no volumes defined), as shown by the Windows Disk Administrator utility (DAS, iSCSI, or FC-SAN). If you already have volumes on those disks that were intended for DPM's use, you should most likely delete them. DPM will create NTFS volumes from the free disk space. Those volumes that have free disk space will appear in the left window of the pop-up screen, and by moving each volume to the right pane, you assign it to DPM, as shown in Figure 4.12.

Adding tape works similarly. After switching to the Tape subtab within the Management function, you will likely see no usable actions in the right pane other than to add a tape device. In general, DPM can make use of almost any tape drive or medium changer that is recognized by the Windows Device Manager under Windows Server 2008 or 2008 R2. This includes not only standalone tape drives and changers, but also synthetic tape devices and virtual tape libraries (including de-duplication appliances that appear as VTLs), as long as they appear correctly in the Windows Device Manager.

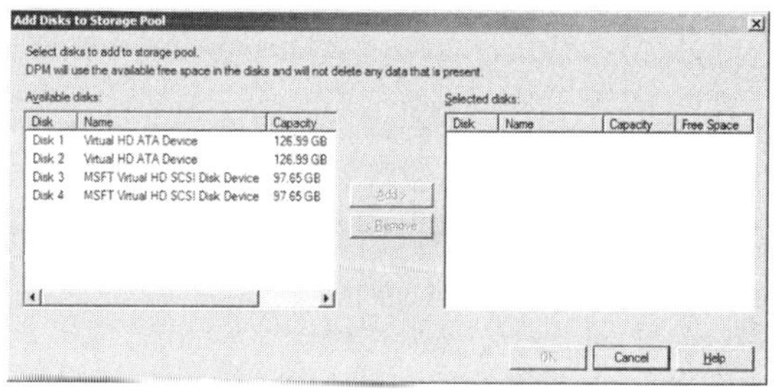

FIGURE 4.12
Adding a disk to the DPM server

Click Rescan, and DPM will inventory what is available from the Device Manager and list the tape drives, media changers, and tape slots within the DPM UI, as seen in Figure 4.13.

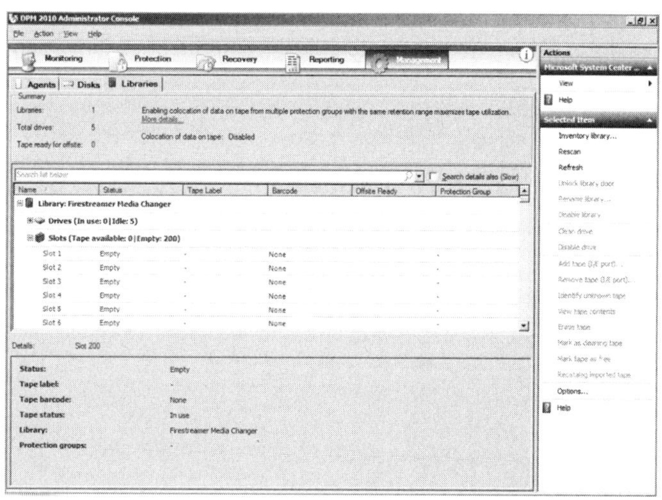

FIGURE 4.13
Adding tape to the DPM server

Firestreamer by Cristalink

A great add-on for DPM is Firestreamer, which is a software-based virtual tape device. You will find it within most of the hands-on labs and other learning venues for DPM because it allows a virtualized DPM server that could not otherwise have a tape device to use one, albeit synthetic.

Firestreamer registers a driver within Windows Device Manager as a tape drive, along with a media changer for changing virtual tapes. And after that registration, DPM uses it like any other tape drive or media changer, as seen in Figure 4.12 earlier. But in the background, Firestreamer creates a big file and treats it like tape.

Normally, as we discussed in Chapter 3, I am a purist about using disk as disk and tape as tape. Disk is a random access device for information that is always mounted, while tape is a sequentially accessed device for information that can be dismounted, transported, or archived. But there are business scenarios (other than running DPM in a learning environment) where synthetic tape is useful, such as being able to use a USB-attached external hard drive with DPM. Removable media cannot be used as DPM disk because 1) the storage pool presumes that all disk is always available since blocks may need to come from it and 2) VSS does not provide the same functions on removable media as it does when it is directly attached. So, a USB hard drive cannot be a DPM disk.

But with Firestreamer, a USB hard drive can be treated as a DPM tape. It can be unplugged, shelved, and archived. With a little creativity, a DVD-RAM tower, remote NAS, remote mount point, WORM (write once, read many) storage solution or de-duplication appliance can all be turned into DPM near line storage (tape) because of my friends at Cristalink (`www.firestreamer.com`).

Task 3: Installing DPM Agents onto the Production Servers

By completing the first two tasks, you now have a working DPM server. It has disk for short-term protection and recovery, as well as tape for long-term retention. Now, we need to put agents on the production servers, so that they can be protected. On the Management tab of the DPM UI, choose the Agents subtab and click the Install Agents task in the Actions pane on the right.

DPM 2007 users will notice a new first screen to the DPM 2010 wizard, which offers two choices, installing agents or adding agents that are already installed, as you can see in Figure 4.14.

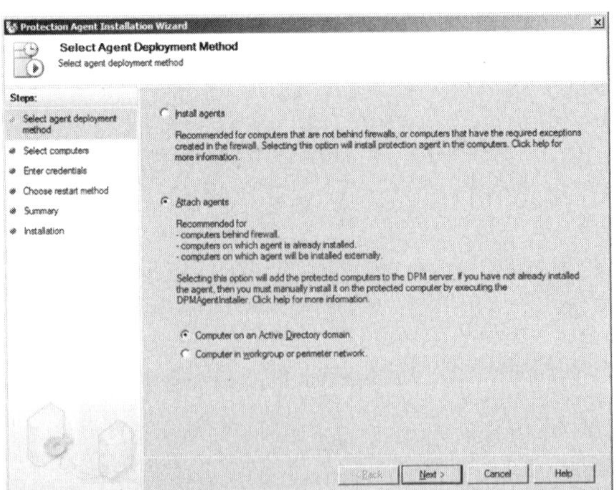

Figure 4.14 Installing agents or adding agents in DPM 2010

Installing DPM Agents from the DPM Server This process is similar from DPM 2007, where we see the list of production servers in the left pane. Moving them to the right pane will select them for agent installation, as shown in Figure 4.15. Next, you will be prompted for a username and password that has rights to install software onto the server. The third screen presents the option of automatically rebooting the server after the agent is installed. A reboot is usually not necessary with most DPM 2010 installations (this is a happy change from DPM 2007). In 2010, this was necessary because the DPM agent's filter driver could only be initialized during OS bootup. In DPM 2010, the filter model changed and a reboot is usually only required when installing a 2010 agent onto a server with an existing 2007 agent already on it. In that case, the reboot is to complete getting the 2007 agent off. On the last screen, you will see the percentage complete status as the agent is copied out to the machines that you moved to the right pane until each one reaches 100 percent or fails. Upon reboot, the servers will appear in the Agents subtab of the DPM UI.

FIGURE 4.15
Push installing the DPM agents from the DPM server

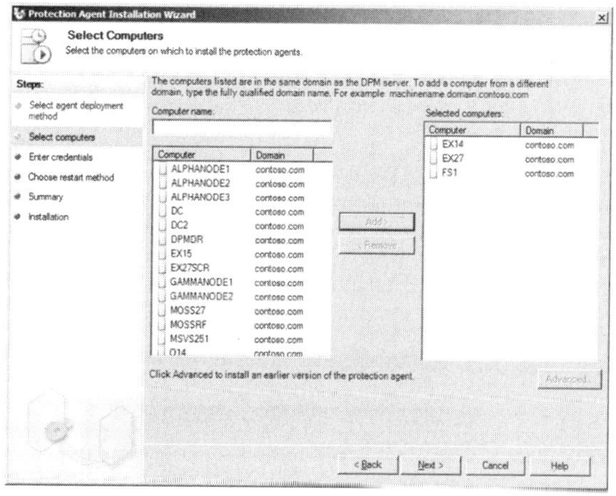

Adding DPM Agents That Were Manually Installed The process of clicking on individual servers to be protected and the DPM agent is usually ideal for small to medium businesses, as well as proofs of concept or evaluations in larger enterprises. However, if you have more than 100 servers or protectable assets in your environment, you may want to automatically install the DPM agent, just like you would manage the rollout of any other application using perhaps System Center Configuration Manager (enterprise), System Center Essentials (mid-sized businesses), or even Active Directory Group Policy (we will cover software deployment technologies in Chapter 10). The agent can even be preinstalled during factory installs or imaging by your hardware vendor.

The DPM agent can be installed via a number of methods using its MSI installation binary. The key difference between installing the agent using the UI and installing the agent manually is that when the UI pushes the agent to the production servers, it installs the agent and creates a connection between the agent and the DPM server that pushed it down. When the agent is manually installed, no connection is created to a particular DPM server because the assumption for a larger deployment is that you wish to install the agent broadly and will have multiple DPM servers available (and not yet know which one will be protecting each production server).

In DPM 2007, you could create the agent-server connection using the DPM Management Shell (PowerShell) by running the `Attach-Production.ps1` script. The script is provided in the `BIN` directory in which the DPM agent was installed and is automatically usable from the Management Shell. It prompts you for five variables, which you can also include in the command line:

- `DPMserver`—The name of the DPM server
- `PSname`—The name of the production server that the agent is installed on
- `Username`—The username (without domain) that has administrator-level privileges on both the DPM server and the production server
- `Password`—Hidden by asterisks
- `Domain`—The domain for the user entered earlier

In DPM 2010, you can still use PowerShell as described earlier. But new in DPM 2010 is the ability to create the same agent-server connection within the DPM UI under the Management Tab and Agents subtab. To create this connection, we will start the Install or Add Agents task. On the first choice screen, we can select the lower choice of Adding DPM Agents that are already installed. The rest of the screens in the wizard are the same as installing the agent: we will be prompted to pick which servers are to be added (and already have the agent installed) and then asked for domain, username, and password. Then, the connection is established.

Regardless of whether you pushed the agents out or manually installed and added them afterward, the result is the same for the Agents subtab shown in Figure 4.16 with agents listed. In this figure, we see several production servers connected to the DPM server. Some of them are unprotected, whereas others have protection already configured.

FIGURE 4.16
The DPM Management tab, Agents subtab

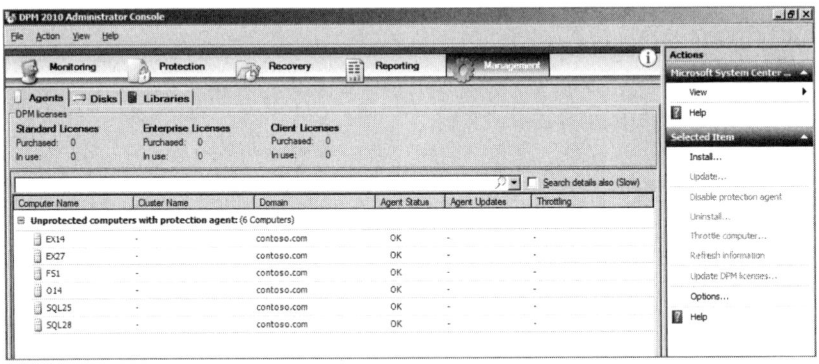

Configuring DPM 2010 Protection

At this point, we have a functional DPM server with disk and tape media, and our production servers have agents installed and connected back to the DPM server. It is time to protect some data. There are four scenarios for protecting data that each requires some explanation and insight:

Server Data Protection The standard for most backup and data protection technologies and a primary focus for DPM 2007 and 2010.

System State and Bare Metal Recovery (BMR) Provides the ability to recover the server itself, as a configuration or complete restoration, respectively.

Virtual Machine Protection This is like bare metal recovery (whole server protection) for machines that are not using physical hardware. It has some extra benefits and considerations.

Client Data Protection This might appear similar to Server Data Protection, except that the nature of more and more client machines is that they are disconnected from the corporate network most of the time. This increases the need for protection but creates additional challenges.

TASK 4: SERVER DATA PROTECTION

As our baseline of understanding, we will use DPM 2010 to protect a variety of production workloads with different kinds of server data, as well as configure protection for system state, BMR, and VMs. Immediately following this task, we look into how some of this data protection takes extra steps to be accomplished.

To begin, we will start in the DPM 2010 Administrator Console and choose the Protection tab from the top ribbon bar. Here, we can see tasks on the right side, including one to create a protection group. A *protection group* is a policy within DPM regarding what should be protected and how the protection should happen.

1. By clicking Create Protection Group, we will start the Create New Protection Group wizard. After the introduction screen, we will see something new to DPM 2010, a radio button selection between protecting servers and clients, as Figure 4.17 shows. We will discuss the differences between server and client protection in Task 5.

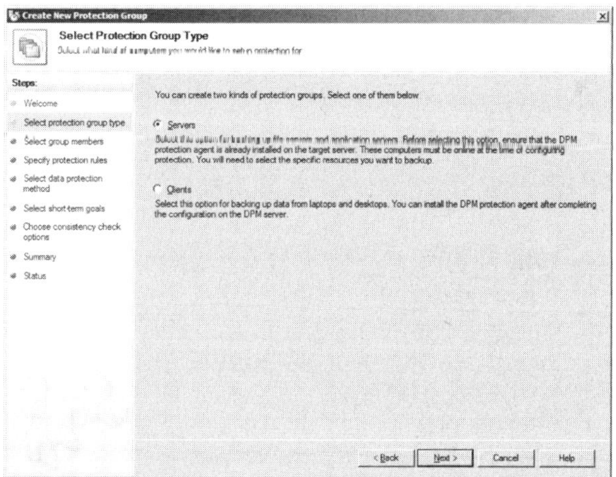

FIGURE 4.17 DPM 2010's Create New Protection Group wizard

2. For now, we will accept the default of protecting servers, but in Task 5, we will choose Clients and see the differences.

3. If we consider a protection group to be a policy of what (should be protected) and how (should the protection happen), then Figure 4.18 shows the what screen, where we choose which servers and data source are to be protected.

The servers in the left pane have a DPM agent installed on them and are connected to this DPM server. By expanding any server, we will see three common protectable data types (as well as applications):

File Shares All the files except for administrative or hidden shares are listed here. For a file server, this is all we need. For application servers, you might protect the share used for storing administrative utilities or other ad hoc material. As discussed earlier in the chapter in regard to DPM storage, DPM allows you to select specific shares, but will locate the actual volume\path on the production server and protect it. This means that DPM administrators do not have to be aware of volume layout for protecting file servers; simply pick the shares that need protecting.

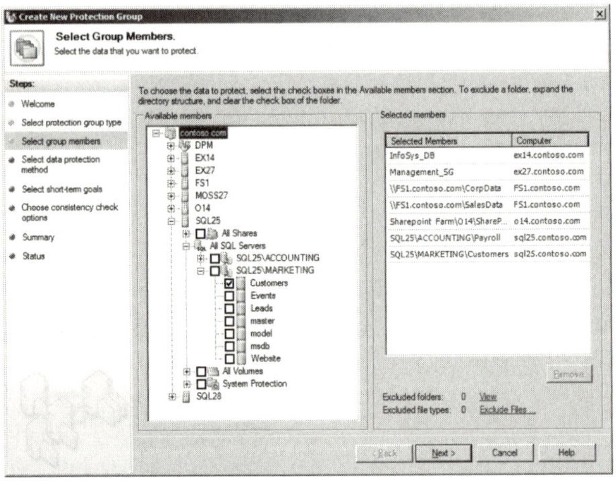

FIGURE 4.18
Selecting what should be protected in DPM

Volumes/Directories Enable you to protect any directory on an NTFS volume within the production server. This is especially useful for protecting application servers where a particular directory holds the configuration information, a database dump, or other metadata.

System State This will be discussed immediately after this task, but is selectable for any production server here.

Along with the three generically protectable data objects per server, any other VSS-based data sources that are supported by DPM will also be displayed here. When first clicking and expanding each production server, the refresh may take between 15–45 seconds. During this time, the DPM server and each DPM agent are inventorying what VSS writers are registered with VSS on the production servers. Essentially, the DPM agent is providing the latest inventory of what can be protected by DPM, including not only the data types via VSS but also the actual data objects that are protectable (as seen in Figure 4.18):

- Exchange Servers will list the storage groups (Exchange 2007) or databases (Exchange 2010) that are protectable.
- SQL Servers will list each instance of SQL Server (2000, 2005, or 2008) that is installed, and then all the databases under each instance.

- SharePoint servers will list the farm (2007 and 2010), as well as the potentially separate index and shared components (2007).
- Microsoft Virtualization hosts will list the virtual machines as they appear, along with what method of backup can be performed. We will discuss this more in detail after this Task, and later in Chapter 9.

Unlike legacy backup products that sell separately purchasable agents for each application, DPM uses a single agent to protect all the supported applications (the Enterprise Data Protection Management License, or E-DPML). For more on licensing, see the earlier sidebar "DPM Agents vs. DPM Licenses" in this chapter. How this affects us is that if one server is running multiple applications that are protectable by DPM, all of the application components will be seen on this screen. For example, Microsoft Office SharePoint Server 2007 uses SQL Server as its content database, so a single server running the entire farm will show both SQL and SharePoint running on the same machine. In that case, we would choose the SharePoint farm for protection.

PROTECTING SQL CONTENT SERVERS WITHIN A SHAREPOINT FARM

When you protect SQL Server, the DPM agent can utilize both VSS block-based protection as well as transactional log replication up to every 15 minutes.

When you protect SharePoint, there is no log (even though it uses SQL Server databases for its content). Therefore, you can only protect the SharePoint farm using Express Fulls. This may be a good reason to protect SharePoint in a different protection group than your SQL servers, where you can do more Express Fulls per day.

Because every server that is part of a SharePoint farm, including the content database servers, must run a DPM agent, it might be tempting to protect them as standalone SQL servers instead of as members of the SharePoint farm. Don't do it.

If you protect a SharePoint content database (SQL) server as SQL, then all that you can restore is the whole database, without any context or metadata. Even if you are only planning for whole-server recoveries, it won't be enough since the database indices won't match the SharePoint metadata.

When you protect the SharePoint farm, you will protect it less frequently because of the lack of transactional log replication, but you can restore individual items, sites, or databases in a way that interacts well across the farm.

In all cases, and similar to the explanation of file shares given earlier, DPM identifies the file-level objects that compose the data sources as they are selected. For example, if a database is selected, the component database file and log files are located. From there, the remainder of the process is as discussed, where the DPM agent identifies the blocks that make up the files, and those blocks are monitored for changes to be synchronized during the next Express Full. And in the case of transactional logs, they are replicated up to every 15 minutes.

With our protection group policy now specifying what is to be protected, the next few screens determine how the protection will occur. Earlier in Figure 4.8, we saw that DPM protects to disk, to tape, and to a remote location.

4. We will cover the remote location in Task 12, but on the screen shown in Figure 4.19, supply a name for the protection group and select your protection method (Disk, for this task).
5. Once you select disk-based protection, the next two screens ask you to configure disk-to-disk protection. The screens won't appear if you don't specify Disk in step 4. In Figure 4.20, we see that disk-based protection has been distilled down to business-driven questions that we will see again when configuring tape in just a few minutes.
   - How long should the data be retained (on disk)?
   - How often should it be protected (to disk)?

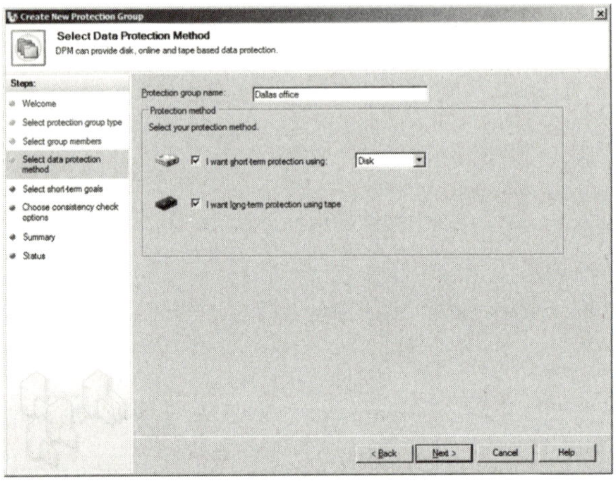

FIGURE 4.19
Select disk- or tape-based protection in DPM.

As discussed earlier in regard to the DPM storage pool, whereas the replica volume stores the complete and most current copy of the data, the recovery point volume stores the block-level changes for as long as the first setting specifies. The second setting—how frequently replication should occur—applies to the transactional logs and can specify up to every 15 minutes.

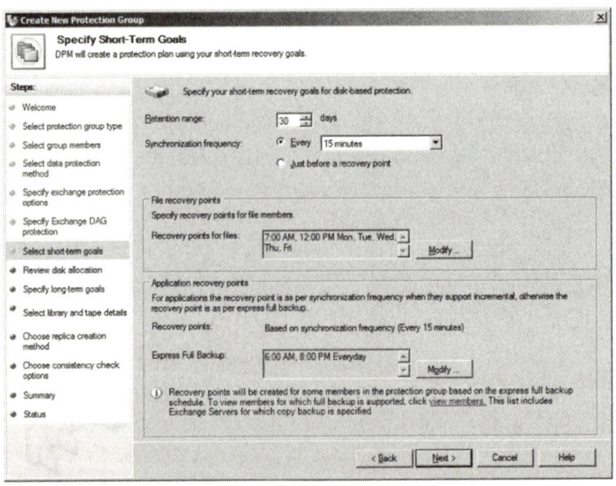

FIGURE 4.20
DPM disk-based retention policy

On the same screen, you can see when the Express Full is scheduled; it defaults to 8:00 p.m. every evening. I recommend that you schedule an Express Full backup at whatever time your legacy backup solution will have finished its nightly operation, perhaps 11:00 p.m. or 2:00 a.m. By clicking the Modify button, you can change not only *when* the Express Full backup happens but *how many* such backups take place. You can specify up to eight Express Full backups per day. Although Express Fulls use VSS and COW (as we discussed earlier), they are not without some I/O consumption. So you must perform a balancing act: do multiple Express Full backups during each business day to achieve faster recovery while ensuring as little I/O impact to the production server as possible. We will discuss the ramifications to application restore scenarios in Tasks 7 and 8. For now, I have chosen three Express Fulls per day at 7:00 a.m., Noon, and 8:00 p.m.. In addition, for this scenario, I have turned off disk-based backups for Sunday, as you can see in Figure 4.21.

FIGURE 4.21
Modifying when Express Fulls occur

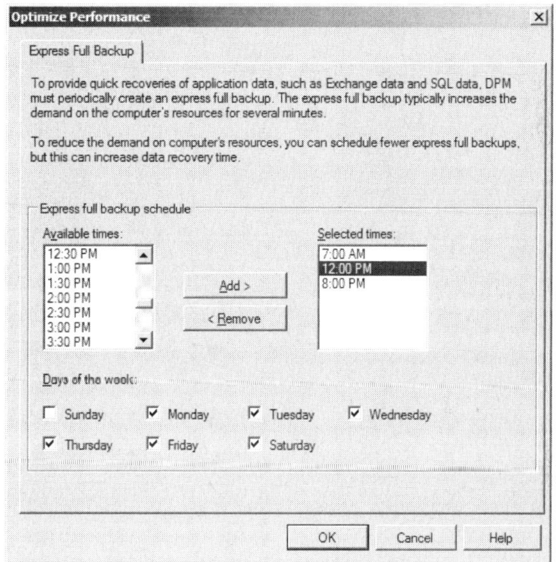

6. On the second disk-based protection screen, you can see how much disk space DPM plans on allocating for protecting the data sources. DPM looks at the approximate amount of file space consumed by the current data sources for the replicas and estimates the disk consumption necessary for the recovery points. Recovery points are configurable settings that you can adjust after using the DPM Storage Calculators found on `http://blogs.technet.com/DPM`. On this wizard screen, we can see that two volumes per data source will be sized and sliced out of the overall DPM storage pool.

7. Now that we've completed the retention policies and media configuration to disk, the next two wizard screens have similar questions and configuration options for protecting to tape. Figure 4.22 shows the same two business questions related to retention time and frequency, and we can tune when the tape backup will occur.

When we select how long to retain the data (for example, 7 years) and how often to do a tape backup (weekly in this case), DPM automatically creates a traditional grandfather–father–son (GFS) rotation scheme of weekly, monthly, and annual tapes:

A weekly backup each week, to be reused each month

Twelve monthly tapes, to be reused annually

Seven annual tapes to be reused after the retention period

FIGURE 4.22
DPM tape-based retention policies

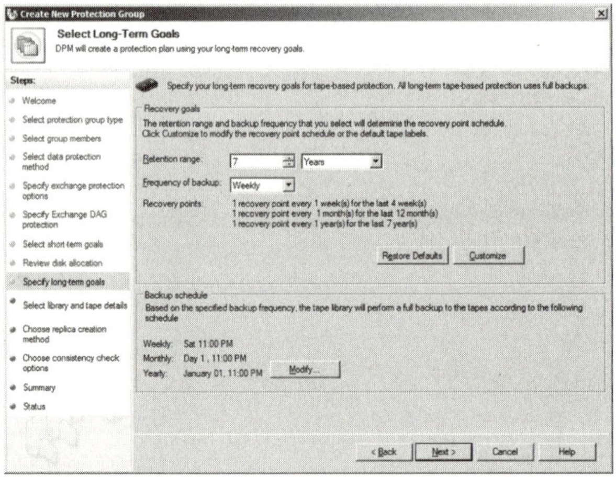

8. On the second tape screen, similar to how we tuned the disk media in step 6, we configure which tape drives or media changers to use. We can also specify whether to encrypt or compress the data on tape. If you are storing tapes off-site, please encrypt the tapes for security purposes. We will discuss offsite tapes and alternatives in Chapter 12. The tape devices shown here are the ones we registered in Task 2, when we added the tape devices and changers that were visible to DPM from the Windows Device Manager.

9. With our policies configured, we now need to determine how and when the initial copy of the data will be transmitted from the production servers to the DPM replica. Our choices are:

Now This option will immediately start sending the baseline copy of the data from the production server to the DPM server.

Later This lets you schedule the baseline to commence after hours.

Manual This option is my favorite for branch offices.

The manual initial replica was first released in DPM 2006 as part of achieving centralized backups for branch offices. The trick is, if your production servers are on the wrong side of a WAN connection, there may never be a good time to do an initial baseline of a few terabytes across a slow connection. Instead, you can make an ad hoc tape backup or just copy the files to a USB hard drive to make the data portable and then ship it from the branch office to the location of the DPM server. At that point, you can simply copy the data from your portable media into a predefined replica volume on the DPM server. Then, when DPM configures the initial protection group, it will discover that it already has a copy of the data within its storage pool and offer to do an *immediate consistency check*, which will compare what is in the DPM storage pool to what is in the production server and only copy over the changes. Therefore, if it took you three days to ship the copy of the data from the branch office to the DPM server, only the blocks of data that changed over the past three days will be transmitted over the wire during the initial copy.

10. The last screen in the wizard provides a summary of the choices that you made. Click OK to confirm, and your protection group is created. You will be returned to the main DPM Administrator Console, as seen in Figure 4.23.

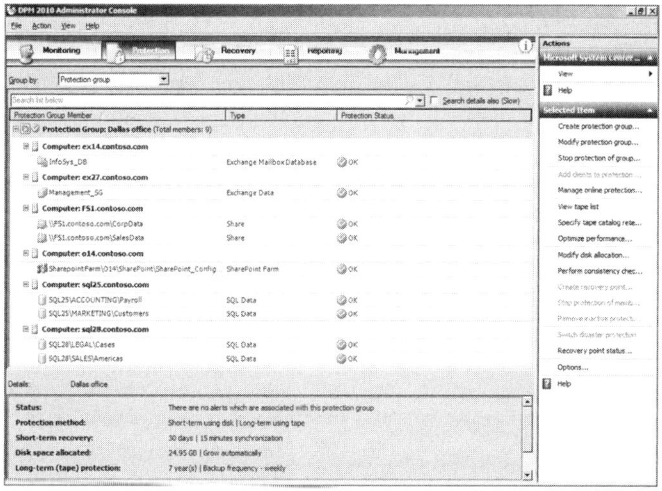

FIGURE 4.23
The DPM console, Protection Tab

It will take several minutes to allocate the storage volumes and then the initial copies of the data for the replica will automatically commence. If you did a manual copy or otherwise invoked an immediate consistency check, you will see each data source initially turn green but then turn yellow as block-level comparisons happen. Each will turn back to green after the consistency checks.

Congratulations; you have now protected most of the key workloads in a Windows datacenter. Now, we will look deeper at a few different kinds of data and learn what is notable about their protection, and later, their recovery.

SYSTEM STATE AND BARE METAL RECOVERY

In Task 4, we discussed protecting the data on a server, using the DPM agent and its interaction with Volume Shadow Copy Services (VSS), as well as the production applications' transaction logs. And for data recovery, that is all that you need. But in some cases, you may wish to recover the whole server. There are two approaches to server-level recovery:

System State *System state* is the collection of Registry entries, core system binaries, and other configuration information necessary to change a clean and generic operating system into the configuration of the server that was already in production. For example, suppose you have 100 branch offices and each one has a single server with similar hardware and OS configuration. To prepare for a server-level failure, you have a couple of spare servers with the same hardware configuration at your corporate headquarters. The spare servers have a generic installation of the same operating system, are maintained to the same patch or hotfix levels, and are called Spare01 and Spare02.

Now suppose branch office server (SVR) 91 fails; you can restore the system state from SVR91 onto Spare02. When the server is rebooted, it will now be SVR91 with all of the original configuration settings, including the system Registry, hardware drivers, machine accounts, domain membership, and all the other finicky bits, exactly like what the original SVR91 had prior to failing. With a newly working SVR91, you can quickly restore the server's data, and the machine will be ready to send out to the branch office.

Bare Metal Recovery *Bare metal recovery* (*BMR*) is not a file-based restore of configuration data. It is a block-based restore of the entire disk partitions for booting and running the operating system and applications. BMR requires an image-based backup of the operating system and application volumes, as well as a utility that can stream blocks back to a new machine with no prerequisite installed components.

For example, assume that SVR91 has a hard drive failure. The remainder of the server hardware is functional, so you can simply replace the hard drive with a new one. But now, the machine does not have a bootable OS or any other operating method. A BMR restoration will boot a small utility whose only function is to apply the blocks from an image-based backup and re-create the OS volume on the new hard disk. Upon rebooting, the machine will have a working OS volume on its new hard disk and will come online as the SVR91 that it used to be.

NOTE A system state–based server recovery presumes that you have a working operating system on similar hardware; that is necessary to restore the configuration only.

A BMR-based server recovery does *not* presume a preinstalled OS. It only presumes similar server hardware and a blank hard drive.

But just because you can do a whole server restore, that may not mean that you want to. In fact, even for a complete server failure, it is often advisable or at least desirable to reinstall the application and then simply restore the data.

For example, Microsoft Exchange servers retain much of their configuration either in Active Directory or between peer-level Exchange servers such as DAG or CCR (see Chapter 7). Recovering a complete Exchange mailbox server can be as simple as setting up a new Windows server with a fresh copy of Microsoft Exchange using a few extra command-line switches, and then restoring the mailbox data from DPM. Along with the simpler restore path, you get the flexibility of not having to use the original hardware; you can use a newer server platform instead. It is worth noting that Exchange 2003 still keeps a lot of stuff in its internal configuration metabase, though, and in Exchange 2007 and 2010, there are still log files and machine-specific configuration details that should be preserved as well.

So, in some cases, you might restore the server by reinstalling the application on any hardware that you want. In other cases, you might choose to use the same hardware but want a fresh start. For example, if a file server that has been in production for two years fails, it may be more desirable to install a clean operating system (perhaps even an upgrade) than to restore the entire machine from bare metal. The benefit of a fresh installation is that the OS is not burdened with 18–24 months of incremental patches and maintenance, but instead has a clean OS with only the patches that are appropriate as of the rebuild.

If you're installing a newer operating system, you might simply re-create the shares and restore the data from DPM. If you're installing the same operating system, you could install the OS and then restore the system state, which includes the Registry and other machine-specific configuration information.

As shown in Task 4, DPM protects three generic data types on all servers: file shares, volumes, and system state. But in actuality, the DPM agent does not directly protect system state—the built-in backup utility does:

- For production servers running Windows Server 2003 or 2003 R2, DPM uses the NT Backup utility.
- For production servers running Windows Server 2008 or 2008 R2, DPM uses built-in OS functionality (similar to the Windows Server Backup utility) that was discussed earlier in the chapter.

In either case, when you select system state protection within DPM, the DPM agent invokes the built-in OS backup utility to deliver the backup itself. The OS's built-in utility is designed with outsourced system state protection as a primary use scenario; the utility backs up the OS in a way that is supported by the OS teams and dumps the backup in a disk-based file (either BKF or VHD depending on the utility). From there, the DPM agent replicates the file from its landing place on the production server into the DPM storage pool.

Because DPM centralizes the management but offloads the execution of system state protection, two recovery scenarios are available:

- For whole-server restorations, the DPM administrator has a copy of the system state for each production server, so that if a server were to fail (especially in a remote location), a new server could be quickly built and sent from the corporate headquarters.
- For configuration rollbacks, the local administrator can utilize the built-in backup utility to restore the server to a previously well-known good configuration, with no need to access DPM.

BMR is also delivered differently, based on whether the production server is Windows Server 2003, 2003 R2, 2008, or 2008 R2:

- For production servers running Windows Server 2008 or 2008 R2, the DPM agent uses the same OS-enabled backup mechanisms as the Windows Server Backup utility does for system state backups. However, the WSB utility does a block-based image backup to locally attached storage (such as a USB external drive) on each production server or a centralized network file share on the DPM server. The management of BMR is still done from the DPM server, but it is executed and stored with each local production server for fast image-based restores.
- For production servers running Windows Server 2003 and 2003 R2, the built-in utility from the OS does not offer a bare metal restore capability. Instead, DPM 2010 provides the same utility originally shipped with DPM 2007, the System Recovery Tool (SRT). The SRT provides a centralized image-level backup of Windows 2003 and XP machines by storing only the unique blocks and partial file elements from the OS and system volumes. BMR efficiently deduplicates the OS blocks, but the restore must happen across the network (instead of from a local copy).

Real World Scenario

EVERYTHING IS PERMISSIBLE, BUT NOT EVERYTHING IS BENEFICIAL

That phrase is one translation of 1 Corinthians 10:23, but I use it most often in meetings with my customers or partners who are looking at new data protection and availability projects.

Sometimes, you don't need to restore the data. You simply need to rebuild a server or its operating system. This is the case for one member or node that is part of failover clustering (Chapter 6), Exchange replication (Chapter 7), or SQL mirroring (Chapter 8).

In some cases, the only thing that you should restore is the data. If the configuration can be re-created easily, then rebuild the server on newer hardware or a newer OS.

In other cases, you would like to use the same hardware and same generation of the operating system, so all that is needed is the data; you then restore the system state, as you'd do with domain controllers.

And finally, you might have some servers that were complex to deploy or that have had incremental patches that must be applied to any new server in exactly the same order. Those servers need a BMR capability.

It's critical that you identify your goals and plan for the right kinds of recovery. Only then can you start picking the right protection options.

VIRTUAL MACHINE AND HOST PROTECTION

We will look more deeply into the specifics for protecting virtual machines and their hosts in Chapter 9. But within the context of DPM 2010, there are three important considerations that we should cover.

In some ways, DPM treats Microsoft virtualization like an application, such as Microsoft SQL Server or Microsoft Exchange. It requires the E-DPML license and exposes the logical data objects to be protected (in this case, virtual machines), much like DPM shows storage groups or databases. The logical objects to be protected (VMs) are then translated by the DPM agent into their respective file objects and the block-level Express Full backups are used to re-synchronize the blocks within the VHDs that change throughout the day.

When selecting VMs for protection using the DPM Create New Protection Group wizard, you will notice that they are listed as being protected either via Saved State or by Child Partition. These two methods can be roughly translated as momentary downtime or no downtime, respectively. We will look closely into VM backups and downtime when we discuss how the virtualization host's VSS writer works in Chapter 9.

And finally, just because you can back up your VMs from the host level, that does not necessarily mean you should. There are benefits, such as being able to protect servers that DPM does not directly support, like Linux machines, because they are encapsulated inside a virtual machine. Another benefit is that you are able to purchase and deploy a single DPM license for the host instead of using one in each virtual machine. But there are also caveats, such as not being able to selectively choose just a subset of files for protection. Essentially:

- The good news of protecting VMs from the host perspective is that you are able to protect the entire virtual machine as a whole.
- The bad news of protecting VMs from the host perspective is that you *have to* protect the entire virtual machine as a whole.

We will look at these and many other considerations in Chapter 9, when we explore how virtualization changes our methodologies for data protection and availability. But for now, as part of Task 4 in protecting server data with DPM 2010, we can treat a Microsoft virtualization host like any other advanced workload that DPM can protect. In Task 11, we will recover a virtual machine with DPM, as well as some individual files from within the virtual machine.

Task 5: Client Protection

Client protection is new in DPM 2010. In DPM 2006, client protection was not possible at all. In DPM 2007, you could protect client workstations using the S-DPML that was intended for protecting file servers. The assumption was that the workstations would be part of Active Directory and reliably connected to the corporate network. A common use case was restaurants or retail stores, where a remote location might only have one PC. The PC might have had server-quality data on it, but as a single machine, it was likely running a desktop operating system.

In DPM 2007 Service Pack 1, a client license (the C-DPML) was added so that those using DPM to protect workstations could do so more economically. But the requirements for well-connectedness still prevailed. In short, DPM 2007 was a good solution for protecting the branch office's single PC but could not easily protect a traveling laptop.

DPM 2010 has made significant investments in the disconnected laptop scenario, which we can see by opening the DPM Administrator Console and creating a protection Group.

Here are the steps:

1. After the introduction screen of the Create New Protection Group wizard, you'll see a screen containing the radio buttons that we first saw in Task 4 when we were protecting servers (see Figure 4.17 earlier). For this task, choose Clients.

NOTE The key difference between server protection and client protection is the assumption of disconnectedness. DPM 2010 assumes that the laptops go home at night or might be traveling for a majority of the time.

2. On the next screen, choose one or more workstations to be protected as data sources, similar to what we did in Task 4 (see Figure 4.18). There are two noticeable differences between server and client backups on this screen:

    - You are only able pick which clients to protect on this screen and not what data sources to be protected (unlike servers that were expandable).

    - You do not have to choose all of your client workstations at this time. You can add additional client machines to this policy later.

3. Now that you have selected some of the machines you want to be protected, click Next so that you can specify what should be protected on them. The wizard provides drop-down lists client-specific data types such as `MyDocuments` or `Desktop` that you can select types for protection. You can also exclude file types that you do not wish to back up, as shown in Figure 4.24.

4. Enter a protection group name and specify whether to protect to disk or tape, as we did in Task 4.

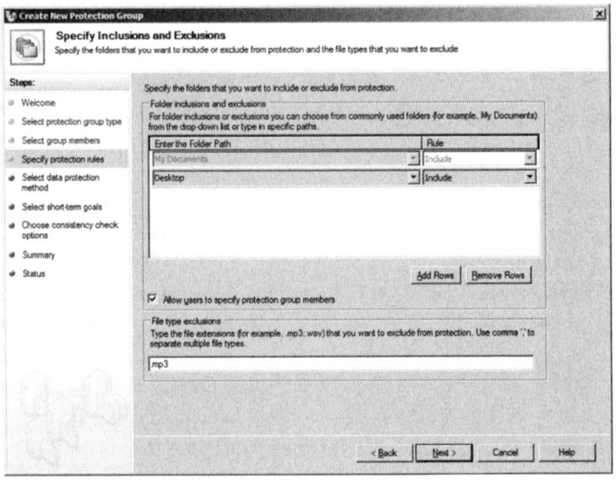

FIGURE 4.24 Choosing what client data should be protected

5. When you start configuring disk-based protection, you'll see a new option specifically for disconnected client machines. Along with the option to indicate frequency of Express Full backups that we saw earlier, there are new options for configuring the tolerance that DPM has for clients that are disconnected. In short, DPM will attempt to protect a client with regularity, similar to how it would a server. But assuming that the client may be traveling throughout the week, you can configure how long DPM will ignore missed backups, as shown in Figure 4.25.

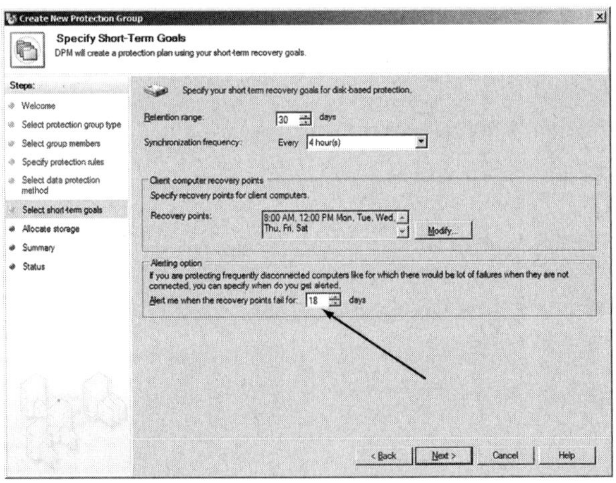

FIGURE 4.25 Settings for handling disconnectedness

In Figure 4.25, we configured 30 days of data retention and a tolerance of 18 days of missed backups. As long as the laptop is protected by DPM at least once during the 18-day window, DPM will be satisfied. If the laptop is disconnected for longer than the specified period, DPM will notify the administrator and issue warnings that the corporate backup policies are not enforced.

Real World Scenario

EIGHTEEN-DAY WINDOW FOR TRAVELING LAPTOPS

An 18-day tolerance window for disconnected laptops provides two weeks plus a three-day weekend holiday. For example, assume that the last day that my laptop is connected to the network is Friday, March 19, 2010, before I travel for two weeks. If I configured DPM for only 14 days, then it will start alerting that I am not compliant to my backup window on Friday, April 1. April 1 is Good Friday (often a company holiday in the U.S.) and it happens to also be my birthday weekend, so I will be off on Monday. Thus, even a 17-day window would not have covered my trip. This is a specific string of circumstances, but some of your users will have stranger ones than that. I could set the alarm for 21 or 30 days, but then I delay being aware of no backups for too long. But configuring 17 days or less runs the risk of too many errors related to three-day weekends. By configuring a nontypical window like 18 days, I can account for a wider variety of traveler scenarios. And my laptop will get backed up without any erroneous alerts on my first day back in the office. Your requirements may be different, but the key is to consider balancing retention requirements with user behavior.

The remaining protection group wizard screens are the same as those we saw in Task 4: allocation of storage, when to do the initial baseline, and a confirmation screen before starting.

Along with protecting client data, the configuration policies from the protection group are also passed to the DPM agent to be done while the laptop is disconnected. The DPM agent uses VSS on the local workstation—in much the same way that the local Windows backup utility does—to provide backups and recovery points on a regular basis, whether or not the node is connected to the corporate network. Thus, if you configure DPM to protect data twice per day, those backups occur when the client is connected to the corporate network (via DPM) or disconnected (using local VSS storage).

To accommodate the dual-backup capability, the DPM agent on client machines also includes a system tray application, shown in Figure 4.26. The DPM client UI lets individual users know of their current protected status and what data is being protected, and enables end users to restore their own data as well as optionally specify additional data directories to be protected. You must first enable this, on a per–protection group basis, within the DPM console. You enable your end users to add directories for protection by clicking the Allow Users To Specify Protection Group Members check box in the Create New Protection Group wizard on the Specify Inclusions And Exclusions screen (see Figure 4.24 earlier).

FIGURE 4.26
The DPM client UI in the system tray

The end user can then use the DPM system tray applet to add the additional directories for protection. Here are the steps:

1. Expand the DPM client from the system tray and choose the Protected Items tab.
2. Some directories will already be checked and bold because they are defined in the protection group policy of the DPM server. Select any directories, and they will be protected along with the data that DPM chose, as you can see in Figure 4.27.

One limitation that many users feel with corporately deployed legacy backup solutions is a lack of flexibility. For example, some technologies might mandate that only a user's My Documents directory be protected. So if the user wants certain data protected, they have to change how their applications work to be sure that the data is stored in the right folder. By enabling your power users to add directories in DPM, you can push down corporate policies that My Documents will be protected but still allow end users to add areas. Once added by the end user, the data is protected on the same retention schedule as the default policies that you defined in the Create New Protection Group wizard.

We will cover client data restoration in Task 12.

FIGURE 4.27
Using the DPM 2010 client UI to select data to protect

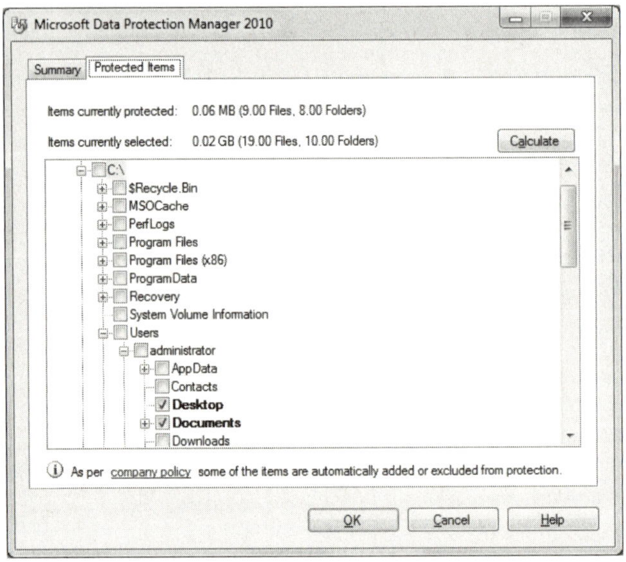

Restoring Data with DPM 2010

No one should deploy data protection. You should deploy the ability to do data restoration. Believe it or not, there is a difference. Some technologies, and even IT regulations (which we will cover in Chapter 12), focus almost exclusively on backing things up. But if you don't regularly test and have an equal understanding of how to restore, then you have missed the point. For the next series of tasks, we will look at restoring a variety of data and discuss the differences between them.

If you are following along with these tasks in your own environment, you may wish to allow data to be protected for at least one or two days prior to attempting the restoration tasks, so that a few days of protected data will be available to you for restoration activities. Tasks 6 through 12 also presume that you have all of the production workloads that DPM is capable of protecting in your environment. Be cautious if you skip reading some of the explanatory text in one of the tasks because it a particular workload may not be your current environment. To minimize redundant text between similar workloads and tasks, I have tried to discuss key ideas that may apply to more than one workload. The process is described in the first workload where it is relevant and then referenced in the subsequent tasks.

How the DPM Storage Pool Restores Data

As discussed earlier in the DPM section, there are two repositories within the DPM storage pool per protected data source—the *replica* volume and the *recovery point* volume. The replica holds a complete copy of the production data as of the latest Express Full block-level synchronization. As blocks in the replica are overwritten during each subsequent Express Full operation, the displaced blocks are stored in the recovery point volume. To recover files of any type, whether they are from a file server, a database, or a virtual machine, the fundamental process is the same. Within the DPM Administrator Console (or via the DPM Management Shell), a data object is selected for restoration along with the point in time that it should be restored to. And for our example, we will assume that the object to be restored consists of eight blocks of data.

If the data to be restored is all held within the replica volume, as in the case of a rebuilding a server that has failed, then the eight blocks that make up the data object are read from the replica volume. The eight blocks are streamed back to the DPM agent on the production server that writes the data back to the production volume.

If a previous point in time is selected, then only some of the eight required blocks may be in the replica volume. The other blocks that make up the file at the point in time that was chosen will be in the recovery point volume. In this case, perhaps five blocks come from the replica, while three blocks have at some point been updated (and overwritten in the replica volume). The original three blocks from the point in time that we want will come from the recovery point volume. But still, only eight blocks are read from the DPM storage pool. Only eight blocks are transmitted across the network. And only eight blocks are written to disk. While this may seem overly verbose, my goal is to emphasize that the DPM disk-based storage pool does not operate on a layering model of full backups and incrementals/differentials layered over the top. If eight blocks are required for the restore, then only eight blocks are read from the DPM disk, transmitted across the wire, and applied to the production server.

Overview of the DPM Restoration Process

To see this in action, go to the DPM Administrator Console and click the Recovery button on the top ribbon. The left pane of the Recovery tab provides a tree-based view of all the production servers that have been protected by our DPM server.

When you expand each of the servers, you will see the same kinds of data objects that you selected in the protection groups. In the next several tasks, we will look at how each application type provides different restore scenarios but the initial activities are the same regardless of data type. Figure 4.28 shows a DPM console with several servers expanded to reveal their various data sources.

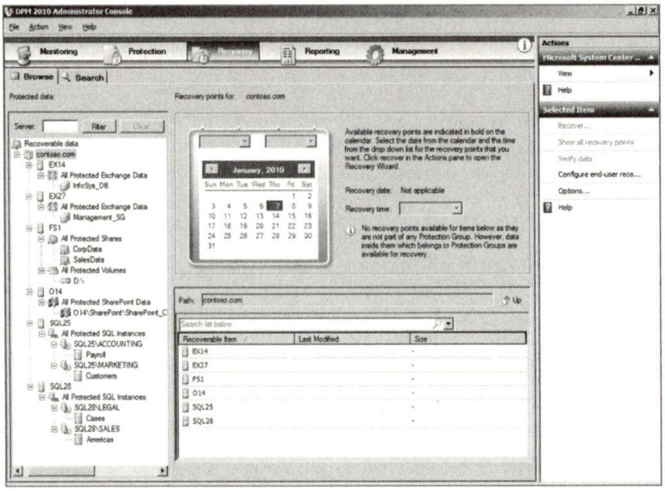

FIGURE 4.28
DPM Administrator Console, Recovery tab

Almost all restores from the DPM server start with the same few first steps:

1. Expand the production server that you wish to recover data from, and then expand the type of data that you wish to recover, such as:
   - Exchange storage group (2007) or database (2010)
   - SQL Server instance
   - SharePoint farm
   - Virtualization host
   - Volume or file share
2. Select the object that you initially chose for protection in the Create New Protection Group wizard. In most workloads, this is a macro or container object with more granular restore capabilities (which we will discuss in Tasks 6 through 11).
3. When you select the container object, the right side of the DPM console changes.
   - In the upper-center portion of the screen, the dates that DPM has recovery points for will appear bold in the calendar.
   - The lower-center portion of the screen will show additional granularity of what can potentially be restored.
4. You can select any bold date on the calendar, and a pull-down menu on the right side of the calendar will the times of day that are available for restoration. If you were doing an Express Full backup only once per day, the pull-down may only show 8:00 p.m. If you are protecting a transactional application such as SQL Server, the pull-down may reveal every 15-minute time slot throughout the entire 24-hour day.

5. Click a desired time, and the details pane in the lower-center screen will update as the granular restore options are verified.

6. Right-click on the object that you wish to restore and select Restore.

Essentially, you can select almost any data object for DPM restoration to any point in time in as few as four mouse clicks:

1. Select the data object from the left tree.

2. Choose the date that you wish to recover to from the calendar.

3. Pull down the point in time that you wish to recover to.

4. Right-click the data object in the lower-center pane, and choose Recover.

This launches the recovery wizard, which we will be using for the next several tasks. After the introduction screen, you see several recovery choices, some of which are specific to the workload being restored and others that are generic to all DPM recovery scenarios. One example is seen in Figure 4.29. In the DPM Recovery Wizards, the last two recovery options are generic across all DPM data sources:

Recover To An Alternate Location The option to recover to an alternate location restores the files that make up your data source to any file share or directory that is accessible from the DPM server. The intent is to provide the files in such a way that an application owner could then act on them.

Copy To Tape The Copy To Tape option is not misspelled although you might expect it to read Copy From Tape. With the Copy To Tape option, the files of the selected data source are restored from the DPM storage pool onto their own tape. This approach is most commonly used for IT environments that periodically ship data offsite to an auditor, vault, or an e-discovery judicial proceeding. Previously, a typical and nonoptimal method of delivering those offsite materials has been to copy an existing backup tape from the nightly library, which includes not only the requested data but also other, unnecessary information. Especially in the case of judiciary proceedings or e-discovery, this is often problematic since whatever is given to the lawyer may be usable against you.

Instead, DPM lets you select only the data object you desire and the specific point in time that the data was at. Then, only that data is restored to its own individual tape. This tape can then be sent off to the auditor, vault, or attorney.

These two restore options are the last two choices in the recovery wizards across all data workloads.

Ignoring the other application-specific options for a moment, the remainder of the recovery wizard offers a few other choices.

Network Bandwidth Throttling Ensures that the restoration activity doesn't overwhelm limited bandwidth segments between the DPM server and the restoration target. For this, DPM provides KBps and MBps settings, including variations for time of day, so you may use partial wide area network (WAN) bandwidth during the production day and all available bandwidth during nonproduction hours.

SAN Recovery Uses a SAN that is shared between the DPM server and the production server. This invokes a SAN-specific script that instructs the SAN to make a mirror of the DPM replica volume within the shared disk array and then remount the mirror on the production server. This can be a powerful feature if the production server(s) and the DPM server are on the same SAN, because terabytes of data can be restored in a matter of seconds.

Notification Uses a Simple Mail Transfer Protocol (SMTP) mail server and notifies the appropriate system administrators when the restoration process is complete.

Following the standardized recovery options, a confirmation screen will display your choices, intended recovery paths, and data source component files. Clicking Restore begins the restoration process.

We will now look at several restore tasks and discuss how the recovery capabilities vary by application.

Task 6: Restoring Files

Building on what has already been explained in the last section, "Overview of the DPM Restoration Process," let's first look at the simplest type of data recovery: individual files. Typically, every data source has the two DPM storage pool volumes: the replica and the recovery point volumes. The same is true for volumes protected by DPM, but this concept needs additional explanation when discussing file share protection.

Imagine a file server (FS1) with an E: drive and three top-level directories:

`E:\APPS`—shared as Applications

`E:\DATA`—shared as Data

`E:\SW`—shared as Software

If DPM was originally configured to protect the entire volume (`E:\`), then everything that we have discussed so far is accurate. There will be a replica volume and a recovery point volume for `FS1-E:\`. And you could select any file or directory for restoration.

If DPM was originally configured to only protect two shares from that volume, such as the Applications and Data shares, then DPM does something to optimize its storage:

- The DPM agent identifies that the two shares are both held on the same production volume.
- The DPM storage pool creates replica and recovery point volumes for the E:\ volume, instead of for each share. But only the paths under `E:\Apps` and `E:\Data` are replicated. Any directories on `E:\` that are not offered under one of the selected shares will not be replicated to the DPM server.

This allows the DPM server to maintain fewer volumes within its storage pool, while still enabling the administrator to identify exactly what should be protected. To restore files using the DPM console:

1. From the Recovery Tab of the DPM console, select either the file share or the actual volume in the left tree.
2. The calendar will adjust to recoverable days, and the pull-down list will be updated with the times of day that were chosen as either Express Full backups or file recovery points in the Create New Protection Group wizard.

3. With the date and time selected, scroll down in the lower-center part of the screen to the folder or file that you wish to recover.
4. Right-click the item to bring up the Recovery Wizard shown in Figure 4.29.

FIGURE 4.29
DPM 2010 Recovery Wizard for files

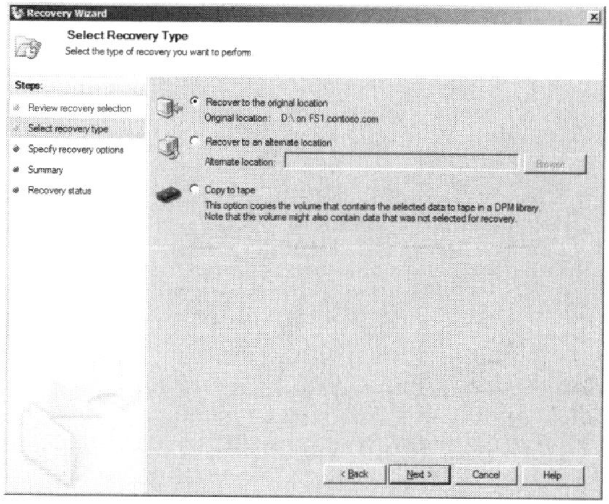

As described in the previous section, the latter two restoration options are available for every DPM protected workload—Restore To File Location and Restore To Tape. When restoring files, there is only one additional option—Restore To Original Location. This is common for most of the DPM protected workloads, where DPM will simply restore the selected items over the location where they were originally protected. This is especially useful for reverting something after it had been erroneously changed or deleted, as well as for whole server or disk recoveries.

TASK 7: ENABLING END-USER RECOVERY OF FILES

As easy as restoring files is from the DPM Administrator Console, it may be more desirable to allow end users to restore their own data.

Real World Scenario

WHAT IF YOU DO NOT TRUST YOUR USERS TO RESTORE THEIR DATA SAFELY?

Some administrators presume that enabling End-User Recovery (EUR) is as dangerous as giving someone scissors and telling them to run with a blindfold on; they can not only hurt themselves but others by restoring the wrong data. But the reality is that users already have the scissors and the blindfold—meaning they already have the ability to delete or overwrite their data and that of their teammates:

- Within their home directories, users can already delete their own data.
- Within team directories, users can already overwrite their peers' data.

EUR does not allow users to restore or overwrite files that they do not already have rights to. So, EUR doesn't create any additional risk or exposure.

What EUR does do is provide a way for savvy users to fix their mistakes without bothering you or the IT help desk. If you still aren't convinced, then filter who can use the EUR application by not installing it via Software Distribution or Active Directory Group Policy. As middle ground, you may wish to enable EUR for managers, but perhaps not for individuals. The key to remember is that for every user that you enable with EUR, there will be fewer restore requests to the IT department.

EUR utilizes the Shadow Copies of Shared Folders (SCSF) functionality that has been available since Windows Server 2003, when VSS was first introduced. At that time:

- Users had mapped network drives to file shares on servers and restored their own data from the file server using an EUR plug-in that enhanced Windows Explorer or Microsoft Office (2003 or better). The plug-in has gone by a few names, such as EUR, the TimeWarp client, and the Previous Versions Client.
- Behind the scenes, VSS was enabled on the local file serving volumes and shadow copies (or snapshots) were scheduled for a few times per day. The shadow copies were stored locally on a hidden percentage of the production volume.

Any user can right-click on a file or folder and select its properties. With the EUR or Previous Versions Client (PVC) installed, an additional tab is displayed in the properties dialog of the file or folder. On the Previous Versions tab, as shown in Figure 4.30, any previous versions of the file can be directly restored to their original location, indirectly restored to an alternate location, or simply opened for viewing.

FIGURE 4.30
The Previous Versions Client for End-User Recovery

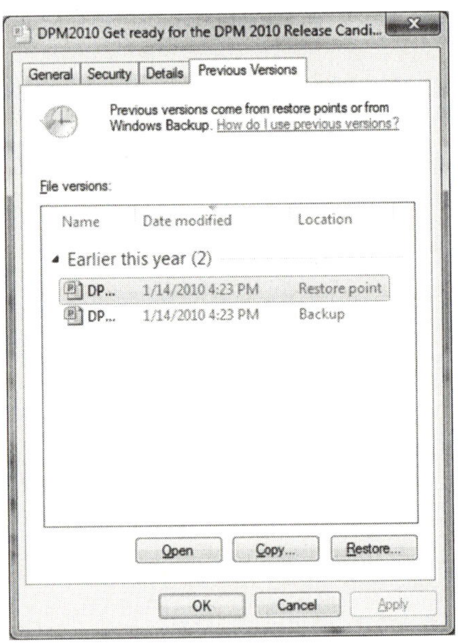

Data might be held on the file servers for up to two weeks in the fixed VSS storage pool on each production server, but a long-term backup is still required. The caveat with this approach is that on a wide array of file servers, the retention range varies dramatically. Some busy servers might only have 4 days' worth of recovery points, whereas other servers might have 20 days, all while consuming incremental disk space on the production volumes.

The original DPM 2006 product was released in part to address this scenario. Instead of each server having additional VSS storage for local shadow copies, the files were protected via DPM and the storage was all centralized in the DPM server. This provided all the servers with a more predictable retention range in a more manageable and centralized place. But to facilitate EUR, DPM utilizes the same PVC but points the PVC to the DPM server instead of local storage on each file server. DPM 2010 continues that methodology.

Enabling EUR requires a few things:

1. The AD schema must be modified (one time per forest) to enable PVCs to be redirected. Initially, the PVC only knows to look for shadow copies of data on the same server as the production data itself. The AD schema needs to be modified so that parameter becomes editable. To do this:

   A. Log into the DPM server using a user account with Schema Admin credentials.

   B. In the DPM Administrator Console, click Tools in the top menu and select Options.

   C. Select the End-User Recovery tab.

   D. Click the Configure Active Directory button, as shown in Figure 4.31.

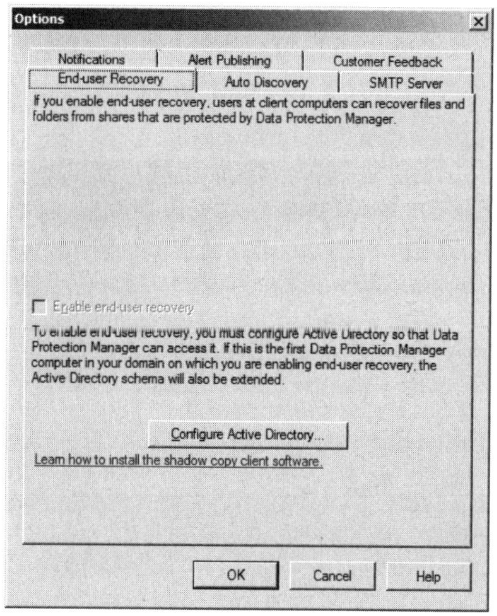

FIGURE 4.31
Enabling EUR within DPM

THE DPM CHANGE TO ACTIVE DIRECTORY SCHEMA

I often hear of DPM administrators who would like to enable End User Recovery, but can't because the Active Directory administrators are concerned about modifying the schema. Initially, the AD attribute that the previous version's client looks at is a non-modifiable setting, which tells the PVC to look for shadow copies on the original production server. The only schema change being made by DPM is to enable that particular AD attribute to be modifiable; no changes are being made to the contents of the AD attribute, just its ability to be updated. That's all. And that is why it only has to be done once per AD Forest.

After that, the PVC continues to reference that AD attribute for determining where to look for shadow copies, based on how you configured DPM:

- **If you enable EUR in Figure 4.31, the DPM server will list itself within the AD attribute so that the PVC looks for previous versions of data on the DPM server (no schema permissions required).**
- **If you do not enable EUR, the AD attribute's contents remain unchanged and the PVC will continue to look for shadow copies on the production server.**

---

2. After allowing some time to be sure that AD has replicated the change across your domain controllers, the AD parameter that the PVC looks for becomes editable. You can enable EUR on a per-DPM server basis. Some file servers may have VSS and SCSF so that their users can restore recent points of time from local VSS shadow copies. Other servers may be protected by DPM, and you can choose to enable EUR for some or all of those servers. To do that, simply select the Enable End-User Restore check box on the End-User Recovery tab.
3. While newer Windows operating systems include the Previous Version functionality already, Windows XP and Windows Server 2003 clients will need to have the PVC installed—ideally using System Center Configuration Manager, System Center Essentials, or another software distribution mechanism such as Group Policy (see Chapter 10 for more on software distribution). Information on installing the client can be found at `http://technet.microsoft.com/en-us/library/bb808818.aspx`.

How DPM Restores Transactional Data

In Task 6, we restored files after first understanding how the DPM storage pool reconstructed previous points in time using blocks from both the replica volume and the recovery point volume. For the transactional data in Microsoft Exchange and Microsoft SQL Server, we need to add in the transactional log replication that occurs up to every 15 minutes.

As discussed earlier in this chapter (see section "How Does DPM Work"), the DPM agent usually invokes between one and four Express Full block-level synchronizations per day. As the DPM administrator, you can configure those operations. Also, throughout the day, the DPM agent will replicate the changes to transactional logs from Exchange or SQL, up to every 15 minutes (as configured by you as well). This configuration takes place in the Create New Protection Group wizard, as seen back in Figure 4.20.

In the DPM storage pool, the replica volume holds not only the copy of the database that is routinely synchronized during the Express Full, but also the log files that are updated every 15 minutes. Using legacy terms:

- The block-based restoration that occurs via the replica and recovery point volumes can be thought of as the restore of a full backup.
- Then, the transaction logs can be replayed through the application, as if they were the differential or incremental backups of that data source.

To illustrate how DPM does this, let's assume that you have been doing an Express Full every morning at 1:00 a.m. and transactional replication every 15 minutes:

1. First, the DPM administrator selects a database for recovery, including the date and time that the data should be restored to. For our example, we are choosing to restore to 3:45 p.m. from last Friday.
2. The replica and recovery point volumes recover the most recent Express Full (whole data object) prior to the desired recovery time—for our example, 1:00 a.m. on the Friday that we wish to recover to.
3. Then, the transaction logs from 1:00 AM until 3:45 p.m. are copied from the DPM server to the production server.
4. The DPM agent instructs the application to play the logs forward.

When the restoration is complete, the database is mounted and has all of its data until exactly 3:45 p.m. on last Friday. With that additional information, let's look at restoring some transactional applications such as Exchange or SQL Server.

TASK 8: RESTORING EXCHANGE MAIL

DPM restoration complies with the Microsoft Exchange support policy for recovering Exchange data per Microsoft Support KB article 904845 (`http://support.microsoft.com/kb/904845`), which outlines the Microsoft support policy for third-party products that modify or extract Exchange database contents. Currently, there is not a supported way to directly recover individual mail items more granular than the Exchange database from a VSS-based backup.

With that in mind, the DPM Recovery Wizard offers different options based on whether the object selected for recovery is at the database level or something more granular. For brevity purposes, we will discuss Exchange in terms of Exchange 2007, which uses Exchange storage groups. These groups in turn hold mailbox databases, which hold mailboxes, which hold folders and items. Exchange 2010 abolishes storage groups but uses the remainder of the hierarchy, starting with databases.

By selecting a storage group or database for recovery with DPM, we see the macro view of the Recovery Wizard, as seen in Figure 4.32.

FIGURE 4.32
DPM 2010 Recovery Wizard for Exchange

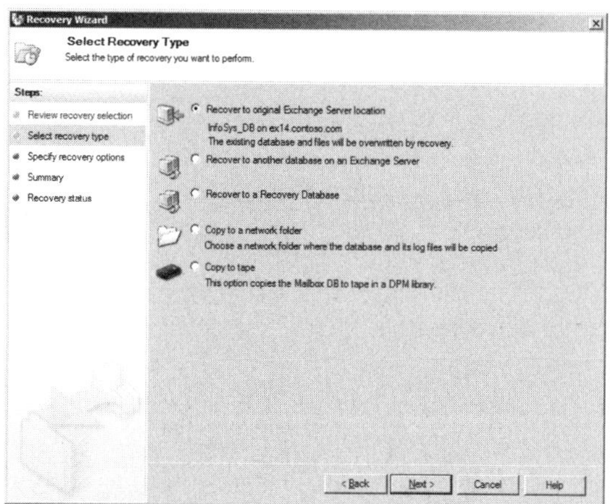

Along with the two standard DPM options, Copy To A Network Folder Location and Copy To Tape, we see several options that are based on storage group and database restores. These options are available based on the level of object you are restoring, as well as timeliness of the restore. The nomenclature also varies slightly between Exchange 2007, which holds databases within storage groups, and Exchange 2010, which deals only with databases. When restoring an Exchange storage group (2007) or database (2010), the text will vary slightly based on your version of Exchange but your restore options are similar, including:

- Restore the SG/DB to the Original Exchange Server
- Restore the Database to A Different Exchange Server
- Restore the SG/DB to the RSG/RDB (discussed later in this task)
- Copy to a Network Folder
- Copy to Tape

After you have selected the restore method, the remaining DPM Recovery Wizard screens will adapt slightly. If you chose to recover the database to an alternate location, an additional wizard screen will allow you to enter the Exchange server or file location you want to restore the data to. The screen containing options for network throttling, SAN restoration, and email notification operates as usual. And the final confirmation screen will show the component files from the Exchange database and logs to be restored.

To recover a mailbox or something smaller than an Exchange database, you can either browse for the item you want to restore or search for it:

- To browse, select the 2007 storage group or 2010 database Exchange container in the left-hand tree view of your Exchange server. After selecting the appropriate date and time, you can browse the lower-center section to see the database and see the mailboxes that are hosted in each database. Right-click on the desired mailbox and select Restore.
- To search, look in the upper-left corner of the Recovery view, above the left pane. There is a subtab that allows you to search. From the Search tab, you can use the pull-down menu to specify that you are searching for file items, SharePoint items, or Exchange mailboxes. After selecting Exchange, you can search by a user's alias or username. The large right pane will list all the recovery points that are available to you. Simply right-click on the mailbox with the date and time that you wish to recover to and select Restore.

In either case, this will invoke a different Exchange Recovery Wizard within DPM that will use the recovery storage group (RSG) in Exchange 2007 or the recovery database (RDB) in Exchange 2010 to recover the database and then pull the mailbox or items that you want out, using Exchange or third-party tools.

Figure 4.33 shows the Recovery Wizard for a mailbox restoration. After the Exchange database is restored to the RSG or RDB, you can use other utilities such as MailRetriever from AppAssure or Recovery Manager from Quest to selectively recover mailboxes, folders, or items.

For more information on Exchange protection and recovery with DPM, refer to `www.microsoft.com/DPM/exchange`.

THE COOLEST RESTORE TIME IS "LATEST"

If you are recovering an Exchange or SQL database and you choose the current day within the calendar for restoration, you may notice an unusual last choice in the pull-down time options. On today's time list, after all the actual times that default to 15-minute increments, is the word "Latest."

FIGURE 4.33
DPM 2010 Recovery Wizard for Exchange mailboxes

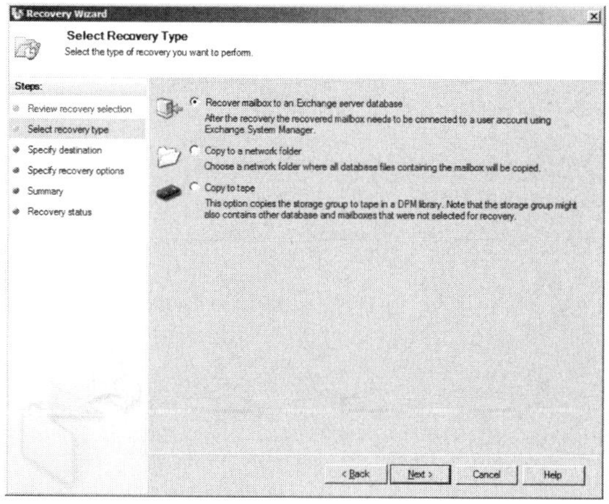

Consider the worst case scenario of a 15-minute replication solution: the production server has a failure 14 minutes after synchronization. To make this clearer, suppose the server hardware failed at 2:59 p.m., which means that the last data that was successfully replicated to the DPM server was from 2:45 p.m..

If you have followed the standard practice of having the databases on one volume and the transaction logs on another volume, you may not lose any data at all. You can put a blank hard drive in where the database volume used to be and DPM will easily restore the data to the last point in time that it has within the storage pool—2:45 p.m..

If you chose Latest from the time listing, after DPM restores all the data that it has, it will look for any surviving transaction logs that remain on the production server volumes starting from that point in time and play them forward. In this case, it would find the logs from 2:45 p.m. until the moment of failure and play them forward to 2:59 p.m.

Literally, when the server comes back online, the database should be within one transaction of when the server failed—hence, the term latest, as seen in Figure 4.34.

FIGURE 4.34
Choosing to restore "Latest" point in time

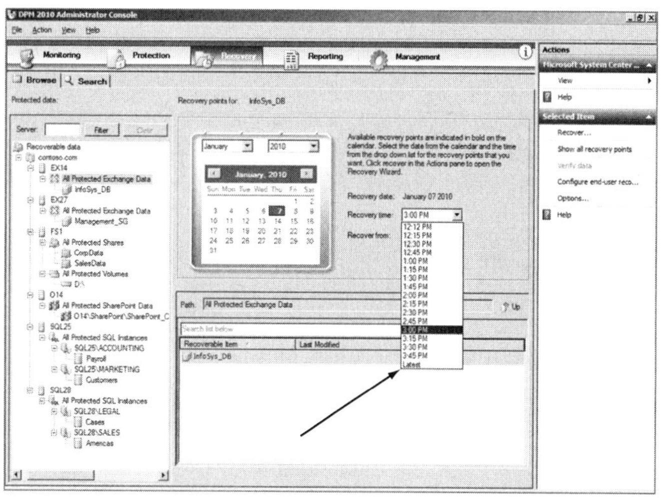

Task 9: Restoring SQL Databases

As discussed earlier, you are able to restore SQL Server databases to any 15 minutes in time by restoring the last Express Full of the database itself and playing forward its transaction log to the desired 15-minute point in time. But there are a few other options that are worth noting with SQL database restorations with DPM 2010.

Like the other workloads discussed so far, when choosing a database to restore, DPM will launch a Recovery Wizard with four choices in this case (as seen in Figure 4.35):

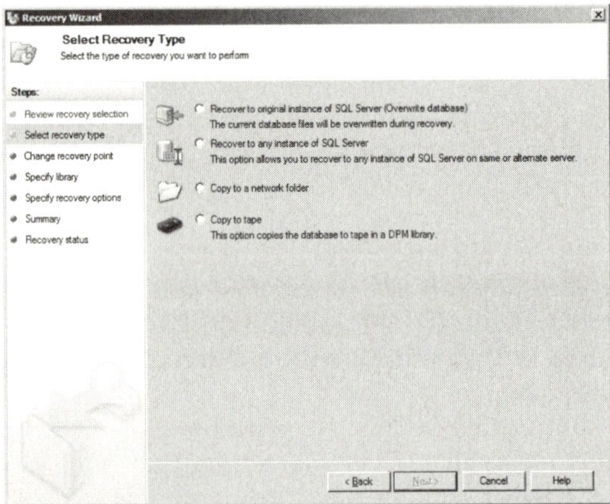

FIGURE 4.35
DPM 2010 Recovery Wizard for SQL databases

- Recover To Original Instance Of SQL Server
- Recover To Any Instance Of SQL Server
- Copy To A Network Folder
- Copy To Tape

The Latest restore option shown in Figure 4.34 is also available to SQL Server 2005 and SQL Server 2008 databases, as described in the section "The Coolest Restore Time Is 'Latest.'" Using the Latest option will first restore a database to the last point in time available with the DPM storage pool, and then the DPM agent will instruct the SQL Server application to play forward its surviving transaction logs so that when the database comes back online, it is within one committed transaction of when the server failed.

To restore a database to the latest possible transaction:

1. Start from the DPM Administrator Console in the Recovery view.
2. In the left pane, expand the SQL server and database instance.
3. Select the database that you wish to recover.
4. After the calendar has updated, select today's date and pull down the time list to the right. "Latest" will appear as the last time slot in the list.

While a DPM administrator can recover a database to any 15-minute point in time, the SQL database administrator can restore data to any point in time. This is because the DPM server can restore the database and logs, but not play the logs forward to a predetermined point in time. An experienced SQL administrator can then use SQL tools to look into the logs and choose a particular transaction to play forward to. This is common when a database has had a significant import of data that has to be reversed. The database administrator (DBA) can simply play the logs forward to the transaction or checkpoint immediately prior to the data import.

To enable a DBA to restore to any transaction in-between 15-minute increments:

1. Start from the DPM Administrator Console in the Recovery view.
2. In the left pane, expand the SQL server and database instance.
3. Select the database that you wish to recover.
4. Choose the date and then pull down the next time slot after the time that you desire. For example, to restore a database to 2:07 p.m., tell DPM to recover up to the 2:15 p.m. time slot.
5. After choosing to restore the database to the original or alternate location, a SQL-specific screen in the Recovery Wizard provides choices of bringing the database up in an operational state or not. Choosing the nondefault option will restore the database to its last Express Full but leave the transaction logs alone so that the DBA can selectively play it forward to a specific transaction, as seen in Figure 4.36.

FIGURE 4.36
Enabling DBAs to restore data to any transaction

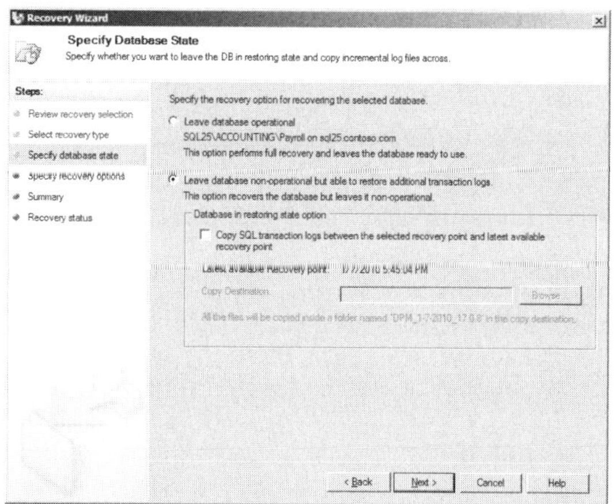

We will look closer at SQL restore scenarios, including a DPM 2010 self-service utility for DBA's to restore their databases from their desktops or the SQL server's console in Chapter 8. For more information on SQL protection and recovery with DPM, refer to `www.microsoft.com/DPM/sql`.

Task 10: Restoring SharePoint Items

Protecting SharePoint uses a methodology called Referential VSS, which essentially means that when the VSS requestor tries to protect one VSS workload, such as SharePoint, part of the process involves being redirected to one or more additional VSS-capable workloads. In the case of

SharePoint, a majority of the data is held within SQL Server databases. In fact, on a single-server SharePoint site, you will find SQL Server and SharePoint both installed. SharePoint handles the metadata and interaction with web services, but the content is held within SQL. For more detail on this, refer to the sidebar "Protecting SQL Content Servers within a SharePoint Farm." This is important to understand because it can affect how we configure protection and recovery.

SharePoint has two recovery modes, depending on the granularity of what is being restored. This is similar to the dichotomy in Task 9 for recovering Exchange databases versus Exchange items, though SharePoint makes it much easier than Exchange. When selecting something in SharePoint to recover with DPM, one of two Recovery Wizards will appear:

- Recovering a farm or database can be done directly from the VSS backup taken by DPM.
- Recovering a site or document is done by mounting a recovered database and selectively moving the desired items into the production database and farm.

To recover a farm or database:

1. Start from the DPM Administrator Console in the Recovery view.
2. Click on the SharePoint server in the left pane to expand the data sources, and then click on the SharePoint data type in the left pane.
3. The lower-center pane will now show the various component parts, including the farm, the shared components, and each content database.
4. Right-click on the farm, shared components, or a database, and selecting Restore will launch the DPM Recovery Wizard for SharePoint, as shown in from Figure 4.37.

FIGURE 4.37
DPM Recovery Wizard for SharePoint

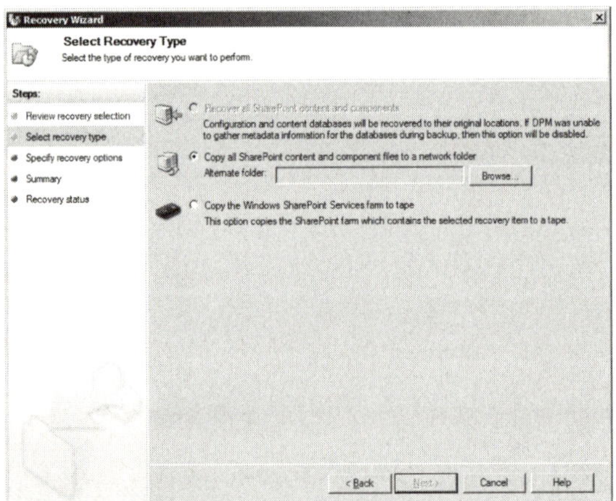

Instead of recovering an entire content database, DPM also provides the ability to recover individual sites or even documents. The mechanism for this varies between Microsoft Office SharePoint Server (MOSS) 2007 and 2010.

- SharePoint 2007 required a recovery farm (RF), which behaved much like an Exchange RSG or RDB (see Task 8). The RF was typically a single server and did not have to match the topology of the production farm. Restoring individual items directly back to the production farm was not supported. Instead, VSS backup solutions needed to restore the content database back to the recovery farm, and then invoke SharePoint APIs for taking the desired site or document from the recovered database and injecting it back into the production farm.

- SharePoint 2010 does not require a SharePoint farm, and instead provides a supported mechanism for backup solutions to restore documents directly back to the production farm.

To restore an individual item or site:

1. Start from the DPM Administrator Console in the Recovery view.
2. Click on the SharePoint server in the left pane to expand the data sources, and then click on the SharePoint data type in the left pane.
3. The lower-center pane will now show the various component parts, including the farm, the shared components, and each content database, just as it did for recovering a component.
4. Double-click into a content database to see the site collections that are hosted in the database. Continue clicking down to the individual site, folder, or document that you wish to recover.
5. Right-click on the document that you wish to restore and click Restore to launch the item-level Recovery Wizard in DPM, as seen in Figure 4.38.

FIGURE 4.38
DPM Recovery Wizard for SharePoint items

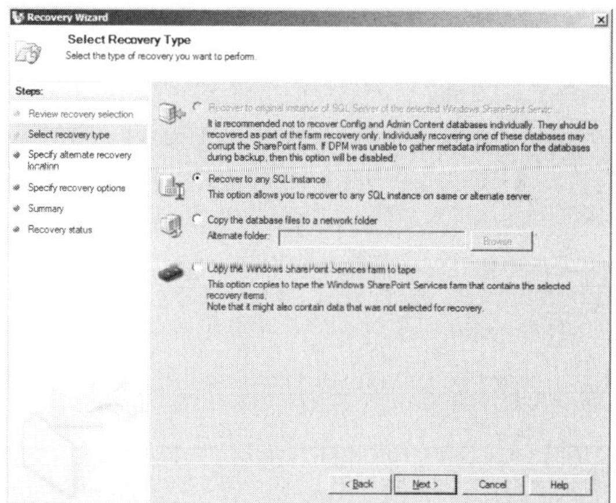

TASK 11: RESTORING VIRTUAL MACHINES

As discussed earlier, DPM treats protecting virtual machines much like protecting an application like SharePoint. Similar to how you choose to protect a SharePoint farm and DPM identifies the component objects and files to be protected, when you choose to protect a virtual machine, DPM identifies the VHD files and virtual machine metadata to be protected. And as you saw in Task 10, where the SharePoint farm was protected as a single object but recovery could be done at much more granular levels, recovery of a virtual machine with DPM 2010 can also be done more granularly.

In DPM 2007, you had to choose between granular recovery and whole VM protection. Previously,

- To recover the entire VM, you needed to do host-based protection of the entire virtual machine.
- To recover files from within a VM, you needed to do guest-based protection from within the virtual machine (meaning, protect it as you would any other server with its own DPM agent).

In DPM 2010, you don't have to choose. In this task, we will do both—recover a whole virtual machine and recover simple files from within the VM.

Recovering an entire virtual machine from a host-based backup essentially provides BMR of the virtual machine. And even better, the hardware is no longer much of a factor, because virtualization abstracts the hardware details. Your original hypervisor host might have been a Dell, but you can recover the VM to an HP host (or vice versa), even with all the variances in network and storage interfaces.

The Best Bare Metal Recovery Is a Virtual One

The challenge with most BMR methods has always been in dealing with disparity of hardware. If your old hardware was two years old when it failed, you likely found newer models when you tried to replace it. Or perhaps your company switched standards from one vendor to another. For every comparative detail that is different between your old and new machines, the risk or complexity of a BMR increases. This is problematic, but can be perceived as desirable. Some innovative products are available whose primary job is to help you migrate machines from one hardware platform to another as part of a recovery or migration scenario.

The good news is that virtualization abstracts almost all the hardware details so that a VM that was running on last year's HP will run on this year's Dell. Perhaps even more interesting is the ability to recover a VM on its own hardware—meaning that if a VM has a catastrophic failure, you can restore the entire VM to what it looked like yesterday, which essentially rolls back or recovers the entire server.

For that reason alone, I recommend virtualizing every server that you can. I even recommend branch office servers be virtualized, even if that virtualization consists of only one VM running on the host in a small server. It empowers new recovery scenarios for very little to no cost. Virtualize everything that you can, and all of your recoveries become more flexible. We'll cover this in more detail in Chapter 9, "Virtualization."

Recovering a virtual machine in DPM 2010 is straightforward:

1. Start from the DPM Administrator Console in the Recovery view.
2. Browse the left pane to expand the virtualization host.
3. Click on the virtualization workload in the left pane to reveal the virtual machines in the left pane as well as in the lower-center pane.

4. Select the date and time that you wish to recover to.
5. Right-click on any of the virtual machines in the lower-center console and select Restore.

Right-clicking on a virtual machine and selecting Restore opens the DPM 2010 Recovery Wizard for virtual machines, as shown in Figure 4.39.

As is typical for DPM, the bottom two options are generic across workloads and allow you to recover the files that make up the virtual machine to either a network or file location, as well as to its own tape for offsite storage. The options specific to the virtualization workload are:

- ◆ Recover To Original Instance
- ◆ Recover To An Alternate Location

New in DPM 2010 is the ability to restore to an alternate host, which will not only restore the VHD files themselves, but also the metadata for the virtual machine definition, so that the virtual machine is already defined within the Hyper-V console and is immediately able to be started on its new host.

FIGURE 4.39
DPM 2010 Recovery Wizard for virtual machines

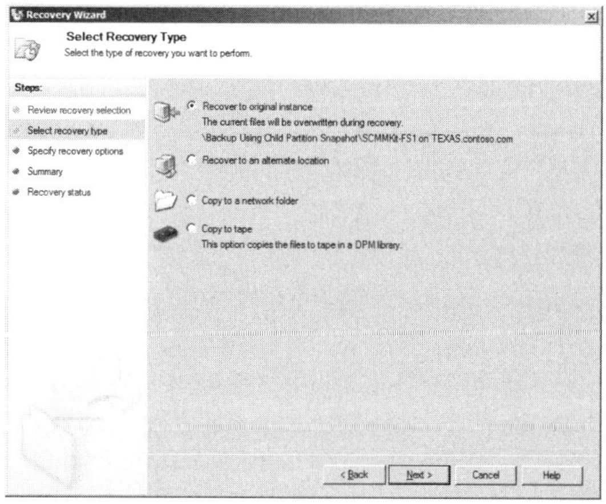

Also new in DPM 2010 is the feature item-level recovery (ILR), which enables you to recover individual file items from within virtual machine backups, without having an agent inside the VM or having protected the VM from the inside. There are some considerations to be aware of:

- ◆ ILR only restores files, not application data such as SQL or Exchange databases. While you technically could recover those various file objects, they would not be restorable as databases; they would be files that an application administrator would need to manually import within the application itself.
- ◆ ILR gives you granular restore capabilities but you are backing up the entire VM. If granular restore is a primary goal, consider running the DPM agent within the virtual machine so that you can select only the file sets that you wish to protect, instead of all the files within the entire VM.

To restore individual files from within a VM, start as you did earlier in this task with steps 1–5. On the DPM Administrator Console in the Recovery tab, browse to the Hyper-V host, select the virtualization workload, and then select the virtual machine in the left pane.

6. By clicking into the VM in the lower-center pane, you display new options that allow you to see each of the VHD files.
7. Expand the VHD files to reveal the file system volumes, such as `C:\`.
8. Now, you can explore the volumes as you would any file servers' volumes and select directories or files for restoration.

Right-clicking on a file or directory will allow you to select Restore, which brings up a Recovery Wizard nearly identical to the generic file Recovery Wizard seen in Task 6 (Figure 4.29).

The DPM workflow for restoring files is similar to Task 6, but the mechanics take a little extra work by DPM. Behind the scenes, the DPM server will mount the VHD (as of the time and date you selected) from within the DPM storage pool as a volume on the DPM server itself. Then, DPM can simply take the file-level items from the mounted volume and copy them to the desired location. Then the VHD volume is dismounted.

NOTE ILR is one of the few scenarios that requires a physical DPM server. In many cases, you might choose to run DPM within a virtual machine. But because ILR requires DPM and its underlying operating system to mount the VHD from within its OS, a DPM server offering ILR cannot currently be virtualized.

Task 12: Restoring Data on Client Workstations

Tasks 6–11 dealt with restoring data from the DPM server's perspective. But as mentioned earlier in the chapter, one of the primary features in DPM 2010 is client-based protection and recovery. If you are recovering client data from the DPM server (say you lost a client workstation or your users are not trained to use the DPM self-service tools), then you can restore client data files the same way as you restore file server data files.

But because the DPM protection policies are also being sent to each client workstation to be enacted even when the machine is disconnected from the corporate network, you can also restore data while disconnected using the previous recovery points on the local machine's storage.

To restore data from the local machine:

1. Right-click on the file or folder that you wish to restore.
2. A list will be presented by the Previous Versions client (as seen earlier in Figure 4.30) that shows the previous versions that exist on both the DPM server as well as the local storage.
3. You can choose to open the file for viewing only, restore the file where it came from, or restore the file to an alternate location.

You can also use the DPM client applet to open a complete point in time for all of your workstation's data on the DPM server. This is especially useful when you have deleted a directory or wish to restore larger amounts of data. By clicking on the Recovery tab of the DPM client applet, you can browse all of the available data sets from the DPM server that is protecting your machine, as seen in Figure 4.40.

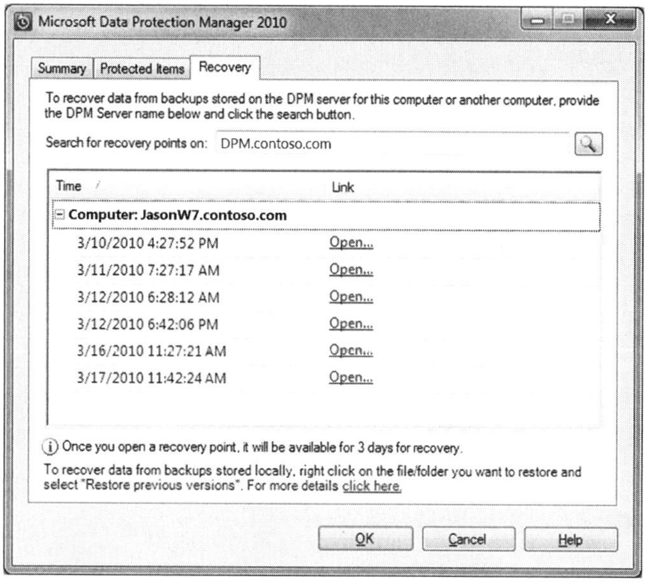

FIGURE 4.40
Restoring data from the DPM client

Using DPM 2010 in Heterogeneous Environments

In the very beginning of the section "System Center Data Protection Manager" we discussed the desire to have a unified disk-, tape- and cloud-based backup solution. And while DPM 2010 can provide these capabilities in an all-Windows environment, it is not able to protect non-Windows-based machines unless they are already virtualized and running within a Microsoft hypervisor. For the wide variety of enterprise-class datacenters that are heterogeneous, this can create a challenging conflict:

- You will still want and need a backup solution that protects more than what DPM is designed for.
- But your heterogeneous backup solution is not optimal or does not support the more advanced Microsoft applications that DPM was designed for.

If you are stuck in this scenario, the answer is to use DPM's disk-based protection to protect the Microsoft workloads with a DPM disk-based backup solution, while utilizing your existing heterogeneous tape-backup solution to back up the DPM server's disk.

Because the DPM storage pool uses NTFS volumes for the replica, the data that you have protected from the production servers is in a natively readable format on the DPM server. In short, the application data is data consistent because of the VSS-based backup mechanisms, but will appear as if the production server had shut down the application. This means that your heterogeneous tape backup solution can back up the DPM volumes as if they were doing an offline backup of the primary application servers. In short, all you need to do is install your third-party heterogeneous backup agent on the DPM server and back up the DPM disk to your heterogeneous tape.

What Is an Offline Backup?

Normally, when you back up something like SQL or Exchange databases, you interface with the application engine, which feeds the backup software with the data. Or more specifically in the case of VSS, the application provides the data to VSS, which provides it to the backup agent. So the data is protected within the context of the application.

You can make an offline backup of applications that do not have a way to talk to the backup software itself. As the name suggests, you simply shut down the application so that the files are not in use. Then, the backup software can back up the files as dormant files without regard to what kind of application was driving them. The good news is that the data is protected. The bad news is that the application services are down during a backup window. So, this method is avoided because of the outage window.

Where the idea of an offline backup is desirable, though, is when you want to integrate DPM's disk-based replica with a third-party tape backup:

1. First, DPM protects the production data sources while they are online and without incurring any outage window. This enables fast restores from DPM disk and uses VSS to ensure a supportable recovery of the application data.

2. Then, the third-party tape backup software can back up the DPM replica, which is dormant like an offline copy, on another schedule. This enables your company to have one set of tapes across the heterogeneous enterprise, while still taking advantage of DPM's application-aware disk-based capabilities.

Backing Up the DPM Server to Third-Party Tape

As stated previously, the DPM storage pool creates two NTFS volumes per data source being protected. One of the volumes is the replica volume, which has a valid copy of the entire data set from the most recent Express Full block-based synchronization. The replica's copy of the production data is suitable for being backed up to third-party tape, so you simply need to install the tape-backup agent from the third-party software.

NOTE The replica volumes to be backed up can be found on the DPM server under `C:\Program Files\Microsoft DPM\DPM\Volumes\Replica`.

The key to remember when backing up the replica volumes is to understand that the NTFS volumes are created but not mounted with a drive letter. However, by navigating through the default file system structure of the DPM installation, we can find them:

1. Start where the DPM software was installed, which by default is `C:\Program Files\Microsoft DPM`.

2. Under the root DPM directory are subdirectories for DPM itself, as well as SQL services if you opted to install them locally. Go to DPM.

3. Under DPM are several directories that make up the DPM installation. The two that matter for purposes of third-party backups are:

   - DPMDB—Holds the SQL database of DPM's configuration. By using a third-party backup solution that can protect SQL databases, you can back up the DPMDB, which will be needed if you wish to re-create a failed DPM server.

   - Volumes—Holds the replicas, as well as other storage areas.

4. Under the Volumes directory is the Replica directory, which is needed for backing up to third-party tape.
5. Under the Replica directory is a listing of VSS data sources, including:
   - File System
   - Microsoft Exchange Writer
   - Microsoft Hyper-V VSS Writer
   - SharePoint Services Writer
   - SQLServerWriter
6. By browsing under any one of these, you can find a list of what at first glance appear to be directories with very long GUID names. But at closer inspection, you should notice that the icons represent a volume mount point instead of a directory. These links go to each of the root of each NTFS replica volume in the DPM storage pool, as seen in Figure 4.41.
7. By clicking on the volume mount point, you will see a single directory with another GUID associated with the actual production volume that the data came from.
8. Under that is a directory named Full, implying a full backup from the Express Full block-level synchronization.

FIGURE 4.41
The DPM Replica volumes as seen in Windows Explorer

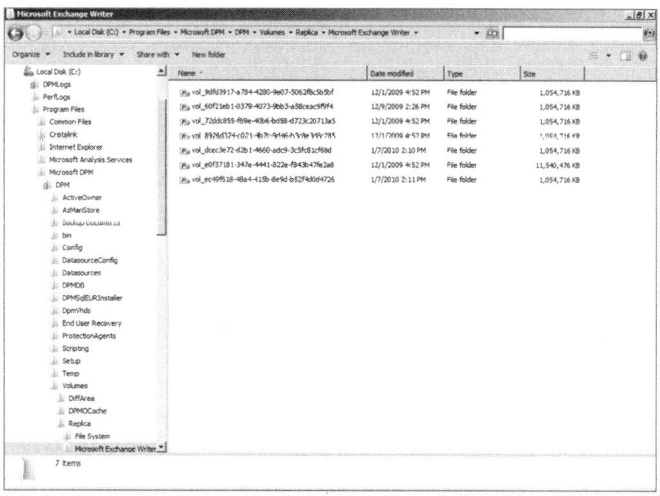

9. Under the Full directory, will be directories for the root of the production volume, named D-VOL if the production data is stored on the D: drive.
10. Everything under the D-VOL (or whatever the root drive letter was) is the actual directory tree from the production server to where the data is stored.

To pull this together, if a production database named Accounting was stored on the production volume under `D:\Databases\Acct.mdf`, then the following tree would hold it on the DPM server:

Every replica volume under the DPM server starts as:

```
C:\Program Files\MicrosoftDPM\DPM\volumes\Replica
```

SQL Server-based protection would add:

```
\SqlServerWriter\volGUID\GUID\Full
```

And the data path on the production server yields:

```
\D-VOL\Databases\Acct.mdf
```

If you have fewer than 23 production data sources protected by a particular DPM server, you can make things much easier for yourself and your backup application by adding drive letters to the volume mount points. This is because you can assume two or three drive letters are taken up by the OS volume, DVD drive, and perhaps one other for the DPM database or application (C:, D:, and E:). This leaves 23 available letters.

To assign drive letters for easier backups:

1. Use the Disk Administrator console from Windows.
2. Every DPM storage pool volume is labeled with DPM as a prefix and includes the production server name and data source name, such as DPM-EX27-SalesSG or something similar. You will find two such volumes. The first one created is usually the replica volume. Browse to locate the Full directory under its root. Or if you are setting this up shortly after setting up protection, one of the volumes will show significant amounts of data consumed after the initial mirror whereas the other one remains empty because it has not started adding recovery points yet. The one with data is the replica volume; the empty one is the recovery point volume.
3. Right-click on the replica volume and select Add A Drive Letter.

Of the 11 directories in the previous example, 7 would be replaced by a drive letter, so that the database can now be found at `X:\GUID\Full\D-VOL\Databases\Acct.mdf`. But because the only data in that volume is in that directory tree, you can point your third-party backup agent at the entire `X:\` of the DPM server (which will only contain the Accounting database from your production SQL server). And in the bigger picture, you might configure your heterogeneous backup solution to back up every drive letter on the DPM server besides C: and D: (if you have fewer than 23 data sources being protected).

ALL THIRD-PARTY BACKUPS OF DPM ARE NOT THE SAME

In general, any third-party backup can do what was just discussed and point at a very long directory tree to find where the data resides and back it up to its heterogeneous tape farm. But some third-party backups do it better than others.

DPM, like most other Microsoft products, offer third parties additional assistance in backing it up in the form of a software developers kit (SDK). The DPM SDK gives third-party backup software the ability to expose DPM's data sources to the third-party backup solution.

In the example paths that we discussed in this section, a third-party backup product's console (that utilized the SDK) might show DPM as the server, and when looking at its data could show `SQL25\AccountingDB` as a data source, with no long filepaths required. When the tape backup administrator picks that data source, the DPM-aware backup agent would traverse the long directory tree to get the data that it needs without adding complex paths or strings.

Disaster Recovery with DPM 2010

In Chapter 12, "Business Continuity and Disaster Recovery," we will go into much more detail about disaster recovery (DR), business continuity (BC), and continuity of operations (CO-OP) in regard to the modern datacenter. But in the context of DPM, we can talk about how to replicate data from one facility to another for *data survivability*.

Earlier in this chapter, you learned that many environments today are protecting their production servers with at least three different technologies:

- Nightly tape backup
- Fast and continuous disk replication throughout the data
- Offsite for data survivability

We also discussed the supportability challenges and interoperability difficulties that come from running multiple data protection agents on the same production server concurrently. To address those challenges, we have looked at using DPM for tape- and disk-based protection of production servers. You can also replicate data from one DPM server to another DPM server in order to provide an offsite capability. This is consistent with the key goal of having a single protection agent on the production server and having a single interface to manage disk-, tape-, and cloud-based protection.

DPM 2 DPM 4 DR

To protect your data offsite may be as simple as replicating from one DPM server to another DPM server for disaster recovery purposes (*DPM 2 DPM 4 DR*). Instead of requiring a completely different replication technology, DPM 2 DPM 4 DR simply uses a DPM agent on the primary DPM server, which makes that primary DPM server a source to a secondary and offsite DPM server, as shown in Figure 4.07.

We will demonstrate this in Task 13. For our purposes, we will call the primary DPM server *DPM* and the secondary DPM server *DPMDR*. Once we install a DPM agent (which requires an E-DPML license) on the primary DPM server, it can be replicated to another DPM server. This creates two loosely coupled relationships:

1. Production servers to DPM
2. DPM to DPMDR

Each pairing has its own protection group settings; which allows for different retention and frequency policies, such as:

1. Protect the production servers to DPM:
    - Every 15 minutes to disk

- 3 Express Fulls per day
- 30 days on disk
- No tape backup

2. Protect the DPM data to DPMDR:
   - Nightly during nonbusiness hours
   - 60 days on disk
   - 7 years on tape, with weekly tape backup

NOTE Notice that in this configuration, the tape backups are being done by the offsite DPM server. The tapes are already offsite, which makes most companies compliant with industry regulations regarding offsite tapes without the operational expense of courier services and the labor requirements of tape handling. We will discuss regulatory compliance and offsite data in Chapter 12.

Using CloudRecovery for DPM

DPM 2 DPM 4 DR requires two sites. Often, both sites are datacenters, but the second site can be something as simple as a branch office with a very good bandwidth to the corporate headquarters. Some companies don't have two appropriate locations, other companies want to outsource whatever they can in regard to backup, and others may have a corporate mandate to have their data maintained by a third-party agency for compliance purposes.

For all of these reasons, Microsoft partnered with Iron Mountain, a leader in offsite data protection and retention. Starting with DPM 2007 SP1, an Iron Mountain agent can be installed onto the DPM server and replicate the DPM replicas to an Iron Mountain datacenter in the cloud via the Internet. This subscription-based service from Iron Mountain is called CloudRecovery.

This model is still consistent with Microsoft's view of a single protection agent on the production servers that results in disk- and tape-based protection with DPM and cloud-based protection by a Microsoft partner. Other partners' cloud-based services may be announced in support of DPM 2010, such as i365's cloud-protection of their DPM2010-based appliance. Information on extending DPM's protection to third-party cloud providers can be found at `microsoft.com/DPM/cloud`. We will discuss the idea of replicating data from an on-premise backup solution to a cloud-based vault in more detail in Chapter 12 as it relates to an overall DR plan.

Task 13: Configuring Secondary Replication for Disaster Recovery

Deploying DPM 2 DPM 4 DR uses many of the skills that you have already learned in this chapter:

- In Tasks 1 and 2, we built a DPM server. We can use the exact same process to build the DPM DR server.
- In Task 3, we deployed a DPM agent from a DPM server. In this case, we push a DPM agent from the DPMDR server to the primary DPM server. In Task 4, we configured protection of several data sources from production servers to the primary DPM server.

With those tasks complete, we can configure secondary replication from the production data sets on the primary DPM server to the offsite DPMDR server. DPM 2 DPM 4 DR is slightly different in DPM 2010 than it was in DPM 2007.

In DPM 2007, you needed to authorize the second DPM server to see what was being protected by the primary DPM server. To do that, you modified settings on the DPM agent. Specifically, you'd go to the DPM 2007 console, select the Management tab, and click the Agents subtab. By selecting the agent on the primary DPM server, you could authorize it to see each of the protected servers' data sources. You could then build a protection group to protect those data sources to a second location.

In DPM 2010, the process is much more streamlined. You simply build a protection group on the DPM DR server with the primary DPM server as a data source. Expand the primary DPM server in the Create New Protection Group wizard to see the protected clients, servers, and the local SQL Server installation (if you configured it as seen in Figure 4.42).

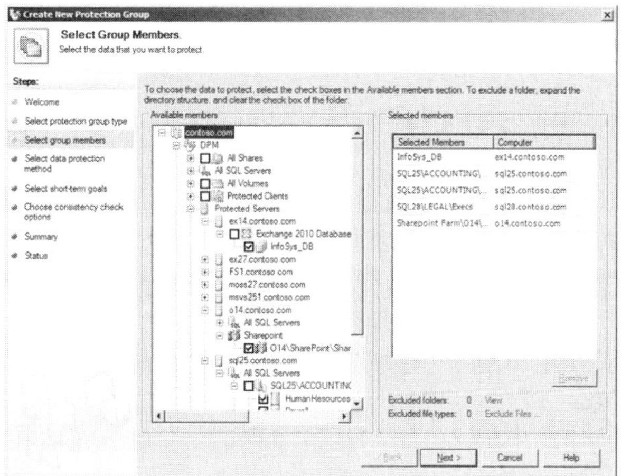

FIGURE 4.42
Configuring DPM 2 DPM 4 DR

Click the Protected Servers icon to see the list of production servers that are protected by the primary DPM server. Expand any of the servers to reveal which data sources are being protected and can be protected again to the DR server.

This provides a way to select which data needs secondary protection. For example, a production SQL server might have 10 databases. Eight of them need some level of protection and may be replicated to the primary DPM server. Three of the eight are critical to the company and therefore warrant secondary replication to the DPM DR server.

The remainder of the Create New Protection Group wizard is typical, with a few minor changes:

- Before leaving this screen, the wizard will prompt you to protect the DPMDB SQL database on the DPM server. The DPMDB is necessary for rebuilding the primary DPM server.
- The disk-to-disk synchronization options start at 1 hour and build up to every 24 hours, instead of down to every 15 minutes on the primary production server. This is in part due to the fact that there are no transaction logs and also because disaster recovery, or data survivability, has a different tolerance for data loss than the production copy.

Summary

In looking at the evolving needs for better backup of Windows environments, Microsoft took three big steps:

1. Delivered Volume Shadow Copy Services (VSS) as part of the Windows operating system, so that application vendors and backup vendors have a common framework for interacting, backing up, and recovering data in a way that is supportable by the applications
2. Reinvented the built-in backup utility that is provided by the Windows operating system, for better system state and bare metal recovery of the OS, as well as ad hoc backups to disk for faster restore
3. Created System Center Data Protection Manager as a full-featured backup solution that assures customers of supportable protection and restore and is focused on key Microsoft application servers and Windows platform technologies

Arguably, one of the best results of DPM is how it is helping Microsoft focus on how backups and restores should be accomplished for application servers. As applications adapt to those needs, every backup solution (from Microsoft or otherwise) will see the benefits. But in the meantime, there is at least one comprehensive data protection and recovery solution that is supported by the production workloads in a Windows datacenter.

With data protection now covered by technologies like VSS and solutions like DPM, the applications can focus on innovating around data availability. In Chapters 5 through 9, we will look at application and data availability, as well as a few more specifics on each of those applications' backup and recovery needs are met.

Chapter 5

File Services

File serving is the number 1 installed role of Windows Server. Because Windows Server is the most widely deployed operating system for most IT environments today, there are a lot of us using Windows File Services. In this chapter, we will look at the built-in capabilities for protecting your file services and making them highly available.

File System Availability and Protection in Windows Server

Technically, file serving is the number 2 function of the Windows Server operating system—with the top function serving as a base for all the other stuff that you can run on Windows Server (for example, SQL Server, Exchange Server, and SharePoint). But think about it. The first "server" that you put into your environment was to share files (and hopefully back them up). I put server in quotes there because many of us started by storing all our data on one beefy Windows desktop (not a server) and then sharing it with the other nodes in our offices or homes. Later, we grew up to our first *real* server—and today, if you have one server operating system in your local environment, it is probably tasked with file sharing, along with other duties.

There are three challenges to increasing the availability and protection of Windows File Services:

- As mentioned earlier, Windows file servers are everywhere. Since it is so easy to spin up a new Windows Server 2008 server and enable file services, chances are you don't know how many of them you have (more on that in Chapters 10 and 11 when we focus on better manageability).
- The data is unstructured and completely unique. Unlike every other kind of data that we could discuss (and will for the SQL and Exchange chapters), file storage does not work on a predictable model of rows, tables, users, mailboxes, or databases. It is a source of capacity that even seasoned IT professionals can find challenging to manage. Windows Server 2008 and its newest offerings in R2 have some great file services management capabilities, but those are outside of the scope of this book. The best ones to look into are File Server Resource Manager (FSRM), which can really change how you manage the server, and File Classification Infrastructure (FCI), which can change how you manage the data.
- The third challenge related to protecting and assuring the availability of file services is not knowing that Windows Server already provides this built-in capability in the Distributed File System (DFS). That is the topic for this chapter.

What Is the Distributed File System?

The Distributed File System (DFS) has been a part of Windows Server ever since Windows NT 4.0. Today, DFS consists of two separate functions in Windows Server—DFS replication and DFS namespace, abbreviated as DFS-R and DFS-N, respectively.

Distributed File System Namespace

Historically, the Windows Server OS has offered DFS as a way to create a synthetic or virtual view ("namespace") that spans multiple file servers and their various file shares. However, the original DFS moniker has been rebranded to be more precise, as DFS namespace (DFS-N), so that DFS-R could be used for DFS replication (which we will cover later in the chapter). Consider this: You may have multiple file shares for your sales department across FS1, FS3, and FS6, as shown in Figure 5.1. Your marketing team has data on FS2 and FS5. The executive team works off FS4. And to make matters worse, those servers may be divided among Los Angeles, New York, and Dallas. Where should you store your data?

FIGURE 5.1
Six file servers (before DFS)

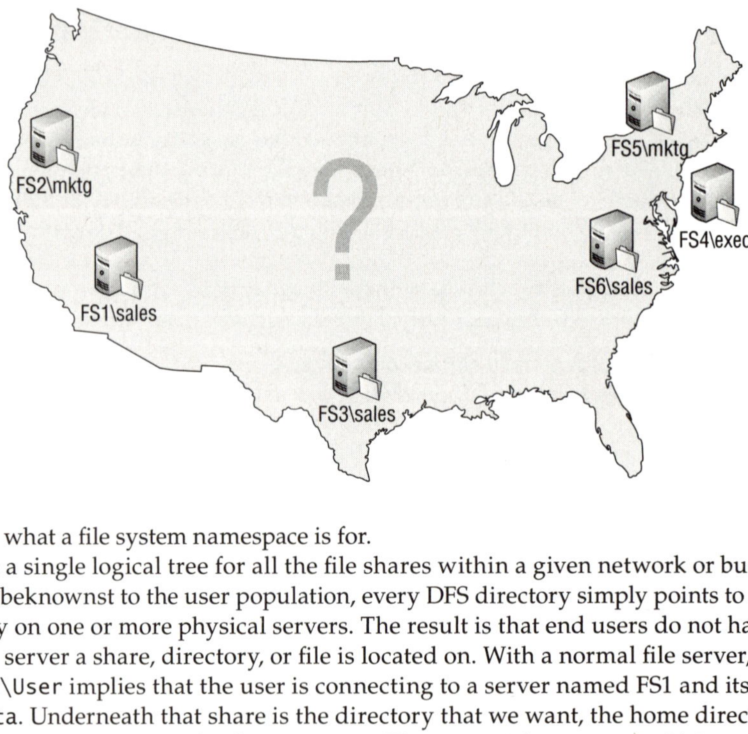

That is exactly what a file system namespace is for.

DFS-N creates a single logical tree for all the file shares within a given network or business function. Unbeknownst to the user population, every DFS directory simply points to a file share or directory on one or more physical servers. The result is that end users do not have to remember which server a share, directory, or file is located on. With a normal file server, the path `\\FS1\Data\User` implies that the user is connecting to a server named FS1 and its file share, named `Data`. Underneath that share is the directory that we want, the home directory named `User`. A DFS namespace works the same way: The user might connect to `\\Contoso\Homedirectories\User`. In this case, `Contoso` is not the name of a particular server, but a namespace that spans many servers. The other layers, `Homedirectories` and `User`, behave like folders but have some special properties that abstract which servers hold those shares and folders.

All Windows-based clients, starting with Windows 95, are natively able to be pointed to a DFS share and will transparently be redirected to wherever the file share exists. To the user population, the DFS namespace appears as simply another file serving network resource with a surprising amount of storage capacity and an impressively intuitive layout of directories (if you do it right):

- In this case, we can start with a DFS *root* as the top of our tree, called `Contoso`.
- Next, all of the file shares from the three sales department teams would be placed under a top-level directory titled `Sales`.
- Similarly, our marketing and executive file shares would be placed under a top-level directory with their departmental names.

The result is shown in Figure 5.2, with the six file servers now offering a single namespace where all the data is able to be located without knowing which servers are hosting the specific files.

FIGURE 5.2
Six file servers using a DFS namespace

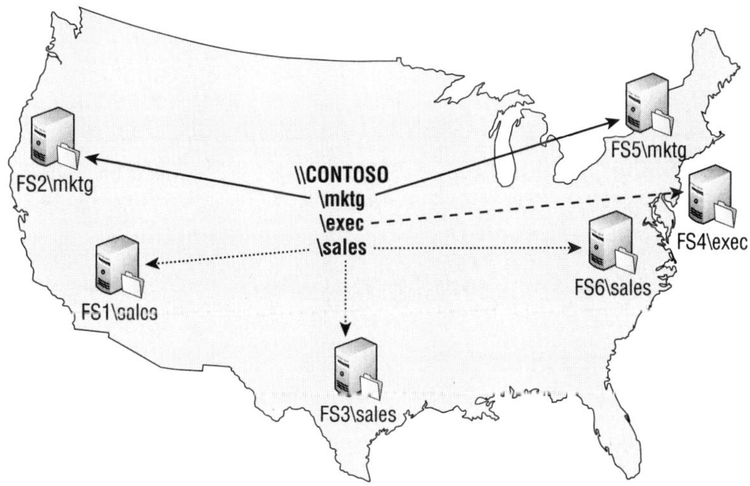

The good news at this point is that users don't care where they are storing their data because they can locate everything easily. The bad news is that the users don't know where they are storing their data and may now be reaching from Los Angeles to New York to get files.

This is where replication comes into the picture.

Distributed File System Replication

Distributed File System Replication (DFS-R) automatically replicates changes between file serving shares. This means that for files that may normally be requested as often in New York as they are in Los Angeles, the data can be duplicated between both sites and stored locally. Users in each locale will easily locate the same data from the same DFS namespace directory, but they will access the copy located closest to each user.

In our case, as shown in Figure 5.3, the marketing team may have enough collaboration that they wish to mirror most of their file shares between both their servers. In addition, the IT department may decide to offer the primary applications that are intended to be installable on most of the company's machines from each of the three locales.

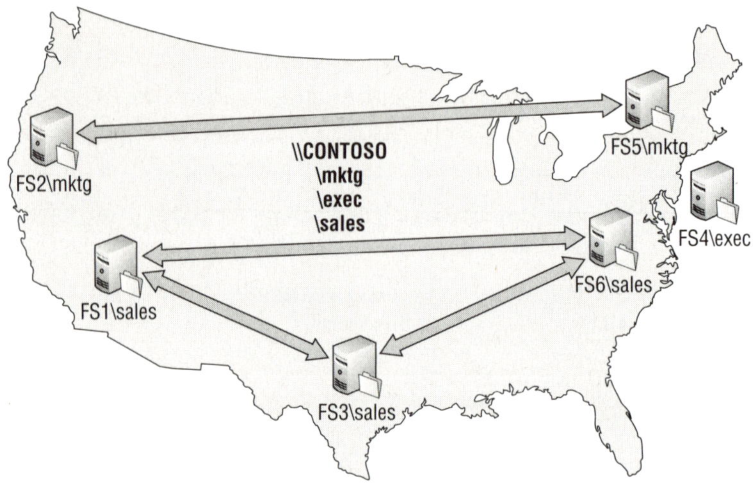

FIGURE 5.3 Six file servers using DFS namespace and replication

We will get into a lot more detail later in the chapter as to how each function works, but this serves as an introduction to the namespace and replication technologies, as well as providing some context for how they are used.

But as an additional overview, Microsoft did a great high-level overview podcast of DFS in Windows Server 2003 R2, which is still valid for Windows Server 2008 R2; see `http://go.microsoft.com/fwlink/?LinkId=39468`.

DFS Terminology

Here are a few key concepts you should understand before deploying DFS namespaces:

Namespace A *namespace* is a logical grouping of file servers and shares in a hierarchy that is easy for users to navigate. It will appear and function similar to a directory, or more specifically, an uber-directory that combines all the real directories in your file servers.

Namespace Server A *namespace server* is a server that hosts the namespace and can be either a member server or a domain controller.

Namespace Root A *namespace root* is the top of a namespace (which is hosted on a server). In our examples, where `\\Contoso\Data` is the path, `\Data` is the root of the namespace. If `Contoso` is a domain-based namespace, then the `\Data` root information is stored as metadata within Active Directory (AD). If not, it is stored on a single server (not something I recommend due to the single point of failure (SPOF).

Namespace Target A *namespace target* is one of potentially multiple servers that hold the root of a namespace. Later in this chapter, when we discuss DFS referrals, we will look at optimizing how clients discover and navigate the Distributed File System.

Folder A folder is simply the logical directory, as seen in the namespace path, which may or may not have any real data or shares behind it. You can create your own hierarchy, regardless of how the servers and shares are organized.

Folder Target A *folder target* is a file share on a file server that is pointed to by a DFS folder.

Enabling DFS on Your Windows File Servers

DFS is part of the File Services feature in Windows Server, but the specifics for enabling it will vary based on which generation of the OS you are running. While some folks are still running Windows Server 2003 (preferably R2), this chapter will focus on utilizing Windows Server 2008 and beyond, but we'll take a brief look back when viable.

Infrastructure Prerequisites

There are a few things that we need to cover before you enable DFS on your file servers:

Active Directory While you are hopefully running Windows Server 2008 (or R2) file servers, if your domain is running in Windows Server 2003 mode, you need to be sure that the DFS replication objects exist in your AD schema. You can install these objects by using forest prepping (`adprep.exe /forestprep`) from the Windows Server 2003 R2 or Windows Server 2008 (or R2) installation media. For instructions on how to update the AD schema, Microsoft provides a straightforward walkthrough with DFS as one of the applicable scenarios at `http://go.microsoft.com/fwlink/?LinkId=64262`.

Antivirus and Backup Software Antivirus and backup software should be DFS aware. This is not as much of an issue as it used to be when DFS replication was first delivered in Windows Server 2003 R2, but it's still worth checking—especially if you leverage an older heterogeneous backup solution for legacy reasons.

Installing DFS on Windows Server 2003 and 2003 R2

DFS is considered a component of the Windows Server operating system, but is also part of the File Server role from Server Manager. DFS replication wasn't available in Windows Server 2003, although a far inferior replication technology called the File Replication Service (FRS) was (more on FRS in the section "Getting Started with DFS-R" later in this chapter). You could still install DFS namespace (called just DFS at that time) in Windows Server 2003.

To install DFS using the Windows Server 2003 R2 Manage Your Server utility:

1. Choose Start ➢ All Programs ➢ Administrative Tools and click Manage Your Server.
   - If this is a new server or you have not yet installed the File Server role, click Add Or Remove A Role. In the Configure Your Server Wizard, on the Server Role page, click File Server, and then click Next twice.
   - If the File Server role has already been installed, click Update This Role For File Server.
2. Either way, in the File Server Role Wizard, choose Replicate Data To And From This server (Figure 5.4) and follow the remaining steps to complete the wizard.

FIGURE 5.4
Use the File Server Role Wizard in Windows Server 2003 R2 to enable DFS.

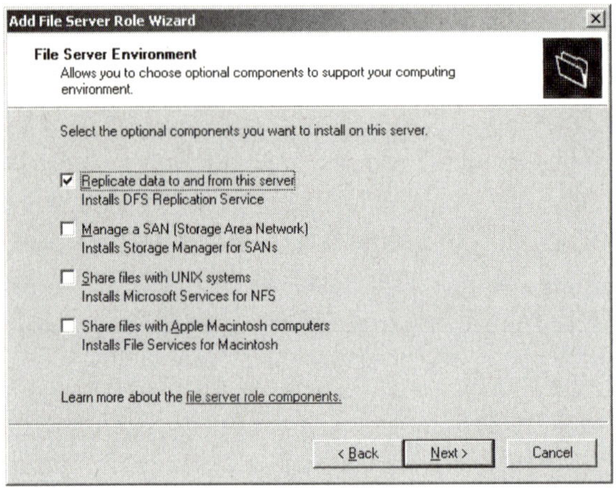

Alternatively, as you can see in Figure 5.5, you can open Control Panel and select Add Or Remove Programs. Then, click Add/Remove Windows Components and scroll down to Distributed File System. Choose all three options and click OK.

FIGURE 5.5
You can also enable DFS as a component of the OS within Windows Server 2003 R2.

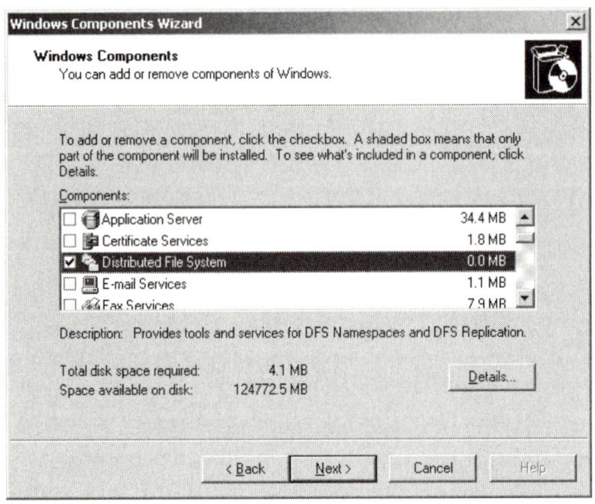

It is important to be familiar with both methods. Although the File Server Role Wizard is a little clearer, the DFS component of Windows is something that can be automated for broad deployments through tools like System Center Configuration Manager 2007. Either way, you will need to have the `\i386` and/or `\Amd64` source directories (or Windows installation media) available.

Installing DFS on Windows Server 2008 and 2008 R2

DFS namespace and DFS replication are both optional components within the File Services role of Windows Server 2008 and Windows Server 2008 R2. To install the File Server role (and therefore DFS as part of it), you can use Server Manager.

You may already have Server Manager already pinned to the Start menu. If not, select Start ➤ All Programs ➤ Administrative Tools and click Server Manager. Then do one of the following:

- If the File Server role has not yet been enabled, click Add Role. In the Add Roles Wizard, click Next on the introduction screen so that you are on the role selection screen, where you will see various installable roles. Click File Server, and then click Next.
- If the File Server role has already been enabled, you should see it on the left part of the roles selection screen as File Services. DFS may already be enabled as well, but to be sure, click the File Services role and scroll down to Role Services. If DFS needs to be installed, click Add Role Services.

Either way, on the Select Server Roles screen of the wizard, you can specify which optional components in File Services that you wish to install. Each of the DFS components is listed (among others). For flexibility later, choose both of the DFS components (see Figure 5.6).

FIGURE 5.6
Enabling DFS in the File Server role of Windows Server 2008 and 2008 R2

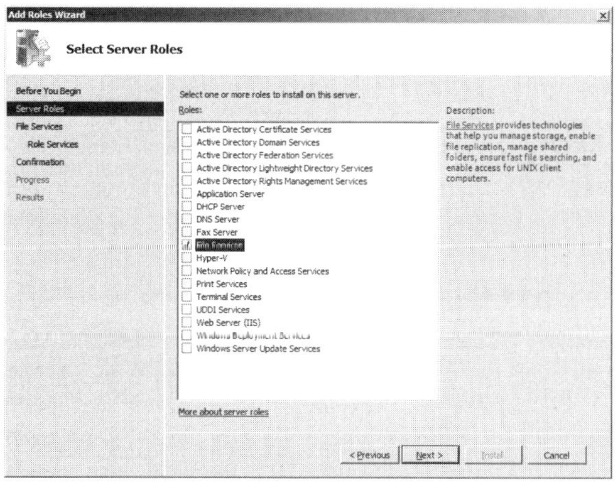

Because you selected to install DFS namespace, a few additional and optional screens will appear. The first screen offers to create a namespace for you. Using the radio buttons, we will choose to create a namespace later using the DFS Management snap-in within Server Manager. If you had chosen to create a namespace, additional screens asking you to supply the type of namespace and its configuration would have followed. But we will cover those concepts and activities in the next section, "Getting Started with DFS-N."

You can accept the defaults to finish the addition of DFS to your File Services without changing any other components that may exist on your server (Figure 5.7).

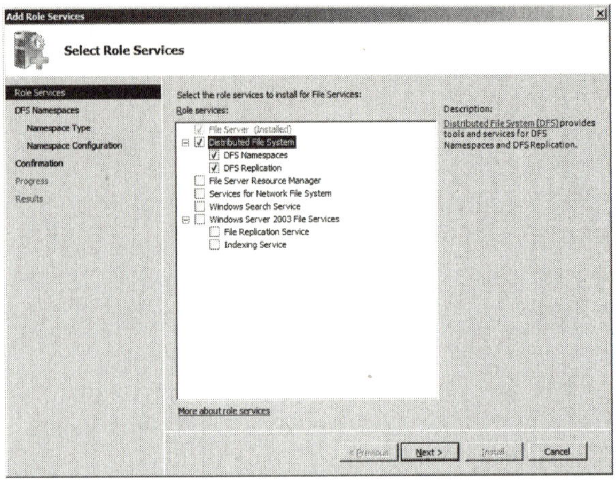

FIGURE 5.7
The File Services role, with DFS enabled, in Windows Server 2008 R2

A reboot should not be required if the only thing you installed is DFS, but for thoroughness, you may want restart the server so that all services are confirmed to start from cold before deploying their functionality. But one way or the other, the DFS Namespace and DFS Replication services should now be running from within the Services applet or Server Manager's viewpoint, and you are ready to start configuring your first DFS namespace, and later DFS replication.

Getting Started with DFS-N

With the DFS components now installed on our Windows file servers, we will start by configuring a namespace in DFS. Later in the chapter, we will add replication.

How a DFS Namespace Works

Normally, a client machine that is accessing a Windows file share goes to a URL or network path that includes the file server name and the share name—such as `\\FS1\Data`. A DFS namespace works in much the same way, but instead of a file server name, the first part of the path is the name of the DFS root—such as `ContosoData` or `SalesTeam`. The latter part of the path, including multiple levels of directories, are simply pointers to shares and directories that exist on real file servers.

In our example, `\\ContosoData` is the name of the DFS root (the top of the tree) and `\Sales-Forecasts` is the share name. `\Sales-Forecasts` points to a real file share on FS1 called `\Forecasts`. But instead of remembering that the sales forecasts are on FS1, users can peruse the distributed (perhaps better named as a unified) namespace. Windows desktops accessing `\\ContosoData\Sales-Forecasts\2009-Q3` will be transparently connected to `\\FS1\forecasts\2009-Q3`.

Everything else, including the ability to set permissions on the shares (above and beyond the file-level access controls), still applies. One caveat to be aware of is that while Windows clients (from Windows NT 4 through all currently shipping Windows servers and client OSs) can resolve a DFS namespace to its physical shares, not all non-Windows clients have this ability. Instead, you may need a third-party software add-on that performs DFS lookups for you. One example is ExtremeZ-IP from Group Logic (`www.GroupLogic.com`), which among other things acts as an effective proxy for Mac clients resolving the DFS namespaces.

DFS for Macs

DFS client support is available within every Windows OS starting with Windows 95. But, environments that rely on Windows Server for file services but use some non-Windows client machines were usually unable to take advantage of DFS. Out of the box, Mac OS X does not provide support for connecting to DFS-N. Then came Group Logic and their ExtremeZ-IP product.

ExtremeZ-IP is a Windows-based software package that implements the Mac's native file sharing protocol, but provides IT professionals with the ability to integrate the Macs properly into the Windows-based IT infrastructure, including DFS-N.

How ExtremeZ-IP Supports DFS-N

ExtremeZ-IP supports DFS-N in three options:

Option 1: DFS Browsing Using the ExtremeZ-IP Zidget

The ExtremeZ-IP Zidget is a user-friendly service discovery tool that is deployed as a Mac OS X Dashboard Widget or as a simple web page. Using the Zidget, users can navigate the full DFS namespace and directly mount any DFS target. In selecting a target, the Zidget works with the ExtremeZ-IP DFS server to handle target selection and site costing so that the Mac user is directed to the optimal share.

Option 2: Finder-Integrated Browsing Using ExtremeZ-IP Virtual Root Emulator

The second option leverages the AutoFS file system technology that is built into Mac OS X 10.5 and later. When Mac users connect to the ExtremeZ-IP DFS server, they are presented with the DFS namespace directly in the Mac OS X Finder and are able to navigate to their target file share directly. The selection of the target share is done dynamically by ExtremeZ-IP, taking into account target availability as well as site costing.

Option 3: DFS Home Directories

Many organizations that use home directories will leverage DFS to provide a single namespace that includes all users' Active Directory home profiles. However, for Mac clients, the Universal Naming Convention (UNC) paths stored in the users' profiles are not recognized as file shares because they are DFS UNCs. ExtremeZ-IP provides a Mac client component that integrates with the Mac OS X login process to seamlessly resolve and mount the appropriate file share.

DFS Namespaces: Domain-Based or Standalone

Two kinds of namespaces are available for deployment:

Domain-Based Namespace A domain-based namespace provides redundancy across multiple namespace servers and is manageable throughout the domain. One big plus of a domain-based namespace running on Windows Server 2008 is the use of access-based enumeration (ABE). There are two modes that the domain can be in for DFS—Windows 2000 Server mode and Windows Server 2008 mode.

NOTE Access-based enumeration (ABE) hides files that you do not have access to open. Without ABE, users can see filenames and file shares, even if they do not have access to the data itself. This can be considered a security problem because filenames may hint as to the confidential content. For example, imagine finding a file called `HostileTakeoverPlanForContoso.doc`. You don't have to be able to open the file to understand what is going to happen to the Contoso company. ABE fixes this, as long as you turn it on.

Standalone DFS Namespace A standalone DFS namespace (see Table 5.1) is hosted by a single server and is easy to set up, but can also be the SPOF since everything will point to it and therefore be inaccessible if the server is down or otherwise offline. However, a standalone namespace can be implemented within a Microsoft cluster (whereas a domain-based namespace cannot).

TABLE 5.1: Standalone Namespace vs. Domain-Based Namespace

	Standalone Namespace	Domain-Based Namespace
Path to namespace	`\\NamespaceServerName\RootName`	`\\DNSDomainName\RootName` `\\NetBIOSDomainName\RootName`
Location of namespace metadata	Namespace server's Registry	Active Directory
Recommended size of namespace	Can be more than 5,000 folders	Windows 2000 mode = fewer than 5,000 folders Windows 2008 mode = can be more than 5,000 folders
Active Directory	AD not required	Windows 2000 mode = Windows 2000 mixed Windows 2008 mode = DCs and DFW servers must be Windows 2008
Redundancy of namespace	Run the standalone namespace within a Microsoft cluster	Multiple namespace servers sharing configuration retained within AD

There's one last, but slightly blurry, factor for determining if the DFS namespace should be standalone or domain-based: whether you will also be using DFS replication. DFS replication requires the servers to be in an AD domain. So, while you could technically run a standalone namespace with domain-joined servers to enable replication, the real reasons to do that were based on scalability prior to Windows Server 2008. Today, there isn't a compelling reason to run standalone unless you have a niche business case.

DFS Namespace: How the Referral Works

With a namespace now established, we can now discuss the elegance of the client experience.

Whenever a client seeks a file share, it begins by looking up the server via name resolution (DNS or WINS). In this case, the client will be pointed to a DFS namespace server, which then gives the client a referral, or a stacked list of file servers that hold a copy of that file resource/shared folder (called folder targets). From here, the client caches the referral and transparently connects to an actual file server or share from within the referral. This will typically be in the same Active Directory site as the client unless no same-site servers exist for the client—or if the administrator has specifically set a priority order. Later, if the primary source were to become unavailable, the client already has the list of alternate locations and will transparently reconnect. Eventually, when the primary server does come back online, a DFS namespace feature called *client failback* enables the client to transparently move from the alternate server back to the originally intended server without requiring a reload of the referral or other manual intervention.

DFS Namespace: Target Priority

By default, the referral provides a list of the folder targets on the various members, without any prioritization or preference. The site costs from Active Directory and the DFS client on the network requester determine which member, from that referral list, that the client will connect to. This is fine for many situations, but if you are defining a particular server as the failover server for others (for example, the centralized headquarters server versus the production servers in several branches), you may wish to explicitly define it as the last (bottom) member of the referral, so that it is only referenced when all other members are inaccessible. Similarly, if you are not managing the concept of sites within your network, you may wish to explicitly define the top (first) member in the referral list as the primary production server.

Configuring a DFS Namespace

For our purposes, the capabilities of DFS-N have not radically changed since Windows Server 2003 R2, though we will be using the interface from Windows Server 2008 R2, which is nearly identical to the Windows Server 2008 interface as well. At the end of this chapter, I will explain the new enhancements for DFS in both Windows Server 2008 and Windows Server 2008 R2.

There are at least four tools you can use to configure a DFS namespace:

- The DFS management console, which is an MMC snap-in installed in the Administrator Tools directory when the DFS service is enabled, as part of the File Services role in Windows Server 2008/Windows Server 2008 R2 or when DFS is installed under Windows Server 2003 R2
- The File Server Resource Manager, which provides a wizard-driven and consolidated view of several file sharing management tools with the Windows Server
- The DFS command-line utilities
- PowerShell

We will be using the DFS Management Console for most of the exercises in this chapter to provide a relatively consistent view from Windows Server 2003 R2, through Windows Server 2008, and into Windows Server 2008 R2.

DFS Namespace Task 1: Create Your Namespace

We will configure a *domain-based DFS root* so that its information will be propagated across the domain and for easier management. To do this, we will use the DFS Management snap-in to first create a namespace and then add a second namespace server for redundancy in the next task.

1. Select Start ➤ Administrative Tools ➤ DFS Management.
2. On the left pane of the tree, right-click the Namespaces group, and then click New Namespace.
3. In the New Namespace Wizard, enter the following:
   - The name of the server that you want to host the namespace.
   - The name of the root of the namespace, such as **Data**. This will be appended to either the server name (standalone) or the domain name (domain-based) as `\\Contoso\Data`. As an interesting side note, when you create a DFS namespace, an empty folder is created on the namespace server (even if there will never be any data in it). Later, as you create links under this point in the namespace, subdirectories will get created within the folder itself. This folder gets shared, so you can set permissions on it, which effectively provides permissions to the entry point to the whole namespace in a manner of speaking, as shown in Figure 5.8.

FIGURE 5.8 Editing settings for the root folder in the New Namespace Wizard

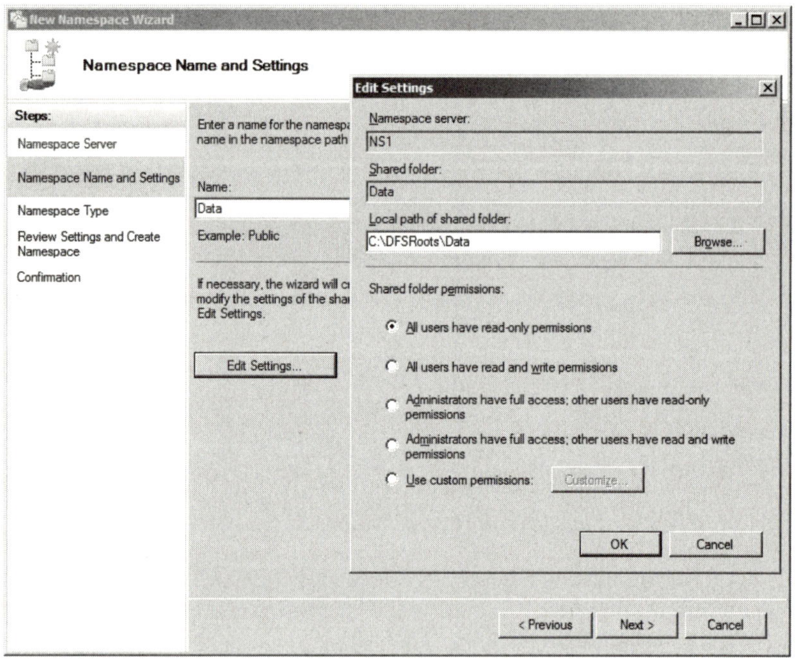

NOTE Remember that Windows uses a policy of compounding permissions, where the most restrictive permissions are in effect. So, be aware of how the permissions of your root folder, the folder targets, and the NTFS permissions will compound. If you manage permissions at every level, your users might find themselves locked out of the wrong data.

- The type of namespace: domain based or standalone. Figure 5.9 shows what the path would look like as a domain-based versus a standalone namespace. In this figure, NS1 is the name of our namespace server, so a standalone namespace would be `\\NS1\Data`. But that is just another name for our users to learn and it has no redundancy unless clustered. So, in our case, we will choose domain based, so the users will access `\\Contoso\Data` across the network. And we've enabled the new scalability and access enhancements of running in Windows Server 2008 mode (described later).

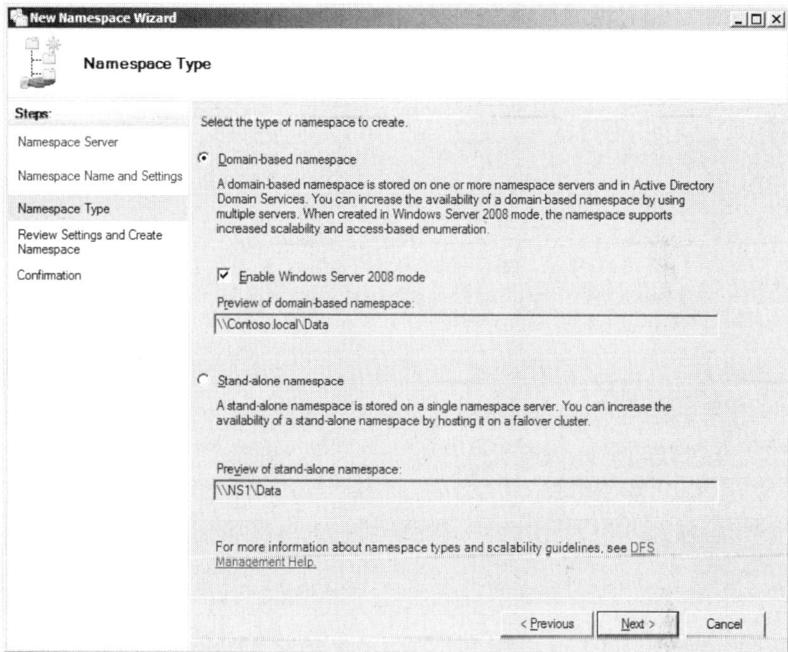

FIGURE 5.9 Specifying the namespace type in the New Namespace Wizard

4. Click Create and then close the wizard.

To confirm this is working, just go to any client machine and browse for `\\Contoso\Data`.

DFS Namespace Task 2: Adding a Second Namespace Server for Redundancy

Since a book on availability should not introduce single points of failure, we will immediately add a second namespace server. As a domain-based namespace, the configuration is within Active Directory, so all we have to do is add the second server to the namespace. If this was a standalone namespace, we would have done the first task of creating a namespace within a Microsoft Cluster Services (MSCS) DFS server instead of a single node.

1. Select Start ➢ Administrative Tools ➢ DFS Management.
2. On the left pane of the tree, expand the Namespaces group.
3. Right-click on the namespace that you just created (`\\Contoso\Data`) and select Add Namespace Server.

4. Enter the new server's name in the Namespace Server text box.
5. Click OK.

When you are finished, the screen should look like Figure 5.10.

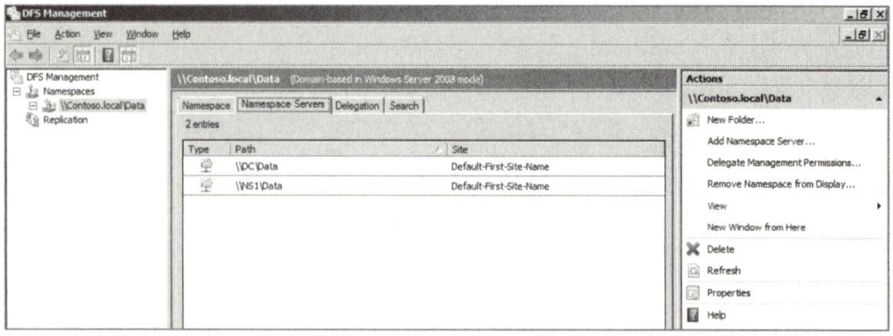

FIGURE 5.10
The DFS console with the namespace defined

On the left, we see the namespace listed. And by clicking on the namespace and then selecting the Namespace Servers tab in the right pane, we will see the two namespace servers that are offering it to our users.

Notice that for this example, we chose both a domain controller and a member server (NS1) that will not be offering files. They are just hosting the namespace. You might choose to host the namespace on some of the primary file servers that will be hosting the file folders themselves—or perhaps use some of the domain controllers in each environment that will obviously already have the domain-based metadata for the namespace within their local information.

DFS Namespace Task 3: Delegation of Management (Optional)

In the DFS Management console, next to the Namespace Servers tab you'll see the Delegation tab, which allows us to enable technical staff to manage this DFS namespace and file services without being a domain administrator. I recommend creating a group within Active Directory (for example, FSadmins) who will be responsible for administering the file services in your infrastructure. By adding users to groups and giving groups permissions, you can easily add and remove IT staff from the FSadmins group as their jobs change.

On the DFS Management console's namespace Delegation tab (Figure 5.11), you can see that Domain Admins already have *explicit* permission to manage this namespace, meaning that it is revocable. Other groups may have *inherited* permissions from Active Directory, and those permissions cannot be changed here.

To add our newly created FSadmins group, simply right-click the namespace (`\\Contoso\Data`), select Delegate Management Permissions, and then enter the **contoso\FSadmins** group name.

DFS Namespace Task 4: Adding Folders and Hierarchy

Now, we have our namespace created and it can be managed by someone other than us, but we don't actually have any data yet.

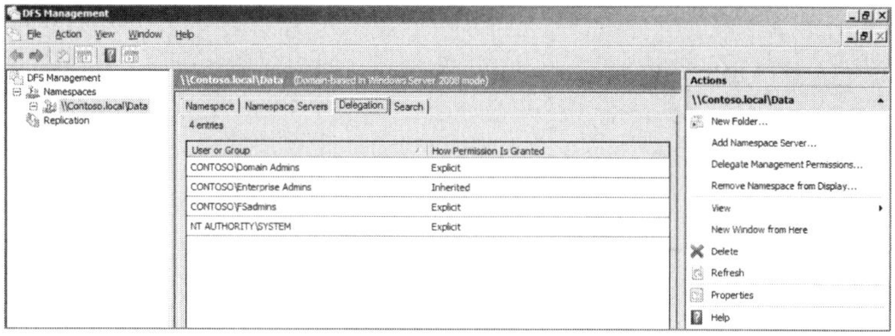

FIGURE 5.11
The Delegation tab in the DFS Management console

We can start by building some top-level folders that may not ever contain files but will provide a hierarchy that makes everything easier for the users. This was the original goal of the namespace in the first place.

1. Select Start ➤ Administrative Tools ➤ DFS Management.
2. Right-click on the namespace and select New Folder, and then enter a few folders to create some structure. In this example, the folders have no bearing on server names or locales, just function:
   - `Engineering`
   - `Management`
   - `Sales`

NAMING STYLES FOR NAMESPACES

Alternatively, we could have created multiple namespaces (`Contoso\Sales`, `Contoso\Engineering`, and `Contoso\Management`). This is mostly a style choice and depends on how big each namespace might be, as well as scaling decisions or where the actual namespace and file servers might be. If a large facility has several file servers supporting engineering, and more notably, all the engineers are in the same geographic location, we might have a namespace just for their servers and data that does not extend outside that locale.

One of our file servers has a file share called `ProjectX` (`\\FS1\ProjectX`). This is a project collaboration folder that our engineers are using, so we're going to connect the real file share to our namespace.

3. Right-click the `Engineering` folder in the namespace, and choose New Folder.
4. Create a new folder object called **`ProjectX`**.
5. Click Add to add a folder target (where the real data resides).
6. Click Browse to open the Browse For Share Folders dialog box.

7. Because the share already exists, browse through FS1, and select the `ProjectX` folder.
   - If the share did not exist, click Create Share to do so. In the Create Share dialog box, define the `ProjectX` share name and the physical location on the server where the directory will reside.
   - If the physical directory does not exist yet, you will be prompted to confirm its creation.

At this point, we have a resilient namespace, because it is hosted on two namespace servers, but the file share itself only exists on FS1. To provide redundancy of the data, we would add a second folder target on this same screen. (If you only have one folder instance, click No at the replication prompt and click OK to complete the folder creation. If you do want a second instance, you should get a better grasp of how DFS replication works, but for this easy example, you can either add the second folder here, or if you clicked OK too quickly, just repeat steps 5–7.)

8. Right-click the folder and choose Add Folder Target; repeat steps 5 and 6 for the second server's folder.
9. Right-click the namespace folder again, and choose Replicate Folder, which will result in a namespace folder similar to Figure 5.12.

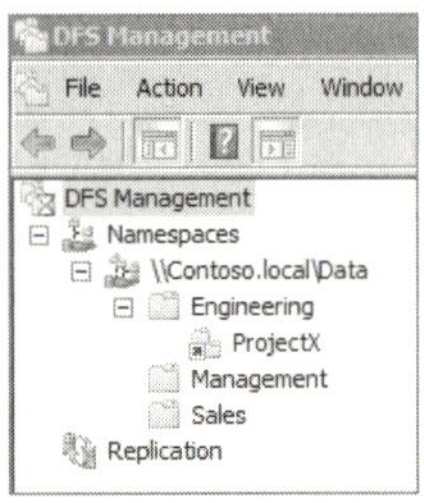

FIGURE 5.12
DFS namespace folder with replication enabled

In the "Key Concepts in DFS Replication" section, we'll discuss a better way to do this long term, but steps 8 and 9 will get you started.

When you finish, the tree on the left should show our new namespace with three functional team directories and one project directory that is tied to one or more production file shares (Figure 5.13).

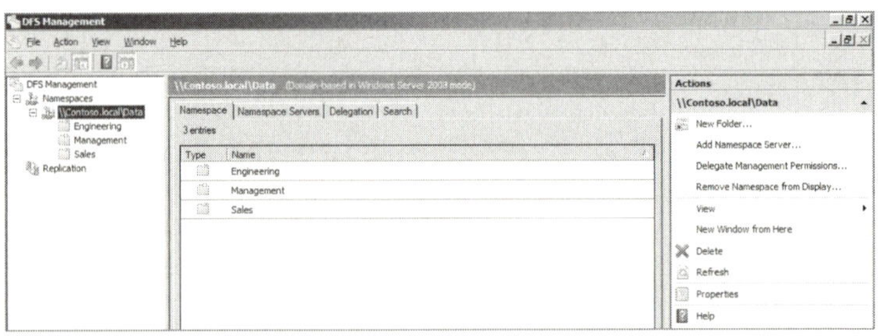

FIGURE 5.13
The DFS namespace after we added our folders and hierarchy

DFS Namespace Task 5: Target Referral Ordering (Optional)

Although we didn't create a replicated folder in step 4 earlier, we will later in the DFS replication tasks add `\\FS2\ProjectX` as a second folder target for the `\\Contoso\Data\Engineering\ProjectX` namespace folder. Now with two folder targets, let's consider optimizing how the target referrals work.

As discussed earlier, when the client machine accesses the namespace, it receive a referral with the list of targets included. The default behavior when a DFS folder has multiple target folders is to use the lowest cost as determined by Active Directory sites across the network. Multiple folders in the same site as the client will be stacked first (in a random order for load balancing), followed by those other folder targets that are not in the same site as the client.

Two typical solutions exist, both of which are best appreciated in branch office scenarios. In both cases, you can modify the target referrals from the DFS Management console and right-click the folder and choose Properties.

- If you want to make sure that all your sites have `\ProjectX` but you don't have the bandwidth to let your New York branch users have access to the London branch's copy, then select Exclude Targets Outside Of The Client's Site.
- If you have slightly more bandwidth and have a centralized copy of the data also at headquarters, you might instead right-click the headquarters' folder target and select Properties. Select the Advanced Tab, click Override Referral Ordering, and select Last Among All Targets.

When you are all done, the proof is in the client experience.

Figure 5.14 shows that a standard Windows client is accessing our `\\Contoso\Data` namespace and we have right-clicked on the properties of the `ProjectX` folder. The DFS tab reveals our referrals and confirms what we are accessing behind the namespace.

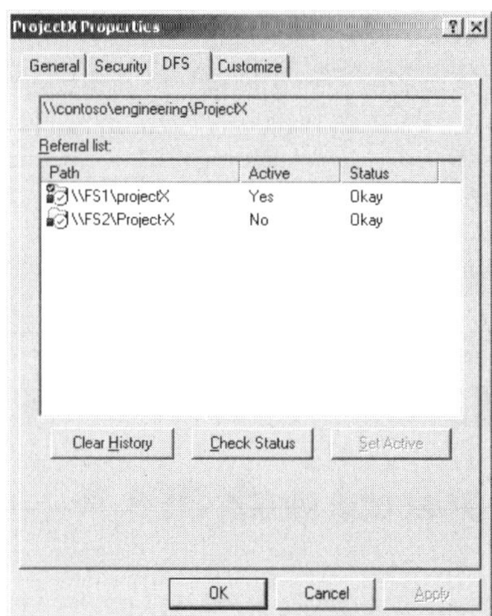

Figure 5.14
The client DFS tab of the `ProjectX` folder's properties

Try disabling the primary file server that the client is currently connected to. If you do, you'll see the client transparently reconnect to the alternate folder target. Going back into the client, the only change is where the client is now being serviced on the DFS tab of the folder's properties (Figure 5.15).

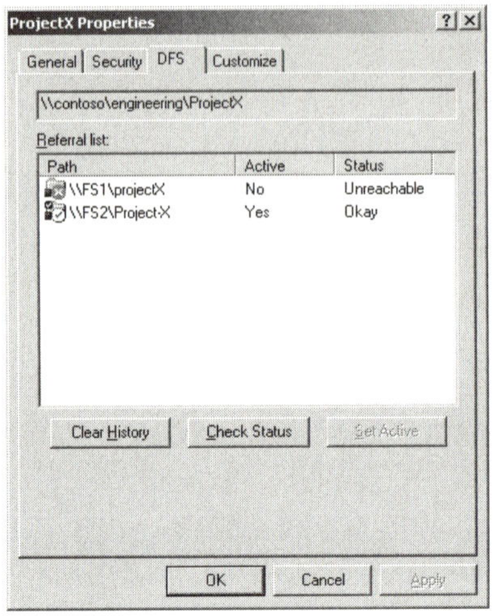

FIGURE 5.15
The client DFS tab after transparent redirection

WHAT'S NEW FOR DFS-N IN WINDOWS SERVER 2008

If you are using Windows Server 2008 to manage Windows Server 2003 or 2003 R2 file servers, you may have noticed some differences between your UI screens and the ones in this book. Along with workflow and cosmetics, here are a few other notable differences in DFS namespace that were introduced with Windows Server 2008:

Access-Based Enumeration (ABE) ABE allows users to see only files and folders that they have rights to see. Prior to Windows Server 2008 and ABE, users could see directories and attempt to click on them, only to get a rights-denied error. This cleans things up so folks only see what they should.

Search The DFS Management console now provides a Search option for finding folders and folder targets within the namespace.

Getting Started with DFS-R

DFS-R is a multimaster replication engine, whereby any of the contributing nodes can synchronize partial-file changes between their peers. The good news is that any of the replication partners can send its updates to the others. The bad news is that any of the replication partners can send its updates to the partners. Because of this, DFS replication enables multiple solutions, with and without DFS namespaces. When used in tandem with DFS-N, the primary business solutions include the following:

Publication Publication, as termed by the DFS folks, is based on a "one-to-many" distribution of files from a primary source to multiple destinations. Examples of this include pushing out standardized forms or other files from a primary headquarters' server out to all of the various branch offices and remote locations across the company. Similarly, if you have installable software that you wish to have in multiple geographies for performance reasons, you might configure replication from the primary IT server out to file shares in the various geographies. Publication is usually deployed by replicating data in one direction from the source to multiple destinations, or by utilizing the new Read-Only Replicated Folders option in Windows Server 2008 R2.

Collaboration Collaboration in a DFS scenario presumes a bidirectional replication between two sites where there are likely active users at each location. This is easy to do but comes with one significant drawback: No locking mechanism is built in between the peer-level replication partners. This means that if two people in different geographies were to each open and make changes to their copy of a file that is being replicated via DFS-R, then the last person to save their file will "win"—and will effectively overwrite any other changes from the other participants. Because of this potential risk, there are two more effective ways to collaborate with file sharing. One alternative is to leverage Microsoft SharePoint or some other document management system whereby a file is checked out for edits, and all other mirrored copies of that file are placed in a read-only state. Another alternative is to use third-party software that offers a blocking manager across multiple file servers so that the first requestor blocks the file to gain exclusive write access while the other replicas are read-only.

High Availability High availability of file shares is a benefit of using a DFS namespace to point to multiple replicated copies of a file share; if a client cannot access the primary or preferred physical share, they are transparently and automatically redirected to the secondary instance of the data. Additionally, since DFS replication is bidirectional by design, the primary share will automatically receive all the updates from the secondary share while the primary was offline. For the purposes of this book, this is the primary implementation of DFS that we will explore.

Centralized Backup of Branch Offices Also called *data collection* in the DFS terminology, centralized backup of branch offices is enabled by providing DFS replication from shares in branch office file servers back to a replica at your headquarters. Along with the availability benefit and potential collaboration described earlier, you gain the additional ability to back up the headquarters copy of the data instead of running separate backup software at each branch location. There are some challenges with this approach that we will describe later in the section "Centralized Backup via DFS-R." But for some environments, this may be an adequate way to centralize all the data and remove tape drives from the remote offices.

Before DFS-R, There Was FRS

While DFS namespace has been part of the Windows Server operating system ever since Windows NT 4 under the name DFS, DFS replication has only been available since Windows Server 2003 R2. From Windows 2000 through Windows Server 2003 (and although the bits technically still exist through Windows Server 2008 R2), a different replication technology called the File Replication Service (FRS) was in the operating system. FRS was a whole-file replication system, meaning that no matter how little or how much a file changed, the entire file would be replicated. In addition, there were bandwidth and performance limitations that effectively negated the use of FRS for the scenarios listed earlier and instead relegated it to the purpose of synchronizing login scripts and other minor small files between the infrastructure or domain controller servers or similar platforms with limited file change rates.

Microsoft was left with a distributed file system namespace to more easily locate files across multiple servers and shares, but no practical benefit of availability, backup, collaboration, or even publication. Because of that gap, many third-party replication technologies began appearing for Windows 2000 through Windows Server 2003 R2. Examples include Double-Take or XOsoft WANSync (see Chapter 3).

As an unofficial historical anecdote, the replication technology in the beta of Windows Server 2003 R2 was originally called FRS2. However, because of the negative perception toward FRS, Microsoft decided to call it DFS-R.

FRS AND DFS-R

The most important thing to know about FRS and DFS replication is that they are not the same—and not even evolutions of each other. They are very different technologies.

Key Concepts in DFS Replication

There are a few more key concepts you should understand before deploying DFS replication:

Replication Group A *replication group* is a set of servers, called members, which are configured to replicate data between them. Note that servers in a replication group must be in the same Active Directory forest.

Replicated Folder A *replicated folder* is a folder that is being synchronized by DFS-R between members of a replication group. The replicated folder does not need to appear in the same location on each member (for example, `D:\Data`). Replicated folders do *not* have to be shared in order to be replicated, but they do need to reside on NTFS volumes.

As changes occur within any instance of a file (within a replicated folder), those changes are identified via Remote Differential Compression (RDC) and replicated between the member servers. The relational bonds between member servers are referred to as *connections*. The overall map of connections, groups, and members is the *topology* of the DFS environment.

The common best practice is to define multiple replicated folders within a single replication group where practical. This allows all the folders within a group to inherit the same topology and settings, including scheduling and bandwidth settings from the replication group. Even within a single replication group, you can still configure individual file settings (such as filters), as needed.

How DFS-R Works: Remote Differential Compression

DFS-R is a multimaster replication engine, whereby any of the contributing nodes can synchronize partial-file changes between their peers. It works by routinely identifying and comparing which parts of files have been updated. By default, this happens after a file closes. DFS-R should not be used on interdependent or transactional files, such as databases with their respective log files, nor with large files that are known to rarely close, such as Microsoft Outlook PST files.

But for traditional Microsoft Word documents, Excel spreadsheets, or PowerPoint presentations, DFS-R provides a highly effective way to replicate only those parts of the files that have changed to alternate locations.

To accomplish this, DFS-R leverages a built-in mechanism in Windows Server called Remote Differential Compression (RDC). RDC is an algorithm that compares one file against another and then recursively parses the file into smaller chunks to identify which pieces of the file are different. This mechanism is particularly ideal for standard documents from Microsoft Office 2003. It is slightly less optimal, though still highly effective, for Microsoft Office 2007 and later documents. To appreciate the benefits of RDC, consider the following common example often referenced by Microsoft in explaining RDC.

Suppose you're changing the title slide of a 3.5 MB PowerPoint presentation. Prior to DFS-R, the next replication of that PowerPoint presentation would transmit 3.5 MB between sites. When you use the RDC algorithm, the file is parsed until only the chunk that contains the new elements of the tile slide is replicated, resulting in perhaps 16 KB of data transfer instead.

How RDC Parses for Changes

Here is another example commonly used by Microsoft when explaining RDC. Say a file originally contains the text "the quick fox jumped over the lazy dog." This file is replicated between the DFS-R sites. Later, a single word such as "brown" is added to the middle of the line.

When one copy of the file is changed, the two files can be compared, and immediately the file can be parsed into large pieces (often called chunks) to identify the section of the file that has been changed. In this case, the middle section will again be compared, parsed, and chunked further to identify the section of the file containing the changes. This process does not occur forever, but it happens often enough to be efficient in determining the scope of the change without adding too much performance penalty or latency. The changed section of the file (including the word "brown") is then transmitted and applied within the replicated instance of the file.

This description gives a word picture that Microsoft often used when first explaining RDC. But in actuality, RDC works by parsing a file into chunks on both the source and target servers (Figure 5.16). For each chunk, a strong hash, or signature, is created. The source then initiates communication and passes the list of the chunks' signatures to the target. The lists are compared to determine which chunks are already on the target and which ones need to be replicated.

FIGURE 5.16
How RDC compares files

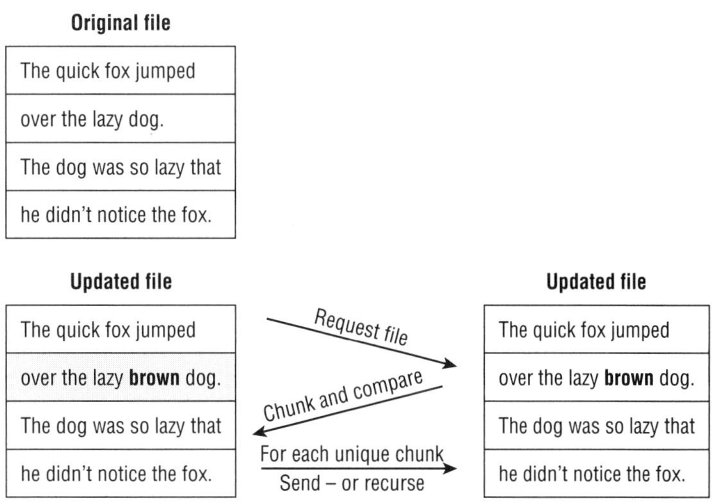

For example, if a file is parsed into six chunks, six signatures will be created and transmitted to the target. The six signatures are compared with six corresponding signatures of the version of the file that already exists on the target. If one of the signatures is different, then depending on the size of the file that one corresponding chunk can be sent from the source to the target. Alternatively, there are scenarios where a larger chunk will be recursively parsed into smaller chunks and the smaller chunks' signatures compared again, to find a more granular view of what was changed.

Cross-File RDC

Additionally, in certain editions of Windows Server, DFS-R can use a function called cross-file RDC. This feature might be the coolest part yet. Essentially, after identifying the partial-file chunks that need to be replicated between nodes, a server using cross-file RDC will determine if any of those file chunks exist in other files already on the local server. If so, the chunks are taken from the local server, thus reducing bandwidth even further.

Cross-file RDC is available only if one of the servers in the replication connection is one of these editions:

- Windows Server 2003 R2, Enterprise edition
- Windows Server 2003 R2, Datacenter edition
- Windows Server 2008, Enterprise edition
- Windows Server 2008, Datacenter edition
- Windows Server 2008 R2, Enterprise edition
- Windows Server 2008 R2, Datacenter edition

How Initial Replication Works

When you first enable replication, you will designate one of the folders as being *authoritative*, meaning that during any conflicts between one folder and the others, this one wins. Aside from that, the topology and replication settings (groups, schedules, throttling) are all maintained in Active Directory. This is both a good thing and bad thing. The good news is that like a domain-based namespace, these settings are natively resilient across domain controllers. Each replicating member simply polls Active Directory for the most up-to-date settings. The bad news involves the polling. Based on the latency during AD synchronization, as well as the individually defined polling intervals by the replicating members, it can take a while before replication setting changes are effectively propagated to all the participants (think hours, not minutes, but not days).

The initial synchronization happens in waves, where the primary member replicates to all of its direct partners. Only when the direct partner has completed its initial synchronization will it then turn around and begin replicating with its second-tier partners. In this way, you can be assured that the authoritative copy propagates all the way through without variation. As the metadata is exchanged:

- Files that are identical between sender and receiver are not replicated.
- Files that are different between sender and receiver are updated to the sender's version via RDC, which determines which parts of the files are different and only transmits those partial file updates.
- Files that exist on the receiving member but do not exist on the sender (authoritative or other upstream sender) are moved to the `DFS-RPrivate\PreExisting` folder.

After the initial replication is complete, the authoritative designation is removed from the original member because all the copies are now considered identical. From this point on, DFS-R works on a "last write wins" principle. Neither side is authoritative. DFS-R works by monitoring file changes within each member. When changes occur, they are replicated to all the other replication partners, regardless of which member started it. This peer level–style replication will begin at the next scheduled replication interval, based on the settings in the replication groups. Peer-to-peer, or what some call multi-master or mesh-style replication, can be both effective and challenging, depending on why you are replicating the data in the first place. Later in the chapter, in the section "Mixing DFS-R and DFS-N for Real-World Solutions," we will discuss several business goals for replication and where DFS-R does or does not fit in each.

Configuring DFS Replication

To configure DFS replication, we will again utilize the DFS Management console (also accessible from the DFS MMC snap-in).

DFS Replication Task 1: Creating a Replication Group

If you skipped ahead earlier and enabled the folder replication when we originally discussed DFS namespace tasks and creating the folder, you likely accepted the defaults and now have a replication group that is the same name as the namespace folder and that has one folder being replicated with two members. That's fine, but you end up with different settings for every folder.

Earlier, we defined replication groups as a set of members that participate in replication together for a series of folders. By first creating a replication group and then enabling the folder replication as part of that group, you ensure that the folders all inherit the settings (such as scheduling and bandwidth controls) of the group, making long-term management much easier. Here are the steps:

1. Select Start ➢ Administrative Tools ➢ DFS Management.
2. Right-click Replication in the left pane and select New Replication Group.
3. In the New Replication Group Wizard, configure the following:

   Replication Group Type: Enter **Multipurpose Replication Group**.

   Group Name: Enter **Team File Servers**.

   Group Members: Select FS1 and FS2.

   Topology: Select the Full Mesh option, as shown in Figure 5.17.

Replication Topologies

The topology options for DFS replication are as follows:

Hub and Spoke Uses three or more servers for a centralized model to and from datacenters.

Full Mesh Everyone replicates to everyone, as seen in Figure 5.17.

No Topology Implies that you will create all your connections later to customize the replication flow.

FIGURE 5.17
DFS replication topology options

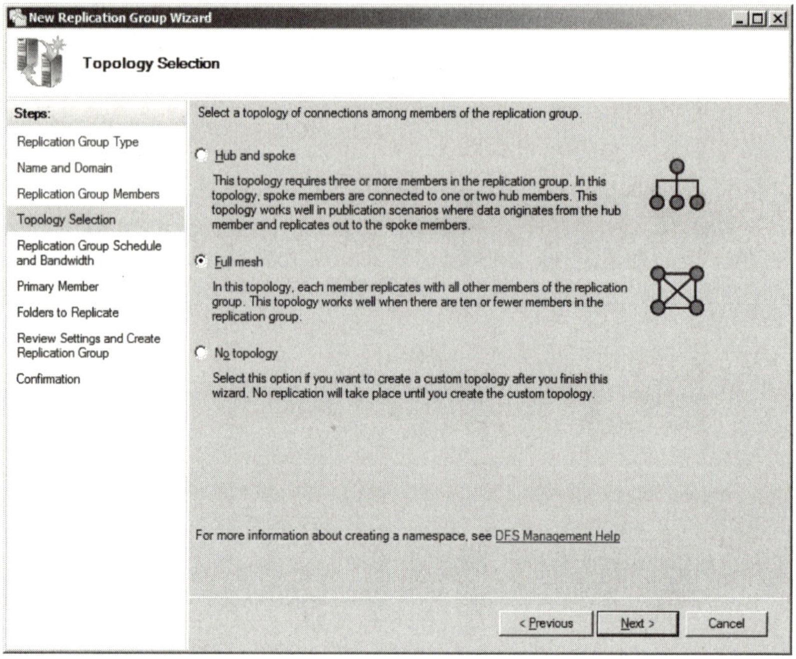

Schedule And Bandwidth: Chose the option of whether replicate continuously using the specified bandwidth, accepting the default choice of Full Bandwidth Usage. We will change this setting in later exercises.

Primary Member: Type **FS1**.

Folders To Replicate: Select a few preexisting physical folders on FS1.

Local Path On Other Members: Choose where the copies of the FS1 folders will reside on FS2, noting that the pathnames do not have to match. After entering each path, click to enable that directory for replication.

4. Click Create, then Close, and then OK to complete the process (Figure 5.18).

DFS-R ISN'T EXACTLY CONTINUOUS DATA PROTECTION

By the strictest of industry definitions, there aren't many mainstream products that are CDP. According to the Storage Networking Industry Association (SNIA), CDP is defined as "a methodology that continuously captures or tracks data modifications and stores changes independent of the primary data, enabling recovery points from any point in the past" (see `www.snia.org/forums/dmf/programs/data_protect_init/cdp/cdp_definition/`).

DFS-R does replicate near-continuously, but DFS-R does not provide the ability to recover to any point in the past, per the CDP definition. DFS-R is focused on providing additional copies that are close to or that match the production copy. So, by our definitions in this book, DFS-R is an availability technology. To have multiple previous recovery points, you will need a disk-to-disk backup solution, as discussed in Chapter 4.

Toward the end of the process, the wizard reminds you that replication will not begin immediately, as we discussed earlier in the chapter. Also, when defining the schedule, note that "replicate continuously" may not actually be continuous replication or the academic term of Continuous Data Protection (CDP), where the replication occurs in real time as a reaction to each new data write. There may be perceived delays based on what else the OS and file system are doing.

FIGURE 5.18
DFS replication group

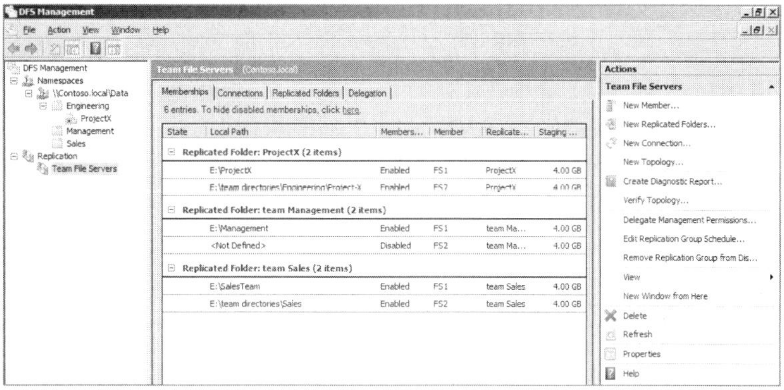

Memberships The Memberships tab shows each of the replicated folders and all of the member servers that are hosting a copy. From here we can go to the members and tune the DFS settings specific to that server.

Connections The Connections tab reveals two one-way replication paths—one for each direction between the replicating pair of member servers. Each connection has its own schedule and other settings. The pair of one-way trusts seen here exists because we selected a multipurpose replication group in Task 1. By selecting a different group type, we would only have replication in one direction, from the source to multiple targets (data publication) or multiple sources to a single target (data collection).

Replication Folders The Replication Folders tab shows us the folders being replicated and whether or not they are in a namespace.

Delegation The Delegation tab allows us to delegate management of this replication group to individuals, similar to how we delegated the namespace management to the FSadmins group in the section "DFS Namespace Task 3: Delegation of Management."

DFS Replication Task 2: Adding Redundancy to a Folder Target

Earlier in the section "DFS Namespace Task 4: Adding Folders and Hierarchy," we created a folder in our namespace (`\\Contoso\Data\Engineering\ProjectX`) that had one folder target pointed to the file share `\\FS1\ProjectX`. While the namespace is natively resilient because we included multiple namespace servers, we also want to make important file shares resilient through DFS replication. This replication would also allow users in separate offices to access the data locally for better performance while ensuring that everyone works from the latest copy.

Depending on how you've done the tasks so far, your replication group may already have FS1 and FS2 happily replicating and the namespace correctly pointing to both of the available folder instances. For this example, we will be adding a new FS3 server to the scenario, where FS1 is at our corporate headquarters, while FS2 and FS3 are branch offices. To do this:

1. Select Start ➤ Administrative Tools ➤ DFS Management.

2. Right-click the replication group and select New Member.
3. Enter **FS3** as the new member.
4. For each folder that is already being replicated with the group, you can choose whether or not the new member server will host a copy. In our example, we have two project directories, but only one of them is relevant to the users that are closest to FS3.
    - For `\ProjectX`: Select the local path on FS3 where the directory will reside.
    - For `\ProjectQ`: Choose Disabled so it is not replicated to FS3.

    Connections This determines with which servers FS3 will replicate. Choosing both by clicking each available member and clicking Add will make a true mesh topology. Alternatively, you might start to optimize the topology of the three servers, where the branches only replicate with the centralized headquarters copy and data doesn't bounce up and down the spokes of the WAN.

    Replication Schedule This allows you to optimize when FS3 will replicate and how much bandwidth it will use during those windows.

    Local Path Of Replicated Folders This lists the currently replicated folders in the replication group, so that you can selectively enable replicas on the new member. In this case, FS3's users need to share some data with FS1 users and other data with FS2 users, so we can add them accordingly.
5. Click Create, then Close, and then OK to complete the process.

The same disclaimer applies: the DFS topology and replication settings will need to be propagated across the domain controllers and then later picked up by each of the participating members, according to their individual poll times. Replication may take an hour or longer to begin, based on AD latency and polling times.

When the steps are complete, you should see something like Figure 5.19. Here all three servers are participating in the replication group, which allows for a consistent schedule and other settings. Each member server may be replicating most, but not necessarily all, the folders in the group.

FIGURE 5.19
DFS replication folders

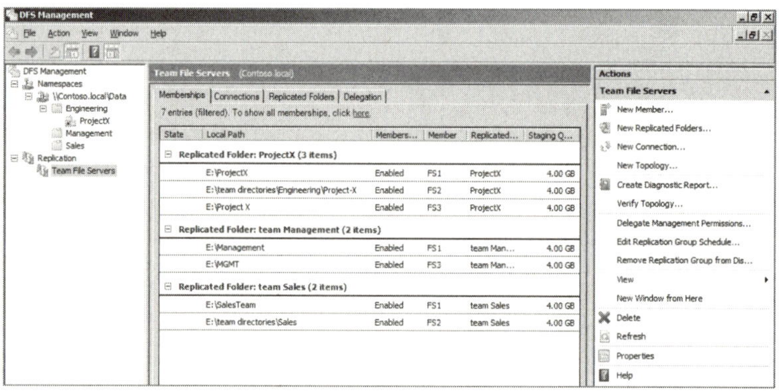

In our scenario, everything is stored on FS1, our primary file server at headquarters—and a subset of the files and shares are replicated to other sites that also need the data on FS2 and FS3. Because of this, we may not want a *full mesh* topology, where every server can replicate to every other server. Instead, we can delete the replication paths from FS2 to FS3, and vice versa. This way, all our data only replicates through our FS1 server at the hub of our intranet, as shown in Figure 5.20.

FIGURE 5.20
Replication group topology in a hub/spoke configuration

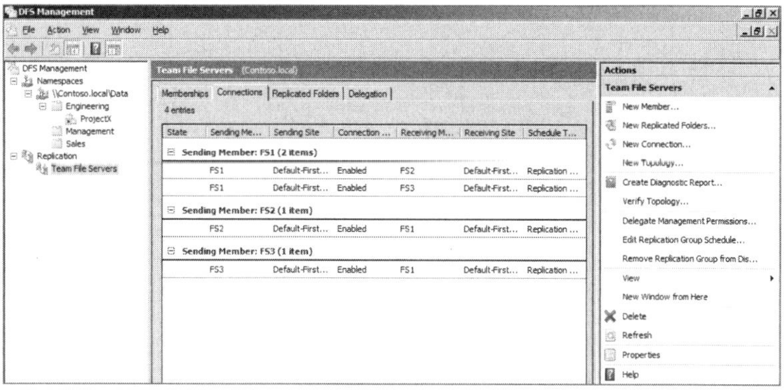

DFS Replication Task 3: Publishing the New Copy of the Replicated Folder in the Namespace

This is somewhat an optional task, depending on why you are replicating. In the earlier scenario, FS1 and FS2 were already replicating the data and both folder instances were listed in the namespace as folder targets, so availability is somewhat already achieved. If we are adding FS3 strictly for collection of the data for centralized backup purposes, then FS3 may have a significantly larger I/O burden and may not be suitable to be an alternate production copy. In this scenario, we do not have to add FS3's folder to the folder target list in the namespace. Users will be able to access either FS1 or FS2, while our backup software has exclusive access to the copy of the data on FS3.

Or, if you do wish to offer the FS3 version, perhaps as the last failover option, you can do that as well from either the namespace viewpoint or the replication viewpoint. To do that, find the namespace folder that was created in the section "DFS Namespace Task 4: Adding Folders and Hierarchy" and edit the folder that has the existing folder targets in it. Right-click on the folder and select Add Target Folder to add the FS3 folder to that mix.

Perhaps a better scenario for this task is one where we were not previously publishing a folder within the namespace. Instead of creating a namespace, then the folder, and then enabling replication, here we've started with building a replicated folder set and are now ready to offer it within the namespace. In this way, we are essentially making sure that our offering is resilient before we connect the users.

1. Select Start ➤ Administrative Tools ➤ DFS Management.
2. Select the Replication object in the tree.

3. Select the replication group and look at the Replicated Folders detail tab.
4. Right-click on the replicated folder and select Share And Publish In Namespace.

   Publishing Method Choose Share And Publish Replicated Folder In Namespace.

   Share Replicated Folders Here you'll define a new shared folder name or select an existing shared folder. Creating a new one also allows you to define which replicated folders to share and adjust share permissions if necessary. In our case, one of our servers already has it shared, but the other does not. DFS will share the folder for us.

   Namespace Path Specify where in the namespace this new folder should go, such as `\\Contoso\Data\Engineering`.
5. Click Share and then click Close to complete the process.

By following these steps, as you can see in Figure 5.21, we have created a `ProjectQ` that is hosted only on FS3 and FS2 and added it to the namespace alongside the others. To finish, delete the `Sales` and `Management` folders from the namespace that we created earlier to help visualize what the namespace would look like—and then click Share And Publish for the respective folders with the same names. Figure 5.22 shows our final deployment with one namespace, one replication group, and various replicated and shared folders.

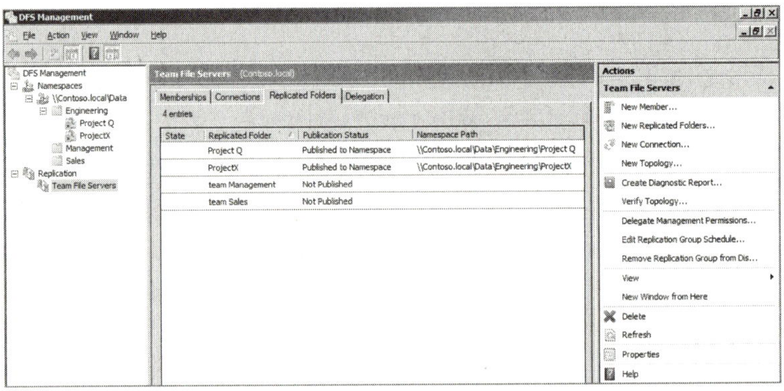

FIGURE 5.21 Updated DFS namespace after publishing replicated folders

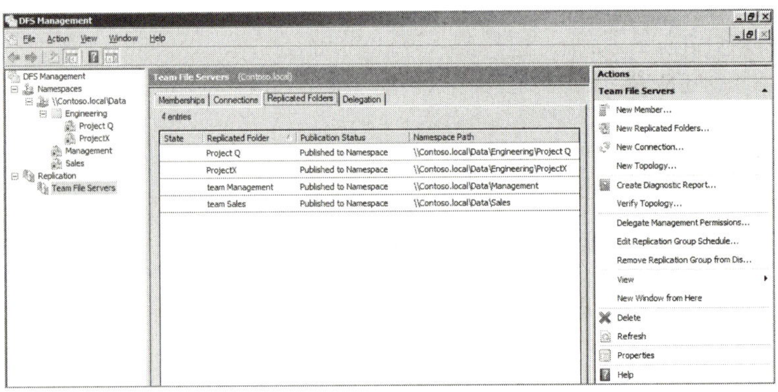

FIGURE 5.22 DFS Management final namespace and replication layout

WHAT'S NEW FOR DFS-R IN WINDOWS SERVER 2008

If you are using Windows Server 2008 to manage Windows Server 2003 or 2003 R2 file servers, you may have noticed some differences between your UI screens and the ones in this book. Along with workflow and cosmetics, here are a few other notable differences in DFS Namespace that were introduced with Windows Server 2008:

Content Freshness DFS replication now prevents an older server that has been offline for a while from overwriting newer data when it comes back after a long outage.

Replicate Now As mentioned earlier, replication changes can take a while to propagate through Active Directory and be polled by the individual servers. This new right-click choice from the DFS Management console momentarily ignores the schedule and forces immediate replication triggers.

SYSVOL Replication Using DFS-R Among other things, SYSVOL stores files such as login scripts, which need to be replicated to all the domain controllers in a domain. In fact, this was an original use for FRS when it was first created, so that the scripts and other items were synchronized across domain controllers. In Windows Server 2003 R2, DFS-R did not support SYSVOL replication, so FRS was still used on the system volume, whereas DFS-R would replicate data areas on the other volumes. In Windows Server 2008, DFS replication was added for SYSVOL. To aid with migration, Windows Server 2008 provided a utility that moved the SYSVOL folders from FRS to DFS-R. Note that the replication behavior of SYSVOL is initially determined when you run the DCpromo utility to promote a Windows Server 2008 machine to a domain controller. If the AD domain functional level is Windows Server 2008 mode, the DC will use DFS-R, but if the mode is lower, the DC will use FRS.

Additional Error Handling and Performance Improvements Windows Server 2008 DFS replication gained significantly better handling of unexpected shutdowns, which often created an I/O burden during resynchronizing.

DFS Replication Options

We've covered all of the basics to get you started using DFS replication, though there are some additional options and tuning that are worth discussing.

DFS Replication: Bandwidth Throttling

DFS replication can be tuned for low-bandwidth environments via two parameters—time and speed.

By default, DFS replicates changes to files as soon as they are closed. DFS can also be configured with start and stop times throughout the day and night, as well as configured to throttle-down the network bandwidth consumed during replication (Figure 5.23). Scheduling is available based on local server time or universal time (UTC). This makes for some interesting scenarios where you might configure limited bandwidth usage during the production day and the full network utilization during afterhours.

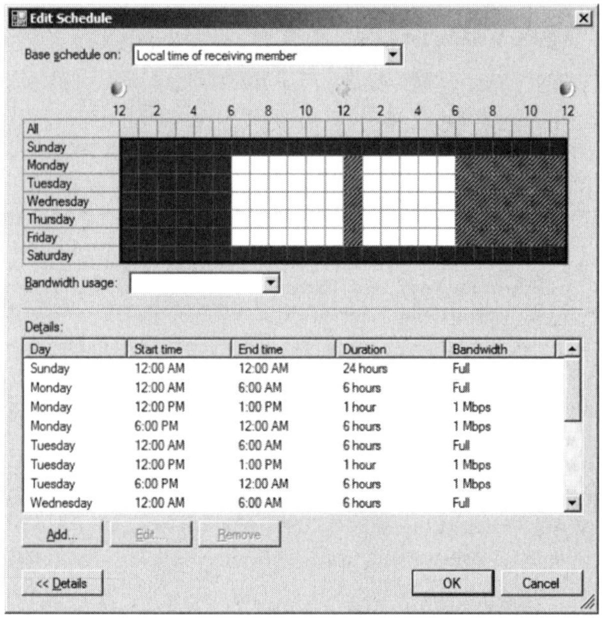

FIGURE 5.23
DFS replication throttling and bandwidth schedule

Bandwidth throttling of DFS replication works but it also causes latency that might not be necessary. Similar to the guidance discussed for configuring disk-to-disk replication in Chapter 3, this form of throttling may incur additional latency. Specifically, if you configure the replication to only use 25 percent of your bandwidth during production hours, but nothing else is using the other 75 percent of the bandwidth, then you haven't saved yourself anything—but you did make your replication take four times as long.

Instead, if your router infrastructure provides for quality of service (QOS) or other packet prioritization, you might choose to prioritize DFS traffic by either the IP address pair (traffic between the server IP and its peers) compared with traffic from another local IP node (presumably a client workstation), or the ports associated with DFS traffic.

This approach is the same one described in the disk-to-disk (D2D) replication and backup sections of Chapters 3 and 4, respectively. The method you choose to manage the server-to-server replication and its throttling may be more political than technical, especially if you have administrators who own the *wire* but not the *servers* or the *applications*. Using DFS or any other D2D throttling solves the problem most definitively, but at the cost of unused bandwidth going unused. Using network prioritization via QOS from the network infrastructure's perspective, makes everyone happy:

- The servers get full bandwidth all the time, as long as no higher-priority process needs it, but they do not impede other traffic that has a higher priority.
- And the networking folks like feeling that they have control of flow.

DFS Replication: Recovery of Replication and Members

This book is on protection, recovery, mitigation—and within DFS are a few things worth noting on the subject.

DFS replication has a *self-healing* database. During the process, replication does not occur between the affected node and its peers. But when the resolution is complete, everything resumes transparently—without administrator intervention. To repair itself, DFS-R scans the file system and re-creates its own database of the metadata for those files. After DFS-R builds its own database, the metadata is compared with that of another replication server. Surprisingly, this is not a lot of data. The metadata (per file) is approximately twice the length of the full pathname and filename plus 144 bytes. For example, the document that this chapter was written from is called `D:\Home\jbuff\projectX\Chapter5-DFS.docx` and has a filename of 40 characters, so the metadata would be around 40   2 (80) + 144 = 224 bytes. If you had exactly a million files on each of your file servers (and are just repairing DFS), this would require sending only around 224 MB to recover the DFS database. If files had changed during this time, those bytes would be additional above the 224 MB, and your servers would use RDC to compare and resynchronize the files themselves.

Additionally, the topology and schedule for DFS replication is stored in Active Directory, as well as cached in a local XML file. If a particular server becomes corrupted, the configuration can be pulled back down after a server recovery, for example. An additional XML file for the server-specific DFS settings is also maintained. This file is protected during any traditional backup of the system state of the Windows Server operating system.

You can monitor the health of the DFS replication through a variety of means, including the built-in DFSR health report, Windows Management Instrumentation (WMI), or a management pack for either System Center Operations Manager or System Center Essentials (see Chapter 11).

DFS Replication: Prestaging the Data

The workflow I just explained showed you how to configure replication, and you already know that RDC will efficiently synchronize the changes thereafter—but what about initially getting the data from source to target, especially for branch offices?

To address this, the folders for DFS replication can be *prestaged*, which means the data can be manually copied, backed up, and restored via any portable medium. For example, to initially get the 800 GB of files from a particular branch office to a headquarters repository, consider getting an inexpensive 1 TB USB drive and copying the data to the portable drive, and then shipping the drive. When the drive arrives at the second site, headquarters can simply copy the drive's contents into the folder that will be participating in the replication. Similar to our discussions of disk-to-disk backup prestaging in Chapter 4, we might presume that the copy-ship-restore process might take three to four business days. At the end, our headquarters' copy has most of the files, but some of them are older than the active production copy within the branch office.

As discussed earlier in the section "DFS Replication: Recovery of Replication and Members," DFS will then build its metadata database of the files at the headquarters location based on the version of the files it has and compare it with the metadata database at the branch to determine what files are different. Then, DFS will use the partial-file technology in RDC to determine which parts of the files need to be replicated.

DFS Replication Metrics

These metrics are consistent from Windows Server 2003 R2 through Windows Server 2008 R2, unless noted:

- Each replication group can have up to 256 member servers and contain up to 256 replicated folders.

- Each server can be a member of up to 256 replication groups, and can have up to 256 connections to other replicated members.
- In Windows Server 2003 R2, a replicated volume could contain up to 8 million replicated files and be up to 1 TB in size. In Windows Server 2008, the tested limit is now over 10 TB of data. Note that this is the tested limit for documentation purposes, not a hard limit in the software, so it won't break at, say, 10.1 TB.

PLANNING A DFS REPLICATION DEPLOYMENT

Here are some factors to keep in mind when planning a DFS deployment:

- RDC is not used on files smaller than 64 KB. Instead, it is more optimal to transfer the whole file instead. Similarly, you may find diminishing value in running RDC between servers on high-bandwidth LAN segments. You can manually disable RDC on a per-connection basis when servers are in close proximity.
- DFS replication only occurs after the file is closed. So using DFS replication on files that are often held open for a prolonged period of time (such as Outlook PSTs and databases) is not practical.
- Replicated folders do not have to be shared (or in a namespace). So, you can replicate key folders as an IT administrator that no user may ever see. Examples are server change-control logs and configuration or asset information.

Mixing DFS-R and DFS-N for Real-World Solutions

DFS is not the whole story when it comes to availability and protection of Windows File Services. Up to this point in the chapter, we've been treating DFS as simply a pair of technologies that could empower a few different availability and protection scenarios. Let's make it real.

Let's put together what we have learned so far and apply it to file services availability. The most classic example is the branch office, where we might have 100 remote offices in different geographies coming back to a single corporate data center. In this example, we can see several implementations of DFS that offer different availability or protection aspects. For these scenarios, let's assume that our corporate datacenter is in Seattle and the branch office that we will be interested in is in Dallas.

Normally, our branch office users in Dallas might normally access a file server named DTX01 with four primary file shares:

- `Users`
- `Team`
- `Projects`
- `Shared`

In this case, `Users` provides individual home directories, `Team` provides a place to share information between peers, `Projects` has subdirectories for each major customer engagement that is ongoing, and `Shared` is a common repository of installation software, corporate templates, and other files that are routinely needed by corporate employees everywhere but stored locally for fast performance.

If we look at how each of these directories is accessed, we can better understand what their availability or protection goals might be:

- An individual home directory underneath `Users` is likely to be accessed exclusively by only one employee who may or may not retain a copy of some or all of the data on their workstation.
- The `Team` directory also likely has some access controls for a subset of the branch office employees, any one of whom may or may not also have separate copies of some or all of the data if they travel with laptops but do not use client-side caching (described in the sidebar "Client-Side Caching").
- `Projects` may be accessed by all the employees in one branch but likely not by many other individuals outside of that specific branch office.
- `Shared` contains a wide variety of material yet likely has no access controls, and similar copies of those files may reside at corporate as well as many other branch offices.

Client-Side Caching

Before you automatically equate "file services" availability and DFS (which often will be the case), you should recognize that there is another potential availability and protection capability that users may already be employing for files—client-side caching (CSC).

CSC has gone by many names over the history of Windows, including My Briefcase, IntelliMirror, and Offline Folders. In its latest incarnation with a Windows XP, Windows Vista, or Windows 7 desktop and a Windows Server 2008 or Windows Server 2008 R2 file server, what you need to realize is that it is easy and reliable for end users to retain a copy of some or all of the file shares that they'd normally access on a file server within their roaming machine.

In some cases, the cached copies of files will be synchronized automatically, such as home directories where a user's `My Documents` directory may be transparently redirected; while users believe they are accessing data locally, they are referencing a directory on a file server. In this case, CSC is automatically enabled so that users are accessing the offline copy of those files when their laptop is disconnected, and they access the synchronized copy of those files from the file server cache when on their corporate network.

In other scenarios, such as shared team directories or project folders, while CSC may not be automatically enabled, it is an easy exercise within Windows Explorer for the end user to manually enable synchronization by right-clicking on a file and selecting Always Available Offline. This allows an end user who is routinely working on a project to select just that particular project directory from the file server and be able to access it online or offline.

In the context and contrast of DFS and file services availability, this provides another layer of resiliency above and beyond what we configure for file services replication and namespaces. In this case, if a file server were to suffer a crisis, those users who have chosen to cache copies of those files or directories would still have them available. Unfortunately, those users who had not opted to enable offline protection of their files or project directories would not have access to them during a server crisis. This brings us back to where DFS should enter the equation.

File Distribution

One of the most traditional uses of file replication technology from within Windows Server is that of distribution, where there is typically a single "source" sending to many numerous "target" servers. In the scenario description we described earlier, the `Shared` directory is a good example where many environments today might still have a manual or batch process of copying corporate directories out to multiple remote locations. These might include standardized documents and templates that should be used corporate-wide, such as human resources (HR) forms or standard PowerPoint logos and graphics. It might also include standard corporate software such as the installable directories for Microsoft Office or perhaps internally developed applications that perform better if locally executed.

DFS replication does not require DFS namespace, though there are benefits for using them together in almost every scenario, including this one. But pragmatically, you could define a few replication groups where the corporate source servers might be:

`\\CORP-IT\Installables`

`\\HRSVR\Standard-docs`

`\\MKTGSVR2\Templates`

These corporate file shares could then be automatically replicated to every remote office server as subdirectories of each file server's `Shared` directory:

`\\DTX01\Shared\Installables`

`\\DTX01\Shared\HRdocs`

`\\DTX01\Shared\Templates`

The power of using DFS replication in this example is that replication only occurs when a corporate share has some new files, and then only the changes within those files are replicated across the WAN. This is ideal when you make minor changes to the PowerPoint template, update some text in an HR document, or stream a patch within an installable directory.

But to make this solution even more elegant, we should embrace DFS namespace. In this example, we could create a namespace called `\\Contoso` with the three root-level directories: `\Installables`, `\HRdocs`, and `\Templates`. The namespace would be placed above the replicated groups so that users in the Dallas office would always access those particular directories under the `\\Contoso` namespace. Because DFS understands the concepts of network sites and topologies, the local copy of those files would always be accessed when a user was running it within the Dallas office. More specifically, when any client attempts to resolve which physical server should be accessed from the namespace referral, the lowest-cost connection, as defined in Active Directory, is used unless a specific priority was preconfigured. This means that if a Dallas user were to visit the Houston office for a day, they would still access the files from `\\Corporate` (the namespace), but the actual copy that they would get is local from the Houston file server, as seen in Figure 5.24.

In a different scenario, if the Dallas file server had some kind of outage where some or all of its files were unavailable, the Dallas office users would be transparently directed to one of the other replicated copies either in another branch such as Houston or the corporate datacenter, depending on WAN link costs and bandwidth.

FIGURE 5.24
How file distribution is transparently masked with DFS

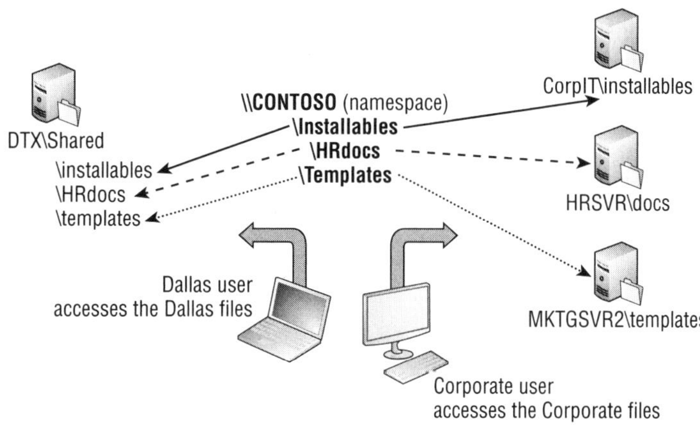

By using a DFS namespace on top of a replicated directory, even though the primary purpose of the replication is distribution, the namespace provides a transparent high-availability capability for those file shares.

Branch Office Availability and Centralized Backup

In the previous example, the replicated data originated at corporate and was sent out bound to the branch offices for better performance due to local access. If we reverse the replication, we see the same benefits but from a different perspective. Instead of replicating corporate contents down to the `\Shared` share on the local file server, let's consider replicating the `\Team` and `\Projects` shares from the file server up to corporate.

First we'll consider just using DFS replication. By replicating these directories from each branch office back to corporate, we gain powerful data protection capabilities.

CENTRALIZED BACKUP VIA DFS-R

By having a continuously (every 15 minutes) replicating copy of the production file sets from the remote offices back to a corporate datacenter, you have the ability to use any tape backup solution and back up the remote office data by backing up the replicated copy that is within a centralized datacenter and, more importantly, not across a WAN. This results in all of the benefits that we discussed in Chapter 3 related to disk-to-disk replication as part of a D2D2T solution. More specifically, you can reduce or eliminate the need for tape drives in remote offices because now all tape backups can be conducted from the corporate datacenter.

DFS replication does not require that directories be shared in order to be replicated. Hence the `\\DTX01\Team` directory might be replicated to `E:\BranchData\DTX01\Team` on `\\CorpFS1` within the corporate environment. To achieve centralized backups, you simply back up the `\\CorpFS1` server's volumes.

It is worth noting that DFS-R is not the only Microsoft method for centralized backup of branch offices in a D2D2T scenario. In Chapter 4, you learned about System Center Data Protection Manager (DPM), which originally was designed exclusively for centralized branch office backup in DPM 2006, and continues to deliver it as a key solution scenario in DPM 2007 and DPM 2010.

Branch File Share Availability

Building on this as an additional benefit, if the production server were to have an outage or hardware component failure of any kind, another copy of those files, presumably with less than 15 minutes of differences, has survived and remains online from the corporate datacenter. Depending on the kinds of data and the mandated recovery scenarios, you have a few options.

You could build a new branch office server in the corporate IT department and quickly copy all the data from the centralized and replicated file directory for DTX01.

Similarly, if another server existed in the Dallas office (such as DTX02), or adequate bandwidth was available between Dallas and Houston, you could copy the Dallas production data to the alternate server so that users could resume business even before their replacement file server was delivered. But in this scenario, we could have already done that. We could have configured replication of the production data from `\\DTX01\Projects` to two target servers: `\\HOU01\DTX_Projects` and `\\CorpFS1`'s `E:\BranchData\DTX01\Projects`. The Houston replica provides an alternate but easily accessible copy of the data to the Dallas users, while the corporate copy could be used for centralized backup. This might seem like overkill to have three copies of branch office data, but as we discussed in Chapter 2, the TCO and ROI of centralizing branch office backups are very compelling and would more than offset the cost of additional storage in the corporate datacenter. Similarly, Chapter 2 taught you that the cost of downtime would also more than justify the additional disk space on the Houston server in order to ensure that the Dallas employees stay productive.

Branch office file share high availability, as well as centralized backup, can be seen in Figure 5.25.

Figure 5.25 Branch office high availability and centralized backup

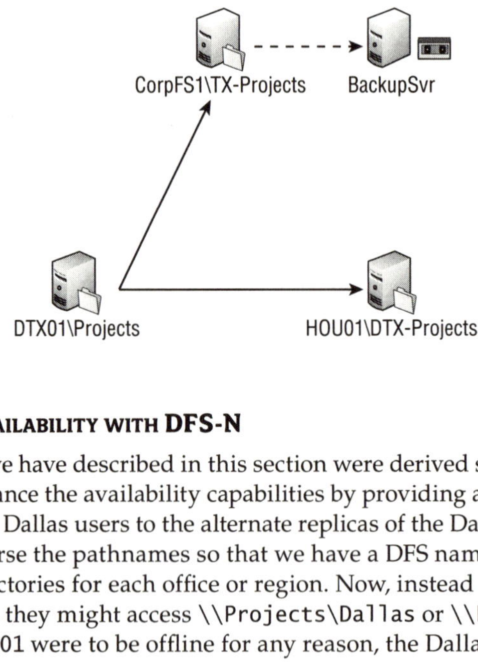

Branch File Share High Availability with DFS-N

So far, all of the benefits that we have described in this section were derived strictly from using a DFS replication. We can enhance the availability capabilities by providing a namespace that will transparently redirect the Dallas users to the alternate replicas of the Dallas data.

In this case, we might reverse the pathnames so that we have a DFS namespace called `Projects` with root-level directories for each office or region. Now, instead of the Dallas users accessing `\\DTX01\Projects`, they might access `\\Projects\Dallas` or `\\Projects\Texas`. The difference is that if `\\DTX01` were to be offline for any reason, the Dallas users would transparently stop using `\\DTX01\Projects` and start using `\\HOU02\Projects` because the namespace would hide which server replica was servicing the end users.

Collaboration Between Branches

There are some potential ancillary benefits that come from this reorganization. For example, suppose the Dallas and Houston branch offices both stored their data within the `\\Projects\Texas` namespace with replicated copies in each local branch office. They would get not only availability, but potentially some collaboration between peers as well.

To enable collaboration between our Dallas and Houston branches, the notable difference from our availability solution is a topology change. In both, our earlier distribution and availability/centralized backup scenarios, the assumption was that only one server was authoritative and creating data, while one or more other servers received replicas. Obviously, for the Dallas and Houston end users to both collaborate, both servers will have data originate on them and be replicated bidirectionally. DFS-R handles this with one important disclaimer—the last write wins.

If those project directories that are originated in and are usually driven from the Dallas office are prefaced with a "D" or perhaps the office number (such as "67"), whereas those project directories originated and managed from Houston have different prefixes, then collaboration is quite easy and without much risk (no more than users within the same office overwriting each other—but hey, they can do that today). However, if the project directories are simply by client name and teammates within both offices, open the project proposal at `\\Projects\Texas\Contoso\project-proposal.doc`, then whichever end user saves the file last will have their changes preserved, while the person who saved first will lose all of their work. For this reason, data collaboration using DFS should be done with caution or with a file system naming convention that mitigates the rest of overriding your peers' data.

When using DFS replication with DFS namespace and branch office deployments, it is a good idea to configure the namespace so that users are explicitly pointed to their local branch copy. Only if the branch copy is unavailable will the users be redirected to a remote copy. If client failback is enabled, the users will transparently redirect back to the branch office copy, after the branch copy is back online and confirmed to be up to date.

Migration and Growth

One of my favorite things about DFS is how easy it makes future growth and migration. Even if you are not ready to do an elaborate namespace and replication plan yet, consider getting your namespace in early. If you start to outgrow a given file server but it is being accessed by a namespace, you can supplement the physical server's storage or even add a second server later—without changing anything for the users. Let's consider if we need to migrate from an older Windows Server 2003 server to a new Windows Server 2008 R2 server:

- Our users can run on the Windows Server 2003 server, while we build our Windows Server 2008 R2 server.
- We can use DFS-R to replicate the file shares from the old server to directories on the new server. By replicating shares on the original server to directories on the new server, we are replicating to unpublished areas on the new server—until we know that they have everything that they need.

- Unlike the old days of weekend projects or scheduled outages, we can build this server during the week. And even if it takes days for the initial replication to happen, our users are still happily using the older server. Everything that they work on will be automatically and transparently replicated to the new server.
- Once the new server has all the directories and contents from the old server, we simply define the shares on the new server and add them as the primary target within the namespace.

Believe it or not, we are done with our migration—with literally no downtime. The users are using the new server's shares and the old server is unscathed, in case we need to revert. If anything is bad about the new server, the users will transparently fall back to the old server—with no user dissatisfaction.

Once we are assured that everything is working and we have a good backup or two, we can decommission the old server. Migrations made easy—all because the users weren't used to going to a *server* like `\\FS1\Data`, but instead to a DFS *namespace* like `\\Contoso\Data`.

DFS Enhancements in Windows Server 2008 R2

DFS has changed considerably since its initial release. As discussed earlier, "DFS" in Windows NT 4.0 through Windows Server 2003 is what we now think of as DFS namespace (DFS-N), the namespace component of DFS in Windows Server 2003 R2 and beyond. More notably, the File Replication Service has been gradually replaced starting in Windows Server 2003 R2 through Windows Server 2008 R2 with what we now call DFS replication (DFS-R), a significantly superior replication engine.

This chapter was written with the Windows Server 2008 administrator in mind.

If you are still on Windows Server 2003 R2, most of the methods described here will work—though there are a few things may not have as much polish or performance or scalability. Table 5.2 shows the performance differences from Windows Server 2003 R2 to Windows Server 2008. The rest of the differences between Windows Server 2003 R2 and Windows Server 2008 are summarized in the "What's New in Windows Server 2008 DFS" TechNet article at `http://technet.microsoft.com/en-us/library/cc753479(WS.10).aspx`.

TABLE 5.2: DFS Performance Differences Between Windows Server 2003 R2 and Windows Server 2008

WINDOW SERVER 2003 R2	WINDOWS SERVER 2008
Multiple RPC calls	RPC asynchronous pipes (when replication with other servers running Windows Server 2008)
Synchronous I/Os	Asynchronous I/Os
Buffered I/Os	Unbuffered I/Os
Normal-priority I/Os	Low-priority I/Os (this reduces the load on the system as a result of replication)
4 concurrent file downloads	16 concurrent file downloads

Source: Microsoft 2009

If you are already moving toward Windows Server 2008 R2, there are a few extras that make everything that we've discussed even better. Along with ever-increasing performance and new versions of the command-line utilities, DFS in Windows Server 2008 R2 saw the following notable updates:

Failover Cluster Support for DFS Replication You can now add an MSCS failover cluster as a member of a replication group. This is a great way to provide resiliency within a given site. You'll learn more about Windows failover clustering in Chapter 6.

Read-Only Replicated Folders This is a great capability for distribution and collection replication models where the targets should not be written to. If you are collecting branch office data for centralized backups, the headquarters copy should not be modifiable since it needs to always match what the production branch offices are sending. In a distribution model where the same data is coming from corporate to all the branches, you should not be able to change something at one branch and everyone get the change.

Before Windows Server 2008 R2, the only way to do this was to manually adjust the ACLs and share permissions—but this was nonintuitive and laborious in larger deployments, especially where the elegance of DFS had smoothed out so many other tasks.

Summary

The most commonly deployed role for Windows Server is that of file services. So, why should it surprise anyone that Microsoft made it so natively resilient? What is more surprising is how easy it is to implement but so few people know about it. What we covered with DFS doesn't even include some of the newest advances with the BranchCache feature in Windows Server 2008 R2. With BranchCache, the first branch office user gets a file across the WAN, and the rest of the branch users get it from their local peer. There is lots of innovation going on for file services, but in regard to availability and protection, it is predominantly around DFS.

- With DFS replication (DFS-R), we can transparently replicate partial-file updates between servers as often as every 15 minutes.
- By using Remote Differential Compression (RDC), the changed files are iteratively parsed into smaller and smaller chunks to identify the components that have been updated—and only those changed areas are replicated.
- With DFS namespace (DFS-N), a convenient alternate directory scheme can be set up so that users do not care which server that their files are on. This increases the ease of normal work, and with transparent redirection between replicated copies, makes file availability easy.

Chapter 6

Windows Clustering

No book on availability in a Windows datacenter would be complete without discussing Microsoft Cluster Services (MSCS).

From its introduction after the initial release of Windows NT 4.0 in the first Enterprise Edition through Windows Server 2003, MSCS was often regarded as nonviable by mainstream IT implementers because of its complexity or because of a few deployment restrictions. But Windows Server 2008 delivered significant improvements in simplifying the deployment and manageability of Windows clusters, and things only get better in Windows Server 2008 R2.

Overview of Clustering in Windows Server 2008 and 2008 R2

This chapter focuses exclusively on Windows Server 2008 and 2008 R2. All references to Windows Server 2008 are intended to reflect the capabilities in both the 2008 and 2008 R2 releases, unless otherwise noted.

The first thing to notice when looking at clustering in Windows Server 2008 and 2008 R2 is that the OS offers two capabilities that are called "clustering":

- Network load balancing (NLB)
- Failover clustering—what most people think of as clustering

Scale Out with Network Load Balancing

Network load balancing (NLB) is usually implemented where the primary goal is to scale out the capacity of a given service. It assumes that all the nodes in the farm or *cluster* have access to the data and usually requires that the clients be stateless, meaning that they could connect/reconnect to different nodes within a given session without impact. Web farms are an example: multiple web servers have equal access to a shared back-end database. The goal of multiple servers is primarily focused on increasing performance or scalability so that the web application can service more users than a single server can.

You could say that there is an availability aspect to NLB: If four servers are participating in the NLB cluster and one of them suffers an outage, the users will be serviced by one of the surviving three nodes. But this kind of recovery is typically unmanaged. In the best-case scenario, as long as the other nodes have adequate bandwidth and resources, the reconnection may be nearly transparent, though it is not technically a failover from the failed node but simply an absorption of the failed node's workload. In the worst-case scenario, a load balancer might just continue to blindly send some percentage of clients to the failed server. As you will see in the rest of this chapter as well as Chapters 7, 8, and 9, there is almost always a better way to handle a failed node that has peers.

NLB is accomplished by changes within the networking stack of the member servers so that all the nodes can share a synthetic MAC address. Depending on how NLB is configured, it can use unicast or multicast in order to provide IP connectivity to the various nodes (each with its own networking ramifications). Behind the scenes, each node has a secondary and unique address so that the nodes can communicate with one another to manage traffic and balance the workloads. The goal of NLB is to provide multiple physical nodes with near identical configurations. Performance and resilience are achieved by masking them together at an IP level and letting each one respond to requests as they are able. An example is a web server front-ending a shared database.

Figure 6.1 shows a typical NLB four-node cluster with shared and private IPs, as well as the common database to facilitate the service. In Figure 6.1, we see that each of the four nodes has its own IP address (left) as well as a shared IP address (right), so that all nodes can service requests. The nodes have their own mechanisms for ensuring that the load is balanced between the nodes. But in this diagram we see a single point of failure in the shared database. With so many users depending on the service, a common practice is to deploy a failover cluster (which is the topic for the rest of this chapter, other than this section on NLB) or a mirrored database (discussed in Chapter 8) for availability of the back end while NLB scales out the accessibility on the front.

FIGURE 6.1
An NLB cluster

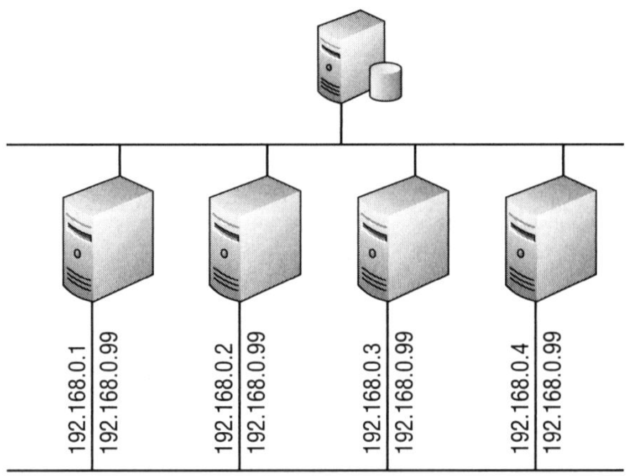

Although NLB does offer a measure of availability, it is only a byproduct of a failed node's workload being absorbed by the surviving nodes (assuming bandwidth is available). Because of this, and its normal niche case use within web services, NLB is outside of the scope of this book in respect to data protection and availability.

WHAT IS AND IS NOT CLUSTERING?

I don't usually think about NLB as clustering, only because I have used the MSCS or Windows Failover Clustering technologies for so long. A dictionary's definition of a cluster usually refers to "a bunch of things that are the same and are together," and within IT there are a few other examples of peer-level objects that are similar, work together, and provide some level of resilience if one were to fail. Perhaps because of these definitions, Microsoft has grouped both NLB and failover clustering under one installation wizard that we will see later in this chapter. So, NLB does count as a cluster, even if some old-school MSCS folks disagree.

Scale Up with Failover Clustering

What most IT administrators, other than webmasters, call "clustering" is more accurately termed "failover clustering" in Windows Server 2008. In NLB, all clustered nodes are considered peers to each other and they share the workload. In failover clustering, some nodes are *active* and offer services, whereas other nodes may be *passive*, waiting for an active node to fail (or be significantly impacted).

THE MANY NAMES OF WINDOWS "CLUSTERING"

In Windows NT 4, the clustering feature was originally called Wolfpack before it was released as Microsoft Cluster Services.

In Windows 2000 and 2003, the clustering feature was termed Server Clustering and offered four-node (2000) and eight-node clusters (2003).

Starting in Windows Server 2008, its proper name is now Windows Failover Clustering (WFC).

Microsoft is pretty consistent with referring the new capabilities within Windows Server 2008 and 2008 R2 strictly by the name *Failover Clustering*, so doing an Internet search on that term will give you the best information on Windows Server 2008 clustering.

The rest of this chapter will focus on failover clustering in Windows Server 2008 and 2008 R2. Clustering creates additional layers that are shared across physical servers and storage.

Failover Clustering Terms and Concepts

Here are some terms used in this chapter:

Standalone Server A *standalone server* refers to a physical server not participating in a cluster.

Server A *server*, for the purposes of this book, refers to a logical server, which may be physical, clustered, or virtual.

Node A *node* is a physical member of the cluster that will host highly available applications, servers, and services.

Virtual *Virtual* refers to the synthetic resources, servers, and services that operate within the cluster. The term *virtual* is not intended to mean a virtualization hypervisor (discussed in Chapters 9 and beyond) is necessary.

Cluster-able *Cluster-able* is used here to mean *able to be clustered*.

In a typical standalone server, we see applications running on an operating system. These applications are installed on physical hardware, utilize unique storage, and access one or more networks, as you can see in Figure 6.2.

FIGURE 6.2
Standalone server stack

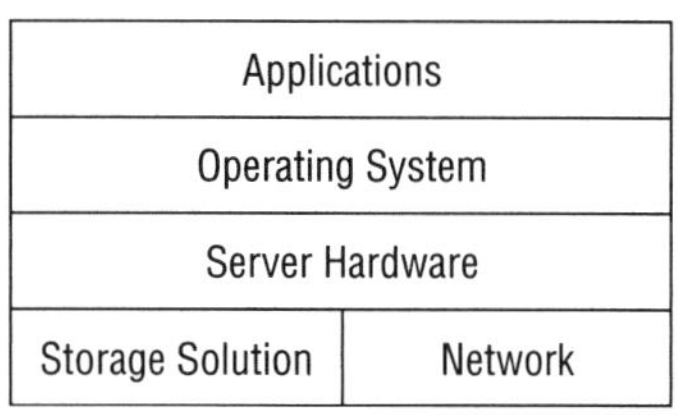

In a simple cluster, two nodes have their own operating systems on individual hardware. The nodes share a common storage solution, participate on the same networks, and facilitate virtualized servers, services, and resources, as seen in Figure 6.3. Here we see that each node has an operating system on top of its own server hardware and its own network access. But what is important in Figure 6.3 is the shared storage at the *bottom* of the cluster and the resource groups, almost like virtualized servers, at the *top* of the cluster.

FIGURE 6.3
Simple two-node cluster stack

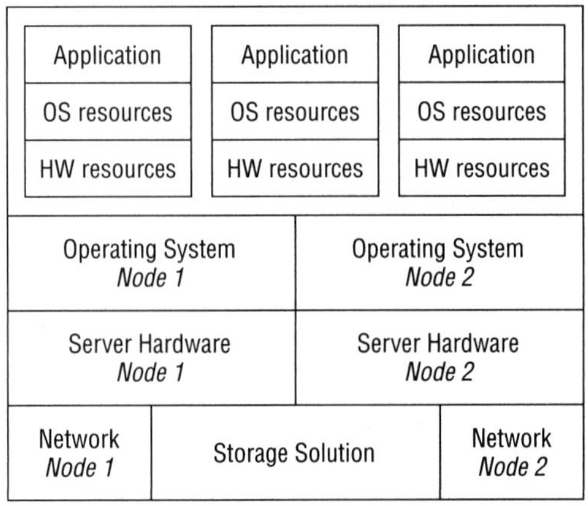

While both physical nodes can access the storage (more on exclusivity later in the section "Start with Shared Storage") and can interact on the same networks, the higher-layer functions—such as offering server names, IP addresses, and running services—are done within the cluster, though they may be fulfilled by one node or the other at any point in time.

The key idea in a cluster is that the virtual server that is created by the synthetic name, IP, and services is what the client machines will connect to. The client machines and their users are completely unaware that their server is not a standalone physical machine. More importantly, they are happily unaware as to whether the virtual resources are running from physical node 1, node 2, or wherever. They simply rely on a server that seems to always be running reliably. That is the goal of clustering.

The Anatomy of a Failover Cluster

Each physical node of the cluster starts out as a standalone machine running either the Enterprise or Datacenter edition of Windows Server. The Failover Clustering feature, also referred to as the high-availability scenario, is only available in these premium editions of Windows Server. With the nodes each having access the same local area networks, as well as shared access to storage, they are ready to become a cluster (covered later in this chapter in the section "Start with Shared Storage").

Initially, we will create the cluster by installing the Failover Clustering software components on both nodes and configuring a shared identity for management. From that point on, we will create virtual servers, not implying the use of a virtualization hypervisor, but using synthetic server names, IP addresses, storage areas, and services.

The term *resource* refers to the individual synthetic items, such as a server name or IP address, that may be delivered by any node within the cluster. Prior to Windows Server 2008, we had the concept of a *group*, which refers to collections of resources that are managed as a single synthetic server—such as a server name, IP address, and one or more services. In Windows Server 2008 and 2008 R2, the term *group* is no longer used—we now call them instances. As we create highly available services and applications, you will still see groups of names, IPs, storage, and application- and workload-specific items that are managed as a single unit, referred to as an instance and delivered by a single node at a time within the cluster.

The main idea is to create one or more groups of resources, which behave as unique synthetic or virtualized servers, and may operate on Node1 for now, but can move and run from Node2 later, or vice versa.

Building Your First Cluster

Shared storage choices are covered later in the chapter. For our initial exercises, we use two virtualized Windows Server 2008 nodes that are sharing three iSCSI LUNs from an iSCSI target running from a Windows Storage Server 2008 appliance. Later in the chapter, we will move from Windows Server 2008 to 2008 R2 to better appreciate the continued enhancements in failover clustering.

WINDOWS STORAGE SERVER 2008 AND ISCSI

Windows Storage Server 2008 is a variation of the mainstream Windows Server 2008 operating system. Here are some characteristics of Windows Storage Server 2008:

- Optimized for file and storage functionality, without the ability to run applications like SQL Server or Exchange
- Delivered exclusively as preinstalled appliances, not as software that can be installed onto generic hardware
- Includes a software-based iSCSI target for delivering block-level storage alongside Windows File Services

Essentially, instead of you taking a normal DVD of Windows Server 2008 and installing it onto your favorite HP or Dell server hardware, those partners and others have preconfigured some of those same models and components, optimized them for storage I/O, and then preinstalled the Windows Storage Server 2008 operating system.

The reason that we are using a Windows Storage Server in this chapter is to provide the iSCSI target for easy shared storage between the clustered nodes.

Start with Shared Storage

For learning purposes, you can download an evaluation ISO/VHD of Windows Storage Server 2008, including an ISO to install the iSCSI target software into your new Windows Storage Server 2008 test box. If you choose to acquire a real Windows Storage Server 2008 storage appliance, that will need to come from Microsoft Storage original equipment manufacturing (OEM) partner such as HP or Dell.

A Quick iSCSI Refresher

SCSI, as we discussed in Chapter 3, is the preferred type of storage for most server infrastructure. One variation is iSCSI (discussed in Chapter 3), which enables storage devices to be connected to servers via IP over Ethernet.

iSCSI Initiator A server (or desktop) operating system runs a software component called an iSCSI initiator, which you can think of as both client software and a disk driver. It communicates via IP to an iSCSI target. The Microsoft iSCSI initiator is included with Windows Server 2008 and later, as well as Windows Vista and Windows 7. An iSCSI initiator can be downloaded and manually installed for Windows Server 2003 and Windows XP.

iSCSI Target An iSCSI target is a storage device that has block-level disk storage in the form of LUNs from its arrays. The target technology offers that storage over Ethernet.

The client component of the iSCSI initiator makes an IP connection to the iSCSI target device. With the connection in place, the disk driver in the initiator connects to the block-storage LUN from the array. At this point, the storage appears to be locally connected to the server (or desktop) that is running the initiator. In almost every practical way, the storage acts as it would if you had physically plugged a disk drive into the server.

The reason that we are using iSCSI in the clustering chapter is because the clustered nodes need to have equal and shared access to the storage. Achieving that with iSCSI is easy by simply configuring the iSCSI initiators on all of the clustered nodes to connect to the same iSCSI target LUNs.

And by using a software-based iSCSI target, found within the trial version of Windows Storage Server, you can do all of the exercises within a virtual environment. In a real production environment, you would more likely use a physical storage solution in the form of a real Windows Storage Server appliance, some other iSCSI appliance, or Fibre Channel–based storage area network (SAN).

iSCSI Pre-setup Task 1: Enable the iSCSI Initiator on Your Nodes

The first thing to do is to enable the iSCSI initiators on your nodes. Technically, you could do this at the same time that you do iSCSI Pre-setup Task 3 when you connect the LUNs to your nodes. But if you do it now, it makes Pre-setup Task 2 easier.

When you click the iSCSI initiator icon in either the Administrative Tools menu or Control Panel, you will see a prompt asking if this is the first time you have configured the iSCSI initiator. You may be prompted to set the iSCSI initiator service to automatically start in Windows.

At this point, it is a client (initiator) without a client, but as a convenience to us, it is advertising itself as a client for discovery on the local subnet.

iSCSI Pre-setup Task 2: Create an iSCSI LUN in WSS08

If you are using another iSCSI target device other than Windows Storage Server 2008, you can skip this step or read along to get the general idea for creating LUNs within your device, and then continue with Pre-setup Task 3.

For the purposes of this book, we will assume that you have installed Windows Storage Server 2008 and the supplemental instructions to install the iSCSI target software. Once you have performed the generic installations, you will also need to successfully connect the Windows Storage

Server 2008 unit to at least two different network paths or segments. For the exercises listed here, we have a CorpNet network that allows users to connect to the servers, and a Backbone network where the servers connect to one another. We can configure the iSCSI LUN that our servers will share to either a dedicated third network, which is preferred, or on our Backbone network to at least keep the iSCSI network traffic from being impacted by user network traffic.

NOTE Windows Storage Server 2008 and the iSCSI Software Target for Windows Storage Server 2008 are both available for evaluation download via Microsoft TechNet (or MSDN), `http://technet.microsoft.com/evalcenter/`.

If you are doing this task with virtual machines for the clustered nodes, you may want to configure a fourth logical network and a dedicated Gigabit Ethernet (or faster) switch for those two nodes. This dedicated network connection will be for your *storage network*. If you are doing this task with real servers, this is still necessary. For education purposes, you can share networks between your storage and the clustered nodes. However, as you increase the I/O within the clustered nodes, performance may suffer. In a real cluster, you would have either a fiber network or dedicated Gigabit Ethernet as your SAN.

Now that we're ready, we need to create a LUN and configure it for sharing. Using the iSCSI Software Target management console of a Windows Storage Server 2008 appliance (or a virtual machine via TestDrive), we will start by creating a target and then adding some storage to it.

The first goal is to create a logical device that will hold all the storage for a particular set of initiator, or in our case, the clustered nodes. Normally, you will create an iSCSI Target for each cluster.

To create the iSCSI target:

1. Right-click on the Targets area of the left pane, and select Create iSCSI Target.
2. Create a logical name for the target. For our two clusters in this chapter, we will have an AlphaDisk and an OmegaDisk as target names (more on naming later in the section "Physical and Cluster Naming").
3. Next, we need to decide what iSCSI initiators will be allowed to connect to this set of storage. If you did the first task and pre-enabled the iSCSI initiators, then click Browse and select them from the list of initiators that are discovered on the local subnet. Otherwise, you can manually add them:
   - The default IQN identifier for iSCSI initiators running on Windows machines is `iqn.1991-05.com.microsoft:FQDN`.
   - For our first node to be added, type **`iqn.1991-05.com.microsoft:alphanode1.contoso.com`**.

This completes the creation of the iSCSI target as a storage repository. But we still have to create the storage itself. The iSCSI Software Target management console included with Windows Storage Server 2008 uses VHDs as the LUNs or volumes being offered.

To create the iSCSI storage:

1. Within the iSCSI Software Target management console, right-click on the Devices item within the left pane and select Create Virtual Disk.

2. Specify the filename of the VHD. For our first volume, name it **Alpha0.vhd**, as it will later be visible as Disk 0 to the Alpha cluster.

3. Specify the size of the volume in megabytes. As a tip, use multiples of 1024 to ensure that it appears the way you expect in other interfaces (for example, a 5 GB volume would be 5 × 1024 or 5120 MB in the iSCSI Wizard).

4. Add a description of what the volume will be. For the first volume in our example, name it **Alpha Cluster - disk 0 - quorum**.

5. Next, assign that storage to the iSCSI target that we created earlier in this task by selecting Add and choosing the AlphaDisk iSCSI target.

As you can see in Figure 6.4, we now have an iSCSI target that is offering storage to our client nodes running the iSCSI initiators. The last step is to attach that storage to the nodes themselves.

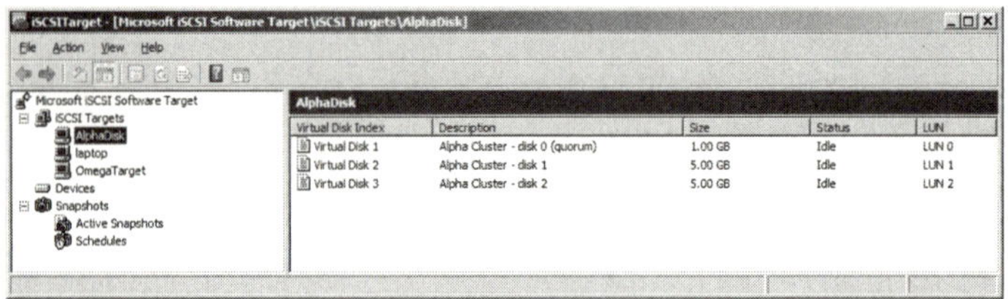

FIGURE 6.4
Our iSCSI target with three LUNs

iSCSI Pre-setup Task 3: Connect Your Cluster Nodes to the SAN

If you skipped Pre-setup Task 1 or this is the first time that you have configured the iSCSI initiator, you may be prompted to set the iSCSI initiator service to automatically start within Windows.

1. In the iSCSI initiator control panel applet, select the Discovery tab, where you can specify where the iSCSI initiator will look for an iSCSI target. Add the IP address of the Windows Storage Server (or other iSCSI appliance).

2. On the Targets tab, click Refresh and you should see the iSCSI target that you defined in Pre-setup Task 2 appear. If so, click Connect and then click Log On.

3. If you are running Windows 2008 R2, a new option called Quick Connect combines the previous steps: you enter the IP address, and Quick Connect will discover the targets, connect, and log on for you.

4. Select the Volumes And Devices tab, as shown in Figure 6.5, and click Autoconfigure to add all the LUNs that are available from that target (which is preferred). You can, of course, also click Add and select them individually.

By creating an iSCSI target for use exclusively by the cluster, we can be sure that all the LUNs offered by the target are appropriate for use by the nodes of our cluster. Repeating this process on each of the clustered nodes will ensure that they all have access to this shared storage across the iSCSI network.

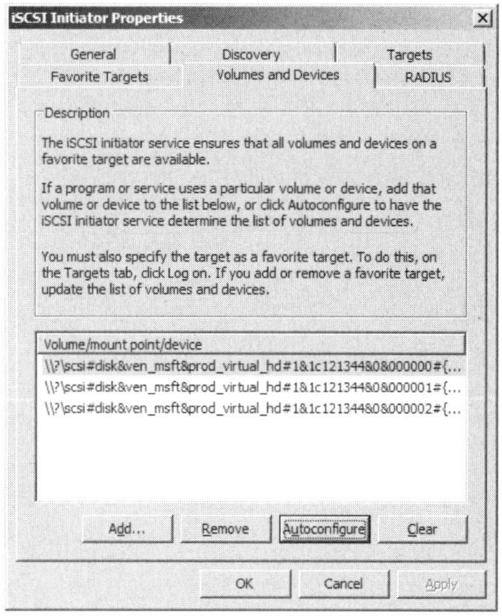

FIGURE 6.5
iSCSI initiator with LUNs

For your own hands-on experience, you could use real physical server nodes and a real SAN (including the iSCSI target within a Windows Storage Server), but I did all of the tasks in this chapter using hypervisors and virtual machines so that you can build your clustering skills without consuming resources.

Creating Your Virtual Hands-on Environment

Perhaps you have two extra physical servers and access to a shared storage array via iSCSI or Fibre Channel already. In that case, you can skip this section. This section is aimed at those new to clustering and interested in getting experience with MSCS by itself, without also navigating the additional complexities of the hardware. So these steps can be done within a single generic computer, acting as a virtualization host with two guests. In fact, every exercise in this book was done using virtualized servers and resources.

This first set of tasks uses strictly Windows Server 2008 Enterprise edition (EE) in three different places: on the host of our hands-on lab machine and within our two virtual clustered nodes. To prepare for this, download the TestDrive VHD from `TechNet.Microsoft.com`, and update each of them via Windows Update (the examples in this book are current as this writing). While not immediately suitable for production, the TestDrive VHDs give you fully configured OSs that are ready to join to your domain and begin learning from.

After you have a running virtualization host, you need to create virtualized resources. For simplicity, I created a directory on my host called `D:\WS08MSCS` for all my virtual machines and resources.

PRE-SETUP TASK 4: CREATING THREE NETWORKS BETWEEN THE NODES

For our nodes to communicate with the rest of the network, as well as each other, we will create three networks between our nodes. If you are not using three separate physical networks, you can do the same thing from within our hypervisor by clicking Virtual Networks and then clicking Create New Virtual Network to create each of the three virtual networks with the following parameters:

Virtual Network 1 We'll use this network to communicate with the outside world; specify these settings:

- Network Name: CorpNet
- Network Adapter: Mapped to the first (perhaps only) physical network interfaces on the host

Virtual Network 2 We'll use this network to communicate between clustered nodes; specify these settings:

- Network Name: Cluster
- Network Adapter: None/Guests Only

Virtual Network 3 We'll use this network for backups and other infrastructure management tasks, without impacting the users; specify these settings:

- Network Name: Backbone
- Network Adapter: Mapped to the second physical network interface on the host if available, or the only network interface if there's only one.

Admittedly, only the first two networks are required, whereas including the third one is a best practice. On any network, it is always advisable to have at least two NICs in every production server. The primary corporate NIC is intended to service the users, whereas a secondary network allows for backups and other infrastructure management tasks without adding network traffic that can impact user productivity. In the case of a cluster, we would not only want those two networks but a third path for the intranode communication.

Pre-setup Task 5: Creating Three Nodes for Our Cluster

We need to create the server nodes for our cluster. In the tasks, we will initially cluster the first two nodes, and then do a later task to add an additional node to the cluster. But first, we have to create them. Each node will have the following:

- Its own memory and CPU
- Three network interfaces
- Individual C: drives for the operating system
- Shared access to the shared storage that we just created

Follow these steps:

1. From the left pane of the Virtual Server administration console, click Create New Virtual Machine and enter these settings:
   - Virtual Machine Name: CLUAnode1
   - Memory: 2 GB
   - When Prompted For A Hard Disk: Choose Attach Disk Later

After the initial virtual machine has been created, we can add the extra pieces that will make it cluster-able:

2. Create three virtual network interfaces:
   - NIC 1: Mapped to CorpNet
   - NIC 2: Mapped to Cluster
   - NIC 3: Mapped to Backbone
3. On the second node, the virtual machine name should be CLUAnode2, but all of the other settings (except the unique IP addresses) should be the same as what you chose for CLUAnode1.

At this point, you have an environment in which you can learn about Microsoft Failover Clustering. Install Windows Server 2008 EE onto each of the nodes' individual C: drives using Windows Server 2008 (or use the TestDrive VHDs), as well as the virtual machine additions or virtualization integration components. Your settings may vary, but here are the specifics of our examples.

The virtual machine (VM) names for the two machines are CLUAnode1 (which is an abbreviation of CLUster A node 1) and CLUAnode2, but when we install the Windows Server operating systems, we will need different computer names. I chose AlphaNode1 and AlphaNode2 as the machine names. The reason for these names will become clearer as we go through the tasks. I specifically did not use the same names that I used within my hypervisor host so that it's clear when we are working with virtual machines. Other than that, you can accept default configurations everywhere. I used the following IP addresses on my nodes (*x* represents node 1, 2, or 3):

CorpNet 192.168.123.*x* (DHCP)

Cluster 10.1.1.*x*

Backbone 192.168.1.*x*

DNS and Gateway Router 192.168.123.254

When you are finished, you will have a logical setup that resembles Figure 6.6.

FIGURE 6.6
Our Cluster A setup

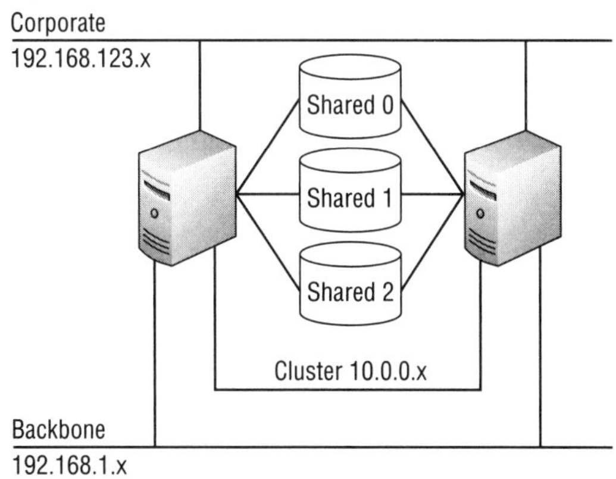

Getting Started with MSCS in Windows Server 2008

With our environment now built, including our Windows Server 2008 nodes that have access to some shared SCSI storage and are members of a domain, we can start installing and configuring our first failover cluster.

Cluster A, Task 1: Installing MSCS in Windows Server 2008

Both forms of clustering that we discussed at the beginning of this chapter (failover clustering and network load balancing) are considered features of the Windows Server 2008 operating system. So, we'll start by going to Server Manager from the console of Node1, clicking Add Features to open the Add Features Wizard, and choosing Failover Clustering on the Select Features screen, as shown in Figure 6.7. After selecting the feature, there are no additional steps other than to wait for the scroll bar.

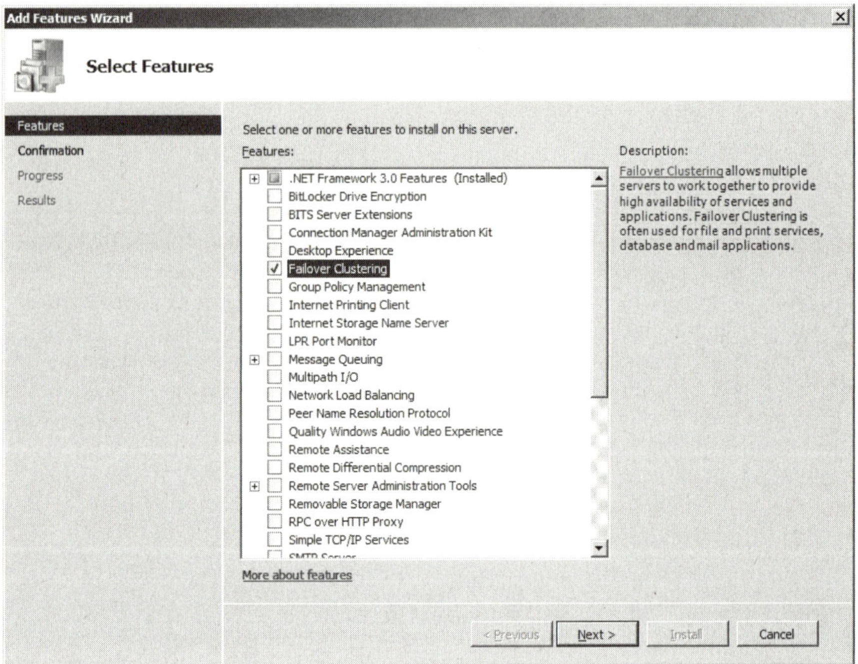

FIGURE 6.7 Installing the Failover Clustering feature

Because we are simply adding the proper software components to Windows Server and not yet configuring a specific cluster, we can go ahead and add the feature to all the prospective nodes to our cluster. In our case, we will install the Failover Clustering feature to nodes AlphaNode1 and AlphaNode2.

You may notice that Failover Clustering is not easily located within the Server Manager. It has its own console called Failover Cluster Management, which can be found in the Administrative Tools area.

Installing MSCS Does Not Require a Reboot... or Does It?

When you're installing the Failover Clustering feature from within Server Manager, it likely will not prompt you to reboot. And while you might be happily surprised to see that this particular feature can be added without a reboot, my personal experience has shown some quirky initial results. A reboot after installing the feature, but before running the Validation Wizard or configuration tool, always seems to fix things.

CLUSTER A, TASK 2: PREVALIDATING THE CLUSTER NODES IN WINDOWS SERVER 2008

Clustering can be a powerful tool in our goal of higher availability, and as a powerful tool, it can be complex. This was certainly true before Windows Server 2008. To make things much easier, the clustering team created a validation tool that will do a rigorous check of our servers to be sure that both nodes have proper networking, storage, and other characteristics that make them suitable for clustering. Prior to Windows Server 2008, Microsoft offered a Cluster-Prep utility (`ClusPrep.exe`) that would help validate some cluster components. But in Windows Server 2008, this utility was replaced with the significantly enhanced validation tool, which is built into the cluster console itself.

When you open the Failover Cluster Management console, look to the center of the interface for the Validate A Configuration link. Clicking this link will bring up the Validate A Configuration Wizard, shown in Figure 6.8.

FIGURE 6.8
The Validate A Configuration Wizard for prospective cluster nodes

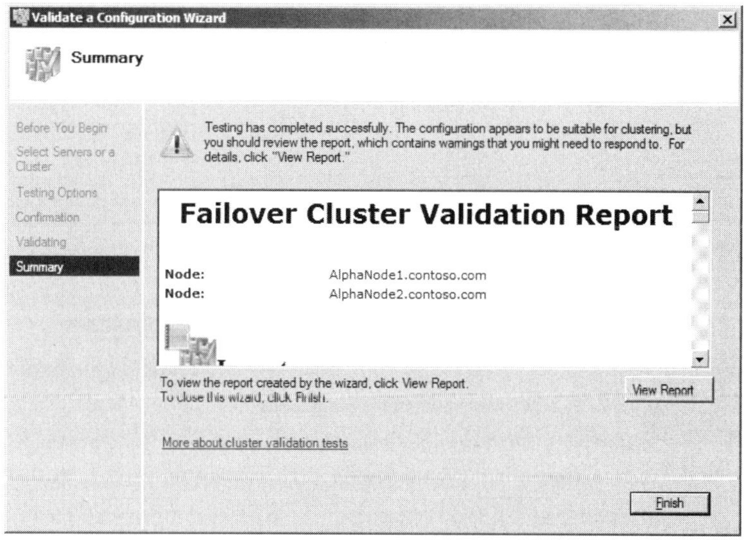

The validation tool will provide an HTML-based report that you can save or send to product support, if necessary. You cannot set a schedule within the tool but you can run it on a periodic basis. This lets you use the tool for troubleshooting as well as adding additional nodes, as you will see later in the section "Cluster A, Task 6: Adding an Additional Node."

With a positive result from the validation test, we are ready to create our cluster across the two nodes that have the Failover Clustering feature installed.

CLUSTER A, TASK 3: CREATING THE CLUSTER IN WINDOWS SERVER 2008

Okay, we're almost ready to create our first cluster.

First, make sure that your first shared disk is online and has been formatted with NTFS. If you do, the cluster will automatically use it for its quorum (see the section "Quorum Models" later in this chapter). If you don't, no suitable shared quorum will be immediately accessible and you'll have to adjust the quorum later.

Going back to the Failover Cluster Management console, click the link Create A Cluster either in the center of the initial screen or in the Actions pane on the right.

The first wizard screen, Select Servers, prompts you to enter all the nodes that are ready to join the cluster (and that have previously been validated using the validation tool). In our case, enter both of them, AlphaNode1 and AlphaNode2, as shown in Figure 6.9.

FIGURE 6.9
Enter all the nodes that are ready to join the cluster.

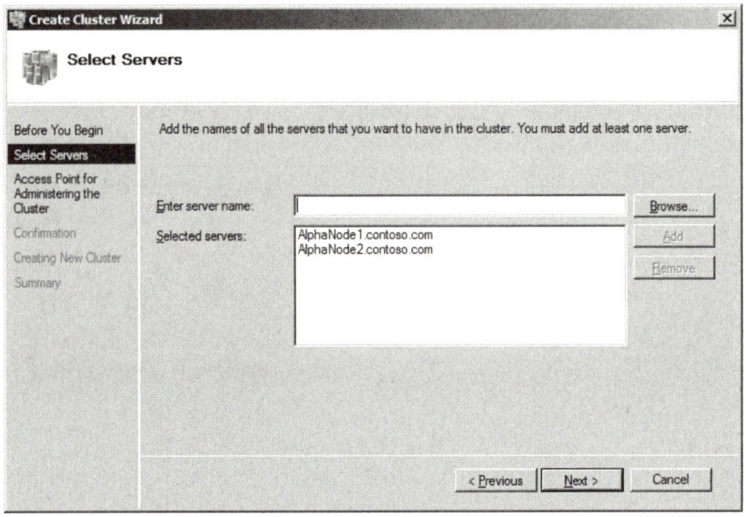

CONFIRM NAME/IP RESOLUTION WHEREVER YOU CAN

To be sure that all the nodes are constantly able to talk to one another in the correct manner, let the names resolve themselves instead of helping.

Specifically, when entering a node name in a wizard, simply enter the short machine name and click Add instead of using the Browse button or entering the fully qualified domain name (FQDN).

If everything is interacting properly, the name should resolve with the FQDN version displayed in the wizard. If not, this is a good sign to stop what you are doing and reconfirm the IP settings and a correctly working name resolving (DNS) system.

Next, we need to create a name for the cluster itself. And in keeping with the best practice of having a name that is relational between our nodes and the cluster itself, we'll name the cluster AlphaCluster, since our nodes are named AlphaNode1 and AlphaNode2.

Surprisingly, that's all that's required. If all your nodes have already passed the Validation Wizard, then the Create Cluster Wizard should complete successfully. During the creation, the wizard will prompt you as to what kind of quorum the cluster will have. We will spend a good deal of time looking at the various quorum models in the next section, but for now, accept the recommended default:

- If you did not format at least one of your shared disks, the wizard will likely prompt you to create a cluster with a Node Majority Quorum.
- If you formatted at least one of your shared disks with NTFS prior to creating the cluster, the wizard will likely prompt you to create a cluster with a Node And Disk Majority Quorum, as seen in Figure 6.10.

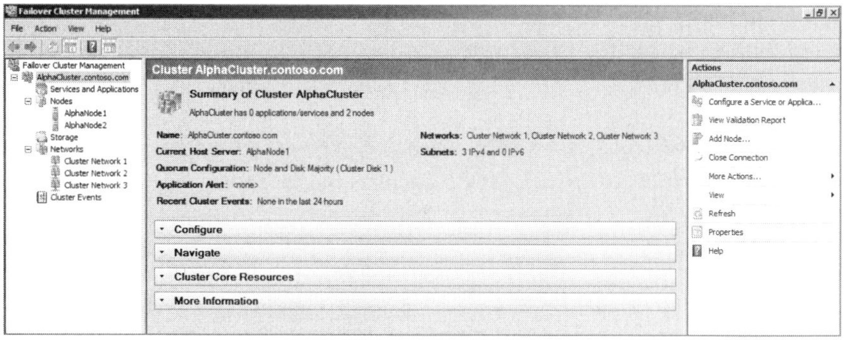

FIGURE 6.10
Our first cluster, with a Node And Disk Majority Quorum

THE FAILOVER CLUSTER MANAGEMENT CONSOLE

With our first failover cluster now operational, we need to orient ourselves within the newly installed Cluster Administration MMC snap-in, which should be available from the Administrative Tools of any of the clustered nodes. This is a far cry from the `CluAdmin.exe` that we had in Windows Server 2003. In the left pane, you can just select the cluster you wish to manage. Choose the cluster that we just created, AlphaCluster, and you will see a tree in the left pane that shows our clustered nodes, as well as a few resources types—just like Figure 6.10 earlier.

Cluster Networking

Initially, the cluster will simply create default names for each of our networks, so I recommend renaming them so that they have more logical clarity:

Cluster Network 3 (Corporate) When we look at Cluster Network 3, it turns out to be the corporate network that will be used by our production clients to connect to our resources. By right-clicking on the network in the left pane and choosing Properties, we can change the properties to something more logical. For this network, we'll change the name, but keep the defaults Network Is Available By The Cluster and Clients Can Connect To The Cluster From This Connection.

Cluster Network 2 (Heartbeat) When we look at Cluster Network 2, we will see the network that we originally determined the cluster would use for its own internal communications. With that in mind, we can rename it as **Heartbeat**, enable it for use by the cluster, and disable the clients from accessing via this method.

Cluster Network 1 (Backbone) This backbone network configuration may vary depending on how you configured your network segments (such as whether you are sharing this network segment with your storage). If you want this network for backup and data protection operations, you'll want to enable it for use by the cluster but prohibit client access. If you are using it for your iSCSI storage network, you will want to disable its use by the cluster since the physical nodes are using it and depend on high-speed and uncongested network access.

When this is all done, your cluster networking configuration should look similar to Figure 6.11. Details of how the physical network cards are bound to the clustered networks appear in Figure 6.12.

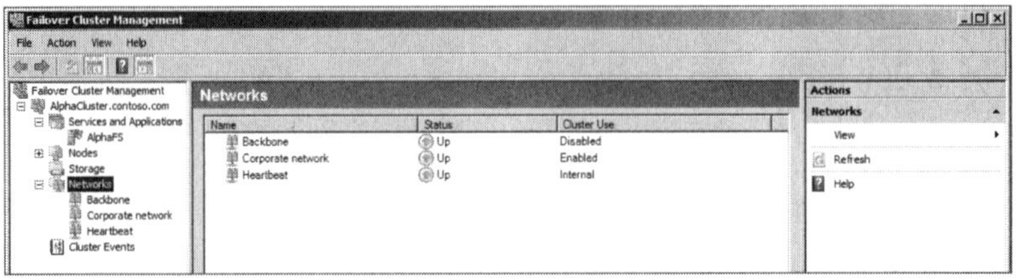

FIGURE 6.11
Our Alpha Cluster networking configuration

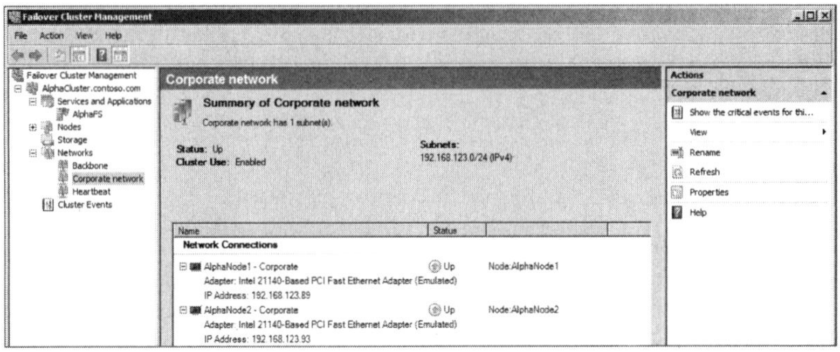

FIGURE 6.12
Our Alpha Cluster networking details

Real World Scenario

IPv6 and Teredo Errors on Your First Windows Server 2008 Cluster Nodes

The first time I started experimenting with Windows Server 2008 nodes for clustering that were hosted on a virtualization host, I encountered several errors. There were duplicate network entries: one set of entries for Internet Protocol version 6 (IPv6) and another for Teredo. This was exasperating since I wasn't using IPv6 anywhere and had disabled it on all my network cards to no avail. So I could continue focusing on Windows Server 2008 clustering, I disabled Teredo and IPv6 (since they aren't required for many environments). Here's how:

Disabling Teredo Open a command prompt that is running with Administrator privileges. Ignore the prompts, and enter the following commands:

- `netsh`
- `interface`
- `teredo`
- `set state disabled`

Source: `http://blogs.msdn.com/clustering/archive/2008/07/26/8773796.aspx`

Disabling IPv6 for the Server Edit the Registry and go to the following key:

```
[HKEY_LOCAL_MACHINE\SYSTEM\CurrentControlSet\Services\Tcpip6\Parameters]
```

Right-click in the right-pane of the Registry Editor and select New – DWORD Value. Set the value of `DisabledComponents` to **FF** and then restart the server for the change to take effect. To enable IPv6 later, simply delete the `DisabledComponents` entry and reboot.

Source: `www.windowsreference.com/networking/disable-ipv6-in-windows-server-20008-full-core-installation/`

Cluster Storage

The Storage item appears in the left pane, though it may not have an expansion button, depending on how you configured your initial storage. By clicking the Storage object itself, your center console will show the current storage, which in this case reflects three shared disks from our iSCSI target. The first one is in use as a witness disk within the quorum (and therefore goes by the drive letter Q) and the other two disks are available for use by clustered applications (which we will configure later). To clarify, and to comply with the common practice of always renaming the default names of resources, you can rename the shared storage resources. This is reflected in Figure 6.13.

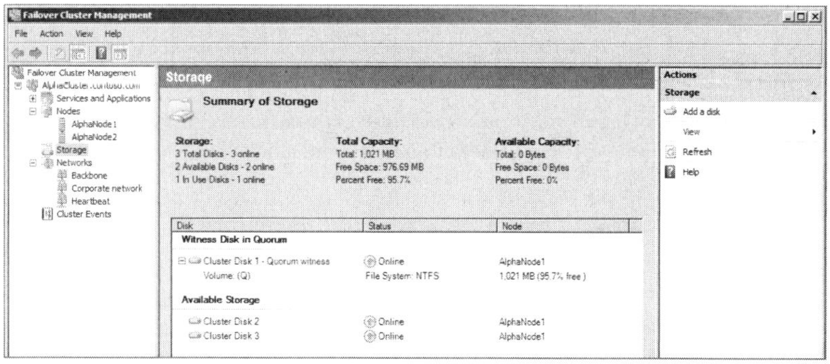

FIGURE 6.13
Our Cluster A storage configuration

Cluster Nodes

You can click or expand the Nodes item in the left pane and select a particular node to see the specifics of the node in the top part of the center console. The lower part of the center console reveals the various storage and network resources being provided, as you can see in Figure 6.14.

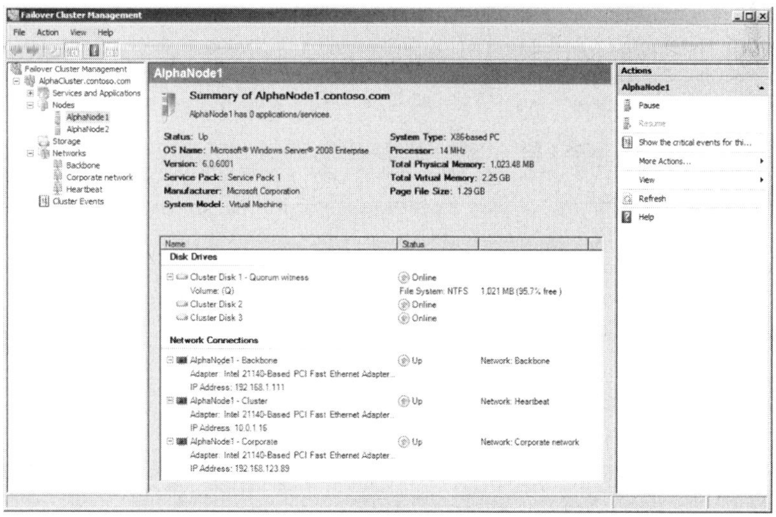

FIGURE 6.14
Our Cluster A Node1 configuration

To complete your first experience with failover clustering, we will create a highly available file server within our new cluster. Each highly available service or application is a set (formerly called a group) of resources, including a machine name and IP for user access, as well as storage and, potentially, application components or other resources.

PHYSICAL AND CLUSTER NAMING

If you are going to have huge clusters with several workloads that are unrelated, this tip may not apply. But if you are building clusters around certain roles or functions, consider a common naming scheme so that you can easily understand when you are working with physical nodes rather than clustered resources.

As an example, for our first cluster, I chose a generic word starting with the letter A—Alpha—as the basis of all the names related to this cluster.

- The logical name of my cluster, AlphaCluster, combines "Alpha" and "Cluster" so that I know I can manage the entire cluster with this name.
- Here are some of the synthetic servers (applications and services) that I will build on this cluster:
  - AlphaFS, for file services
  - AlphaDFSN, for DFS namespaces
  - AlphaDB, for SQL databases
- The physical nodes are called AlphaNode#, with # representing the number of the node (1, 2, 3...).

Using this kind of naming will ensure that all the resources show up in Active Directory or a browser next to each other, and I will easily understand what the cluster name is, who the nodes are, and the resources being offered. So, when a user asks about an issue with AlphaFS, I will know exactly where to go to manage it.

As a variation on this, if I wanted to create a large database cluster, I might name the cluster FruitCluster, with the nodes FruitClusterNode1, FruitClusterNode2, and so forth. Each of my clustered resource groups might be named for a different fruit, such as AppleDB, BananaDB, or CherryDB.

If you have a few cities in your environment, you might have a few clusters in Austin, Texas, that each start with a word beginning with A, whereas Dallas servers start with a word beginning with D. But if you find your creative energies waning, more generic names like cluster CLU33, with nodes CLU33A and CLU33B and resource groups CLU33DB1 and CLU33DB2 might be appropriate as well. Find a naming scheme that prefaces the logical cluster name, the node names, and the resource machine names with a common prefix.

CLUSTER A, TASK 4: CREATE A HIGHLY AVAILABLE FILE SERVER

To create a file server, you will need some shared storage that can host the files. So, you'll leave the Failover Cluster Management console and manage the disk from the Disk Administration utility on either physical node. To start the Disk Administration console, open Server Manager, expand Storage, and click Disk Management.

In the Disk Administration console, you should see the local disk for the node, as well as the shared storage volumes. Likely, the local disk is C and the first shared storage is Q for the quorum witness. The remaining volumes show a different status than we are used to (online or offline). Here, you see which shared storage volumes are available or reserved since they are controlled by the Failover Clustering service. But you can still format them, so do so by selecting one and creating a new simple volume; for this example, label it as F:.

As always, let's begin within the Failover Cluster Management console. In the left pane, the top option underneath the cluster itself is Services And Applications. Right-click and choose Configure A Service Or Application. This will start the High Availability Wizard.

The High Availability Wizard begins by listing all the built-in services or applications (analogous to roles within a normal server) that can be deployed within this cluster. For this task, you will create a file server.

The remaining wizard screen options will reflect the role, service, or application that you choose. This wizard is one of the most significant clustering changes in Windows Server 2003 and makes clustering much more viable for mainstream environments.

When configuring a clustered file service, you'll be prompted for the logical file server name and storage that the file service will use. The default is to append the cluster name (AlphaCluster) with a role designation like FS, resulting in AlphaClusterFS. But as a common practice, I prefer to not pick the defaults, so let's change the name to **AlphaFS** just because we can (and make it easier on our users).

Because the IP addresses of the two physical nodes on the corporate network are using DHCP assigned addresses, the cluster will automatically enable the virtual file server to use a DHCP assigned address as well. If the network cards on the clustered nodes were using static addresses, you would have the option of entering a static address for the AlphaFS server.

Next, you should see any available shared storage and specifically, the F: drive that you created at the beginning of this task. If your wizard does not show any shared storage, close the wizard, format an NTFS partition within one of your shared storage volumes, and repeat this task.

This should result in a confirmation screen. Click Next, and you should see a report showing the successful completion of the clustered file service. To complete the process of creating a clustered file service, rename the storage resource (similar to how we did the quorum witness disk) to reflect what service it is associated with.

You also need to create some production file shares for our users. By expanding the Services And Applications item in the left pane, you will see the newly created AlphaFS service. Clicking this service will show the summary of the Alpha File Server, and in the right pane, you can click Add A Shared Folder. Adding a shared folder will invoke the same Provision A Shared Folder Wizard that is run for a nonclustered file server. The wizard will walk through the following choices:

Shared Folder Location This is where you see the available F: volume and can either browse to an existing location or type the path specifically. If the folder does not exist, the wizard will prompt and offer to create it for you.

NTFS Permissions Here you can assign permissions for access. You likely already have an Active Directory group that has all your appropriate users in it, and you can choose only that group to have access to this team directory.

Share Protocols Here you can define the SMB and NFS share names.

SMB Settings Here I recommend you click Advanced and select Access Based Enumeration, which enables a new feature in Windows Server 2008 where the share is not visible for users who do not have rights to access it.

SMB Permissions Here again, you would normally have a team group in Active Directory and enable that group to have modify permissions within this share. Otherwise, the default is read-only access to the share, regardless of the file system NTFS permissions.

DFS Namespace Do not enable this setting now; we will revisit it in Chapter 5.

After a final confirmation screen, you will see an acknowledgment that the share has been created. You can repeat this process for a few other team directories. Then, you can go back to the Failover Cluster Management console, expand the Services And Applications item, and click AlphaFS. Figure 6.15 shows our clustered file service.

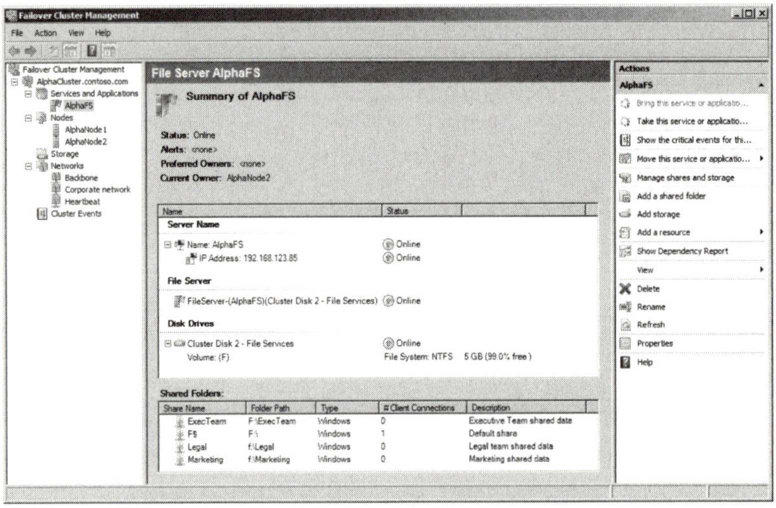

FIGURE 6.15
Our clustered file service

CLUSTER A, TASK 5: TEST IT FROM A WINDOWS CLIENT

None of this stuff counts if the clients can't take advantage of it. So, to be sure that you've created a highly available file server, go to a Windows client, select ➤ Start ➤ Run, and type **\\ALPHAFS**. This is the name of the file server that the users will see, without knowing whether or not it is clustered. If you did it correctly, you will see our file shares, as shown in Figure 6.16.

Notice that in Figure 6.16, the left pane shows some of the other servers in the network, including the two nodes within our cluster, AlphaNode1 and AlphaNode2. Browsing those nodes does not reveal the file shares that you created, because those shares come from the AlphaFS file server, not one of the physical nodes in the cluster.

FIGURE 6.16
Our clustered file shares from the client perspective

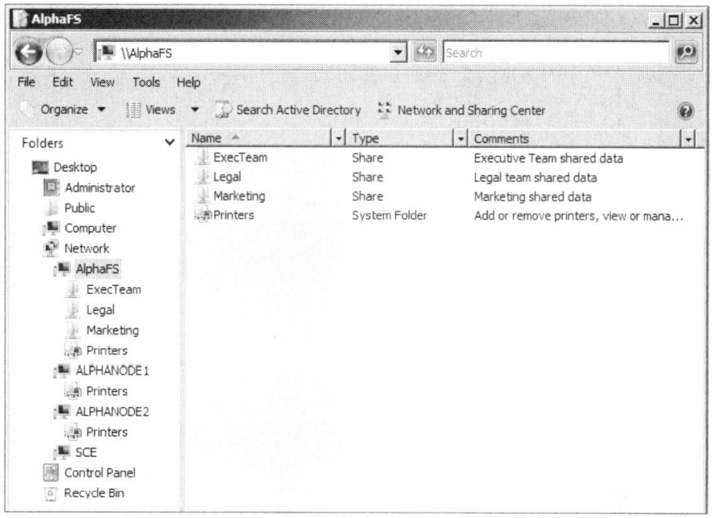

How Failover Clustering Works

Thus far, you've created at least one cluster. It has multiple physical nodes and has at least one highly available service deployed. Up until this point, this may seem like just a complicated standalone server. So, let's look at how a failover cluster really works.

The Cluster Heartbeat

When you first configured the cluster, you defined a private network segment for exclusive use by the clustered nodes. In a two-node configuration, you could even use a cross-over cable, though a best practice is to still use a network switch. As part of the self-diagnostics of the cluster, each node will occasionally check the health of the other nodes by sending or receiving a heartbeat. With a two-node network, the network between the two nodes could be as simple as a crossover cable or a small workgroup hub. The hub is preferred because you can see status information from a hub's front panel. Having an isolated and reliable network switch becomes increasingly important as the number of nodes increases within a cluster, so that they can all maintain awareness of one another's status.

This interconnect is also used for other control traffic between the nodes, such as configuration changes and status/connectivity to the Failover Cluster Management console.

When Failover Occurs

When the administrator intentionally moves a resource group or when a failover condition (such as missed heartbeats) is met, the cluster will move the resource group to another suitable node. To do this, all the resources in the group are taken offline. Because some resources are dependent on others, less dependent resources go offline first. In a clustered file server, this happens quickly and may not appear to matter, but with application servers, it does matter more.

In the case of a clustered file server moving between nodes:

1 The file shares quickly go offline.
2. The shared storage itself goes offline.
3. The IP/networking goes offline.
4. The server name goes offline.

Now that the resources are offline, their ownership can be modified. We will discuss methods of establishing a quorum in the next section. But for now, the quorum can be thought of as a very small database that tracks which resources are being delivered by which physical nodes. You may think of the quorum as a two-column table. The left column lists all the resources (such as the IP address, name, and shares). The right column indicates which clustered node is currently chartered to deliver it. So, when failover occurs, it is almost a matter of bringing a set of resources down on Node1, changing the ownership (column 2) attribute from Node1 to Node2, and then Node2 will bring the resources back online.

There is a little more to it than that—but first, let's see how the quorum works.

Quorum Models

Perhaps the most significant architecture change for Windows Server 2008 and 2008 R2 failover clusters involved changes in the *quorum*. Before Windows Server 2008, the quorum was a single point of failure, so a critical component of your high availability solution could bring it down. In Windows Server 2008 and 2008 R2, we now have four models for the quorum. In all configurations, the idea is to create a majority within the participants in order to determine how the cluster should handle an outage.

Understanding Split-Brain Syndrome

When multiple nodes are ready to resume services for their peers during outages, what happens when things are cut in half?

This is a common concern for asynchronous replication technologies that offer failover (see Chapter 3), as well as two-node clusters with their own copies of the storage. If the solution is split such that each node thinks that the other side is down, but each node has all the storage and networking access to resume services, each node might pick up where the other left off. The result? Both sides are now running the same applications. Some users are changing data on the left copy, and other users are changing data on the right copy. Merging them back together later may be all but impossible.

This is the reason why quorums work with a majority that is best delivered with an odd number of participants—three, five, or seven votes.

Before Windows Server 2008 and 2008 R2, there was a concept called majority node sets, where the quorum was stored on multiple file shares and kept in sync so that you could have three file shares. If the two nodes were to be separated, the likelihood was that one split-brain node would be able to see a majority (two) of the three shares, while the other split brain-node would only see one. The node seeing only one of the shares would know that as a minority, it had the outage. Meanwhile, while the node seeing two shares would understand that with a majority, it was the survivor, and it would resume services for the failed node.

In Windows Server 2008 and 2008 R2, the concept of majority quorums has evolved. But keep in mind that you still should have an odd number of voting members so that you don't have split-brain syndrome.

Witness Disk (Only)

The Witness Disk (Only) model is essentially how the quorum was handled in most clusters prior to Windows Server 2008. The nodes are all dependent on the shared and single quorum on a shared disk volume between the clustered nodes (as a legacy scenario similar to Windows Server 2003 and 2003 R2 clusters). If any node fails, the remaining node(s) look to the quorum, which unilaterally decides if or what resources will fail over and to where.

As you can see in Figure 6.17, the Witness Disk model has a single point of failure for our high-availability solution in the quorum itself. For this reason, the additional quorum models were created in Windows Server 2008—and this is not a recommended configuration for most Windows Server 2008 failover clusters.

FIGURE 6.17
Witness (legacy) quorum model cluster

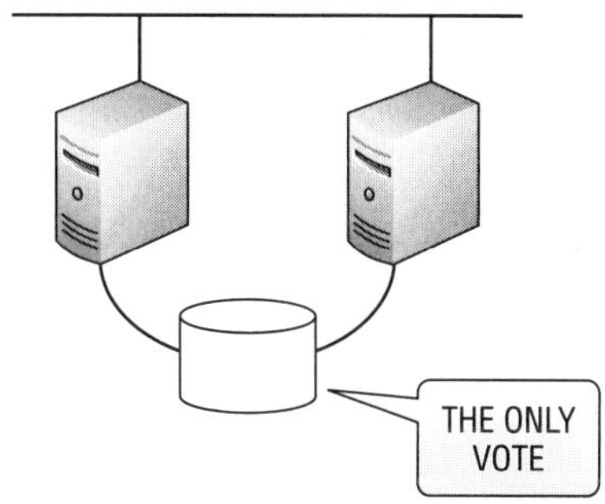

Node and Disk Majority

In the Node and Disk Majority Quorum Model (see Figure 6.18), decisions about the health and response of the cluster are gathered by a majority of the voting members. Each node gets a vote, and the quorum (shared drive) gets a vote. So, in a typical two-node cluster, there are three potential votes. With three votes available, any two votes will determine the outcome of the cluster, which in this case, is probably one surviving node plus the quorum drive. What is also important to note is that in this new model, the flaw from two-node Windows Server 2003 clusters is resolved, which is the single point of failure in the quorum itself. With Windows Server 2008 and 2008 R2, the cluster can survive a failed quorum because two of the three votes are still available (the two nodes themselves). This is therefore an ideal configuration for two-node clustering.

FIGURE 6.18
Node and Disk Majority two-node cluster

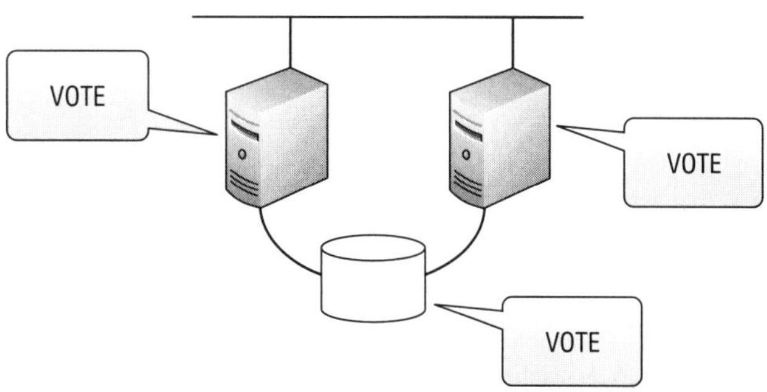

Also notable here is what happens without a majority. If one node and the shared storage were to go offline, the remaining node will "take a vote" and realize that only one of the three nodes is participating. At this point, the surviving node knows that it does not have the votes to continue and will not try to resume services.

NOTE "Node and Disk Majority" is the preferred quorum model for clusters with *even* numbers of nodes, since the quorum witness disk adds one more vote for a clear majority.

Node and File Share Majority

The Node and File Share Majority model works similarly to the Node and Disk Majority model, except that file share majority quorums lack a shared disk, so this option is not intended for shared access scenarios like a clustered file server. Instead, for service-based solutions that do not require a shared disk, such as Exchange 2007 CCR (see Chapter 7), a copy of the quorum is stored on a file share that should be accessible by all the nodes of the cluster. The server outside the cluster that is offering the file share is called a *witness server.*

The file share witness server is simply another server, perhaps a domain controller, an infrastructure server like DHCP/DNS, or another member server. The job of the witness server's file share and its data is to cast a third vote alongside the two votes of the cluster nodes. This enables you to create two-node clusters without a shared disk, such as *geo-clusters* (geographically distributed clusters), between sites.

As you can see in Figure 6.19, the witness server has a file share and acts as a third voting member to help determine how the cluster should react during a node outage.

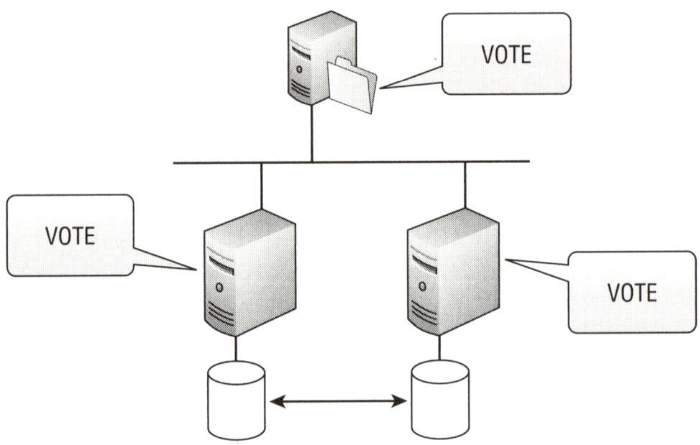

FIGURE 6.19
Node and File Share Majority-based cluster

Two additional notes on file share witness quorum configurations:

- Because the file share is very small and not I/O intensive, the witness server can provide the file share witness offering to several clusters simultaneously.
- This configuration is ideal (and partially designed) for geographically distributed clusters with autonomous storage.

Node Majority

In the Node Majority model, the nodes still get a vote like in the previous scenario, but the quorum disk does not. The key to the Node Majority configuration is that each node has its own copy of the storage, which is replicated via third-party replication, such as the host-based asynchronous replication or array-based mirroring solutions that we discussed in Chapter 3.

Assuming a three + node configuration, the remainder of the scenario works the same as the Quorum Majority model: if any node fails, the N-1 nodes vote to determine how the failover recovery should be handled. In a three-node scenario, the surviving two nodes confirm that they still have a majority of control and begin resumption of the services of the failed node (see Figure 6.20).

GEO-CLUSTERING IN WINDOWS SERVER 2008 AND 2008 R2

Around the time of Windows Server 2003 and 2003 R2, geographically distributed cluster nodes started growing in popularity—as long as each node had its own storage, which was replicated via asynchronous host-based replication or array-based mirroring (see Chapter 3).

But for many environments, it wasn't practical before Windows Server 2008 because of two hard limits of cluster services:

- Windows Server 2003 R2 (and before) required the nodes to be in the same IP subnet.
- Windows Server 2003 and 2003 R2 had a maximum heartbeat timeout of 500ms.

Between these two limitations, geo-clustering was desirable but not particularly practical across long distances without a VLAN or other unorthodox routing configuration for the IP addresses. And even then, the solution still had a maximum distance due to the heartbeat.

Starting in Windows Server 2008, failover clusters no longer require the same IP subnet across all nodes and the heartbeat became configurable, so geo-clustering has become viable.

FIGURE 6.20
Three-node cluster in Node Majority configuration

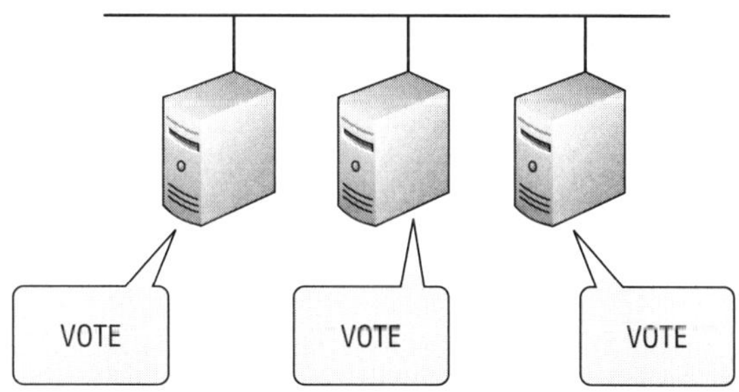

NOTE Node Majority is the preferred quorum model for clusters with *odd* numbers of nodes.

Since there is already an odd number of votes, no external witness disk or file share is needed in order to determine a clear majority. The next section expands upon this idea.

RECOMMENDED QUORUM CONFIGURATIONS

Here are my recommended quorum configurations:

- For clusters with an even number of nodes, use Node and Disk Majority, since the witness disk provides an additional vote for a clear majority.
- For clusters with an odd number of nodes, use Node Majority, since no additional votes are needed for a clear majority.
- For geographically distributed clusters with autonomous storage, use a File Share Witness.
- Disk-only quorums are not recommended.

What Changes with the Third Node and Beyond

For many deployments, a simple two-node *active/passive* cluster is fine. In an active/passive scenario, one of the nodes is relatively idle while the other node performs the production tasks. You might also choose to deploy an *active/active* cluster, where each node is delivering some of the production resources, such as file services, from one node and a SQL Server database on the other. This is typical in a small office where dedicating a two-node cluster to each workload may be impractical.

The challenge with active/active type deployments is that you have to presume that any single node has enough processor, memory, networking and storage I/O to handle the collective tasks if the other node were to go offline. This effectively caps every node at under 50 percent performance capacity, in order to ensure that resources are available during times of crisis. For this reason, it is logical to add a third or perhaps fourth node, with N-1 of the nodes active and one passive node shared among the cluster. This scenario is similar to having a single spare tire for your car, even though you have four tires in production. The assumption is that you won't have more than one flat tire at a time, so one spare is almost always sufficient. In the case of an AAAAP (four active/one passive) cluster, we would have one completely available node—and hopefully three nodes would be able to handle all of the production requirements if two were to fail in a similar timeframe.

With those scenarios in mind, we will do two more tasks with our AlphaCluster, first adding an additional node and then changing the quorum type to optimize for a three-node cluster.

Cluster A, Task 6: Adding an Additional Node

For this task, I built a third machine that is also running Windows Server 2008 and has three network interfaces. However, because I am adding this third node later in the deployment, I intentionally have changed some names, such as the network objects, just as you might if you installed the third (or fourth) nodes later due to increasing demand within the cluster.

Here's the list of steps for creating and adding a third node:

1. Install Windows Server 2008 EE on similar hardware—with the name AlphaNode3.
2. Join the same Contoso domain, within the same OU in Active Directory.
3. Ensure that each of the three network cards is attached to the correct networks as the other nodes:
   - Corporate/Internet
   - Cluster/Heartbeat
   - Backbone/Storage
4. Ping the other two nodes and DC to confirm proper IP connectivity, including the multiple subnet routes.
5. Configure the iSCSI storage:
   - Set the iSCSI target for the cluster to accept connections from the new node.
   - Configure the iSCSI initiator on the new node to connect to the iSCSI target for the cluster.
   - Confirm that the three clustered disks are visible within the Disk Administration console on the new node.
6. Install the Failover Clustering feature and ensure that Windows Update is current on the new node.
7. Reboot the new node.

With the new node now cluster-able, configured, and ready, we need to start by rerunning the Cluster Validation Wizard from the Failover Cluster Management console. This is another advantage of the Failover Clustering Management console compared to Windows Server 2003's `ClusPrep.exe` utility. The Validation Wizard can be run on an active cluster, not just during a cluster's initial setup.

My recommendation is to run the wizard from one of the nodes that is already within the cluster. Run it twice, once on just the new node (by itself) in order to test its individual viability, and then run the validation test again including all the nodes (existing and new), to confirm no anomalies. Interestingly, when you select any node within the cluster for validation, the wizard will select the other nodes that are already within the cluster as well.

THE VALIDATION WIZARD CANNOT TEST ONLINE STORAGE

One difference when running the Validation Wizard on an active cluster is that the clustered disks that are currently servicing highly available applications or services cannot be tested. You should be see a prompt that lists active cluster services or applications and be given the choice to either leave those applications running (and skip the tests of those storage resources) or take the applications offline so that the storage can be tested. Because we are designing a solution for high availability, a rigorous testing of all resources is prudent, so the best practice is to take the services offline and perform the complete test.

Taking the complete cluster offline may not be immediately practical, based on the business or political environments. So, a test without the storage is better than no test at all. In fact, it will still validate most of the aspects (including patches and networking).

Say you don't perform the complete test and you add the node, having passed all other tests, to the cluster. But when a failure happens, you learn that the new node cannot access the shared storage and the failover does not occur because you didn't plan ahead well enough. Ninety-nine times out of 100 it is worth checking everything.

With the Validation Wizard reporting no issues across all three nodes, the process of adding the node becomes easy.

1. From the Failover Cluster Management console on one of the existing cluster nodes, expand the Nodes area under the cluster itself.
2. Right-click on the Nodes item and select Add Node.
3. The Add Node Wizard asks you for the name of the new node and then will begin joining the node to the cluster. No other user inputs are required. When the progress bar finishes, the cluster will now have an additional node.

It is that simple—except that by adding a third node, you have reduced the high availability because of the quorum.

CLUSTER A, TASK 7: CHANGING THE QUORUM TYPE

The quorum should have an odd number of voting members so that a clear majority can be determined. With our initial two-node cluster, we created a quorum by using a shared disk witness for the third vote. This approach allows the cluster to tolerate an outage by either node because the surviving node plus the disk witness provides two of the three votes and the cluster will continue.

However, if you just completed Task 6 and added a third clustered node, the automated report from the console should provide a warning similar to this: "The cluster has an odd number of nodes and a quorum disk. A quorum disk in this scenario reduces cluster high availability. Consider removing the quorum disk."

With an odd number of clustered nodes, a majority can already be clearly determined without the need for the witness disk.

To change the quorum type, right-click on the cluster name in the left pane, and select More Actions ➢ Configure Cluster Quorum Settings. Again, with the strong emphasis in Windows Server 2008 and 2008 R2 on making clustering easier, another wizard will spawn: the Configure Cluster Quorum Wizard.

When you first enter the wizard, the four quorum types are offered as radio buttons, with the current configuration selected as the default. Because the cluster was previously a two-node cluster, the Node and Disk Majority model is already selected, but consider the recommendations to the right of each option. In our case, because we now have three nodes, the wizard will correctly recommend a Node Majority configuration, as shown in Figure 6.21. This effectively eliminates another potential point of failure in the shared storage, though you might also have the storage natively mirrored at an array level. It is worth noting that the wizard will allow you to pick a nonoptimal quorum type. For example, if you know that you will be removing or adding more nodes later, you might select the quorum type for your eventual number of odd/even nodes, even though you are not yet at that number.

FIGURE 6.21
Configure Custom Quorum Wizard

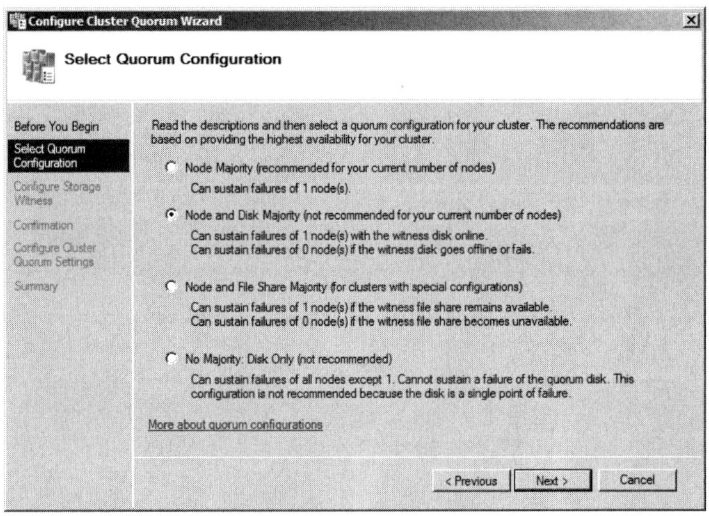

If you select the Node Majority, the nodes will vote among themselves (two of three winning). No other options are presented with this choice, and the report at the end will notify you that the disk that was in use for the quorum witness disk has now been returned to the cluster for other storage needs.

Windows Server 2008 R2 Failover Clustering

To get us completely up to date, we will look at what has changed in failover clustering from Windows Server 2008 to 2008 R2 and then build a second cluster using Windows Server 2008 R2.

What's New in Failover Clustering (Windows Server 2008 R2)

Windows Server 2008 brought the most significant changes to clustering since it was first released with Windows NT 4. The changes center primarily on simplified setup and management, as well as improvements for storage, shared folders, and networking. For a complete list of enhancements in Windows Server 2008, see `http://technet.microsoft.com/en-us/library/cc770625(WS.10).aspx`.

Windows Server 2008 R2 builds on the enhancement in Windows Server 2008 and includes the following:

- Validation reporting has become even more robust. With Windows Server 2008, we saw significant proactive testing compared to `ClusPrep.exe`, but the validation feature primarily tested the nodes of the cluster for cluster-ability. With Windows Server 2008 R2, Microsoft released a configuration analysis tool for the entire cluster and introduced additional best practices. Also, the reporting is richer; dependency reports and embedded diagrams for the dependencies are featured.
- The migration tools in Windows Server 2008 were from Windows Server 2003. In Windows Server 2008 R2, we can migrate:
  - From Windows Server 2003 and 2003 R2, for those who never updated to Windows Server 2008 and want to go straight to 2008 R2
  - From Windows Server 2008 (the most common scenario)
  - From Windows Server 2008 R2, for those who want to move resources and services from one 2008 R2 cluster to another
- Failover Clustering can now be managed via a PowerShell command-line interface, instead of `Cluster.exe`. `Cluster.exe` is still available in Windows Server 2008 R2 for legacy purposes and convenience (but for the last time, according to Microsoft). PowerShell support is included within Windows Server Core (new in Windows Server 2008 R2). Everything you could do in `Cluster.exe` is available in PowerShell, along with much of the automation found in the easy-to-use wizards.
- Support for DFS Replication is included. In one common scenario, you create a hub spoke, with all the branch offices (spoke) coming back to a corporate (hub) file server. Prior to Windows Server 2008 R2, this hub server could not be highly available via failover clustering. With Windows Server 2008 R2, DFS-R is supported so that the hub can be resilient.
- Other roles that received enhancements include:
  - Print serving
  - Remote desktop brokering
- Several enhancements give better insight and improve maintenance:
  - Management Pack for System Center Operations Manager 2007
  - Performance counters
  - Enhanced logging
  - Read-only access to monitor the cluster while maintaining security
- Network enhancements are included for better self-healing logic and network customization, including optimizations for the new Hyper-V R2 cluster-shared volumes (CSVs).

And most importantly, if your hardware works with Windows Server 2008 clustering today, it will work with 2008 R2.

Building Your Second Cluster Using Windows Server 2008 R2 in Hyper-V

In our first cluster, we used Windows Server 2008 with Virtual Server 2005 R2. For our second cluster, we will use Windows Server 2008 R2 with Hyper-V, but still use iSCSI shared storage from a Windows Storage Server appliance.

As in the previous set of tasks, we will start with a generic installation of the operating system, with three network interfaces:

- Corporate/Internet
- Cluster/Heartbeat/Interconnect
- Storage/Backbone

To follow along with our tasks, download the TestDrive VHDs for Windows Server 2008 R2 EE from `http://TechNet.Microsoft.com/EvalCenter`. After importing the VHDs into your Windows Server 2008 R2 with Hyper-V host, change the name of the machines to OmegaNode1 and OmegaNode2, configure the networking as shown earlier, and run Windows Update.

Cluster B, Task 1: Preparing Windows Server 2008 R2 Nodes

While the experience is relatively similar between Windows Server 2008 and 2008 R2, there are enough enhancements that it is worth going through the revised setup in 2008 R2.

Again, for this chapter, I used TestDrive VHDs so that you can follow the exact steps, if you choose to. After importing the VHDs into Hyper-V on your host (or you can install your own Windows Server 2008 R2 servers), prepare them for clustering:

1. Name the nodes using our convention, **OmegaNode1** and **OmegaNode2**.
2. Connect them to the correct IP networks:
   - CorpNet, which in our example includes our iSCSI storage, though you would normally run iSCSI on its own gigabit or faster switch
   - Cluster as a private two-node network with explicit IP addresses
3. Join them to the same Active Directory forest, within the same OU.
4. Enable the iSCSI initiators to connect to an iSCSI target with two or more LUNs. For our examples, continue to use the iSCSI target provided with your Windows Storage Server appliance. One notable change with Windows Server 2008 R2 is the option for a *quick connect* within the iSCSI initiator; when you enter an IP address, it discovers the iSCSI target, connects to it, and logs on within a single click.
5. Run Windows Update on them (or use System Center Configuration Manager or System Center Essentials to update their patches).

Cluster B, Task 2: Enabling Clustering in Windows Server 2008 R2

The experience is relatively similar in both Windows Server 2008 and 2008 R2, though there are enough enhancements that again it is worth going through the revised setup in 2008 R2.

Enabling the Failover Clustering feature from the Server Manager is the same as in Windows Server 2008, with no configuration options required (though a reboot is still recommended).

Again, I highly recommended that you run the validation tool before creating the cluster. One subtle but nice enhancement in Windows Server 2008 R2 is the ability to create a cluster as the last step of successfully running the Validation Wizard. Notice in Figure 6.22 the link Create The Cluster Now Using The Validated Nodes in the lower right of the result screen of the Validate A Configuration Wizard.

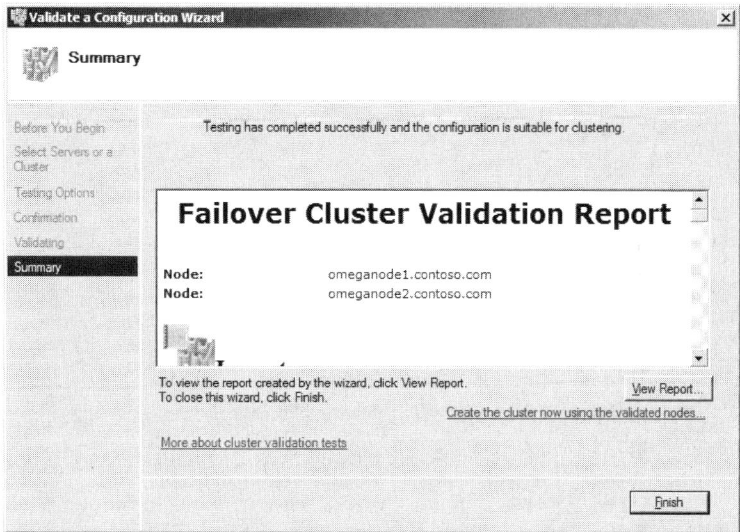

FIGURE 6.22
Windows Server 2008 R2 Validation Wizard with the create cluster option

Clicking this link takes you directly into the Create Cluster Wizard. The first screens of the Create Cluster Wizard are prepopulated with the names of the nodes that you submitted for validation. All that's left to do is to name the new cluster, adjust the networking, and wait a few seconds.

Migrating to Windows Server 2008 R2 Failover Clusters

One of the enhanced areas for Windows Server 2008 R2 and failover clustering is the migration tools. There is no upgrade (in place) for clustering, but Windows Server 2008 R2 does provide the ability to migrate from Windows Server 2003, 2003 R2, Windows Server 2008, and 2008 R2 clusters into 2008 R2. The ability to migrate to a failover cluster using Windows Server 2008 R2 is a new feature based on feedback from customers wanting to move resources from one cluster to another, even if both are of the current OS version. You can learn more at `http://go.microsoft.com/fwlink/?linkID=142796`.

To follow along with this task, create a Windows Server 2003 R2 cluster called Gamma, and we will migrate the file services from the Gamma cluster into our newly created Windows Server 2008 R2 Omega cluster. While most of this book presumes that you have little experience with the data protection and availability technologies covered here, the task of migrating to Windows Server 2008 R2 is best appreciated when migrating from a legacy solution like Windows Server 2003 R2.

Optional Task: Building a Windows Server 2003 R2 Cluster Using Virtual Server 2005 R2

A step-by-step guide to creating the legacy Windows Server 2003 R2 cluster is outside the scope of this chapter, but here is an overview of creating the legacy storage for 2003 R2.

I have intentionally created all of the tasks in this chapter, and most of the book, using virtualization along with OS images available on Microsoft TestDrive VHDs so that you can repeat the tasks without expensive hardware.

To simulate a legacy Windows Server 2003 R2 cluster, I chose to use a shared SCSI storage volume in Virtual Server 2005 R2, which is not possible with Microsoft Hyper-V. Incidentally, this form of shared storage, which effectively behaves like parallel SCSI drives with two PCs linked into the same SCSI chassis and bus, is not supported with Windows Server 2008 R2 because it does not support SCSI persistent reservations.

Running Virtual Server 2005 R2 on Windows Server 2008

While Windows Server 2008 includes its own and far-superior hypervisor, Hyper-V does not allow us to create a shared SCSI volume that two or more virtual servers can share. Because of this, we can install the earlier Virtual Server 2005 R2 on our Windows Server 2008 host, instead. To do this, download and install the following in this order:

- Virtual Server 2005 R2
- Virtual Server 2005 R2 Service Pack 1
- Virtual Server 2005 R2 KB948515 (to provide compatibility with Windows Server 2008)

For better performance, you may wish to install Windows Server 2008 x64 on your host, along with the x64 versions of Microsoft Virtual Server (MSVS) 2005 R2, along with its service pack and any necessary hotfixes. However, Virtual Server 2005 R2 only allows for 32-bit guest operating systems. So for convenience, you may want to install Windows Server 2008 x86 (and the x86 virtualization components), so that you are only dealing with one version of the operating system.

After you have a running Virtual Server 2005 R2 host, we need to create our virtualized resources. For simplicity, create a directory on your host called `D:\WS03MSCS` for all your virtual machines and resources.

Creating a Shared Storage Volume Within Virtual Server

To create the shared storage for our clustered nodes, open the Virtual Server console. On the left side, click Virtual Disks and then click Create ➢ Fixed Disk. Use the following parameters to create your disk:

Location: `D:\WS03MSCS` (wherever you want it)

Filename: `D:\WS03MSCS\shared0.vhd`

Size: 1 GB

The first disk will be for the quorum. Repeat the steps to create a data disk named `Shared1.vhd` with 5 GB.

Note that shared SCSI disks in virtual servers must be a fixed size. When working with virtual servers in test environments, I am sometimes tempted to use dynamically expanding disks in my virtual machines to save on space within my test servers. However, shared SCSI disks in Virtual Server must be fixed disks. If you try to be frugal during this step, you will have to repeat it. I did.

Creating a Windows Server 2003 Cluster

Step-by-step guidance on creating a legacy cluster is not in the scope of this chapter, especially in consideration of the 21 steps to do it in Windows Server 2003 compared with essentially three clicks in Windows Server 2008 R2. But the main steps are similar:

1. Configure the networking for public and private connections for CorpNet, as well as the cluster heartbeats.
2. Install Windows Server 2003 or 2003 R2 Enterprise edition on each node.
3. Install the clustering components.
4. Create a cluster with one node.
5. Add the other node to the cluster—unlike Windows Server 2008, where the cluster can be created with all nodes simultaneously.
6. Create a file serving group, with the appropriate name, IP, storage, and share resources.

Now that you've built it, and you can appreciate just how much better Windows Server 2008 and 2008 R2 failover clustering is, let's migrate off the old cluster that you just built.

While there is no such thing as an *in-place upgrade*, there is the idea of an *in-place migration*. In this case, in-place means that we will be using the same node hardware before and after, but we will not be uplifting the nodes themselves. For our discussion, imagine a simple two-node cluster with shared storage, with Node1 on the left and Node2 on the right.

STEP 1: EVICT NODE 2 FROM YOUR EXISTING CLUSTER

Start with your old cluster (perhaps Windows Server 2003 R2—if you were brave or inherited it from another administrator—Windows Server 2008, or a test 2008 R2 cluster) and prepare to evict a node. You might normally do this when a node has failed and you know that it will not be coming back.

In our case, because we can evict a node in a controlled and patient manner, we will use a change window with a few requirements:

- We have confirmed a reliable backup of our cluster that includes the system state of all the nodes, as well the data sources. By confirming this, we have successfully restored a simple data object to another location. This is a book on data protection, so obviously we are zealous about backing up and testing our restores using a supported backup solution that can back up the clustered nodes in a VSS-supported manner. If you are unsure whether your backup solution is reliable for backing up the system state and cluster data sources, consider one of the backup technologies, such as DPM (discussed in Chapter 4).
- You have limited to no users on the cluster.
- You have management agreement that the cluster can be less highly available, since you will be taking a node offline indefinitely.

If you have met these conditions, you are ready to decommission a node from the legacy cluster by first moving all the cluster resources (groups in Windows Server 2003 R2 and instances in Windows Server 2008 R2) to the primary cluster node, or what will be the only remaining node.

With all of the resources gracefully moved to Node1, you can evict Node2 from the cluster by right-clicking on the cluster and selecting Evict Node.

Step 2: Build a Single-Node Cluster out of Node2

Now, we will build a single-node cluster out of the decommissioned Node2 with Windows Server 2008 R2 Enterprise or Datacenter edition:

1. I recommend pulling the C: hard drive out of Node2 and putting a fresh drive in place. This gives you a quick way to get back to a good state if you had to. But either way, install Windows Server 2008 R2.

NOTE In this step, we're pulling and inserting drives in a physical node that should be clustered. We will discuss this more in Chapter 9 when we explore virtualization, but for now keep in mind that yet another benefit of virtualization is the ability to do this kind of operation without a concern for hardware. One VHD can be swapped with another in just a few seconds.

2. Make it a real server within your environment:
   - Join your Active Directory domain and verify connectivity to your infrastructure management servers (DC, DNS, Backup, and so forth).
   - Use Windows Update or your patch management system, such as System Center Configuration Manager (for enterprises) or System Center Essentials (for midsized businesses), as well as the relevant monitoring tools, such as System Center Operations Manager. You'll learn more about these tools in Chapters 10 (management) and 11 (monitoring).
3. Configure the networks for your intended cluster design for heartbeats, backbones, iSCSI storage, and so forth.
4. Create a single-node cluster, using the methods that we discussed earlier in the chapter:
   - A. Enable the Failover Clustering feature within Windows Server 2008 R2.
   - B. Run the Validate A Configuration Wizard.
   - C. With a successful validation, create a cluster from the single node.

With everything done correctly, you should end up with two nodes: one is Windows Server 2003 R2 and the other is Windows Server 2008 R2.

Step 3: Migrate the Cluster Configuration

Run the Migrate A Cluster Wizard from the Failover Cluster Management console on the Windows Server 2008 R2 clustered node, as Figure 6.23 shows.

For some clustered application types, a particular and separate migration method may be required (such as Exchange 2007 CCR), but for many of the built-in functions, the Migration Wizard takes care of moving the configuration, including virtualized machine names, IPs, and resource definitions, but not the data.

Step 4: Move the Data

This is arguably the one step where in-place has some different connotations. If your legacy cluster uses a form of shared storage that is supported by Windows Server 2008 R2 clustering, then you might just move the LUNs from the legacy Node1 to the newly created Node2.

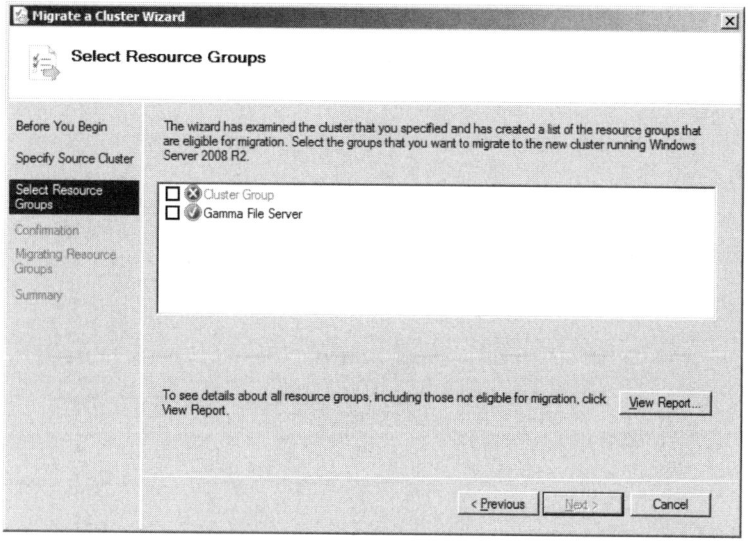

FIGURE 6.23
The Migrate A Cluster Wizard in Windows Server 2008 R2

It may benefit you to allocate different storage and copy the data so that your old node still has its copy for now, and the new copy has its own copy. Again, this gives you fallback options if everything does not go well. This is easiest if you have a SAN that can snap a copy of the LUNs within the storage array and split them, so that the original LUNs remain on the legacy Node1 and the new LUN copies are mounted to Node2. This is shown in Figure 6.24, where we have chosen to leave F: on the old cluster and use a new clustered disk within the new cluster after migration.

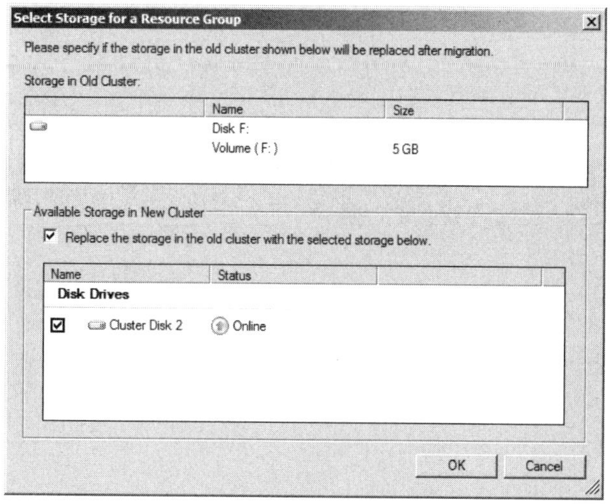

FIGURE 6.24
Storage migration choices

You might also consider allocating new storage to your Node2 and then doing a full restore from your backup solution. This strategy presumably gives you back the same data, but it also gives you the opportunity to rigorously test your recovery capabilities in a non-production environment. If the restore fails, you know that your backup has other issues that need to be investigated, but you haven't lost anything since the legacy Node1 still has the original data.

But one way or another, get the data onto the new Node 2 and begin verifying that your single-node cluster is viable, with the correct configurations (from the Migration Wizard) and data.

If You Don't Want to Duplicate the Storage During Migrations

In a migration scenario, an organization may believe that it cannot afford the duplicated storage for the data volumes or even the spare C: drives for the nodes.

However, not duplicating the C: drives can be thought of as *penny wise, pound foolish*. For a few hundred dollars, you provide a significant recovery capability. Nine times out of 10, you won't need this capability and everything will work. But after a long history of server upgrades and migrations, with more than a few mishaps, I can assure you that the one time that you will need this capability, it may save your job.

There is nothing quite like being six hours into an eight-hour change window and realizing that you need to roll back, and you can't do it in the remaining two hours.

When the migration is done, you can take those two spindles and keep them as spares, add some internal storage to a server, or use them as the duplicate drives for the next cluster to be migrated.

If you have significant data volumes across expensive SAN storage, I challenge you to not assume that you can't get the storage. In today's economy, storage vendors are willing to do aggressive things to show their partnership with you and keep you as a long-term customer. With that in mind, it is not unreasonable to ask for additional storage or evaluation units for 60 days so that you can complete your migrations. If your current SAN vendor won't loan you the incremental storage, you likely can find a competitive SAN vendor who would happily loan you storage for your new cluster in hopes that you'll use them side by side and decide that the new stuff is better.

The power of additional recovery options, as well as reduced stress during the migrations, is worth pursuing duplicated storage.

Depending on how you handled the data, you may have already brought the legacy cluster Node1 down. But if you were able to use a duplicated storage scenario, you will need to manually bring down the legacy cluster resources on Node1 and manually bring up the migrated resources on the new cluster Node2.

When the migration wizard runs, the resources are defined but placed in an offline state, so that no duplicate conflicts happen on the network, as seen in Figure 6.25. Here the services and shares have been migrated but the resources are offline within the new cluster. This approach ensures that you do not have a name or IP conflict until you are ready to switch over.

Once the old resources are brought offline, you only need to right-click on the GammaFile instance (or group) and click Bring Online.

Step 5: Decommission Node 1

Once you are satisfied that the new cluster is performing correctly, it's time to decommission Node1 (and the legacy cluster) and add that node to the new cluster with a fresh Windows Server 2008 R2 installation.

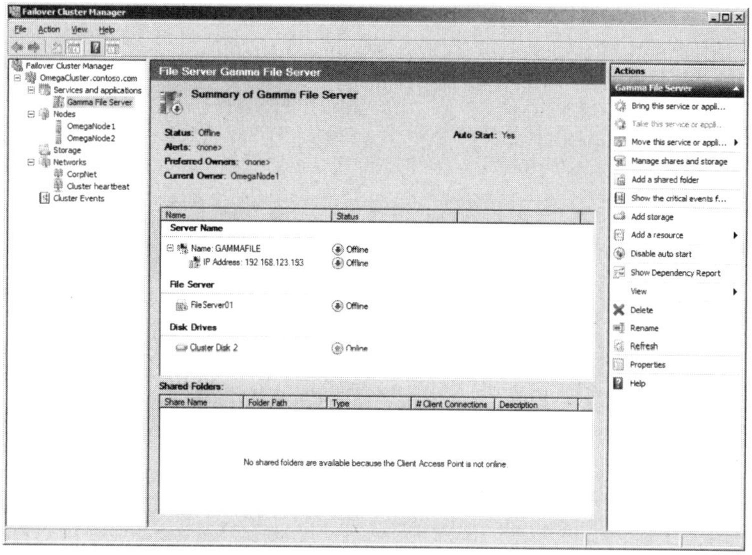

FIGURE 6.25
Dormant new file services after migration

You may choose to first decommission the cluster, which will clear out its entries within Active Directory; remove the Node 1 from the domain; and then reformat the hardware. But another method that I recommend is to remove the hard drive from Node1 while it is still configured as the surviving node of the legacy cluster and put it aside, as I recommended with Node 2 earlier in this section. Again, this provides a fast way to go back to a known-good configuration if you need to.

If you start with a clean hard drive, build a new Windows Server 2008 R2 server that will eventually join your new cluster as a second node using the method described earlier in the section "Cluster A, Task 6: Adding an Additional Node."

Considerations That Make Migrations Easier

Another option is to use a third node instead one of the two in the existing cluster. While a true in-place migration of a two-node cluster has its merits (especially on a budget), if you have one additional server that you may be planning to stage for a new application or test server, things get easier. Or if your cluster farm upgrade is a focused project within your team and there are other items required, purchase another server as part of the migration so that you can leap-frog through your clusters and you'll have a cold spare node when the migrations are over.

This way, you keep a highly available cluster running on what is presumably important data and service assets today, but you can start building your new clusters that take advantage of what is provided in Windows Server 2008 R2 failover clustering.

Summary

You cannot seriously look at improving the data availability of your Windows datacenter without taking a fresh look at failover clustering in Windows Server 2008 and 2008 R2.

All of the old adoption blockers are gone, including:

- Complexity of setup
- Complexity of operations
- Complexity of support
- Inflexibility on certified hardware
- WAN limitations around IP addresses and heartbeat timeouts
- Storage difficulties with SCSI lockups and array connectivity

The short version is that clustering is cool and now it is easy.

We will also see failover clustering as the basis for other data availability scenarios, such as Exchange CCR and DAG (see Chapter 7).

For more information on failover clustering in Windows Server, see `www.microsoft.com/windowsserver2008/en/us/failover-clustering-main.aspx`.

Chapter 7

Microsoft Exchange

There is a phrase in my house that "If momma isn't happy, then nobody is happy."

In today's datacenter, one might say, "If email is down, then everybody is down."

Microsoft Exchange Server is one of the most common email platforms that run on Windows Server for most datacenters. Similar to the history we discussed in Chapter 6 regarding the complexities of early clustering, the availability and data protection methods for the early releases of Exchange (4.0 through 2000) had been considered by many to be challenging. But the last few generations have seen the product go from being a well-behaving MSCS clustered resource to having a complete portfolio of built-in availability mechanisms that are now part of the core product.

In this chapter, we will start by looking at Exchange Server running with a Microsoft cluster and then explore the various replication and availability technologies within Exchange 2007 and Exchange 2010.

Exchange within Microsoft Cluster Services

This chapter will focus on Exchange 2007 and 2010. But to appreciate why these Exchange products are delivering the availability technologies that they are, we need to take a brief look back. Prior to Exchange 2007, the Exchange team did what every other normal application team did that wanted high availability in a Windows world; they deployed within a Windows Failover Cluster solution (see Chapter 6). So, let's start with looking at Exchange Server running in a failover cluster.

Single Copy Clusters

As discussed in Chapter 6, the operating model of a Windows failover cluster is to have two or more nodes running Windows Server Enterprise Edition or higher, and sharing storage, either physically or mirrored. At least for Exchange, there's always shared storage in a single-copy cluster (SCC). *Cluster resources,* also sometimes called virtual resources, are created for logical server names and IP addresses, in order to create synthetic servers, services, or applications within the Microsoft cluster that will be used in production. Applications such as Exchange Server are then installed into these highly available and virtualized servers (also called resource groups or instances), so that a virtualized Exchange server might be running on cluster node 1 or node 2, typically without the application itself being aware of (or caring) which node it is running on, as shown in Figure 7.1. Essentially, clustering packages the virtualized application (like Exchange Server) along with its logical server name, IP, and storage allocation, and has the potential of moving it around within the clustered nodes, based on the resources under it.

FIGURE 7.1
Single-copy cluster

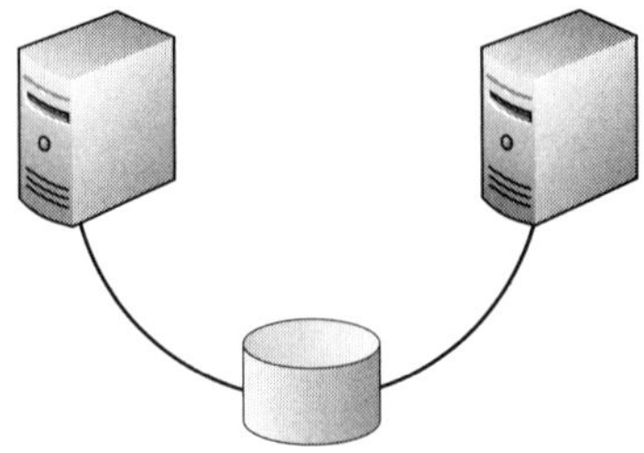

For the clustered Exchange server to work, you have to be sure that regardless of which physical node the virtual Exchange server was operating on, it has to have assured access to the storage. In this case, Microsoft Cluster Services (MSCS) is built on a shared storage solution. This allows all of the physical nodes to have physical connectivity to the same shared storage array, while only one node (at a time) has access to the particular storage LUN with the single instance of the Exchange databases, hence the name *single copy cluster* (SCC).

Getting Started with SCCs

We will be starting where we left off in Chapter 6 on clustering, with a functioning Windows failover cluster. For our Exchange solution, we will be installing Exchange onto one *active node* and then again onto a *passive node* (which will take over if the active node fails), whereby only one node will be actively running Exchange services. If the active node were to fail, then a passive node could resume service, as discussed shortly. As the cluster grows beyond two nodes, N–1 of the nodes might be active, with a single passive node for the cluster, similar to having a single spare tire on a car that has four wheels. In your car, the probability is low that more than one of the tires will fail simultaneously—hence a single spare. Similarly, a five-node cluster might be considered AAAAP, where four of the nodes are active, and one spare is passive. Or, the same five-node cluster might be AAAPP, where three of the nodes are active and two are passive.

Building on top of the cluster that we built in Chapter 6, we have:

Cluster AlphaCluster

Two Physical Nodes AlphaNode1 and AlphaNode2

Shared Storage The cluster has multiple iSCSI-based shared volumes, one of which will be used as shared storage for the Exchange mailbox databases.

Over the next few pages, we will talk about why SCC-based Exchange solutions do not provide as good a high-availability solution as CCR (described in the next section). We will show how to deploy Exchange 2007 clustered mailboxes in Tasks 2 through 5 (later in this chapter), but in the meantime the abbreviated steps are as follows:

1. Enable the prerequisite Windows component roles and features to support Exchange 2007 clustered mailbox servers, which we will discuss in Task 2, later in this chapter.
2. Install the active clustered mailbox role on the first node of the cluster (AlphaNode1, in our case), which is covered later in Task 4.
3. Install the passive clustered mailbox role on any additional nodes of the cluster (AlphaNode2, in our case), which is covered later in Task 5.

NOTE Using the same hardware you might use to build an SCC configuration, you can build a CCR configuration, which provides a higher level of availability for not only the Exchange services but also the Exchange databases; hence the abbreviated discussion regarding SCC deployment steps. We will cover the same mechanisms and installation steps later in the chapter, but with the additional context for Exchange replication.

Failover Behavior

With the Exchange cluster now operating, we have one or more nodes that are actively hosting Exchange resource groups, which are effectively virtualized Exchange servers with access to some of the cluster shared storage, and running Exchange services.

Two types of movement between clustered nodes can occur within an Exchange SCC or failover cluster:

- Planned switchovers
- Unplanned failovers

Planned Switchovers with Clustered Exchange

In a planned outage, such as a rolling upgrade for a service pack or other node-level maintenance, you can choose to simply "move" the resource group from the currently active node to another operational passive node. To do this, right-click on the resource group for your Exchange services and choose Move Resource To Another Node; then choose which node the resources will move to.

What occurs during an intentional move is that the resources within the group are systematically shut down, according to any resource dependencies that the resources might have (see Chapter 6). So the Exchange services shut down in an order that is approximately the opposite of how they started up.

1. First, the services are shut down and then the clustered resources such as the Exchange server name and IP address are taken offline.
2. Next, the ownership of the resources is switched from the currently active node to the new node.
3. The resources are brought back online again.

All of these steps are covered in more detail in Chapter 6. For our discussion here, the failover can happen within seconds for the cluster resources but will take longer for the Exchange services and its data operations (mounting the databases, for example).

Unplanned Failovers with Clustered Exchange

For an unplanned failover, there is no graceful shutdown of the active node. Instead, the assumption is that the physical node, its underlying operating system, or a critical component has been compromised, so the cluster has to recover.

To do this, the cluster will validate that the active node has in fact failed and that the remaining nodes are suitable to resume service (as described in Chapter 6). What is important to remember for our discussion is that the Exchange databases are potentially not in a data-consistent state due to the hard outage of the original node. When the new clustered node brings the Exchange services back online, it will gain access to the clustered storage, bring the network name and IP address online, and then begin restarting the Exchange services. But when the Exchange services start, they will likely find the databases in the same state as if you had a single physical, nonclustered, Exchange server and simply powered it off without shutting down first. Perhaps the databases are completely valid or perhaps not. Either way, the file system may need to invoke CHKDSK to validate the file system blocks, before the Exchange databases can attempt to be mounted. After that process, which can be lengthy on its own, Exchange may need to validate the integrity of the databases (refer to the sidebar "How Exchange Logs Work—for Consistency's Sake"). After the databases are confirmed as consistent and the available transaction logs are played forward, the remaining Exchange services can start and the failover is "complete."

How Exchange Logs Work—for Consistency's Sake

Like other database application servers such as SQL Server (Chapter 8), it is primarily because of Exchange's sensitivity to abrupt service outages that it has a transactional database to begin with. This means that all the physical operations of the Exchange databases are first written to the Exchange database log files. Then, on a regular schedule and as I/O allows, the records in those log files are played into the active database itself.

In this way, when the services resume after a hard outage, the last transactions with the database can be compared with the last entries in the log files. If there are discrepancies, perhaps the last entries in the log should be "played forward" into the database or the database can be "rolled back" to ensure consistency with the logs. Once the database and the logs are consistent, and `Eseutil.exe` assures the services that the database has integrity, the Exchange store can come back online.

Challenges with SCC

There are admittedly some challenges with assuring the availability of Exchange with an SCC. Many of these stem from the architecture of the failover cluster or MSCS itself, namely the single instance of the data within the shared storage.

NOTE When we refer to a single and shared instance of storage within a Windows failover cluster, it is intended to mean the single LUN that is presented to the cluster. Certainly, with mirrored arrays at the storage layer, or using asynchronous replication, there might be more than one physical copy of the data. But because mirroring and replication always ensure that the copies are in sync, there is always only one logical instance of the data and it is only visible to one of the clustered nodes at a time. The punch line is that if that one shared Exchange database becomes corrupted at a database level, then any storage-based mirrors will not help you because your only instance (all storage copies) of the data is invalid.

Failover Challenges with SCC

As described earlier in this chapter, the process of moving ownership of the clustered resources from one node to another can happen in milliseconds (ms). Bringing up core resources like the synthetic server name and IP will also usually take less than a few seconds. Unfortunately, the actual amount of time it takes storage to come online and the clustered Exchange instance to start does not always have a finite and predictable value, which can affect your RTO and SLAs (see Chapter 2 for recovery time objective and service level agreement guidance). Reasons for the unpredictable amount of time to bring the database online can potentially include CHKDSK for the file system, ESEUTIL for the Exchange database itself, and the play-forward of any available transaction logs. Not every Exchange recovery will require the use of either CHKDSK or ESEUTIL, but they will all require log file playback, and that in turn has an unpredictable effect on failover time because the number of pending logs will vary according to when the last backup was done, how busy the server was, and several other factors.

While Exchange is self-healing in many scenarios, the actual amount of time for SCC failover within a failover cluster can be unpredictable and is therefore less desirable. Compounding that challenge is the growing size of mailboxes and supported users that are being offered with Exchange 2007 and 2010. With that increase in scale, the overall recovery time during a cluster failover becomes even less predictable.

Storage Challenges with SCC

It is the shared (storage) resource underneath the cluster that causes some of the challenges and in fact the name "single-copy cluster"—there is only one instance of the data (regardless of the number of clustered nodes).

Unfortunately, this causes a single point of failure (SPOF). If the shared storage array were to fail or becomes corrupted, all the clustered services and virtualized Exchange servers are impacted. The single copy of the data is not available, regardless of what physical node the virtualized Exchange server is attempting to run on. Because of that, it is common to make the storage array redundant by block-level array mirroring (and usually with multipath I/O and dual network switches), as seen in Chapter 3.

The challenge, even with all the storage redundancy, is the single logical copy of the data that is available to the Exchange, regardless of whether the actual blocks are mirrored across arrays or spread across spindles. Within an SCC, there is still only one copy of each Exchange database. And if that database were to become corrupted, all of the storage redundancy in the world is simply assuring the availability of a corrupted database. And as more and more users retain more of their information in their inboxes, the size of mailboxes and Exchange databases continues to increase, which exacerbates the potential impact to your end users due to database corruption in our single copy.

The only answer to addressing corruption concerns in the past was a good backup solution, with robust checking of the integrity of the database using ESEUTIL or other means. It is outside the scope of this book to talk about ESEUTIL, other than acknowledging its role as an integrity checker and what was discussed in Chapter 4 (concerning Microsoft backup technologies such as Data Protection Manager and its use of ESEUTIL in the backup process).

Location Challenges with SCC

The other caveat of running Exchange, or any other application, within a traditional failover cluster is that the entire multinode solution must usually reside within a single datacenter and is therefore susceptible to site-wide crises. To overcome this, you can physically separate the clustered nodes across some distance, with a few considerations:

- Cluster heartbeat
- Disk mirroring
- Disk replication

As discussed in Chapter 6, prior to Windows Server 2008, while you could physically separate the two clustered nodes, there was a nonconfigurable heartbeat that had to connect the clustered nodes with a 500 ms timeout value. While one-half second is short for us, it is an eternity for clustered nodes and was the first trigger for determining server failover conditions. With the previously nonconfigurable heartbeat value, there was a short practical limit to how far the nodes could be separated, even with high-bandwidth connections, such as across a campus or downtown. The heartbeat timeout became configurable with Windows Server 2008, though the recommended best practice is still under 250 ms between clustered nodes.

If the nodes are separated, you also need to contend with ensuring that each node has its own copy of the storage. Without that replication, one node would have the shared storage in close proximity but the other node would not, as shown in Figure 7.2.

FIGURE 7.2
A split cluster with nonduplicated storage

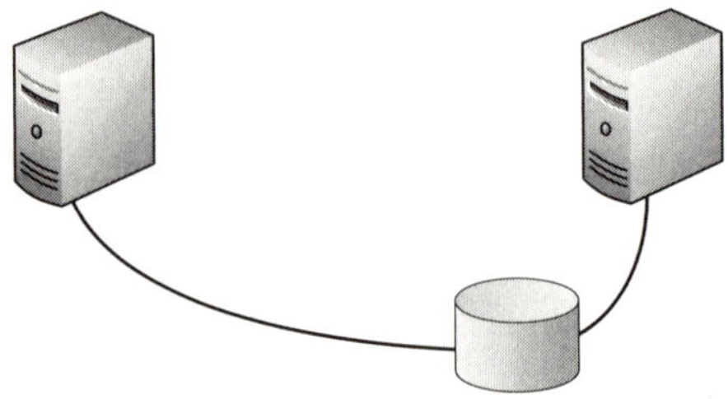

In Figure 7.2, if the left node were to fail, everything would be okay since the surviving node on the right has the clustered storage available. But if the right side of the solution were to have a site-level crisis, the surviving node on the left has no data. Because of this, physically separated SCC environments should always use completely redundant storage arrays and switches, as you saw earlier in Figure 7.1.

Unfortunately, synchronously mirrored storage, as discussed in Chapter 3, has a finite limit to how far the storage arrays can be separated without degrading the responsiveness of the storage solution and thereby the performance of the Exchange server. For this reason, you might initially consider geo-clustering the solution, as discussed in Chapter 6, where a software-based asynchronous replication solution is used to replicate the "shared storage" from a host level. The cluster and the SCC implementation of Exchange still see a single logical copy of the data, but unbeknownst to even the cluster services, the storage is actually locally stored instead of shared, with a copy on each physical node, as seen in Figure 7.3.

FIGURE 7.3
Geo-clustered Exchange using host-based replication

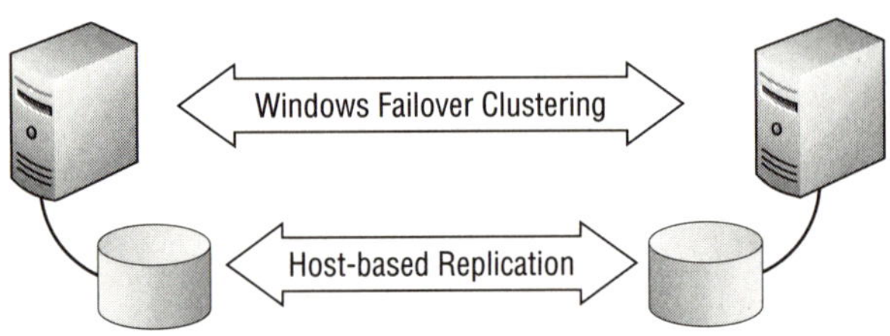

The geo-clustering option in Figure 7.3 may look interesting at first glance, but you can use it only at the risk of some supportability challenges. As we will see in the rest of the chapter, there are much better ways to stretch Exchange across sites than this.

SINGLE-COPY LIMITATIONS OF SCC

Many of the limitations of running Exchange within clustering still come back to the heartbeat and other characteristics of running within Windows Server cluster services. Even with the recent configurability of that heartbeat after Windows Server 2008, the reality of all SCC configurations is that a single logical copy of the Exchange databases exists.

NOTE Ultimately, you could deploy redundant storage on expensive arrays with multiple clustered nodes, and a corruption of the single and shared database could keep the entire solution offline. You really aren't providing high availability for the Exchange data, only the Exchange service. For that reason, Microsoft has stopped supporting SCC configurations after Exchange Server 2007.

Exchange 2007 Continuous Replication

As we just mentioned, due to the challenges with SCC and the reality of a single logical copy of the Exchange databases, where potential corruption trumped all the other likely server outage issues, SCC is supported in Exchange 2007 but gone as of Exchange 2010.

With Exchange 2007, the push began to solve the availability issues within Exchange via built-in replication. This is great evidence supporting one of our core concepts from Chapter 1 on the evolution of data protection and availability. Originally, the high availability needs of email might be met externally to the application (Exchange Server), via Microsoft clustering (Chapter 6) or asynchronous replication (Chapter 3) with failover. But as the original product evolves, those data protection and availability needs are addressed by the original product. In the case of Exchange Server 2007, three built-in continuous replication methods were provided to address three kinds of availability needs:

- LCR—Local continuous replication
- CCR—Cluster continuous replication
- SCR—Standby continuous replication (introduced in Service Pack 1)

How Does Continuous Replication Work?

In all three cases, the foundation of Exchange replication is the log files for the Exchange databases. By replicating the log files to other Exchange hosts with additional copies of each database, corruption within one physical instance of a database is not passed on to the other copies, as it would be with file- or host-based or storage- or block-based replication, as discussed in Chapter 3. As a happy coincidence, it turns out that replicating the Exchange logs is also the most efficient way to replicate the Exchange data—more than block-, byte-, or file-based replication technologies. In those other methods, both the log elements and the database elements have to traverse the network. In the case of Exchange replication, only the log elements regularly traverse the network (not including the initial database seeding). Updates to the databases are done by replaying the logs into each local instance of the database after the replication is complete. To be more specific, after the database is initially seeded and replication is enabled, this is how Exchange replication works:

1. The Microsoft Exchange Replication service on the source server hosting the active copy of the database creates a read-only, hidden, and secure share for the database's log directory, which enables the other target mailbox servers that host a passive copy of the database to copy the log files from the source server.

2. The Microsoft Exchange Replication service on the target server subscribes to Windows file system notifications on the source share, and it is notified by the file system when a new log file exists.
3. The target's Log Copier copies the logs from the Source Log directory into the Inspector directory.
4. The target's Log Inspector rigorously inspects each log, ensuring that the log was not physically corrupted during transmission, and can retry the replication request up to three times if necessary. After passing inspection, the log then drops into the Replica Log directory.
5. The target's Log Replayer then applies each log to the local instance of the database, also called the passive database copy.

Seeding a Database

Throughout this chapter, we will talk about how Exchange database replication works by continually pushing or pulling transaction logs between replication partners and applying those transactions to the secondary copies of the database. But we should acknowledge we're assuming that the secondary database is ready to receive the changes.

Seeding is the process by which the secondary copies of the database are created on the secondary servers and initially populated with data. Often, this is done automatically when creating a new database on the primary and its copies on the secondary servers. There are a few scenarios where you may wish to manually seed the database instead (especially if you are configuring replication across a slow network connection).

For the initial replication and creation of the new database copies in Exchange 2007, if the first log that created the original database is still on the replication source, the initial replication will copy that log and the replay will create the new database at the replication target. This approach makes it easy for new databases that include replication.

If the initial transaction log no longer exists because the initial database has been in use for a while, then you can use the `Update-StorageGroupCopy` cmdlet.

For more information on database seeding, check out:

Exchange 2007 `http://technet.microsoft.com/library/bb124706.aspx`

Exchange 2010 `http://technet.microsoft.com/library/dd335158.aspx`

Local Continuous Replication (LCR)

The "L" in LCR stands for "local" in local continuous replication. LCR refers to replication within a single Exchange server, whereby a single physical Exchange server has two disks that will each have their own copies of the Exchange database and logs.

How LCR Works

As described in the last section, the logs are replicated between the instance of the database on one disk and the instance on the other disk (within the same server). After each instance of the database has new and valid logs, each will apply the logs to its copy of the database in short order. The result is two disks within the same server, each with its own copy of the Exchange database.

At first glance, this might appear to be software-based mirroring of two disks. Is it really that much different than letting the OS mirror two spindles or arrays? Yes, because if you mirror at the storage or disk level, only one logical database exists. The single database may reside on a disk that now has redundancy in its actual blocks and spindles, but if the database were to become corrupted, the Exchange server is done. By using LCR, you can survive a spindle-level failure (like what mirroring delivers), but also a physical database integrity issue. Figure 7.4 compares what a simple two-spindle solution looks like in an LCR configuration (on the left) and a disk-mirrored pair (on the right). Of course, on a real Exchange server, there might be separate spindles and RAID configurations for the database and log areas. But for this example, what is important is to understand what LCR is attempting to solve for—physical database corruption and single-spindle failure within a server.

FIGURE 7.4
Local continuous replication (LCR) in Exchange 2007, compared with disk mirroring

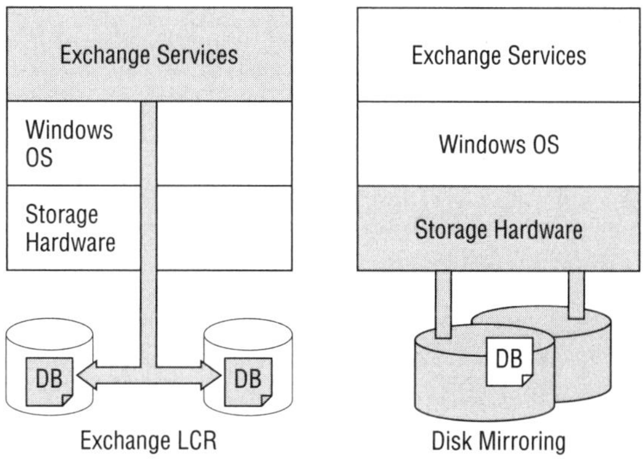

NOTE Be aware that LCR is only available in Exchange 2007. LCR was not available in Exchange 2003, and LCR is not available in Exchange 2010.

TASK 1: GETTING STARTED WITH LCR

Enabling LCR within an Exchange 2007 server is straightforward. In this example, our initial production environment has two Exchange servers running, one with Exchange Server 2007 SP2 and the other with Exchange 2010. We will be using the Exchange 2007 server, which has three storage groups.

From the Exchange Management Console (EMC), go to a storage group that you wish to make resilient, in this case, the Accounting Storage Group.

1 In the left pane, expand the Server Configuration ➤ Mailbox containers in the tree.

2. In the upper box, select the Exchange 2007 server that you wish to manage (in our case, the only one).

3. In the lower part of the console, we can now see the three storage groups, and we can see that each of them has one database, as shown in Figure 7.5.

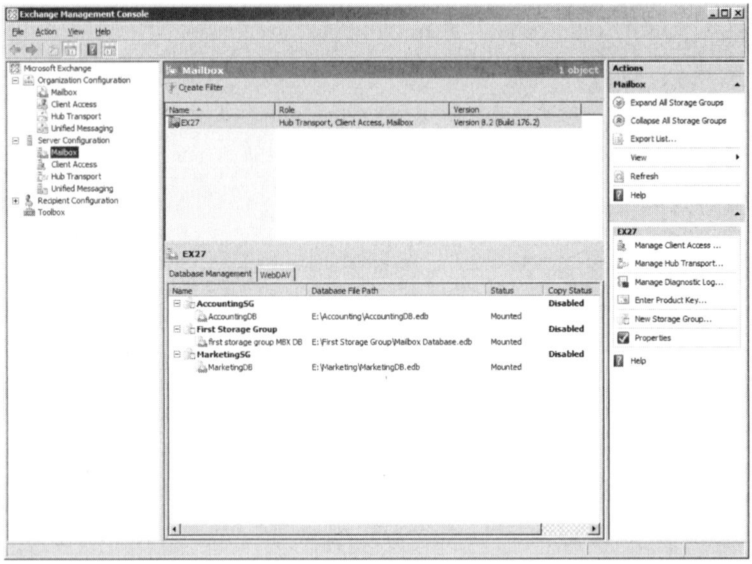

FIGURE 7.5
An Exchange 2007 server with three storage groups

4. By selecting the storage group that we wish to manage, we will see storage group–specific actions in the right pane. One of those options is Enable Local Continuous Replication. Alternatively, you can right-click on the storage group that you wish to replicate. One of the options in the context menu is Enable Local Continuous Replication.
5. Either method brings us to the LCR wizard for Enabling Storage Group Local Continuous Replication, where we can see the AccountingSG storage group, which contains the AccountingDB database, which is held in the `E:\Accounting` directory on my server.

NOTE Traditionally, a best practice for Microsoft Exchange and other transactional database servers is to have a minimum of three disks or arrays: one for the operating system and binaries, one for the databases, and one for the logs. Because LCR will have a second set of databases and a second set of logs, add two more disks or arrays to an Exchange server using LCR.

6. On the second screen of the wizard, the LCR wizard will default to putting the replicated files to a buried subdirectory under the C: drive. To change the defaults, click the browse button next to each of the prompts, and select where the LCR replicated copies will be. Initially, we are selecting where the replicated system files and logs will be.
7. On the third-screen of the wizard, we specify where to store a replicated database, as shown in Figure 7.6.
8. The fourth screen simply confirms our selections. Click Enable. If there are no errors, the Accounting Storage Group and its associated database are now enabled for LCR.

Now back within the EMC and with our Mailbox server still selected in the top-center box, we can see a fourth column within the lower-center box for our storage groups and databases that shows us the Copy Status. For our LCR-enabled storage group, Accounting, we should see a status of Healthy, whereas the other storage groups display a status of Disabled, as shown in Figure 7.7. Notice in the lower-right corner of Figure 7.7, we see controls for the replication in the Task menu. These controls are also available by right-clicking on the LCR replicated storage group.

FIGURE 7.6
Defining the LCR secondary database

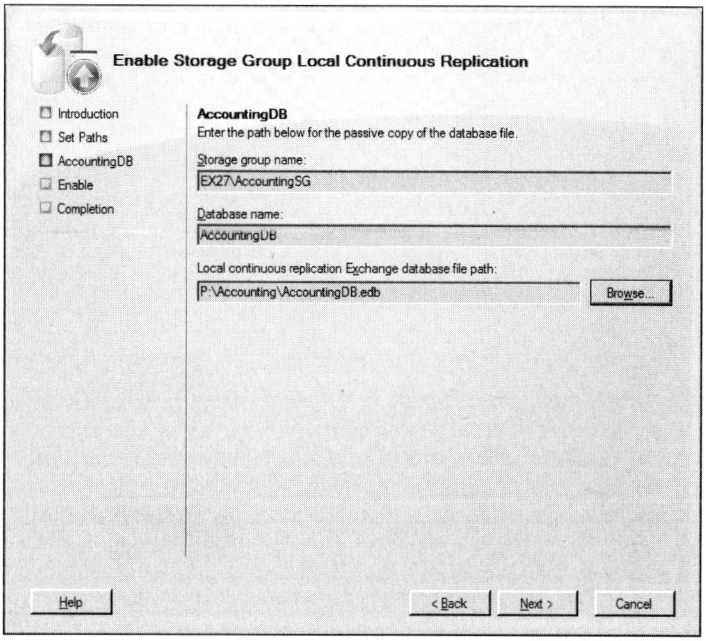

FIGURE 7.7
Exchange console, with LCR active

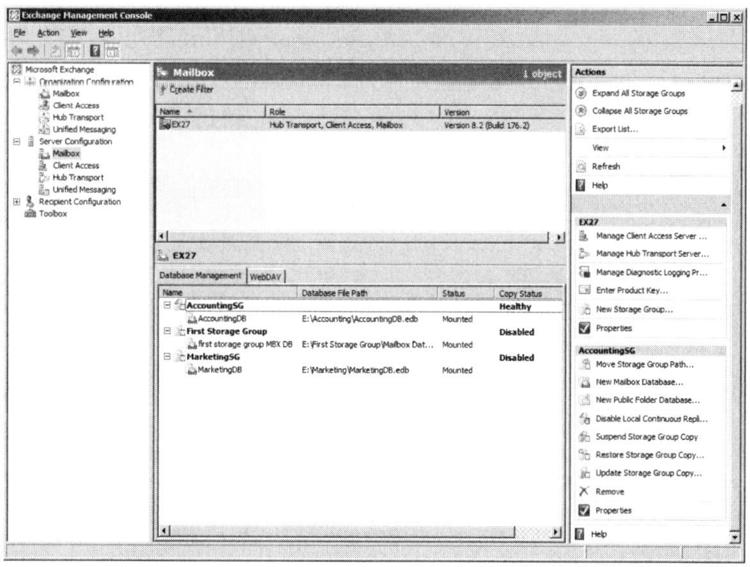

For more information on the state of the LCR mirror, we can right-click on the storage group and click Properties. The only other tab for the SG properties is the LCR Status, which will reflect not only whether the copy is healthy, but also its current status, queue lengths, and event times for replication.

With everything now operational, we have two databases on two separate disks in the event of spindle or corruption issues with the primary storage. To test this, we can use the Exchange Management Shell (PowerShell) to switch the active database by first dismounting the database and then using this command: `Restore-StorageGroupCopy -Identity "AccountingSG" -ReplaceLocations`.

Notice that since LCR knows of the pair already, the only real parameter is the name of the storage group being switched, `AccountingSG` in this case. If the Exchange Management Shell confirms for us that no errors occurred, we can mount our database to complete the switch.

Cluster Continuous Replication

In the last section, we discussed local continuous replication (LCR), which replicated the Exchange logs and maintained two databases within a single Exchange server. The goal was database availability, as well as being able to survive both database corruption as well as a storage-level failure.

Cluster continuous replication (CCR) uses a similar log replication model but does so between two separate Exchange servers. CCR provides the same type of database corruption protection because only the logs are replicated and therefore physical corruption on one database would not be replicated to the other. But instead of protecting within a single server (LCR) and offering availability against storage-layer issues, CCR protects against whole-server and data failure issues.

How CCR Works

CCR combines two very different availability technologies in order to provide an effective high-availability solution for Exchange Server 2007:

- Microsoft clustering
- Exchange log replication

As discussed earlier in the chapter, the legacy Exchange cluster, also referred to as an SCC, utilizes Microsoft Cluster Services (MSCS) to provide failover resiliency for the clustered Exchange services. But as we mentioned, there is a significant flaw in the SCC clustered model: the single copy of the database. The single copy of the database makes SCC susceptible to a variety of scenarios that could bring down the whole server, including database corruption (of the single database) and an outage of the shared-storage solution.

Interestingly, physical database corruption and storage issues are the two protectable aspects of Exchange log replication, so CCR uses this replication to mitigate the two flaws in SCC and provide a more resilient Exchange cluster.

As shown in Figure 7.8, the *top* of a CCR configuration is a Microsoft cluster using MSCS to provide failover capabilities of the Exchange services. The *bottom* of the CCR configuration shows Exchange log replication to ensure that each node of the cluster has its own copy of the database, which is isolated from corruption from the other node and does not have a SPOF.

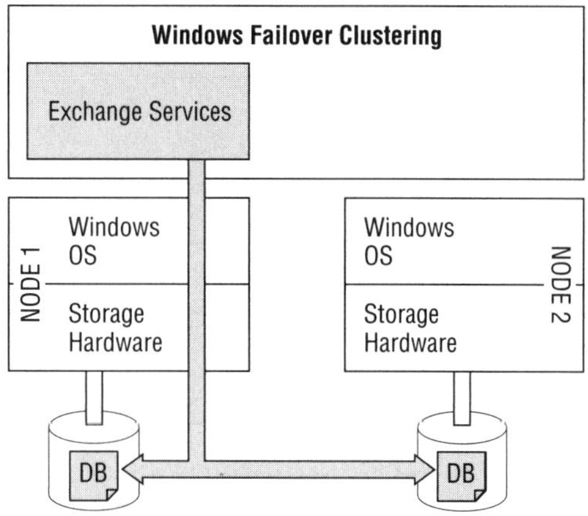

FIGURE 7.8
Cluster continuous replication

Prior to Exchange 2007, and even in its early days before IT implementers understood why CCR was compelling, you could achieve similar results by using MSCS "on the top" and third-party, software-based replication technologies (see Chapter 3) to replicate the storage. But CCR is superior to those application-agnostic replication mechanisms because while the host-based replication does provide each node with its own copy of the storage, they are linked in real-time replication so that logical database corruption is passed from the active node to the passive node(s). In addition, those third-party solutions might take several minutes to completely fail over, because they have to clean up the database during the resumption of clustered service on the secondary node. Exchange log replication updates the passive databases in its normal transactional method, so the database is almost always in a consistent state and suitable for near immediate resumption of service, if required. In addition to the capability differences described earlier, third-party asynchronous replication of Exchange databases is not supported by Microsoft (see `http://support.microsoft.com/kb/904845`).

For those reasons, many environments that may have chosen to utilize third-party asynchronous host-based replication for their Exchange 2003 availability needs are now using the built-in availability solutions for Exchange 2007 and 2010.

Task 2: Preparing to Install CCR into a Windows Server 2008 Cluster

To deploy CCR in an Exchange 2007 environment, we would normally start by walking an Exchange administrator through what may be an unfamiliar task of building a Windows failover cluster. In a CCR configuration, there is no shared storage.

Each node of the cluster needs to have a few features, roles, and dependent elements installed that are similar to the prerequisites of most Exchange 2007 installations:

- Feature: Failover Clustering
- Feature: Windows PowerShell
- Feature: Windows Process Activation Service
- Role: Web Server (IIS), plus a few nondefault additions:
  - Application Development: ISAPI extensions

- Security: Basic Authentication
- Security: Windows Authentication
- IIS 6 Management Compatibility: IIS 6 Metabase Compatibility
- IIS 6 Management Compatibility: IIS 6 Management Console

Optionally, you can install the prerequisites using Windows PowerShell. The following command lines can be run in a single batch file to consistently configure the Exchange server clustered mailbox server role prerequisites:

```
ServerManagerCmd -i PowerShell
ServerManagerCmd -i Failover-Clustering
ServerManagerCmd -i Web-Server
ServerManagerCmd -i Web-ISAPI-Ext
ServerManagerCmd -i Web-Metabase
ServerManagerCmd -i Web-Lgcy-Mgmt-Console
ServerManagerCmd -i Web-Basic-Auth
ServerManagerCmd -i Web-Windows-Auth
```

Or, if you prefer, the Exchange team has provided XML answer files for each of the Exchange 2007 server roles (using `ServerManagerCmd`) at `http://msexchangeteam.com/files/12/attachments/entry448276.aspx`.

Our clustered nodes are now ready to host Exchange Server 2007 and the Clustered Mailbox Service role within our Exchange environment.

NOTE The Clustered Mailbox Server (CMS) role is the only role that is cluster-able in Exchange 2007. The other Exchange roles, such as Hub Transport or Client Access, will need to be deployed on standalone servers and can be made highly available by load balancing across multiple instances.

Task 3: Building the Windows Failover Cluster

For our purposes, we will create a new two-node cluster using the same methods described in Chapter 6. Refer to the section "Building Your First Cluster" in Chapter 6 and its related tasks for more detail on how to build a Windows Server 2008 failover cluster.

To build the initial Windows failover cluster:

1. Start with two domain-joined physical nodes that have both public and private networking, for the corporate network and cluster heartbeats, respectively, and at least one additional storage volume besides the OS drive each:
   - EX27CCR1
   - EX27CCR2
2. Start the Failover Cluster Manager from the Administrative Tools menu.
3. Validate both nodes at the same time, using the Validate A Configuration Wizard. The wizard should finish by reporting that the nodes are able to be clustered, except that some of the storage tests will likely fail with an informational warning that no cluster-

suitable shared storage was found (which is correct for a CCR configuration), as shown in Figure 7.9.

FIGURE 7.9
Validate A Configuration Wizard

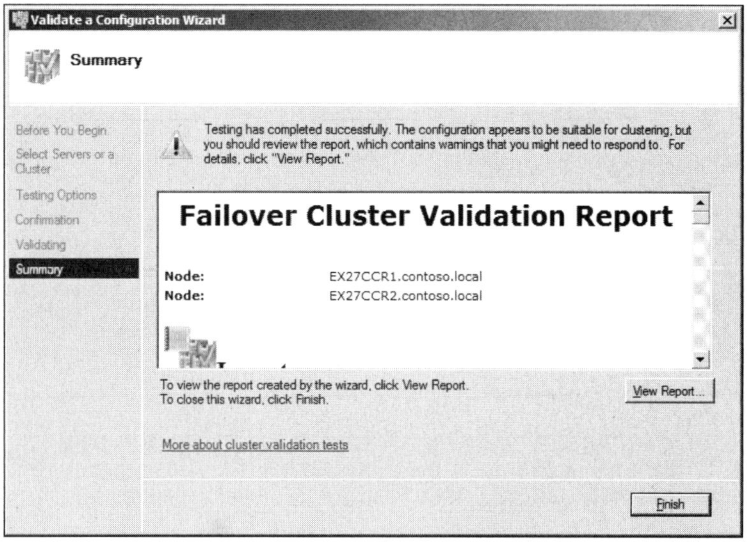

4. Build a Node Majority cluster with the two nodes, which in my case is named EX27CCRcluster.

NOTE When you initially finish building the cluster, it will show an informational warning because you do not have an odd number of voting members in the quorum. In a shared-storage cluster (like an SCC discussed earlier), you would have a shared quorum drive as the third voting member. In this case, we will build a file-share majority set so that the CCR configuration has no shared dependencies.

5. Create a file share on a node outside of the cluster, which will serve as the third voting member of our cluster. For this example, I created a file share off the local domain controller: `\\EDC\Ex27ccrQ`.
6. To modify the cluster configuration so that it will use the new file share, right-click on cluster in the left pane of the Failover Cluster Manager and select More Actions ➤ Configure Cluster Quorum Settings.
7. In the Configure Cluster Quorum Wizard, advance to the Select Quorum Configuration screen and choose Node And File Share Majority, as shown in Figure 7.10.
8. On the next screen, type in or browse to the file share that you created.
9. A confirmation screen will appear; after you click Finish, the cluster will be modified to use the file share as a third voting member of the cluster. The result will be a resilient Windows failover cluster (Figure 7.11) that is ready for Exchange 2007 CCR deployment.

With a functioning cluster built, we still need to prepare the nodes for running Exchange Server 2007. Two last steps should be done to prepare for CCR:

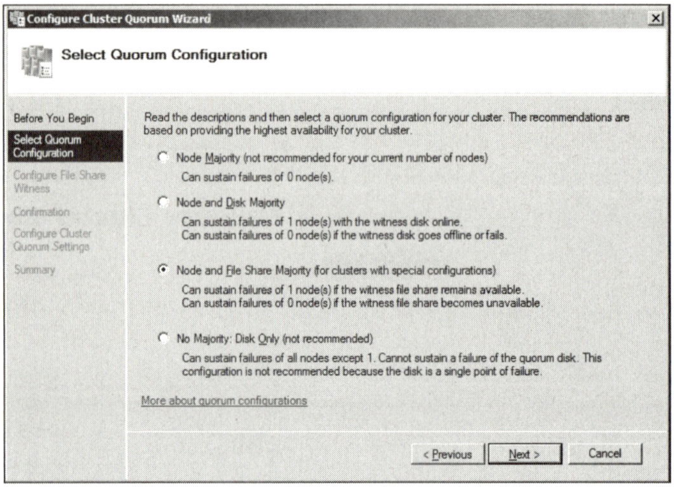

FIGURE 7.10 Configuring the cluster quorum for file share majority

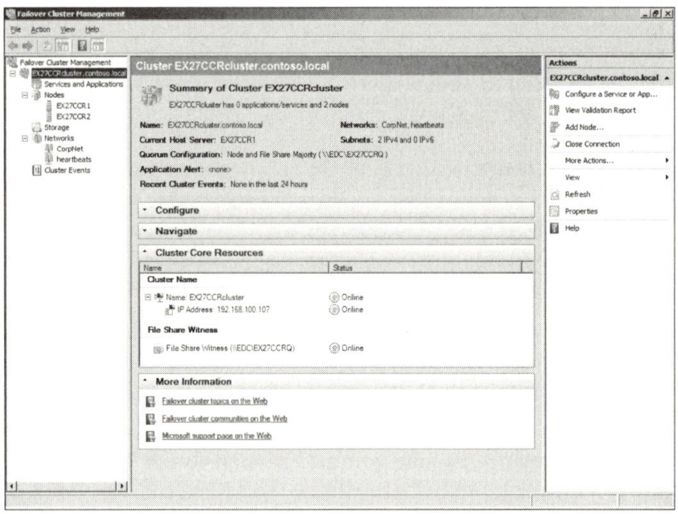

FIGURE 7.11 Our Windows failover cluster, ready for Exchange

10. Be sure that each node has additional (nonshared) storage with the same drive letters. In my configuration, each node has:
    - C: for the OS and binaries
    - E: for the Exchange databases
    - L: for the Exchange logs
11. Run the Validate A Configuration Wizard on the cluster again to be sure that the cluster is completely ready on its own.

TASK 4: INSTALLING CCR ONTO WINDOWS SERVER 2008 CLUSTER NODE 1

On the first node that will be running Exchange 2007, confirm that the node is fully patched for Windows Server and then run SETUP.EXE from your Exchange installation media. For this example, I am running the evaluation edition of Exchange 2007 with SP2.

NOTE If installing into production or on multiple servers, you can slipstream the Exchange service packs, meaning that the SP components can be intermixed with the original server installation media on a file share, so that you do not have to update the Exchange install afterward. The evaluation software that was used in these exercises was Microsoft Exchange Server 2007 with SP2 already included.

With the prerequisites installed (and confirmed by the Exchange installer splash screen), select Install Microsoft Exchange Server 2007. After the introduction and licensing screens, as well as the offer to enable error reporting, we are finally presented with an Exchange Setup screen with two choices:

- Typical Exchange Server Installation
- Custom Exchange Server Installation

At this point, follow these steps:

1. Select a Custom installation.
2. For our first node, choose Active Clustered Mailbox Role, as shown in Figure 7.12. On this screen, you can optionally also choose a different location for the Exchange Server application binaries.

FIGURE 7.12
Installing the CCR Active Clustered Mailbox Role

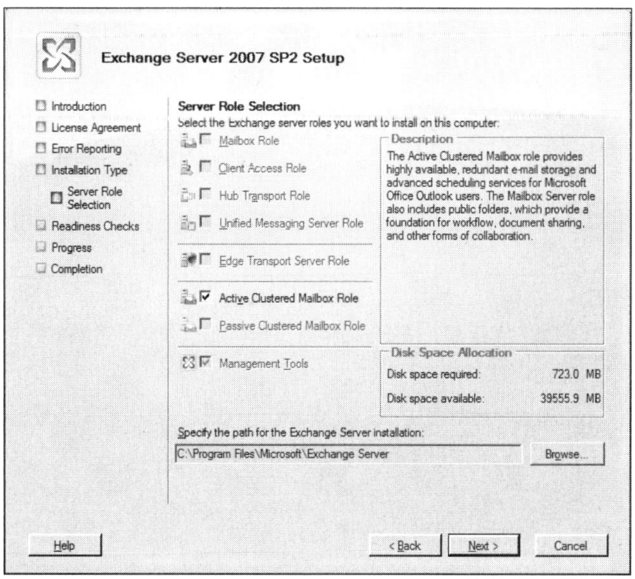

3. Because you have selected a clustered installation, you are asked which kind of cluster you will be installing:

   - Cluster Continuous Replication
   - Single Copy Cluster

   Choose Cluster Continuous Replication (CCR).

NOTE Earlier in the chapter ("Getting Started with SCCs"), we stated that SCC and CCR have similar installation steps, which are covered in Tasks 4 and 5.

If you are installing an SCC deployment of Exchange 2007, the steps are the same except that in step 3 above, for SCC configurations choose shared storage within the cluster, while for CCR configurations choose local drives whose drive letters match between the nodes.

4. On the same screen, choose the name of the mailbox server. This is the logical name that the clients will connect to.
5. Still on the same screen, choose the drive and directory where the database files will reside. In our case, each of our nodes has an E: drive with an `E:\ExecMail` empty directory. We will specify that directory, as shown in Figure 7.13.

FIGURE 7.13
Exchange 2007 CCR cluster setup

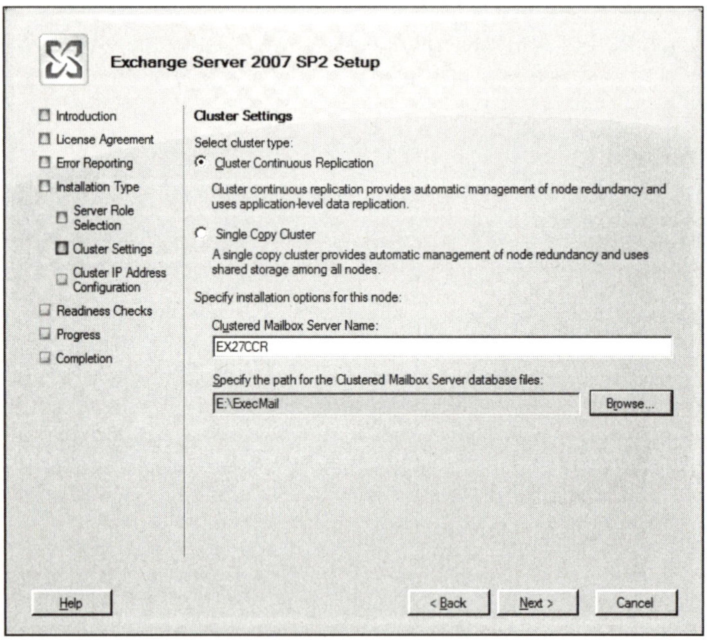

6. The next screen prompts you for the Cluster IP address. You have the option of using a static address (recommended) or a DHCP address within our IPv4 network, as well as using an IPv6 network. If your normal server deployment method is to use DHCP for the server IPs (perhaps with reservations), you can choose DHCP for the clustered mailbox server. You will be prompted for the name of the clustered network you want to use, such

as Corporate, Heartbeat, or Backbone from our Chapter 6 installation. Otherwise, select a static IPv4 address as you would for any other production server, as shown in Figure 7.14.

FIGURE 7.14
Exchange 2007 CCR networking

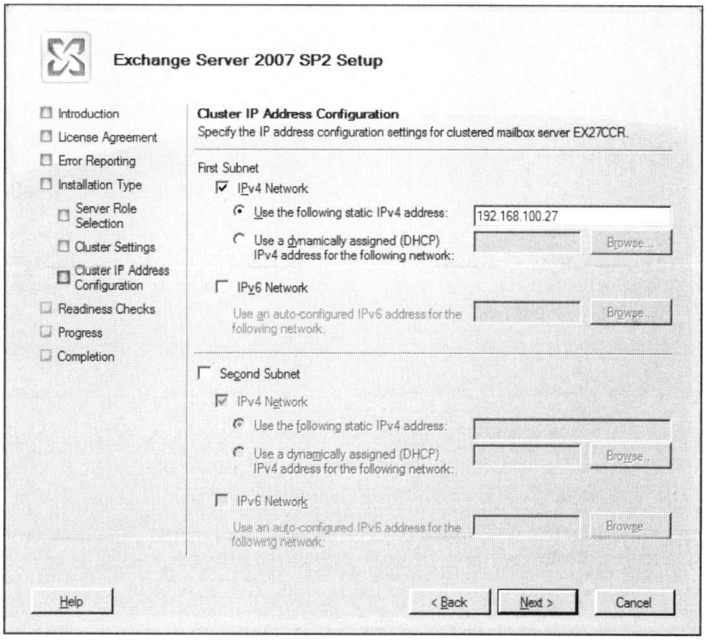

NOTE While IPv6 is the future, I recommend disabling it for these sample exercises, as I found it problematic during setup of Windows Failover Clustering. For details on how to disable IPv6 and the Teredo networking functions, refer to the sidebar "IPv6 and Teredo Errors" n Chapter 6.

7. The installation wizard will then scroll through several prerequisite checks and install components. When complete, the Clustered Mailbox Server will be installed onto our first node.

One thing to note is that if you check what has happened within the Failover Cluster Management console, you will find that the virtual Exchange service has been created, with the appropriate name, IP, and Exchange services. However, Node1 is the only potential owner of the CMS role because the other node(s) do not have access to the application binaries or configuration. For this reason, we need to install Exchange onto each node that will be a potential host for this service.

TASK 5: INSTALLING CCR ONTO WINDOWS SERVER 2008 CLUSTER NODE 2

The Exchange CCR installation requires a separate but very abbreviated installation onto each node of the cluster. Start by ensuring the node is up-to-date with Windows patches and then running `SETUP.EXE` and moving through the licensing and other screens:

1. Select Passive Clustered Mailbox as the role, and specify the same path for the installation directories as the first node (`C:\Program Files\`).

2. After the prerequisites are confirmed, click Install to begin installing Exchange onto the passive node.

Because this is a passive node within a cluster, the installation will simply install the proper Exchange Server binaries onto the node so that it is suitable for becoming the Clustered Mailbox Server (CMS) role. Additionally, node 2 will now be added as a potential owner or host of the clustered Exchange instance and its cluster resources.

When everything is complete, both nodes should be rebooted, verified again for patches from Windows Update, and potentially rebooted again, starting with the passive node. This ensures that the CMS remains running on the active node while the passive node is updated. When everything is complete on the passive node, use the Exchange Management Console to switch the active and passive nodes, and then repeat the maintenance process on Node 1, now that it is passive.

The result is a CMS, as seen in the Failover Cluster Management console in Figure 7.15.

FIGURE 7.15
Failover Cluster Management view of Exchange 2007 CCR

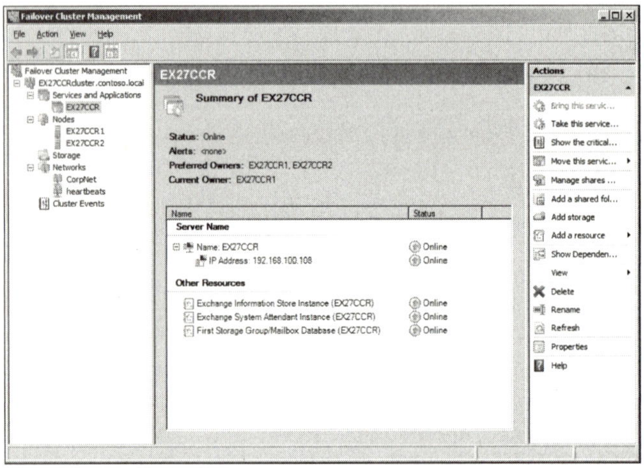

You will actually manage the CMS instance from the Exchange Management Console (GUI) or the Exchange Management Shell (PowerShell). Within the Exchange Management Console, expand the Server Configuration and then Mailbox, and then right-click on the CMS and choose Manage Clustered Mailbox Server. The action is also available in the Actions pane on the right side of the UI if a clustered mailbox server is selected. In either case, the result is a new wizard for managing CMSs within the Exchange 2007 management console. The wizard offers three key tasks:

- Move the clustered mailbox server to a different node
- Start the clustered mailbox server
- Stop the clustered mailbox server

To appreciate the difference between WFC's view of EX27CCR (Figure 7.15), notice how the Exchange Management Console simply sees it as another Exchange server in Figure 7.16.

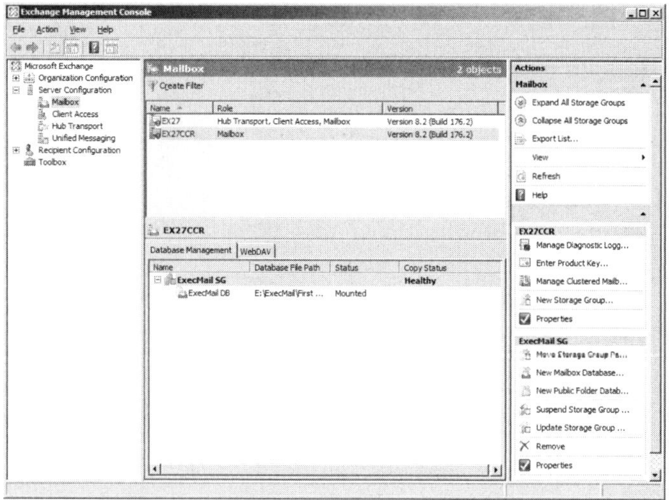

FIGURE 7.16
Exchange Management Console view of CCR

DATA PROTECTION AND BACKUP CONSIDERATIONS WITH CCR

Because a CCR environment provides us with two copies of the same mail database, there are some special considerations when backing those database instances up—assuming that your backup solution supports them. Microsoft System Center Data Protection Manager (Chapter 4) supports the Exchange 2007 CCR backup requirements in both DPM 2007 and DPM 2010. Other backup solutions that leverage Volume Shadow Copy Services (VSS) may also, but many do not so check with your specific backup vendor.

Figure 7.17 shows the data selection screen of DPM 2010 in protecting both a standalone Exchange 2007 server as well as the CCR cluster that was just built.

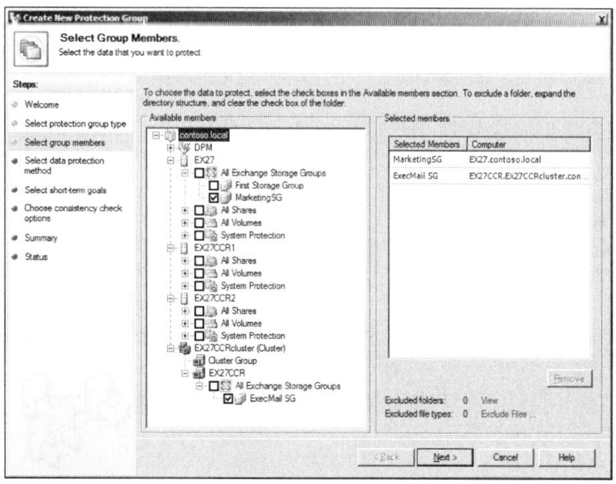

FIGURE 7.17
Exchange data protection in DPM 2010

In examining Figure 7.17, notice the differences between the four server objects for protection:

With EX27 (the standalone server), there are four types of data that can be protected:

- Shares
- Volumes
- System protection
- Exchange storage groups

With EX27CCR1 and EX27CCR2 (the two cluster nodes), there are only three types of data to protect:

- Shares
- Volumes
- System protection

EX27CCRcluster (the Windows failover cluster) shows each of the clustered resource groups. Expanding the EX27CCR group, we can see only the Exchange Storage Groups that are clustered:

- Exchange storage groups

After choosing at least one storage group from the standalone Exchange server and the CCR cluster (as shown in Figure 7.17) and clicking Next, we can see the other Exchange-specific screen for DPM 2007 or DPM 2010.

There are typically three behaviors, and a twist, for backup applications that are fully CCR and VSS aware. These enable you to specify whether to:

- Back up the active node of a CCR pair
- Back up the passive node of a CCR pair
- Back up a specific node of a CCR pair, regardless of the active/passive role

The choice of protecting a node by its role as either active or passive is primarily due to your consideration of impacting the production users during the backup. Also, the built-in online maintenance window for the active database might be a factor that drives you to backing up the passive node. Backup applications that can perform Exchange 2007 CCR backups do so with relatively little I/O impact, but it is not zero impact. On heavily utilized Exchange servers, any additional I/O may be undesired. Because of this, your backup solution should provide you with the ability to configure backups from the passive node's database. In this way, your users on the active node will not be impacted while the passive node services your backup.

However, because the passive node is consistently replaying logs from active node, it may not be up to the same point in time for its data. Therefore, your backup may be several minutes behind what is actually on the active node. It is worth noting that even though the database in your backup of a passive node may be behind the active copy's, the backup also gets the log files—so you have not lost data. But after restoring the backup of a passive node, more logs will have to be played forward to bring the database online. The only concern would if there was a large copy queue length and the passive copy were many logs behind in replication. That is the choice that you should make when selecting active or passive backups (if your backup solution supports it).

Alternatively, if your CCR pair is physically separated between buildings with reduced bandwidth between the sites, you may wish to specify a particular physical node to be backed up because the backup server is in the same site, regardless of whether that node is currently active or passive. Most administrators prefer to back up the CCR node that is on the same gigabit switch as their backup server, rather than back up the other CCR node that is across a lesser network connection.

Earlier, I mentioned that CCR-capable backup solutions may offer up to three choices, plus a twist. The choices are active, passive, or node-specific. The twist is the behavior of the backup application if you chose to protect a passive node and later there isn't one due to a failover. If you are configured to protect the passive node in a two-node CCR but one of the nodes has failed, then the surviving node is "active" and there is no passive node for the backup application to reach out to. Some backup applications will offer an additional behavior choice for when the passive node is unavailable:

- Back up the active node
- Let the backup job fail

As an example, these choices are available in Data Protection Manager (Chapter 4), as shown in Figure 7.18.

FIGURE 7.18
Data protection options for Exchange 2007 CCR

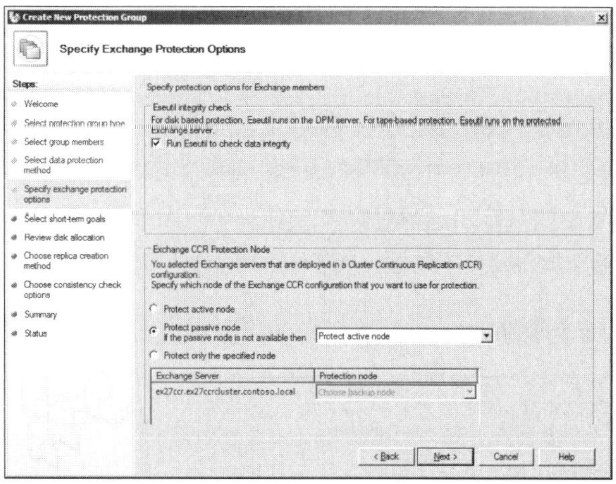

Although there is no universally accepted best practice on whether to protect the active, passive, or specific node, the general consensus when both nodes are in the same IT facility is to back up the passive node (and back up the active node when the passive is not available). You should assess the balance of the backup I/O impact on the production server (likely what encouraged you to target the passive node originally) versus any compliance/recovery mandates that you have of ensuring that your backups continue. Also consider your recovery time goals if you are backing up a passive node that is likely to have a long queue of replication logs to play through.

When and How to Truncate Logs after the Backup

In a standalone Exchange server, the full backup operation always triggers the Exchange server to update its database and truncate its logs. The same process occurs with backups of CCR environments with a slightly different workflow when backing up the passive node of a CCR configuration. The passive node cannot modify the contents of its database other than to replay the log files that have been replicated to it from the active node. Instead, when the Exchange VSS writer is notified of a successful backup from the backup application and its VSS requester, the Replication service on the passive node notifies the Information Store service on the active node of the successful backup. At this point, the active node will note the backup within its own logs, and assess a few criteria for its copy of each log file for the backed-up database:

- Has the log file been backed up?
- Is the log file below the database checkpoint (meaning that the transactions from the log have been successfully applied to the database)?
- Do all other copies of the database copy agree with deletion?

After assessing which logs meet the criteria, the active node is ready to update its database as having been successfully backed up, and the following occurs:

- The Information Store service on the active node will truncate its logs. The truncation will be written as a system event record in the database's log stream.
- Similarly, the passive node will receive the replicated logs that include log truncation records. After the normal inspection process, the passive node will replay the truncation commands, which will update the passive database and truncate the logs on the passive node.

Standby Continuous Replication

So far, we have seen LCR use replication within a single Exchange server to protect against a disk failure. We also saw how to use CCR to protect against a disk, server, or network failure. SCR was introduced with the first Service Pack 1 for Exchange Server 2007 to add a third replication layer of protection for disaster recovery scenarios, such as a complete site failing.

How SCR Works

We again see the same log replication technology used in LCR and CCR to provide another redundant copy of the Exchange database. Like the other replication modes in Exchange 2007, once the SCR node is initially seeded with its database, SCR replicates just the logs between Exchange servers. Then, each Exchange server applies the transactions to its own database, which ensures that database corruption within one database is not propagated to the other instances.

Unlike the members in CCR, which participate in the same failover cluster, SCR sources and targets are specifically not members of the same cluster, nor do they have to be clustered at all. An *SCR replication source* can be:

- A standalone mailbox server
- A clustered mailbox server (CMS) within an SCC cluster
- A clustered mailbox server (CMS) within a CCR cluster

An *SCR replication target* can be:

- A standalone mailbox server, not running LCR on any of its storage groups
- A node of a failover cluster where the CMS role has not been configured anywhere in the cluster

Essentially, the SCR replication target is constantly receiving and replaying log files, similarly to the passive node of a CCR pair. Typically, SCR is usually thought of for long-distance replication and therefore can tolerate a certain amount of latency or lag behind the primary copy of the data on the source. You, as the Exchange administrator, can induce a replay lag in order to have a copy of the mailbox database that is intentionally delayed. This replay lag provides another layer of data restore where changes that might have been enacted on the production source would not yet be propagated to the replication target (like logical corruption of the database, for example).

NOTE CCR is for *server* resiliency; if a server or one if its databases fails, CCR will recover it to a surviving node. SCR is for *datacenter* resiliency.

However, the SCR node is by design always passive and will not automatically fail over. As discussed in Chapter 3 and as we will cover in much greater detail in Chapter 12, that is the difference between a *disaster recovery* (DR) scenario and a *business continuity* (BC) or *high availability* (HA) scenario—automated failover. In fact, because SCR is only a replication model without failover, it supports one-to-many replication, where one source can replicate to multiple targets, even at different locations. SCR is intended for disaster recovery to ensure that the data survives a site-level crisis, but it will require some specific effort to resume service. For that reason, SCR is most often implemented in combination with the automatic HA solution of CCR, as shown in Figure 7.19.

FIGURE 7.19
CCR combined with SCR in Exchange 2007 SP1 or above

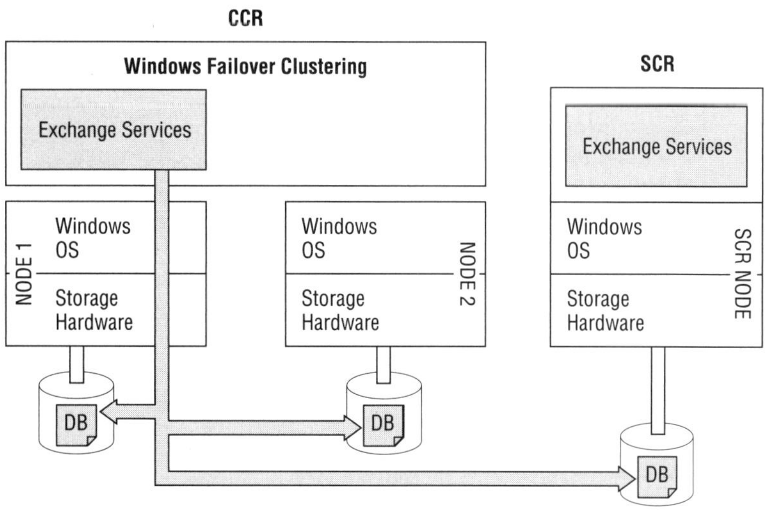

We will first protect our production data sources with SCR in Task 6, and then resume service in Task 7.

Task 6: Getting Started with SCR

First, we will be adding SCR protection to some storage groups on the Exchange servers that we have already been working with in the other tasks of this chapter:

- On our standalone Exchange 2007 server (EX27), we protected the Accounting database with LCR to provide resiliency of that department's mail locally in Task 1. We will protect the Management database with SCR.
- After creating a Clustered Mailbox Server (CMS) on our CCR cluster named EX27CCR in Task 4, we created an ExecMailSG storage group and ExecMailDB database, which we will also protect with SCR.

Along with these existing production Exchange servers, we will need an Exchange 2007 SP1 server or later with the mailbox role installed as our SCR target. As usual, I built these exercises using the TestDrive Windows Server 2008 operating system, the prerequisites listed earlier in Task 2 (except for failover clustering), and the evaluation download of Exchange Server 2007 with Service Pack 2. All of this can be found at `http://TechNet.Microsoft.com/EvalCenter`. In the exercises, this node is called EX27SCR.

NOTE Be sure that the same paths as the production databases and logs are available on the SCR targets. If the database in production is at `D:\MGMT\MgmtDB.edb` and the logs are at `L:\MGMT\`, the `D:\MGMT` and `L:\MGMT` directories must exist on the SCR targets as well.

SCR was delivered in SP1 of Exchange 2007 as a command-line only function, so there are no screens or mouse clicks to deal with. Instead, we will launch the Exchange Management Shell, which is based on Windows PowerShell. The command used is `Enable-StorageGroupCopy`, with a few parameters:

```
-Identity <SourceServer\StorageGroup>
-StandbyMachine <name of SCR target server>
```

This command will enable the copy process, but some configurations may still require seeding of the initial replica. To do this, we can use a similar command, `Update-StorageGroupCopy`, with the same parameters. There are many other parameters and commands related to enabling, disabling, pausing, and resuming replication, all of which have documentation available at `http://technet.microsoft.com/en-us/library/bb124727(EXCHG.80).aspx`.

The previous two commands do not have output that provides a status, other than if an error occurs, so we can use the `Get-StorageGroupCopyStatus` command (with the same parameters again) to view the replication status. Thus, our commands are as follows:

```
Enable-StorageGroupCopy EX27\ManagementSG -StandbyMachine EX27SCR
Get-StorageGroupCopyStatus EX27\ManagementSG -StandbyMachine EX27SCR
```

NOTE Note that the status may take up to 3 minutes to change; see `http://blogs.technet.com/timmcmic/archive/2009/01/22/inconsistent-results-when-enabling-standby-continuous-replication-scr-in-exchange-2007-sp1.aspx`.

In our case, we would run these commands for each of the storage groups that we wish to replicate to our SCR server, so our cluster would be protected with the following:

```
Enable-StorageGroupCopy AlphaMail\ExecutiveSG -StandbyMachine EX27SCR
Get-StorageGroupCopyStatus AlphaMail\ExecutiveSG -StandbyMachine EX27SCR
```

TASK 7: PREPARING THE SCR SERVER FOR RECOVERY

Technically, you could do these steps as part of the actual recovery, or what SCR refers to as activating the copy. But as we will cover in Chapter 12 on disaster recovery and business continuity, we should try to do as much prep work as possible before the crisis. In this case, we will create the temporary recovery objects in Active Directory that will later point to the replicated databases during activation at our DR site. The syntax here provides the DR objects for our Management storage group and database from EX27.

1. Using the Exchange Management Shell, we will start by creating a new storage group on the SCR server, along with a mailbox database.

```
New-StorageGroup -Server EX27SCR -Name drMgmtSG -LogFolderPath ➥
L:\drMgmt -SystemFolderPath L:\drMgmt

New-MailboxDatabase -StorageGroup EX27SCR\drMgmtSG -Name drMgmtDB ➥
-EdbFilePath  D:\drMgmt\drMgmtDB.edb

Mount-Database drMgmtDB
```

2. Next, we will dismount the database and delete the files that were created:

```
Dismount-Database drMgmtDB -Confirm:$False

Del  L:\drMgmt\*.*  /F/Q
```

This gives us the disaster recovery objects that we will use for failing over the Management storage group and database later in the chapter.

TASK 8: ACTIVATING THE SCR COPY

In this last Exchange 2007 exercise, we will assume that our production server or CCR cluster has failed, likely as part of a site-level crisis that occurred at our production facility. To do this, we will open the Exchange Management Console, choose Server Configuration ➢ Mailbox, and click on the production server to dismount the database that will be failing over to the SCR server (in our case, `EX27\ManagementDB`).

Now, we need to bring the SCR copy of the data online and then move the storage group and database paths of the recovery object to point to the correction location:

1. From the Exchange Management Shell, restore the storage group and then check the integrity of the database:

```
Restore-StorageGroupCopy EX27\ManagementSG—-StandbyMachine EX27SCR
```

2. Next, run `ESEUTIL` on the database to dump the database header. Note that if the storage group prefix is the same for the SCR source and the target storage group that will be used, then you don't have to run `ESEUTIL` in Recovery mode.

```
ESEUTIL /mh d:\Mgmt\ManagementDB.edb
```

3. By scrolling up through the output, we will likely see that the database was not properly shut down. To clean this up, look in the log files and note the generation number of the log file. For example, by typing `DIR L:\Mgmt\E??.LOG`, we may see `E05.log` returned.

4. Go into the log directory from the Exchange Management Shell and run ESEUTIL with the /R Exx switch (where xx is the number from the log file, 05 in our case). The /R switch runs ESEUTIL in Recovery mode so that the transaction logs are played back into the database.

    ```
    ESEUTIL /R E05
    ```

5. Run the command on the database again, as we did in step 2:

    ```
    ESEUITL /mh d:\Mgmt\ManagementDB.edb
    ```

6. This time, by scrolling up through the output, we should see that the database is now in a clean shutdown state.

Now that we have a database in a clean shutdown state, we simply need to update Active Directory with the new paths for the storage group and the database, and then mount the database. Pay special attention in the following script that we are essentially pointing the storage group (drMgmtSG) and database (drMgmtDB) on the SCR or disaster recovery server to where the replicated production database is and then mounting the database:

```
Move-StorageGroupPath EX27SCR\drMgmtSG -LogFolderPath L:\Mgmt ➥
-SystemFolderPath L:\Mgmt -ConfigurationOnly

Move-DatabasePath EX27SCR\drMgmtSG\drMgmtDB ➥
-EdbFilePath D:\Mgmt\ManagementDB.edb -ConfigurationOnly

Set-MailboxDatabase EX27SCR\drMgmtSG\drMgmtDB -AllowFileRestore:$True

Mount-Database drMgmtDB
```

Our last activity is simply to move the users over by re-pointing them in Active Directory for all users' mailboxes (except system or attendant) that were in the ManagementDB on the production EX27 server, and point them to the drMgmtDB database on the EX27SCR server, using the following command:

```
Get-Mailbox -Database EX27\ManagementSG\ManagementDB | ➥
Where {$_.ObjectClass -NotMatch ''SystemAttendantMailbox' | ➥
ExOleDbSystemMailbox)''} | Move-Mailbox -ConfigurationOnly ➥
-TargetDatabase EX27SCR\drMgmtSG\drMgmtDB
```

This command notifies Active Directory about the new server that is hosting this storage group. Specifically, the `-ConfigurationOnly` switch indicates that we are moving the configuration (only) but not asking Exchange to move the data (because the data already resides on this server). For more detail on the specific Exchange PowerShell commands and their respective options, see the Exchange TechCenter for PowerShell Cmdlets (`http://technet.microsoft.com/en-us/library/bb124233.aspx`).

At this point, Active Directory has been updated so that those users whose mailboxes were in `EX27\ManagementDB` are now recognized as being in `EX27SCR\drMgmtDB`. Client access may not be initially restored, based on the latency of Active Directory replication, but the users will be up shortly after their domain controller sees the changes. Depending on the version of Outlook that each user is running, their experience will vary between a completely transparent switchover, to asking the user to log in again, to a pop-up notifying the user that "Your Exchange administrator has made a change that requires you to restart Outlook."

To fail back, we would want to repair the production server and use SCR to replicate the data from EX27SCR back to EX27 while the users were still at the DR site. After EX27 was repopulated, we would perform the same process in a more controlled fashion to point the users back at EX27 and complete the failback.

Backup Considerations with SCR

Similar to the additional capabilities that some backup applications provide for CCR, special scenarios are also available for SCR configurations. For the CCR scenario, we discussed the benefits of protecting using the passive node in the pair so as not to impact the production users. This is not as easy in SCR because the mechanisms that provide VSS-based backup software with access to the CCR's passive copy do not provide the same functionality to the SCR copy; therefore, a typical backup solution cannot simply be pointed at the SCR node. However, a few backup solutions are capable of using the SCR node for backups by temporarily pausing the continuous replication so that the backup software can safely back up the SCR copy of the database and its related logs. The result is a backup of the Exchange server from the offsite SCR node.

The compelling reason for doing this is that nothing can replicate Exchange data offsite more efficiently than the Exchange services themselves. Disk-to-disk (D2D) backup solutions, as well as host-based replication technologies (both covered in Chapter 3), will both replicate not only the logs that Exchange replicates but also parts of the ever-changing database. In addition, host-based replication alternatives will replicate corruption between copies, whereas SCR will detect physical corruption and prevent it from replicating to the database copies. Thus, the ideal model is to only have Exchange replicating its logs, with no additional traffic from disk based backup or host-based replication between the sites.

Does this mean that we no longer need disk-based backup or host-based replication for Exchange 2007 deployments using SCR? The answer is twofold:

- No, backups (disk- and tape-based) are still necessary because Exchange replication is focused on near-real-time replication with the goal of availability. Backup is about previous recovery points, coming back to our initial guidance from Chapter 1 when we recommended that you ask yourself whether you are trying to solve for *availability or protection*, because they are not the same and will likely require two different technologies.
- Yes, SCR often negates the need for other replication technologies within Exchange deployments, though there may be other applications that do not have built-in replication and still warrant after-market replication/failover.

As of this writing, very few backup solutions are utilizing VSS for protecting Exchange 2007 in such a way as to back up from the SCR node. More products offer options for CCR deployments, though still not a majority of the mainstream backup products. As discussed in Chapter 4, Microsoft Data Protection Manager does provide the CCR options and the capability to back up from the SCR node in both DPM 2007 with SP1 as well as DPM 2010. For other backup solutions, you should check with your particular backup vendor.

Exchange 2010 Database Availability

Like any other software product, each generation builds on the last. So while Exchange 2007 made some significant advances in high availability with CCR and disaster recovery with SCR, there were some limitations:

- The Clustered Mailbox Server (CMS) role cannot coexist with other roles on the same Exchange 2007 machine, such as the hub, client access server (CAS), or unified messaging (UM), so deploying a CCR pair necessitates other servers.
- CCR has a dependency on understanding and maintaining a Windows failover cluster. While Chapter 6 shows us that clustering has become much easier, it still requires more effort than what an Exchange administrator might wish to do when they are already maintaining a large enterprise of Exchange services.
- SCR is a command line–only offering, so while you might manage everything else between the Exchange Management Console and the Failover Cluster Manager, you have to use PowerShell for implementing and remotely activating the disaster recovery database instance. In fact, one of the goals for Exchange 2010 over 2007 in regard to high availability is eliminating the need to use even the Failover Cluster Manager—the Exchange management tools are the only ones necessary to manage the entire Exchange environment (whether the components are clustered or not).
- In the event of a database issue, the whole server and its services has to be failed over, not just the database.
- SCC and LCR still have single points of failure, which is counterintuitive for solutions intended for higher availability.

For these reasons, Exchange 2010 has eliminated SCC and LCR, while combining and improving CCR and SCR into the *database availability group (DAG)*.

Database Availability Group

As a simple explanation, we can compare DAG with CCR:

- CCR is a Windows failover cluster offering a Clustered Mailbox Server and utilizing replicated Exchange data.
- DAGs are replicated Exchange databases that utilize some failover clustering components behind the scenes.

Essentially, the DAG functionality in Exchange 2010 dramatically reduces clustering aspects of high availability and manages the solution from a replicated database perspective, instead of the CMS perspective. Along with this philosophy shift are a few other changes:

- There are no storage groups in Exchange 2010. In Exchange 2003, we saw a few storage groups with multiple databases. In Exchange 2007, we saw storage groups that usually had one database each. And now, storage groups are gone. The database is the primary area of focus.

- Failover is at a database level, which is managed by Exchange 2010, instead of server-level failover, which was managed by Windows Failover Clustering (WFC) with Exchange 2007, 2003, 2000, or even 5.5.
- With WFC not being the core of the solution, an Exchange DAG can be easily stretched across sites without the constraints of geo-clustering that were discussed in Chapter 6. More importantly, DAG does not require interaction with WFC or its management tools. In fact, trying to configure your cluster settings using the WFC tools will likely break the DAG. When you create a DAG, all the necessary WFC objects are automatically created and initialized for you.

The Mailbox Server role is not the only role that changes with this paradigm shift. The client access server (CAS) also takes on more focus in high availability (other than being load balanced) in that it is responsible for transparently redirecting clients to whichever copy of a given mailbox database is active at a point in time. In Exchange 2010, the CAS connects the client to the instance of the database that is currently active. If the DAG changes which copy of a mailbox database is active, the clients will start accessing the new active instance because they are connecting through the CAS and not directly to the mailbox servers. This creates an architecture like the one shown in Figure 7.20.

FIGURE 7.20
CAS and DAG in Exchange 2010

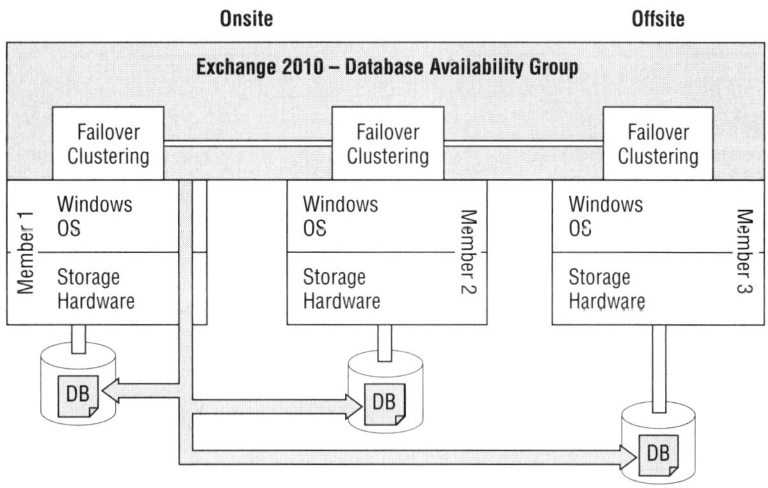

What Is a DAG?

The DAG itself consists of up to 16 servers that are running the Mailbox Server role and is the boundary for replication, where a database can have one or more copies. Unlike Exchange 2007, where you could replicate CCR within a cluster and SCR outside the cluster (perhaps to a second cluster), all replicated copies of a database reside within a single DAG. The DAG can span multiple IP subnets, although all members of a DAG must be in the same AD domain.

The DAG replicates the databases via Exchange continuous replication and then utilizes components of WFC behind the scenes. WFC is literally so far behind the scenes that an Exchange 2010 administrator using DAG may never need to open the Failover Cluster Management console. The only elements of WFC that DAG uses are the cluster heartbeats, node management, and the cluster group database. In fact, there is no Clustered Mailbox Server (CMS) role in Exchange 2010. Instead, the cluster's resource components are replaced by active managers.

DAG Active Manager

A new role on the Exchange 2010 Mailbox Server is the *Active Manager* (AM). AM is defined and runs within the Microsoft Exchange Replication service and is key to Exchange's high availability because it determines which database instance is currently active. AM also communicates with the CAS and Hub Transport servers so that they know which database to communicate with when moving mail or connecting clients.

One AM is the *Primary Active Manager* (*PAM*):

- The PAM is responsible for determining which database instance is active.
- If an active database fails, the PAM decides which passive copy is most suitable to become active.
- The PAM writes its data to the cluster database to affect changes to the WFC resources.
- The PAM receives topology notifications from Active Directory, such as user and mailbox connections.

All other Active Managers are Standby Active Managers (SAMs) and maintain read-only copies of the topology, which can be queried by the Active Manager client components running on the Client Access and Hub Transport servers. If the PAM fails, one of the SAMs will become the PAM for the DAG.

DAG Databases

With the database now the focal point of the Exchange high-availability architecture, you should know a few new terms and concepts:

- Each database is globally unique within Active Directory, instead of being part of a storage group and specific to a mailbox server. Because of this, all database names must be unique. If all of your Exchange server storage groups have a database with the default name of "mailbox database," you will need to rename the databases prior to introducing Exchange 2010 into the environment.
- Databases can be *active* or *passive*.
- Only one instance of each database can be active at a time, and it services clients.
- All other instances are passive until the active fails, at which time one passive instance will become active.
- No server can have more than one copy of a database—which means no LCR.

DAG Replication

Although we refer to databases as active or passive, we refer to the participants in DAG replication as being either a source or a target. Interestingly, while it is true that normally the active database will also be a replication source, there are scenarios where one passive database copy can be used to update another passive copy (such as seeding or re-seeding), where a server hosting a passive database might still be a replication source.

One big takeaway on DAG replication is in comparison to the workflow of CCR replication. In Exchange 2007, the source server was the catalyst for replication. The passive node would get the file system notifications by subscribing for alerts in those directories, and then its Replication service would copy the files from the source directory, inspect them, and replay them into the passive server's database.

In Exchange 2010, the replication trigger is reversed. Instead of the source server deciding what should be replicated, each target already knows what is in its database, so it knows what should be coming next and will actively request it from the source server. In response, the source sends what each target requests, utilizing built-in encryption and compression. The remainder of the workflow is consistent with Exchange 2007, with rigorous inspections before replaying the log into the other database instances. The inspection includes:

- Checking the physical integrity of the log file.
- Confirming the header is correct for the database.
- In case the replication target with its passive database had previously been active, it looks for legacy `Exx.logs` and moves them before the new log (with potentially the same name) is applied.

If there are any errors during inspection, the log is moved to the directory that will have it be replayed into the passive database. In Exchange 2007, the Replication service performed the replay, but in Exchange 2010, this is handled by the Information Store service instead.

Also notable is that Exchange 2010 replication is TCP based, instead of SMB based as in Exchange 2007. And finally—but perhaps the most noticeable change related to replication in Exchange 2010—is that with the removal of storage groups, some of the PowerShell cmdlets for use in the Exchange Management Shell have changed:

In 2007, we used `Get-StorageGroupCopyStatus`.

In 2010, we use `Get-MailboxDatabaseCopyStatus`.

The management console also displays more status and configuration choices for DAG replication and failover.

DAG Initial Seeding

Earlier in this chapter (see *"Seeding a Database"*), we discussed how Exchange 2007 required the first log file for a database so that it could replay that log on the secondary servers, which would invoke the Create Database command and facilitate the secondary copies.

Exchange 2010 no longer requires the first log file in the database. Instead, Exchange 2010 can explicitly seed any database copy, regardless of whether the log file contains the `createDB` record.

If the initial transaction log does not exist (such as when you deploy DAG using some existing Exchange 2010 standalone servers), use the `Update-MailboxDatabaseCopy` cmdlet. One difference between this cmdlet and the 2007 equivalent (`Update-StorageGroupCopy`) is that you can seed from a passive copy to a new passive copy by specifying which copy to use as the source. In Exchange 2007, the update command always replicated from the active copy.

Alternatively, you can manually copy the database from an alternative copy or use third-party replication software if it uses the built-in Exchange 2010 API for third-party replication. In all cases, the new replica needs to be in the same directory path on the new Exchange 2010 host.

DAG Failover

With a DAG, *failover* (unplanned) and *switchover* (planned) happens at either the database level or the server level. Here is how DAG works:

- If an active database fails, another instance of that database becomes active instead.
- If an entire mailbox server that is running active databases fails, the same process happens for each active database on that failed server. For each active database, another database instance on a different server simply becomes active.
- If the mailbox server that fails happens to be running the Primary Active Manager, a new Primary Active Manager is selected and the active databases from that server are reactivated elsewhere.

The Primary Active Manager (PAM) determines which of the passive database copies to bring online. All currently unreachable copies, as well as those that are explicitly blocked from activation by the Exchange Administrator, are ignored from consideration. For the remaining passive databases that are candidates for becoming active, the databases are sorted based on how current they are to the active copy in order to minimize data loss:

- In order to further reduce data loss, Exchange 2010 uses a process called *ACLL* (*Attempt To Copy Last Logs*). ACLL will reach out to the passive database servers and try to collect all the log files that would allow at least one of the passive copies to become completely current, and thereby not lose data when becoming the active copy.
- If no passive copy of the database can be mounted without zero data loss, the AutoDatabase MountDial setting is used to determine whether one or more of the databases can be mounted with an administrator-predetermined amount of acceptable data loss.
- In case two or more passive copies meet the same criteria and are equally viable to become the active instance, each database copy has an Activation Preference value, which by default is the order in which the copies were created (first copy = 1, second copy = 2, etc.). This value can be changed but is used only to break the tie when two copies are equally viable to become the active.

The PAM will recursively assess the passive copies using degrading criteria either until a database is acceptable for activation or until it determines that none are acceptable and the DAG fails. But if any of the passive databases can be brought online, then:

- The mounted database will generate new log files using the same log generation sequence.
- The transport dumpsters on each Hub Transport server in the relevant Active Directory sites will be contacted by the newly active database host to recover any mail contained in the transport dumpster that hasn't yet been delivered to the recipient's mailbox. If the new

active database is at a different site, Exchange will query the transport dumpsters in both the old and new sites.

And after the new database is mounted, the PAM will update the Hub Transport and Client Access servers to resume servicing email users.

DAG Failback or Resync

There is usually not a reason to fail back to the original host or original primary database copy, but eventually, the server and its database copy that used to be active will be brought back into the DAG. At this point, the Active Manager on that node will see that that copy of the database is no longer active and an incremental resync is necessary.

As an example, consider a DAG with three copies of the same mailbox database, which we will refer to here as DB1, DB2 and DB3:

1. DB1 is current active, but its server, SRV1, fails.
2. DB3 becomes the active copy.
3. SVR1 with DB1 on it comes back online.
4. Now, DB1 is in a different state than DB3 (which is still active) and needs to be resynchronized as a passive copy of DB3.

To resynchronize a previously active copy to the currently active copy, the log files are compared until a point of divergence is found:

- If the new active copy was brought up with no data loss, there should not be a point of divergence.
- If the new active copy was brought up with incremental data loss, it will have created new log files, including those that perhaps have the same generation number as uncommitted or nonreplicated log files on the original copy (DB1).

Once divergence is found, any diverged log files on DB1 are discarded and the authoritative log files from the current active copy (DB3) are replicated across to update DB1 to the current state. If too much divergence has occurred, such as if SVR1 and DB1 had been offline for a significant period of time, then a full reseed of the database may be required, instead of an incremental resync from the new active copy.

Getting Started with DAG

One of the coolest aspects of Exchange 2010 DAG is a concept called *incremental deployment,* which is the ability to evolve your solution from standalone to highly available to disaster recoverable at your own pace. In Exchange 2007, you would build a CCR solution from bare metal with clusters and replication, and then move the mailboxes into the highly available clustered mailbox server databases. In DAG, implementing high availability and site resilience features can be done after Exchange has been installed and the mailbox servers and their standalone databases have been active for a while. In addition, DAG uses the same workflow for each additional member, regardless of whether those members are nearby for high availability or remote for site resilience—and it all can be done from a single UI, instead of requiring scripts.

To demonstrate the incremental deployment nature of DAG, we will start this exercise with an existing Exchange 2010 server named EX14 and replicate its production databases to a new Exchange server named EX15. Both servers are running the evaluation download of Exchange 2010 and are part of the same domain as all the Exchange 2007 servers and clusters that were discussed earlier in this chapter.

In Figure 7.21, we see the new Exchange 2010 console showing EX14, with its production databases, as well as a new EX15 server.

FIGURE 7.21
Exchange 2010 console

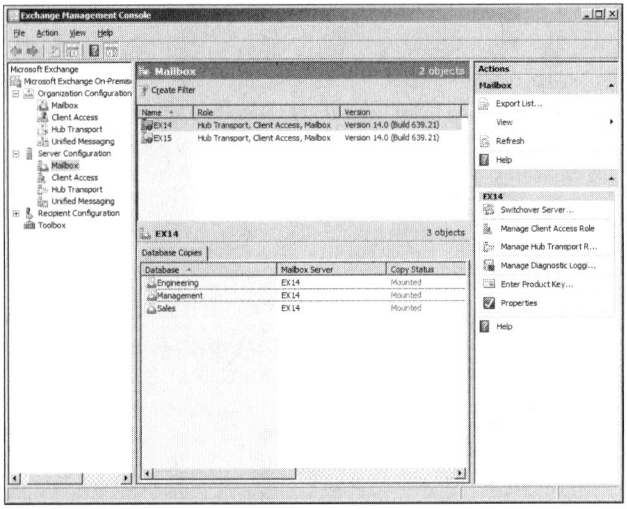

TASK 9: PREPARING THE SERVERS FOR EXCHANGE 2010 AND DAG

To install Exchange 2010 on a new server, you must install a few prerequisite software packages (which you are prompted to do during the initial setup screen), as well as several roles and features. As in our earlier discussion on Exchange 2007 prerequisite components in Task 2, you can use a `ServerManagerCmd` script (shown here) to install all the required roles and features and use an XML answer file delivered in the `\Scripts` folder of the Exchange 2010 installation media.

```
sc config NetTcpPortSharing start= auto
ServerManagerCmd -ip Exchange-Typical.xml -Restart
```

After issuing these two commands, you should be able to install Exchange 2010 onto your new servers, including at least the Mailbox role and at least one Exchange 2010 CAS, but also the Hub and additional CAS roles, if desired.

NOTE For more information on installing Exchange 2010's prerequisite software, features and roles, visit `http://technet.microsoft.com/en-us/library/bb691354.aspx`.

Although it is not necessary to preconfigure a Windows failover cluster prior to deploying DAG, the WFC feature must be added to each machine. If the WFC feature is not already enabled on the local server that is running the New Database Availability Group wizard, the wizard will attempt to enable it for you. Since we are already using scripts to ensure that all our Exchange servers have exactly what they need in advance (and so we can create the DAG from any node that we choose), it is recommended that you add the WFC feature as we have added all of the other features and roles:

```
ServerManagerCmd -i Failover-Clustering
```

TASK 10: CREATING THE DAG

With Exchange 2010 now deployed on at least two servers, we are ready to create our DAG. Again, because incremental deployment allows us to deploy high availability and site resilience after the initial install of Exchange, I have preconfigured some production mailbox databases (Sales and Management) on EX14, as if it had been a standalone Exchange 2010 server for a while, as shown in Figure 7.22.

FIGURE 7.22
A production server and database, before DAG

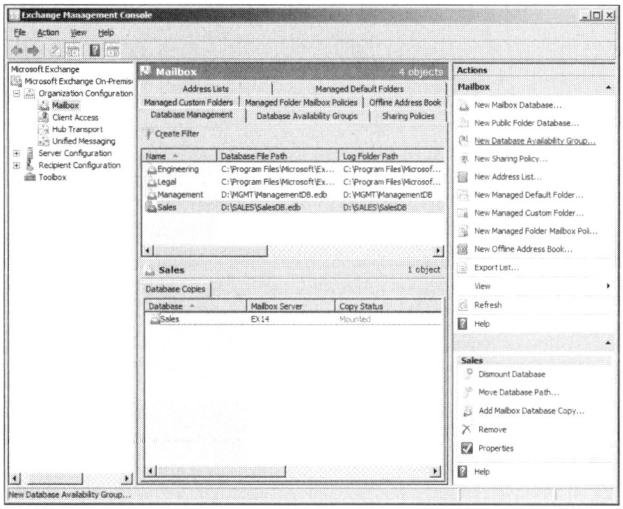

Creating the DAG itself is easy:

1. From the Exchange Management Console, as shown in Figure 7.22, go to the Actions pane in the upper-right corner and click New Database Availability Group.
2. The New Database Availability Group wizard will immediately prompt you for three pieces of information:

   DAG Name This will become the network name that the mailbox databases will be accessed through.

   Witness Server Choose a server that will not be part of the DAG, which will host the file share used for a file share and node majority quorum (see Chapter 6), similar to the file share that we created for our Exchange 2007 CCR configuration. For my example, I chose a local domain controller to offer the file share.

   Witness Directory This is the directory on the witness for the file share. If it is not yet created, the wizard will create it.

Figure 7.23 shows the New Database Availability Group wizard with our DAG name and witness information included. Clicking Create will create the DAG. Yes, it really is that simple.

FIGURE 7.23
Exchange 2010's New Database Availability Group wizard

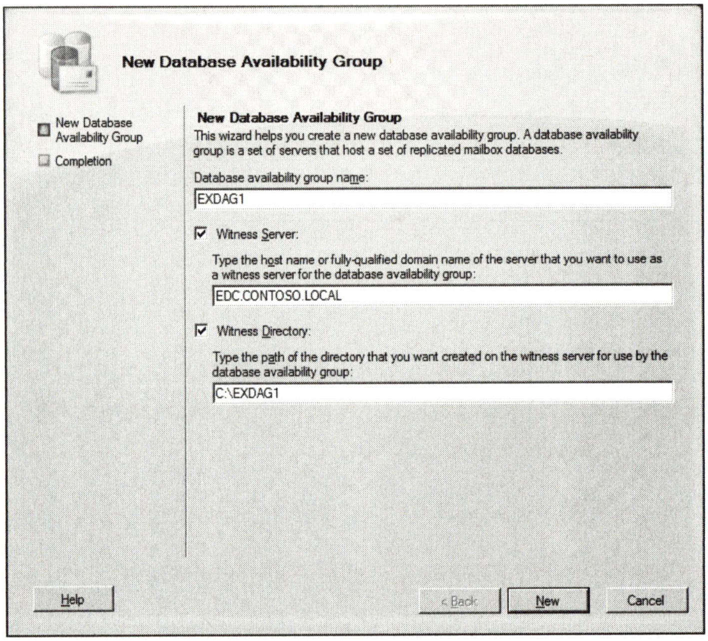

The DAG is initially just an empty container, to which we will later add mailbox servers and databases. When the first member server is added, a Windows failover cluster is created behind the scenes. Because creating a DAG is creating a Windows failover cluster, the prerequisites and recommendations of clustering from Chapter 6 still apply, including:

- The OS must support clustering, including the Enterprise and Datacenter Editions of Windows Server 2008 or 2008 R2.
- Nodes should have both public (CorpNet) and private (cluster heartbeat) network segments for the cluster to operate correctly.

Although DAG does use components of WFC, it is not necessary to preconfigure these components for the cluster itself. The name of the DAG that you chose in Task 10 becomes the cluster resource network name. The DAG will also create the networking cluster resources and either prompt you for an IP address or use DHCP, based on what the physical network cards in the DAG member servers are using.

The DAG will also register the network name to DNS and Active Directory, and configure the failover clustering components as required, including the quorum model:

- If the DAG has an odd number of members, the failover cluster will use a node-majority model, where only the member servers are needed to determine the quorum.

- If the DAG has an even number of members, the failover cluster will use a file share and node majority model, where the file share also has a vote (thus providing an odd number of votes and thereby a clear majority).

NOTE In my own first experiences with Exchange 2010 and creating a DAG and databases, I came across an error message that told me I could not create a database. According to `http://support.microsoft.com/kb/977960`, this error can be due to Active Directory replication latency and is resolved in SP1 for Exchange 2010. Using the following command resolved it for me:

```
Set-ADServerSettings -PreferredServer <DC-FQDN>
```

Task 11: Adding Member Servers to the DAG

As mentioned earlier, when the first member server is added to the DAG, the failover cluster is created and any mailbox databases are associated with the DAG.

As additional member servers are added to the DAG, they are added to the failover cluster (which will update the quorum model), they are registered within Active Directory as members of the DAG, and their databases are also registered with the DAG.

To add member servers to the DAG:

1. Right-click on the DAG that you created in Task 10 and select Manage Database Availability Group Membership.
2. Select each of the servers that you wish to add. For this example, I am adding my EX14 and EX15 servers to the DAG we created called EXDAG1, as shown in Figure 7.24.
3. Click Manage to add the servers to the DAG.

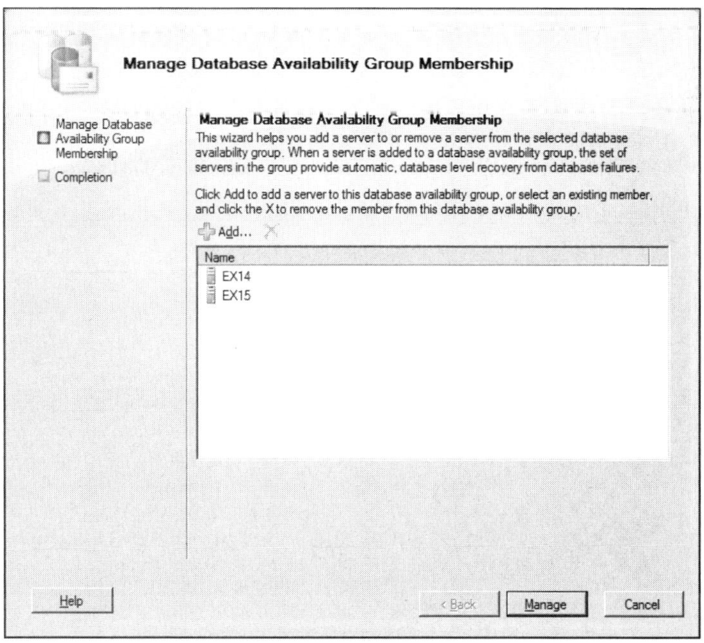

FIGURE 7.24
Adding Exchange 2010 servers to the DAG

You could also have used the Exchange Management Shell to add each of the two servers to the EXDAG with the following commands:

```
Add-DatabaseAvailabilityGroupServer -Identity 'EXDAG' -MailboxServer 'EX14'
Add-DatabaseAvailabilityGroupServer -Identity 'EXDAG' -MailboxServer 'EX15'
```

TASK 12: REPLICATING DATABASES IN THE DAG

For the scenario that we have been using in these exercises, EX14 is an Exchange 2010 server that has been in production, whereas EX15 is a new Exchange 2010 server that we have built so that we can start taking advantage of DAG for high availability and site resilience. Because of this, EX14 has a few mailbox databases already, but EX15 does not.

To create a copy and establish replication between the DAG members:

1. Start the Exchange Management Console.
2. Expand the Organization Configuration and then the Mailbox container. This will show all the databases within your environment.
3. Right-click on a database that you wish to replicate and then choose Add Database Copy, which launches the wizard shown in Figure 7.25.

FIGURE 7.25
Exchange 2010 DAG: adding a database copy

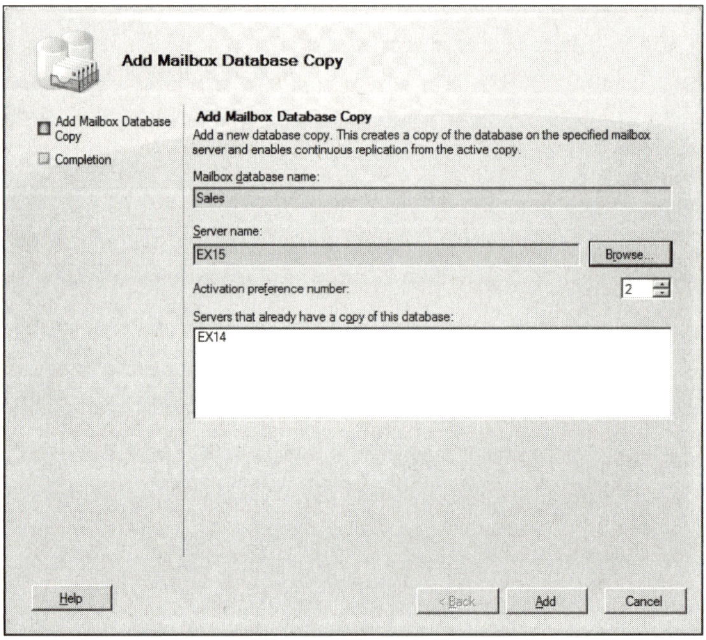

4. The server that has the active copy of the database is already filled in within the wizard, so clicking the Browse button will allow you to choose which server will host the additional copy of the database, as shown in Figure 7.25, where we are adding a copy of the Sales database from EX14 onto EX15.
5. Click Add (accepting the other defaults).

The wizard will then create the database on the second server, and initiate all the processes for seeding the copy and enabling continuous replication. You could also have used the Exchange Management Shell to do this with the following command:

```
Add-MailboxDatabaseCopy -Identity 'SalesDB'  -MailboxServer 'EX15'
```

The Exchange Management Console in Figure 7.26 shows the two copies of the database, with the copy on EX14 as Mounted (meaning it is the active copy), and the copy on EX15 as Healthy (meaning it is a passive copy that is successfully synchronizing).

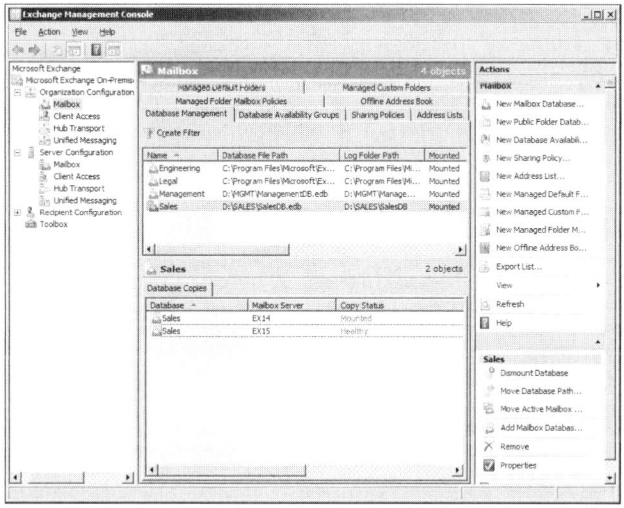

FIGURE 7.26 Exchange 2010 Management Console, showing DAG

TASK 13: SWITCHOVERS IN DAG

As we have seen in the other Exchange 2010 tasks, almost everything in DAG can be done with a right-click and single screen wizard in the Exchange Management Console or a single command line from the Exchange Management Shell. Switching between copies of the database is no exception.

To switch database copies:

1. Go to the Exchange Management Console.
2. Expand the Organizational Configuration ➤ Mailbox container to see the global list of databases.
3. From the Database Management tab on the top half of the screen, select the database that you wish to switch over so that the two database copies are seen in the lower part of the screen.
4. Right-click on the passive copy that is currently listed as Healthy, and select Activate Database Copy from the context menu, as shown in Figure 7.27.

A dialog box will appear, allowing you to select whether you want to override the mount settings for cases where you may need to force a database to mount, even if some data loss might occur. Accepting the default will cause the passive and active databases to switch roles.

FIGURE 7.27
Activating the passive copy of a DAG

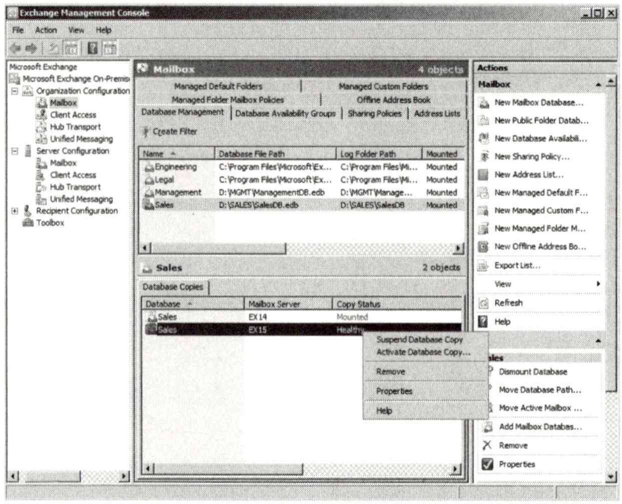

Alternatively, you could also run a command from the Exchange Management Shell to activate the copy of the SalesDB mailbox database on the EX15 server instead of the server that it was on (and no override to the mount, as done before):

```
Move-ActiveMailboxDatabase  SalesDB  -ActivateOnServer EX15 ➥
-MountDialOverride:None
```

GLOBALLY UNIQUE DATABASE NAMES

In Task 12, we went to the Organization Configuration container instead of the Server Configuration container that we would have in Exchange 2007, because databases are now considered global objects in Exchange 2010. Because of this, every database must have a globally unique name across your Active Directory forest. So if you have multiple servers with the default "First Storage Group" and "Mailbox Database" objects, then you need to rename the databases prior to an Exchange 2010 deployment. You can ignore the storage group names since storage groups are not relevant in Exchange 2010.

For example, you might rename the executive mailbox database in your existing Exchange 2007 server from MailboxDatabase to ExecMail2007, and the new Exchange 2010 database as ExecMail. Then, when you move the users' mailboxes from one server to another, there is an obvious correlation and a practical name to the database moving forward.

Data Protection Considerations with DAG

One important change for backing up Exchange in 2010 is the removal of the streaming backup APIs that were available in Exchange 2007. Technically, the APIs are still there (they are used for initial database seeding), but they aren't usable by backup applications anymore. Instead, if you are going to back up Exchange 2010, it must be done using a VSS-based backup solution.

Even then, these capabilities will vary based on how well your backup vendor leverages the VSS writer and APIs that are available with Exchange 2010.

Similar to how Exchange 2007 storage groups appeared under the EX27CCR cluster (and not the individual nodes) in Figure 7.17, Exchange 2010 databases appear under the EXDAG1 object (not the member servers), as shown in Figure 7.28. You can optionally still protect file shares, directories, or system information about the Exchange 2010 member servers, but the databases are selectable for protection from the EXDAG1 container (regardless of whether they are replicated or singular).

FIGURE 7.28
DPM 2010: Exchange 2010 DAG protection

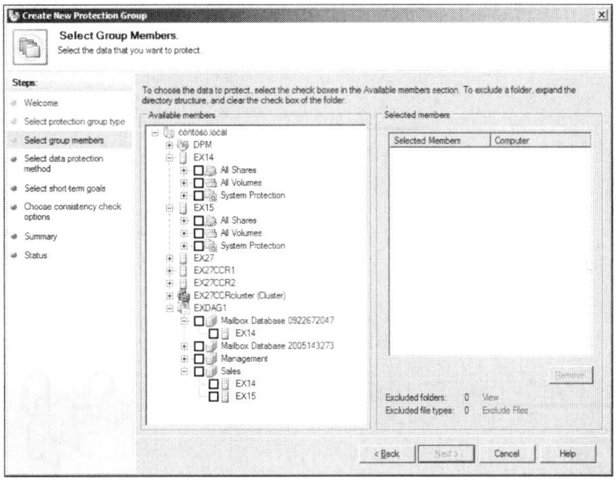

DAG offers backup capabilities similar to those for CCR environments, where you can back up a particular node or choose to protect an active or passive instance. Additionally, you can choose to do full backups, which will later result in log truncation, or database copies, which leave the logs untouched. For example, Microsoft's Data Protection Manager 2010 offers full backups or copies within a DAG group, as shown in Figure 7.29.

FIGURE 7.29
DPM 2010: Exchange 2010 DAG options

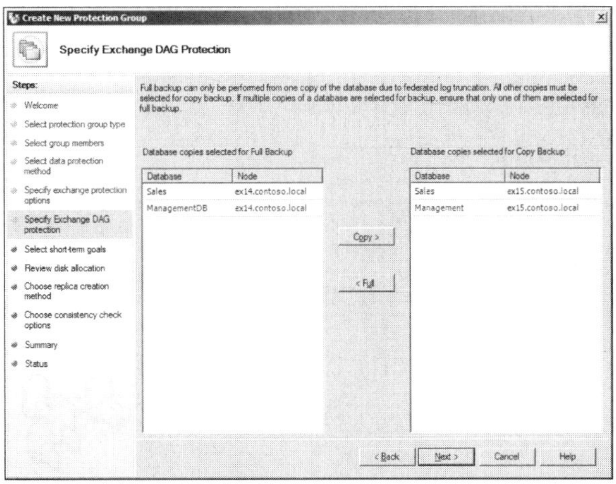

Because storage groups are not part of Exchange 2010, there is no *recovery storage group* (RSG). Instead, there is an equivalent *recovery mailbox database*. By using a VSS-based backup solution, you can restore mailbox databases back to their original host, to an alternate host, or to a network folder or share. Figure 7.30 shows the DPM 2010 Recovery Wizard for Exchange. For more information on protecting and recovering Exchange with DPM 2010, see Chapter 4 or visit `www.microsoft.com/DPM/exchange`.

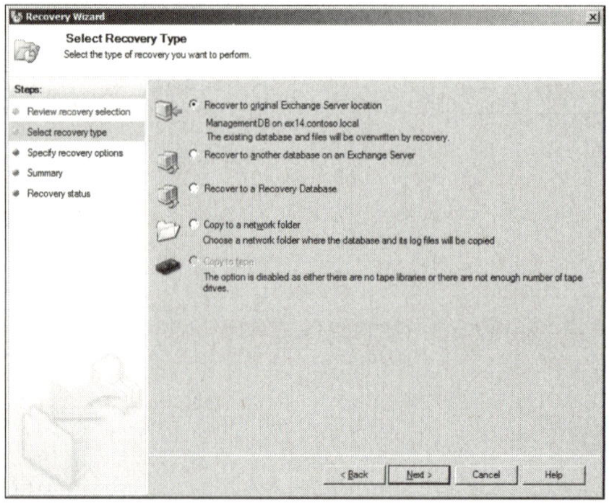

FIGURE 7.30
DPM 2010: Exchange Recovery Wizard

Alternatively, Microsoft offers guidance in cases that Exchange 2010 does not require backups. In that discussion, if your primary recovery goal is due to server failure and the DAG maintains three or more copies of a database, traditional backup may not be necessary since the other DAG copies could rebuild a failed server. That is assuming that you are backing up in anticipation of a restore due to database failover. In the bigger picture, some Exchange 2010 guidance says that there are three scenarios where you might normally back up:

- Site/server/disk failures
- Archiving/compliance
- Recovering deleted items

But in Exchange 2010:

- DAG addresses most site/server/disk failures.
- Email archiving addresses archiving/compliance.
- The enhanced dumpster enables recovery of deleted items.

NOTE For more information regarding how backup mechanisms work in Exchange 2010, refer to `http://msdn.microsoft.com/en-us/library/dd877010.aspx`.

There will likely be some Exchange environments where these data protection mechanisms address your needs. In the bigger picture, there are some additional considerations concerning data protection that will need to be addressed outside of Exchange 2010:

- Most IT environments are averse to protecting some workloads one way and other workloads in different ways. File services, databases, and the myriad of other workloads will still be protected via disk- and tape-based protection. Supplementing the built-in capabilities of Exchange 2010 with the same data protection mechanism protecting the other Windows platforms is usually operationally efficient.

- Most larger companies have some form of compliance and retention requirement, often for 5, 7, or 10 years. In most environments, that length of retention will necessitate tape in some manner, as discussed in Chapters 3 and 4.

SPLITTING THE DB AND LOG LUNS

Exchange 2003 and 2007 advocated the common best practice of keeping databases and logs on separate volumes, based on their performance characteristics. A great in-depth article on Exchange 2007 storage guidance can be found at `http://msexchangeteam.com/archive/2007/01/15/432199.aspx`.

For Exchange 2010, Microsoft now advocates putting databases and logs together, with one spindle or LUN per database. And for performance reasons, they are probably right. However, you may gain some additional data recovery capabilities if you separate the database and logs. If you lose only the physical database volume (but your log volume survives), backup software like Data Protection Manager (Chapter 4) can recover the database and then play forward the surviving transaction logs to return your Exchange server to the last transaction available within the logs. Of course, if you are using DAG, you have other choices. But if you are not yet able to use DAG, keeping the database and logs split may give you additional recovery options.

Summary

Exchange has evolved considerably from its early days on top of Microsoft Cluster Services (MSCS), when MSCS and many of the first generation of cluster-able software were considered challenging (see Chapter 6). Today, both Exchange Server 2007 and Exchange Server 2010 have built-in replication technologies that are designed to provide wholly supported and reliable resiliency to the point that older third-party replication methods may be regarded as obsolete in regard to Exchange.

- SCC (single-copy cluster) was well behaved with Exchange 2003, but its use was discouraged in Exchange 2007 and it is not available in Exchange 2010.
- LCR was only available in Exchange 2007 and only effective for a niche scenario.
- CCR within Exchange 2007 utilizes the best aspects of Microsoft clustering, while addressing MSCS's usual challenge of shared storage through continuous replication of the Exchange logs.
- SCR provides disaster recovery for Exchange 2007 by replicating the Exchange data to additional servers (up to 50) that are at remote sites. DAG in Exchange 2010 blends the functionality of SCR and CCR, while reducing the role of "clustering" from MSCS. The result is a seamless availability solution that is truly part of Exchange 2010 and not bolted onto the side.

Although CCR, SCR, and DAG now offer high availability that is built into Exchange Server, the need for long-term data retention should still be met with an Exchange-supported backup and recovery solution.

Chapter 8

Microsoft SQL Server

In our earlier workload-specific chapters on file services (Chapter 5) and Exchange (Chapter 7), the workloads each directly delivered a service to end users. Microsoft SQL Server is a platform as much as it is a workload, meaning that other applications are installed on top of it. Specifically, SQL Server is a data repository that is used by thousands of Microsoft and third-party applications from well-known industry applications like SAP to home-grown applications that you have written yourself. Even other Microsoft applications often rely on SQL, such as Microsoft SharePoint farms and the System Center management technologies discussed in Chapters 4, 10, and 11.

In this chapter, we will first look at the built-in capabilities for ensuring higher availability of SQL Server. Then, we will look at the considerations for backing it up.

SQL Server Built-in Resiliency

Microsoft SQL Server 2005 or 2008 include many built-in resiliency features, including:

- Support for Windows Failover Clustering, including geographically distributed clusters
- Database mirroring
- Log shipping
- Replication

The first several sections of this chapter go into depth on each of these topics. The goal of this chapter is *not* to teach you how to become a SQL database administrator. I assume that you have a basic knowledge of installing Microsoft SQL Server on a Windows server OS, after which some other database administrator takes over.

Instead, the goal is to show you how to make the SQL platform more highly available and better protected than a standalone server might be, so that the database and applications have the best possible platform to run from.

SQL Terminology

The only two things that you should be sure to understand is how SQL Server is installed and what files are necessary:

Instance An instance of SQL Server is an installation of the Microsoft SQL Server software on a Windows OS. It is common to have multiple instances of SQL installed on a single physical server, each with its own name. For example, a SQL server that I will be using in the tasks included in this chapter is called SQL28 and has two instances of SQL Server 2008 installed on it—named Legal and Sales. This means that I ran the installation process twice. The first time that I was prompted to use a default instance name of Microsoft SQL Server or a custom name, I chose Legal. The second time that I ran the installation, I used the name Sales. This installs most of the key SQL Server services twice, as shown in Figure 8.1.

FIGURE 8.1
Multiple instances of SQL Server, as seen in the Services control panel of Windows

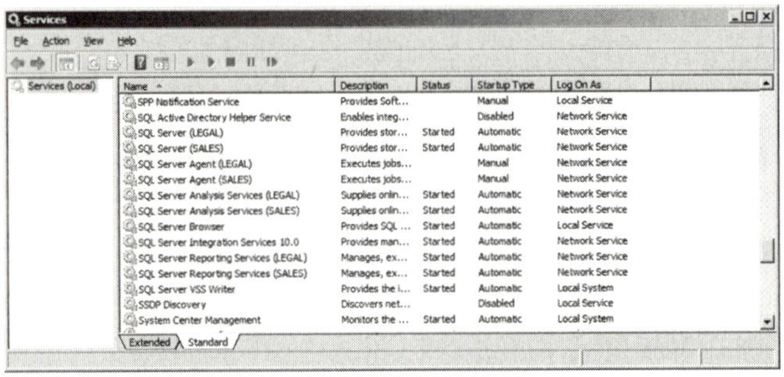

A few common modules of SQL Server are shared by all the installed instances, including the management console, online books and documentation, and so on.

Database Underneath each instance of SQL are a few default databases, such as Master, which provides administrative support for that instance. Other databases are created in support of applications that will be installed and configured later. Each database has a main database file (with the extension `.mdf`) and a log file (with the extension `.ldf`). For an accounting database:

`D:\ACCT\Accounting.MDF` is the main database file.

`L:\ACCT\Accounting.LDF` is the transaction log.

Database Recovery Modes Databases can typically be in one of three recovery modes, which determines factors such as performance, consumed space, and potential data loss or recovery: Simple, Full, or Bulk-Logged. Each has different capabilities for protection and recovery, which we will explore as we look at the various resiliency features within SQL Server.

Clustering or Mirroring?

The next sections of this chapter cover deploying SQL Server within a Windows Failover Clustering, as well as database mirroring and failing over individual SQL Server databases. By the end of the chapter, things will be much clearer to you, but for now a starting choice of clustering or mirroring can be summarized like this:

Clustering SQL Server Provides a complete failover solution for not only the databases, but also logins, SQL jobs, and so forth. However, Windows Failover Clustering has only one logical copy of the database, which can be accessed by two or more clustered nodes. Even if the storage underneath the cluster is mirrored (see Chapter 3), it is one logical copy whose multiple physical copies will be simultaneously written to by the cluster. It is ideal for protecting against machine component-level failures, but does not protect against database corruption.

Mirroring and Failing-Over Databases Provides protection on a per-database perspective. The mirroring mechanism ensures that physical corruption in one instance of the database will not affect the others, and in fact, the mirrored database can restore some page-level corruption transparently. However, it is only the actual database that gets mirrored. If you require more than Windows-authenticated logins or use jobs to actively maintain and manipulate the data, you will need to handle this outside of the database mirroring and failover mechanisms.

SQL Failover Clustering

Microsoft SQL Server was one of the original applications to be clustered by Windows, when their versions were Windows NT 4.0 Enterprise Edition and SQL Server 4.21. Today, Windows Server 2008 and 2008 R2 and SQL Server 2008 and 2008 R2 are more integrated and easier than ever to deploy into a failover cluster configuration.

We will start with what we learned in Chapter 6 on Windows Failover Clustering. To that end, I have built a new cluster with the following physical nodes and clustered services:

DeltaCluster, the logical cluster

DeltaNode1, a Windows Server 2008 node of the cluster

DeltaNode2, a Windows Server 2008 node of the cluster

The cluster is using iSCSI storage for its shared volumes and is running as a Node and Disk Majority cluster because it has an even number of machines, so a tie-breaking disk quorum is needed (Figure 8.2). For more information on how we built this, refer back to Chapter 6.

FIGURE 8.2
Failover Cluster Management console

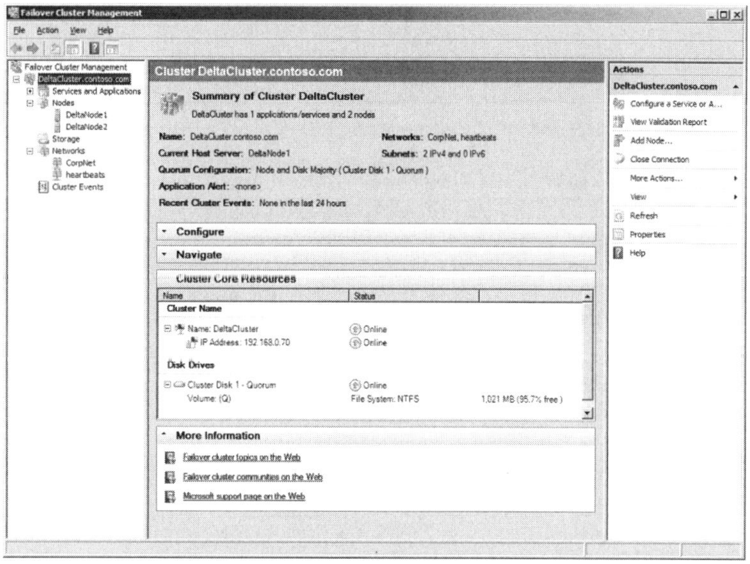

CLUSTER NAMING AND IP ADDRESS CONSISTENCY

In Chapter 6, we discussed the best practice of prefix-naming and ranges of IP addresses within each cluster. For the cluster configuration used in this chapter, I have reserved the entire range of 192.168.0.70–79 and will be prefacing every name resource with the word *Delta*. This results in the following IP and name pairs:

192.168.0.70 for DeltaCluster, the logical name of the cluster

192.168.0.71 for DeltaNode1, a physical node of the cluster

192.168.0.72 for DeltaNode2, a physical node of the cluster

192.168.0.73 reserved for DeltaNode3, in case it is added later

192.168.0.74 reserved for DeltaNode4, in case it is added later

With the logical cluster (for administration) and up to four nodes covered, the upper five IP addresses in this block will be used for application services in the cluster. In this chapter, we will eventually add:

192.168.0.75 for DeltaClusterDTC, distributed transaction coordinator

192.168.0.76 for DeltaDB, the network name for the clustered SQL Server instance

Preparing to Cluster SQL Server

When planning to cluster SQL Server, the key is to use the same storage planning that you would for a standalone SQL server. In a standalone SQL server, you typically will have at least two different storage volumes: one for the database file and another for the log file, each with its own performance requirements. The disk LUNs that you provide as shared storage for the cluster need to have the same performance considerations. And if you are going to run multiple instances of SQL Server, with a variety of databases and applications, then the storage LUNs should reflect the performance considerations of each of the databases and transaction log files.

For a simple configuration, I have added three additional iSCSI LUNs to the cluster to allow the databases and transaction logs to be on separate volumes with different performing storage. These shared disks have been renamed as SQL-DB, SQL-LOG, and DTC, respectively, as seen in the Failover Cluster Management console in Figure 8.3.

FIGURE 8.3
Shared storage within a SQL failover cluster

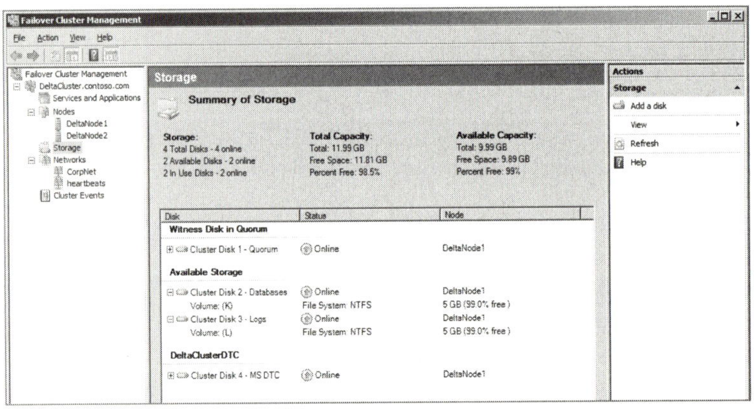

Before you install SQL Server onto these nodes, they need to be prepared for serving databases, which means that you must install the Application Server role on both nodes.

1. Open the Server Manager and select Roles ➢ Add Roles.
2. Add the Application Server role.
3. You'll see a prompt telling you that this action will require the Windows Process Application Service. Click OK.

4. Within the options for the Application Server role, you need to enable two components (Figure 8.4):
   - Incoming Remote Transactions
   - Outgoing Remote Transactions
5. Click Next and then Finish to complete installation of the Application Server role on this node.
6. Repeat this process (Steps 1–5) on each of the other nodes within the cluster.

   That prepares the node to be part of a SQL Server cluster. But we also need to prepare the cluster to handle the databases. To do this, we need to make the Microsoft Distributed Transaction Coordinator (MSDTC) highly available within the cluster.
7. Open the Failover Cluster Manager (this assumes that you have already built your cluster, based on the principles taught in Chapter 6).

FIGURE 8.4
Installing the Application Server role for the nodes of the cluster

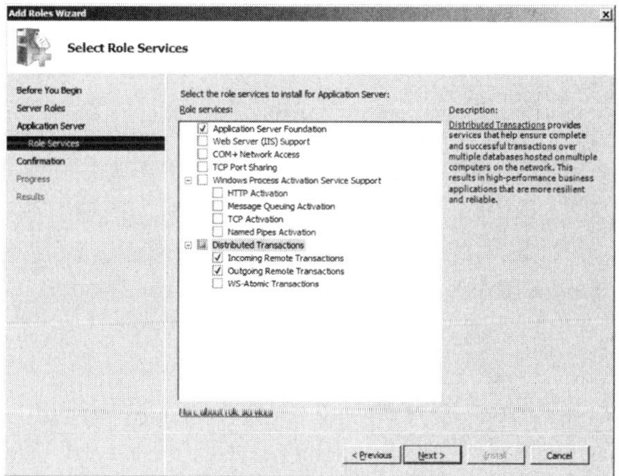

8. Expand the left-pane tree, select your cluster, and then right-click on Server And Applications and select Configure A Service or Application, which will launch the High Availability Wizard.
9. Select Distributed Transaction Coordinator (MS DTC) and click Next.
10. You will be prompted for the Client Access Point name and IP address for the clustered MSDTC instance. This access point is how applications like SQL Server connect to the DTC. In this case, I used the naming and IP convention discussed earlier:

    Client Access Point name DeltaClusterDTC

    IP address 192.168.0.75
11. Add a shared disk resource, and then click Next to finish deploying the DTC. The complete configuration of the DeltaClusterDTC can be seen in Figure 8.5.

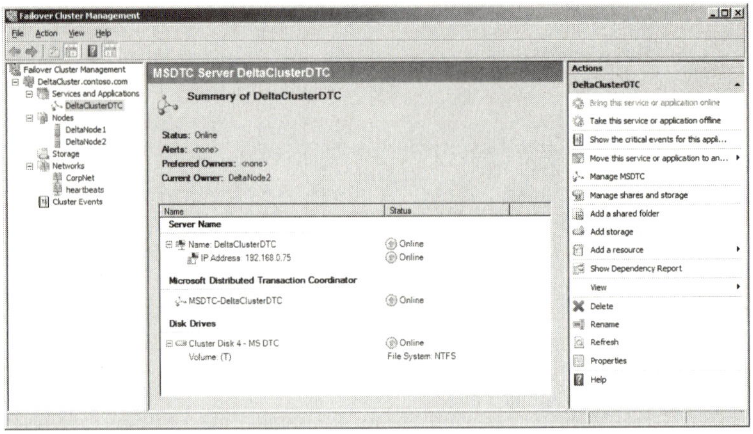

FIGURE 8.5 The clustered Distributed Transaction Coordinator

Now, you are ready to deploy SQL Server into a cluster. Doing this in SQL Server 2008 is a two-step process, with a different workflow for installing the first node versus installing SQL Server on the second node.

NOTE Before installing a new application like SQL Server, it is always prudent to run Windows Update and confirm that the base server or cluster node in this case is completely up-to-date. In addition, try rebooting one node at a time so that you can confirm that the cluster services are correctly able to move between nodes in a reliable fashion. Now, with both nodes updated and agile within the cluster, you are ready to install your application.

Task 1: Installing SQL Server onto the First Clustered Node

As with the earlier chapters, all of the exercises in this chapter are done with evaluation software and/or TestDrive virtual machines that are available for download from the Microsoft website. In this case, the clustered nodes are virtual machines created from TestDrive VHDs, and we will be using SQL Server 2008 Enterprise evaluation software that you can also download from the Microsoft evaluation center : `http://TechNet.Microsoft.com/EvalCenter`.

NOTE All exercises in Task 1 involve only the first node of the cluster that will be receiving SQL Server. This is very important for two reasons. The installation process for subsequent SQL Server nodes is different. Also, if you have to reboot the first node, you need to be sure that the other node is undisturbed so that the cluster remains operational.

Upon first running the SQL Server setup, you may be prompted to install additional prerequisites, such as the .NET 3.5 Framework or an updated Windows Installer. But once you complete those requirements, and potentially rebooting, you are ready to install SQL Server 2008. As of this writing, Service Pack 1 (SP1) was the latest available for SQL Server 2008, and SP2 was imminent (as well as the release of SQL Server 2008 R2). As always, staying up-to-date is important. If you are installing SQL Server 2008 into a Windows Server 2008 R2 cluster, SP1 (or better) for SQL Server 2008 is mandatory and you will get a compatibility alert from Windows Server 2008 R2. SQL Server 2008 without SP1 is not supported on Windows Server 2008 R2. The installation process will work, but you need to apply a SQL service pack immediately after (and you probably should anyway).

To install SQL Server onto the first node of the cluster, follow these steps:

1. If this is a new cluster with no other user activity, a best practice before this kind of staged installation is to move all the resources to the first node so that the installer already has controlling access to the resources. In this case, the simplest way is to simply reboot the second node, which will force all resources and groups to the first node.

2. From the node 1 console, run `Setup.exe` from the installation media, which will launch the SQL Server Installation Center.

3. From the left pane, choose Installation Center. In the right pane, choose New SQL Server Failover Cluster Installation, as shown in Figure 8.6.

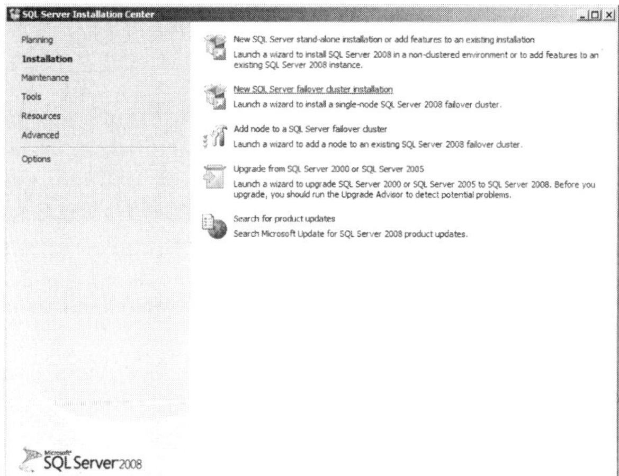

FIGURE 8.6
Installing SQL Server onto node 1 of the cluster

4. The SQL Support Rules tests will initially run. It is important to verify that all these tests pass before moving ahead. If acceptable, click Next.

5. Enter a SQL Server product key or evaluation edition, and then click Next through the licensing agreement and the Setup Support Files installation.

6. On the Feature Selection screen, choose which components you wish to be installed. Note that the directory used for these features can go to the default location on the C: drive or any other local disk. Later, we will choose where the shared databases are stored. Click Next.

7. On the Instance Configuration screen (Figure 8.7), enter the network name of the SQL Server that clients will connect to. Using our naming convention, this would be **DeltaDB**. You have the option of using the default name of the instance, which is MSSQLSERVER, or creating your own named instance (I have chosen ACCOUNTING). This screen will again be installed locally, since you will go through an installation process for the other nodes later. If there were other instances of SQL Server within the cluster, we would see them listed at the bottom.

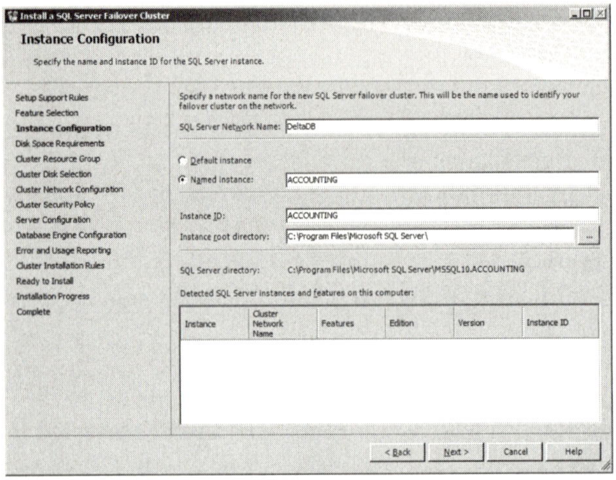

FIGURE 8.7
Creating the clustered SQL Server network name and instance

8. On the Cluster Resource Group screen, choose or create the name of the resource group that will appear in the left tree of the Windows Failover Cluster Management console. This is not a name that clients will see, so it can be whatever is useful to you when managing the cluster. I adapted the default to show the application, the network name, and the instance. If you have already created a resource group, you can choose it from the list of resource groups in the FCM console. Notice that none of the existing resource groups are capable of hosting the SQL Server instance. Otherwise, you could pick one of them instead.

9. On the Cluster Disk Selection screen, choose which shared disks will be used. In this case (Figure 8.8), I had preconfigured two shared disk for the cluster—one for the databases and another for the transaction logs. Those disks will appear green, meaning that they are suitable for inclusion in this clustered SQL Server instance. Other shared disks that are in use elsewhere will appear red, such as the quorum witness disk.

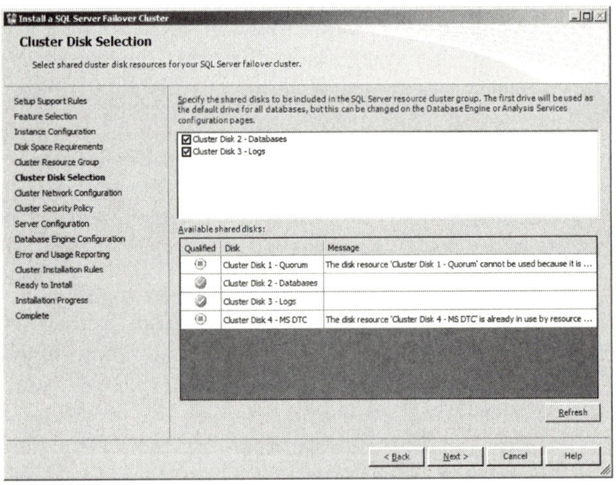

FIGURE 8.8
Choosing the shared disks for the clustered SQL instance

10. On the Cluster Network Configuration screen, configure the IP address of the SQL server that the users will connect to. Using our best practice, I chose from the same range as the other addresses in the cluster, as seen in Figure 8.9. Click Next to continue, followed by Next again on the security policy screen to accept the recommended default.

FIGURE 8.9
Configuring the network address for the clustered SQL Server

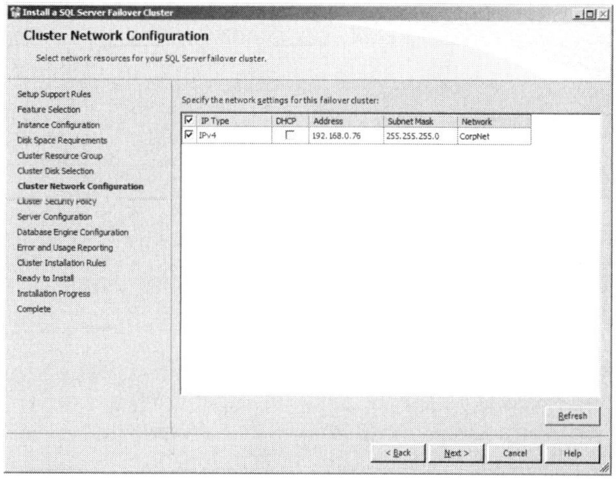

11. On the Server Configuration screen, set the user account to be used by the SQL Server components. Notice that the startup type is set to Manual and cannot be changed (Figure 8.10). The cluster will handle this later.

FIGURE 8.10
SQL Server Configuration service settings

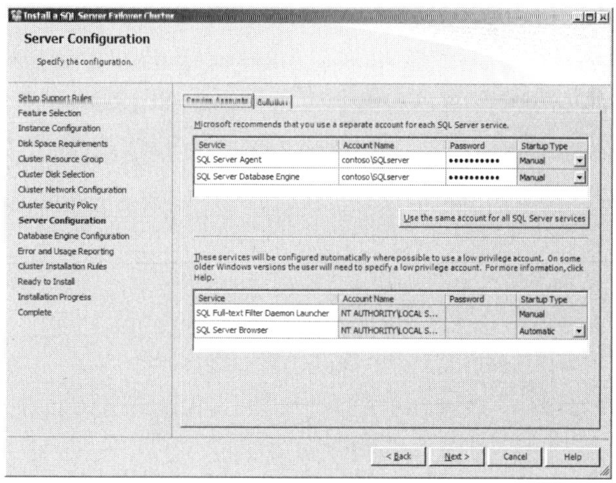

12. Choose the file locations on the Database Engine Configuration screen, all of which should use the shared storage volumes that we chose earlier, including the user database, TempDB, and the backup location.

The Cluster Installation Rules will test the configuration, after which you click Next to see the Summary screen. Click Next again to start the installation. The scroll bar will show progress for a while, and the eventual result is a single-node clustered SQL Server. When complete, the Failover Cluster Management console will show the new SQL Server instance in the Services And Applications area of the left pane (Figure 8.11).

FIGURE 8.11
Clustered SQL instance, as seen in the Failover Cluster Management console

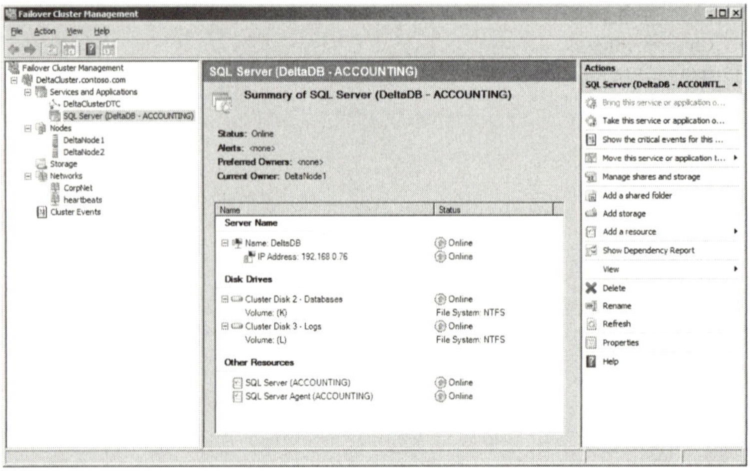

The process for installing the subsequent clustered nodes is far less complicated (or time consuming), because Windows Failover Clustering will retain the configuration, as well as what is stored in the SQL databases. All that is left is to get the binaries installed on the additional cluster nodes.

Task 2: Installing SQL Server onto the Second Clustered Node

Installing application software on the second (or additional) node of a cluster often follows a similar model, where the application is primarily installed and configured on the first node. Then, the binaries are installed on the second node with an abbreviated setup process, because the shared data and Windows Failover Clustering maintains the rest. We saw this for Exchange 2007 in Chapter 7 and it is similar for SQL Server as well.

To install SQL Server onto an additional node of the cluster:

1. From the node 2 console, run `Setup.exe` from the installation media, which will launch the SQL Server Installation Center.

2. From the left pane, choose Installation Center. In the right pane, choose Add Node To A SQL Server Failover Cluster.

   The first few steps are the same as we saw in Task 1 for the first node, including the SQL Support Rules tests, product key, and licensing agreement. After that, we will see that the Add A Failover Cluster Node wizard has far fewer options to work through.

3. On the Cluster Node Configuration screen, you can choose which SQL Server instance that this node should be added to. In a clean configuration, there is only the instance that we just installed on node 1 (Figure 8.12), but in a larger cluster, we might have several choices. Here, we can see the Accounting instance of a clustered SQL Server named DeltaDB, which is currently hosted on DeltaNode1.

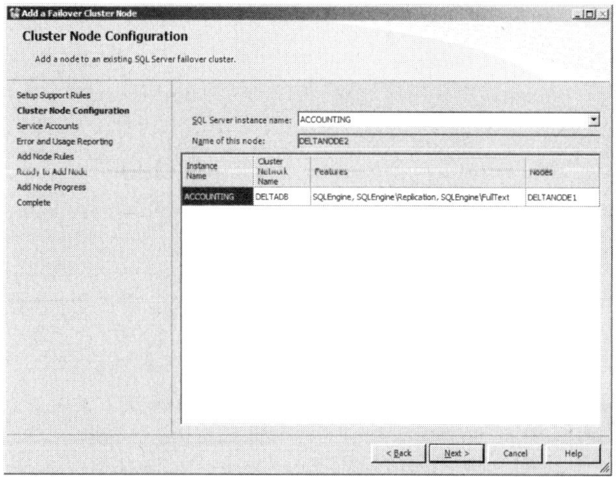

FIGURE 8.12
Choose which instance to install the second cluster node to.

4. On the Service Accounts screen, we see the same services that we configured in Task 1, but notice that the service account names are also grayed out because they are not configurable on the additional nodes. On this screen, enter the password for each account (Figure 8.13) and click Next.

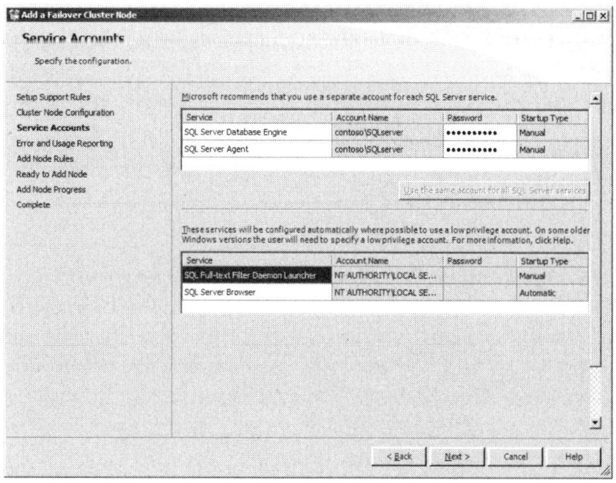

FIGURE 8.13
Confirm the service accounts' passwords.

5. The wizard then does some additional Add Node Rules testing, provides a summary of the installation choices, and installs SQL Server onto the node.

Congratulations, you now have SQL Server clustered across the two nodes. But we are not done yet. Don't forget the service packs. Start by updating the node that does not currently have the database (node 2). This provides two safeguards:

- If anything changes in the data because of the software update, you aren't trying to move from the newer version (which understands the change) to the older version (which doesn't).
- If the service can't move over, at least the data is still on a machine that knows how to serve it.

Applying a SQL service pack is relatively straightforward. It does do more proactive checking than most user-based applications or OS service packs, but there are no configuration steps, so a few extra Next clicks and the passive node (the node not currently serving the database) will be updated.

NOTE In the previous two tasks, I used the evaluation download of SQL Server 2008, which comes as an ISO file (and thereby is convenient to use in a virtual machine), and then updated it with SQL Server 2008's SP1 download. A better suggestion in production environments is to do a slipstream install of SP1 into the installation directories of SQL Server 2008. This means that the original SQL 2008 bits are replaced by the SP1 updated versions, so that you only have to do one install. Not every application and its associated service packs support slipstreaming, but when they do, it is a beautiful thing.

Here is a good blog post on slipstreaming SP1 with SQL Server 2008:

`http://blogs.msdn.com/buckwoody/archive/2009/04/09/slipstreaming-sql-server -installations-and-the-sp1-controversy.aspx`

When you've applied the service packs to the passive node, I recommend running Windows Update, to be sure that it is all completely up-to-date, and then rebooting one last time. After all, everything is running from the other node, anyway.

When the passive node is completely back online, use the Failover Cluster Management console (Figure 8.14) to move the clustered SQL Server instance from the currently active Node1 to Node2. To move an instance between clustered nodes, follow these steps:

1. Expand the left tree of Services And Applications.
2. Right-click on the SQL Server instance and choose Move This Service Or Application To Another Node ➢ Move To Node DeltaNode2.

After confirming that the SQL instance is online from node 2, you can apply the SQL service pack and Windows Updates to node 1. Reboot node 1 to get a fresh start. And as a last step, move the SQL instance back to node 1. The reason for moving things back again is not because it runs any better from one node or another. After all, the nodes are equal, which is the whole idea of a cluster—it shouldn't matter which node an application is being served from. The reason that you should move the database one last time is to be sure that it can move. The worst thing that could happen is to walk away thinking that everything is running fine, better not knowing that something broke during the last updates.

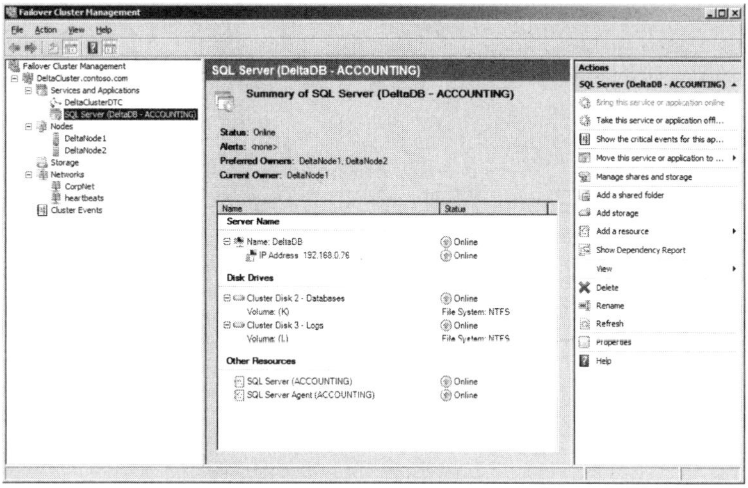

FIGURE 8.14
The Clustered SQL Server instance within the Failover Cluster Management console

What Happens When a Database Changes Nodes?

Switching an application, whether it is SQL Server, Exchange, or something else, is very rarely seamless when switching between nodes. The time involved may be very little, but it is not zero. Let's first look at the behavior of a planned move between nodes, such as what we did during our rolling upgrade to SP1.

When you click to move a database, here is what happens:

1. The database is shut down. In our brand-new cluster, it likely doesn't take any time at all. But in a very busy production environment, it may take a few seconds to commit the data that is in memory and do the final disk writes to the database files.
2. The SQL Server application services are shut down.
3. The cluster resources' ownership has changed within the cluster, including:
   - The network name
   - The IP address
   - The two storage volumes
   - The two or more services
4. The ownership of each one is flipped from Node1 to Node2, or vice versa.
5. Once the ownership of everything is confirmed by the new owning node, the disks are brought online, the network name starts being offered, and the IP address becomes active.
6. The application services start up and the database is mounted.

Most things in high-availability scenarios are predictable, and one of the reasons that most IT environments can set more rigid service-level agreements (SLAs; see Chapter 2) after they have deployed high-availability solutions. But in the last workflow that we described, steps 1 and 6 can be slightly more unpredictable, based on what was going on with the database and its applications at the time that the move was invoked.

Now, let's assume an unplanned outage like a hardware or component failure in the active node. Steps 1 and 2 didn't happen. The node just died.

Here is what happens when the active node dies (hard):

1. The active node dies, without warning.
    - The databases are not cleanly shut down.
    - The higher functions just unexpectedly stop writing to the files, no matter what state they were in.
2. The cluster calculates quorum to determine if it has a majority to keep operational.
    - In a two-node cluster, like the one we built, the surviving node and the witness disk make up two of the three votes, and therefore have a majority.
    - In a three-node cluster, if the other two nodes are still operational, they have a majority.
    - For any cluster larger than that, the same principles apply for determining if a majority is still in communication.
3. With a majority confirmed, the cluster resources' ownership is changed to that of the surviving node, including:
    - The network name
    - The IP address
    - The two storage volumes
    - The two or more services
4. The ownership of each resource as recorded in the quorum is flipped from Node1 to Node2, or vice versa. If the failed node was hosting other applications or the cluster's configuration itself, those groups will also be moved to the surviving node.
5. Once the ownership of everything is confirmed by the surviving node, the disks are brought online. But because disk I/O had been unexpectedly halted on the original node, a check of the integrity of the file system and data may be required. This process can be quick unless there was some damage that requires repair. The greater the amount of active I/O at the point of failure on the original node, the greater the likelihood that some level of repair may be necessary. This can affect your planned RTO and SLA because this step is somewhat unpredictable. At some point, the disks do hopefully come online and the process continues.
6. After the validated disks are brought online, the network name starts being offered and the IP address becomes active.
7. The application services start up and an attempt is made to mount the database.

Steps 5 and 7 bring unpredictability to any cluster of a transactional application. Prior to Windows Server 2008, the checking of the disk in step 5, also known as the CHKDSK process, could be appreciably long. On large data volumes that were extremely busy at the time of a node crash, the disk volume could take *hours* to be mounted. Similarly, if there was a significant amount of inconsistency between the database and the log, step 7 could take time.

Of course, between Windows Server 2008 and SQL Server 2008 (including their respective R2 versions), things are much better. They are better because of how they handle their file I/O and transaction logs, so that failover is more resilient and the unpredictability is reduced (but not eliminated).

Should You Cluster SQL Server?

Here are two reasons why a clustered SQL Server is not ideal:

Single Instance of the Data Not to be confused with an instance of SQL Server, there is only one instance or copy of the database within the cluster. If this one and only copy of the database were to experience either data corruption or a failure in the shared storage array, the two or more clustered nodes have no data and the high-availability solution has failed. If clustering SQL Server is otherwise desirable, you may want to consider replicating the databases to another instance outside the cluster. A few methods for this are discussed later in this chapter, in the sections "SQL Database Mirroring" and "SQL Log Shipping and Replication."

Failover RPO and RTO When a Windows cluster has to fail over SQL Server services, the normal behavior of switching control of the resources from one node to another must occur; then the services must start, and the database has be recovered from what is usually an abrupt stop. This may result in data loss and (as we just stated in the previous section), recovery time can be unpredictable.

Because of these two circumstances, many administrators' preferred solution for SQL Server high-availability scenarios is to use database mirroring with automatic failover, which will be discussed in the next section, "SQL Database Mirroring." Database mirroring provides two copies of the database that are on separate servers, and the replication can be configured so that there is little to no data loss between the copies. These are the same reasons why we saw Exchange move from single-copy clusters (SCC) to CCR in 2007 and DAG in 2010 (see Chapter 7).

SQL Server database mirroring began in 2005 and continues to be a popular availability solution in SQL Server 2008 and 2008 R2.

So why not always use database mirroring instead of clustering? Here are two reasons:

Legacy Applications Not all of the applications that you will install on top of SQL Server are able to utilize mirrored databases. If the application is not able to follow the mirrored pair when they switch roles, the database will still appear to be broken to the application, even though it is available from the mirror.

Failing Over non-Database Components As you will see in the next section, database mirroring and failover is only for the database itself. If you need logons (other than those done through Windows authentication) or jobs that need to run, those elements are not included in the failover of a mirrored database. By using a cluster, everything within the instance fails over.

SQL Database Mirroring

As we just mentioned, the other high-availability solution for SQL databases is database mirroring, provided the applications that will be built on SQL Server are able to utilize the mirrored configuration. Mirroring is done on a per-database level and is ideal when only the database itself needs protection (instead of an entire application ecosystem or the whole instance of SQL Server).

In a mirrored configuration, we will have two instances of SQL Server that will facilitate the mirrored pair (preferably on separate machines), as well as a potential third SQL Server instance to enable automated failover:

Principal In a mirrored database configuration, the principal database is the copy that is actively serving the data to the applications and users.

Mirror In a mirrored database configuration, the mirror database is the copy that is continually receiving replicated log information from the principal and applying it as a secondary copy. It can be thought of as a *hot standby* or a *warm copy* of the data, depending on whether automatic failover has been enabled or the data is ready but something must be done (manual failover) before it can be accessed.

The mirror database cannot be accessed directly by anything except the principal database. Instead, when a connection is attempted to the mirror database, SQL Server attempts to transparently redirect the connection request to the principal database instead.

Witness In a mirrored database configuration, an optional third instance of SQL running on a third computer is called the witness. The witness is used to determine which of the other instances should be the principal or the mirror during failover scenarios. We will look closely at the witness later in this chapter, but as a short introduction, the witness acts as a third vote, similar to the quorum in a failover cluster, to determine whether failover between the principal and mirror should or should not occur. Collectively, the three can be seen in Figure 8.15.

The terms *principal* and *witness* primarily refer to their role in the database mirroring relationship as the sender and receiver, respectively. The machine running the instance of SQL Server that currently owns the principal role is termed the principal server within the pair, and it hosts the principal copy of the database. Similarly, the machine running the instance of SQL Server that owns the mirror role is called the mirror server within the pair, and it hosts the mirror copy of the database.

FIGURE 8.15
The principal, the mirror, and the witness

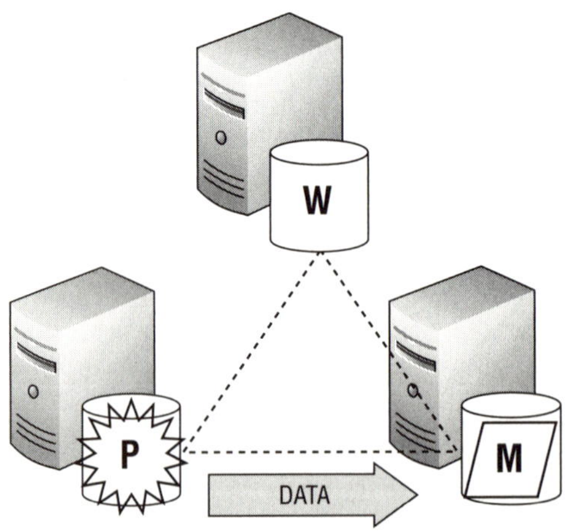

For most of this chapter, we will use the terms principal and mirror as generic nouns that refer to the sending and receiving server, instance, and database configurations, respectively. It is also worth noting that because the relationship and descriptors are most accurately applied per database, some databases could be principals on Node1 and be mirrored to Node2, while other databases could be principals on Node2 and be mirrored to Node1. But for simplicity's sake, we will use the SQL terms in the broader sense of presuming one direction from the instance of SQL that is serving the principal copy of the database to the instance of SQL that is receiving and maintaining the mirror copy of the database.

NOTE Only databases that use the Full-Recovery mode can be mirrored because of how the transaction logs are used. Databases that use Simple-Recovery mode cannot be mirrored, but they can be clustered.

Starting the Mirror Session

To begin database mirroring, the mirrored copy of the database is seeded, often from a backup of the active database, which is referred to as the principal. Once the mirrored instance is ready, a *database mirrored session* is started that creates the relationship between the principal, the mirror, and potentially, a witness. As part of the mirroring session, each instance begins tracking communication and exchanging status with the others.

With the session established, the mirror must immediately ensure that its database is current compared to what is in the principal. To do this, the mirror instance determines the log sequence number (LSN) of the last transactions that were applied to the mirror database. The mirror sends its LSN to the principal, so that any transactions latter than that can be sent from the principal to the mirror. Specifically, logs of the transactions after the LSN, as well as any future transactions, are placed in the send queue on the principal server. The *send queue*, as the name implies, is a holding area for logs to be sent from the principal server. Logs in the send queue of the principal are transmitted to the redo queue of the mirror. The redo queue on the mirror server holds the received logs. From there, the mirror instance will immediately apply those transactions to the mirrored copy of the database.

How Mirroring Works

In a normal and standalone SQL Server, the application service serves the logical database information either directly to users with SQL client connections or to a server-based application. But as changes happen within the database, those instructions are:

1. Immediately written to the transaction log
2. Later applied from the log to the database file

In database mirroring, both the principal and the mirror are responsible for applying the changes to their own database files. So, when a client changes data on the principal, the process begins the same way and then mirroring begins:

1. Changes are immediately written to the transaction log on the principal.
2. The changes are put into the send queue on the principal, which will cause those logs to be sent to the redo queue on the mirror. Note that as of SQL Server 2008, the transaction logs are compressed for better network efficiency between the principal's send queue and the mirror's redo queue.

3. The principal server will commit the transaction to its own database but may not yet confirm the commit, depending on how database mirroring is configured:
   - If *synchronously mirroring*, the principal will *wait* for confirmation from the mirror that the transaction has been successfully written into the redo queue of the mirror before the principal instance confirms the transaction commit to its principal database.
   - If *asynchronously mirroring*, the principal will confirm the transaction commit to its database *without waiting* for confirmation that the mirror has successfully written to its log.
4. Either way, the mirror will commit the transaction to its database, as quickly as possible.

We will go into much more detail on *synchronous* and *asynchronous* mirroring in the next section. But the general behavior of database mirroring is that starting from the oldest LSN record, the mirror will redo, or replay, each transaction into its own database. The mirror database behaves exactly as the principal database does, with every insert, delete, or update operation applied to the mirror in the same way that they were applied to the principal. Any changes to the principal database, including log truncation or other maintenance operations, are captured within the transaction log of the principal, transmitted to the mirror instance, and eventually enacted on the mirror database as well.

NOTE **Even in synchronous mirroring, the principal only waits until the logs are written to the mirror's redo queue, not the actual mirrored database itself. So, it is possible that at any given moment, the mirror database is behind the principal database—even in a synchronous configuration. This is okay because the redo queue is played forward and emptied out before any failover occurs, so there is still no data loss.**

Depending on who you talk to, SQL Server's database mirroring has either two modes or three scenarios. The two mirroring modes are:

High Performance Mirrors asynchronously

High Safety Mirrors synchronously and may or may not include failover

To better clarify these, many folks describe three scenarios instead:

High Performance Mirrors asynchronously

High Safety Mirrors synchronously and does *not* include automatic failover

High Availability Mirrors synchronously and does include automatic failover

The operating mode for database mirroring is determined by the transaction safety setting. We will do most of the exercises in this chapter using the SQL Server Management Studio to configure mirroring and failover. However, if you use Transact-SQL, you will want to modify the `Safety` property of the `ALTER DATABASE` statement. Safety will be set to either `FULL` or `OFF`, for synchronous or asynchronous mirroring, respectively.

Synchronous Mirroring for High Safety

When you set `Transaction Safety` to `FULL`, the databases will mirror synchronously. As described earlier, synchronous mirroring is achieved by the principal database not committing the transactions from its own log until it receives a confirmation from the mirror server that the transactions have been successfully written to disk in the log destined for the mirror database (Figure 8.16).

FIGURE 8.16
Synchronous database mirroring

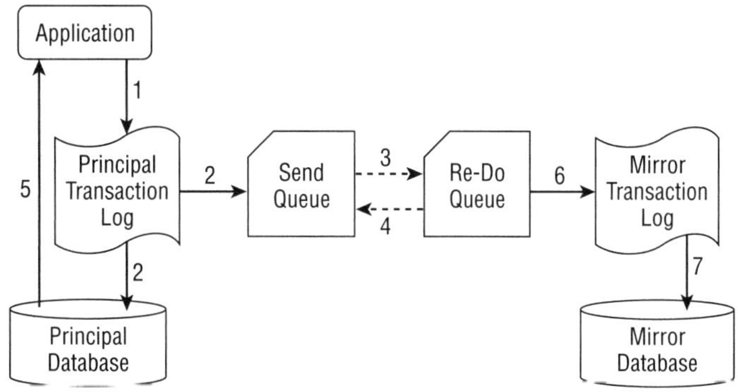

Because the mirror server has confirmed the disk write of the transactions going to its redo queue, it is a near guarantee that they will be applied very soon into the mirror database, or at least before the database is brought online as a new principal during failover.

In the section "SQL Database Failover" later in the chapter, we discuss doing a manual failover between the principal and mirror, as well as an automatic failover that utilizes the principal, the mirror, and a witness.

The challenge of synchronous database mirroring, like the other synchronous storage technologies discussed in Chapter 3, is that as distance or network latency increases between the principal and the mirror, the general performance of the production (principal) server and its applications will suffer. Because of this, synchronous mirroring may be ideal for high availability of SQL databases within a datacenter or corporate campus, but is suboptimal for distance-based protection such as across a major metropolitan area, or larger disaster recovery and business continuity scenarios (which will be discussed in Chapter 12).

Asynchronous Mirroring for High Performance

When you set `Transaction Safety` to `OFF`, the databases will mirror asynchronously. As described earlier, asynchronous mirroring is achieved by the principal database freely committing the transactions from its own log, without waiting for a confirmation from the mirror server that the transactions have been successfully written to disk in the log destined for the mirror database. Instead, as soon as the transaction is transmitted from the send queue on the principal, the transaction is confirmed to the client as having been written (Figure 8.17). By not introducing the latency of the mirror's confirmation, performance on the production (principal) server is increased.

By mirroring asynchronously, higher performance can be achieved by the production SQL Server that is serving the principal database—because the SQL applications and clients do not have to wait on the verification by the mirror disk. Asynchronous mirroring is an effective data protection and availability scenario that still uses only the built-in technologies. Used just for data protection, it is usually superior to other replication-only technologies that are not SQL-specific, such as the host-based or storage-based replication technologies discussed in Chapter 3. In most cases, sending only the changes from within transaction logs is the most efficient and most granular replication model for most transactional applications. In this way, SQL database mirroring is similar to Exchange 2007 SCR or Exchange 2010 DAG as an ideal way to move granular changes across copies of large databases.

FIGURE 8.17
Asynchronous database mirroring

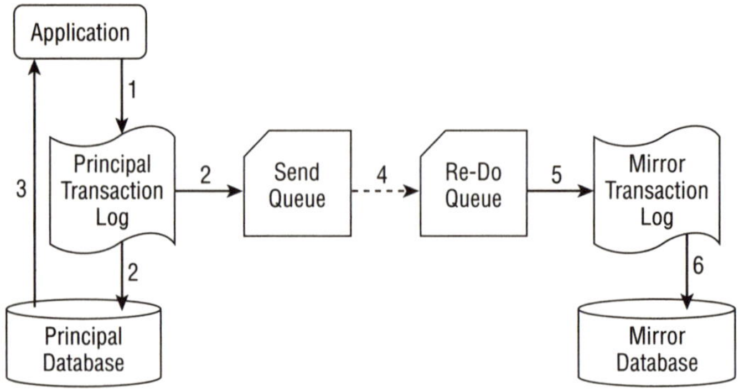

However, for appreciable distances needed in disaster recovery scenarios, SQL log shipping (discussed later in this chapter) is often preferable to asynchronous database mirroring.

PAGE-LEVEL SELF-HEALING

For some database issues, failing over is not the best answer. In the case of minor I/O or data page errors, the better answer is to simply repair the principal from the mirror.

One of the additional benefits of database mirroring in SQL Server 2008 and 2008 R2 is automatic resolution of some errors related to reading a data page. If the data cannot be read from the principal and the databases are running in a synchronized state, the principal will request the page from the mirror to determine if it is readable there. If the data page can be read from the mirror, the mirror's page automatically overwrites the principal's to resolve the issue.

CONFIGURING ENDPOINTS FOR DATABASE MIRRORING

There is one last concept to cover before getting started with database mirroring: the idea of *endpoints*. Endpoints are objects within SQL Server that facilitate network communication. Database mirroring requires a dedicated endpoint, which is not used by any other communication, including client connections.

Database mirroring endpoints use a unique and administrator-defined TCP port number to communicate with the other instances of SQL Server to listen for network messages related to database mirroring. All database mirroring connections will use a single endpoint per instance of SQL Server.

The network address that the database endpoint creates includes the fully qualified domain name of the server, as well as the TCP port number. So, a SQL server named SQL28 in the contoso.com domain and using port 7077 as its endpoint would be reachable via `TCP://SQL28.contoso.com:7077`. Notice that neither the instance name nor a particular database name is listed here. The entire instance will use port 7077 as its database mirroring endpoint, whereas if the server had a second instance of SQL Server, the second instance would use a different TCP port.

Endpoints have several security considerations that are worth noting:

- Any firewall will need to allow inbound and outbound traffic on this TCP port for the SQL Server.
- By default, there is no database mirroring endpoint. This must be set up by the administrator when configuring database mirroring, so that a hole is not available until it is needed.

- Authentication occurs between the principal and mirror endpoints, using either Windows authentication (NT LAN Manager or Kerberos) or certificates, in order to authorize communication using the endpoints.
- By default, database mirroring endpoints have encryption enabled.

Task 3: Preparing the Database Mirror

To get started with database mirroring, we must first create the mirror database on a second instance of SQL Server. We will create the mirror on the secondary server by doing a backup from the primary (principal) server and manually seeding the database into the secondary (mirror) server. In my examples, SQL28 is my current production server, while SQL27 is my new server that will be the mirror. Both of them have a SALES named instance of SQL Server 2008 SP1.

Backing Up the Principal Database Using the UI

Start from the SQL Server Management Studio, and connect to your server and instance. In my case, the principal is at `SQL28\Sales`, as seen in Figure 8.18.

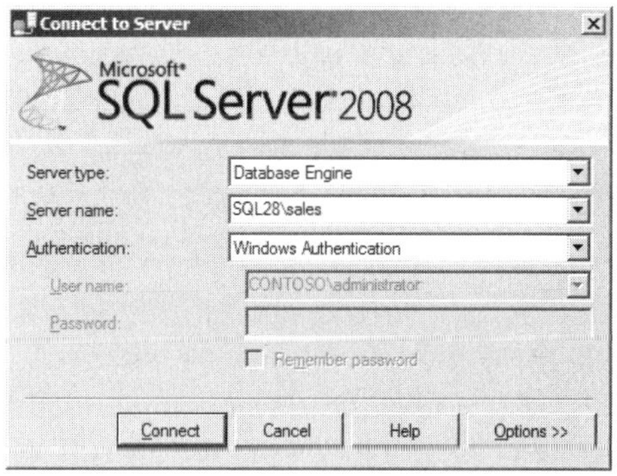

Figure 8.18
Connecting to a SQL server instance

To back up the database on the original (principal) using the Management Studio:

1. Expand the Object Explorer left pane to see the databases on your instance and locate the one that you will be mirroring.
2. Right-click your database and select Tasks ➤ Back Up, which will launch the Back Up Database UI (Figure 8.19).
3. You can accept the defaults for most, but the key fields to confirm are as follows:

   Database This field is prepopulated with the database that you right-clicked, though you can choose any database from the pull-down list.

   Backup Type Keep this set to Full.

   Backup Component Select the Database radio button.

   Backup Set You can amend the prepopulated name and description if you like.

   Backup Set Expires Expiration determines when SQL can overwrite this particular backup, so the default of 0 days (meaning it can be overwritten whenever you like) is typically fine.

Alternatively, you might set this for 30 days, so that SQL couldn't overwrite it for a month, but delete the file from Windows Explorer tomorrow.

Destination Make sure the Disk radio button is selected, and click Add to set a location (Figure 8.20). I chose `L:\Sales\Customer.bak`.

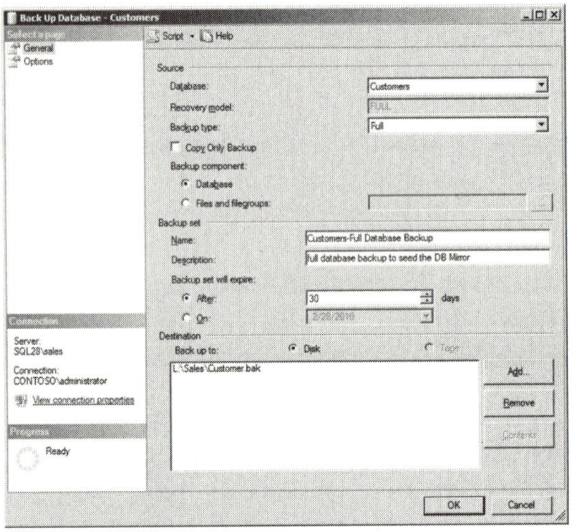

FIGURE 8.19
The SQL Back Up Database UI

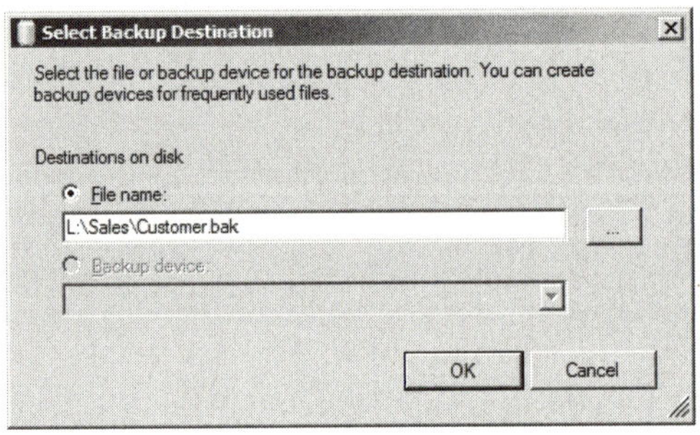

FIGURE 8.20
Specifying where to back up your database

4. Click OK to do the full backup of the database. A dialog box should pop up notifying you of success.

5. To back up the transaction log, which we will also need, repeat steps 2, 3, and 4. But in step 3, change the following:

   Backup Type Change it to Transaction Log.

   Backup Set The default name should change to reflect the Log backup instead of the Full database backup.

6. Click OK to perform the backup of the transaction log. A dialog box should pop up notifying you of success.

7. To confirm, repeat step 2 to start the process again. But this time, simply go to the bottom of the UI and click the Contents button to see what is in the backup media file that you have been using. You should see two items: one for the full backup and one for the transaction log, as seen in Figure 8.21.

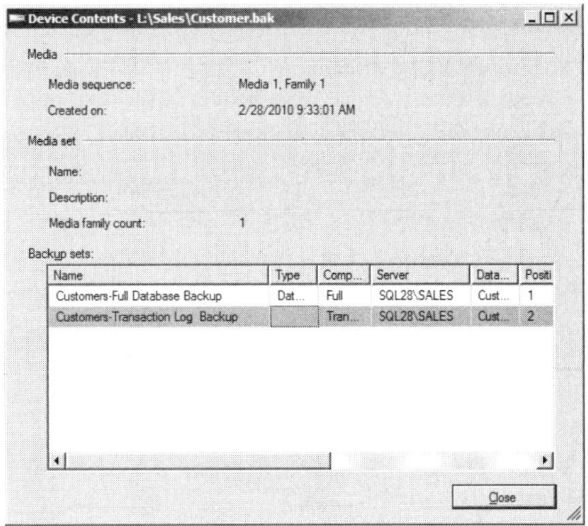

FIGURE 8.21
These two items should be in your backup file to seed the mirror database.

BACKING UP THE DATABASE AND LOG USING TRANSACT-SQL

Alternatively, there is a reason that the L in SQL is Language. Click the New Query button at the top of the Management Studio, after you have connected to your instance of SQL in step 1. Using Transact-SQL (the language), here is the script to do the backup of not only the database (which can be done from the UI), but also the transaction log that we will need in a few minutes:

```
BACKUP DATABASE Customers
    TO DISK = 'L:\ Customers.bak'
    WITH FORMAT
BACKUP LOG Customers
    TO DISK = 'L:\ Customers.bak'
GO
```

This does the same type of full backup of the database. The `FORMAT` command overwrites the file, so it does not contain anything else. Immediately after the database backup, the log is backed up. Because `FORMAT` was not specified in the second backup command, it is appended within the backup media file. If you followed both examples listed here (the UI and the script), you will have two backup media files because I put them in two locations.

CREATING THE MIRROR DATABASE

Now, we need to go to what will be the mirror server. We will be copying over the backup file from the principal server, creating an empty database by the same name and then restoring the backup into it.

Start from the SQL Server Management Studio and connect to your *mirror* server and instance. Because we are now working on the mirror, I connected to the SQL27 server and SALES instance (similar to Figure 8.17 earlier).

1. Create the database, being careful to use the same paths wherever possible. In my case, the Customers database is stored in the same locations for both servers:

   Database `D:\Sales\Customers\Customers.mdf`

   Transaction Logs `L:\Sales\Customers\Customers_log.ldf`

Restoring the Principal Database into the Mirror Using the UI

Now we need to do a restore, using the No Recovery option, which essentially leaves the database in a state where additional recoveries can be done after this one. This is important because the mirror database will be constantly recovering what is being replicated to it from the principal.

2. Right-click on the Customers database and choose Tasks ➤ Restore ➤ Database. This will bring up the Restore Database interface.
3. Under Destination For Restore, the Customers database should already be selected, but you will need to change Source For Restore to From Device.
4. Click the browse button to the right of the From Device field and select the BKF file that you created on the principal server and copied to the mirror server. Click OK, and the Restore Database interface will look like Figure 8.22.

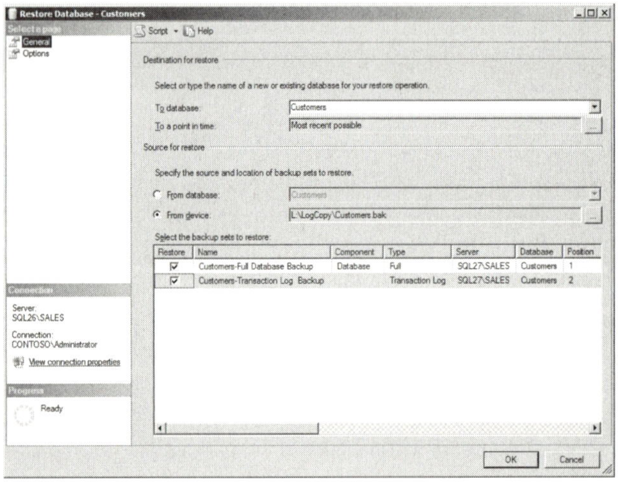

FIGURE 8.22
The Restore Database interface

5. Check both boxes to choose the recovery of both the database and the log file, but do not click OK.
6. Move from the General page to the Options page by clicking Options in the upper-left corner.
7. At the top of the Options page, choose to overwrite the existing database, since you are doing a restore.
8. Toward the bottom of the screen, under Recovery State, you must click the middle choice to restore with no recovery. This allows additional transaction logs to be restored, which will start coming from the principal server later, after we have set up mirroring.

Restoring the Principal Database into the Mirror Using SQL

Alternatively, you could use the following Transact-SQL method:

1. After connecting to the mirror server and instance (`SQL27/Sales`), click the New Query button in the upper-left corner of the SQL Server Management Studio.

2. Use the following Transact-SQL script:

```
RESTORE DATABASE Customer
   FROM DISK = 'L:\Customers.bak'
   WITH NORECOVERY
GO
RESTORE LOG Customer
   FROM DISK = 'L:\Customers.bak'
   WITH FILE=1, NORECOVERY
GO
```

Task 4: Getting Started with Database Mirroring

With the database and log backed up at the principal server, let's continue from the mirrored server. Figure 8.23 shows the left pane of the SQL Server Management Console, with the principal SQL28 server on the top and the mirror SQL27 server on the bottom. Notice that the Customers database on the mirror server on the bottom is in a Restoring mode. This is because of the NORECOVERY option that we used during our restore process.

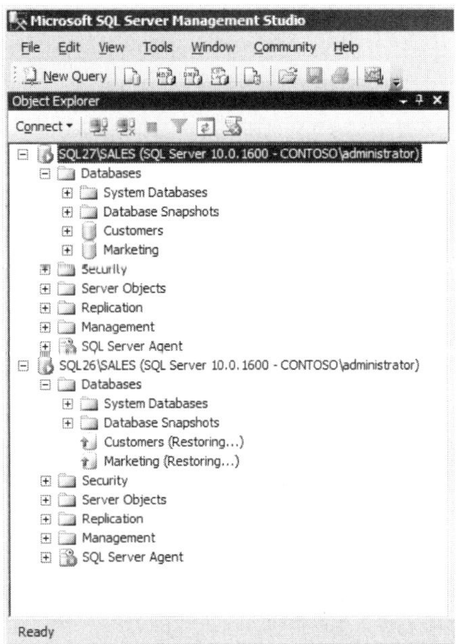

FIGURE 8.23
The SQL Management Console, with the principal and mirror, ready to go

Now we can configure database mirroring. To do that, start from the SQL Server Management Console, expanded as seen in Figure 8.23:

1. Expand the tree in the left pane of the Object Explorer to find the principal server instance.
2. From the principal instance, expand Databases and find the database that you wish to mirror.
3. Right-click on the database and choose Tasks ➤ Mirror, which will open the Database Properties dialog box to its Mirroring page.

4. Click the Configure Security button to start the Configure Database Mirroring Security (CDMS) Wizard.
5. The CDMS wizard will help you create the database mirroring endpoints.
   - When asked whether to configure a Witness at this time, say No.
   - The principal will already be selected, along with a proposed TCP port address. Click Next.
   - When prompted for the Mirror, click Connect to choose the instance on the Mirror server, and click Connect again.
   - Leave the accounts blank, and click Next for the summary; then click Finish to create the endpoints.
   - A dialog box will confirm that the endpoints are created. Of the two buttons—Start Mirroring and Do Not Start Mirroring—choose Do Not Start Mirroring.
6. Instead of step 5, you could also have run this script on both the principal and the witness. Note that in step 5, the wizard offered a port number and configured it on all the participants. If you're using a script, be sure to choose an unused and non-firewalled port on the participants yourself (preferably the same on all participants, but not required):

```
CREATE ENDPOINT Mirroring

    STATE=STARTED

    AS TCP (LISTENER_PORT = 5022)

    FOR DATABASE_MIRRORING (ROLE = PARTNER)

GO
```

7. With the security wizard complete and the endpoints set up, we will see the Mirroring screen populated with the principal and mirror servers (including the port numbers that we chose for their endpoints). In the lower part of this screen, we can choose one of three modes for database mirroring:
   - High Performance (asynchronous) Replication
   - High Safety without automatic failover (synchronous)
   - High Safety with automatic failover (synchronous) (notice that this one is grayed out because we did not configure a witness earlier, which we will explain in the next section)
8. Choose High Safety without automatic failover (synchronous) and then click Start Mirroring.

Your principal is now replicating with your mirror.

Because we chose Synchronous, the two databases will be the same for any future failovers that we want to do. This is the same kind of relationship that we saw in Chapter 5 with DFS namespace and DFS replication. Database mirroring, like DFS replication, is a data movement mechanism, and there are practical benefits of just doing the mirroring on its own. However, to achieve high availability using the replicated data, we needed DFS namespace to point people to the replicated files in Chapter 5. And here in Chapter 8, we need to point clients to the mirrored databases, using database failover.

SQL Database Failover

Database mirroring on its own is just that—mirroring or replication of the databases between a primary and a secondary copy. Failover is how you can use the secondary copy (mirror) to resume service when the principal has failed. To facilitate automatic database failover, you will need a third vote to help the two mirrored database copies determine who should be serving up the data. This is called the witness.

Can I Get a Witness?

A witness is a third instance of SQL Server (strongly preferred to be on a third physical machine), which acts as a third vote, along with the principal and mirror SQL instances, to determine who should be serving up the data. The witness does not actually run the database. The witness's only job is to help determine when the principal-mirror partners should automatically fail over the database, so its performance characteristics can be less than what would be required by the principal or mirror instances. In fact, the witness can even run on a lesser version of SQL Server, such as Workgroup or Express editions. In addition, a witness server can act as the witness for several principal-mirror pairs, as seen in Figure 8.24.

FIGURE 8.24
Witnessing multiple principal-mirror partners

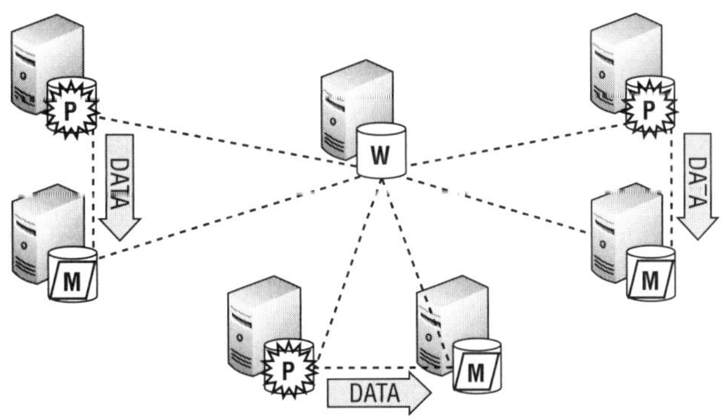

Technically, the witness can be a lesser version of SQL Server and run on lesser hardware than the principal–mirror partners. However, if you use the same SQL Server version and hardware specifications, then you have an additional recovery scenario. If Node1 was the principal and fails, Node2 as the mirror can fail over.

- If you know that Node1 will be down for an extended period of time, you could convert your Node3 witness server into the new mirror so that your database remains protected. It won't provide automatic failover, but it will ensure that the data remains protected.

WITNESSES ARE FOR HIGH SAFETY MODE ONLY

The witness should only be used in automatic failover scenarios, where the databases are configured for High Safety mode, meaning that the two databases are synchronously mirroring. A witness for automatic failover should *never* be used in High Performance mode, where the two databases are asynchronously mirroring.

Because a witness enables a completely automated failover configuration, it should not be used during asynchronous mirroring. Otherwise, upon determination to fail over, the mirror will begin serving data without all of the original data from the original principal. Not only will the data be lost, but it may appear to have vanished from the outside client's perspective. The client will have originally believed that their data was applied (on the original principal), but after failover, the data may not be there anymore (on the new principal) because it had not yet been asynchronously mirrored.

In addition, asynchronous configurations may assume that that the principal and mirror may occasionally be separated due to slow or intermittent network connectivity. In a two-node, principal-mirror configuration, that is fine. But in a three-node, principal-mirror-witness configuration, the principal must be able to see either the mirror or the witness. If it doesn't, the principal may erroneously believe that is no longer supposed to be serving the data and actually go offline, even though nothing else is wrong.

To create a witness for a mirrored database scenario, we will repeat some of the steps that we did in Task 4, "Getting Started with Database Mirroring," earlier in this chapter.

Task 5: Adding a Witness to the Mirroring Configuration

Start from the SQL Server Management Console (Transact-SQL is an option, too) to add or replace a witness. Adding a witness in Management Studio also changes the operating mode to High Safety mode with automatic failover.

1. Browse the Object Explorer in the left pane to select the principal server instance (connecting to the principal server if needed).
2. Expand Databases and select the principal database that you want to add a witness for.
3. Right-click on the database and select Tasks ➢ Mirror to open the Mirroring page of the Database Properties dialog box.
4. On the Mirroring page, click Configure Security to launch the Configure Database Mirroring Security Wizard.
5. Unlike when we configured mirroring without failover in Task 4, this time, when prompted with Include Witness Server, choose Yes and click Next.
6. On the next screen, as we did before, you can accept the preconfigured choices for the principal and its port selection.
7. Next, you may be prompted to connect to the mirror; if so, the normal SQL connection UI that we saw in Figure 8.16 will let you connect and authenticate to the Mirror instance.

8. On the next screen, you will be prompted to connect to the witness using the normal SQL connection UI that we saw in Figure 8.16 so that you can connect and authenticate to the witness instance.
9. Next, using the best practice that all the SQL servers should use the same domain-based account, you can leave the service accounts blank.

When you return from the Configure Security wizard, you will be back at the Database Properties dialog box where the witness information is now filled in and the High Safety Without Automatic Failover (Synchronous) option is no longer grayed out, but in fact is automatically selected (Figure 8.25).

To enable the witness and change the session to high-safety mode with automatic failover, click OK.

FIGURE 8.25
Database mirroring properties, with a witness and failover enabled

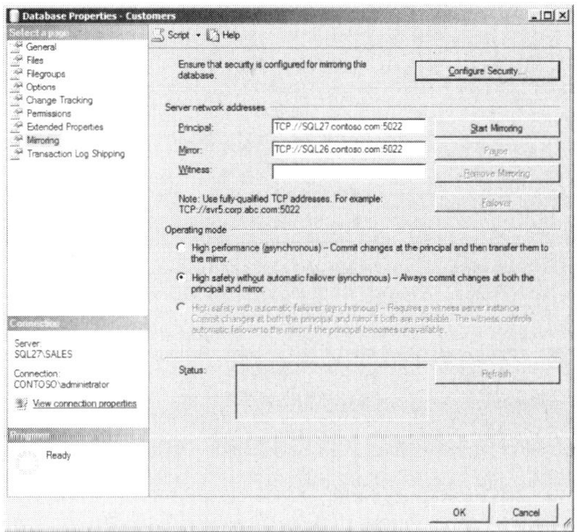

SQL Quorum

In high-availability technologies like clustering or database failover, *quorum* is just a fancy word meaning "majority rules." In other words, in a three-node solution—just like a three-node Windows Failover Cluster (Chapter 6) or a principal-mirror-witness configuration—each participant gets a vote to determine whether failover will occur. Two out of three votes is a majority, which gives them the ability to determine how the solution will behave.

Full Quorum Full Quorum is the default configuration of three nodes that can all communicate with each other, as seen in the left of Figure 8.26.

Partner-Partner Quorum If the witness were to become disconnected, then the principal and mirror maintain the quorum between themselves, as seen in the right of Figure 8.25. No failover has to occur since the principal is still serving data, but Automatic Failover (described in the next section) is no longer possible. This is because if the principal were to fail while the witness is not available, the mirror is the only node remaining.

FIGURE 8.26
Full Quorum and Partner-Partner Quorums

Witness–Partner Quorum If either the principal or the mirror becomes disconnected, the remaining partner and the witness maintain quorum, as seen in the left diagram in Figure 8.27.

FIGURE 8.27
Witness–partner and dual witness–partner quorums

If the principal and witness remain, the principal continues to serve up data.

If the mirror and witness remain, automatic failover may be initiated (see the next section).

Dual Witness–Partner Quorums If the principal and mirror become disconnected from each other (right side of Figure 8.27), but both still have connectivity with the witness, then the mirror, believing that the principal has failed, will try to initiate automatic failover. This situation might lead to something called split-brain, where both halves of a failover solution believe that they are the only one operating and begin serving data. Split-brain scenarios can be very difficult for any failover solution to consolidate back to a single data source. Instead, in SQL database mirroring and failover, when the mirror and witness interact in order to confirm that a quorum majority still exists, the mirror will be notified by the witness that the principal is still online—and no failover will occur.

Lost Quorum When all three nodes become disconnected from one another, none of the nodes have quorum. The principal will stop serving data because it is no longer in a quorum. The mirror will not fail over, because it is not in a quorum either. Now, the database is offline everywhere. The order that the nodes reconnect with one another and reestablish a quorum will determine whether or not the database comes back online automatically.

If the principal and either the mirror or witness reconnect first, the principal will confirm that it was the last principal in the solution. This is important because if the principal went offline first, the mirror may have failed over and changed the database before the quorum was completely lost.

If the principal was, in fact, the last principal in the partnership, then quorum is reestablished and the principal will bring the database back online.

If failover had occurred, the original principal will rejoin the quorum as a mirror, but the database will not come back online until the last principal rejoins—as shown in Figure 8.28.

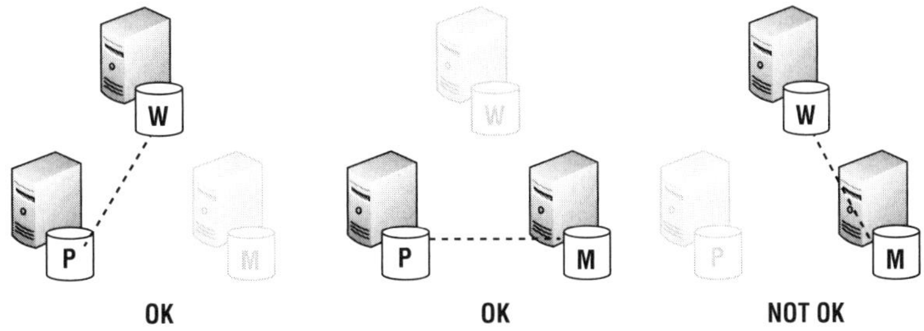

FIGURE 8.28
Recovery scenarios from lost quorum

If the principal is not reconnected to one of the other nodes, and instead the mirror and witness reconnect to reestablish a quorum, then automatic failover will not occur because the mirror may not have all the data. A manual failover is possible, or the configuration will wait until the principal has reconnected before it brings the database back online.

NOTE If your witness is going to be offline for an extended period of time, consider removing it from the mirroring session. Without a witness, automatic failover cannot happen anyway, so you haven't lost anything. But by removing the witness, you can ensure that your surviving partner-partner quorum doesn't become a lost quorum. In a lost quorum, the principal stops serving the data. But by converting the three-node solution back to a two-node solution, the principal will keep serving the data, even if it loses connectivity to the mirror.

Automatic Failover

Automatic failover involves the mirror and participant roles being switched, so that the database is now served from the opposite partner within the pair. Automatic failover requires high safety (synchronous) mirroring. This usually occurs due to an unrecoverable error on the original principal.

All three participants—the principal, the mirror and the witness—monitor the connection status between themselves and the other two instances. Typically, the decision to invoke automatic failover begins by a synchronized mirror server losing connection with the principal. At this point, the mirror talks to the witness to determine if the witness has also lost connectivity to the principal.

- If the witness *has not* lost connection with the principal, the mirror will be notified that the principal is still operating and no failover will occur. While no failover occurs, the principal will set its database status to `DISCONNECTED` and suspend replicating its transactions until the mirror server reconnects with the principal. Instead, it will queue those transactions, so that the mirror will be able to catch up upon reconnection.
- If the witness *has* lost connection with the principal, the mirror and witness will confirm with each other that they have a degraded witness-partner quorum and the mirror instance immediately initiates automatic failover to become the new principal and begin serving the data. More specifically:

  1. The mirror determines that it cannot communicate with the principal and confirms with the witness that the witness has also lost communication with the original principal.
  2. Both the mirror and the witness agree that the mirror is now officially the new principal. This is important, so that when the original principal comes back online, it will be notified by the other quorum members that a new principal is in effect.

3. The redo queue from the principal is played forward into the mirror database. Remember, automatic failover only occurs if the partners are synchronously mirrored, which ensures that all the data that was written to the original principal database was also confirmed as received by the redo queue on the mirror. This ensures that no data was lost.

4. The mirror database comes online to begin serving users as the new principal database.

Meanwhile, when the principal discovers that it has lost connectivity with both the mirror and the witness, it knows that it is no longer in the quorum and stops serving the data. Typically, each node remembers what its role in the configuration is and will attempt to reenter the quorum in the same role. However, when the principal does rejoin the quorum, it will find that the mirror has failed over and is the new principal. The original principal will become the mirror and begin resynchronizing itself.

Manual Failover

Manual failover still requires high safety (synchronous) mirroring. Manual failover does not require a witness server because the failover is not automatic. Instead, a database or system administrator will choose to reverse the principal and mirror roles.

Manual failover is not just for situations when automatic failover is not feasible or when using asynchronous mirroring. You may wish to configure synchronous mirroring to ensure that no data is lost, but you may not want any failover to occur by itself. Instead, as long as both partners are connected and mirroring status is seen as `SYNCHRONIZED`, you can easily invoke a manual failover without a witness.

Here is how a manual failover works:

1. The principal server disconnects clients from the principal database. Usually, this step isn't needed in an automatic failover because the principal has gone offline. But in this case, we need to notify the clients to disconnect so that we can switch roles.

2. The principal sends any last transactions since the last synchronization to the mirror as a tail log backup. A *tail log backup* is a backup of only those transactions since the last successful backup log.

3. The mirror instance processes any remaining items from the redo queue, makes note of the LSN as of the last transaction that it processed within its logs, and then compares that with the tail log backup to ensure that it has as much data as possible.

4. With the mirror database now fully up-to-date, it becomes the principal database and begins serving data.

5. Similarly, the original principal database becomes the mirror database and in so doing will purge any unsent logs and synchronize itself with the new principal. When the resynchronization is complete, the failover is finished.

Manually Failing Over a Database

From the SQL Server Management Console:

1. Connect to the principal server instance.

2. In the left side of the Object Explorer pane, expand the server with the principal server instance.

3. Expand Databases and select the database to be failed over.
4. Right-click the database, and select Tasks ➤ Mirror.
5. On the Mirroring tab of the Database Properties dialog box, click Failover.

A confirmation dialog box appears. Upon confirmation, the principal server will begin to connect to the mirror, using either Windows Authentication or a prompting for a Connect To Server dialog box. Upon authentication, the roles will reverse and the previous mirror server will start serving data to client connections.

To fail over the Accounting database (as an example) using Transact-SQL:

1. Connect to the principal server and set the database context to the master database (with the `USE master` command).
2. On the principal server, issue the following:

```
ALTER DATABASE Accounting SET PARTNER FAILOVER
```

Using Failover as Part of a Rolling Server Upgrade

When we think about high availability and failover, it should not always be in the context of an unplanned crisis or error. When looking at upgrading or maintaining servers, the database mirroring and manual failover methods provide a great way for upgrading the server without downtime.

To accomplish this in principle (pun intended), you simply update the server that is hosting the mirror first, while the users continue to operate from the principal. Then, manually fail over the database to the mirror server. Now, while the users are running off the upgraded server, you can update the original principal. And because the two servers are usually identical, there isn't a need to fail back. You are already done.

Here are some suggestions for best results with using database mirroring and failover as part of an upgrade plan:

1. Without having upgraded anything yet, invoke a manual failover. This enables you to verify that the failover works, as is. Otherwise, if the failover doesn't work before you get started, you might do the work to upgrade one of the servers and when the failover doesn't work, you won't know if it was because of the upgrade. Do a manual failover beforehand, and then you'll know that the database can move before upgrading either side.
2. Similarly, if a pair of SQL servers is performing different roles (principal, mirror, or witness) for different databases, try to manually fail over all databases so that one server is preferably hosting all principals and the other server is hosting all mirrors.
3. Ideally, the two databases should be in High Safety mode (synchronous mirroring without failover) before doing the failover and upgrade plan.
    - If the mirroring is currently asynchronous (high performance), consider changing the mirroring mode to synchronous.
    - If the mirroring is currently synchronous with failover enabled (high availability), consider removing the witness so that a manual failover without data loss can be done, without the potential to accidentally fail over automatically during the upgrade.

NOTE To remove a witness, follow the steps in Task 4, "Getting Started with Database Mirroring," and simply remove the TCP address of the witness server from within the CDMS wizard (in step 5).

4. Manually fail over the database to the upgraded mirror server.
5. After failover, the upgraded server is the principal. So, before resuming mirroring in the opposite direction, be sure to check the principal database using `DBCC CHECKDB`.
6. Upgrade the original principal (which is now the mirror).
7. If you had changed the mirroring state, change it back:
   - If previously mirroring asynchronously, change it back.
   - If previously mirroring synchronously with automatic failover, upgrade the witness as appropriate and then add it back into the configuration.

Other Recovery Methods

But just because you can fail over, do you want to? Maybe not.

If you have been synchronously mirroring between two servers with equal performance characteristics, you can use the automatic failover described earlier or invoke a manual failover.

If you have been asynchronously mirroring, you may wish to fail over to the mirror instance. Of course, with asynchronous mirroring, there is the potential for disparity between what data is on the principal and what data is on the mirror. If so, you have a few choices:

- Fix the principal server. Sometimes, the best recovery is just to address the primary issue. Maybe it is just a service that has to be restarted. If you can repair the server, restart the service or reboot the machine, and the original principal with all its data comes back online, that may be your best plan. You will have a potentially longer recovery time (RT), but you shouldn't lose any data since you are using the original principal (RP).
- If the principal server is running and just a database appears lost, then try to get a *Tail Log backup*. This is usually done before restoring a database, but in this case, it conveniently captures what is likely missing between the original principal and the mirror copies. By restoring the tail log onto the mirror, you may not lose any data at all—even from an asynchronously mirrored pair.
- Force the mirror into service. This is not considered the same as a manual failover, which is supported in synchronous replication scenarios only. The next section will discuss forcing service in more detail.

Maybe it is OK to lose a small amount of data. If it wasn't OK, this database should not have been configured for asynchronous mirroring. It should have been configured for synchronous instead.

Forcing Service

Forcing a resumption of service from the mirror in an asynchronous mirroring configuration will likely cause some data loss. In fact, Microsoft considers this as a disaster recovery method only—meaning that it should only be used during dire circumstances, because data will almost inevitably be lost.

That being said, uptime (RTO) is often justifiably more important than a small amount of lost data (RPO). So, let's take a look at what data could be lost, and then how to force service, if it is necessary and justified.

Why Could Data be Lost?

The primary use scenario for forcing service with data loss is when you have been asynchronously mirroring a database and the principal has gone offline. If you had been running synchronously, both copies would be able to recover to the same point in time. But presumably because of performance considerations, often as part of mirroring across a longer distance, you were mirroring asynchronously. This means that the principal server likely has logs in its send queue that had not yet been transmitted to the redo queue on the mirror server. If the principal were to be down only a few minutes, you are better off to expedite the principal's return. When it comes back up, the data that was queued will transmit and no data loss will occur. But if the principal is offline, and the right business decision is to bring the mirror instance online, then you will have to force service.

When you force service, the mirror database will become the new principal and immediately begin serving data. When that happens, any queued transactions from the original principal are no longer applicable. The original mirror stops being in Recovery mode and so it is no longer able to receive any additional changes from the original principal. This is the data that will be lost.

When the original principal comes back online, it will attempt to rejoin the mirrored pair with its original mirroring partner. At that time, it will find that the original mirror has become the new principal, so the old principal will demote itself to become a new mirror. But, the remirroring does not automatically restart. Instead, the mirroring session is automatically suspended, without the new principal overwriting what is on the original principal. This allows you, or another database owner, to determine if the unsent data on the original principal is too great to be lost.

In some cases, it may be worth the extreme effort to break the mirror, somehow identify what data had not yet been replicated from the original principal to the original mirror, and pull a copy off. Later, the data may be able to be reinserted into the new principal, but this does not occur easily or frequently.

More often, the data is not salvageable or not worth the effort. Instead, the mirroring session can be reenabled. At that time, whatever is in the send queue is flushed as the original principal fully becomes the new mirror in Recovery mode only. The database on the original principal is rolled back to the point that the new principal took over, and then any new transactions from the new principal are applied forward as in a regular database mirroring pair.

Forcing Service with Data Loss

To force service with data loss, connect to the server with the mirrored database and use the following command (Customers is the sample database):

```
ALTER DATABASE Customers
   SET PARTNER FORCE_SERVICE_ALLOW_DATA_LOSS
   GO
```

Client Connectivity

With the database now mirrored and able to fail over, let's spend a moment learning how a SQL client connects to a mirrored pair. The goal of this section is not to teach you to program SQL clients, but simply to complete your awareness of how the client behavior changes when connecting to a mirrored set, compared with a standalone server.

When the initial connection is attempted, the client has a connection string, which includes the name of the server instance and the database name that it is attempting to connect to. The name in the connection string should be the name of the principal instance and is also termed the initial partner name. Optionally, a failover partner name can also be included in the connection string, which should be the mirror instance.

The native SQL client or the .NET Framework data provider, running on the client, populates the initial partner name and failover partner name and attempts a network connection to the initial partner. One of two things will happen:

- If the initial partner is able to be connected to and it has the principal database, the connection is established.
- If the initial partner is not able to be connected to, a connection is attempted to the failover partner. If the failover partner can be connected to and it has the principal database, the connection is established and the data provider updates its records as to who is the mirror.

In this manner, if the client attempts to connect but the database has reversed its roles compared with what the client expected, the connection is still made and the current roles are updated to the data provider for that client.

Later, if the principal fails and the mirror has to fail over for it, the data provider will attempt to reconnect to the server that it was previously connected to. If the connection attempt fails, it will attempt to connect to the failover partner. If either of these reaches the principal database, the connection is reestablished. There are some specifics that must be addressed within the client-side application in handling the reconnection, as well as determining whether the last transaction from the client appears to still be in the newly connected principal database. But that is out of scope for this server-centric availability and protection book.

CONNECTION AND MIRRORING STATUS

The principal, mirror, and witness (when configured) monitor one another to ensure a connection. Literally, this means that they maintain a state of `CONNECTED` or `DISCONNECTED` for each pairing, which helps determine which failover mechanisms are applicable.

In addition, the principal and mirror maintain a status condition for the health of the mirroring itself:

`SYNCHRONIZING` is used during the initial seeding or when the mirror needs more data than just what is actively changing, implying that the mirror needs to catch up.

`SYNCHRONIZED` indicates that the principal and the mirror are actively communicating. As data is changing on the principal, it is transmitted to the mirror. This does not imply a synchronous mirror—just that both partners are actively communicating in a timely manner.

`SUSPENDED` means that the principal is not actively communicating with a mirror. This may mean that the mirror is offline, or that the principal had been offline and the mirror has now failed over (hence no mirror is online). Instead, transactions are queuing in the send queue on the principal with the intent to begin resynchronizing when the mirror comes back.

SQL Log Shipping and Replication

So far, we have covered the primary high-availability solutions that are built into to SQL Server. However, there are two different replication technologies that can be manually utilized to provide additional availability mechanisms:

- SQL log shipping
- SQL replication

What is most notable about these is that they can have more than one secondary copy of the data. Therefore, no automated failover solution is available. After all, during a failure, which of the potentially multiple secondary copies should take over?

Introducing SQL Log Shipping

SQL log shipping performs scheduled backups of the transaction logs on the production server and ships them to one or more secondary servers, which then independently apply them to their own databases. In this kind of scenario, there are three kinds of participants and four jobs to be aware of:

Primary Server and Primary Database The production server where your clients connect and the data originates from

Secondary Server and Secondary Databases The alternate servers that receive and store the copies of your production data

Monitor Server An additional server that tracks key events throughout the log shipping process and alerts the participants to error conditions

Backup Job Runs on the Primary Server regularly (default every 15 minutes) to back up the transaction log, clean up old backups, and notify the primary server and the monitor server when necessary

Copy Job Runs on each secondary server to transfer a copy of the backups to the secondary server from whatever location that the backup job dropped them in

Restore Job Runs on each secondary server to apply the transaction logs to its own copy of the database

Alert Job Runs on the monitor server to notify the primary and secondary servers about changes or errors in the log shipping process

That's really all there is to log shipping. On a loosely coordinated schedule:

1. The backup job on the primary server backs up the transaction logs on the primary database
2. The copy jobs on each secondary server transfer a copy of the log backups from the primary server or network location.
3. The restore jobs on each secondary server apply the log backup to their own secondary instance and database.

It is not an availability solution in the same way that Windows Failover Clustering or database mirroring is. However, log shipping does provide a one-to-many replication model that can be leveraged to provide reporting from the secondary sites (some limits apply).

Task 6: Getting Started with SQL Log Shipping

In this task, we will do a few activities, including preparing the primary server to offer its log backups, setting the backup schedule, and selecting the secondary servers.

1. From the Windows Explorer of the primary server:
   - Create a folder where you will be backing up your transaction logs to, such as `L:\LogShip`.
   - Create a file share (such as `\\SQL27\LogShip`) for it so that the secondary servers can go get it.

2. Switch to the SQL Server Management Console, and connect to the primary server instance.
3. Right-click on the database that you want to begin log shipping and then click Properties.
4. In the left pane of the Database Properties dialog box, select the Transaction Log Shipping page, which will appear similar to Figure 8.29, though we still need to fill in our data.

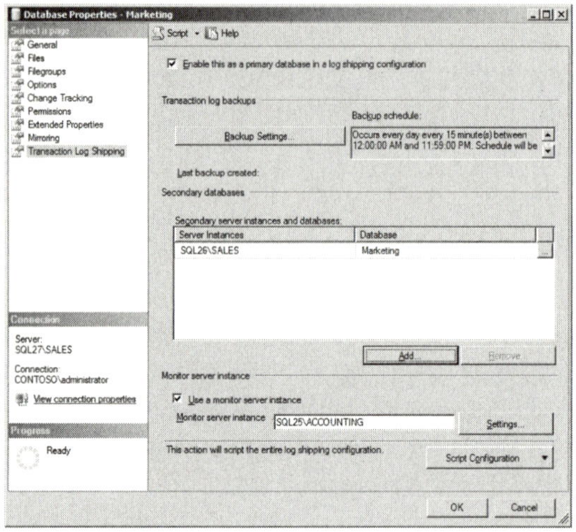

FIGURE 8.29
Configuring log shipping

5. Check the "Enable this as a primary database in a log shipping configuration" check box.
6. Click the Backup Settings button to access the Transaction Log Backup Settings screen (Figure 8.30).

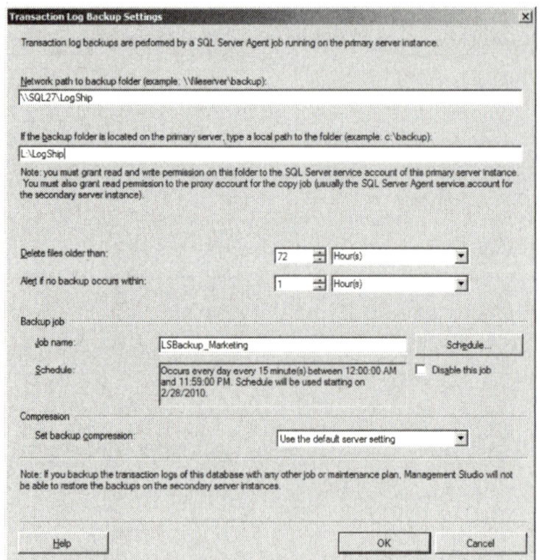

FIGURE 8.30
Transaction Log Backup Settings

7. Enter both the network share and the local directory that you created in step 1. In my example, those were:

   Network Path to the Backup Folder `\\SQL27\LogShip`

   Local Path to the Backup Folder `L:\LogShip`

8. Accept the other defaults for now relating to the schedule and compression, and click OK.

9. Returning to the database properties' Log Shipping screen, you can now determine the secondary server instances and databases. Click Add.

   We need to configure what the secondary database servers and instances are, as well as the copy jobs and restore jobs, and how the initial seeding of the secondary databases should be done. To configure the secondary servers and their jobs:

10. Click Connect and connect to an instance of SQL Server that you want to use for your secondary database.

11. On the Secondary Database Settings screen, pick an existing database or type a new database name.

12. On the Initialize Secondary Database tab (Figure 8.31), you can choose how the secondary database is initially seeded. It may be tempting to let Management Studio create the secondary database for you, but that is only convenient in the short term. If Management Studio creates the database, it creates the database in the same directory as Master, which is likely not where you would prefer to keep your replicated production databases. Instead, create the database yourself on the secondary instance, and then return to this screen. You may also choose to initialize the database yourself, using the steps that we covered in Task 3 to back up the primary database and transaction log, and then restore them into the secondary database, using the No Recovery mode.

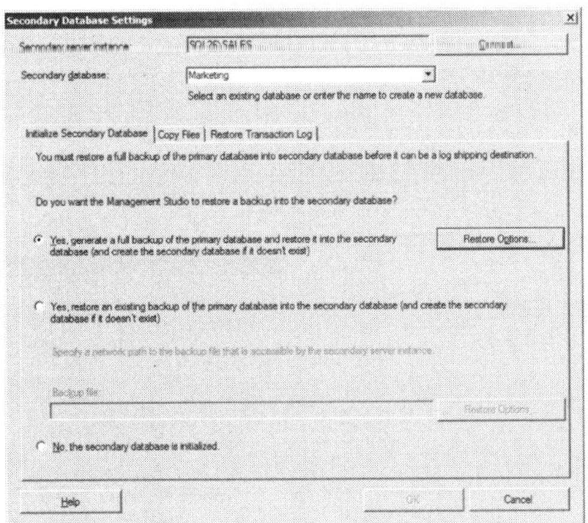

FIGURE 8.31
Initialize Secondary Database tab

13. On the Copy Files tab (Figure 8.32), you can customize the copy job that the secondary servers will do to get the data from the primary:

    - For Destination Folder For Copied Files, select the folder on the secondary server where the files will be copied to. I had previously created an `L:\LogCopy` folder and I entered it here.
    - You can customize the copy schedule, but the typical goal is to keep it approximately in sync with the backup schedule, so that shortly after each backup is complete, the copy will fetch it.

FIGURE 8.32
Where the log shipping copy will come from

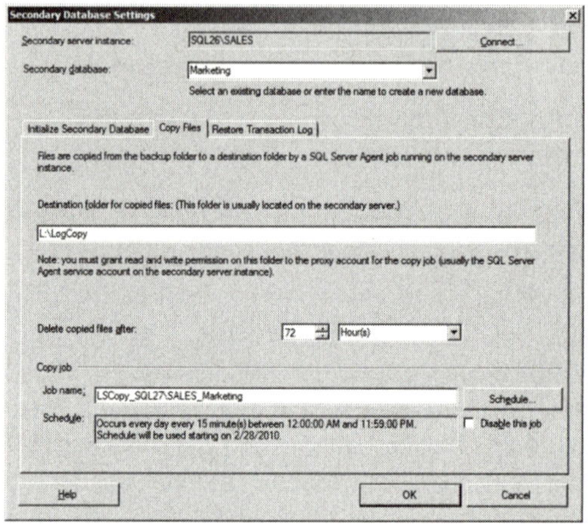

14. On the Restore Transaction Log tab (Figure 8.33), you can configure the restore jobs that will apply the logs to the secondary database:

    - The Database State When Restoring Backups setting will most often be No Recovery Mode.
    - You can tune the restore timing, but the same advice is true as with copy jobs. The typical goal is to have a restore happen shortly after each copy, which hopefully happens after each backup job.

FIGURE 8.33
How the secondary servers restore the data

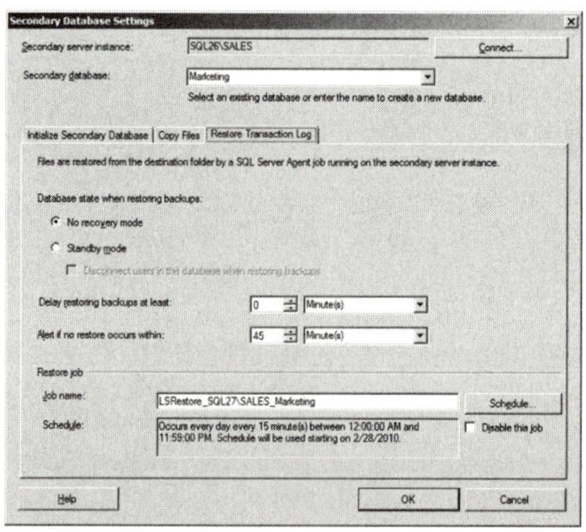

15. Click OK to complete the Secondary Database Settings dialog box.

    Next, we need to configure the monitor instance of SQL, which will collect event notifications from the primary and secondary servers to confirm that log shipping is working properly. To configure the monitor instance and its jobs:

16. Click Monitor Server Instance and type the name of the instance of SQL that will be monitoring.
17. Click the Settings option to the right of the monitor instance, which will open the Log Shipping Monitor Settings dialog box.
18. Click Connect and choose your monitor. In my case, I chose an older server in my environment and its instance, `SQL25\Accounting`.
19. Additional settings, such as how the instance will connect to the database as well as tuning the schedule, can also be done here. Click OK to return to the main log shipping screen.

With all of the options completed, the Transaction Log Shipping screen should appear similar to Figure 8.29. Click OK to commence log shipping.

Introducing SQL Replication

There is a fourth and final SQL technology that merits discussion relating to potential availability solution: SQL replication. SQL replication can replicate in a manner that is somewhat similar to database mirroring, but only for a subset of the data. If whole database protection is required, database mirroring is more efficient.

SQL replication uses different terms:

Publisher The database server that is sending its changes

Publication The data items that the publisher is offering, as a subset of the databases

Articles The specific data items, such as tables, within a database or stored procedure

Subscriber A database server operating a warm standby of the data

Subscription The data, schema, and rules of the publication

SQL replication is designed to operate in low-latency, high-output configurations in order to provide a subset of its databases to one or more standby servers that can be programmatically called on to activate the data or leverage in other publication or distribution manners. It does not include any built-in failover solution for availability.

Which SQL Server HA Solution Should You Choose?

We have lots of choices for high availability and replication of SQL Server 2005 and 2008, including:

- Windows Failover Clustering (WFC)
- SQL database mirroring (DM)
- SQL log shipping (LS)
- SQL replication (REPL)

There are a few questions that we can pose to clarify which options are applicable to your availability and protection goals:

What part of your data do you need to be available?

- If you only need a particular database, database mirroring is your best and most flexible choice.
- Log shipping works at the database level as well. It can't replicate as consistently (frequently) as database mirroring, but it is usually a better performer across low-bandwidth links.
- If you need more than just databases, failover clustering provides resilience for an entire instance of SQL.
- If you want less than a database, replication allows granular data at a table level.

How many copies do you want?

- Failover clustering only offers one copy of the data, even across multiple-server nodes. Even if you use array-based storage mirroring to ensure that the disk is not a single point of failure, there is still only one logical copy of the data. And if it becomes corrupted, you are done.
- Database mirroring provides two copies: the principal and the mirror.
- Log shipping and SQL replication can provide two or more copies.

Do you want to automatically fail over?

- Failover clustering can handle that, even providing multiple nodes to fail over to in a four-node cluster, for example.
- Database mirroring provides one alternative server to fail over to (the mirror), but also requires a third instance to act as the witness.
- Log shipping and replication do not offer failover.

We could go on and nitpick them each, but those are the big ideas. The Microsoft SQL Team has a complete list of considerations and limitations in "Selecting a High Availability Solution" at `http://msdn.microsoft.com/en-us/library/bb510414.aspx`.

You can also mix solutions. Here are a few examples:

Failover Clustering Participating in Database Mirroring In this configuration, the first level of failover happens between the nodes of the cluster. The entire cluster would be considered the principal of the mirrored pair. Ideally, failing between nodes happens fast enough that the witness and mirror do not react before another node can bring it back online. Preferably, both the principal and the mirror are independent two-node clusters, as seen in the left side of Figure 8.30.

Database Mirroring and Log Shipping Database mirroring provides a second synchronously mirrored copy and built-in failover. But if you need more copies, you can add log shipping to the mix. In that case, the principal (DM) is primary copy (LS). When the scheduled log backups are done from the primary, they should be stored on a server other than either of the DM partners, such as the witness. This ensures that the file share that all of the log shipping secondary servers are looking to will not change. In short, the DM principal (either node) needs to back up its logs to a share on the DM witness. The secondary servers will grab the log backups from the share on the witness and replicate them to the various other servers, as seen in the right side of Figure 8.34.

FIGURE 8.34
Combining SQL availability and replication technologies

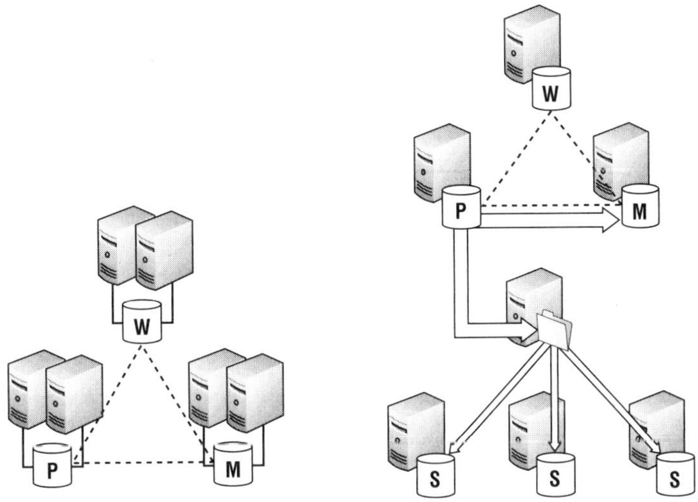

Backing Up SQL Server

SQL Server is a popular platform for building other applications on. Several vendors offer various backup solutions. In Chapter 4, we discussed one of the primary driving concerns of third-party backups: supportability. If the restore fails, who will be on the line to ensure that the databases are served again?

SQL Server has its own backup and restoration capabilities, as you know from Task 3. It includes the ability the back up to a flat disk file or to a directly attached tape drive. In SQL Server 2008, compression was added for better efficiency. The database can get a full backup, a differential backup, or just the transaction logs.

The Most Important Rule in Backing Up SQL Server

The most important rule in backing up a SQL Server is that only one technology should touch the transaction logs. This is because most applications that would use the transaction logs as part of their data protection will truncate them when their operation is complete. SQL's own log shipping is a good example. After every 15-minute log backup, the logs on the primary are truncated. SQL does this so that 15 minutes later, it knows exactly where to start (with the only log that is left).

Because of this, well-mannered backup software programs are dynamically aware of databases that are doing log shipping, and will automatically disable their own use of log files. Those backup products will treat log shipped databases as simple recovery-mode databases (that do not have log files). Bad-mannered backup or replication software will be oblivious to the log files and truncate when they want to. Then, the log shipping does its thing and truncates the logs. A few minutes later, the backup comes in and truncates afterward. At the end of the day, neither the log shipping secondary server nor the backup platform has the entire data set.

So, be careful when you know that your transaction logs are being touched for anything, other than by your primary database.

The Other Most Important Rule in SQL Server Backups

The second most important rule is to use Volume Shadow Copy Services (VSS), as discussed in Chapter 4. As we discussed in that chapter, VSS provides a consistent set of interfaces, including a VSS writer that is developed and maintained by the SQL Server product team. It essentially provides a gateway of how the SQL server would like to be backed up. If you use a backup product that utilizes the SQL Server VSS writer, you can be assured of not only a reliable backup but one that will be supported later. If you do not use a VSS backup, you are assuming additional risk if a SQL server fails and the backup is unable to restore correctly.

One VSS-based backup solution we covered in Chapter 4 was System Center Data Protection Manager (DPM). In Chapter 4, we discussed how a VSS-based backup is used to do block-level disk-to-disk synchronization of the database files from the SQL server to a DPM server. In between those block-level Express Full operations, which might occur every 4 to 24 hours, are transaction log backups every 15 minutes (except where log shipping is active).

Chapter 4, Task 9, takes you through the steps of a basic SQL database restore to any 15-minute point in time and to any of the following locations (Figure 8.35):

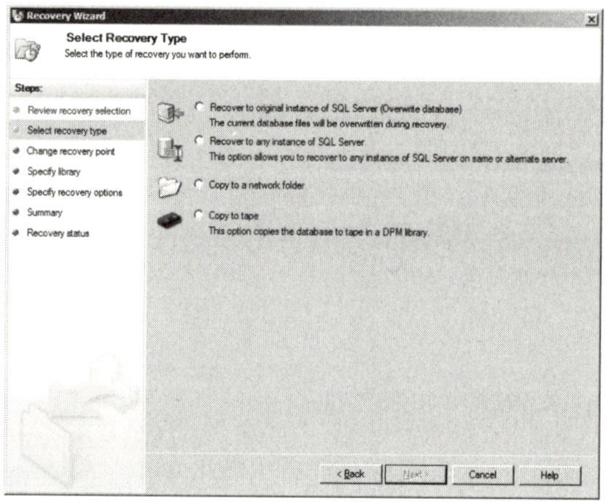

FIGURE 8.35
SQL Recovery Options from DPM 2010

- To its original location
- To any other SQL instance
- To a network folder
- To its own tape

You also have the ability to recover the SQL database without committing the logs; that way, you can use the SQL tools to selectively apply the log to any single transaction.

Restoring Databases with DPM 2010

In Chapter 4, we discussed backing up and restoring SQL Server databases with System Center Data Protection Manager 2010. In that chapter, we specifically protected various data sources (including databases) in Task 4, and then we restored a SQL database in Task 9.

New in DPM 2010 is a self-service restore utility that enables SQL Server DBAs to restore databases without using the DPM console. The SQL Server Self-Service Restore (SSR) utility from DPM 2010 enables DBAs to restore their own databases from the console of a SQL server, or even from their desktop. To enable this process we must first do two things:

1. Configure self-service restores in the DPM console.
2. Install the SQL SSR onto the database administrator's desktop or SQL Server console.

Configuring Self-Service Restores in DPM Console

From the DPM 2010 Administrator Console, click Configure Self Service Restore in the right pane's list of actions. This will launch the configuration tool for the SQL SSR, which will initially be a blank window.

1. Click Create Role to grant a group of DBAs permission to restore databases themselves. This ensures that only certain DBAs are able to restore data.
2. On the top of the tool, type the role name, which is definable by you, as well as a description that further clarifies who this group is. At the bottom, you can type the names of security groups that are already defined in Active Directory, as seen in Figure 8.36.

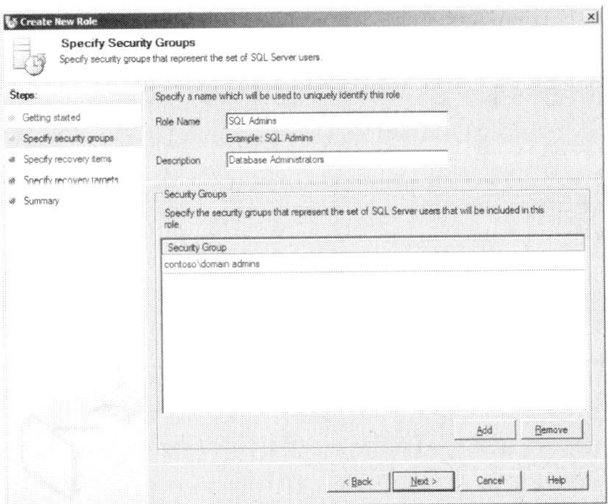

Figure 8.36 Authorizing a group to restore SQL databases

3. On the Select Recovery Items screen, you can select which instances of SQL Server that this group that you are creating has rights to restore from. Type the name of each server and instance on the left side of each line, and optionally includes the names of particular databases on the right. By leaving the database side blank, this group is able to recover any of the databases in the instances that you have specified, as seen in Figure 8.37.

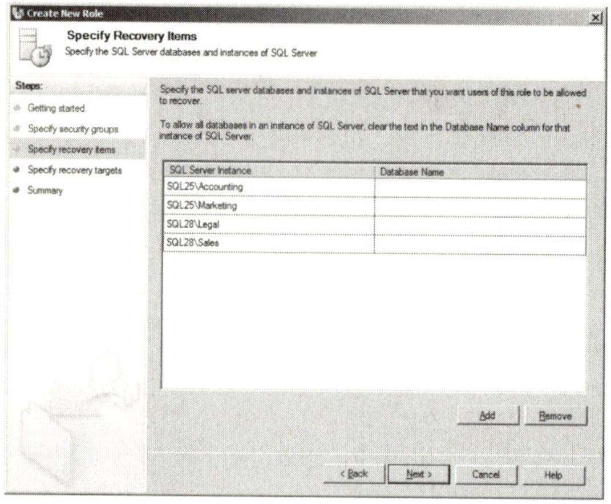

FIGURE 8.37
Selecting which instances can be recovered

4. On the Recovery Target Locations screen, you can enable this group to recover the databases directly back to instances of SQL Server. If you do not check the box, then you can only restore as files to a network location, where you could then manually mount the data within SQL. By selecting this option, you can again list server and instances as you did in the previous screen. This enables you to authorize DBAs to restore to only a test server or less encumbered server instead of recovering back to a busy production server.
5. By clicking Finish, you create the new group within DPM and users logging on as members of that group will be able to restore databases as you specified.

INSTALLING THE SQL SSR UTILITY

Off the root of the installation media of DPM 2010 is a directory named `DPMSqlEURinstaller`. There are two installation executables: one for x64 and the other for x86. They can be installed on most Windows workstations (such as the DBA's desktop) or servers (such as a SQL server). There are no options or configuration choices.

RESTORING YOUR OWN DATABASE

A new icon for the restore utility will be created on the desktop after the installation is complete. Double-clicking on it will launch the DPM Self-Service Recovery Tool (Figure 8.38).

1. Click the Connect To DPM Server button and enter the DPM server name that you wish to restore from. This will pass your current domain credentials to the DPM server and confirm that you are part of a predetermined group that is able to initiate self-restores.
2. This screen is actually a status screen showing current or past recovery jobs that were initiated from it. Click New Recovery Job at the bottom of the tool to start the Recovery wizard.
3. Using the pair of drop-down boxes, you can choose which instance and which specific database to restore, as shown in Figure 8.39.

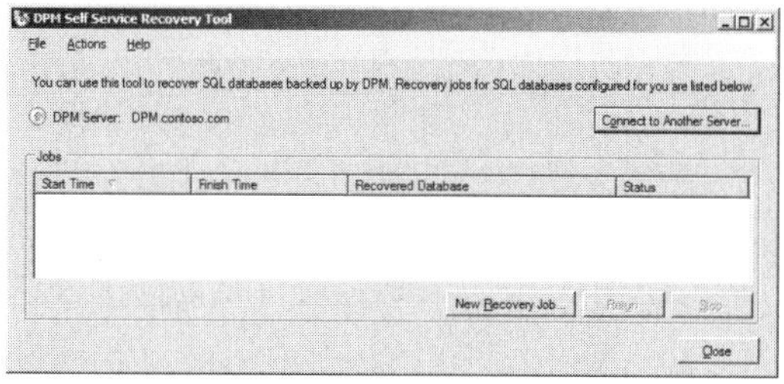

FIGURE 8.38
The SQL Self-Service Recovery utility from DPM 2010

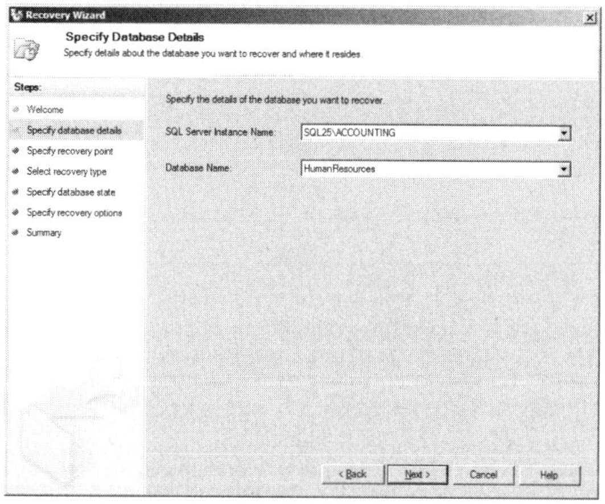

FIGURE 8.39
Specify which database to restore

4. Choose the date and time to restore the database to. Similar to what you saw in Chapter 4, the bolded dates within the calendar indicate recovery points are available for that date. When you select a date from the calendar, the pull-down on the right will reveal which 15-minute points in time are available for restoration (Figure 8.40).

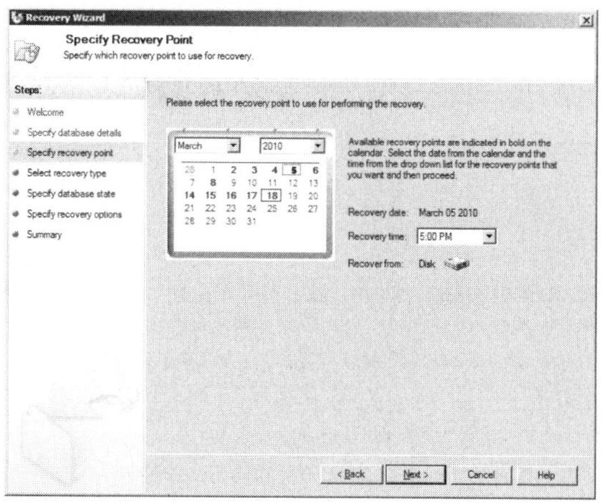

FIGURE 8.40
Specify a recovery date and time

5. Choose whether to restore the database to an instance of SQL Server or to restore the database files to a network folder. Your ability to restore to an instance of SQL may be grayed out if you did not check the box to enable this when configuring the DPM server group in step 4 in the previous section, "Configuring Self-Service Restores in DPM Console."

   - If you choose to restore to a network folder, you are prompted for what folder to restore to.
   - If you choose to restore to an instance of SQL Server, the next screen allows you to select which instance, as well as the new database name and the path for the database files (Figure 8.41).

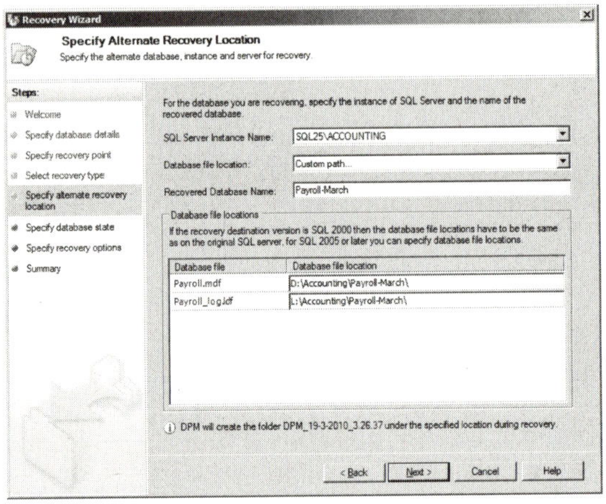

FIGURE 8.41
Specify the recovery location

The remaining screens will look similar to the SQL Server database recovery options in Task 9 of Chapter 4:

- Whether to bring the database online after recovery
- Whether to notify via email when the recovery is complete
- A confirmation screen of the choices that you selected

By clicking the Restore button, you submit the job to the DPM server. The database will first be restored to the most recent Express Full (see Chapter 4) prior to the selected time, along with the incremental transaction logs to whichever time you selected. After all the files are restored to the SQL server, DPM will instruct SQL Server to mount the database and play the transaction logs forward to the point in time selected in the Recovery wizard. You will see when the recovery is complete either by receiving an automated email courtesy of step 7 or when the SQL Self-Service Recovery utility indicates the job is complete (Figure 8.42).

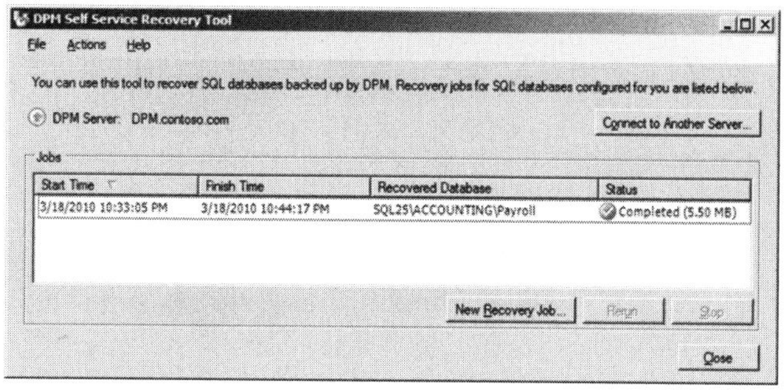

FIGURE 8.42
The SQL Self-Service Recovery tool, with completed recovery

Summary

While the built-in backup will provide you with ad hoc backups in cases where you need to prestage a database mirror or log shipping, you will need a full-fledged backup solution (such as System Center Data Protection Manager 2010) that uses VSS for data consistency and supportability for your data protection goals.

In combination with a reliable data protection solution, you have lots of options for easily ensuring the availability of your SQL Server platforms and databases. More importantly, what you need for availability is built in. Now, you just have to choose:

- Failover Clustering with SQL Server provides a straightforward way to fail over whole instances of SQL Server, but it doesn't protect against data corruption or disk-level failures.
- Log shipping and replication both provide one-to-many replication for multiple redundant copies, but they do not offer a failover capability.
- Database mirroring is becoming an all-around favorite, because it offers synchronous and asynchronous replication as well as manual and automated failover. But it only works for databases themselves. If your application has lots of moving parts, clustering may work better for you. And if long distance is important, log shipping might be most effective.

The good news is that you have options, and most of them are in the box!

Chapter 9

Virtualization

In the first few chapters, we looked at the big concepts and decision points for data protection and availability. Then, we moved into tactical and pragmatic implementation guidance on several data protection and availability technologies in the modern Windows datacenter.

In this chapter, we'll change gears and look at how virtualization changes what we have learned so far. We'll discuss how to protect and recover virtual environments, as well as how to ensure that our virtualization infrastructure stays highly available. Finally, we'll step away from the traditional concepts of availability and protection of virtualization and look at other capabilities that can be gained by combining data protection and virtualization.

Virtualization Changes Everything

With a firm understanding of various data protection and availability technologies that are available in the modern Windows datacenter, it is time to switch gears and explore how server virtualization changes what we have learned so far. There are several varieties of virtualization within the IT environment today, including:

Application virtualization, which abstracts how the application is delivered to the desktop

Desktop virtualization, which moves the processing requirements from the local desktop to a back-end server, and only requires graphics, keyboard, and mouse in the user experience

Storage virtualization, which blurs how storage capacity is attached to servers in a way that it is often more scalable and resilient but with an additional layer of complexity and cost in the implementation

Server virtualization, where operating systems are encapsulated and compartmentalized into virtual guests that utilize a percentage of the CPU and memory of a virtualization host

This book focuses on server virtualization, and will refer to it as simply virtualization, as a means of delivering autonomous OS and application deployments that share resources from one or more host computers. Everything that we have discussed in the book until now has primarily involved physical servers (with an understanding that the servers could be physical or virtual). Now, let's take a much closer look at what it takes to deliver data protection or availability to a virtualized platform.

Protecting Virtual Machines

Backing up virtual machines offers unique challenges compared to backing up physical servers. Most physical server backups happen by installing a backup agent into the operating system that is running on the hardware. The agent interacts with the operating system, file system, and potentially applications running on the OS. Because the agent is running within the OS, it is aware of the state of the file system and applications in order to ensure that the backup is done in a way that provides the best chance for a reliable restore. That awareness is lost when backing up virtual machines from the outside—in other words, a host-based backup of virtual machines.

Challenges in Virtual Machine Protection

Without an agent running inside the virtual machine, it is nearly impossible to discern if the data inside the virtual machine is in a state that is suitable for backup. More importantly, if the guest OS is running a transactional application such as SQL Server or Microsoft Exchange, it is important that the database and transaction logs be protected in a consistent manner. Also, it is important to ensure that whatever is currently in the virtual memory or virtual processors is not lost during the backup. Three methodologies are available for backing up by VMs running on a hypervisor (Microsoft's or otherwise):

- Shut down the virtual machine and then back it up.
- Snapshot the storage in the host.
- Do a VSS-based backup (only available in Microsoft virtualization hosts).

The first choice is obviously the least ideal. If you can't reliably protect a virtual machine while it is running, you could shut it down. Of course this incurs downtime, but it technically is a choice that ensures nothing is lost from CPU or memory (because the machine is dead).

The second, somewhat more popular choice, is to use SAN-based storage to do a snapshot of the array or volume that the virtual hard disks are in. The idea is to take a snapshot of the storage LUN that the virtual disks are part of, and then move a copy of the storage LUN to another Windows server. The secondary Windows node will see the new storage as additional disks, with data conveniently already on it. Then you simply take any legacy backup software and back up dormant virtual hard disks from the secondary LUN.

Most storage-based approaches to backing up virtual disks, including LUN snapshots as well as host-based replication, often miss a key quality differentiator for virtual machine backups—crash consistency versus data consistency. Consider the following scenario:

- A transactional application is running within a virtual machine.
- Eight transactions are streaming through the application, of which:
    - Items A and B have been successfully committed to the database.
    - Items C, D, and E have been written to the transaction log
    - Items F, G, and H are in the memory of the application.
- A replica of the storage LUN containing the virtual hard drive (VHD) is taken using either SAN mirroring or host-based replication.

In most cases, the copy of the VHDs is presented to a legacy backup solution will include a VHD with a database and transaction log that collectively have five of the eight transactions. The remaining three items (F, G, and H) that were in flux between application processes and memory are lost. But if you attempt to recover the virtual machine, it will boot its OS and start the application to find that it has uncommitted data. The application then has to recover itself in the same way that it recovers from a hard power failure, by attempting to reconcile between the database and transaction log and hopefully roll the transaction log updates forward into the database. This scenario is caused by the fact that the application was not involved in the backup. Some call this a *crash-consistent backup*, meaning that the data that is preserved (the five of the eight) will be usable when the restoration processes are complete.

One variation of this is to leverage enough direct application APIs or VSS to notify the application to prepare itself for backup. In this case, the application has time to at least commit any data that is in memory to either the transaction log or the database. However, this usually requires some additional logic within each guest operating system. And when delivered in support of a storage array or host-based replication solution, that additional software component is often expensive.

The last and best choice is to use application-aware backup technology that was designed for virtual environments. In Microsoft virtualization environments, this is the VSS writer. The Hyper-V (or Virtual Server 2005 R2) VSS writer provides two different experiences for backing up virtual machines from the host, depending on whether or not the guest operating system is VSS capable.

NOTE The mechanisms for backing up VMware-based machines vary greatly from those used for protecting Hyper-V–hosted machines. This chapter focuses on the Hyper-V as the virtualization host. VMware mechanisms are not covered.

VSS-Based Backups of Virtual Machines

In Chapter 4, "Better Backups," we discussed how VSS enables backups of Microsoft workloads such as SQL, Exchange, or SharePoint. The Microsoft virtualization hosts, namely Virtual Server 2005, Hyper-V, and Hyper-V R2, also have VSS writers to enable supported backups.

In Figure 9.1, we see how a VSS -based backup works. There are four basic operations that occur:

FIGURE 9.1
How VSS facilitates backups

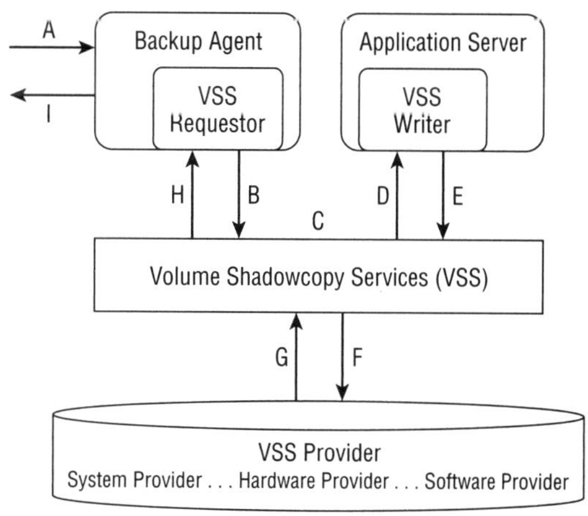

1. The backup agent includes a VSS requester, which communicates with Volume Shadow Copy Services (VSS) and the enumerated VSS writers, as seen in Figure 9.1, actions A, B, and C.

2. The VSS writer for the application to be backed up then invokes application-centric instructions to prepare its data for backup (Figure 9.1, action D).

3. The VSS writer notifies VSS, which in turn notifies a software or hardware-based VSS Provider to take a shadow copy, or snapshot, of the data (Figure 9.1, items E and F).
4. The quiesced copy of the data is provided to the VSS requester and backup software (Figure 9.1, items G, H and I).

The key idea is that VSS facilitates a conversation where the requester (backup agent) and the writer (production application) work together to get a copy of the data in a manner that is supported by the application.

NOTE This section describes how a VSS-based Hyper-V backup *should* be done. Each backup vendor chooses to what degree that they leverage VSS within their backup methodology. One example of a backup vendor that does fully utilize the Hyper-V VSS writer is System Center Data Protection Manager (covered in Chapter 4). There may be other vendors that utilize a similar or subset of these methods.

The VSS writer in Microsoft virtualization hosts works similarly. In fact, it does the process twice—once outside on the host, and again inside the guest. Let's look again at the four-step process listed earlier within the context of Hyper-V:

1. The process begins as discussed before, with the backup agent acting as a VSS requester that talks to VSS and the VSS writer of what it wants to back up (Hyper-V in this case).
2. Hyper-V internally prepares a VM for protection, which we will discuss in more detail.
3. Once Hyper-V has prepared the VM for backup, its VSS writer notifies the VSS Provider to take a shadow copy or snapshot.
4. The image of the VHDs is then made available to the backup software.

The host-based backup process of a virtual machine has the same basic flow that takes place with any other VSS-based workload being backed up, with the power happening in step 2. What makes a virtualization host's backup special is what happens in step 2 and what happens after step 4. As mentioned in Chapter 4 regarding Volume Shadow Copy Services, the actual process that each application uses to prepare its data to be backed up in step 2 will vary by the application. SQL does it one way and Exchange does it differently. The method that Microsoft virtualization hosts use will vary based on whether the guest operating system is VSS-capable.

Protecting VSS-Capable Virtual Machines

If the guest operating system is also VSS-capable (meaning that it is running Windows Server 2003 or above), Hyper-V prepares the guest for backup. Essentially, the same four-step VSS process between the backup agent (VSS requester) and the Hyper-V host (VSS writer) will be done a second time within the guest. At the host perspective, steps 1 and 2 from the VSS process occur, and then things jump into the guest. After the guest finishes its process, then the host steps 3 and 4 conclude.

Here is a closer look at what happens inside the guest during this recursive VSS process:

A. In a host-based backup scenario, it is assumed that there is no traditional or separate backup agent running inside each guest. But in fact, one of the technologies inside the Hyper-V

Integration Components (HV-IC) is a VSS requester. The HV-IC VSS requester does what any VSS requester does: it talks to VSS in the operating system of the guest, and requests a backup of whatever VSS writer–based applications are running within the guest.

B. The applications within the guest, such as SQL or Exchange, prepare themselves for backup like they normally would during any VSS-based backup, such as applying their transaction logs to their databases.

C. Once the applications are in a data consistent state, the application VSS writers notify VSS and the VSS provider inside the guest OS, and a snapshot is taken of the applications and file system.

D. The snapshot is then offered to the VSS requester, which is the HV-IC. Normally, after a traditional backup agent gets its data, it transmits the data to the backup server. In this case, the HV-IC (acting as a backup agent or VSS requester) notifies the hypervisor that the VM has been internally backed up, courtesy of the guest-based VSS provider.

The remainder of the host-based process' steps 3 and 4, that we described earlier, can then resume. Putting these two recursive processes together:

1. The backup agent uses its VSS requester to start a backup with the Hyper-V host and its VSS Writer.
2. The Hyper-V host gets its data ready for backup by doing steps A-D inside the guest:

   A. Within the guest, the HV-IC acts as a backup agent and uses its VSS requester to initiate a VSS-based backup within the guest.

   B. The VSS writers within the guest-based applications are instructed to get their data consistent for a backup.

   C. With the application data now consistent, a VSS snapshot is taken within the guest, using a VSS provider within the guest Windows OS.

   D. The snapshot is offered to the VSS requester (backup agent) within the HV-IC. The HV-IC notifies the hypervisor that the guest is now suitable to be backed up.

3. Now, the Hyper-V host has data that is ready to be backed up—namely, a VHD set that has recently been internally snapped.
4. The VSS provider on the Hyper-V host then snaps the storage on the host and offers this to the VSS requester (real backup agent), as seen in Figure 9.2.

The result provided to the backup agent is a snapshot of a VHD (which recently had a snapshot taken within its file systems). As a key point, there is a slight time difference between when the internal snapshot within the guest was taken and when the external snapshot of the VHD was taken. If the backup application were to protect the external VHD as is and then later restore it, there would be similar disparity. Instead, the shadow copy instance of the VHD would become temporarily mounted on the Hyper-V host and the snapshots aligned by removing anything in the external snapshot that occurred after the internal snapshot was taken. This process would result in a consistent image that could be protected and reliably restored.

FIGURE 9.2
Hyper-V VSS backup workflow

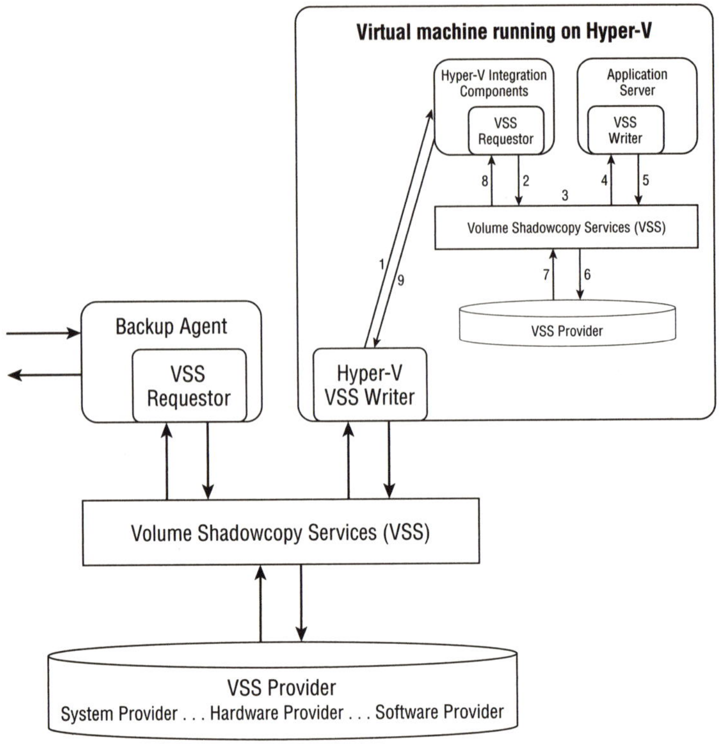

INTERNAL AND EXTERNAL VHD CONSISTENCY

VHDs appear and function as disk volumes, but they are really containers. Imagine that you have purchased a present. You put it in a box that was built to hold it perfectly. This box is like the logical file system and its shadow copy from the inside of the guest.

Then, you take that box and put it in a bigger box along with a good amount of padding, such as newspaper or foam peanuts. The bigger box is like the external shadow copy provided by the host and to be given to the backup software.

The cleanup activity that occurs after a Hyper-V backup is complete is similar to getting rid of all the extra padding so that the outer box is fitted to be exactly the right size for snugly wrapping around the inner box. Now, it is just a box within a box, with your precious item inside. In this case, your data, which is application consistent from SQL Server or Exchange or File Sharing, is ready to be given like a present to the backup application.

PROTECTING NON-VSS-CAPABLE VIRTUAL MACHINES

In the previous section, we discussed how the backup occurs if the guest OS and its applications are VSS capable. However, if the Hyper-V VSS components determine that the guest OS or its applications are not VSS-capable, a different method must be used to protect the VM. The interaction between the backup agent and Hyper-V is the same: the agent requests a backup and Hyper-V provides a shadow copy of the VM's virtual hard drive files to be leveraged for protection. But in the previous discussion, the guest had done its own VSS requester, writer, and provider backup. If the guest is not VSS capable, Hyper-V is stuck with nearly the same issues as any other hypervisor that wants to back up a guest-based OS without access to its internal and active memory or CPU state.

How this is handled will vary by backup application. For example, System Center Data Protection Manager (DPM) uses a saved state approach (see Chapter 4). In this case, the non-VSS virtual machine is put into a saved state, which dumps the memory and CPU information into a file and temporarily hibernates the running guest. Now, with the guest in a still state, a VSS shadow copy is made of the file system for the volumes that hold the VHD components. As soon as the shadow copy is complete, the VM is resumed from its saved state and the guest is completely unaware of what happened, other than its internal clock will have missed a few minutes and should update itself upon resumption.

Although not every backup solution offers this functionality, those that do can then utilize the shadow copy of the hibernated VM. DPM performs a block-checksum on the blocks of the VHD versus what is already in the DPM storage pool, and then sends only the changed blocks. This allows DPM to replicate only the changes within the VHD. Other backup software may transmit the entire hibernated VM to their backup engine. In any case, the process is done from the shadow copy, so that the VM was only offline for a few minutes to save state, create a snapshot, and resume service. While still incurring a minor amount of downtime, it is a significant improvement over the VM being offline for the entire backup.

Host-Based vs. Guest-Based Backups

So far, protecting VMs from a host-based backup solution may sound appealing.

"Everything is permissible, but not everything is beneficial." Just because you can protect virtual machines from the host perspective does not mean that you should. While there is certainly some efficiency gained by doing host-based backups of virtual machines, you must be aware of the trade-offs.

Benefit: Deployment and Manageability

One key benefit for host-based protection is the ability to deploy and manage a single data protection agent on the virtualization host. In this way, any number of VMs can be protected with the same ease that any number of databases can be protected on a SQL server. The VMs appear simply as data objects. In addition, the single backup agent on the virtualization host will almost certainly cost less than purchasing and deploying agents for each guest operating system that is running.

Benefit: Heterogeneous Backups

Host-based backups can allow backup software to protect server resources, which would not be possible if the production machine was physical. For example, DPM only protects current Windows machines, such as Windows Server 2003 and Windows Server 2008, as well as Windows XP, Vista, and Windows 7 clients. It is unable to protect Linux machines or legacy Windows NT or

Windows 2000 servers. However, DPM (or any other Hyper-V capable backup solution) can perform a host-based backup of VMs, no matter what operating systems are running inside the guests. The Hyper-V components, not the backup software, determine whether or not each guest operating system is VSS capable. If so, a recursive VSS-based backup is performed. If not (as is the case for Linux or Windows NT), a saved-state backup is performed, as discussed in the previous section.

In this way, a Windows-only backup solution like DPM can protect the Linux servers in a predominantly Windows datacenter.

Benefit: Whole Server Recovery

In Chapter 4, we discussed the benefits of bare metal recovery (BMR), which allows you to recover an entire machine starting from a clean disk. The BMR process can be challenging for most physical server recoveries, unless restoring onto the same hardware or at least the same model system as the original. While BMR can be a desirable recovery capability, its complexity often precludes its use. But all of the complexities are due to the variances in hardware between the original machine and the equipment that the restoration will be performed to. Those variances are all mitigated with virtualization. No matter which server vendor has manufactured the Hyper-V host hardware, the guest operating systems all see the same kind of network card, the same storage interfaces, and even the same hardware abstraction layer (HAL). With that in mind, a virtual machine that was originally running on a Dell Hyper-V host can easily be brought online with an HP Hyper-V host. Moreover, with some understood migration mechanisms, a virtual machine that was originally running on VMware ESX can be made to run on a Hyper-V server. With those limitations no longer valid, BMR is a natural byproduct of host-based backups. The VM can simply be restored to the same or an alternative host, without concern for what the bare metal might actually be.

Challenge: Whole-Server Recovery

Whole-server recovery is both a benefit and a challenge. Although it is advantageous for scenarios where you might want BMR to do a whole server recovery of a virtual machine, there are likely many more times when you only wish to restore a single file or data object. In most cases, a host-based backup requires a whole-server recovery. There are exceptions to this rule:

- For VMware environments, only a few backup vendors offer the ability to protect a VM with a host-based backup but restore an individual item. As mentioned earlier, the mechanisms used for VMware host backups are very different from Hyper-V mechanisms and are not covered in this chapter.
- For Hyper-V environments, the only solution known to provide single-item-level recovery from a host-based backup is System Center Data Protection Manager 2010 (Chapter 4), as of this writing.

It is worth noting that even these exceptions are for file-based data. For application-centric data such as a SQL database, all that is recoverable from a host-based backup are the actual files that make up the database. To result in any kind of SQL-centric database recovery, where the database and transaction log files are logically linked and interact, the backup has to take place directly with the application from within the guest—not from a host-based backup.

Challenge: Whole-Server Protection

When you back up the whole virtual machine, you normally get everything, including:

- The data that you want
- The data that you don't want
- The application binaries
- The operating system

In the case of the host-based VM backups, you will get everything listed above for each and every virtual machine that you protect. Unless you are protecting to a near-line disk solution that can do de-duplication of the common Windows blocks after the fact, then your backup pool may be significantly larger than you want because of all the additional files being protected. Here are the two factors you should consider:

- If you don't mind protecting everything or want to back up every whole VM in preparation of a whole virtual machine restoration, the additional storage makes sense for your recovery goals.
- If you wish to granularly select data for protection, it must be done from a backup solution that runs inside each guest.

Challenge: iSCSI Storage Within Guest OSs

Windows Server 2008 and later has made *iSCSI* storage easy to deploy. In guest operating systems, it can be tempting to use iSCSI storage: the virtual machine boots from a typical VHD that holds its `C:\`, but all of the production data volumes are iSCSI mounted from an external storage solution. If you choose to do this—and it can be a very strong solution—you will want to follow the best practice of having at least two gigabit Ethernet or better networking interfaces in your Hyper-V host:

- One network interface and related virtual network for the normal networking connectivity between VMs and the rest of the production network
- A separate network interface and related virtual network for the iSCSI storage networking traffic

With those deployed, your VMs can use actual storage that is scalable and perhaps more convenient to deploy and manage than VHDs. But you will not be able to do a host-based backup of the entire virtual machine. The connection to the iSCSI storage is within the guest and is not visible by the host. Therefore, all the iSCSI storage volumes will be missed when a host-based backup is attempted on that virtual machine. Some backup software will not back up the VM at all, because it cannot back up the iSCSI volumes. Other backup software will back up the VHD volumes and may offer an error alert or not.

Similarly, you cannot normally perform a host-based backup of a virtual machine that is using pass-through disks for the same reason. The host-based backup agent cannot follow the storage to the pass-through location.

Guidance: Deciding Whether to Protect from Guest or Host

The choice of whether to protect your virtual environment from the host or from the guest comes down to your recovery goals:

- If you are using pass-through disks or iSCSI storage in your guest OS, you cannot do a host-based backup and must protect the machine from a guest-based solution that can access all the storage.
- If you wish to protect only certain files as part of saving storage, and thereby choose not to recover other files (such as the Windows operating system), you will need to do guest-based protection.
- If you wish to restore individual files, you will likely need to have guest-based protection—unless you are using a backup solution that allows for item-level restore (ILR), such as DPM for Hyper-V.
- If you wish to restore transactional data, such as a SQL database, you will need to have first backed it up using an application-aware agent from within the guest.
- If you wish to recover an entire virtual machine, choose host-based protection.

Restoring Virtual Machines

Restoring VMs is a straightforward process, as long as you remember that a virtual machine is more than restoring just the VHD files themselves. A virtual machine also includes the metadata definition of the machine itself, such as:

- The number of processors
- The amount of memory
- The number of network cards, and which hypervisor networks they are connected to
- The kind of storage controllers, and which VHDs are connected to each

Most backup software that is designed to protect virtualization hosts will capture the XML file that maintains each virtual machine's configuration, as well as the VHD files for the storage. With this in mind, you have at least three recovery scenarios:

- Whole-VM recovery
- Single-VHD recovery
- Item-level recovery (ILR)

Whole-VM Recovery

This is a simple case of restoring what you backed up. In its basic form, the backup application allows you to restore the virtual machine back to the virtualization host that it originally resided on. This is considered easy, as long as the virtual networking has not been changed and the virtual NICs are connected to the proper virtual segments. In this scenario, the XML file is used to restore the configuration, while the VHD files are placed back where they were originally backed up from.

A variant of this approach (which not all backup software packages offer) is the ability to restore a VM to a virtualization host other than the one it came from. This is more complicated than it might initially sound, because the VM has to be effectively imported into the new host. Normally, this might require you to export the VM from the original host and then import it on the new host. In fact, as an example, DPM 2007 could not restore to an alternate host, but DPM 2010 added that capability. DPM 2010 captures the metadata that defines the VM (and would normally be exported) while the VM is being backed up on the original host. DPM then uses that metadata when restoring the VM to a new host, as if it was importing the VM.

Single-VHD Recovery

To a VM, this process is like restoring a failed hard drive—only easier. In a physical machine, you would replace a failed hard drive with a new one and then restore the data back onto it. In a virtual machine, the VHD is the container with the contents already included. After restoring the VHD, you may have to reconnect it to the VM from the hypervisor's console or your virtualization management UI, such as System Center Virtual Machine Manager.

Item-Level Recovery

As mentioned earlier, the ability to recover a single file or folder item from a host-based backup is not common in VMware backed up environments and in Hyper-V environments is unique to those using DPM 2010. To perform ILR, the backup solution effectively mounts the VHD from within its storage pool, so that it has intimate access to the file systems that are stored within the VHD. This forces two requirements on the DPM server:

- The DPM server must be a physical server, instead of being virtualized, so that it can also run the Hyper-V role. This is necessary so that it can mount the VHD file.
- The VHD must have FAT or NTFS file systems. Non-Windows virtual machines that are running a nonrecognizable file system will not be able to have individual files restored.

With those two prerequisites met, the backup software internally reconstitutes the VHD to the point in time selected for restore, but instead of copying the VHD to another location as a typical restore, it temporarily mounts it as an additional volume on the backup server itself. After the volume is mounted, it can browse the file system to find the desired file or directory, and then does a file-based restore to whatever destination has been selected.

Availability of Virtual Machines

If you are going to put all of your eggs in one basket, then it better be a good basket.

That thought is certainly true when considering virtualization. Normally, you would already be concerned about using high-quality server and storage hardware, as well as ensuring proper software maintenance, to ensure good uptime for a typical physical server. And for key workloads, like those discussed in Chapters 5–8, you might also deploy various high-availability solutions for even better assurance. But when considering running several production (virtual) servers within a single physical host, the requirements for uptime become even more important. If a single component of a virtualization host were to fail, several production resources and hundreds or thousands of users could be affected.

The initial approach for high availability within Microsoft virtualization environments is to use Windows Failover Clustering (Chapter 6) between two hosts, so that the virtual machines can easily move between two physical hosts. In this way, using the clustering methods described in Chapter 6, as well as the storage mirroring capabilities in Chapter 3, no single point of failure exists within the virtualization host(s). Microsoft refers to this as a *Quick Migration.*

Quick Migration in Windows Server 2008 and Hyper-V Server 2008 was a good solution for moving VMs between hosts, but it was not a perfect scenario. The flaw in Quick Migration is the downtime between when a virtual machine goes offline from NodeA and when the failover cluster is able to resume the virtual machine on NodeB. Specifically, the Quick Migration process includes three relatively quick steps:

1. Save the virtual machine's state.
2. Move the virtual machine's component files and state information between hosts by changing the ownership between the clustered hosts for the storage LUN that the VM resources reside on.
3. Restore the virtual machine.

A Quick Migration is quick, but it isn't transparent. Because of that, a newer methodology called Live Migration was introduced in Windows Server 2008 R2.

NOTE Unlike most of the chapters in this book, where I've tried to address not only the most current version but also one revision back for folks who cannot always move to the latest and greatest, this section, "Availability of Virtual Machines," is specific to Windows Server 2008 R2 and Hyper-V Server 2008 R2.

Live Migration (LM) is a new feature in Windows Server 2008 R2 and Hyper-V Server 2008 R2 that lets you move VMs from one host to another without any perceived disruption of service or connectivity from the clients. I used the word *perceived* because there technically is a momentary interruption, but because a Live Migration completes in less time than most TCP timeout settings, the clients will not lose connection; thus the perception is that the VM moved transparently.

The ability for VMs to transparently move from one host to another enables scenarios that Microsoft virtualization could not offer before, including:

Scaling Up or Down Instead of Hyper-V hosts being allocated based on presumed or maximum resource allocation, they can be allocated based on real usage. As a datacenter's need for virtualization resources grow, new hosts can be brought online and the VMs transparently moved for better utilization. Similarly, if hosts are underutilized, VMs can be consolidated to fewer hosts so that some hardware can be powered down to save on power and cooling.

Host Maintenance Bringing down a virtualization host for maintenance used to cause significant downtime because all the VMs running on the host would have to come down as well. Instead, VMs can be transparently moved from the host needing maintenance to another, so that hosts can be taken offline and later returned to service without affecting the VMs. For more on deployment, maintenance, and management, refer to Chapter 11.

How Live Migration Works

LM works by copying the memory of the VM across to the new host node before the migration actually begins. With the memory prestaged and the storage now shared (via Cluster Shared Volumes, which we will discuss next), the migration of the virtual machine takes a significantly shorter amount of time. When you use the Management console or Windows PowerShell to initiate a live migration, five steps occur:

Step 1: LM Initiated When an LM is initiated, the existing host starts a connection to the new host, preferably over a dedicated LM network segment. The configuration of the virtual machine is relayed to the new host. The new host then creates a synthetic VM and allocates the appropriate amount of memory.

Step 2: Copy the Memory to the New Host All of the memory that is allocated to the virtual machine is tagged into what is called a working set. The first step of the Live Migration is to flag all of these memory blocks as of a point in time and then begin copying them from the existing host to the designated new host—into the allocated memory for the synthetic VM that was created in step 1.

The VM is still active on the existing host, so the working set is monitored for changes. Any 4 K memory pages that are updated will be flagged so that they can be sent after the initial copy is complete.

Step 3: Copy the Changed Pages With the majority of memory already copied, the memory pages that had changed while the initial copy was happening are then sent across. This process can occur recursively, with fewer pages needing to be copied each time.

NOTE Copying the memory is what takes most of the time during an LM, so it is strongly encouraged that the cluster have a separate network dedicated to LM interaction that is at least 1 GB Ethernet or faster. This ensures that the memory information is replicated without any other traffic for the fastest possible LM.

Step 4: Reassign the Storage Handle for the VM VHDs By using Cluster Shared Volumes (CSV), the new host can already see the VHDs. But it doesn't have write-level ownership for those files. In step 3, the file handle is changed from the original host to the new host.

This is similar to how multiple users can open a Microsoft Word document simultaneously. The first user gets the file in a read/write state, while the other users get a read-only version. When the first user disconnects, another user can take ownership. CSV file handles for VHDs work the same way.

Step 5: The VM Is Brought Online from the New Host At this point, the host has read/write control of the storage and the VM is preloaded with all the memory and state information from the original instance, so the VM can simply resume processing from the new host.

As part of resuming service the VM will have the same IP address that it had before, but the MAC address of the NIC will be different because it is running on a separate host. This is inconsequential for clients on other subnets, but the clients and router interfaces on the same subnet need to be refreshed. This is done by doing an unsolicited Reverse ARP, which updates the ARP (MAC address) cache for nodes on the local subnet. It is a transparent and low-level network function, but it improves network resumption with the VM.

How ARP and MAC Addresses Work

Most IT administrators understand that when you request access to a network address like www.JasonBuffington.com or \\FS1, there is a name resolution that has to occur, using DNS or WINS. The name resolution looks up the logical address that you entered and translates it to an IP address such as 10.1.1. 4. From there, the routers between you and your destination figure out how to get you from 192.168.123.2 (source) to 10.1.1.4 (destination).

This process works great between subnets and will get your network packets from your client to the NIC on the router of the subnet you want to get to, such as 10.1.1.x. But then, how does the router get the packets from its interface (10.1.1.1) to the server that you intended (10.1.1.4)? The answer is Address Resolution Protocol (ARP).

ARP is a low-level networking function, where a network interface on the *local* 10.1.1.x subnet sends out a packet, which then asks, "Who has IP address 10.1.1.4?"

The NIC on the computer with that IP address responds with "I have that IP address and my MAC address is 00–1D-36–8D-61–7A."

The initiator records that MAC address in a simple table, called an *ARP cache,* which lists IP address 10.1.1.4 going to MAC address 00-1D-36-8D-61-7A. And all future network packets that come off the router to that IP address will be electrically transmitted to the NIC with that MAC address.

This works great until a server fails over and the MAC address changes. Network packets on the local subnet will be sent to the old MAC address and rejected until the ARP timeout occurs (usually a few minutes later). At that time, the initiator will send out a new ARP request, hoping that perhaps something has changed. In that case, the new server would respond with its new MAC address and everything would be OK. Failover would work this way, but there would be a few minutes where the network connectivity would fail.

Some failover techniques, including Live Migration, move an IP address between machines where the IP stays the same, but the MAC has changed. Part of cleaning up the network stack is for the new host to do an Unsolicited Reverse ARP. Unsolicited means that the server is not responding to a request but doing it proactively. Reverse ARP means that the server sends a shout-out saying, "I know you didn't ask, but I have IP address 10.1.1.4 and my MAC address is 00–1D-36–9E-72–8B."

Any NIC on the local subnet, including the router, will update their ARP cache with the new MAC address, so that all new packets will go to the new server. This happens as part of the failover process, so that nothing has to time out and the network appears to function seamlessly.

The process of how LM works is summarized in Figure 9.3.

Defining Clustered Shared Volumes

The key to LM is assuring instant storage access to multiple Hyper-V R2 nodes that could potentially host the virtual machines. The answer is an extension in the Windows Server 2008 R2 file system called *Cluster Shared Volumes* (CSV).

FIGURE 9.3
How LM works

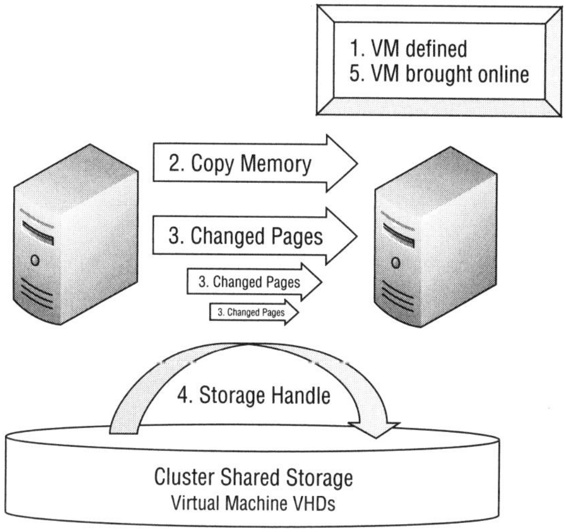

CSV allows multiple clustered nodes to each have read/write access to a shared volume of storage that is housed on a SAN. CSV provides multiple benefits, including:

- Failover of individual virtual machines
- Easier storage management because it does not require individual LUNs per VM
- Better storage utilization because the VHDs can make better use of the storage space
- Resilient storage by handling server-storage connectivity issues within the cluster via redirected I/O

Before CSV, Windows Failover Clustering assigned individual nodes with exclusive access to the underlying storage LUNs and volumes. Thus, part of the failover process was switch control of the storage LUNs from one clustered node to another. Similarly, prior to CSV, only one VM was usually placed in a storage LUN, so that its failover and move to a different clustered node would only impact that VM. Putting multiple VMs in a single LUN before CSV would force all VMs to have an outage and move whenever any VM had to move.

If Node1 were to fail, the software-based resources on Node1 would be taken offline, the related storage and resources would be reassigned ownership to Node2, and the storage and resources would be brought back online on Node2. Conceptually, this might look like Figure 9.4.

FIGURE 9.4
Conceptual view of clustered Windows Server 2008 (not R2) nodes and storage stack

NODE 1	NODE 2	NODE 3
Server OS	Server OS	Server OS
File System	*not accessible*	*not accessible*
LUN	*not accessible*	*not accessible*
Storage Array		

CSV creates an additional logical layer in the storage stack that allows the file systems of all the clustered nodes to have access to the shared storage volume, while still preserving ownership and data integrity by the active node(s), as conceptualized in Figure 9.5.

FIGURE 9.5
Conceptual view of clustered Windows Server 2008 R2 nodes and storage stack with CSV

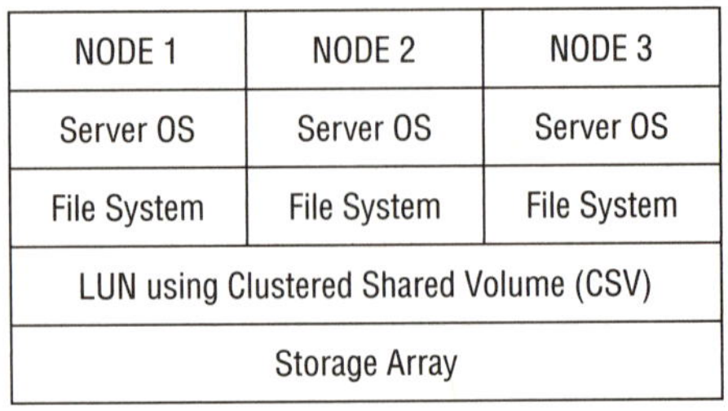

Because access to the storage does not have to be moved from one clustered node to another, the failover process can be much quicker. And with the clustering capabilities of Hyper-V R2 and the awareness of CSV, the higher-layer virtualization functions are ready to almost immediately rehost a virtual machine when its initial host goes offline.

Requirements for LM and CSV

As we've mentioned before, there are some specific requirements for deploying Hyper-V and failover clustering:

Operating system (one of the following)

- Microsoft Hyper-V Server 2008 R2
- Windows Server 2008 R2 Enterprise
- Windows Server 2008 R2 Datacenter

Networking

- A public network for corporate network access, where all cluster nodes must be on the same subnet, so that the virtual machines can retain their original IP addresses
- A private network for cluster heartbeats
- Dedicated 1 GB or better private network for Live Migration, so that the LM memory transfer and CSV controls occur as quickly as possible
- A separate network if you are using iSCSI storage
- Possibly additional network interfaces for the virtual machines to access to the corporate network

Hardware

- All server, storage, and networking hardware must be certified for Windows Server 2008 R2. For more information, go to `http://WindowsServerCatalog.com`.
- All processors must be from the same manufacturer and preferably with the same feature set. It is important to note that the new *Processor Compatibility Mode* supports

variations within an architecture, so differences between Intel processors might be accommodated, but not migrating a VM between an Intel host and an AMD host, or vice versa.

- The entire cluster (as a whole) must pass a validation test from the Failover Cluster Manager (FCM) to be supported.

Configuration Essentials

- All OS installations within a cluster must be the same type (either Full Installation or Server Core) and should have the same role within an Active Directory domain (preferably member servers).
- If your storage is supported for regular Windows Server 2008 R2 failover clustering, it will support CSV.
- Each cluster can include up to 16 hosts.
- Each host can support up to 64 VMs.

Getting Started with CSV

To get started with LM and deploying CSV, we will begin with what we learned in Chapter 6 on building a failover cluster with Windows Server 2008 R2 and then integrate Hyper-V R2 into it.

Task 1: Building the Cluster Nodes

Build between two and sixteen Windows Server 2008 R2 nodes with a configuration that is suitable for clustering and with the performance characteristics that are appropriate for hosting virtual machines.

1. Configure the multiple network paths of a LM/CSV cluster, as described in the previous section. All node network paths must be on the same respective subnets, so that the virtual machines' IP addresses can remain the same.
2. For the cluster's storage, a CSV-enabled Hyper-V cluster can use any storage that a normal cluster can use, including iSCSI, SAS, and Fibre Channel, as long as the volumes are formatted NTFS. For this exercise, I have added two iSCSI-based LUN's to the server:

   Q: (100MB) as a small quorum drive

   H: (50GB) for the virtual machines

   In my example, my first node was already a Hyper-V host, so it also had a 500GB V: drive with several production virtual machines already deployed and operational, as seen in Figure 9.6.
3. With the hardware properly configured, use the Server Manager on each node of the cluster to install the required software components:
   - The Hyper-V role
   - The Failover Clustering feature

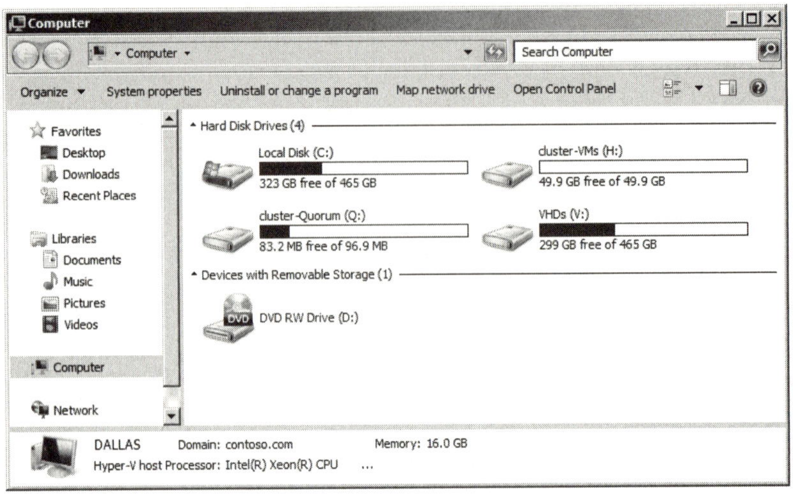

FIGURE 9.6
Example storage as seen on a node, prior to clustering and CSV

TASK 2: CREATING A CLUSTER

Using the same methods that we covered in Chapter 6, let's create a Windows Failover Cluster.

1. From the Start Menu, go to Administrative Tools and select the Failover Cluster Manager, as seen in Figure 9.7.
2. Validate the prospective nodes to be sure that they are cluster-able. You can choose to validate each node separately, but the better method is to validate all of them in the same wizard so that the interconnecting network paths are also tested. This will also affect the default creation choices in the next step.

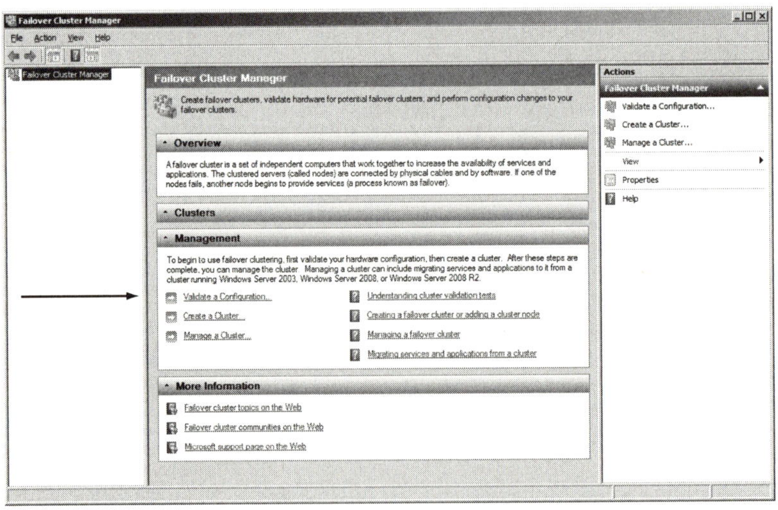

FIGURE 9.7
The Failover Cluster Management

3. After confirming that the nodes are cluster-able, create the cluster. You can do this by clicking the link on the last screen of the Validation Wizard or from the FCM in Figure 9.7.

4. Enter the cluster's name and an IP address for cluster management, as shown in Figure 9.8.

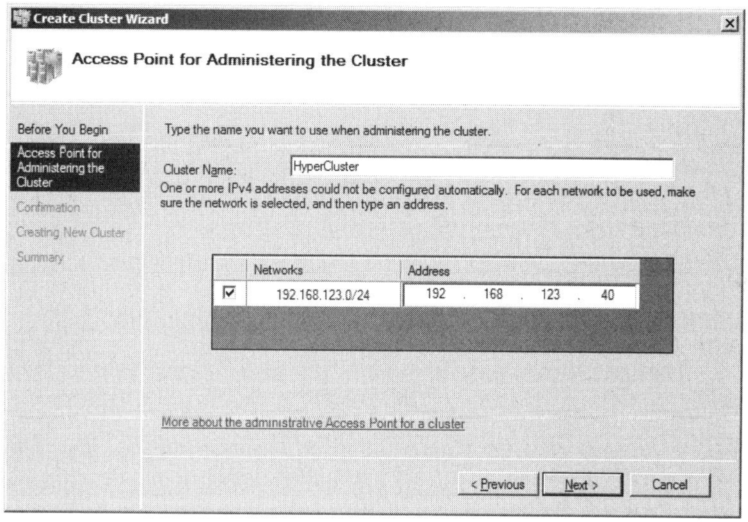

FIGURE 9.8
Create Cluster Wizard

5. After confirming your intent, Windows Server will create the cluster (Figure 9.9).

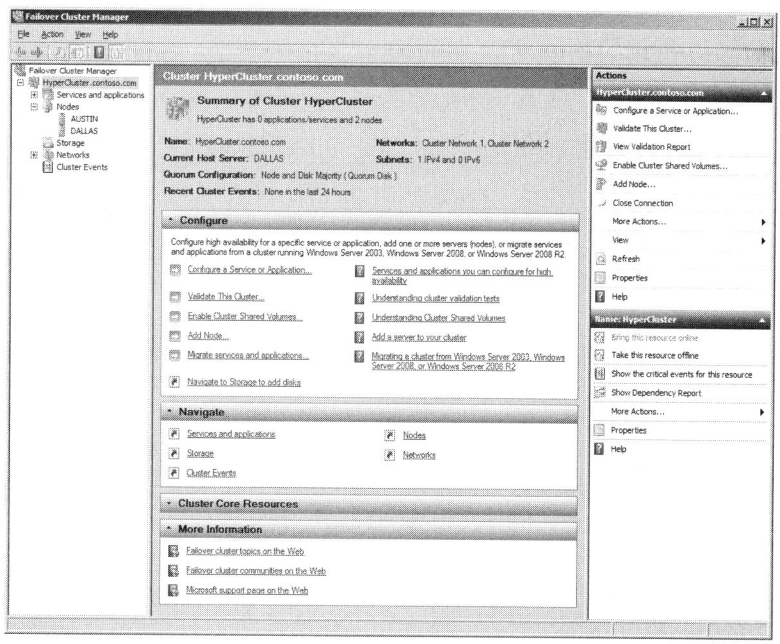

FIGURE 9.9
Our new Hyper-V cluster

TASK 3: ENABLING AND CREATING CSVS

Here comes the fun part, and the easy part for that matter.

1. From within the FCM, click on the cluster in the left pane and then select Enable Cluster Shared Volumes (either right-click the cluster and choose that option from the context menu or select it from the right-side Actions pane).
2. A dialog box will appear, as seen in Figure 9.10, to confirm that CSV is only for use within the Hyper-V role. Attempting to use the CSV volumes for anything else is unsupported by Microsoft and could potentially result in data corruption.

FIGURE 9.10
Disclaimer on enabling Cluster Shared Volumes

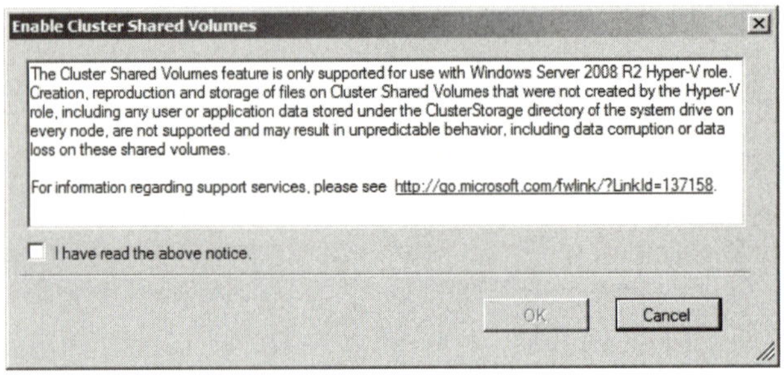

After acknowledging the support disclaimer, a new branch titled Cluster Shared Volumes will appear in the left pane's tree. This is a container for storage objects, like the original container for storage objects that are normally part of the cluster, so we will need to create some clustered disks in this new container, using LUNs that are accessible from the cluster-able storage array.

3. Before creating CSVs, we should confirm that our storage is visible to the cluster. From the left pane, click on the Storage branch of the tree to see the clustered disks. These will have generic disk names by default, so change them to be meaningful, such as Quorum-disk and VM-disk, as shown in Figure 9.11.
4. Now, we can go to the newly created branch of the left-pane tree (Cluster Shared Volumes), and select Add Storage from the right-side Actions pane.
5. The Add Storage dialog box will present any shared storage volumes that are NTFS formatted and not participating in the File Majority Quorum. In our case, there is only one. Click on each LUN that you wish to use by Hyper-V and CSV, as shown in Figure 9.12.

Notice that after the LUN is added to the CSV list, the volume's path changed from having a drive letter (I: in my case) to a directory path of `C:\ClusterStorage\Volume1`. When you enable CSV, the cluster will create a directory named `ClusterStorage` on the root of the `%SystemDrive%`, which in most cases will be `C:\ClusterStorage`. This path exists on every member of the cluster, which is how the hypervisor can find the VMs and VHDs. Underneath this root will be volume mount points to whichever disks are enabled with CSV.

NOTE As a best practice, be sure that the OS is installed to the same drive letter in every node (such as `C:\`), so that the `%SystemDrive%` paths will be the same on all clustered nodes.

FIGURE 9.11
Our clustered storage

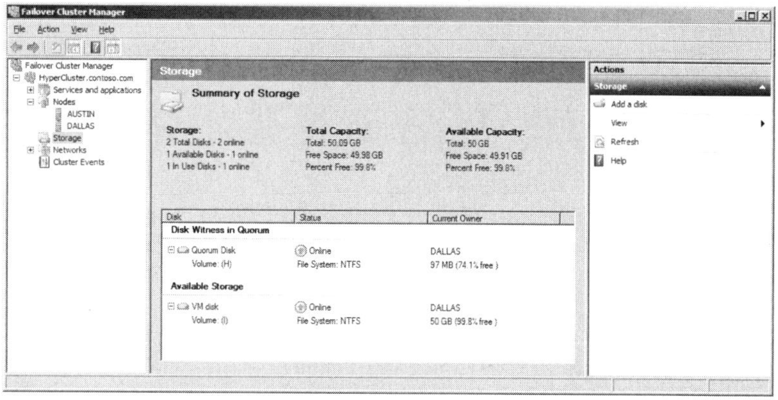

FIGURE 9.12
Adding storage to our Cluster Shared Volumes

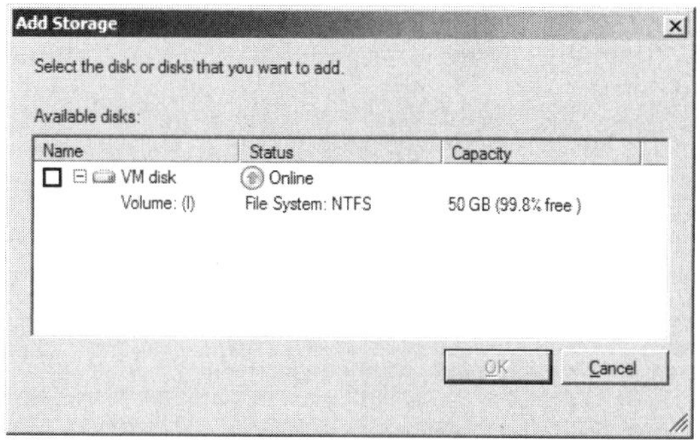

The C:\ClusterStorage root directory name cannot be changed, but you can change the names of the volume mount points underneath it. By going to Windows Explorer, you can rename the directory to whatever you wish. I changed the directory name to VMdisk, which will also be reflected in the FCM in Figure 9.13.

FIGURE 9.13
Our CSV storage

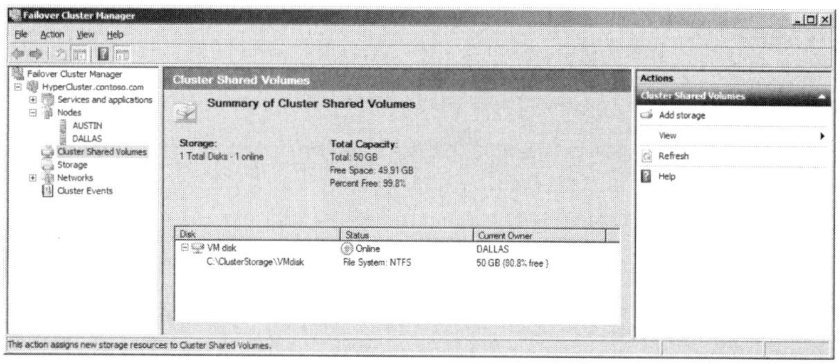

TASK 4: CREATING THE VIRTUAL MACHINES

We now have a Windows Failover Cluster that has Hyper-V enabled on multiple nodes and has shared storage. It is time to get back to virtualization by copying over the VHDs or creating a new VM. For our example, I copied a VHD into C:\ClusterStorage\VMdisk (or whatever your volume mount directory is named). The VHD can be fixed size, dynamically expanding or differencing based, but it must be a VHD and not use pass-through disks.

Creating a highly available virtual machine requires two tasks—creating the virtual machine and then making it resilient. Creating the VM can be done in Hyper-V or the Failover Cluster Management console. For the first one, let's use the console that we are already familiar with, the Hyper-V Manager.

1. From the node that currently owns the CSV storage that you just created, open the Hyper-V Manager and create a new virtual machine.
2. When asked where to store the VM configuration, you must check the box to store the VM in a different location and then choose the CSV shared storage, such as `C:\ClusterStorage\VMdisk\LOBapp`, as shown in Figure 9.14.

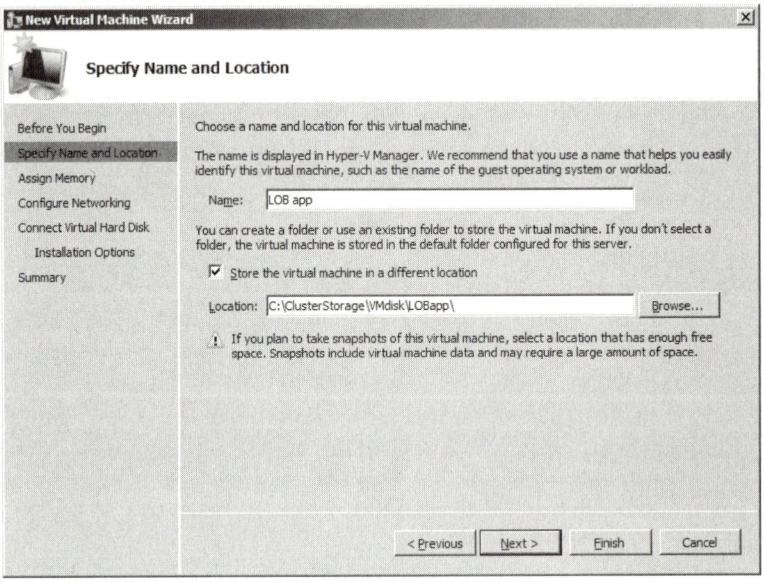

FIGURE 9.14 The Specify Name And Location screen of the New Virtual Machine Wizard

3. Configure the memory and networking as you normally would.
4. When asked about a virtual hard drive, you must choose to create a new VHD or use an existing VHD that will be stored in the same CSV shared storage, such as `C:\ClusterStorage\VMdisk\LOBapp`, as seen in Figure 9.15.

You obviously still need to deploy your VHDs across storage volumes in accordance with the best practices of storage I/O. CSV does not change this. In fact, it exacerbates the need for proper storage planning since the I/O requirements of a CSV volume are the aggregate of the I/O needs for every VHD that is running on it. Here are some factors to keep in mind:

- If you have multiple VMs with relatively low I/O requirements, you may be able to put several of their VHDs within a single CSV LUN.

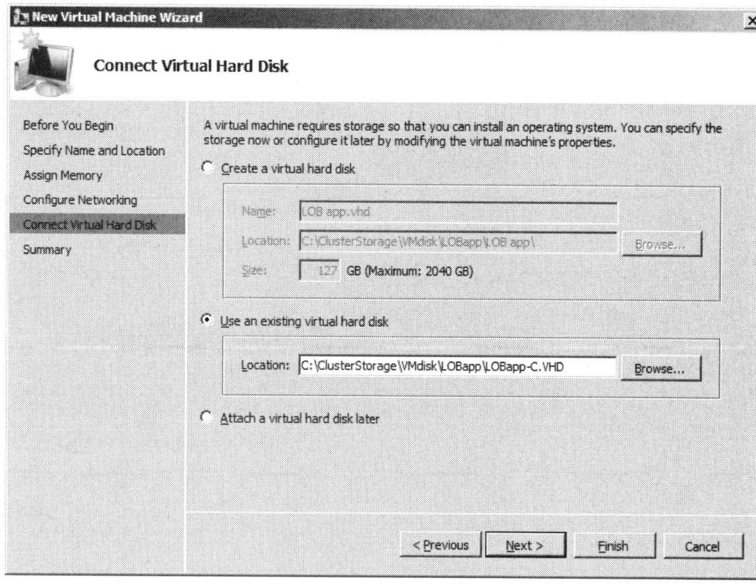

FIGURE 9.15
The Connect Virtual Hard Disk screen of the New Virtual Machine Wizard

- On the other hand, if you have some VHDs with very high I/O requirements, they will still necessitate high-performance storage and likely use dedicated CSV LUNs.
- A common recommendation is to presume that if you would normally use two physical disks on a physical server (binaries and data), then you should use two VHDs for a virtual server—each potentially in a different CSV LUN based on performance.

Just because you can put multiple VMs' VHDs in a single CSV LUN does not mean that you necessarily should.

NOTE Do not start the virtual machine yet. The VM has to be off before it can be configured for high availability in the FCM.

TASK 5: MAKING YOUR VMS HIGHLY AVAILABLE

In the previous task, we used the Hyper-V Manager to create a VM. In this task, we will use the FCM to make the VM highly available. The process is similar to creating any other highly available resource within a cluster (see Chapter 6 for a more thorough explanation of creating and managing clustered resources).

1. In the left pane of the FCM, click on Services And Applications. You can either right-click or use the actions pane on the right to select Configure A Service Or Application. This will open the High Availability Wizard, as seen in Figure 9.16.
2. Select Virtual Machine.

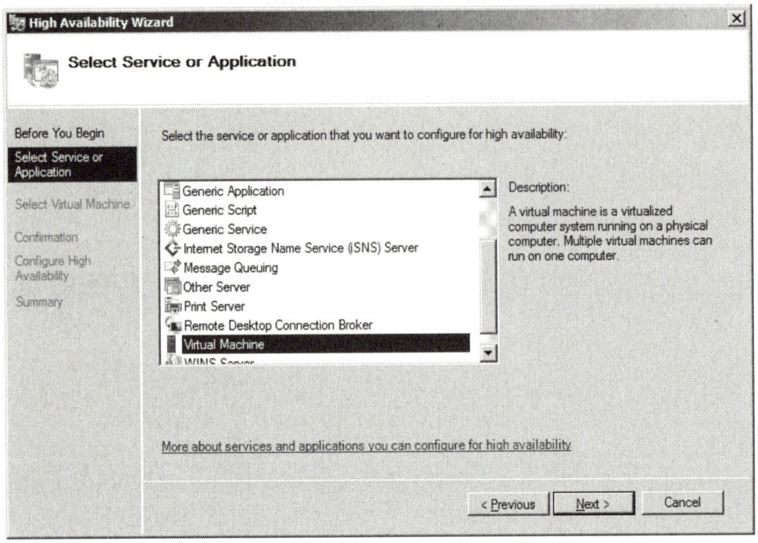

FIGURE 9.16
Defining a virtual machine in the High Availability Wizard

3. You will see a list of every VM listed in Hyper-V on either of the hosts, with the hostname that it was initially created with on the right side, as shown in Figure 9.17.
4. Choose any virtual machines whose configuration and VHDs reside under the `C:\ClusterStorage` directory tree and are shut down.

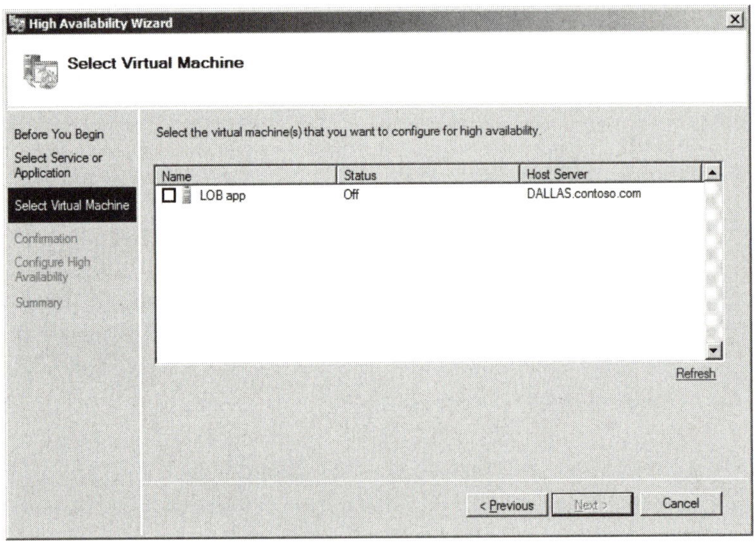

FIGURE 9.17
Selecting virtual machines for high availability

5. The wizard will complete with a report (Figure 9.18) of whether Failover Clustering was able to absorb the VM as a clustered resource.

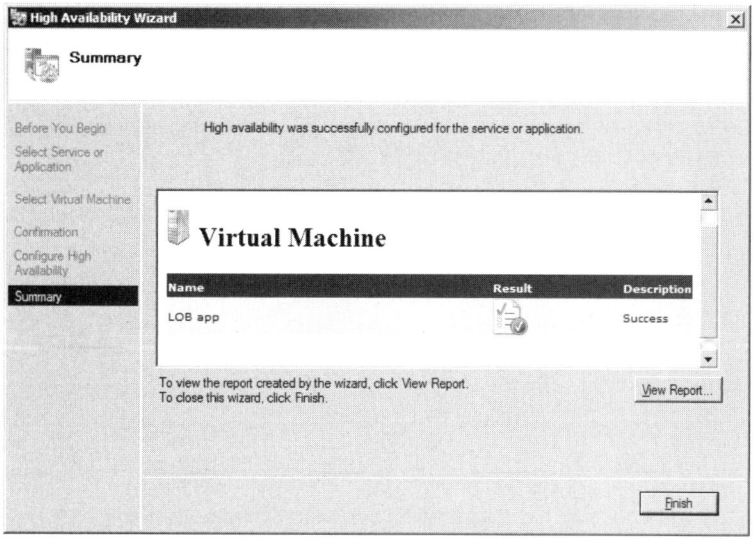

FIGURE 9.18
Successful configuration of a VM for high availability

6. When you finish the wizard, you will see the virtual machine listed in the Services And Applications area of the Failover Cluster Manager.

   As an optional last step, you should explicitly choose which network path will be used for LM. As discussed earlier, the speed of the migration is greatly dependent on having fast connectivity between the existing and new hosts, so the best practice is to have a dedicated network for LM.

7. To configure the network for LM, select the VM in the left pane and then right-click on the VM within the center window and select Properties. One of the tabs in the resulting dialog box is called Network To Live Migration, which will include all cluster interconnects by default. Here, you can reorder the paths' preferred order and deselect any paths that you do not wish to use during migration.

NOTE From now on, you must manage highly available virtual machines from within the Failover Cluster Manager and not from the Hyper-V Manager. If you change the configuration of the VM within FCM, the cluster nodes will be aware of it. If you change the VM configuration from within Hyper-V, you need to refresh the virtual machine in the FCM to pick up what you changed in Hyper-V.

From this point on, you will manage the VM from the cluster console, not the Hyper-V management console. To aid you in this, most of the normal virtual management tasks are available in the Actions pane on the right.

By double-clicking on the LOBapp from either the left tree pane or the LOBapp object within the Services And Applications window, you will get more details on the virtual machine, along with actions similar to Hyper-V to shut down or turn off the VM.

Of course, the most exciting action is the ability to Live Migrate the VM from one node to the other without client disruption. To do that, simply click Live Migrate Virtual Machine To Another Node in the actions pane on the right, as shown in Figure 9.19.

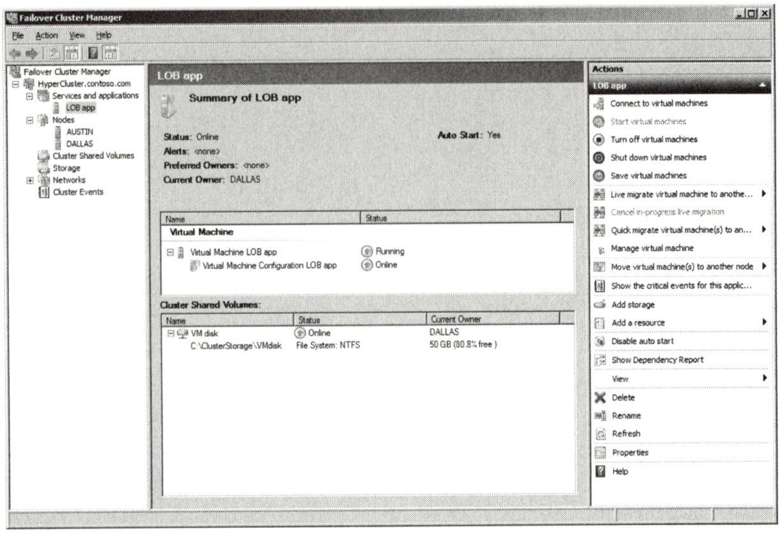

FIGURE 9.19
Managing a VM from within the FCM

Backing Up CSV Configurations

As we have discussed in Chapters 5–8, high-availability solutions like clustering and replication can significantly increase uptime for key resources. Unfortunately, data-availability configurations also tend to create challenges for data-protection technologies.

Specifically, backing up CSV configurations created challenges for all legacy backup solutions that were developed prior to Windows Server 2008 R2. Depending on the backup vendor's release schedule, some vendors began changing their agents to be CSV aware, while other products that were imminently releasing their next version adjusted for CSV in their next release. System Center Data Protection Manager (Chapter 4) did the latter—DPM 2007 did not support CSV—but the newly released DPM 2010 offered a beta at the time of Hyper-V R2's release. DPM 2010 released to market at about the same time as this book was published.

The primary reason why CSVs caused a challenge is that the only supported way to back up a Hyper-V node is by using VSS (see Chapter 4). Unfortunately, based on which node the backup agent was running on (and invoking VSS) versus which node was actively writing to the virtual hard disks, a significant performance penalty could be incurred by the cluster. While most legacy backup solutions may have visibility to the shared CSV file systems, only solutions that are designed to be CSV aware and leverage VSS should be used to protect Hyper-V R2 clusters that are enabled for Live Migration.

The other key consideration for backing up CSVs relates to handling a backup during a Live Migration. When a VSS-based backup is initiated on a VM that is currently being migrated, the Hyper-V VSS writer will wait for the migration to complete before continuing with the backup. The backup from the primary node will continue as a copy instead of a full backup, which may have ramifications for any postbackup cleanup processes.

You can find more information on the requirements and methods of protecting Hyper-V with VSS at `http://technet.microsoft.com/en-us/library/ff182356.aspx`.

CSV Redirected I/O Mode

Typically, the node of the cluster that is offering a particular virtual machine has direct access to the VHD within CSV. However, one of the benefits of CSV is resiliency within server-to-storage communication. That way, if a direct connection is not possible, the I/O is redirected through the CSV network path to another node that does have access to the storage. This enables an additional aspect of fault resilience but does put higher demand on the CSV network.

Redirected I/O Mode is also used for host-based, or parent-partition-based, backups. This ensures that backups can be done from one node in the cluster while another node is actually hosting the VM.

For these reasons, a fast and dedicated network for LM/CSV communication is recommended.

How Virtualization Makes Data Protection and Availability Better

For most people, server virtualization is a way to consolidate underutilized servers. Many experts estimate that the average physical server runs at 15 percent of its potential and therefore wastes power, cooling, and space in datacenters. The acquisition and maintenance costs of the physical hardware itself should be taken into account as well. Virtualization allows IT administrators to run multiple virtual servers on one or more physical servers to maximize power, cooling, space, and physical resources.

But there are some nontraditional benefits of virtualization that can significantly improve your data protection and availability capabilities, including:

- Disaster recovery staging
- Bare metal recovery
- Server rollback

Disaster Recovery Staging

For just a moment, let's forget about virtualization and look at what disaster recovery staging requires for physical production server farms. If your production server farm uses mostly physical servers today, you normally have two choices: *business continuity* or *disaster recovery* (BC/DR) to a secondary site.

NOTE Disaster recovery and business continuity will be covered in Chapter 12. But for now, we will treat the two terms as similar methods for having a secondary datacenter at a remote location—in case the primary facility were to have a catastrophic failure.

Legacy Options for Physical BC/DR sites

Before looking at how virtualization can be leveraged, let's outline three common legacy approaches for creating disaster recovery or business continuity secondary sites for physical production servers.

Legacy Option 1: Physical One-to-One (1:1) Replication

The most traditional approach for ensuring the BC/DR of a key physical server is to build a second and usually identical physical server at the remote location. With a second server at the remote site, the burden becomes to replicate the data to the secondary location. This can be done using either array-based mirroring or host-based replication, as discussed in Chapter 3. Now, you have two identical servers and the secondary location has some version of the data, which may be identical or slightly delayed, depending on your distance and replication method. The last step would simply be to bring up the server and resume services. The methods and automation options will be addressed in Chapter 12.

The obvious challenge with this method is the exorbitant costs associated with the redundant physical hardware, as well as the power, cooling, and space required at the secondary site. For the vast majority of production servers and computing environments, the costs are not justifiable. This is one of the main reasons that many environments do not have adequate BC/DR preparation today.

Legacy Option 2: Physical Many-to-One (M:1) Replication with Total Failover

An option that was pioneered by the host-based replication vendors was the idea of many-to-one replication. In this case perhaps 5 or 10 physical servers' data and configurations would be replicated to a single replication target at the secondary location. This would reduce the number of physical servers at the secondary location, but not as much as you might think.

Often, the replication targets needed to be super-servers with significant amounts of memory, processing power, and storage devices that were in actuality bigger than the aggregate characteristics of the production servers being protected. That's because the replication targets had to be able to offer all the production services that the collection of production sources would run. So far, this sounds like virtualization, but the point is that those replication technologies didn't use virtualization—they faked it:

- Replication technologies using this method would fail over by spoofing additional machine names and IP addresses on the secondary server.
- They offered the file shares that were the same as those being offered by the primary file servers. However, this meant that file share names had to be unique across the production file servers. Otherwise, `FS1\data` and `FS2\data` would conflict with each other when they both failed over to the same replication target. Alternatively, you could configure a different replication target for each file server in the production farm. Neither of these was flexible.
- They would have previously installed each application into the single OS running on the secondary server. This means all applications in the production servers had to be compatible to run on a single OS in the target—meaning that you could not protect a SQL server and an Oracle server to the same target. Nor could you protect an Exchange 2007 and an Exchange 2010 server to the same target.

But discounting those limitations, many-to-one replication did provide a more cost-effective scenario than the one-to-one scenario.

Legacy Option 3: Physical Many-to-One Replication with Partial Failover

A common variation of Legacy Option 2 was to not provide a failover capability for all the production servers being replicated. Instead, key servers might have 1:1 or M:1 failover configured, but the other production servers were only configured for data protection, not availability. After a disaster had occurred, new servers would have to be built for those who did not initially fail over.

This method reduced the complexity of spoofed failovers and concurrent application installation, but at the cost of reduced agility in failing over to the secondary site.

Potential Option 4: Application-Specific Replication with Failover

As discussed in Chapters 5 (DFS), 7 (Exchange), and 8 (SQL Server), some applications have their own replication and failover mechanisms. The first three legacy options do not make any assumptions or workload prerequisites for what is being staged at the disaster recovery site, and neither do the recommended methods discussed next. For those reasons, we are putting aside the workload-specific long-distance replication mechanisms for now. We will reexamine the potential of using them as part of a larger disaster recovery plan in Chapter 12.

Using Virtualization for Physical Server Business Continuity

When considering the evolving legacy options, a key goal was to replicate from multiple production servers to a reduced number of secondary servers at a remote location. The challenge was to reduce the number of servers without sacrificing the agility to fail over in a timely manner. *This is a great scenario for virtualization.*

As readers of this book, you know that virtualization offers the ability to dramatically reduce the number of physical servers in an environment, in order to save on cooling, power, space, and hardware costs. Normally, we might use migration utilities to help us convert our physical servers into virtual servers as part of a onetime migration process. But we can also use those same migration tools to stage a secondary business continuity server at our remote location that is virtual instead of physical.

Physical-to-Virtual (P2V) Utilities

Normally used for migrations, P2V tools work by running an agent on the production physical server that effectively does two things:

- A onetime disk-to-disk backup of the production server volume(s)
- Translation of the network, storage, and other hardware drivers

The result is a nearly identical OS with the original operating system and applications installed, along with the original Registry and everything else that is unique to the server. The difference is the hardware-specific drivers have been switched out to the virtual network, virtual storage, and virtual graphics drivers provided by the hypervisor. During this process, the original IP addresses and all data volumes can be retained, even though the hardware has changed.

Instead of running a P2V utility once, as part of a migration, you can schedule it to run perhaps every weekend to refresh the VM that will be used for BC purposes. The P2V utility provided with Microsoft System Center Virtual Machine Manager can also be invoked from a command line, using the `New-P2V` PowerShell cmdlet.

This cmdlet and its various parameters can then be inserted into any automation or scheduling tool so that it routinely refreshes the VM that may be required for BC. Depending on your network topology, you may wish to run the P2V utility to secondary server that is in the same geography as the primary production server—and then use a replication technology to send it to the remote disaster recovery facility.

Using the P2V utilities, you can easily create dormant VMs that mirror your physical production servers. But you aren't done yet. You will also want to protect the data within those physical servers, and you'll want the data protection to happen much more frequently than how often you run the P2V process. You will also have to decide what level of failover and automation is appropriate for your environment.

Because the P2V process can be intensive, I recommend that you run it only during off-hours and on a less frequent schedule, such as each weekend. This is okay because the machine configuration should not radically change that often. If you have a few physical production severs that appreciably change more frequently than that, you may wish to incorporate a P2V step within your change process so that those changes are captured in the VM as often as they are applied to the production server.

Protecting the Physical Servers' Data

You will almost certainly want the data at your disaster recovery site to be more frequently updated than once per week. In this case, you can utilize either a host-based replication technology that can replicate the data to a location of your choosing (as discussed in Chapter 3) or a backup technology that utilizes disk-to-disk protection (such as DPM, covered in Chapter 4).

Depending on which method you use for replicating the data, there are multiple ways that you can recover the data to the virtual copy at the remote site:

- If you want to use the storage to mirror the data, consider using a SAN that offers iSCSI connectivity, so that the iSCSI initiator can be configured within the VM to immediately connect to the storage volumes.
- If you want to use a file-replication technology, such as host-based replication discussed in Chapter 3, you will need to somehow attach the VM to the storage after the recovery.
- If you want to use a disk-to-disk backup technology, the easiest method is to simply attach clean VHD data volumes to the VM and do an automated restore from the backup pool.

One trick that might help for disk-to-disk backup and replication methods is to create VHD volumes on the replication target and mount them natively, and then replicate the data into those volumes. Then, when you need to connect the data to the VM, you simply have to dismount the VHDs from the host OS and add the VHDs to the guest OS that needs the data. Alternatively, if your backup server or replication target is using a SAN, you may be able to move the LUN that received the data from the replica area to somewhere that the VM can directly attach to.

Bringing the Virtual Machines Online

When a disaster really strikes, you will want to have as much automated as possible—except the actual kick-off of the recovery itself. We'll explain more on that in Chapter 11, but for now we will assume a manual initiation of the recovery and look at how we can automate everything after the decision.

We can use a batch file or an embedded task in a management system such as System Center Operations Manager to invoke our recovery process. Both Hyper-V and the Virtual Machine Manager (VMM) that we used for P2V is command-line controllable via Windows PowerShell. The script to bring a virtual machine online is as simple as this:

```
Start-VM -VMMServer localhost -VM "LOBapp" -RunAsynchronously
```

Once the virtual machine is online, you will need to restore the data based on the method chosen for protection in the previous section. In addition, you will need to address whether the recovery site will use the same IP address ranges or not. If you use the same address ranges, then the VMs will come right online, but you will have fewer options for testing the configuration, since you may incur IP conflicts between sites. If you use different IP address ranges at the recovery site, then the VMs' original IP addresses will not work on the new segments right away. One approach would be to assign DHCP addresses on the NICs within the production server but use DHCP reservations at both the primary and secondary facilities. This way, the server has relatively fixed IP addresses for troubleshooting purposes, but it will easily move between sites and network segments.

As a last step in bringing the virtual machines online, the IP addresses and DNS registration may eventually spread the updated IP address to all the appropriate clients. You can accelerate the process by registering the new IP address with all the relevant DNS servers and gateways when extranet clients are involved. Most gateways and DNS servers have a command-line capability, such as `dnscmd.exe`, which enables you to directly edit its address data.

Recovering Back to the Original Site

The discussion until now has focused on failing over to the secondary site. But equally important is failing back to the primary site. There are two methods of resuming operations from the primary site, depending on whether you want to resume operations virtually or physically:

- It may be that you failed over all the production servers to their virtual copies and everything has been running for a while. In that case, you might consider staying virtual. You simply make a copy of the virtual machines and run the VMs on hosts at the primary facility. The copy is so that you can facilitate virtual-to-virtual (V2V) protection and recovery later—see the next section.
- It may be that you want to resume operation with physical production servers. Unfortunately, while System Center provides a P2V utility, it does not provide a V2P utility to migrate machines from virtual back to physical. Instead, be sure to also back up the system state of the production physical servers on a regular basis, perhaps as often as you do the P2V exercise. Then, when you want to rebuild your physical production server farm, you can use the system state protection mechanism to re-create the physical servers.

Failing Over Less than a Whole Site

Thus far in our discussion on disaster recovery staging, we have focused on site-level failures. But what if the whole site hasn't failed? Or as a more common scenario, what if you don't want to maintain the resources at the secondary site to fail over the entire production farm en masse?

Earlier, we talked about two scripts:

- Using VMM to bring up the virtual machine
- Using DPM or other disk-to-disk to restore the data

But instead of thinking of this as two massive scripts that incorporate the actions for all your production servers, create a single script that does this per production server. Now, you have perhaps a five-line script called `dr-sql25.bat` for bringing up a SQL server named SQL25. For each production server, create a similar script with the first line invoking VMM to bring the VM online and the latter lines restoring the data. Now, you can bring your whole data center online with a simple script like the following:

```
DR-SQL25.BAT
DR-SQL26.BAT
DR-SQL27.BAT
DR-EX14.BAT
DR-EX15.BAT
DR-FS1.BAT
DR-FS2.BAT
```

More importantly, you may only have the virtualization hosting horsepower to run less than half of your production farm at your secondary site. If so, you can immediately run a smaller script for your truly business-critical servers:

```
DR-SQL25.BAT
DR-EX14.BAT
DR-FS1.BAT
```

Upon declaring a disaster and activating those scripts, you could then make immediate arrangements to expedite more virtualization host hardware to your secondary site—perhaps as a prenegotiated drop ship, or just an overnight purchase. When the additional host(s) arrive, they simply need to have Windows Server with Hyper-V installed on them. You can either:

- Restore the VHDs using DPM to the new host, which will preserve the machine configurations.
- Copy the VHDs from the replication target to the new host, and then manually define each machine.

Either way, the rest of your virtual machines come online within a day of the disaster. Technically, you could even bring only one server online, because it failed in the production site. But the first line of defense should be a more integrated data availability solution:

- If it is a file server, use DFS-R and DFS-N—see Chapter 5.
- If it is cluster-able, use Windows Failover Clustering—see Chapter 6.
- If it is Exchange, use CCR/SCR (2007) or DAG (2010)—see Chapter 7.
- If it is SQL Server or SharePoint, use database mirroring and load balancing—see Chapter 8.

But there will be circumstances that preclude the use of these. So yes, you can simply run the batch file to bring that virtual machine and its data online. And if the two sites are in close proximity, you've just migrated from physical to virtual—so don't go back.

Using Virtualization for Virtual Server Business Continuity

If you didn't just do it, read the section "Using Virtualization for Physical Server Business Continuity," and then imagine how much easier it would be if the servers were already virtualized in the primary production farm. In the previous section, we described the four phases of physical-to-virtual BC/DR:

1. Use P2V utilities to stage the BC/DR servers.

2. Protect the data and prepare for data restoration.
3. Bring the virtual machines online.
4. Recover back to the original site.

And in those four phases, a great deal of the work involved the physical-to-virtual conversion, and vice versa. Remember, one of the benefits of virtualization is that all the VM guest operating systems are accessing generic storage, network, video, and other hardware drivers that are provided by the hypervisor. This makes the virtual servers very portable.

By putting either a disk-to-disk replication (see Chapter 3) or a disk-based backup and recovery (see Chapter 4) solution in place on the production hypervisor hosts, you can replicate the VMs and all their data volumes to a secondary site. With this in mind, the four phases reduce down to two steps:

1. Bring the replicated VMs up on the secondary site.
2. To fail back, use the same replication technology in the opposite direction. Take down the secondary VMs and bring up the primary VMs.

Bare Metal Recovery

In a Windows Server 2008 or 2008 R2 environment, there are two common ways to do a *bare metal recovery* (*BMR*) on a physical server:

- Utilize the Windows Server Backup (WSB) utility's bare metal recovery capability, either directly or indirectly (such as how DPM centrally manages BMR schedules and triggers WSB to actually do it).
- Use an unsupported, block-level, third-party utility.

The WSB method utilizes an external hard drive (something preferably outside the disk array that your server primarily uses) to store the block-based images of your server storage. The process can be done by the WSB utility itself, or can be initiated by a centrally located management system like System Center Data Protection Manager (see Chapter 4). With a physical production server, your methods are limited because the logic to capture the disk blocks has to run within the operating system that it is trying to protect. Technically, you could argue that booting from a SAN that supports snapshots of the system volume might be considered a BMR as well. But in that scenario, the disk is not actually in the server, so it isn't a recovery from bare metal—it is simply leveraging a resilient storage medium for the server disk.

By leveraging virtualization, we get new BMR capabilities because the protection of the OS can be taken from outside of the OS, as a host-based backup of a guest. By protecting the outside of a virtual machine, the VHD preserves the hard drives themselves. And because the hypervisor already uses synthetic, and more importantly generic, drivers, a VM that was originally hosted on a Dell host can be brought back online from an HP host (or vice versa). In fact, machines that were originally running on a VMware ESX host can be brought online within a Microsoft Hyper-V host (by programmatically exchanging one hypervisor's generic driver set for the other hypervisor's generic driver set).

Server Rollback

A variation of the mechanics of BMR that provides better capability is rolling back a server. This involves easily, and almost immediately, bringing the virtual machine back online from a previous point in time. With a physical server, protecting a server in preparation of rollback is essentially the same function of Windows Server Backup (WSB) or a third-party utility that delivers BMR. The difference is that BMR assumes that something catastrophic has happened to the production server and it needs to be rebuilt from the beginning. The goal of BMR is to bring newly repaired server hardware back to what it looked like immediately before the outage. In contrast, the goal of server rollback is to take a functioning server from its current configuration to a previous configuration that is more desirable. There are two methods of preparing and achieving a server rollback—using either the hypervisor or a virtualization-aware and VSS-capable backup solution.

Hypervisor VM Rollback

The first is to utilize the hypervisor itself. Again, because the hypervisor has an external view of the virtual machine and the storage is held within the virtual hard drive files, the VHDs can be periodically copied using either shadow copies or snapshots. In Microsoft Hyper-V, this is done by simply right-clicking on a virtual machine within the Hyper-V Management console or System Center Virtual Machine Manager console and selecting Snapshot.

The disk blocks that currently make up the VHD files of the virtual machine can be identified and logically frozen. Instead of those physical blocks being overwritten during data changes, the blocks are written to different locations on the physical disk, so that both the old block and the new block persist. If several days have passed since the snapshot was taken, there may be a significant number of new blocks that the virtual machine is using that are different from those that were frozen in the previous point in time. This can be done routinely, as long as disk space is available in the host. Figure 9.20 shows a snapshot tree of previous recovery points.

FIGURE 9.20
A snapshot tree of previous recovery points for a VM with Hyper-V

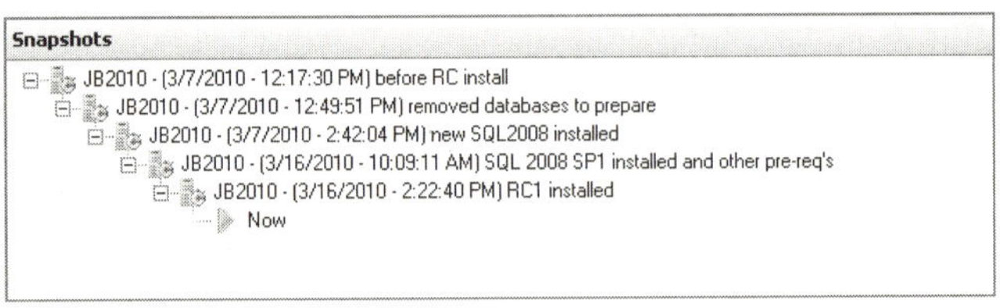

After a few more days, you may decide that you need to roll back the VM to the previous point in time. You can do this by going back into the Hyper-V Management console and selecting Revert. Revert will discard the newer blocks that were made after the snapshot was taken so that the VHD files are literally what they were when the snapshot was invoked. The VM will then come back online in its previous state.

Unfortunately, using snapshots in Hyper-V is done on a VM as a whole, which means that while it may be desirable to restore the VM's system volume to a previous state, the data volumes will also be reverted. Reverting the entire VM is a good method to use when you are about to install new software or make another appreciable change inside a VM. If the installation or other change does not work out, you can immediately reverse it without attempting to uninstall and potentially leave yourself in a broken state. This can easily be done in a short time window when you are not likely to have much data change. If, however, you wish to revert one VHD or virtual machine volume while leaving the other volumes unscathed, a better approach is to use a virtualization-capable backup.

Reverting a VM Using Backups and Restores

If you use a VSS-based and Hyper-V capable backup solution, the VHDs can be protected while the virtual machine is still running. The VHD set and metadata for the virtual machine configuration are then stored within the backup software. Most backup software with this capability offers the ability to restore the entire VM or a single VHD file. With System Center Data Protection Manager (see Figure 9.21), just a single VHD, such as the one containing the OS volume, can be restored back to the virtualization host without impacting the VHDs that store the data volumes.

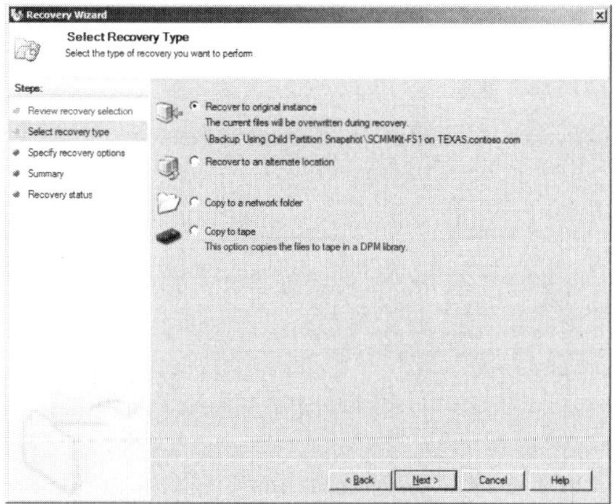

Figure 9.21
DPM restore wizard for virtualization

For more information on the process of restoring individual VHDs or even files within the VHDs, refer back to Task 11, "Restoring Virtual Machines," in Chapter 4.

Real World Scenario

Single-Role Virtualized Servers

To me, the capability of quickly rolling back a virtual machine to yesterday is worth its weight in gold. And being able to restore an entire VM from last month is just as cool, because it gives you some recovery scenarios that are much more flexible than going after last night's tape backup.

For that reason, I recommend virtualization for small branch offices with single servers. The only thing on the hardware itself is Hyper-V and DPM. The file server runs as a virtual server. And since even the standard license of Windows Server includes one host instance and one virtual instance, there is no additional cost. But if the file server has an issue, a branch manager can restore the VHD or the whole VM in just a few minutes, and it is effectively like recovering the whole file server.

As the small branch becomes a bigger branch, they can simply deploy a second VM within the same host, instead of getting a second server and figuring out space, power, cooling, or even just where to put the second monitor (or buy a KVM switch). Chances are that the first server had I/O to spare anyway.

One of my favorite deployments, whose name I cannot mention, has hundreds of remote sites in some of the furthest reaches on the planet. Many of the sites are even mobile, so space is an absolute premium. Their hardware runs just Hyper-V. Each host has at least a virtualized file server and a virtualized Exchange server, as well as DPM. If anything weird happens, the first reaction is to roll back the VM. The second reaction is to restore the image from DPM. And because DPM can replicate from one DPM server to another, all of those remote sites replicate their data back to locations in the United States via satellite, so that no data would be lost if the remote site were to have a catastrophe.

Summary

Windows Server 2008 R2 and Hyper-V Server 2008 R2 provide some strong new availability capabilities in Live Migration for ensuring that your virtual servers remain highly available in ways that application-specific availability technologies (such as those described in Chapters 5–8) cannot. However, the Cluster Shared Volume (CSV) technology that supports Live Migration can offer challenges to legacy backup solutions and must be protected using a VSS-capable solution that is CSV aware.

Other than CSV challenges, virtualization (for the most part) makes data protection easier because it provides the ability to protect the production servers from the outside, or host perspective. This includes not only traditional protection and recovery of production servers, but also whole-server protection and disaster recovery scenarios. Even the smallest of environments can benefit by combining virtualization and data protection in some innovative ways.

Chapter 10

Management and Deployment

Throughout this book, we have looked specifically at technologies and product features designed to raise the protection or availability of key services and applications, including backup, clustering, file services, email, databases, collaboration, and virtualization. But sometimes, the key to running a better datacenter is not additional platforms or technologies, but managing what you have in a more proactive and holistic way.

This chapter on management (and the next on monitoring) will discuss the importance of maintaining what you have to a higher quality bar, as well as providing a view of your now highly available and better-protected systems. Specifically, we will look at management and deployment in enterprise datacenters, midsized organizations, and virtual infrastructures.

Well-Managed Systems for Higher Uptime

Let's consider some of the implementations that we have covered in previous chapters:

- Replicated and highly available file shares
- Replicated and highly available Exchange mailboxes
- Replicated and highly available SQL databases

Now, imagine what will happen if:

- One of the file servers has a different service pack than the other, so it is consuming inordinately more bandwidth to stay in sync than it should.
- One of the Exchange servers never receives security hotfixes and is exposing the environment to vulnerabilities.
- One of the mirrored SQL database servers is routinely rebooting, but nobody notices because the other takes the load.

Although these examples may appear farfetched, the point is that unless your systems are well managed, consistently deployed, and routinely maintained, the other availability and protection methods won't be as effective as they should. In addition, we should be thinking about rolling up all the various availability and protection technologies within a management infrastructure so that even the protection technologies can be consistently deployed and maintained.

Management of computer systems is a very important, and potentially time-consuming, task for today's organizations. The number of computer systems is increasing in most environments, which makes it hard to keep the systems up-to-date with software applications, software updates, and operating systems while adhering to corporate standards.

In this chapter, we will look at three key scenarios and examine tools that can help with manageability and deployment in each:

- Large enterprises
- Midsized organizations
- Virtual datacenters

How Manageability Fits into a Backup and Availability Book

If you were reading a book on how to get more performance out of your car and add after-market additions to it, the book would not be complete without also emphasizing that one of the most important aspects to better car performance is regular maintenance. A high-powered engine won't help you if you never change the oil.

Similarly, a book on raising availability and improving data resiliency should talk a bit about server maintenance (or more specifically about deployment and manageability). A well-maintained server (courtesy of security updates, software hotfixes, and new drivers) is almost always more resilient than a server left in its initially deployed or ad hoc–patched state. This is especially true when considering that not all server workloads have built-in availability mechanisms like those discussed in Chapters 5–9. Sometimes, maintaining or raising the quality of your existing server is the only resiliency choice that you have.

Large Enterprise Deployment and Manageability

Large enterprises have significant challenges in deploying and maintaining even the things that some folks may consider basic, such as Windows or Windows Server. With so many units, it is important to drive consistency not only in the initial deployment but all throughout the lifecycle of the computing assets.

Even turning on the features for availability can be a challenge when you are dealing with 2,000 SQL databases or 1,200 servers that need to be backed up. For enterprises needing manageability and deployment consistency, Microsoft offers System Center Configuration Manager.

Introducing Microsoft Systems Management

Microsoft released its first true systems management product back in 1994 as a product called Systems Management Server (SMS) 1.0. Through the next few years, the product was updated to include versions 1.1, 1.2, and 2.0. In 2003, the next version of the Systems Management Server product was released as SMS 2003. This release was a major update to the previous Systems Management Server products and included new capabilities from the prior releases, including a new client designed for mobile scenarios.

With the creation of the System Center brand of management products from Microsoft, the current release of the product is called System Center Configuration Manager 2007, which released to the market in the year 2007. Configuration Manager 2007, or as it is referred to by its shortened name ConfigMgr, is a product upgrade from the previous version, SMS 2003. As of this writing, Configuration Manager 2007 is at a Service Pack 2 release, on top of which you can install the Configuration Manager 2007 R2 update. The R2 update is not an update, as a service pack provides, but is a set of feature add-ons to the Configuration Manager 2007 SP1 or SP2 base version.

System Center Configuration Manager 2007 R2 and R3

ConfigMgr is a member of the System Center family of products, and is designed to help organizations manage their Windows-based systems with numerous ConfigMgr features. The various management scenarios for ConfigMgr include:

Discovery Before you can effectively manage systems, you must know what systems need to be managed. ConfigMgr can automatically discover computer resources and add them to the ConfigMgr database. The primary source of computers, users, and groups for ConfigMgr is Active Directory Domain Services. Once you have discovered computer systems, you will install them as clients so that they can be managed.

Inventory One of the first actions a client will do is generate inventory information. ConfigMgr clients automatically generate detailed information about the system's hardware and software assets. This inventory data is valuable for administrators to manage corporate computer assets, and often is used to provide data for targeting of software distributions.

Application Deployment Administrators wind up spending a significant amount of time deploying software to systems. ConfigMgr provides a centralized and automated software delivery system that is commonly used to deploy new or updated applications to client computers. Configuration Manager 2007 R2 adds the capability of deploying virtual applications through integration with the Microsoft Application Virtualization technology.

Updates One of the most important tasks you must do is manage software update compliance of systems. ConfigMgr integrates with Microsoft's Windows Server Update Services (WSUS) to help identify missing updates (such as security updates). It provides you with the ability to identify systems missing updates and the ability to manage the deployment of appropriate updates to clients.

Operating System Deployment Computer systems constantly require deployment of operating systems. ConfigMgr assists you with the deployment of operating systems, either new versions or reinstallation of the operating system in a break-fix scenario. Automating OS deployment using ConfigMgr can save you a significant amount of time.

Consistency Compliance Ensuring that your computer assets are configured to your corporate standards can be a time-consuming and difficult task. ConfigMgr allows you to design (or import) rules that will identify systems that are, and are not, compliant with corporate guidelines. You can then use Configuration Manager's software distribution feature to return systems to the desired compliance state.

Windows Mobile Devices The population of nonpersonal computers is increasing in corporate environments today. These systems need to be managed just as personal computers do. ConfigMgr provides discovery, inventory, and software deployment to Windows Mobile systems, including the ability to deploy configuration settings to the Windows Mobile clients.

Security Assurance In addition to deploying appropriate security updates to systems, ConfigMgr can help prevent clients from accessing your corporate network until the updates have been deployed. If the required updates have not been deployed, clients are not allowed to join the corporate network until those updates are deployed.

Configuration Manager Site System Roles

To provide these features to clients, the ConfigMgr environment must be installed. This environment consists of at least one site (often multiple sites in disperse locations) and various site system roles. A site consists of one main ConfigMgr server, called the site server; potentially additional Windows servers (called site systems) that offload site services from the site server for managing clients; and the clients that are managed by the site server. There are many site system roles that can be installed in a ConfigMgr site, whether on the site server itself or on remote site systems.

This section lists the site system roles available in Configuration Manager 2007, including whether or not there is any support for Windows cluster, Windows Network Load Balancing clustering, multiple installations of the same site system role per site, or those scenarios where you are only allowed one computer running the specific site system role per site.

There are a core set of infrastructure components, also referred to as site system roles. These site system roles provide support for all feature areas of the Configuration Manager 2007 product, and include:

Site Server There is one site server per site, and it is created by running Configuration Manager Setup on the server. This role cannot be moved to a different site after installation without uninstalling or reinstalling the site installed on the original site server.

Site Database Server This is the Microsoft SQL Server 2005 SP2 or SQL Server 2008 computer that stores the ConfigMgr site database. If this is a remote SQL Server installation, with no other site system roles co-located on the computer, this role can be run in a clustered environment using the Windows Cluster service. This is the only site system role that is supported in a Windows Cluster environment. This role can also be moved to a different server after initial installation of the site using a site reset.

SMS Provider Computer This is a site system that runs the SMS Provider. The SMS Provider is a special security layer that sits between the ConfigMgr administrator and the site database, validating that the administrator requesting to access data or perform some specific action has the rights to do so. This would normally be installed on the site server, or the site database server, but could be installed on a third computer in the environment if the site database is hosted in a clustered environment. This role is assigned during site installation, although it can be moved during a site reset process.

Management Point This is the primary point of contact between ConfigMgr clients and the ConfigMgr site. Management points can be part of a Windows Network Load Balancing cluster if you require redundancy, load balancing, or scalability beyond 25,000 clients in a single ConfigMgr site. The original management point role can be assigned to a different computer after installation.

Reporting Point This site system provides the ability to run reports for ConfigMgr from either the console or a specific URL. A site can have multiple reporting points to help distribute the load between various people running reports. There are no reporting points assigned to a site by default; they must be added to the site by the administrator.

Reporting Services Point This is a Microsoft SQL Server Reporting Services (SRS) server that has been integrated with ConfigMgr to allow reports to be run in an SRS context instead of the traditional reporting mode using reporting points. A site can have multiple Reporting Services point site systems to help distribute the reporting load for report execution. There are no Reporting Services points assigned to a site by default; they must be added to the site by the administrator. This site system role is only available in a ConfigMgr site that has installed the Configuration Manager 2007 R2 or R3 add-on.

To provide support for the Configuration Manager 2007 software distribution and software update features, the following site system roles are required. These roles provide files to clients to be run or installed locally, as well as a location to scan for applicable software updates:

Distribution Point This is the site system that clients use to access software distribution, software updates, and operating system image packages. A site can have up to 100 distribution points to help provide multiple sources to access package content from. A distribution point site system role is installed on the site server during site installation, though it can be removed from the site server and added to different servers (making them distribution point site systems) after installation.

Branch Distribution Point This is a ConfigMgr client that provides content to other ConfigMgr clients as a distribution point. Branch distribution points are preferred over standard distribution points when clients are located over slower WAN links from the rest of the site systems. A site can have up to 2,000 branch distribution points to provide content to clients in remote locations in those remote locations. There are no branch distribution points assigned to a site by default; they must be added to the site by the administrator.

Software Update Point This is a WSUS server that is configured to integrate with ConfigMgr in order to provide software updates to ConfigMgr clients. Software update points can be part of a Windows Network Load Balancing cluster if you require redundancy, load balancing, or scalability beyond 25,000 clients in a single site. There are no software update points assigned to a site by default; they must be added to the site by the administrator.

Deploying operating systems in Configuration Manager 2007 has many scenarios and thus many site system roles that may be required. In addition to some of the roles mentioned earlier (management point, distribution point, and branch distribution point), operating system deployment can use the following site system roles:

PXE Service Point This site system role is installed on a Windows Deployment Services (WDS) server to provide operating system deployment (OSD) services to bare metal systems or other systems that perform a network boot. A site can have multiple (the current support statement is up to 10) PXE service points to support remote locations and provide multiple locations for servicing network boot requests. This site system role is not installed in a site and must be added by the administrator.

State Migration Point This site system role provides a secure server for moving user state information from a user's current computer to the user's new computer in an operating system deployment computer-replacement scenario. A site can contain any number of state migration points. There are no state migration points assigned to a site by default; they must be added by the administrator.

As detailed later on in this chapter, you can use numerous methods to deploy ConfigMgr clients. Depending on the method used, there are various site system roles that would be required to support the deployment method. These roles include:

Server Locator Point This site system role allows client computers to validate the site they are to be assigned to and helps clients find the default management point. This site system role is only required if the site is not publishing data to Active Directory or in environments where there are systems that cannot access the site's data that is published to Active Directory. This role is not installed by default and must be added by the administrator. You can install as many server locator point site systems in your site as you feel necessary for your environment.

Fallback Status Point This site system role allows ConfigMgr clients to generate state messages related to the client deployment process. These state messages generated during the ConfigMgr ager client deployment process are sent to the fallback status point, which in turn provides the state messages to the site server to be processed into the site database. You can have multiple fallback-point-site systems in your site, although clients will only use the specific fallback status points that they are configured to use. No fallback status point is installed in the site by default, and one must be added by the administrator if desired.

In addition to the site system roles mentioned here, there are other site system roles that can be implemented if you want to implement the specific feature in your environment. These roles include:

Asset Intelligence Synchronization Point This site system allows the central site in a ConfigMgr hierarchy to connect to System Center Online, either on a scheduled basis or on demand, to download any updates to the Asset Intelligence catalog to the site. This connection also allows the requesting for identification of software discovered locally that is not already included in the database. Any updates downloaded from the central site are replicated to primary sites in the hierarchy. This site system role is not installed by default in the central site and must be added by the administrator. This site system role is only available in Configuration Manager 2007 Service Pack 1 or 2 sites.

Out-of-Band Service Point This site system role is used to integrate with Intel AMT vPro enabled systems to provide out-of-band management to those systems. This site system role is not assigned in the site by default, and the administrator would need to add this role to the appropriate computer. You are only allowed to install one out-of-band service point per primary site. This site system role is only available in Configuration Manager 2007 Service Pack 1 or 2 sites.

System Health Validator This site system role is installed on a Windows Server 2008 server that is installed with the Network Policy Server role to provide integration with the Network Access Protection feature of the Windows Server operating system. This role is not assigned to the site by default and would need to be added to the site by the administrator. One system health validator site system can support a hierarchy of up to 100,000 clients, or you can have a separate system health validator in each site in the ConfigMgr hierarchy.

The Configuration Manager Console

To provide these management features to clients, including setting up the various site system roles, you use the ConfigMgr console. The console is the primary tool that administrators use to manage their sites, as well as any child sites in the hierarchy. You can install the ConfigMgr console on multiple computers to allow numerous administrators to share the administrative load or perform unique duties.

The ConfigMgr console is divided into sections, each providing a unique set of capabilities—management of the site, management of clients, monitoring status, and so on. The UI is divided into three panes, as shown in Figure 10.1. The left section is referred to as the tree pane, the middle section is the results pane, and the far-right section is referred to as the Actions pane. These references will be used in the step-by-step instructions included in this chapter to walk through various ConfigMgr features.

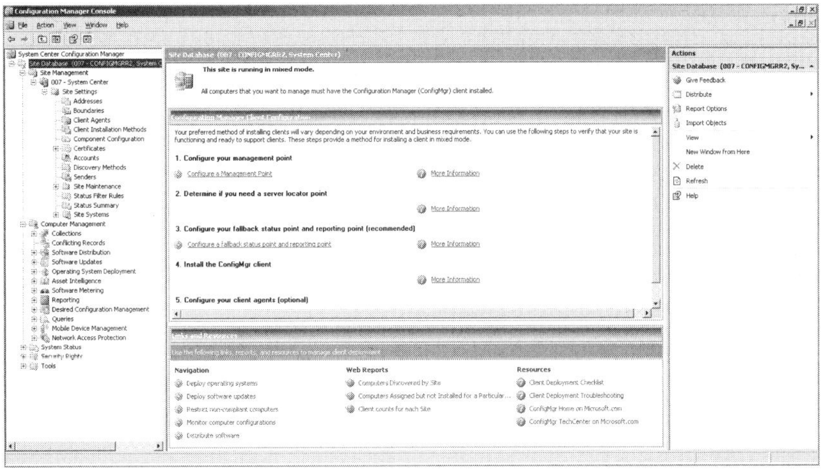

FIGURE 10.1
The ConfigMgr console

To begin, choose Start ➤ All Programs ➤ Microsoft System Center ➤ Configuration Manager 2007, and then click ConfigMgr Console.

When the ConfigMgr console window appears, as shown in Figure 10.1, it will display the home page, with the System Center Configuration Manager node selected. If the computer that the ConfigMgr console is running on has access to the Internet, the results pane will display the Configuration Manager TechCenter site. If the computer does not have access to the Internet, it will display a static text page. From here, you can can begin to administer your ConfigMgr environment:

- To administer the site, start by expanding nodes in the tree pane. Expand Site Database, expand Site Management, expand the local site code (in the screen shots included in this chapter, the site code is 007), expand Site Settings, and then you can configure settings for the local site.
- To administer the clients in the site, expand Site Database, expand Computer Management, and then use the appropriate node for the feature to be implemented.

There are step-by-step sections in each of the feature areas provided throughout the remainder of this chapter for your reference. All of these step-by-step sections will assume that the ConfigMgr console has already been started.

Now let's take a look at some of the features and how to use them to manage your systems.

Asset Identification and Agent Installation

One of the first things that you want from a management product is to identify your assets. The initial process is to discover the available systems in the environment. The primary discovery method used in most ConfigMgr environments is Active Directory System Discovery. This discovery method queries Active Directory for computer systems, which are then added to the site database. Included in this discovery method is basic data about the resource, including the Active Directory site membership, the computer name, IP address, IP subnet, installed operating system, and domain the system is a member of.

Hands-on Learning with Configuration Manager

A management solution like ConfigMgr requires installing not only the management platform itself but also the various production servers that would be managed, such as Windows Server, SQL Server, or Exchange Server, as well as an Active Directory deployment. Because of this, it is less practical for this chapter to start from the beginning with a clean install and build up an enterprise management architecture.

Instead, you can gain hands-on experience with System Center Configuration Manager, as well as System Center Essentials, by using the TechNet Virtual Hands-On lab environments. Virtual labs provide you with a private environment to learn in for a few hours, using just your web browser and connecting to a large lab farm at Microsoft. Virtual labs for ConfigMgr can be found at `www.microsoft.com/systemcenter/configurationmanager/en/us/virtual-labs.aspx`.

Using the virtual labs, you will have the chance to try a wide range of tasks that are described in this chapter, including:

Asset intelligence: Task 1

Software deployment: Tasks 2–8

Software updating: Tasks 9–12

Desired state compliance: Tasks 13–16

Deploying operating systems: Tasks 17–20

Preventing unsecure system access: Task 21

Installing the Configuration Manager Agent

After the systems are discovered, they need to be installed as ConfigMgr clients so that they can be managed. There are several methods that can be used to install the ConfigMgr client on appropriate systems. These methods include:

Client Push Installation This method can automatically install the ConfigMgr client on discovered resources initiated remotely from the site server, or only deploy to systems you decide to install the client on.

Software Update Point Installation This method will install the ConfigMgr client on systems from a software update point (which is installed on a Windows Server Update Services computer) as the computer completes a scan against the WSUS server for applicable updates.

Group Policy Installation This installation method installs the ConfigMgr client on systems targeted with a Group Policy object created for the Group Policy Configuration Manager client installer.

Manual Installation This installation method installs the ConfigMgr client when initiated from a command prompt, logon script, or other manual process. Manual installation is usually only used to install individual clients instead of a large number of clients, which the previously described installation methods are designed for.

Software Distribution This installation method is used to upgrade existing Systems Management Server (SMS) 2003 or ConfigMgr clients to the current version of ConfigMgr. This installation method does not install brand-new clients but upgrades existing clients.

After installation of the ConfigMgr client software, additional information about the client can be collected through the ConfigMgr inventory process. ConfigMgr collects information about the hardware attributes of clients (such as the amount of memory, processor speed, free hard disk space, and so on) as well as information about software installed (primarily the applications that are installed). Asset Intelligence is the primary method that is used to identify applications that are installed on a client. When Asset Intelligence is enabled, this data is collected automatically through hardware inventory, and viewed either through the ConfigMgr console or ConfigMgr reports (70 Asset Intelligence reports are included in the console).

TASK 1: ENABLING ASSET INTELLIGENCE

The ability to identify and manage software assets through the Asset Intelligence feature is not enabled by default in ConfigMgr. However, it is a simple process to enable Asset Intelligence data collection so that clients begin to report the details regarding the software applications that are installed on the client. The following step-by-step task will guide you through the process to enable Asset Intelligence data collection in your site (Figure 10.2).

FIGURE 10.2
The Asset Intelligence page

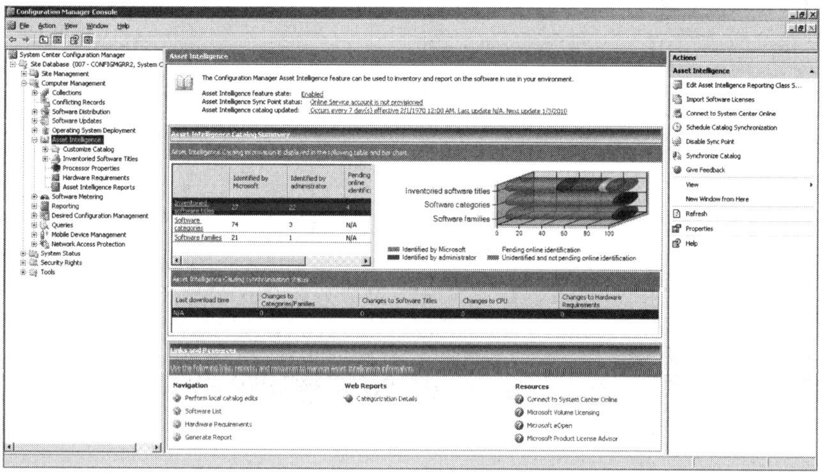

From the ConfigMgr console:

1. In the tree pane, expand Site Database, expand Computer Management, and then click Asset Intelligence.

   The *Asset Intelligence* page will appear in the results pane. By default, Asset Intelligence is not enabled in the site, so the Asset Intelligence Feature State option will display Disabled in the top section of the results pane.

2. In the tree pane, right-click Asset Intelligence, and then click Edit Asset Intelligence Reporting Class Settings.

   The Asset Intelligence Reporting Class Settings dialog box appears allowing you to enable all Asset Intelligence classes or just selected classes. Unless you are going to create your own reports to display additional data that Asset Intelligence can collect, there is no need to enable all classes.

3. Click the option "Enable only the selected Asset Intelligence reporting classes." Then click the check box to select each class that you want to collect data for. If you hold the mouse pointer over the class, a tooltip appears displaying the built-in Asset Intelligence reports that will use the data for the class the mouse is pointing to. You will notice that all classes are used by built-in reports, with the exception of `SMS_InstalledExecutable` and `SMS_SoftwareShortcut`.
4. After you have selected the classes you want to enable, click OK and then click Yes to the message box that is presented to confirm you want the classes enabled.

   Clients will then begin reporting Asset Intelligence data after their next policy retrieval process (which is hourly by default) and the next hardware inventory cycle (which is weekly by default). Both of these actions can be manually initiated on clients for testing purposes if needed.

Centralized Software Deployment

To deploy software using ConfigMgr, you will need to create a few specific objects. These objects include:

Collection This is the target recipients for the software distribution. For example, you might create a collection that uses a query to group all ConfigMgr clients that have 1 GB of memory, 2 GB of free disk space, and a 1 GHz processor, and that don't have a specific application already installed. All of this data can be collected from hardware inventory. There are a number of built-in collections in ConfigMgr, though often you will create your own collections based on the grouping of systems, users, or groups that you want to use for the targeting of software, software updates, or operating system deployments.

Package This is the set of files that you want to make available to the collection members. Often this would be the files used to install an application (including `Setup.exe`). For example, you could create a package that would deploy the Data Protection Manager backup agent. The files that comprise a package are referred to as the package source files. Often packages are created from a package definition file, which is a single file you can import that will provide all the details about the package, though you can manually create a package if you don't have a package definition file (such as an MSI file) to import for the specific package you need to create.

Program This is the command line that you want to execute from the package source files. An example program could be similar to `Setup.exe` or `msiexec.exe /q /i` *`msisetup`*`.msi`. A single package can have multiple unique programs that would launch different command lines for various options, such as a typical install or an unattended install, or to uninstall the software. In addition to installing software, the purpose of your program could be to launch a program that has already been installed, such as to initiate an on-demand backup process. If your package was created by importing a package definition file, the package definition file also will have included at least one, possibly multiple, programs that are created automatically for you.

Distribution Point This is the site system (very often there will be multiple distribution points available in a single site) that contains the package source files from which targeted clients retrieve the package files from in order to run the program. If the package contains source files, the package must be on at least one distribution point that is accessible to each client in order to successfully run the program.

Advertisement This object ties everything together. The advertisement references the collection, package, and program, and in effect says "The members of this collection are to run this program from this package at this time." Clients retrieve the advertisement and then act on it as instructed. Without the advertisement, the client would not know anything about the package or program. The advertisement does not dictate which distribution point the client will use, but the client will intelligently determine the best distribution point to use to access the package source files from the best source given the client's current location.

Once an advertisement has been created, status for the advertisement can be viewed directly in the ConfigMgr console or via reports launched from the console, as shown in Figure 10.3.

FIGURE 10.3
The Software Distribution page

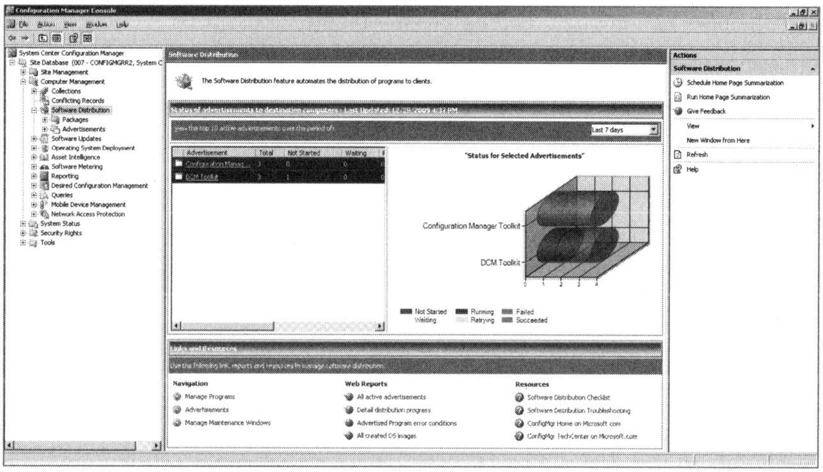

TASK 2: CREATING A PACKAGE FROM A DEFINITION FILE (MSI FILE BASED)

As mentioned earlier, a package is the set of files that you want to make available to your clients to run or install. Packages can be manually created in the ConfigMgr console, or you can automate the creation of a package by importing a package definition file. The following step-by-step task will guide you through the process to create a package by using a Windows Installer file as a package definition file.

In the tree pane, expand Site Database, expand Computer Management, expand Software Distribution, and then click Packages. There are no packages created by default with ConfigMgr.

1. Right-click the Packages node, and then select New ➢ Package From Definition.
2. Complete the Create Package From Definition Wizard using the following information:
   - On the Welcome page, click Next.
   - On the Package Definition page, click Browse, and then open the package definition file (this procedure assumes an MSI file is used for the package definition file).
   - On the Source Files page, click "Always obtain files from a source directory," and then click Next.
   - On the Source Directory page, specify the appropriate UNC or local file path to the source files, and then click Next.
   - On the Summary page, click Finish.

The new package will appear in the ConfigMgr console under Software Distribution/Packages.

Task 3: Viewing the Programs Created from Importing a Definition File (MSI File Based)

A ConfigMgr program is the command line that you want your clients to run from the package source files. Programs can be manually created in the ConfigMgr console, or you can automate the creation of programs by importing a package definition file. The following step-by-step task will guide you through the process to create six programs by importing a Windows Installer file as a package definition file.

To view the programs:

1. In the tree pane, expand Site Database, expand Computer Management, expand Software Distribution, expand Packages, and then expand the package that was just created.

   The nodes for the package will appear in the tree pane. One of those package nodes is Programs.

2. In the tree pane, click Programs.

   The programs that were created for this package appear in the results pane. If you created the package by using an MSI for the package definition file, there should be six programs created: three for targeting of computers and three for targeting users (Figure 10.4).

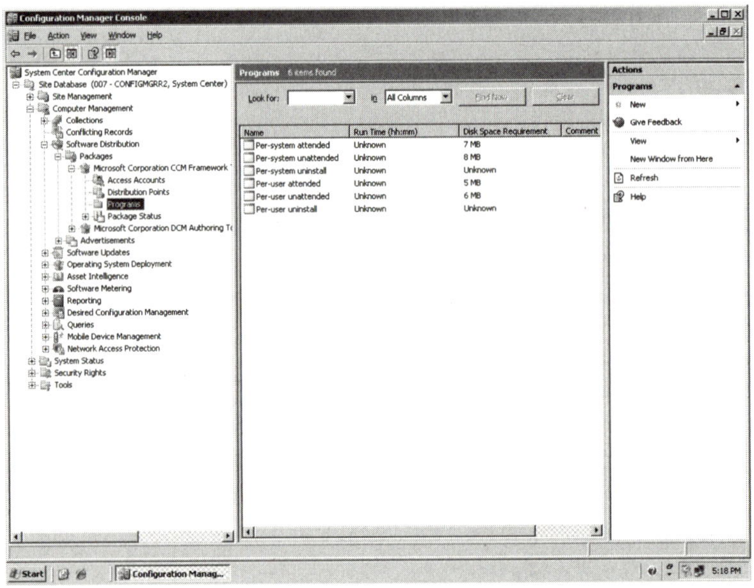

Figure 10.4
ConfigMgr console programs

The next step in the process is to add the package to a distribution point so that clients can access the package source files.

Task 4: Distributing the Package Source Files to a Distribution Point

Before clients can successfully run the appropriate program, the package source files must be distributed to at least one ConfigMgr distribution point that the clients have access to. ConfigMgr clients only access package source files from a distribution point, unless the source files the program refers to already exist on the client computer, such as a virus-scanning program or other operating system utility. The following step-by-step task will guide you through the process to distribute a package to a distribution point.

1. In the tree pane, expand Site Database, expand Computer Management, expand Software Distribution, expand Packages, and then expand the package that was just created.

   The nodes for the package will appear in the tree pane. One of those package nodes is Distribution Points. By default, no distribution points are added to this package automatically.

2. In the tree pane, right-click Distribution Points, and then click New Distribution Points.
3. Complete the New Distribution Points Wizard using the following information:
   - On the Welcome page, click Next.
   - On the Copy Package page, select the distribution point(s) that you want the package source files to be copied to, and then click Next.
   - On the Wizard Completed page, click Finish.

Depending on how large the package source files are, how many distribution points you added to the package, and the network access from the site server to the distribution point(s), it may take several minutes or longer to copy the package source files to the distribution point(s). You can use the Package Source node under the package to determine when the distribution process has completed. A status of Installed indicates that the files have been copied to the distribution point and are ready for clients to access.

The final object that must be created in order for clients to run the advertised program is the advertisement. You also need a target collection; however, you can also use any of the built-in collections to target the package and program to.

Task 5: Creating an Advertisement

ConfigMgr clients learn about a program to be run through an advertisement. The advertisement instructs the client (through the target collection) which program to run, from which package, and when it is to be run. The following step-by-step task will guide you through the process to create an advertisement to instruct a client to run a specific program from a specific package.

1. In the tree pane, expand Site Database, expand Computer Management, expand Software Distribution, and then click Advertisements.
2. In the tree pane, right-click Advertisements and select New ➢ Advertisement.
3. Complete the New Advertisement Wizard using the following information:

   A. On the General page, supply the following information:
      - A name for the advertisement
      - An optional comment
      - The package that is to be accessed by the client
      - The program the client is to run from the package source files
      - The collection the program is targeted to

B. On the Schedule page, click the New button (the icon resembles a starburst) if you want the advertisement to be run automatically at a specific time, and then click Next. If you want the advertisement to be optional (only run when the user decides to run it), do not set a schedule, and simply click Next (Figure 10.5).

FIGURE 10.5
Advertisement scheduling

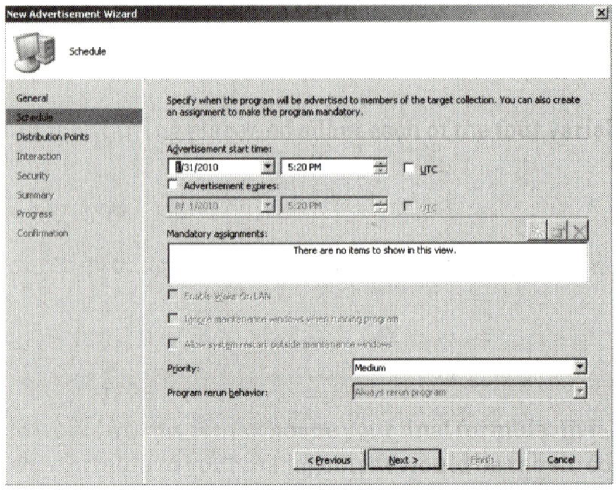

C. On the Distribution Points page, normally you can leave the defaults, and then click Next.

D. On the Interaction page, normally you can leave the defaults, and then click Next.

E. On the Security page, add appropriate accounts and rights if necessary, and then click Next.

F. On the Summary page, click Next.

G. On the Wizard Completed page, click Finish.

The new advertisement appears in the results pane. Clients will retrieve the new advertisement on their next policy polling interval (hourly by default). If you want to speed up the process, you can force the client to retrieve policies more immediately.

TASK 6: FORCING THE CLIENT TO CHECK FOR POLICIES MORE QUICKLY

The client will normally check for updated policies hourly by default, though the administrator can configure clients to check more or less frequently. But you can force the client to update sooner:

1. In Control Panel, start ConfigMgr. The Configuration Manager Properties dialog box appears open to the General tab.
2. In the Configuration Manager Properties, click the Actions tab. The available actions for the client are displayed.
3. In the list of actions, click Machine Policy Retrieval & Evaluation Cycle, and then click Initiate Action.
4. Click OK to close the message box that appears indicating that the action may take a few minutes to complete.
5. Click OK to close the Configuration Manager Properties dialog box.

The client will then request new policies, which includes advertisements, from its management point. After the policy has been retrieved and evaluated, a balloon and icon should appear in the system tray. If the advertised program was scheduled, and the scheduled time has been reached, the balloon and icon will indicate that an assigned program is about to run, and will count down from five minutes. After the countdown completes, the assigned program will run automatically. If this is an optional program, you can follow the steps in Task 7 to run the program.

TASK 7: RUNNING AN OPTIONAL ADVERTISED PROGRAM

Not all software deployments push the programs to every desktop. Instead, the software can be offered on-demand, so that those client machines that need it can be easily select it from their own desktop. This ensures that those that get the program will get it consistently deployed, without mandating that every desktop receive it.

1. From the client machine, in the system tray, double-click the "A new program is available to be run" icon. This will start the Run Advertised Programs window, which can also be started from Control Panel.
2. Click the advertised program you wish to run, and then click Run. Depending on the advertisement configuration, there may be an additional dialog box that appears (Program Download Required) indicating that the content needs to be downloaded before the program can run (Figure 10.6).

FIGURE 10.6
Running advertised programs

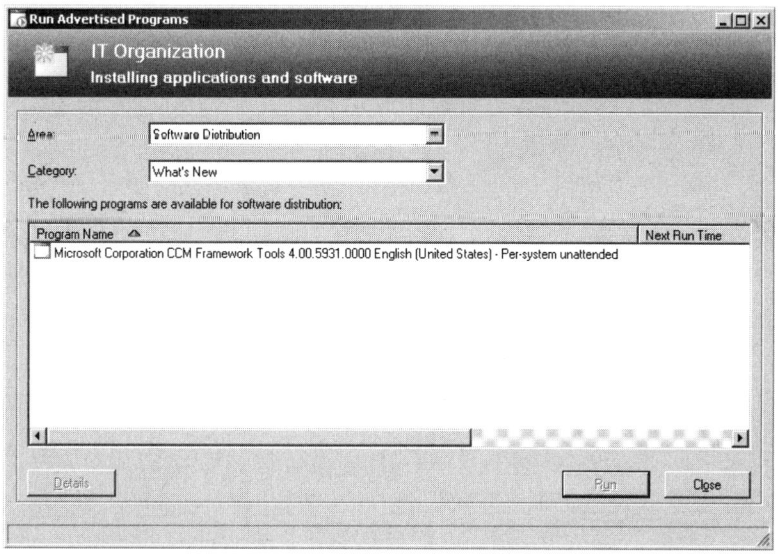

3. If a download is required, select "Run program automatically when download completes," and then click Download. The package source files are downloaded to the client computer, and then the advertised program will start automatically.

If the advertised program was an unattended install, as is often the case, you will not see any user interaction for the program run. If it is an attended install, you will then have to complete some sort of user interface to successfully finish the program run.

After the program has been run, the easiest way to validate success is via the ConfigMgr console's Software Distribution page.

Task 8: Validating Advertisement Success

You can use the ConfigMgr console to verify the status of your advertised programs. You can do so in two main ways—one is to run reports to view advertisement status, and the other is to view the Software Distribution page results. The following step-by-step task will guide you through the process of forcing the Software Distribution page to update its status to display the most recent status information from clients.

1. In the ConfigMgr console, expand Site Database, expand Computer Management, and then click Software Distribution. The Software Distribution page displays data based on a schedule that runs hourly. So the current advertisement may not appear yet.
2. In the tree pane, right-click Software Distribution, and then click Run Homepage Summarization. It takes a moment to complete the process.
3. In the tree pane, right-click Software Distribution, and then click Refresh. The Software Distribution page updates to reflect the updated status.

The Software Distribution page displays a table in the left side of the results pane and a chart in the right side. You can use the table to view statistics on the number of targeted systems, the success and failure, and so on. In the chart, you will see the results of the advertisement using colors. Success is indicated by green.

Securing Resources with Software Update Management

Deploying software updates is similar to deploying software. So if you understand the concept and process for deploying software to clients, you will have a great start at understanding the process for deploying software updates. Software updates require a target collection, a deployment package (essentially a package of updates that are made available to clients just like package source files for software distribution), and distribution points. However, instead of a program, software update deployment uses the Windows Update Agent from the Windows operating system to determine which updates are available and install them. Software updates use deployments rather than advertisements. A deployment is essentially an advertisement.

To determine which updates are applicable to clients, you first synchronize your software update point with the Microsoft Update website. Then at the scheduled time (weekly by default) clients scan against the software update point, and identify compliance for the updates that have been synchronized with the software update point. The client then sends its compliance data to the ConfigMgr environment. You run reports to view the compliance data, or view update compliance directly in the ConfigMgr console (Figure 10.7).

Once you have identified which updates are applicable to clients, you add the updates to be deployed to a deployment package. Clients will then install the applicable updates based on the deployment. Compliance information is then returned to the site after any applicable updates have been installed.

The integration of ConfigMgr and WSUS provides a few more benefits to administrators than using WSUS on its own. The primary advantage of ConfigMgr software update deployment is that software update deployment through ConfigMgr offers additional scheduling capabilities and control over when the deployments occur on clients. This is beneficial to control deployment of updates to ConfigMgr collections, including the use of maintenance windows to designate windows for deployment. ConfigMgr also provides over 30 reports specific to software update deployment.

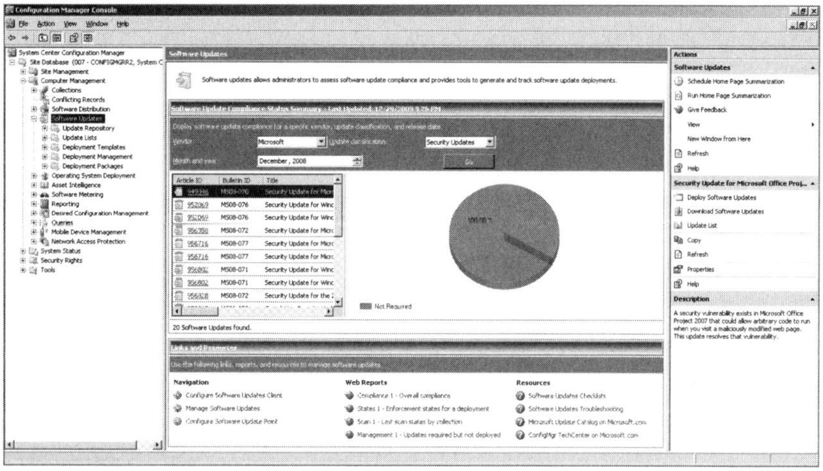

FIGURE 10.7 The Software Updates page

TASK 9: FORCING SOFTWARE UPDATE POINT SYNCHRONIZATION

ConfigMgr clients check their compliance against available software updates from the software update point site system. This site system would normally check for new updates every week from the Microsoft Update website. However, you can also force the software update point to check for an updated catalog of software updates on demand. The following step-by-step task will guide you through the process to force the software update point to synchronize with its update source, which is usually Microsoft Update.

1. In the ConfigMgr console, expand Site Database, expand Computer Management, expand Software Updates, and then click Update Repository. If the software update point had previously successfully synchronized with its update source, the appropriate update categories (such as critical updates and security updates) would appear in the results pane. If no categories appear in the results pane, no synchronization has been successful.
2. In the tree pane, right-click Update Repository, and then click Run Synchronization.
3. Click Yes to confirm the request to force a synchronization process. This process could take hours for the first synchronization process, depending on the number of classifications and products configured to be synchronized with this site.

You can validate the successful synchronization by looking for a status message with an ID of 6702 for the SMS_WSUS_Sync_Manager component. You can also refresh the Update Repository node of the console to see if new classifications have been added (assuming they were not present previously).

After a successful synchronization, clients need to scan against the software update point to identify their software update compliance. This will happen automatically after the next policy retrieval process (hourly by default) and the next software updates scan cycle (weekly by default). However, both of these processes can be initiated manually on a client to speed up the process for testing purposes.

Task 10: Forcing Software Update Scan by a Client

After the software update point has synchronized its catalog, ConfigMgr clients can then scan against the software update point for compliance. This would normally occur every week, but you can also force clients to scan for software update compliance on demand. The following step-by-step task will guide you through the process to force a client to initiate a scan immediately, instead of waiting for it to occur on its own.

1. In Control Panel, start ConfigMgr. The Configuration Manager Properties dialog box appears displaying information on the General tab.
2. In the Configuration Manager Properties, click the Actions tab. The available actions for the client are displayed.
3. In the list of actions, click Software Updates Scan Cycle, and then click Initiate Action, as seen in Figure 10.8.

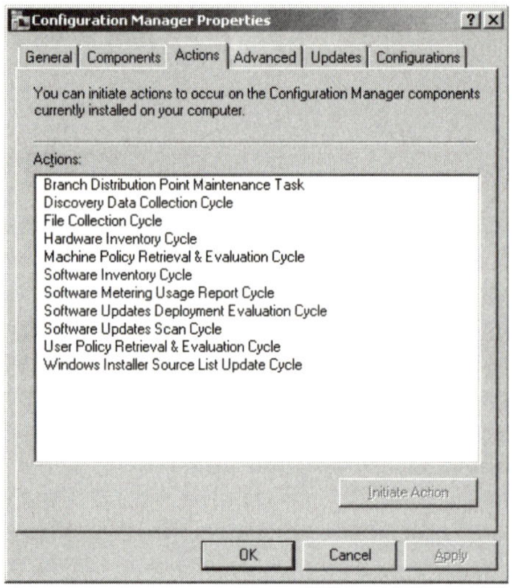

Figure 10.8
Configuration Manager client actions

4. Click OK to close the message box that appears indicating that the action may take a few minutes to complete.
5. Click OK to close the Configuration Manager Properties dialog box.

The client will then initiate a scan against the software update point. After the scan, the client will send its software update compliance data to the site via state messages. By default, state messages are sent from the client every 15 minutes.

Once the client software update compliance has been processed by the site server, you can validate the compliance in reports or the Software Updates page.

Task 11: Viewing Software Update Compliance

Before you can effectively deploy software updates, you need to know what updates are required by your ConfigMgr clients. You can view this compliance status through reports or via the console directly. The following step-by-step task will guide you through the process to update the Software Updates page to display current software update compliance information.

1. In the ConfigMgr console, expand Site Database, expand Computer Management, and then click Software Updates. The Software Updates page displays data based on a schedule that runs every four hours. So the current compliance data may not appear yet.

2. In the tree pane, right-click Software Updates, and then click Run Homepage Summarization. It takes a moment to complete the process.

3. In the tree pane, right-click Software Updates, and then click Refresh. The Software Updates page updates to reflect the updated status for the configured vendor, update classification, and date. These can be changed as necessary, but the default values will display update compliance for Microsoft security updates for the current month.

The Software Updates page displays a table in the left side of the results pane and a chart in the right side. You can use the table to view statistics on the number of targeted systems, the number of compliant systems, the number that require specific updates, and so on. In the chart, you will see the compliance with the highlighted update using colors. Compliance with the highlighted software updates is indicated by blue.

After you have determined which, if any, updates need to be deployed to clients, you can begin the update deployment process.

Task 12: Deploying Required Software Updates

ConfigMgr clients learn about software updates that might be applicable for installation through ConfigMgr policies. The policy that provides information about available software updates comes from a deployment, which is created by the administrator. The following step-by-step task will guide you through the process to deploy software updates using the Deploy Software Updates Wizard.

1. In the ConfigMgr console, expand Site Database, expand Computer Management, expand Software Updates, expand Update Repository, expand the update classification that you need to deploy (such as Security Updates), and then click All Updates. The software updates in that specific classification appear in the results pane, including the current compliance information.

2. In the results pane, right-click the update you want to deploy (you can multiselect updates if more than one is to be deployed), and then click Deploy Software Updates.

3. Complete the Deploy Software Updates Wizard using the following information:

   A. On the General page, supply the following information:

      - A name for the deployment
      - An optional comment

   B. On the Deployment Template page, select the deployment template you wish to use (if one had previously been created) or select the option to create a new deployment template. If you create a new deployment template, there will be numerous additional wizard pages not covered in this step-by-step procedure.

C. If the Collections page appears, click Browse to select the desired target collection, and then click Next.

D. On the Deployment Package page, you can add the selected updates to an existing deployment package or create a new deployment package. If you choose to create a new deployment package, supply the following information (shown in Figure 10.9):

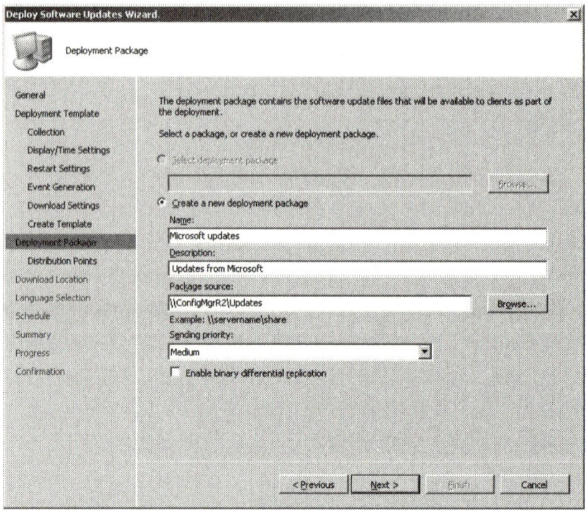

FIGURE 10.9
Deploy Software Updates Wizard, Deployment Package page

- A deployment package name
- An optional comment
- A package source directory (this is where the updates are downloaded to and prepared for replication to the distribution point(s)

E. On the Distribution Points page, click Browse, and then select the distribution points you want this deployment package replicated to.

F. On the Download Location page, designate to download the updates from the Internet or to copy them from a location they were previously downloaded to.

G. On the Language Selection page, select the appropriate languages of updates that you want to be added to this deployment package.

H. On the Schedule page, configure the appropriate settings for when you want the updates to be deployed to the clients. These settings would override the settings from the deployment template.

I. On the Summary page, click Next. The deployment package and deployment are created, and the deployment package is then copied to the designated distribution point(s).

J. On the Wizard Completed page, click Close.

You can view the new or updated deployment package, as well as the new deployment, in the appropriate nodes under Software Updates. Clients will learn about the deployment when they next retrieve policies from the site. They will then install any required updates as appropriate according to the mandatory schedule of the deployment. You can then view the updated software update compliance in the Software Updates page or via reports as you initially identified compliance.

Identifying Desired State Compliance

ConfigMgr provides the ability to identify systems that are compliant, as well as not compliant, with specific guidelines you define. These guidelines can be for applications that are required to be installed, applications that should not be installed, Registry settings, software update compliance, regulatory compliance, or drift from a desired state.

To identify compliance, you will create, or import from Configuration Packs, configuration items and configuration baselines. Configuration items are the rules that you want to scan for—such as application installation state, Registry setting, result of a script, and so on, and what is considered compliant. Once you have created or imported configuration items, you then create configuration baselines. A configuration baseline includes at least one configuration item and could include more. The configuration baseline is then assigned to a collection of target clients for evaluation according to the schedule specified in the configuration baseline.

The ConfigMgr console includes the ability to validate compliance for configuration baselines directly in the console or via reports (see Figure 10.10).

FIGURE 10.10 The Desired Configuration Management page

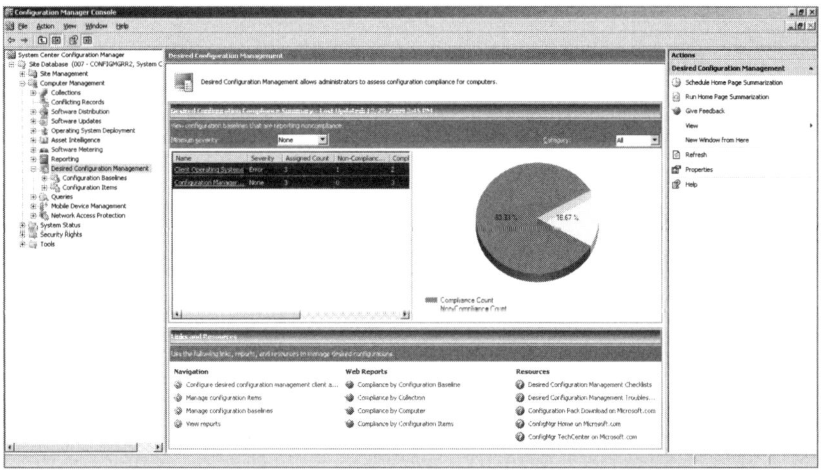

TASK 13: CREATING AN APPLICATION CONFIGURATION ITEM

Before ConfigMgr clients can report compliance for desired state, you must create or import configuration items to identify what condition the client is to validate compliance against. The following step-by-step task will guide you through the process of creating an application configuration item.

1. In the ConfigMgr console, expand Site Database, expand Computer Management, expand Desired Configuration Management, and then click Configuration Items. The list of configuration items appears in the results pane. There are no configuration items created by default.

2. In the tree pane, right-click Configuration Items, then select New ➤ Application Configuration Item.

The pages of the wizard will be different depending on the type of configuration item you create. The following steps will describe an application configuration item.

3. Complete the Create Application Configuration Item Wizard using the following information:

   A. On the Identification page, supply the following information:

      - A name for the configuration item
      - An optional comment

   B. On the Detection Method page, supply the following information:

      - Select the option Use Windows Installer (MSI) Detection.
      - Click Open, and then open the MSI file that you want to validate installation of (for example, you could use `\Program Files\Microsoft Configuration Manager\Client\i386\Client.msi`), as shown in Figure 10.11.

   C. On the Objects page, you can just leave the defaults, and then click Next.

   D. On the Settings page, you can just leave the defaults, and then click Next.

   E. On the Applicability page, if you want the configuration item to be validated on all clients, you can leave the default, and then click Next.

   F. On the Summary page, click Next.

   G. On the Wizard Completed page, click Finish.

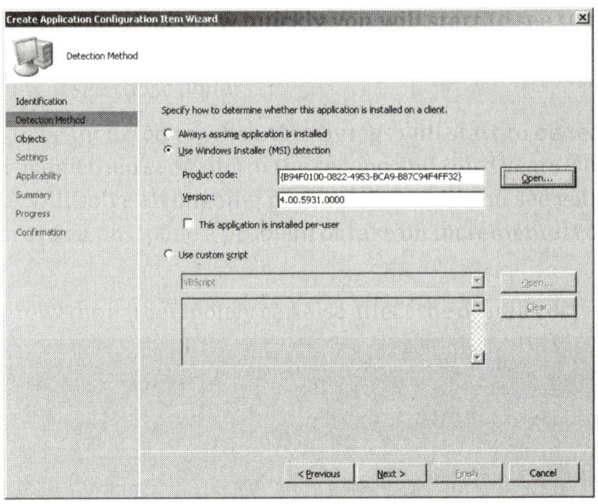

FIGURE 10.11
Create Application Configuration Item Wizard, Detection Method page

The new configuration item appears in the results pane. You now need to add the configuration item to a configuration baseline before clients can validate compliance against this item.

TASK 14: CREATING A CONFIGURATION BASELINE

After the configuration item(s) have been created or imported, you then add the appropriate configuration item(s) to a baseline. The following step-by-step task will guide you through the process of adding the application configuration item to a configuration baseline. This baseline will then be assigned to a collection of clients in the following task.

1. In the ConfigMgr console, expand Site Database, expand Computer Management, expand Desired Configuration Management, and then click Configuration Baselines. The list of configuration baselines appears in the results pane. There are no configuration baselines created by default.
2. In the tree pane, right-click Configuration Baselines, and then click New Configuration Baseline.
3. Complete the Create Configuration Baseline Wizard using the following information:
   - A. On the Identification page, supply the following information:
     - A name for the configuration item
     - An optional comment
   - B. On the Set Configuration Baseline Rules page, click Applications And General.
     - In the Choose Configuration Items dialog box that appears, select the appropriate configuration item(s), and then click OK.
     - Click Next on the Set Configuration Baseline Rules page.
   - C. On the Summary page, click Next.
   - D. On the Wizard Completed page, click Close.

The new configuration baseline appears in the results pane. You now need to assign the configuration baseline to a target collection before clients can validate compliance against this baseline.

Task 15: Assigning the Configuration Baseline to a Collection

After the configuration baseline has been created or imported, you can then assign the configuration baseline to a collection of clients. Clients in the targeted collection will then scan for compliance against the configuration baseline. The following step-by-step task will guide you through the process of assigning the configuration baseline to a collection.

1. In the ConfigMgr console, expand Site Database, expand Computer Management, expand Desired Configuration Management, and then click Configuration Baselines. The list of configuration baselines appears in the results pane.
2. In the results pane, right-click the appropriate configuration baseline, and then click Assign To A Collection.
3. Complete the Assign Configuration Baseline Wizard using the following information:
   - A. On the Choose Configuration Baselines page, if you only want to assign the selected configuration baseline, click Next. If you want to add an additional configuration baseline to this assignment, click Add, and then select the additional configuration baseline(s).
   - B. On the Choose Collection page, click Browse, and then select the desired target collection.

C. On the Set Schedule page, if you want to use the default schedule of reevaluating the configuration baseline on a weekly schedule, click Next. If you want to set a different schedule, configure the specific simple or custom schedule, and then click Next.

D. On the Summary page, click Next.

E. On the Wizard Completed page, click Close.

The configuration baseline will be evaluated by clients after the next policy retrieval cycle (hourly by default). Once evaluated at a client, each client will send the results to the site via state messages (sent by the client at 15 minute intervals).

After the configuration baseline has been evaluated, the easiest way to validate compliance is via the ConfigMgr console's Desired Configuration Management page.

Task 16: Validating Configuration Baseline Compliance

As with software distribution and software update compliance covered earlier, the compliance information for desired configuration can be viewed in either ConfigMgr reports or via the Desired Configuration Management page. The following step-by-step task will guide you through the process of viewing the updated compliance data for the Desired Configuration Management page.

1. In the ConfigMgr console, expand Site Database, expand Computer Management, and then click Desired Configuration Management. The Desired Configuration Management page displays data based on a schedule that runs hourly. So the current configuration baseline results may not appear yet.
2. In the tree pane, right-click Desired Configuration Management, and then click Run Homepage Summarization. It takes a moment to complete the process.
3. In the tree pane, right-click Desired Configuration Management, and then click Refresh.
4. In the results pane, in the Minimum Severity box, click None. The Desired Configuration Management page updates to reflect the updated status.

The Desired Configuration Management page displays a table in the left side of the results pane and a chart in the right side. You can use the table to view statistics on the number of clients in the collection the configuration baseline was assigned to, the number of compliant as well as noncompliant systems, and so on. In the chart, you will see the results of the assignment using colors. Compliant systems are indicated by green.

Deploying Operating Systems

ConfigMgr allows you to update the operating system on systems in the environment, as shown in Figure 10.12. The operating system deployment feature of ConfigMgr allows operating systems to be installed through various methods:

In-Place Upgrade This deployment method is used when the computer to receive the new operating system is an existing ConfigMgr client. This method uses the ConfigMgr software distribution feature to install the new operating system image on the targeted client(s).

Network Boot This deployment method is used for bare metal deployment of systems with no operating system installed. This method uses a ConfigMgr PXE service point site system to install the operating system image through the computer's network boot process.

Boot Media This deployment method is used for systems that have network access but are not able to use network boot. The operating system deployment installation process starts from boot media, and then continues from ConfigMgr distribution points on the corporate network to access the required image and package files.

Standalone Media This deployment method allows a client to be installed completely from media, such as a set of DVDs or CDs, that contain the images and package files necessary to complete the operating system and ConfigMgr client installation. After the operating system has been installed, the installed computer would be moved to the corporate network to be managed by ConfigMgr.

To deploy operating system images with ConfigMgr, there are a number of objects that you must have available in the site:

Boot Image This is a Windows Preinstallation Environment (WinPE) image that is used when preparing the target system to receive a new operating system. ConfigMgr includes two boot images—one for 32-bit systems and one for 64-bit systems. In addition, you can create your own boot images to use with ConfigMgr in the Windows Imaging (WIM) format.

Network Access Account This is a ConfigMgr account that is used with operating system deployment when the target system is running the boot image. This is required as WinPE does not have domain membership and there is no user context in order to access a ConfigMgr distribution point to download the operating system image and any other required packages.

Operating System Image This is the new operating system you want to deploy to the target system. This file is in a Windows Imaging (WIM) format. It is created by capturing a reference system into the operating system image file and then importing it into ConfigMgr.

Task Sequence This is the set of instructions that are to be carried out on the target system in order to deploy the new operating system. You will likely create multiple task sequences to control operating system deployment in various scenarios, deploy unique operating systems, install different ConfigMgr packages, and so on. The task sequence will specify the boot image the target system will initially boot, how to prepare the target hard drive, the operating system image to install, how to install the ConfigMgr client, which domain to join, and so on.

Configuration Manager Installation Package This is required because when ConfigMgr deploys an operating system image, it automatically installs the ConfigMgr client on the target system. As a result, when an operating system image is deployed to a system, that system will become a managed client by ConfigMgr.

There are additional objects that you might use with ConfigMgr operating system deployment, depending on the scenario of the deployment. In the majority of environments, the ConfigMgr operating system deployment process will include drivers, driver packages, and normal ConfigMgr packages to be deployed as part of the operating system installation process. Additionally, it is common to use a ConfigMgr package for the User State Migration Tool (USMT). This package allows for migration of user state, such as documents, spreadsheets, presentations, and other data files, to be migrated from an old computer and operating system to a new computer and operating system.

After all the objects are prepared, the last step is for the task sequence to be advertised to the target system. If this is a bare metal system, and not in the ConfigMgr site database, ConfigMgr supports deployment to unknown systems. Once the target system has the task sequence (provided through the various deployment methods discussed earlier), it will boot a boot image, prepare the hard drive, install an operating system image, install any drivers dynamically identified by the target system, join the designated domain, install the ConfigMgr client, install any specified

ConfigMgr packages, install targeted software updates, and complete any additional steps configured in the task sequence. When the process has completed successfully, the client will be a managed ConfigMgr client with the new operating system.

FIGURE 10.12
The Operating System Deployment page

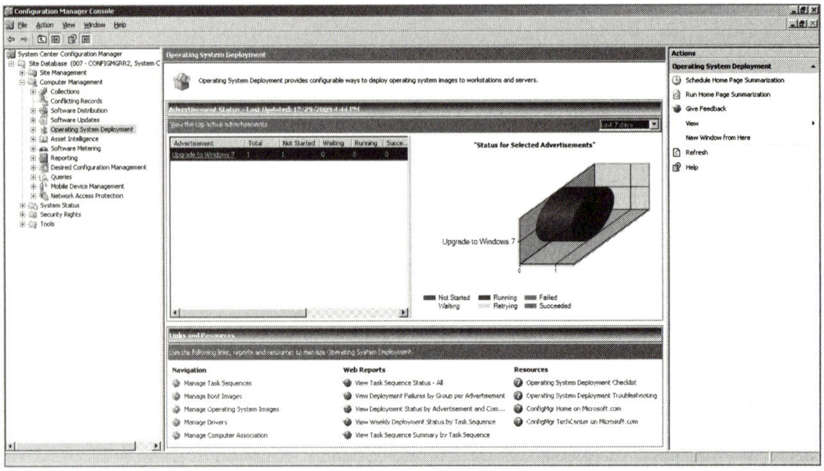

TASK 17: DISTRIBUTING THE BOOT IMAGE TO A DISTRIBUTION POINT

In all the operating system deployment scenarios, the target system must boot to a boot image. In some of these scenarios, such as the in-place upgrade of an operating system by an existing ConfigMgr client, the boot image is accessed from a ConfigMgr distribution point (similar to how clients access package source files or software updates from distribution points). The following step-by-step task will guide you through the process of adding the boot image to a distribution point.

1. In the tree pane, expand Site Database, expand Computer Management, expand Operating System Deployment, expand Boot Images, and then expand the appropriate boot image (x64 or x86).

   The nodes for the boot image will appear in the tree pane. One of those nodes is Distribution Points. By default, no distribution points are added to this boot image automatically.

2. In the tree pane, right-click Distribution Points, and then click New Distribution Points.
3. Complete the New Distribution Points Wizard using the following information:
   - On the Welcome page, click Next.
   - On the Copy Package page, select the distribution point(s) that you want the package source files to be copied to, and then click Next.
   - On the Wizard Completed page, click Close.

Depending on how large the boot image is, how many distribution points you added to the boot image, and the network access from the site server to the distribution point(s), it may take several minutes or longer to copy the image to the distribution point(s). You can use the Package Source node under the boot image to determine when the distribution process has completed. A status of Installed indicates that the boot image has been copied to the distribution point and is ready for clients to access.

The next object that must be created in order for clients to install a new OS is the operating system image. Operating system images can be created through numerous processes, including ConfigMgr. Once you have created the operating system WIM file, you must import it into the ConfigMgr console.

Task 18: Importing an Operating System Image

Before ConfigMgr can make new operating system images available, they must be added to ConfigMgr through an import process. The following step-by-step task will guide you through the process of importing the captured operating system image to ConfigMgr.

1. In the tree pane, expand Site Database, expand Computer Management, expand Operating System Deployment, and then click Operating System Images.

   The operating system images appear in the results pane. By default, there are no operating system images included with ConfigMgr.

2. In the tree pane, right-click Operating System Images, and then click Add Operating System Image.
3. Complete the Add Operating System Image Wizard using the following information:
   A. On the Data Source page, enter the network path to the WIM file, and then click Next.
   B. On the General page:
      - Supply the desired name for the operating system image.
      - Supply the appropriate version.
      - If desired, supply an optional comment, and then click Next.
   C. On the Summary page, click Next.
   D. On the Wizard Completed page, click Close.

Once the image has been added, you need to distribute the operating system image to at least one distribution point in order for systems to access it. You can use the previous step-by-step procedure to add a distribution point to this operating system image.

The next object that you will need is a task sequence. There are many options that can be configured in a task sequence, depending on the scenario you want to complete. Due to the number of options in task sequence creation, only a quick overview of the process is included here.

Task 19: Creating a Task Sequence for Deploying an Operating System Image

Very much like how a program instructs a ConfigMgr client what action to take on the package source files that have been advertised to it, the task sequence instructs the target system how to complete the operating system deployment process. There are many, many more available actions in a task sequence than there are with a software distribution program, but the analogy can be helpful in understanding task sequences. The following step-by-step task will guide you through the process of creating a simple task sequence to deploy an existing operating system image.

1. In the tree pane, expand Site Database, expand Computer Management, expand Operating System Deployment, and then click Task Sequences.

The task sequences appear in the results pane. By default, there are no task sequences included with ConfigMgr.

2. In the tree pane, right-click Task Sequences and select New ➢ Task Sequence.
3. Complete the New Task Sequence Wizard using the following information:
   - **A.** On the Create A New Task Sequence page, select the Install An Existing Image Package option, and then click Next.
   - **B.** On the Task Sequence Information page (Figure 10.13):

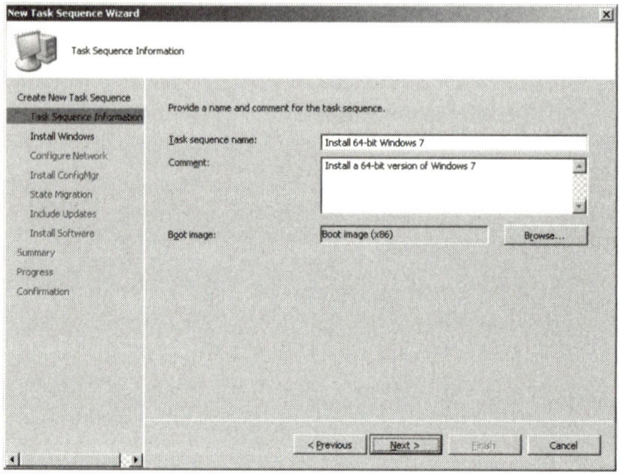

FIGURE 10.13
Task Sequence Information wizard page

     - ◆ Supply the desired name for the task sequence.
     - ◆ Supply an optional comment.
     - ◆ Click Browse, and then select the appropriate boot image.
   - **C.** On the Install Windows page (Figure 10.14):
     - ◆ Click Browse, and then select the appropriate operating system image.
     - ◆ Specify the image to install from the WIM file.
     - ◆ Configure the partitioning and formatting of the target hard disk as appropriate.
     - ◆ Specify the product key and licensing information.
     - ◆ Configure the target administrator account.
   - **D.** On the Configure The Network page:
     - ◆ Configure the appropriate workgroup or domain to join the target computer to.
     - ◆ If joining a domain, configure the administrator account to use.
   - **E.** On the Install The ConfigMgr Client page, specify the ConfigMgr package created to install the ConfigMgr client, as well as the desired command-line parameters.

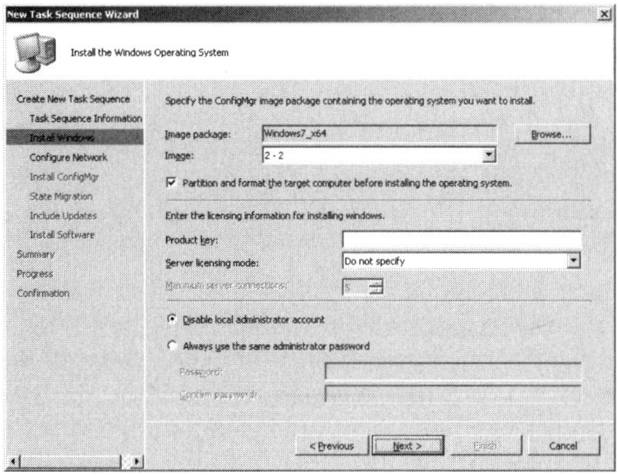

FIGURE 10.14
Install Windows wizard page

F. On the Configure State Migration page:

- Specify the ConfigMgr package created for USMT, if appropriate.
- Select or clear the options to capture the user state, network settings, and Windows settings as appropriate.

G. On the Install Updates In Image page, configure the appropriate setting for software update deployment to the target system.

H. On the Install Software page, add any desired ConfigMgr packages to be deployed after the operating system image has been installed.

I. On the Summary page, click Next.

J. On the Wizard Completed page, click Close.

The last step in the process is to advertise the task sequence to a target collection. There are a number of options available for the advertisement process, depending on the desired deployment scenario.

TASK 20: ADVERTISING THE TASK SEQUENCE

Just as an advertisement is used to instruct target clients what program to run from the available package source files, the task sequence is made available to the target system through an advertisement. The process is similar to that of software distribution, but it does have few unique options specific to operating system deployment. The following step-by-step task will guide you through the process of advertising a task sequence to a collection of systems.

1. In the tree pane, expand Site Database, expand Computer Management, expand Operating System Deployment, and then click Task Sequences. The list of task sequences in the site appear in the results pane.
2. In the results pane, right-click the task sequence to be deployed, and then click Advertise.
3. Complete the New Advertisement Wizard using the following information:

A. On the General page, supply the following information:

- A name for the advertisement
- An optional comment
- The task sequence that is to be accessed by the client
- The collection the task sequence is targeted to
- Whether or not the task sequence is available in a PXE or boot media scenario

B. On the Schedule page, click the New button (the icon resembles a starburst) if you want the advertisement to be run automatically at a specific time, and then click Next. If you want the advertisement to be optional (only run when the user decides to run it), do not set a schedule, and simply click Next.

C. On the Distribution Points page, normally you can leave the defaults, and then click Next.

D. On the Interaction page, normally you can leave the defaults, and then click Next.

E. On the Security page, add appropriate accounts and rights if necessary, and then click Next.

F. On the Summary page, click Next.

G. On the Wizard Completed page, click Close.

The tracking process is completed using the Operating System Deployment page. You will need to update the page manually if you want more up-to-date status than will appear by default (the Operating System Deployment page updates hourly by default). Previous step-by-step processes have shown how to manually update pages. Those procedures can be used for the Operating System Deployment page also.

Preventing Unsecure System Access

Another feature of ConfigMgr that helps secure your network and clients is its integration with the Windows Server feature called Network Access Protection (NAP). NAP prevents clients from accessing resources on the corporate network until the clients have passed NAP security checks. The NAP feature of the operating system allows you to configure security settings such as the Windows Firewall, port configuration, antivirus signatures, and so on. When integrated with ConfigMgr, NAP extends to support restricting network access until the client has installed required security updates. The integration of NAP with ConfigMgr requires that both features, NAP and ConfigMgr software updates, be configured and working properly.

This feature has specific configuration requirements that are more restrictive on the environments that the feature can be used in. NAP requires a computer configured as a Network Policy Server, which is only available with the Windows Server 2008 operating system. It requires an enforcement method, such as DHCP, 802.1x, IPSec, or VPN. For additional information on the Network Access Protection feature, which is out of scope for this book, visit the Network Access Protection area on the Microsoft TechNet website (`http://technet.microsoft.com/en-us/network/bb545879.aspx`). In addition to the NPS, you need to configure policy settings, have appropriate remediation capabilities, and have NAP-enabled clients.

Once the NAP infrastructure has been configured and works properly, you enable NAP integration in ConfigMgr. To do so, you simply:

- Add the system health validator role to the NPS computer.
- Ensure that your ConfigMgr site is publishing data to Active Directory.

- Enable the Network Access Policy Client Agent, which is disabled by default.
- Configure the software updates you want required for NAP compliance.

Once configured successfully, ConfigMgr clients will include their compliance regarding the NAP-enabled software updates in the NAP evaluation, and not allow the client to access the full corporate network until those NAP-enabled software updates have been installed on the client.

Task 21: Deploying NAP-Enabled Software Updates

As you have already done the step-by-step for deploying software updates, this step-by-step procedure will provide a quick overview of the process. Start the Deploy Software Updates Wizard and use the following information:

1. On the General page, provide a name for the deployment and an optional comment.
2. On the Deployment Template page, select the deployment template you wish to use.
3. If the Collections page appears, select the desired target collection, and then click Next.
4. On the Deployment Package page, you can add the selected updates to an existing deployment package, or create a new deployment package.
5. On the Distribution Points page, select the distribution points you want this deployment package replicated to.
6. On the Download Location page, designate the location to retrieve the updates from.
7. On the Language Selection page, select the appropriate languages.
8. On the Schedule page, configure the appropriate schedule.
9. On the Set NAP Evaluation page:
    - Select Enable NAP Evaluation if you want this update to be required in the client's NAP evaluation.
    - Configure the schedule for when you want this update to be NAP enabled.
10. On the Summary page, click Next.
11. On the Wizard Completed page, click Close.

The update will be required for NAP evaluation as of the schedule you set in the deployment.

Virtualization Management

In Chapter 9, we looked at a virtualization host as a platform that needed protection and assured availability, just as we looked at Exchange, SQL Server, or File Services platforms in earlier chapters. If you have only one virtualization host in your environment, you can likely manage it from its own console, and that would be fine. But in this chapter, we are looking at managing the complete infrastructure as the sum of its parts. So far, ConfigMgr has shown how we can manage the physical aspects of the virtualization host, including the operating system, software updates, and the hardware itself. But virtualization is more than that.

To put this in the context of protection and availability, we can (in some ways) treat the virtual machines that are running on virtualization hosts as the service or data that must be protected and made highly available, similar to how we looked at Exchange storage groups, or SQL databases, or Windows file shares. In earlier chapters, you learned how to manage just SQL or just Exchange, for higher availability or protection for just that platform. In these later chapters, we are looking for what we can do to maintain the entire infrastructure—holistically.

That being said, as virtualization deployments grow larger and larger in enterprises, a standalone virtualization management solution is needed. In the System Center family of products, Virtual Machine Manager (VMM) 2008 R2 is that solution.

VMM 2008 R2 is designed to be a heterogeneous virtualization management solution, covering the day-to-day tasks that a virtualization administrator performs. The focus of VMM is slightly different than other virtualization management solutions. In many proprietary virtualization solutions, the management software must perform all the work associated with the VMs, including backup, recovery, monitoring, and updates.

The System Center tools recognize the fact that VMs are machines first, virtual second—meaning that administrators must perform many of the same management tasks for virtual machines as they do for physical machines, along with virtualization-specific tasks. Since many of those tasks are covered by the other System Center tools, VMM works with and integrates with those tools to create a seamless physical and virtual management experience.

Overview of VMM 2008 R2

Virtual Machine Manager is another part of the System Center family of enterprise management products that includes not only Configuration Manager but also Data Protection Manager (Chapter 4) and Operations Manager (Chapter 11).

VMM provides centralized management of virtual machines and their hosts, including:

- Windows Server 2008 and 2008 R2, with Hyper-V
- Microsoft Hyper-V Server 2008 and 2008 R2
- Microsoft Virtual Server 2005 R2
- VMware Virtual Infrastructure 3 and vSphere 4

Figure 10.15 shows the architectural layout of VMM.

Starting at the top of Figure 10.15:

- VMM is manageable by two interfaces:
    - The VMM Administrator Console is a standalone application that can be run from the VMM server or another platform, and is the primary way to manage VMM and thereby the various virtualization hosts throughout the environment.
    - A role-based, self-service, web-based portal is also available. This is not a web-based administration console, per se, but a resource for authorized users to be able to provision and monitor their own VMs.
- Both of these interfaces are built on top of Windows PowerShell, which can also be used to manage VMM via command-line or script.
- The VMM server application itself runs on a Windows Server 2008 or 2008 R2 64-bit server and requires a database, hosted by SQL Server.

FIGURE 10.15
Architectural layout of VMM

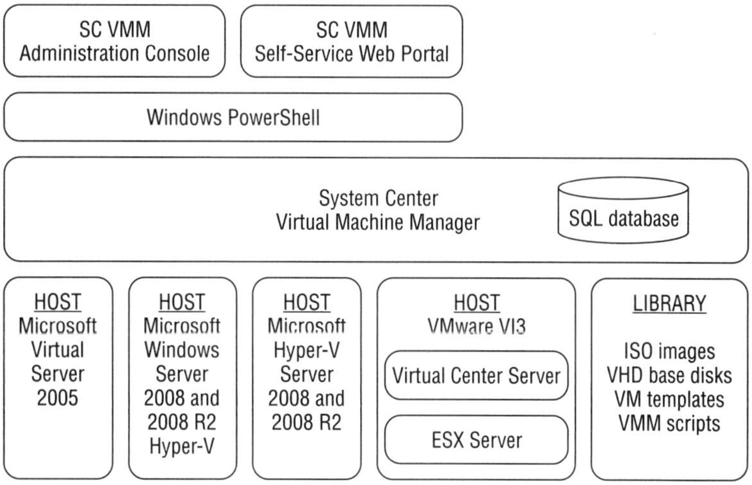

- VMM then communicates via VMM management agents to the various virtualization platforms that were listed earlier in this section.
- In addition, VMM can leverage one or more VMM libraries, which include:
  - ISO images of CD and DVD media for use by the VMs
  - VHD files as base hard drive images for new VMs
  - Templates for new VM configurations
  - Scripts for automating additional tasks related to VMs

NOTE Notice the blank area in the upper-right corner of Figure 10.15. System Center Essentials (SCE) 2010 (discussed later in this chapter) utilizes a subset of the capabilities found in the enterprise VMM 2008 R2 product. The SCE interface theoretically would fit in this blank area as another interface into the VMM engine. But SCE does not manage the standalone VMM product; it does, however, manage the VMM components that are part of SCE 2010, which you will see in Task 28, "SCE Virtualization Tasks."

VMM Management Interfaces

The various graphical interfaces (VMM console, self-service portal) do not interact directly with the VMM server. Those interfaces interact with Windows PowerShell, which in turn submits instructions to the VMM server. Any function of the VMM Administrator Console can be done solely through PowerShell, and in fact, you'll enjoy greater functionality and level of granularity via the PowerShell command compared to using the Admin Console.

VMM uses the System Center or Microsoft Outlook–style interface in the Administrator Console. The VMM Administrator Console is not an MMC snap-in, but is an application built using the Microsoft .NET Framework and is built on top of Windows PowerShell. Each multistep process, or wizard, in the Administrator Console has a View Script button that when clicked shows the associated Windows PowerShell script for the command about to be run. View Script action opens these scripts in Notepad, so you can easily edit them right from VMM. This allows for quick storage and reuse of the PowerShell script, along with a great tool to learn how to use VMM PowerShell commands within the context of the Administrator Console.

The PowerShell cmdlets work across virtualization platforms, so that cmdlets like `New-VM` work on both Microsoft and VMware systems. IT administrators can use one set of cmdlets to manage Virtual Server, Hyper-V, and VMware hosts.

VMM Database

VMM does not require a dedicated SQL server, although it does need its own database from either SQL Server 2005 or SQL Server 2008. This means that VMM can share a common SQL server with Data Protection Manager (Chapter 4) or Operations Manager (Chapter 11), each of which has separate databases.

VMM and Other System Center Components

As mentioned earlier, VMM requires a database from Microsoft SQL Server, which might also be offering databases to other System Center family members, including DPM (Chapter 4) or Operations Manager (Chapter 11). While the databases do not interact, there are other interaction points between the products:

- You can use DPM along with VMM (and particularly its physical-to-virtual migration features) as part of a disaster recovery scenario, as we described initially in Chapter 9 and will look at in more detail in Chapter 12.
- A connector is available so that Operations Manager and VMM can share information, allowing a more comprehensive view of status information across your physical and virtual machines.
- The most integrated scenario is in SC Essentials (discussed later in this chapter), where parts of VMM are completely embedded within SCE 2010, which also includes parts of Operations Manager and other management technologies.

Hosts Managed by VMM

The bottom half of Figure 10.15 shows the virtualization hosts that are managed by VMM, including not only those from Microsoft but also VMware.

Microsoft virtualization hosts are managed using the Windows Management Interface (WMI) and Windows Remote Management (WinRM). When initially designating a Windows Server to be managed by VMM, VMM will check to see if the Microsoft virtualization software is already installed and enabled on the prospective host.

- If a Windows Server 2003 or 2003 R2 server is not yet a virtualization host, VMM will install Microsoft Virtual Server 2005 R2 with SP1 and any relevant hotfixes.
- If a Windows Server 2008 or 2008 R2 server is not yet a virtualization host, VMM will enable the Hyper-V role on the server.

After the virtualization components are enabled, VMM will add the server to its list of managed hosts.

VMware management is accomplished through VMware VirtualCenter (vCenter) and its VMware Web Services API. Because of this, a vCenter server is still required as an intermediary when managing VMware hosts from VMM. In fact, because VMM is intended to manage multiple virtualization platforms, it can provide centralized management across all the virtualization hosts in the enterprise, including multiple vCenter servers (and their ESX hosts), as well as the range of Microsoft virtualization platforms. The result is that Microsoft customers running VMware do not have to immediately move from VMware to Hyper-V in order to gain the unified physical and virtual management benefits of System Center.

Key Features of VMM 2008 R2

VMM 2008 R2 provides a single view across all your virtualization hosts and guests, as seen in Figure 10.16, including those from Microsoft or VMware and regardless of what operating systems are running inside the virtual machines. VMM then performs all the key functions of those hosts and VMs that a virtualization administrator would expect. It creates new VMs, moves VMs, deletes VMs, and even stores VMs for deployment or reconfiguration. When creating new VMs, VMM can create the VM from new VHDs, from clones of existing machines, and even from preconfigured VMs, using templates. VMM will perform the SYSPREP functions on a VM and make it available for deployment, allowing VMM to deploy the resulting VM and automatically complete the initial configuration, including setting the machine name and joining the VM to a domain.

FIGURE 10.16
The VMM 2008 R2 console's main screen

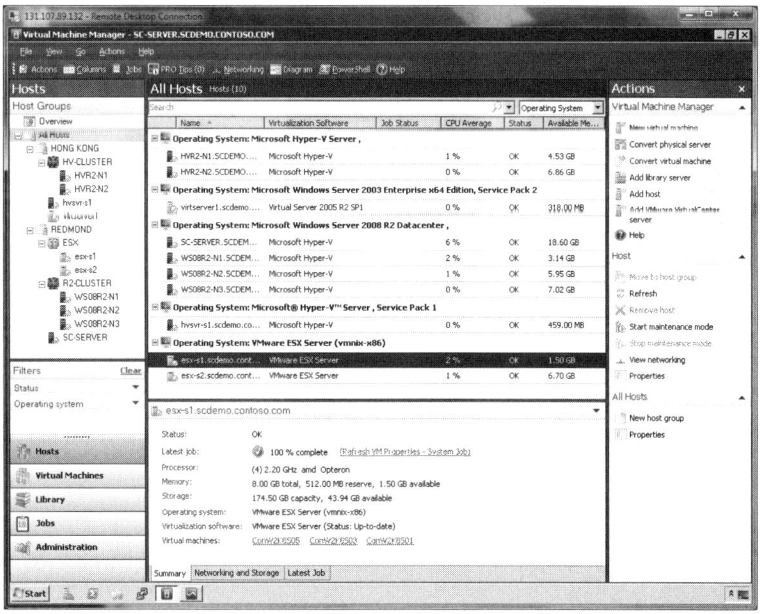

There are a few key capabilities in VMM 2008 R2 that are especially worth noting; let's take a closer look.

Physical-to-Virtual (P2V) Migration

A key aspect of embracing virtualization is migrating legacy physical systems into virtual machines. This feature has been in VMM for a while and continues to get better. The main idea is to decommission physical servers that are underutilized by consolidating them onto one or more virtualization hosts. To do this, the P2V functions of VMM:

1. Send an agent to the physical server that captures the hardware characteristics of the physical server, such as memory, processor, storage configuration and networking
2. Create a similarly configured virtual machine
3. Replicate all of the physical OS, applications, and data in such a way that the VM configuration is identical except for the hardware; ideally, while the physical server continues to run without interruption
4. Adjust the networking configuration, so that the VM has the same IP addresses
5. Bring down the physical machine and bring up the virtual copy

We will learn more about this later in *Task 23, "Physical to Virtual Migration."*

Virtual-to-Virtual (V2V) Migration

As mentioned earlier, VMM is intended to manage both Microsoft and VMware virtualization hosts. However, because many companies can save costs and gain additional capabilities by moving from VMware to Hyper-V, VMM provides a virtual-to-virtual (V2V) migration capability from VMware VMDK-based machines to Microsoft VHDs. Migrating from VMware to Microsoft can be done while the VMware-based VM is running or shut down.

The V2V process requires the VM to be shut down so that the actual VMDK virtual disk files can be converted to the VHD format. After that, the internal VMware guest-software components are replaced by Hyper-V integration components as drivers for the virtual hardware (video, networking, storage).

If the VM cannot be shut down, you can use the P2V process described earlier. Yes, it's true—you can P2V a VM, meaning that the physical-to-virtual migration tools can be used on a server that is actually hosted as a VM on a VMware server. Just like any other P2V process, the storage is copied from the existing disks (virtual or physical) to a new set of VHD disks, and then the drivers are converted from what they were (physical or virtual) to the new Hyper-V equivalents.

Hyper-V R2 Live Migration

As discussed in Chapter 9, one of the newest and most exciting features in Windows Server 2008 R2 with Hyper-V, as well as Microsoft Hyper-V Server 2008 R2, is Live Migration (LM). VMM 2008 R2 (but not VMM 2008) is required to manage LM clusters.

Intelligent Placement for VMs

When you have only one or perhaps two virtualization hosts, you probably have a pretty good idea which VMs will be running on which hosts. But as you start deploying more virtualization hosts and thereby many more VMs, you will eventually start to lose track of which VMs are where or where new VMs should go.

VMM includes a capability called Intelligent Placement, which is leveraged during migrations as well as new VM creations. It compares the virtual hardware requirements of the new VMs to the available resources on each and every virtualization host within your environment, and then recommends which virtualization hosts are most suitable for hosting your new VM. You can also define prioritization rules and preferences, so that you have more control over VMM's recommended placements. This allows you to prioritize the assessments of the hosts toward key characteristics, such as available memory or processing power. It will also filter the available hosts based on hosting requirements such as only placing 64-bit guests on 64-bit hosts.

If the selected action is a migration, Intelligent Placement will tell you if the movement is Live or may require downtime and will also analyze processor compatibility, ensuring that the VM that is moved will properly run on the destination hardware. After all the variables are analyzed, the Intelligent Placement feature will then make a star-based recommendation on which host is the best for the VM. You can even ignore the recommendation and place the VM on any of the available hosts.

Integration with Operations Manager

In Chapter 11, we will look at Operations Manager's management packs (MPs), which provide workload-specific knowledge and embedded tasks. These MPs are usually created by the workloads themselves. For example, the SQL Server team wrote the SQL Server management pack. Because of this, the original workload team can define all the pertinent counters and events to be monitored and know how to handle problem resolutions moving forward.

A software-based connector links VMM and Operations Manager so that status information can flow between the two monitoring tools. An extension of this collaboration is a feature called Performance and Resource Optimization (PRO), which enables Operations Manager to create alerts within VMM, based on monitoring parameters found within the Operations Manager MPs. These PRO-enabled management packs (sometimes called PRO-packs) extend the depth of workload-, hardware-, or module-specific awareness of MPs with virtualization-specific actions that VMM can utilize or invoke.

Task 22: Deploying the VMM Agent

As with many management technologies, VMM uses an agent to assist in managing the hosts and VMs. Like DPM, VMM uses a host-based agent to manage the host and access the VM. You do *not* need to install a VMM agent inside each VM to manage or control it. The VMM agent deployment is done at the host level only.

While the VMM agent installation can be done manually, it is most easily done through the VMM Administrator Console:

1. From the main Administrator Console, under the Actions panel in the upper right, choose Add Host.
2. On the Select Host Location screen (Figure 10.17), select the type of host you want to manage, and then enter the proper credentials to access the host. In this example, we will add a host that is in the Active Directory. Adding a VMware host to manage with VMM does not result in an agent installation.

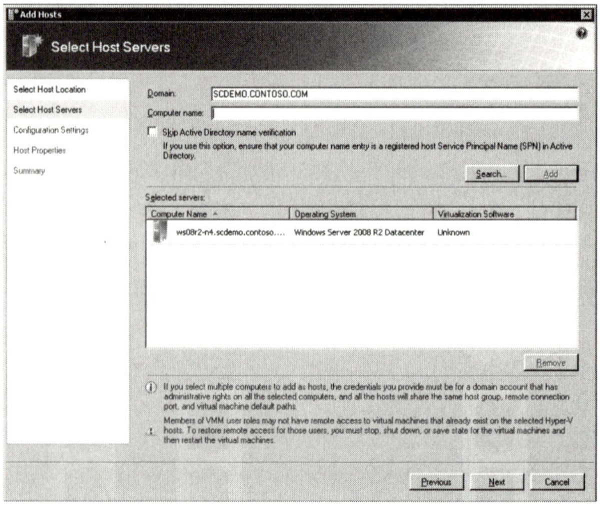

FIGURE 10.17
VMM Add Host wizard: choosing the host type

3. Next, on the Select Host Servers screen, enter the server name manually and click the Add button, or click Search and search for the host in the Active Directory. Once the host-name has been added, the host will be listed, along with the operating system and any virtualization software installed.
   - If the selected host is Windows Server 2003, 2008, or 2008 R2 and the host has no virtualization software, the VMM agent install will also install or enable the appropriate virtualization software:
     - For Windows Server 2003, VMM will install Virtual Server 2005 R2 SP1.
     - For Windows Server 2008 or 2008 R2, VMM will enable the Hyper-V role on the servers.
   - If the selected hostname is a cluster name or the host is part of a cluster, the entire cluster will be added to VMM.
   - Also, if any of the hosts on the cluster do not have virtualization software, VMM will automatically enable or install the virtualization software on all the cluster hosts, as described earlier.
4. The next screen is the Configuration Settings screen (Figure 10.18), which configures the hosts in the VMM console. You can select the host group that the host will be placed into, which allows you to create logical groups of hosts. Also, you can enable Host Reassociation, which will reassociate the host with this VMM server. Each host can be managed by only one VMM server. Therefore, this setting is useful if you need to transfer control of a host from one VMM server to another.
5. The wizard continues to the Host Properties screen, which is used to configure the local paths to store the VMs. VMM automatically discovers the default and custom paths that are already configured on hosts and allows you to add additional paths.
6. Finally, a summary screen is presented with all the work to be done, along with the View Script option that lets you see the PowerShell script associated with this action. Click Add Hosts to complete the wizard.

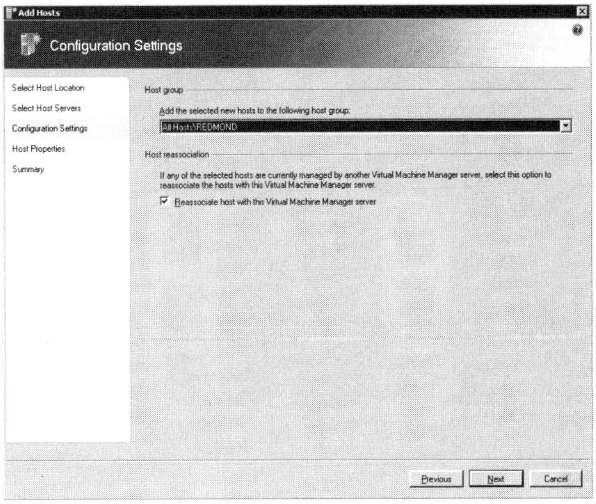

FIGURE 10.18
VMM Add Host wizard: configuration settings

You can view the progress of the addition and the agent installation through the VMM Jobs window.

TASK 23: PHYSICAL-TO-VIRTUAL MIGRATION

As we noted earlier, VMM can perform a conversion of a physical machine's OS and configuration into a virtual machine, which is usually referred to as P2V. This process is nondestructive, so the physical machine is not affected by the process. While P2V is normally associated with server consolidation, moving machines permanently to the virtual world, there is also a great application for backup and recovery.

The P2V process can be used to create a point-in-time snapshot of a running physical system. The resulting VM can be used as a backup image but an image that doesn't require the matching hardware. Thus, multiple VMs could be staged on a backup site, without the need to buy and maintain the matching physical hardware. If a disaster event occurred, the VMs could simply be turned on and the differentials between when the P2Vs were performed and when the last DPM backup was done could be restored. This gives flexibility to the recovery process and an alternative backup method, using the power of virtualization.

There are several requirements for the physical machine that will be converted. First, the physical machine must be on a network that the VMM server could contact. Second, the source machine must be running a supported operating system. The supported operating systems for P2V are Windows Server 2008 R2, Windows Server 2008, Windows Server 2003 SP2 or later, and Windows 2000 Server SP4 for server operating systems and Windows XP Professional SP2, Windows Vista SP1, and Windows 7 for client operating systems. For the P2V process, VMM uses the Volume Shadow Copy Service (VSS), which was covered in Chapter 4, to unobtrusively freeze, replicate, and consolidate the hard drives and stream the data into virtual hard disks. This allows the machine to be converted without any downtime, so that you don't have to schedule downtime for the server just to create the P2V image. If the physical server runs Windows 2000, an offline P2V image creation is done and there will be downtime.

To perform the P2V conversion, we use the VMM Administrator Console. The P2V process is started by choosing Convert Physical Server under the Actions pane in the upper-right portion of the Administrator Console. This brings up the Physical to Virtual Migration wizard:

1. The first page is the Select Source screen, where the machine to be converted is identified. Enter the DNS name or IP of the physical machine and the appropriate administrator credentials to connect to and manage it. Hint: Enter the full DNS name for the host, not just the machine name.

2. The next page is the Virtual Machine Identity screen, which allows you to give the VM a name, assign an owner, and give a description to the resulting VM (Figure 10.19). A few hints on this:

   - The name of the VM is the name for reference in VMM. It is not the actual machine name of the converted VM. For example, the actual machine name might be EX14, whereas the VM could be called ExchangeSvr for ExecTeam.

   - This is a good place to fill out the Description field with information about when this P2V was done and what this VM represents. The information will be available when you manage the VM later.

FIGURE 10.19
P2V wizard: VM identity options

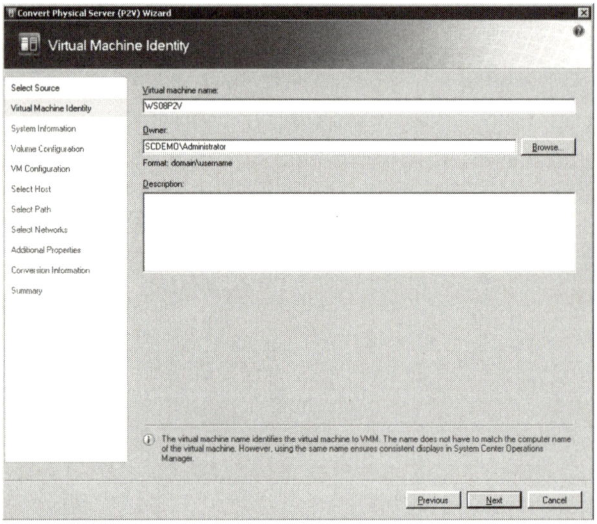

3. On the System Information screen, the wizard starts the process of gathering information from the source machine. When you click the Scan System button, VMM will temporarily install the VMM P2V agent onto the physical machine. The P2V agent will retrieve the necessary information about the source machine's operating system, hard drive, and network adapters. The information is then displayed for review, as shown in Figure 10.20.

4. In the next step, the wizard presents the Volume Configuration screen, which allows you to select the hard drive partitions to convert. By default, the boot partition is always

selected and any other partitions that are present are made available. You can choose which partitions will be kept as part of the conversion.

- Each select partition can be made as a fixed-sized VHD or a dynamic VHD (a dynamic VHD file only takes up the room of the occupied data whereas the fixed VHD's file size is always the same as the configured disk). For best performance, choose a fixed VHD.
- The P2V is a smart copy process, pulling over only the data on the specified partitions, as opposed to a fixed transfer of an entire hard drive image and size. This minimizes the time it takes to perform the P2V.
- This screen also has an option for the conversion settings, including online or offline conversions and an option to shut down the source machine when the P2V is done. This is helpful if you plan on using the P2V VM as the primary system after the conversion.

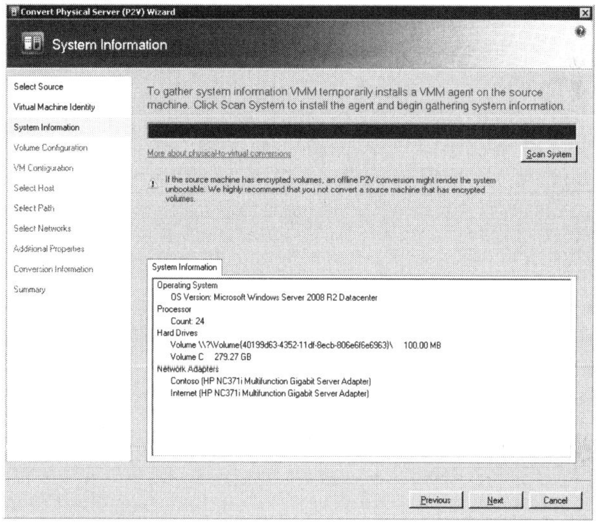

FIGURE 10.20
P2V wizard: system information options

NOTE The option to automatically shut down the source machine, after the P2V conversion is done, is a powerful choice that should obviously be used with care. Certainly, you do not want the VM to come online while the physical server is still running, but you may wish to manually shut down the production server after the conversion so that you can do a last backup or other operational tasks. Just be sure that no data is changed between the time the P2V is done and when the physical machine is powered down and the VM is brought online.

5. The wizard continues with the Virtual Machine Configuration screen, which allows you to configure the number of processors and the amount of memory the VM will be configured with. This screen also presents an opportunity to increase the amount of memory available to the machine, potentially even more than the physical machine was configured with.
6. Next, the Select Host screen, also known as the Intelligent Placement screen (Figure 10.21), appears. As described earlier in this chapter, VMM will evaluate a series of parameters

to recommend the best host to place the converted VM on. A host must be selected, as the VMM P2V process uses a host to process the VM. If you choose a host that is in an HA cluster, VMM will automatically make the VM highly available and configure it for use in the cluster, as described in Chapter 9.

FIGURE 10.21
Intelligent Placement choices

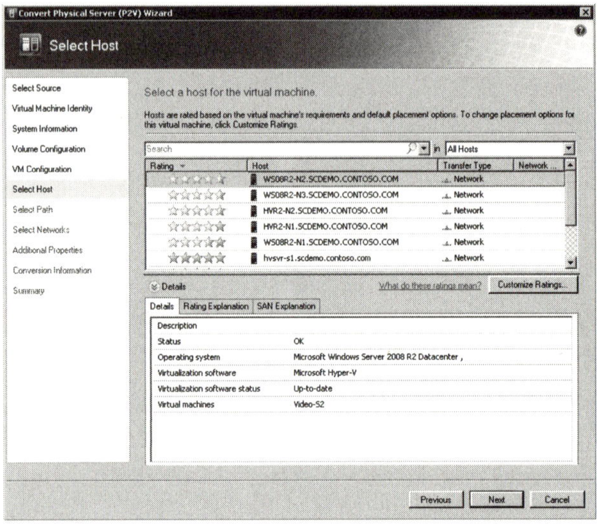

Once the conversion is done, the converted VM does not automatically start. You can decide to store the VM in the VMM library, store it in an offsite location, or even move the VM to the backup site or alternate operations site. Along with converting physical servers to virtual machines for consolidation purposes, in Chapter 12 we will see how storing the converted VM in a secondary site will help us stage a disaster recovery facility, without the hardware expenditures.

7. Next, you will be asked to select a path for the VM. This is the file system location for the VM. The file system referenced can be local paths or SAN-based paths.

8. On the Select Networks screen, you can configure the VM for the potential networks that are available on the designated host. This will allow the VM to see the available networks and is critical for maintaining the proper network connections for the converted machine.

9. Next is the Additional Properties screen, where you configure the actions that occur to the VM when the physical server starts or shuts down. This allows the VM to automatically start when the host starts and enables the VM to gracefully enter a saved state (similar to hibernate on a laptop) when the host shuts down.

   Once all the parameters for the P2V are configured, VMM does a final validation of the conversion to verify that there are no known issues to prevent conversion. If there are, possible resolutions are presented.

10. Finally, a Summary screen (Figure 10.22) is presented with all the information gathered, along with the View Script button. Click this button to view the entire PowerShell script for the conversion. Also, you can configure the converted VM to start after the conversion is done.

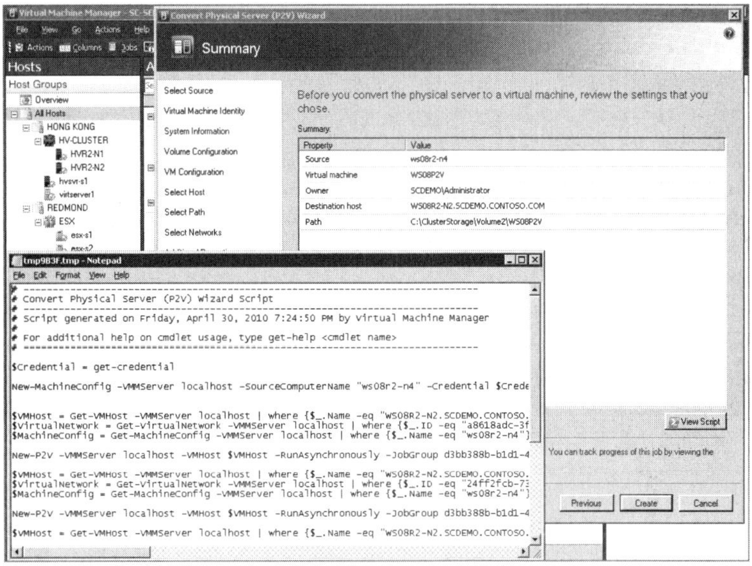

FIGURE 10.22 Summary of P2V choices, including the PowerShell script that will actually do the work

By default, newly converted VMs will not start automatically (they are converted to a Stopped state), nor does the P2V process shut down or change the running status of the source machine. As noted before, this is a nondestructive P2V process. Because the new VM will have the same computer name, IP address, and even MAC address of the original server, that machine must be shut down before the VM can be started. If you want the source machine shut down or the newly converted VM to start automatically, those settings should be set in the wizard. As a general best practice, it is a good idea to perform the P2V and then run the resulting VM in a test environment, making sure that everything converted successfully.

11. Click the Create button, and VMM will start the P2V process. You can view the progress by opening the Jobs window in VMM, which will track each step in the process and give estimated times.

Task 24: Understanding New Virtual Machine Provisioning

One of the most overlooked tasks in virtualization management is the deployment of new virtual machines. Often overshadowed by more advanced capabilities such as Live Migration, new VM provisioning is a key task of virtualization management. VMM is designed to make the creation and deployment of new VMs as easy as possible.

With VMM, there are several ways to create and deploy a new VM. These include the following:

Using a Blank VHD Allows you to install the OS manually.

Using an Existing VHD Allows you to reuse an existing VHD but configure a new VM configuration.

Cloning an Existing VM Allows you to take an existing VM that is stored in the VMM library and create a copy from it. This creates a new VM using an existing VHD and VM configuration.

Using a VMM Template Allows you to create a new VM using a preset VHD and VM configuration, while allowing for guest OS configuration.

In this example, we will use a *VMM template*. A VMM template consists of a VHD, on which you've run Sysprep, and an associated VM configuration, which includes the OS configuration. When the template is chosen, the resulting VM will be deployed and the initial configuration of the guest OS is automatically completed based on the configuration set during the deployment wizard.

NOTE Sysprep is a tool that can be run on a configured Windows operating system that removes the machine-specific settings, such as the machine name and Registry identifiers. The next time the OS is booted up, a mini-setup routine will ask for that information. This approach is common in cloning a physical machine to several identical copies, such as in a classroom or a server farm. It is ideal as part of preparing a VM template to be the master image for deploying new virtual machines.

To perform a new VM deployment using a template, use the VMM Administrator Console. Start the new VM process by choosing New Virtual Machine under the Actions pane in the upper-right portion of the Administrator Console. This brings up the New Virtual Machine Wizard:

1. The first screen is Select Source, where you are given the options to use an existing virtual machine, template, or virtual hard disk, or create a VM from a blank virtual hard disk, as shown in Figure 10.23. Select Browse, which will open a listing of available objects in the VMM library. The objects are sorted by the type, starting with Templates. Select the desired template and proceed with the wizard.

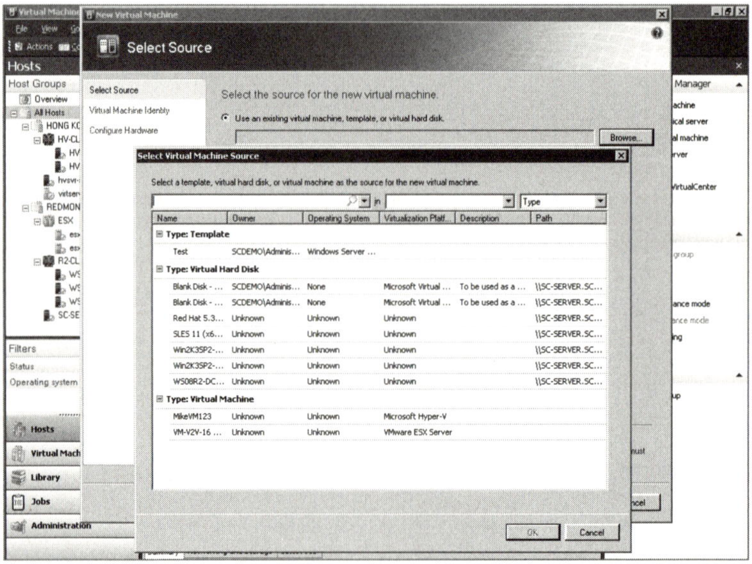

FIGURE 10.23
New Virtual Machine Wizard: Select Source

2. Next is the Virtual Machine Identity screen, which allows you to give the VM a name, assign an owner, and give a description to the resulting VM, similar to what we saw in Figure 10.19. As with the P2V wizard, the name of the VM in this step is the name for reference in VMM—it is not the actual machine name within the converted VM. For example, the actual machine name might be EX14, while the VM could be called ExchangeSvr for ExecTeam. All of this test information will be available when you manage the VM later.

3. On the next screen, Configure Hardware, you are given the opportunity to configure the hardware configuration of the VM. This includes key configurations, including processors, memory, hard drives, and network adapters. Note that all the parameters are preconfigured based on the template but you can change any parameter, as shown in Figure 10.24.

FIGURE 10.24
Configuring hardware for the new VM

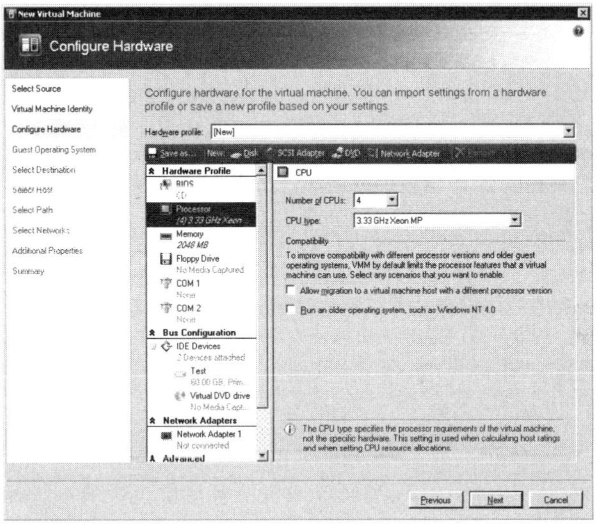

4. The next step in the wizard is the Guest Operating System screen, which allows you to configure the guest OS. Again, as with the hardware configuration, the template provides some preconfigured parameters. In this step, there are several required parameters that must be configured, including Computer Name (the actual computer name inside the VM), Full Name, and Product Key (Figure 10.25). You can also configure the VM to join a domain or even additional postinstall configurations. This step essentially fills in the settings that were stripped away during the Sysprep operation to the template VM.

FIGURE 10.25
Guest OS–specific options in the new VM

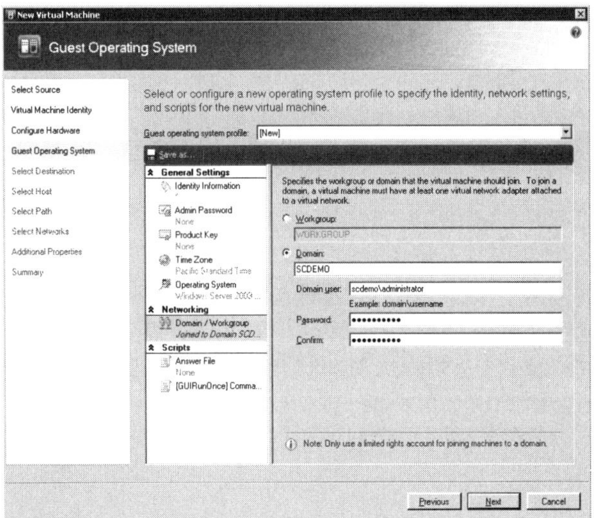

The next few options are similar to what we saw in the P2V wizard. Previously, in Task 23, the P2V wizard captured the machine-specific information, as well as the disks and networks to be converted. Here in Task 24, the New Virtual Machine Wizard just allowed us to enter those machine specifics, and will be using the preconfigured VM for much of the rest. What is left is to actually determine where the VM will reside on which host's storage and network connections, as well as tweak the startup and shutdown behavior of the VM.

5. The Select Destination screen only allows for one option in a new VM deployment, which is to place the VM on a host. Then, the Select Host screen appears. As described earlier, this step is also known as Intelligent Placement, as seen in Figure 10.21. If you choose a host that is in a high availability cluster, VMM will automatically make the VM highly available and configure it for use in the cluster.
6. Next, you will be asked to select a path for the VM. This is the file-system location for the VM. The file system referenced can be local paths or SAN-based paths.
7. On the Select Networks screen, you can configure the VM for the potential networks that are available on the designated host. This will allow the VM to see the available networks and is critical for maintaining the proper network connections for the converted machine.
8. Next is the Additional Properties screen, where you configure the actions that occur to the VM when the physical server starts or shuts down. This allows the VM to automatically start when the host starts and allows the VM to gracefully enter a saved state (similar to hibernate on a laptop) when the host shuts down.
9. Finally, a Summary screen is presented with all the information gathered, along with the View Script button, which allows you to view the entire PowerShell script for the deployment. Also, you can configure the new VM to start after the conversion is done.
10. After you click the Create button, VMM will start the creation process. You can view the progress by opening the Jobs window in VMM, which will track each step in the process and give estimated times.

Midsized Management: Physical and Virtual

As we saw in the previous sections, management and deployment in large enterprises can be a complex thing, so thankfully there are advanced toolsets available to help. When we looked at the various data protection and data availability solutions in Chapters 5–9, they were applicable for datacenters of all sizes (even the one-rack closet in a small business). But IT systems management is different in that there are different toolsets, based on the size of the organization.

In large enterprises with datacenters using physical and virtual infrastructure, we saw two Microsoft offerings:

- System Center Configuration Manager (ConfigMgr)
- System Center Virtual Machine Manager (VMM)

In midsized businesses with up to 500 PCs or 50 servers, the goals of better manageability and deployment for both physical and virtual IT resources are the same—but the tools are different, and in fact are unified in System Center Essentials (SCE).

Introducing SCE 2010

For midsized organizations, SCE 2010 provides many of the same capabilities as System Center Configuration Manager and System Center Virtual Machine Manager, but delivered in a way that is optimized for midsized organizations:

- Asset inventory
- Updates
- Software deployment
- Virtualization deployment and management

Earlier in the chapter, we discussed the many different roles and server components that are part of a ConfigMgr deployment. In true enterprise-scale deployments, all of these components would work together to support the deployment and management of tens of thousands of machines. However, in an environment with only up to 500 PCs, a single SCE server is all that is required (or allowed).

In the next few sections of this chapter, we will look at some of the same deployment and management activities discussed earlier in the chapter, but with the SCE equivalent actions to achieve them.

WHY TALK ABOUT SMALL IT IN A DATACENTER DATA PROTECTION BOOK?

The title of this book uses the words *Virtual Datacenters*, which are meant to relate to enterprise datacenters that are utilizing virtualization technologies. However, in a midsized company that has 500 users and perhaps only 25 servers, those 25 servers are the difference between that whole company running or not running. Sometimes, a virtual datacenter can mean a single server rack in the closet of a small business, or the one room in the back of the building with the noisy air conditioners.

Moreover, small and midsized organizations have the same needs for server uptime and data protection that larger companies do, but often do not have the expertise or budget that larger IT staffs may have. In some ways, this book was written as a way to provide expert-level guidance on enterprise availability and protection technologies to folks without experts onsite.

Getting Started with SCE 2010

SCE 2010 uses what many refer to as the Outlook interface (Figure 10.26), with a left pane that provides a tree view in the upper left, a context-sensitive middle area, and a list of tasks and other resources on the right side. Also notable is that all the various function areas appear as a stacked list in the lower-left corner.

We will use the SCE 2010 UI to perform a few of the functions previously accomplished in ConfigMgr and VMM. As with most of the earlier software exercises, a publicly available evaluation download from `www.microsoft.com/SCE` was used to build our SCE 2010 server.

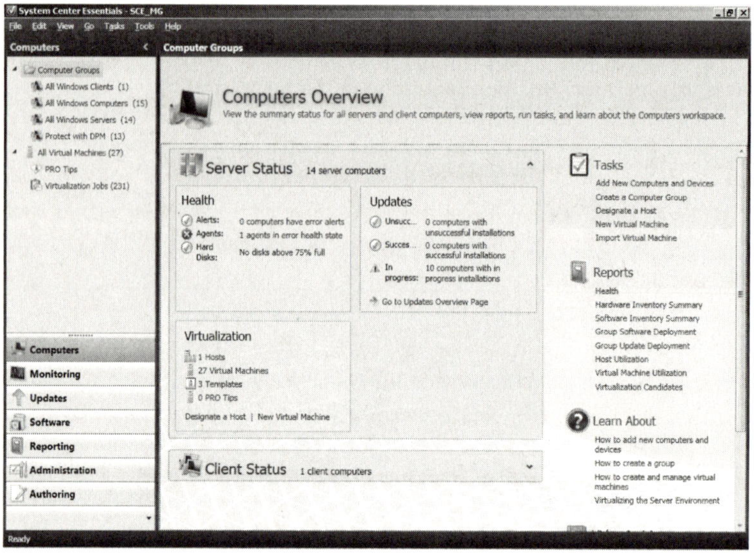

FIGURE 10.26
The SCE 2010 console

When first getting started with SCE, we need to discover the computers in our network, which will be managed by System Center. *Discovery* is a process in SCE that searches for computers and network devices to be managed. You can then browse the list of discovered objects and choose which computers will receive a SCE management agent.

Discovery can be done from the Computers screen of the SCE console, as seen earlier in Figure 10.26. The right side shows several common tasks; one of the tasks, Add New Computers And Devices, will launch the Computer And Device Management Wizard. This wizard is used to discover the computers within your environment, and then install an agent onto each one that you wish to manage.

After the initial deployment, new discoveries can be done by either running Wizard again, or by scheduling Discovery to occur automatically (once each day) from the Administration screen of the SCE console.

TASK 25: TAKING INVENTORY OF ASSETS WITH SCE

In Task 1, we used ConfigMgr to enable Asset Intelligence so that we could collect data on what machines are in our environment, and what is installed on them. In SCE, agents that are installed onto managed computers will inventory the software and hardware. On a configurable basis, SCE will scan the local environment to discover new machines, after which it will (or you can) install the SCE management agent. Once each day, the management agents will synchronize their updates and send the inventory. Afterward, you can run a report of the inventoried data, which includes the following categories:

Hardware: CPU, BIOS, and manufacturer/model

Hardware: Storage (physical disks and logical drives)

Hardware: Networking (NIC and IP information)

Hardware: Peripherals

Software: Operating system

Software: Installed applications

To generate an inventory report, start from the Computers screen of the SCE console. On the right side, you will see a variety of reports, providing information on hardware, software, updates, and so forth. But to really appreciate how everything comes together, try the Health report, as shown in Figure 10.27.

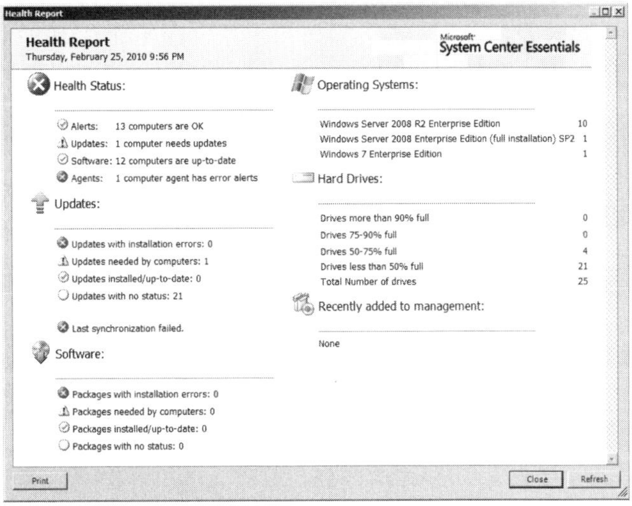

FIGURE 10.27
The overall Health Report within SCE

TASK 26: PATCHING PCs WITH SCE SOFTWARE UPDATES

One the most significant things that you can do to maintain the availability, and protection, of an IT infrastructure of any size is simply to maintain the software updates. That is what most of the patches are for—to ensure uptime and quality of service. Earlier in the chapter, Tasks 9–12 showed you how to do a variety of update work using ConfigMgr. SCE does not use technologies from ConfigMgr to deliver software updates. Instead, it uses technologies derived from Windows Update Services (WSUS) but delivered within SCE.

The updates features of ConfigMgr, WSUS, and SCE are all designed to provide a central point within your network to download and manage the updates for your entire environment, instead of requiring each and every machine to download them individually. There are three categories of updates (in priority order):

Updates Required by Essentials Ensure that the machine stays well managed (and updated)

Security Updates Protect the operating system and applications

Updates Resolve a known issue with an application or operating system

These kinds of updates are important for ensuring high uptime, which is a focus of this book. It is so important that Microsoft makes significant investments in the Windows Update services, which is what SCE uses. SCE takes the inventory of what it already knows is running on your network, and then downloads everything that those computers will need from Windows Update so that it can push the updates out to your managed computers for you.

To manage updates in SCE, go to the Updates screen in the SCE console. In the main area, you can see which software updates are needed by which managed computers, as well as invoke tasks to approve or deploy new updates.

For SCE to update your managed computers, three things have to occur:

1. SCE must initially synchronize with Windows Update, so that it can download the updates to a local cache.
2. The computers must be managed (running an agent) and be part of a *computer group* (logical grouping of machines within the SCE console).
3. The updates must be approved for that computer group.

Initially, SCE must connect with Windows Update and download information about the available updates. Then, it will compare that with the criteria that you have defined and download the actual updates to a local cache.

NOTE The default location for the updates within SCE is off the SCE server's OS system drive. The updates will very quickly take up a good amount of space, so a best-practice recommendation is to change the location of the cache from the default when running the initial wizard of the SCE setup.

With the updates now stored locally within the SCE server (so that every computer doesn't have to download them individually and consume bandwidth), SCE provides a list of these updates to be approved per computer group (Figure 10.28).

FIGURE 10.28
Approving software updates

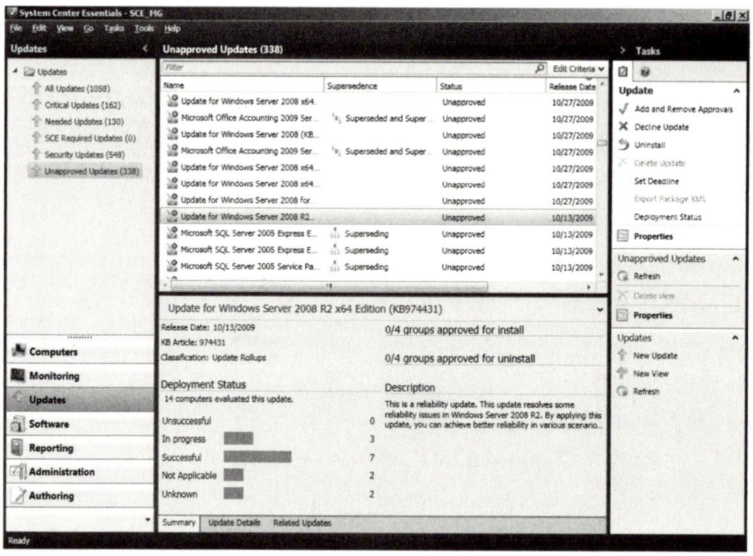

Along with manually approving some updates, you can choose to *automatically approve updates* of a certain type and to a certain computer group, such as security updates. This ensures that any updates that are specifically intended to protect against vulnerabilities are automatically applied in the next cycle after they are received, without any interaction or potential delay. After the initial synchronization, SCE can be configured to automatically return to Windows Update and seek new updates on a regular schedule.

It is worth noting that the automatic updates choice in SCE is to approve them for distribution among the clients. The behavior of how the clients receive the software will be determined by the Updates policy on the local machines (which can be mandated via a Group Policy setting done by the SCE server).

- If the local machine is configured to automatically download and apply updates, then it will—from the SCE server. The machines will check for new updates from the SCE server by default, at least once per day.
- If the local machine is not configured to automatically apply updates, the installable updates will be available when the local machine does access updates.

At any point in time, you can return to the Updates screen of the SCE console to check the status of how many machines were successfully updated, how many machines are in progress, and if any machines are not yet updated (Figure 10.29).

FIGURE 10.29
Checking the status of updates in SCE

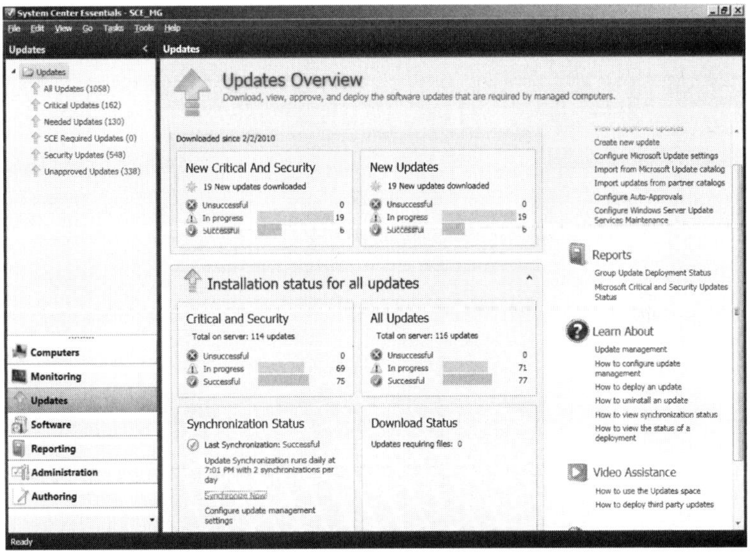

TASK 27: DEPLOYING SOFTWARE WITH SCE

If you like the idea of centralized software deployment, as we saw it in the Tasks 2–8, but in a smaller environment would prefer the ease of use that we saw in the SCE software updates feature, then you have come to the right place. In this way, we can be assured that all the machines (servers and clients) are receiving the same versions of software, and that they are installed in a similar manner. This, again, results in higher reliability (as well as interoperability) throughout the environment.

Software deployment, even in an easy-to-use wizard designed for small businesses, cannot be covered in just a few pages, but the key to getting started is understanding three deployment concepts (refer to Tasks 2–7 for more in-depth insight):

- What makes up a software installation
- How to build a software installation package
- How to push a package out to the PCs

There are three kinds of installable software you should be aware of:

EXE Applications Applications that are invoked from an executable, with other possible files in the same directory

MSI Installations Software that uses the Windows Installer and provides additional relevant information about the software package (covered in the next section) directly into the deployment tool of SCE or ConfigMgr

EXE-MSI A Windows installer application that is invoked from the EXE file, which again provides the additional information about the package, courtesy of the MSI, as well as some additional flexibility through the EXE

Building a Software Package

To build a software package, you need to specify the location of the installation files, as well as any additional switches or options that are necessary to install the software. Follow these steps:

1. On the Software screen of the SCE console, click Create New Package in the tasks area on the right.
2. Type or browse to the setup file location.
3. Enter a convenient package name that might include your customizations, language choices, platforms requirements, etc. If you are installing from an MSI, these details may be prepopulated.
4. Type a description for the package, and then click Next.
5. You can specify what OS versions, which architectures (x64, x86 or IA64), and which languages of clients can receive the package, as shown in Figure 10.30.
6. Click Next to see additional screens where you can:
   - Customize the return codes that would indicate a successful or unsuccessful deployment.
   - Add install or uninstall command-line options.
7. A summary screen will display your choices; click Create to form the package.

On the last screen, you'll see the "Show deployment options when this wizard closes" check box, which is selected by default. If you leave it selected, SCE will display the deployment and publication options when the New Software Package Wizard is complete.

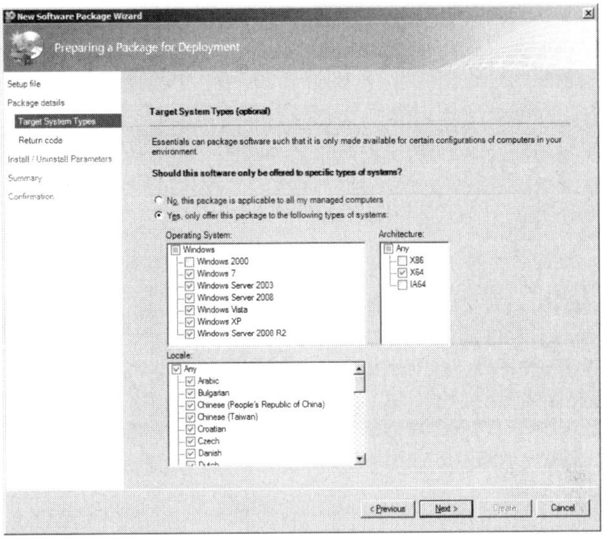

FIGURE 10.30
Choose OS, architecture, and languages for new software packages.

APPROVING PACKAGES FOR DEPLOYMENT

If you left the "Show deployment options when this wizard closes" check box selected in the New Software Package Wizard, then it brought you directly into the Add And Remove Approvals dialog box.

If not, then you can choose to approve and deploy a defined software package on the Software screen of the SCE console by clicking the Deploy An Existing Software Package task on the right side of the console. This will bring up a list of the packages that are defined. Select one and click OK to access the Add And Remove Approvals dialog box, shown in Figure 10.31.

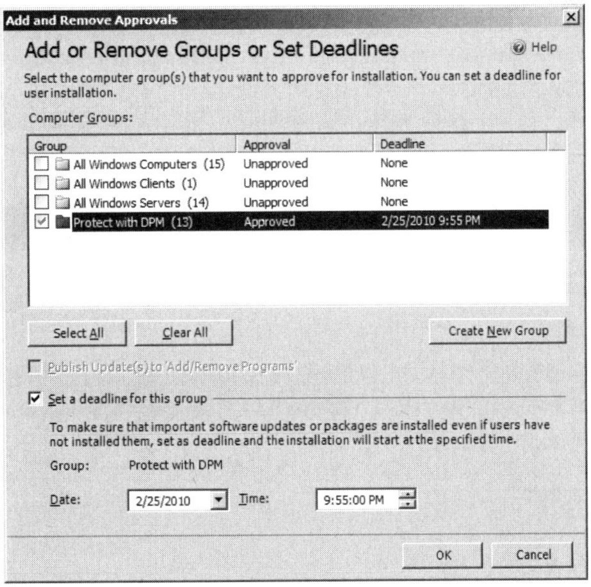

FIGURE 10.31
Add and Remove Approvals dialog box

By using this dialog box, you can do the following:

- You can choose which computer groups should receive the package, or create a new group to receive it.
- You can choose to have the installation be optional and simply included in each local machine's Add/Remove Programs list. If listed, the software must be manually installed from the Control Panel of the machine by someone who has local administrator privileges on that machine.
- You can choose whether to set a deadline for when the software must be installed by using the Date and Time pull-down boxes. If a deadline is set, the software will be automatically installed at that time or at the next opportunity.

NOTE In my example, I created a software package for the DPM 2010 backup agent so that I could automatically deploy it across my environment. So, in this step, I created a group called Protect-with-DPM and approved the package for it. Now, any managed computer (server or laptop) that I put in the group will receive the agent so that I can back up the data.

Task 28: Performing SCE Virtualization Tasks

Earlier in the chapter, we looked at deploying and managing virtualized resources with SC VMM. One of the big changes from SCE 2007 to SCE 2010 was the addition of virtualization management for midsized environments. With that in mind, the VMM tasks that we did earlier (Tasks 22, 23, and 24) on deploying agents to virtualization hosts, performing P2V migrations, and creating new VMs via templates can also be done in SCE 2010.

Designating a New Virtualization Host

Designating a new virtualization host for SCE to manage is similar to VMM Task 22. You can choose a machine to become a virtualization host, running either Hyper-V (WS08 and WS08R2) or Virtual Server 2005 R2 (Windows Server 2003 and Windows Server 2003 R2).

1. On the Computers page of the SCE console, navigate to Computer Groups and select the All Windows Servers group.
2. In the tasks pane on the right, click Designate A Host.
3. In the wizard that launches, select a computer to use as a host, and then supply your administrative credentials. Click Next to continue.
4. You may be warned that designating the computer to be a host may require the computer to be restarted; click Yes.
5. An optional screen will display the progress as the machine receives a virtualization management agent and a hypervisor is confirmed or installed (see Task 22 for more details on this process). When the progress is complete, or if you deselected the option to monitor the progress, click Finish to leave the wizard.

Now that we have one or more virtualization hosts within our midsized organization's IT environment, we need to deploy some virtual machines—either by migrating some physical machines into VMs (P2V) or deploying new virtual machines from templates.

PHYSICAL-TO-VIRTUAL MIGRATION

Migrating a physical server to a VM with SCE is similar to Task 23 and uses much of the same P2V technology found in VMM.

1. On the Computers page of the SCE console, navigate to Computer Groups and select the All Windows Servers group.
2. In the tasks pane on the right, click Convert To Virtual Machine to launch the Copy Server wizard.
3. Enter your administrative credentials for the physical server that you will be doing a P2V conversion of. You can click Test to verify the credentials or Next to continue.

   Similar to Task 23, a P2V agent is temporarily installed onto the production server, and the configuration details of the physical server are populated into the wizard for acceptance or tuning.
4. Click Change Properties to adjust the memory, CPU, and other hardware characteristics of the VM, as shown in Figure 10.32. Click Next to continue.

FIGURE 10.32
Adjusting the hardware in a P2V conversion

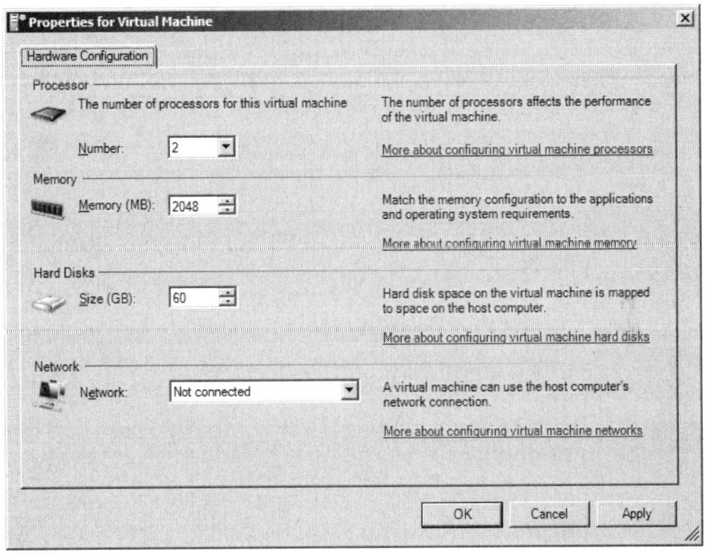

5. SCE will identify one or more virtualization hosts that have adequate resources to host the VM, as you defined it. Choose which host that you prefer and click Next.
6. The next page allows you to give the VM a name and give it a description, similar to what we saw earlier in Figure 10.18. The name of the VM in this step is the name for reference in VMM—it is not the actual machine name within the converted VM. For example, the actual machine name might be EX14, whereas the VM could be called ExchangeSvr for ExecTeam. You can also specify where to store the VM configuration files.

7. Click Next to go to the Summary page and confirm your settings.
8. Click Create to convert the VM and also automatically shut down the physical production server after the VM is created.

You will be notified when the new VM is complete. At that time, you have the choice of whether or not to start the new VM immediately. Click Close to leave the wizard.

Creating a New VM from a Template

Creating a new VM from a template in SCE is similar to Task 24, where you can start with a default profile and build a VM using a wizard.

1. On the Computers page of the SCE console, navigate to Computer Groups and select the All Virtual Machines group.
2. In the tasks pane on the right, click New Virtual Machine.
3. In the New Virtual Machine wizard, you can choose which template that the new VM will be based on. Preconfigured options include:
   - Basic server
   - High-end server
   - Recommended configuration

   Beyond the preconfigured profiles, you have the option of changing the hardware configuration of this particular VM (as seen earlier in Figure 10.32), including:
   - Processors
   - Memory
   - Storage
   - Networking
4. You can choose how the OS inside the VM will be set up (Figure 10.33):

   Install From Network This option uses a centralized OS deployment mechanism.

   Install From DVD This option uses a physical DVD drive on the hypervisor host.

   Install From Available ISO Images This option allows you to use ISOs from a library of OS installation media.
5. Click Next to continue.
6. Choose which host will be running this VM from the list of hosts that have sufficient available resources based on your virtual hardware configuration. Click Next.
7. The next page allows you to give the VM a name and a description, similar to what we saw earlier in Figure 10.19.
8. The Summary screen lists the choices that you made; click Create to build the virtual machine.

FIGURE 10.33
OS installation options for a new VM

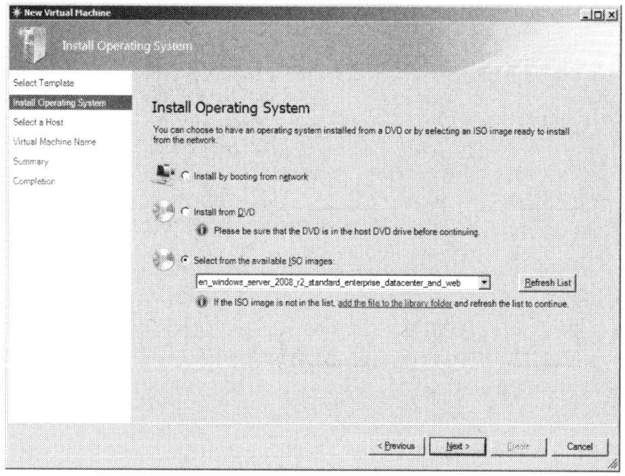

Once the virtual machine is created, SCE will automatically start the virtual machine and connect you to it.

Summary

Sometimes, the best way to keep systems highly available is to simply ensure the quality of the primary systems themselves. In this chapter, we looked at some enterprise and midsized tools for better software deployment, patch management, and inventory.

We also looked at pure virtualization management, including how to create new servers and move physical servers into a virtual datacenter. In our next chapter, we will discuss monitoring and problem resolution.

Chapter 11

Monitoring Systems

Similar to the discussion on management that we had in Chapter 10, sometimes the best way to ensure availability of systems is proactive monitoring. Long gone are the days of simply being aware whether or not a system is running. A quiet or busy phone in the help desk will tell you that.

In this chapter, we will look at monitoring tools designed to provide insight into how well the datacenter is running. As in Chapter 10, we will first look at an enterprise-centric view and then a midsized organization perspective.

The Need for Monitoring

It has been said that software is put in place within an organization for one of two purposes: to make money or to save money. When it comes to software that is intended for use by multiple people, whether internal or external customers, one of the first concerns is deploying that software, since we probably all know of situations where procured software remains as shelfware. Deployment was covered in Chapter 10, using technologies such as System Center Configuration Manager and System Center Essentials. But once a line-of-business application is deployed, the primary concern becomes knowing that the system is running and that it is responding to end-user requests in a timely fashion.

To help manage application health and performance, many organizations have started to implement operational frameworks such as what Information Technology Infrastructure Library (ITIL), `www.itil-officialsite.com`, and Microsoft Operations Framework (MOF), `http://technet.microsoft.com/en-us/library/cc506049.aspx`, prescribe. These frameworks help drive the process in how applications are managed—such as security, backup and recovery, patching, and so on—as well as expectations concerning levels of service of those applications and escalation paths. Most of the time these expectations and commitments are agreed between the owner of the service (for example, the Exchange messaging platform) and the entity hosting the service (for example, the datacenter), and formulated into operational and service level agreements (OLAs and SLAs), as we discussed in Chapter 2.

A core focus of any OLA or SLA is the availability and performance of the applications that are the subject of that agreement. To take an example that defines what we mean by availability and performance, let's examine the situation of a Microsoft SharePoint portal that is used to share key sales information to sales teams across your organization. Normally, an end user would type the URL of the portal into their web browser, and the portal would appear in that browser in a matter of seconds. Let's take two possible scenarios:

- A critical network switch in the London office, where the SharePoint portal is hosted, fails, resulting in end users across the organization being unable to connect to the SharePoint portal. This would be seen as an availability incident, since (from the perspective of the end user) it is not possible to access the portal at all.

- After a recent sales promotion, the SharePoint portal is experiencing significantly heavy load, resulting in an average wait time to serve incoming requests of over one minute. This would be seen as a performance incident, since while the portal can be reached, the perspective for the end user is that it takes too long for the pages to appear.

One of the first questions that must be answered is how to ensure that an application is up and running, since if an outage does occur there may negative consequences, such as the following:

- The IT support resources of the organization become inundated with requests for assistance.
- End users switch to unapproved applications, with possible security ramifications, if incidents persist for long periods of time or occur too frequently.
- The hosting service suffers financial penalties if defined service levels are not achieved.

Additional funds can be put into ensuring the high availability and performance of applications and IT services. However, the goal is to proactively understand when there is significant risk of an outage and to act as soon as possible, or identify the root cause of the outage so that it can be quickly mitigated to restore service. This falls into the realm of monitoring.

From a technical perspective, there are numerous approaches to determining if an application is both available and performing, from the manual to a more automated approach. Manual approaches may involve having someone connect to the application and perhaps run a few actions to verify that everything is working as expected. This approach does not scale well across multiple applications and IT services. A manual approach is also subject to errors in that it only gets the perspective of the individual performing the test and not of the wider audience. As such, this is a possible approach for applications with a small, localized user base but not for enterprise scale.

To approach validating the availability and performance of applications across a larger scale, many have elected more automated approaches. This might entail anything from implementing their own testing infrastructure (from the writing of simple scripts to the implementation of larger, in-house engineered approaches), to purchasing software that claims to do the job, to outsourcing the operation to some third party.

Throughout this chapter we'll explore some of the challenges that organizations face when implementing a monitoring solution as part of maintaining a high level of availability across the systems. We'll also discuss various Microsoft technologies that can deliver an effective monitoring solution that will scale across datacenters of all sizes.

Challenges in Monitoring

Anyone who has tried to implement an enterprise-wide monitoring infrastructure will likely have come across a number of challenges, both technical and human related. In this section, we will explore some of these challenges, but it is by no means a full investigation of the space.

The nature of the environment that you are trying to monitor can also create challenges. As organizations grow in size and geographical coverage, and as they implement increasingly complex architectures, the challenges of successfully monitoring that environment dramatically increase as well. Examples of such challenges include the following:

Traversing Active Directory Trust Boundaries Many organizations run with numerous Active Directory domains, and often with different trust relationships between those domains. Traversing those security boundaries and expanding the scope of those concerns to monitoring locations across nontrusted network connections or in demilitarized zones (DMZs) are all challenges that can break many applications—and challenges that any good monitoring application must attempt to overcome.

Communicating Through Security Perimeters Managing communications through security devices and software such as firewalls, as well as across nontrusted networks, also create challenges in ensuring the success, integrity, and security of monitoring data transmitted from computers into any monitoring application. Particularly when dealing with strict security policies, monitoring software must be able to adapt or deploy to fit within the resulting architecture.

Working in Heterogeneous Environments In larger organizations, it is rare to find situations where the organization has standardized on a single type of platform. Most often there is a mix of Windows, Unix, and Linux, and often some other technologies such as mainframes, across which different lines of business applications operate. In many situations, older hardware will remain just because the cost to transfer the software to a new platform cannot be justified.

Working in Clustered Environments Especially difficult from a monitoring perspective is when an application is deployed within a Windows cluster. Understanding the health of the cluster can be relatively straightforward, but determining the health and performance of applications running on clustered environments has to be taken into consideration by the monitoring software (for example, identifying when an application is migrated to a different cluster node).

Monitoring Across Virtual and Physical Environments Particularly with the rapid adoption of virtualization technology, and running systems on both physical hosts as well as within virtual machines, monitoring solutions do not always take into consideration the complete picture. Being truly effective requires a grasp of the health and performance of the hardware platform (the virtualization host), the operating system and workloads running on that hardware platform, the VMs running on that machine, and the workloads running within those VMs.

Scaling up the Monitoring Infrastructure Being able to scale is important when an organization wishes to monitor a large number of computers, as well as when determining the volume of monitoring data that needs to be collected. Although much of this can be determined by architecting the solution correctly at the outset, adequate planning is a step that is often not carried out as thoroughly as possible.

As mentioned earlier, human-related issues can also be a challenge when implementing a monitoring infrastructure. Concerns such as security, invasion of space, invasion of privacy, micromanagement, loss of autonomy, and other related human blockers can disrupt the smooth deployment of monitoring capabilities. These kinds of challenges can be approached through the creation of a monitoring-based policy, also referred to as *organizational governance*; education of IT service owners who can determine how monitoring can help ensure uptime and reduce management costs; and overall communication. Such approaches will be received with varying levels of success, but they are challenges that must be overcome—whether through amicable measures or through strict adherence to policy and governance.

Enterprise End-to-End Monitoring

System Center Operations Manager 2007 is the product within the System Center Suite that delivers end-to-end health and performance monitoring of your enterprise environment: monitoring systems and their workloads, line-of-business applications, and IT services.

Operations Manager 2007 is the third generation of Microsoft's enterprise monitoring solution, and builds on the successes of its predecessors: Microsoft Operations Manager (MOM) 2000 and MOM 2005. In fact, Operations Manager 2007 delivered a significantly redesigned architecture that added new capabilities and extensibility over MOM 2005. One of the most significant additions was that rather than focusing on the health of individual systems and workloads, Operations Manager 2007 added an additional dimension to enterprise monitoring through distributed application monitoring. This allows Operations Manager to evaluate health and performance across the often-complex interrelationships and operational integrity of distributed applications, and therefore helps you determine the integrity and delivered level of service of line-of-business applications and IT services running within organizations. A full comparison of the differences in features and capabilities between MOM 2005, Operations Manager 2007 SP1, and Operations Manager 2007 R2 can be found at `www.microsoft.com/systemcenter/en/us/operations-manager/om-compare-products.aspx`.

The core health and performance monitoring and management scenarios that Operations Manager 2007 delivers include:

Import and Configuration of Predefined Monitoring Intelligence The rules and monitors that are required to determine the type of system being monitored, the workloads operating on that system, as well as the ability to monitor and manage the system or workloads, are encapsulated within management packs that are created by Microsoft and its partners. These management packs can be selectively downloaded into the Operations Manager database, ready to use for discovery and monitoring activities. Where required, operators can also "override" individual settings to customize how an entity is monitored, as well as create new monitors and rules to apply to different systems and workloads.

Integrated Identification of Systems to Monitor Operations Manager assists you in identifying systems to monitor by using automated discovery of all Windows-based computers joined to an Active Directory domain, by scanning Active Directory using advanced queries, or by browsing Active Directory by computer name. Unix and Linux systems can be discovered using IP address or DNS name.

Automated Discovery of System Configurations and Workloads Upon discovery, an Operations Manager agent will normally be deployed to that discovered system so that it can be managed by Operations Manager. This agent will automate the discovery of the configuration of the system that it is monitoring, as well as the workloads running on that system.

Automated Distribution of Monitoring Intelligence Once the exact type of system and its workloads are determined through discovery, Operations Manager will then download the rules, monitors, and any required security information to the agent so that the agent can perform the monitoring and management of the system and its workloads. Any updates to this monitoring intelligence are redistributed at the first opportunity.

User-Definable Applications User-definable distributed applications allow operators to define their own health model for applications that do not have their own management pack, including the selection of the components to monitor, and the creation of new monitors where required.

Alerts for Health and Performance Incidents If a monitor or rule identifies a nonoptimal situation, Operations Manager can raise a warning or critical alert to operators, as well as notify them through a number of mediums such as email, instant messaging service, and SMS.

Embedded Knowledge Embedded knowledge enables operators to quickly investigate the most likely root cause of a situation identify possible causes and leverage recommended actions to remediate that incident. This knowledge is embedded within management packs, and can also be extended by customers.

Management Tasks Management tasks allow operators, where permitted, to instruct Operations Manager to proxy an administrative task on behalf of the operator. This may be to validate a situation or to perform some remediation activity.

Synthetic Transactions Through its agents, Operations Manager is able to run a predefined sequence of actions (known as *synthetic transactions*) against websites and databases. These transactions are generally used to verify the operation and responsiveness of a monitored object.

Introducing Operations Manager 2007 R2

The latest iteration of the product, Operations Manager 2007 R2, helped address many requests that Microsoft was hearing from customers and the market. A number of improvements were implemented in the product (see the Microsoft TechCenter for additional details on changes implemented in Operations Manager 2007 R2); two of the most significant new capabilities are:

Monitoring Beyond Microsoft Technologies With the addition of the ability to monitor Unix and Linux systems such as SUSE and Red Hat Linux, Sun Solaris, IBM AIX, and HP-UX, as well as the workloads running on those systems, Microsoft leveraged the OpenPegasus (`http://openpegasus.com`) framework to successfully monitor across Unix and Linux. In addition to joining the OpenPegasus Steering Committee, Microsoft has released much of its code into the open source community so that others can easily extend the capabilities beyond what Microsoft and its partners have done.

Service Level Tracking The service level tracking capabilities introduced in Operations Manager 2007 R2 enable distributed applications to be tracked against service level commitments set against them. By adding the ability to define service level expectations against existing monitors and new reports to show how current performance and availability metrics map to those desired levels, it can be quickly determined where service levels are trending toward service level violations for the various distributed applications and IT services that Operations Manager is monitoring.

Operations Manager Architecture

The core construct of any Operations Manager deployment is the Management Group, which defines all the computers of which Operations Manager is aware, along with the monitoring data that is being collected from across those computers and their workloads. The management group is defined during the installation of the initial Operations Manager deployment. The systems and workloads monitored within that group are discovered and managed during the lifecycle of the Operations Manager implementation.

At a minimum, an Operations Manager deployment will include the following required components:

Operations Manager Database The Operations Manager database is a Microsoft SQL database that stores the configuration information for the management group and all monitoring data collected by the Operations Manager infrastructure.

Root Management Server (RMS) The RMS is the first management server installed within a management group and is the primary control point of the Operations Manager deployment. While other management servers (including gateway servers) may be deployed to help manage the collection of data, the RMS is where the configuration, administration, and core communications infrastructure resides.

Operations Console The Operations Console provides an integrated interface for administering the management group, as well as monitoring and managing the computers and workloads within. Leveraging a role-based access capability, operator access can be granularly controlled to access monitoring data, authoring tools, reports, and more within the console.

Operations Agents Agents are deployed to computers that you want to monitor, and they discover elements running on those computers that you wish to monitor, as well as collect information about those elements. Agents can also act as proxies, with the ability to receive data through agentless technologies such as SNMP. An operations agent will be assigned to a management server; from this server, it will receive management updates or actions (to perform on the computer or application that it is monitoring). The agent will then transmit the monitoring information it gathers to that management server. To adjust for high-availability situations, agents can be multihomed to different management servers, allowing the agents to continue monitoring through a secondary management server in case their primary management server becomes unavailable.

Management Packs Management packs are containers (packaged in the form of XML files) that are downloaded into the RMS that instruct Operations Manager on how to discover a computer, component, or application; what to monitor to determine health and performance of that monitored element; and the views and reports that are presented to the operator through the console. As of this writing, more than 100 management packs are available for Operations Manager, including management packs for Exchange Server 2010 and Office SharePoint 2010. We will discuss several such management packs, their applicability, and some of their specific counters and functionality later in the section *"Monitoring the Health and Performance of Key Workloads."*

The following are additional server roles and components that you can install, either at initial deployment or at a later stage, to further enhance the power of your monitoring infrastructure:

Windows PowerShell Command-Line Interface An optional PowerShell command-line interface provides a number of PowerShell cmdlets through which several management tasks are exposed. You can leverage these tasks via individual PowerShell-based calls or through scripting.

Management Servers Management servers deliver the management scalability of the Operations Manager infrastructure by managing a subset of the computers within the management group. Taking its instructions from the RMS, a management server manages the communications to and from operations agents within its span of control, such as propagating rule updates and sending management commands. Management servers are also responsible for receiving monitoring information from the agents it manages and then forwarding that data to the RMS. For high availability, a management server can also be promoted to an RMS in case its RMS becomes unavailable.

Gateway Servers Gateway servers are a special version of management server that can be deployed into environments that are outside the trust of the Active Directory forest within which the RMS is installed, in order to manage systems that reside in that nontrusted domain. Examples of such situations might be where an organization has systems operating within

DMZ networks or a branch office. The gateway server performs the role of management server for those systems that are part of the nontrusted domain into which the gateway server has been deployed. The gateway server enables those systems to be monitored and managed centrally through the RMS via a secure and authenticated certificate-based connection. The gateway server can communicate securely with the RMS over nontrusted network connections.

Web Console Server A web console server delivers a web-based management console through which operators can view the monitoring data and tasks to which they are permitted access. This console does not provide the full functionality available through the Operations Console—only the monitoring, favorite reports, and My Workspace views.

Data Warehouse Whereas the Operations Manager database is optimized for the rapid collection and recording of monitoring data, the Data Warehouse is a Microsoft SQL database that is optimized for the long-term storage and analysis of that monitoring and alert data. An optional component of any Operations Manager deployment, the Data Warehouse aggregates data from multiple management groups on an hourly basis, and is the database queried for both reporting and for the analysis of possible trends.

Reporting Server The Reporting Server leverages Microsoft SQL Reporting Services to present the reports that it builds from data queried from the Reporting Data Warehouse.

Audit Collection Services (ACS) ACS provides a centralized aggregation of events written to the Security event log on monitored computers. This capability includes the installation of the following:

ACS Database The ACS database is a Microsoft SQL database that stores the aggregate security events from across systems within the management group.

ACS Collector Server ACS collector servers extend the capabilities of management servers to aggregate Security event log data from agents that have the ACS Forwarder capability enabled. The ACS collector server filters and preprocesses that data before writing it to the ACS database.

ACS Reporting The ACS Reporting feature can be installed alongside or separately from the Reporting Server, and it provides a number of audit reports.

As with any enterprise architecture, the exact type of deployment needs to meet the monitoring requirements of the organization. Microsoft details three types of deployment:

Single Server, Single Management Group In this deployment, all Operations Manager 2007 core roles and configurations are implemented on a single server. For most examples in this chapter, our reference system has been deployed using this model.

Multiple Servers, Single Management Group Through this deployment, the various Operations Manager roles are distributed across a number of servers.

Multiple Management Groups This is the most complex deployment type; multiple management groups are deployed alongside and work together to deliver the desired level of monitoring.

We won't discuss these various deployments, so for additional guidance on which advanced scenarios are best for your environment, consult Microsoft resources such as TechNet and the Operations Manager 2007 Deployment Guide (`http://technet.microsoft.com/en-us/library/bb419281.aspx`).

User Roles in Operations Manager

The most-often used interface to Operations Manager is the Operations Console, which caters to the key audiences for Operations Manager. By default, Operations Manager is installed with six types of operator:

Operations Manager Administrators Operations Manager Administrators are granted full privileges to Operations Manager.

Operations Manager Advanced Operators Advanced Operators are able to edit (override) the configurations of rules and monitors within their scope of control and access.

Authors Authors are permitted to create, edit, and delete monitoring configurations (tasks, rules, monitors, and views) within their scope of control and access.

Operators Operators are permitted to interact with alerts, tasks, and views that are within their scope of control and access.

Read-Only Operators Read-Only Operators are permitted read-only access to alerts and views that are within their scope of access.

Report Operators Report Operators are permitted to run and view reports within their scope of access.

By adding and removing Active Directory users and groups to these default user roles, as well as through the creation of new user roles based on these defaults, you can granularly control who has the ability to monitor, manage, and report on which objects within the management group.

NOTE Appreciating a management solution like Operations Manager requires installing not only the management platform itself but also the various production servers that would be managed, such as Windows Server, SQL Server, or Exchange Server, as well as an Active Directory deployment. Because of this, it is less practical for this chapter to start from the beginning with a clean install and build up. Instead, you can gain hands-on experience with System Center Operations Manager, as well as System Center Essentials, by using the TechNet Virtual Hands-On lab environments. Virtual labs provide a private environment to learn in for a few hours, using just your web browser and connecting to a large lab farm at Microsoft.

Virtual labs for Operations Manager can be found at `www.microsoft.com/systemcenter/operationsmanager/en/us/virtual-labs.aspx`.

Getting Started with Operations Manager

To start the Operations Console, choose Start ➢ All Programs ➢ Microsoft System Center Operations Manager 2007 R2 ➢ Operations Console. The first time the Operations Console window appears, it will display the Monitoring Overview page, with the Monitoring area selected, which provides a summary view of computer and distributed application health. Subsequent restarts will display the screen that was last displayed when the console was closed.

The Operations Console is divided into sections. Each section provides a defined set of capabilities—administration of the management group, monitoring of the management group, authoring of new monitoring configuration items, and execution of available reports. The Operations Console is divided into the following parts (as shown in Figure 11.1):

Menu and Toolbar Lets you interact with the menus and available toolbar icons.

FIGURE 11.1
The Operations Manager Console

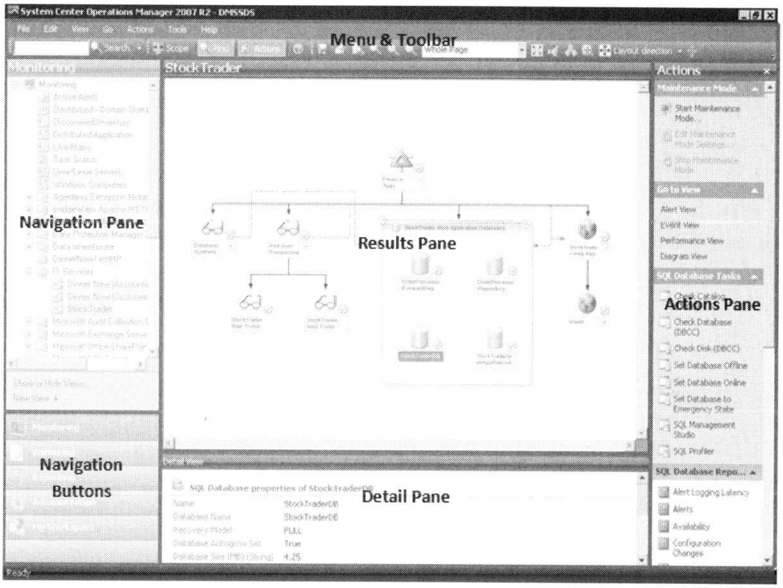

Navigation Pane Allows you to navigate the available views, reports, or options, based on the selected area of focus (that is, Monitoring, Authoring, Reporting, Administration, and My Workspace).

Navigation Buttons Sometimes referred to as the WunderBar, these buttons allow you to navigate to a selected area of focus (that is, Monitoring, Authoring, Reporting, Administration, and My Workspace). The list of buttons available is dependent on whether you have been granted access to that area.

Results Pane Displays the results from the navigation tree, or from some search action.

Detail Pane Presents detailed information about the object selected within the results pane.

Actions Pane Lets you select any available management tasks, reports, or additional resources.

We'll refer to each of these areas of the console throughout the remainder of this chapter.

Next we'll look at some of the Operations Manager features and how to use them to monitor your environment.

Discovering Systems to Monitor

When you first install Operations Manager, you effectively have an environment that is ready to start monitoring but with nothing to monitor. The first step is to discover the computers you wish to monitor, and add them to the management group. The process that Operations Manager uses to perform this identification of systems to be managed is called discovery.

Understanding Run As Accounts

Before you can use the monitoring system to discover the systems and workloads that you wish to monitor, it is important to understand how Operations Manager will attempt to manage and monitor the computer and workload characteristics. Any action that Operations Manager performs on a computer or workload—whether to read a performance counter or event log—requires that the *Operations Agent* have the correct permissions to be able to view that information and, where necessary, issue commands to manage a target. These credentials are stored and accessed by Operations Manager as the following:

Run As Accounts *Run As Accounts* are the credentials that are used to execute commands on a particular entity or server, and provide support for a number of different authentication methods (for example, basic authentication and digest authentication).

Run As Profiles *Run As Profiles* are logical containers of one or more Run As Accounts, and are leveraged by Operations Manager to perform some action on the target system. For example, the SQL Management Pack defines a SQL Run As Profile that is used whenever actions are performed on SQL Server instances.

When installing an agent on a managed computer, the default option is to install that agent to operate under the LocalSystem account, since this account possesses extensive privileges on the computer and thus is ideal to be able to monitor across all services and workloads running on that computer. However, organizations may wish an agent to run with fewer privileges, or even run within a least-privilege model, in which case the agent can be installed using a domain account (either created across all monitored systems or unique to one or a group of machines). In general, unless a Run As Account is specified for some particular action, the agent will always default to using the credentials under which it was installed to gather monitoring information, or attempt to execute a command on that managed computer.

Although manual installation of agents is possible, the ideal approach to deploying operations agents across your environment is to use the Discovery Wizard (Figure 11.2). To launch this wizard, click the Administration navigation button and click the Discovery Wizard link at the base of the Navigation pane.

1. First, select the type of system you're looking to discover, whether it is a Windows computer, Unix, or Linux computer, or network device.

   - Discovery of Windows computers leverages Active Directory System Discovery. Users can have Operations Manager automatically discover computers registered with Active Directory, write custom queries to discover computers of some particular type or classification, or add individual computers by their DNS or IP information.

   - Discovery of Unix or Linux computers is slightly different in that the operator will enter an IP address, DNS name, or IP address range to discover target systems, and Operations Manager will then attempt a secure connection (using the Secure Shell protocol) to each system to verify its existence and that the credentials provided to access that system are correct.

   - Managing network devices enables discovery by IP address, for subsequent management via SNMP.

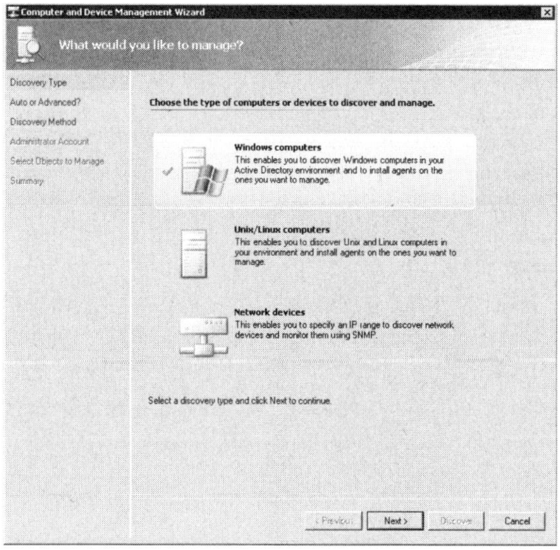

FIGURE 11.2
The Discovery Wizard

2. Once discovered, you can elect to manage that computer via an operations agent installed on the system, or through proxy-based (agentless) management via an existing agent-managed computer or management server. For most cases, the installation of an operations agent is the recommended approach as it provides the greatest degree of monitoring and management capabilities, with the added advantage that if the computer on which it is installed becomes disconnected temporarily from the network, it will continue to monitor and retain collected data until it can communicate again with its management server.
3. You then have the option to install the agent to run with Local System privileges (for Windows computers), or to run it under a domain or local account, as discussed in the sidebar "Understanding Run As Accounts."

After installation of the Operations Manager agent software, the agent will immediately download discovery rules from the management server that installed it and initiate a *discovery* of the system configuration, as well as of any workloads running on that system.

As different elements are discovered, the agent will then download the monitors and rules for each discovered element, and start to feed that data back to its management server. This monitoring information will start to be represented within the console as one of the following types of information:

Health State The health state view indicates the health rollup of the different monitors that represent the health and performance of an entity. The different states are healthy, warning, and critical. What is displayed in the results pane may actually represent the rollup of a number of health monitors, and operators have the option to launch the Health Explorer against any particular health indicator (see later in this list).

Performance Charts Performance charts show performance counter data against time, allowing you to view possible trends. These charts can be customized to change the representation (between line and spline chart types), timeline, and axis scales.

Diagram Views Diagram views show a graphical representation of IT services and distributed applications, and allow you to drill into that representation and view the health state of each object. An example is shown in Figure 11.3

FIGURE 11.3
Diagram view of a distributed application

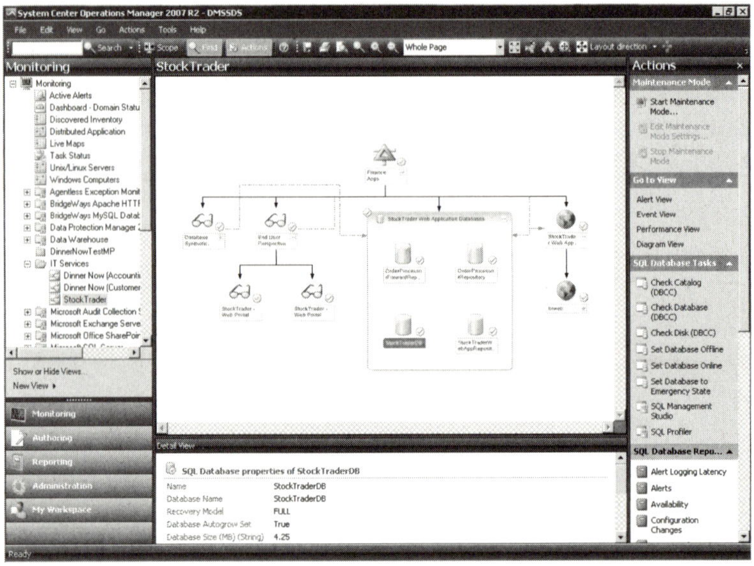

Health Explorer The Health Explorer presents all the individual monitors that together determine the health of a particular object, along with in-depth information regarding the potential cause and remediation should a particular monitor enter a warning or critical state. If available, inline tasks may also be presented in the Health Explorer that you can execute to provide additional diagnostic information or remediate an issue.

IMPORTING MONITORING KNOWLEDGE

The real power of Operations Manager is in the knowledge that is found in the monitors, rules, reports, views, and context-specific information that can be imported into its framework via management packs. Many of these management packs have been created by Microsoft product teams and can be located by visiting the Microsoft Pinpoint website at `http://pinpoint.microsoft.com/en-US/systemcenter/managementpackcatalog`.

Microsoft partners, system integrators, members of the Operations Manager community, and even customers have also created management packs to deliver monitoring and management capability for an entity. Once created, management packs can be easily imported into the product using the Import Management Packs wizard via the Operations Console (see Figure 11.4).

There are essentially two methods through which management packs can be imported:

Import From Disk Operations management packs can be downloaded or copied to a disk that is local (and accessible) to the Operations Console.

Import From Catalog Approved operations management packs are published to an online catalog that can be browsed and imported. This feature was introduced, and is only available, with Operations Manager 2007 R2.

FIGURE 11.4
The Import Management Packs wizard

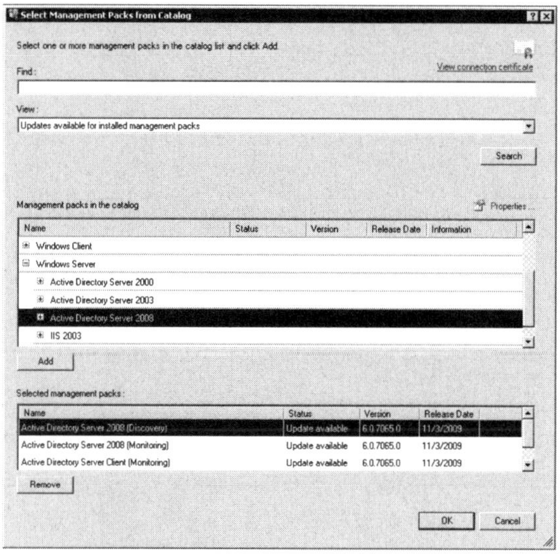

An advantage of importing management packs from the online catalog is that a number of views are available to help you focus on the management packs you need. Those views include all the available management packs, updates available for installed management packs, all management packs released in the past three months, and all management packs released in the past six months. An additional benefit of the online import is that Operations Manager automatically handles the download, import, and cleanup of download files.

When Operations Manager is first installed, a number of management packs are automatically imported and available for use, such as the MP that delivers self-monitoring capabilities for the product. Importing new management packs through the Operations Console is a straightforward process:

1. In the navigation buttons area, select the Administration pane.
2. In the Navigation pane, select Management Packs. All the currently installed management packs and their respective versions will appear in the results pane.
   - If the Actions pane is open, click Import Management Packs.
   - Otherwise, right-click on the Management Packs node in the Navigation pane and select Import Management Packs from the context menu.
3. In the Import Management Packs Wizard:
   - **A.** Click Add to open the drop-down list of import options, and select Add From Catalog.
   - **B.** From the View drop-down list, leave the default, All Management Packs In The Catalog, selected and click Search. The list of available management packs will be displayed in the Management Packs In The Catalog section.
   - **C.** Browse through the list of available management packs, and select one or more to download. Note that multiple selections can be made by holding down the Shift or Ctrl key for multiple or individual selection, respectively.

D. Click Add to add the desired management packs to the list of selected management packs for download.

E. Click OK. Operations Manager will then present the import list and allow you to select to automatically resolve any dependencies by clicking the Resolve link located next to the management pack with that dependency.

F. Click Install and Operations Manager will automate the download and installation of that management pack.

G. On the summary page, click Close.

Changing the Default Monitoring Settings

It is important to remember that no two IT environments are the same, and so monitoring software needs to allow organizations to tune the configuration of their monitoring configuration to their needs. As a rule of thumb:

- The greater the level of detail collected, the greater the impact on local and network resources required to collect and communicate those metrics back to your monitoring control center.
- The more detail that is collected, the greater the opportunity for operators to be inundated with alert and monitoring information—also referred to as *monitoring noise.*

For example, it may be desirable to obtain processor, disk drive, and memory metrics on your core database servers to watch for potential situations that could decrease server (and database) performance, or risk the availability of those databases. Being able to tweak the frequency that those metrics are gathered, or even being able to set different collection configurations based on the target database server and performance parameter being monitored, can help balance the monitoring requirement against the impact of setting those configurations settings.

In Operations Manager, management packs are shipped with a number of configuration settings exposed for organizations to configure. The process of changing a default configuration—such as changing the value of a monitoring parameter, changing the group against which a monitor is enabled, or disabling a monitor completely—is referred to as *overriding.* In fact, many management packs today are being shipped with several of their monitors in a disabled state, or with collection capabilities significantly tuned down, so that installation of a new management pack does not overload operators with monitoring noise. This approach also allows organizations to tune the monitoring capabilities accordingly.

There are a number of ways to override a monitor; here's one:

1. In the navigation buttons area, select the Authoring pane.
2. In the Navigation pane, select Authoring ➤ Management Pack Objects ➤ Monitors.
3. In the results pane, enter **Logical Disk Free Space** in the Look For box and click Find Now.
4. Browse the returned results in the results pane to find the Windows Server 2008 Logical Disk group. Select Logical Disk Free Space.
5. In the Actions pane, select Overrides ➤ Override The Monitor ➤ For All Objects Of Class: Windows Server 2008 Logical Disk. The Override Properties dialog box will appear.
6. Click the check box to the left of the parameter Error % Threshold For System Drives and enter **4** in the Override Value column.

7. Click Apply and you will see the Effective Value field for that parameter updated accordingly. Compare this to the Default Value and Override Value fields.
8. Close the dialog box.

Creating New Monitors

There will often be times where you want to create a new monitor for a specific purpose that is not covered by an existing management pack. Operations Manager provides built-in authoring capabilities that dramatically simplify the ability to create new custom monitors, leveraging templates and a wizard-based interface to walk you, step by step, through the process. Out of the box, the following monitoring templates are provided:

OLE DB Data Source This monitor type allows you to monitor any database by defining a provider to construct a connection string (for example, Microsoft OLE DB Provider for SQL Server), and Structured Query Language (SQL) calls to test connectivity and (optionally) measure connection time, query time, and fetch time performance metrics.

Process Monitoring This monitor type allows you to monitor for processes you want to be running (for example, SQL Server running on your database servers), as well as for processes that you do not want to be running (such as Microsoft Office running on your domain controller). When monitoring processes you do expect, the monitor can also configured to monitor for:

- The minimum and maximum number of instances of a process that should be running at any one time
- Processes running longer than an expected duration, such as checking that an antivirus scan does not run for longer than 10 minutes
- Impact on processor and memory, ensuring that a process does not consume more resources than expected

TCP Port A TCP port monitor allows you to monitor a TCP port running on a target computer.

Unix/Linux Log File This monitor type allows you to verify the existence of a log file on either a single or across a group of Unix or Linux computers, and you can use regular expression matching to test for the existence of a particular string within that log file.

Unix/Linux Service Similar to a Windows service, a service running on Unix or Linux is often referred to as a *daemon*. This monitor allows you to confirm that a daemon is running on one or more Unix or Linux computers in your enterprise.

Web Application A web application monitor is one of the more extensive monitors available to you. At its basic level, it allows you to define a Uniform Resource Locator (URL) that Operations Manager will test for responsiveness. More advanced uses include using a built-in web recorder to record a macro against a website that Operations Manager will replay every time the monitor is executed. In this way, you can test actions such as logging into a web portal and validating expected responses, confirming that the web portal and any related components (for example, a back-end database) are responding as expected.

Windows Service This monitor type allows you to confirm that a selected Windows service is running on one or more target computers.

You can create a new monitor by launching the Add Monitoring Wizard (see Figure 11.5).

FIGURE 11.5
The Add Monitoring Wizard

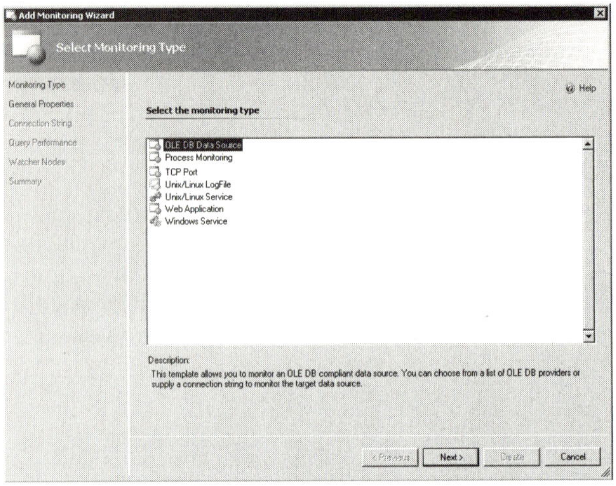

To monitor the presence of the Windows Volume Shadow Copy (VSS) Service (Chapter 4):

1. In the navigation buttons area, select the Authoring pane.
2. At the base of the navigation pane, select the Add Monitoring Wizard link to launch the Add Monitoring Wizard.
3. Select Windows Service and click Next.
4. On the General wizard screen:
   - In Name, enter a suitable name for the monitor, such as **VSS**.
   - In Description, optionally enter some information relating to the monitor.
   - For Management Pack, it is best practice to not put all new objects into the Default Management Pack. This allows you to compartmentalize objects based on an IT service or grouping of similar monitor types, which aids with subsequent export and management of objects within that management pack. Select a management pack you have created, or click New and follow the prompts to create your own new management pack.
5. Click Next.
6. In the Service Details screen, complete the following, then click Next:
   - Next to Service Name, click the browse button and select the computer you wish to use as your reference. Doing so displays all the services currently running on that computer. Select the service you want to monitor; for this example, select the Windows Volume Shadow Copy Service.
   - Next to Targeted Group, click the browse button and specify the computers against which you wish to target this monitor. Click Search to return all available groups, or enter search criteria in the Filter By and Management Pack fields. Select your target computer or group of computers and click OK.

7. The Performance Data screen allows you to set performance thresholds for processor utilization and memory usage. You can also specify the number of samples, over what time interval you want to gather these metrics, and where sampling should be used to average the results to avoid false positive alerts. Click Next.
8. Review the Summary screen and click Create to generate and deploy the monitor.

Creating Your Own Distributed Application Diagrams

While downloading the available management packs will cover most of your monitoring needs, there are situations where you may want to monitor an application for which a management pack does not exist. For example, say the application was custom-built by your own development team, or perhaps the application is not well known. In the same way that you can create new monitors, you can also create your own application health model using the Distributed Application Designer (DAD), all without having to have knowledge of how to write a management pack!

The DAD is a drag-and-drop user interface that allows you to define and group the various components that together comprise your application. It also allows you to identify interrelationships between each component group. This mapping effectively creates a "description" of what needs to be monitored to determine if your application is healthy, and also determines how the health status of one component affects the health of the whole application. When these mappings are saved, Operations Manager will create the health monitors and default reports for your application. You can also create a link to the diagram view for your distributed application in the monitoring pane.

A thorough introduction to the DAD is outside the scope of this book, but Figure 11.6 shows an example of creating a basic web application health model.

Figure 11.6
The Distributed Application Designer

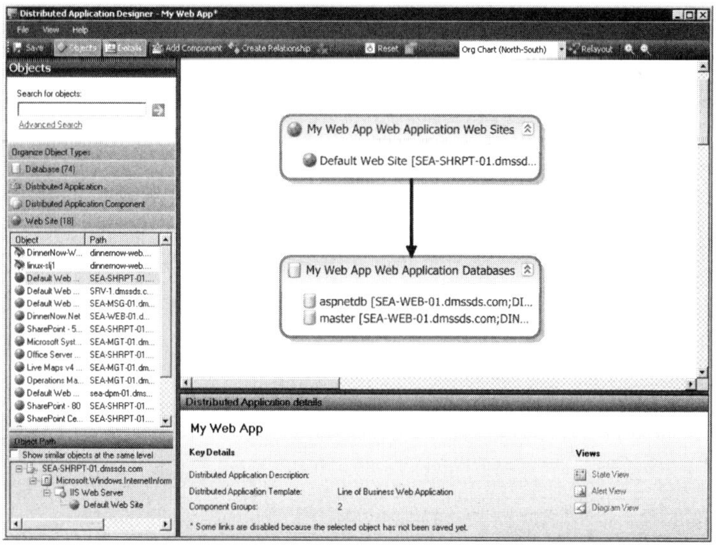

To create a simple health model for a web application, follow these steps:

1. To launch the DAD, click the Authoring pane and select the New Distributed Application link at the bottom of the Navigation pane.

2. In the dialog box, enter a name for your distributed application as well as an optional description, and click the Line of Business Web Application template. Select the management pack in which to store this distributed application, and click OK.

3. The DAD will now appear with a basic framework for web applications. In the left-hand column:

   - Click Database to display all the databases that have been discovered.
   - Click and drag the database(s) of choice into the Application Databases component group. Note that if you attempt to drag it into the Application Web Sites, the designer will not let you complete the action.
   - Click Web Site to display all the discovered web servers.
   - Click and drag the website(s) you want into the Application Web Sites component group.

4. Click Save.

Monitoring the Health and Performance of Key Workloads

This chapter started with the position that one of the best ways to ensure high availability and data resiliency was to proactively monitor the production systems themselves. We have looked at how this can be done in the enterprise datacenter.

There are hundreds of management packs available for use with System Center Operations Manager 2007 and 2007 R2 as well as System Center Essentials 2007 and 2010, which we will discuss later in this chapter. But along with monitoring the health of the general platforms (such as Windows) and applications (such as SQL Server or Microsoft Exchange), we should also be aware of how to proactively monitor the health of the additional high availability, business continuity, and data protection technologies that we have discussed in Chapters 4 through 9, including:

Chapter	Technology
4	System Center Data Protection Manager (DPM)
5	Distributed File Services (DFS)
6	Windows Failover Clustering
7	Exchange Replication
8	SQL Server Database Mirroring
9	Hyper-V R2

NOTE Management Packs are available for download from `http://pinpoint.microsoft.com/en-US/systemcenter/managementpackcatalog`.

Monitoring Data Protection Manager

When monitoring the protection envelope that DPM provides, it is essential to monitor both the DPM servers as well as the data protection activities on the computers protected by DPM. The monitoring intelligence presented in this section is incorporated into System Center via the management pack for DPM.

Monitoring the DPM Server

At the heart of the DPM infrastructure, the key areas of the DPM Server that must be monitored include:

- Validating that the core DPM server services, such as DPM (`msdpm.exe`) and DPM Writer (`DpmWriter.exe`), are running and responding.
- Checking that the databases that DPM uses are healthy and available. While the management pack for DPM provides basic health monitoring of the database, if you have deployed DPM with a Microsoft SQL Server database, additional monitoring can be gained by also utilizing the SQL Server management pack.
- Ensuring that all disks within the DPM storage pool can be accessed by the DPM server, and that protected volumes are configured correctly.
- Monitoring core operating system performance characteristics, such as processor and memory utilization, to ensure that the operating system is performing within expected boundaries.

Monitoring Data Protection Activities

Providing that the DPM Server is operating as expected, the next question that has to be answered is whether the computers within the protection realm of DPM are being fully protected. Some of the monitoring activities that must be performed here include:

- Validating that the DPM server is able to connect to the DPM agents installed on protected computers
- Identifying if any protection groups have synchronization or consistency check failures that require additional attention
- Confirming the integrity of protected data within the DPM storage pool against its data source, and when a recovery operation is performed

While the validation, identification, and confirmation activities can be performed from within the DPM console, they are automated through the DPM management pack so that any issues can be raised through the Operations Manager console for a centralized and appropriate level of response.

Monitoring Distributed File Services

When thinking about monitoring DFS, there are two areas you must consider: DFS namespace (DFS-N) and DFS replication (DFS-R).

Monitoring DFS Namespaces

DFS namespace (DFS-N) enables shared folders located on different servers to be grouped virtually into a namespace that, when accessed from a computer, gives the impression of being a unified set of folders. Ensuring the health and performance of your DFS-N implementation requires the following:

- Confirming that the DFS service is running on namespace servers and identifying any errors during its operation
- Ensuring connectivity of namespace servers to Active Directory and that the DFS metadata is accessible
- Monitoring the DFS namespace metadata, including its integrity, and that the namespace, DFS folders, and DFS folder targets are represented correctly.
- Ensuring the availability of DFS folders and folder targets from computers

These capabilities and more are incorporated into the management pack for DFS namespaces, which can be downloaded from the Microsoft PinPoint catalog listed earlier.

Monitoring DFS Replication

DFS Replication (DFS-R) keeps folders synchronized across servers using an approach that only transfers the differential of data within those folders between servers with a DFS-R relationship. For example, DFS-R is used to replicate Sysvol between domain controllers.

Successfully monitoring DFS-R requires the following:

- Confirming the health and availability of the DFS-R service on computers where that service is installed and enabled
- Discovering and monitoring replication groups
- Discovering and monitoring volumes hosting replicated folders, including the size of memory allocated
- Monitoring the integrity and availability of replicated folders across computers
- Identifying replication backlogs and the average time to clear those backlogs
- Identifying the number of replication conflict files that have been reported, and monitoring the amount of space being used to store those replication conflicts

For full monitoring of your DFS-R environment, System Center provides end-to-end monitoring through its management pack for DFS-R.

Monitoring Windows Failover Clustering

To provide high availability, Windows failover clusters use a variety of nodes, networks, resource groups, and storage to ensure that applications continue to be available in case one of the cluster nodes becomes inoperative. Ensuring the health and performance of Windows failover clusters requires monitoring across the failover cluster components, such as the following:

- Validating the configuration of the hardware of each node in the cluster, and ensuring that the cluster service has been started and is operational
- Checking that permissions required to operate the cluster are correctly configured

- Confirming network settings and availability so that the cluster can operate successfully and that applications running on the cluster can be successfully communicated with
- Ensuring the viability of the cluster storage, confirming that it is available, performing, and mounted correctly on each cluster node

System Center delivers a comprehensive set of monitoring for Windows failover clusters through the Failover Clustering management pack.

Monitoring Exchange Replication

As you learned in Chapter 7, Exchange 2010 delivers a number of enhancements in its approach to high availability that dramatically simplify the planning and deployment of Microsoft's latest messaging technology. Exchange 2010 introduces database availability groups (DAGs) as a collection of up to 16 mailbox servers, each hosting copies of mailbox databases from the other mailbox server in the DAG. If one mailbox server fails, its mailbox data can be recovered and accessed via another mailbox server in the DAG.

To monitor the health of Exchange 2010 replication, the following PowerShell cmdlets are provided as part of the Exchange installation:

`Test-ReplicationHealth` `Test-ReplicationHealth` is run against any mailbox server in the DAG and provides a thorough series of tests to validate that replication is healthy and active and that the Active Manager is available. It also confirms the health of the underlying cluster service, quorum, and network components.

`Test-MRSHealth` `Test-MRSHealth` tests the health of the Exchange Mailbox Replication Service that runs on client access servers.

The management pack for Exchange 2010 provides thorough monitoring of your Exchange 2010 deployment by System Center, and includes extensive and detailed monitoring of individual mailbox databases as well as of its replication capabilities. For more information and to download this management pack, visit the Microsoft management pack download site listed earlier.

Monitoring SQL Mirroring

SQL Server stores mirroring status information within a table in the MSDB database, which is updated (by default) once per minute. Information stored in the table can be queried using one of two tools:

Database Mirroring Monitor The Database Mirroring Monitor can be found in SQL Server Management Studio on Standard or Enterprise editions of SQL Server. It allows you to view the current operational health of the mirror, configure warning thresholds against performance counters, and view information reported by those performance counters.

Stored Procedures SQL Server provides a set of `dbmmonitor` system stored procedures that interact with the mirroring status table. The system stored procedure `sp_dbmmonitorresults` can be used to view the status table, as well as to trigger an update of the status table.

The type of status information that you can obtain from the table includes:

- Confirmation that the principal database and mirror database are both online and running
- Validation that the mirror is operational and successfully moving data from the principal database to the mirror database
- Identification of any backlog between the principal database and the mirror database

- The ability to compare performance trends and identify any issues or bottlenecks
- The operating mode (high performance, high safety without automatic failover, or high safety with automatic failover) of the mirror

System Center provides detailed monitoring of your SQL Server deployment through the management pack for SQL Server.

Monitoring Virtualization

In Chapter 9, we discussed how virtualization can solve data protection and availability challenges in new ways. At the same time, virtualization platforms must also be protected and made highly available.

In Chapter 10, we explored the differences between managing and deploying physical resources with System Center Configuration Manager and virtual resources with System Center Virtual Machine Manager (VMM). But monitoring virtualization can be done through multiple tools, including not only VMM, but also Operations Manager (discussed earlier in this chapter) and SC Essentials (discussed in the next section).

Monitoring virtualization workloads is more complicated than observing other applications since it enables containers (VMs) of applications, which in turn require management and monitoring. Without proper monitoring of the operating system and applications inside each VM, you will have a restricted view of overall system performance and status. Internal VM monitoring aside, there are important performance counters worth observing to check the health and stability of your virtualization platforms.

With the increasing use of virtualization, specifically the Hyper-V role on Windows Server 2008 and Windows Server 2008 R2, understanding the health of the Hyper-V service is a critical piece of ensuring the health of virtualized guests and networks running on a Windows Server virtualization host.

Windows Server 2008 and 2008 R2

As part of understanding the health of Hyper-V, it is also important to assess the health and performance of the server that is acting as the virtualization host, as follows:

Availability Ensure that core operating system services are operational, that the system is configured correctly, that there are no device or networking issues, and that hard drive and memory capacity is not approaching a critical low.

Performance Monitor the performance of the system processor, the performance of physical and logical disks, the availability and performance of local memory, and the load on physical network adapters.

For full monitoring capabilities, System Center provides the management pack for Windows Server, which delivers detailed monitoring and knowledge across availability, performance, security, and configuration categories.

Hyper-V Host Role

Monitoring for the health of the Hyper-V role is primarily focused on ensuring that the following services are started and operational:

- Hyper-V Image Management Service (`vhdsvc`)

- Hyper-V Virtual Machine Management Service (`vmms`)
- Hyper-V Networking Management Service (`Nvspwmi`)

Two sets of performance counters specific to Hyper-V provide the fundamental components for monitoring:

Hyper-V Virtual Machine Health Summary Includes two counters: Health OK and Health Critical

Hyper-V Hypervisor Provides insight into the number of logical processors the system can see, the number of VMs running, and the total number of virtual processors presented to them

As with other performance and health measures, the processor load on a physical system is a critical indicator. It can, however, be complicated and less than intuitive to capture and measure. It is also important to monitor the status of the free space and free memory available on the virtualization host, especially when VMs have been configured with dynamically expanding virtual disks, and to ensure that sufficient memory remains for future VMs.

Typical performance indicators visible in Task Manager for things like storage (queue depth) and available memory should be evaluated in much the same way as other Windows-based systems, as they are visible within the parent operating system partition. It is interesting to note that processor utilization is not as easy to view—the processor load of a VM is more complicated to view.

NOTE Tony Voellm has a great blog where he discusses Hyper-V performance tuning and monitoring at `http://blogs.msdn.com/tvoellm`.

System Center delivers this monitoring through the management pack for Hyper-V, which also discovers the virtual networks and VMs that are running on hosts as well as their state (running, suspended, or stopped). Figure 11.7 shows one of the views available in the Hyper-V management pack.

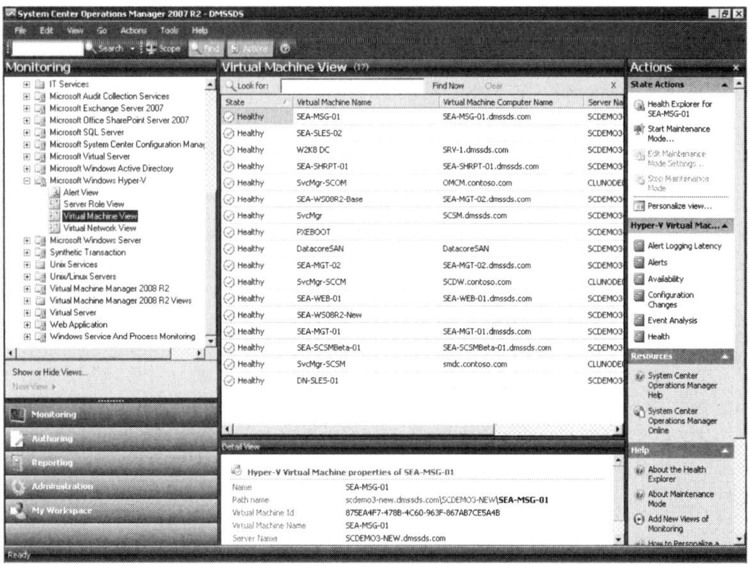

FIGURE 11.7 View from the Hyper-V management pack

Monitoring in Midsized Organizations Using System Center Essentials

In Chapter 10, we discussed systems management and deployment from both an enterprise perspective and for midsized organizations, as well as what was unique in regard to virtual infrastructure components compared with physical ones. In that chapter, we used:

- System Center Configuration Manager for systems management in enterprises
- System Center Virtual Machine Manager for virtualization hosts and guests

We also mentioned that many of those same capabilities were also available for midsized organizations through a unified tool called System Center Essentials (SCE) 2010. SCE 2010 also includes a subset of the monitoring tools found in System Center Operations Manager, which was discussed earlier in this chapter. The goal is to provide a complete tool for physical and virtual deployment, management, and monitoring for environments with up to 500 PCs and 50 servers.

Throughout the book, we've recommended data protection and availability technologies that were equally applicable to datacenters, as well as small and medium businesses. Systems monitoring is needed in these virtual datacenters, but it should be available without the complexity necessary for monitoring tens of thousands of computers.

So, for the rest of this chapter, we will look at monitoring systems using the methods discussed in the first part of this chapter but that are applicable to smaller environments.

Introducing SC Essentials 2010

SCE 2010 provides a single UI that manages all its deployment and management (Chapter 10) functions, as well as discovery and monitoring, as shown in Figure 11.8.

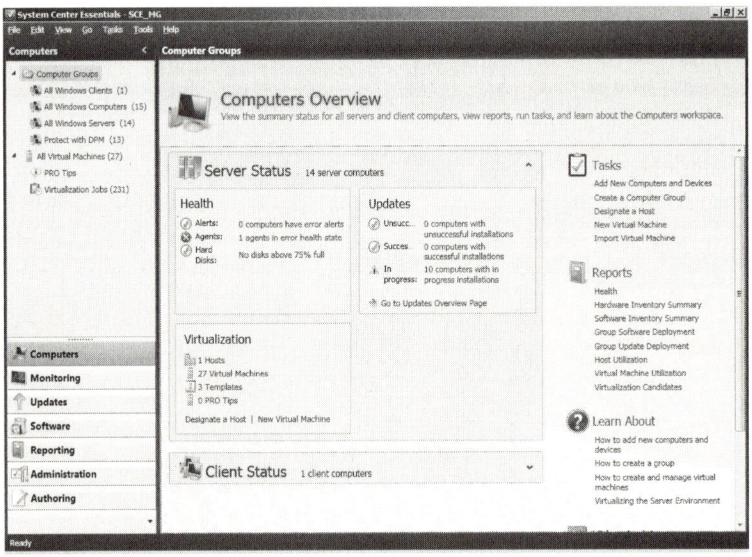

FIGURE 11.8
The SCE 2010 management console

In this chapter, we will look at the administration and monitoring functions.

Discovering Midsized Resources

Similar to Operations Manager, SCE can regularly reach out to your production environment to find new computers that should be monitored and managed. To configure this, select the Administration tab in the lower-left corner of the SCE console, as shown in Figure 11.9.

FIGURE 11.9
SCE 2010, Administration tab

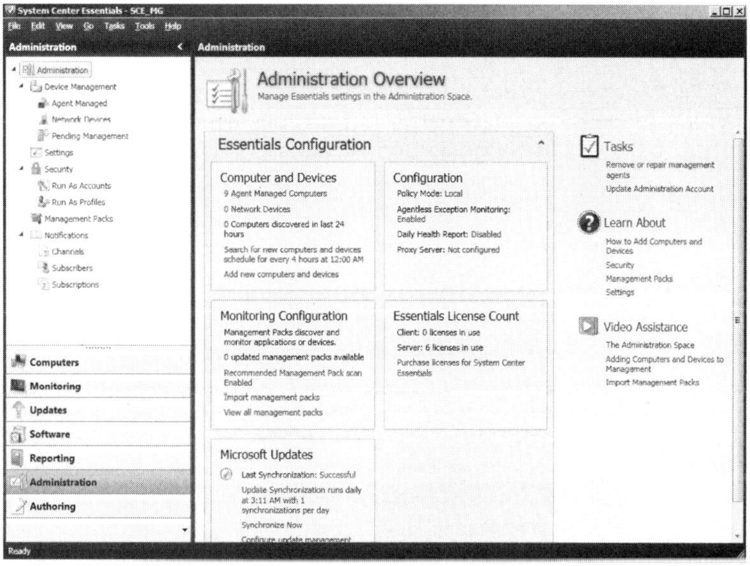

On the Administration page, notice the Computers And Devices box in the upper-left corner. When you first installed SCE, you configured it to search for new machines each day. To manually force a search:

1. Click the Add New Computers And Devices link under Computers And Devices.
2. On the first screen of the Computer And Device Management Wizard, you can choose to discover either Windows Computers or Network Devices. If you are following along from a trial installation of SCE 2010, click Windows Computers.
3. On the Auto or Advanced? screen of the wizard, you can choose to have SCE search your entire Active Directory domain automatically, or do an Advanced Discovery to let you search for specific machine types, such as servers or clients.
4. On the Discovery Method screen, you can let SCE search the entire Active Directory for the machine types that you just chose, or you can browse for or type computer names. By clicking the Browse button to the right of the wizard, we manually entered the names of two of the SQL servers that we used in Chapter 8, as shown in Figure 11.10.
5. Enter the credentials of an account with Administrator privileges on the local machines that you selected so that the agent can be installed.

FIGURE 11.10
Choosing new machines to begin managing with SCE 2010

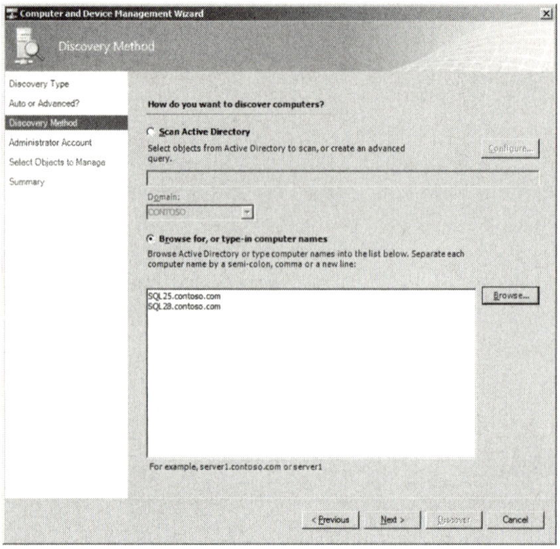

6. A list of the machines will appear for confirmation in the Discovery Results screen of the wizard. If you chose for SCE to automatically discover the machines, this screen will present the findings, and you can select the machines you want to add. If you manually entered the machines, they will appear here in their fully qualified domain names.
7. Click Finish and a task will be launched to install the agent on each machine. You can watch each one complete, or close the Task Status box, which will continue even if you close the status screen.

When the agents have successfully installed, you will be able to see the new machines in the list of Agent Managed machines by expanding the tree in the left pane and clicking Administration, Device Management, and then Agent Managed.

With the devices now managed by SCE 2010, we can begin monitoring their health and application service availability.

Monitoring Midsized Environments

To monitor the health and condition of your midsized IT organization (up to 500 PCs and 50 servers), simply start up the SCE management console and go to the Computers tab, as shown in Figure 11.8 earlier.

There is a great deal of information available from the main screen area, which is divided into a few sections:

Server Status Shows the health status of the machines running Windows Server (see Figure 11.11).

The Server Status window is divided into three areas of information:

Health Within the health area, four kinds of information are displayed, with links directly to additional screens that can offer more information:

- Alert Conditions, so that you can immediately click on any machines that are actively flagging new alerts that need attention

FIGURE 11.11
The SCE computer view, server status

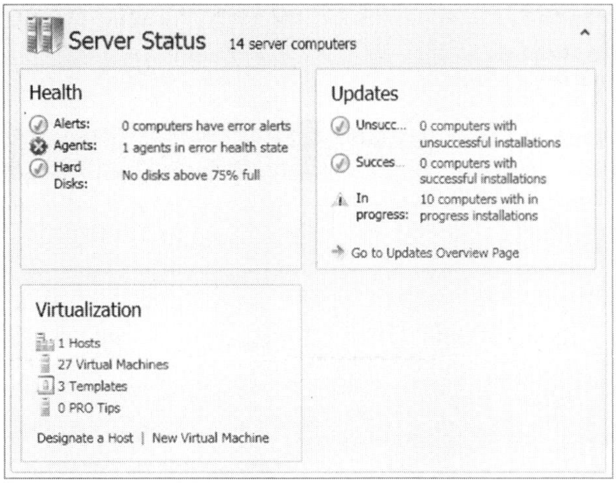

- Agent Status, regarding the health of the monitoring agents themselves on each machine
- Hard Disks, showing if any hard disks are full past the set threshold of 75 percent by default
- Unmanaged, indicating if there are any machines that are discovered but not yet under management by SCE

Updates Provides a quick overview of the software updates that have been successfully or unsuccessfully deployed throughout the environment, as discussed in Chapter 6:

- Unsuccessful lists and links to any machines that failed to receive their software updates
- Successful lists and links to the machines that did receive their software updates
- In Progress lists and links to the machines that are pending software updates at the present time

Virtualization In the Virtualization area, you can see:

- How many hosts are managed by SCE
- How many virtual machines exist across all the hosts
- How many virtual machine templates are available for new VM deployments
- How many Pro Tips are installed

You can also designate a new server as a virtualization host, as well as create a new virtual machine.

Client Status Indicates the health status of the Windows client machines, as well as their software updates status, with the same kinds of information as the Server Status window.

Action Bar The bar on the right side, which includes common tasks, reports, and videos so you can learn more.

In the left pane, the all-up view is the top of the tree. However, by clicking one of the groups of computers, such as All Windows Computers, you can see a list of the machines in your environment and their specific alerts, agents, and other status information, as shown in Figure 11.12.

FIGURE 11.12
Computer details list

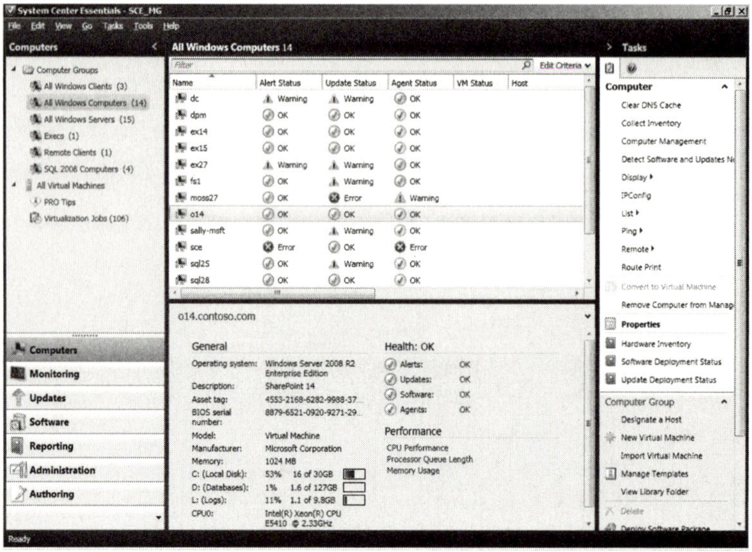

Almost everything on this page is a link to specific guidance or deeper information on the topic at hand. It is that deeper knowledge that makes this level of systems monitoring extensible and practical not only for large enterprises, but also midsized organizations.

Knowledge Applied to Midsized Scenarios

Earlier in the chapter, we discussed the management packs that Operations Manager uses to monitor the health and the various applications and services in your environment. The MPs are usually built by the development teams of those products or other relevant experts in the community. For example, the Exchange 2010 development team wrote the Exchange 2010 management pack. This is the same for SQL Server, SharePoint, Windows, DPM, and so on.

And as we mentioned earlier, the MP contains not only which metrics should be monitored, but all the embedded knowledge to isolate why something may be broken and recommend resolutions for it.

USING SYSTEM CENTER MANAGEMENT PACKS WITH SCE

One of the design goals of System Center management packs is to utilize the same embedded knowledge and monitoring models of the MPs for both enterprise and midsized organizations. Because of this, almost all management packs that are usable by System Center Operations Manager 2007 and 2007 R2 are also usable by System Center Essentials 2007 and 2010.

There are a few minor differences:

- Most MPs by design can be more or less verbose, so that enterprise (SC Operations Manager) users can gain extra insight into the details of their environments, whereas midsized IT administrators (SCE) are not overwhelmed with too much information that likely doesn't apply to smaller environments. As an option, you can enable the additional verbosity and detail within SCE, if desired.
- SC Operations Manager, by default, ships with a wide range of MPs and makes the rest available via an online catalog at Microsoft.com. SCE auto-discovers the MPs that are relevant to your environment after building an inventory of what is running on your computers, and then offers to download only those MPs that apply.

By clicking the Monitoring tab in the lower-left corner, you can see the Monitoring Overview, as shown in Figure 11.13.

FIGURE 11.13
SCE 2010, Monitoring Overview

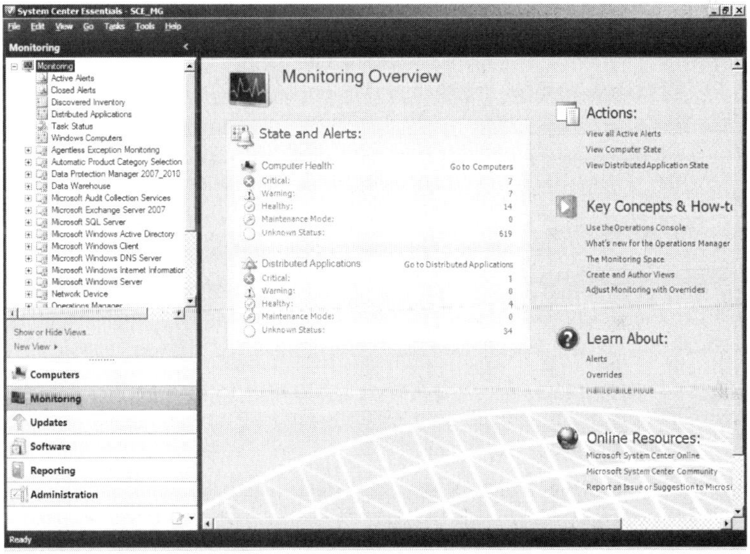

This presents us with SCE screens that are similar to those in Operations Manager. By expanding the tree on the left pane, you can see all the MPs that are currently installed, as well as the rich information that is available within each.

By double-clicking on the error alert of a machine, you are launched into the Health Explorer for that machine. The Health Explorer in SC Essentials behaves like the Health Explorer in Operations Manager by aggregating all the relevant knowledge into a tree-based view, which expands on any error condition. The result is that you can easily find the root causes of most system problems, along with the likely cause and recommended resolution, as shown in Figure 11.14.

FIGURE 11.14
SCE 2010, Health Explorer

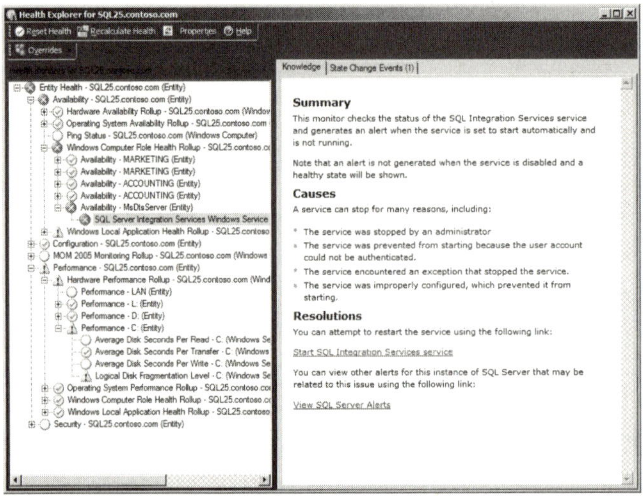

Virtualization Monitoring in Midsized Datacenters

Because virtualization management is considered a key aspect of systems management in midsized organizations, many of the capabilities from System Center Virtual Machine Manager 2008 R2 are included within SCE 2010. This can be seen in three aspects.

Computers View: Server Status In Figure 11.11, you saw the Server Status window of the Computers view; one of the three main sections was Virtualization. This section provides an overview of the number of VMs in the environment, the number of managed hosts, and the number of templates available for deploying new VMs.

Computers View: Computer Details List In Figure 11.12, you saw the list of machines managed by SCE, with specific status for alerts, agents, and so on. If the machine is in fact a virtual machine, then additional details regarding which host it is running on are also be displayed.

Computers View: Machine Details Finally, by double-clicking on any machine, you open a pop-up with at least two tabs, which are standard for any machine.

The first tab includes overview information, including hardware details as well as links to the same alerts, agent status, and other links that we have discussed so far.

The second tab lists the software installed on the machine. This should be the same as the installed programs list of the machine's Control Panel.

If the machine is a virtual machine, a third tab is present with the virtual hardware characteristics that were configured using SCE, VMM, or the Hyper-V console, as shown in Figure 11.15. If the machine is powered down, these settings can be configured directly from here. For more information on these virtual hardware settings, see Chapter 10.

FIGURE 11.15
Machine Details: Virtual Hardware configuration

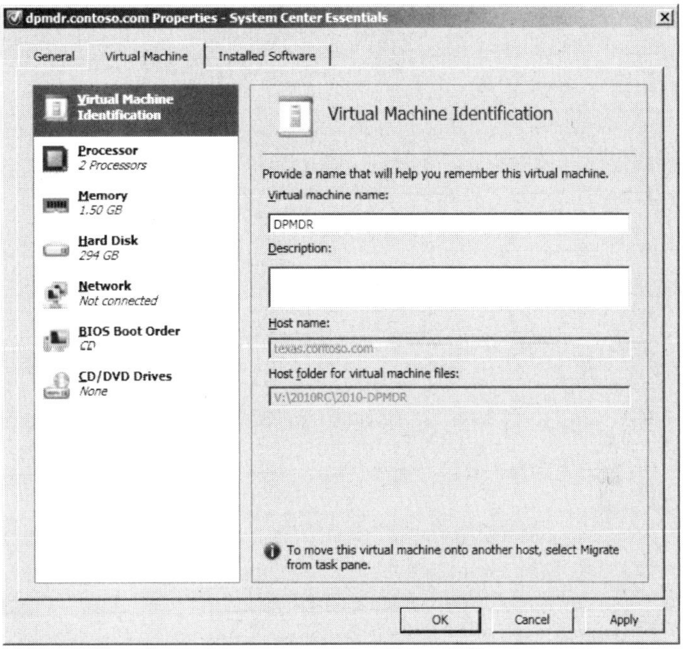

Summary

System Center provides a rich set of monitoring capabilities that can extend across the dynamic range of today's datacenters.

System Center Operations Manager covers the most challenging and complex of environments, including monitoring of Windows, Unix, and Linux computers and their workloads, as well as monitoring of network devices. With an extensive set of partners, the monitoring reach of Operations Manager extends across nearly every vendor and deployment type.

System Center Virtual Machine Manager addresses the special monitoring requirements of the virtualized components of your environment, including Hyper-V as well as VMware.

System Center Essentials brings together the most applicable aspects of these enterprise technologies, along with some of the deployment and maintenance aspects of System Center Configuration Manager, as a unified tool for midsized organizations.

Whether you are an enterprise (using SCOM and SCVMM) or a midsized organization (using SCE), the goal is to start looking beyond solving point problems like Exchange availability or SQL protection, and begin monitoring and managing your environment in a consistent way.

Chapter 12

Business Continuity and Disaster Recovery

Get your data out of the building.

That is the introduction to this chapter. It will also be the closing words in the summary, and one of the main themes in between.

We'll talk about why, both from an operational perspective as well as a regulatory perspective. We'll explore various methods for doing it. And we'll share some anecdotes on how to validate it. But for our final chapter, the most important thing to think about is getting your data out of the building.

What Makes BC and DR So Special?

For many, the concept of backup has been considered a tactical tax, while *disaster recovery* (DR) and *business continuity* (BC) have been thought of as either strategic or lofty and unattainable. Those are extremes descriptions, where the reality of BC/DR often lies somewhere in the middle. Most of this book has focused on pragmatically understanding and deploying protection and availability technologies. We will do the same for various aspects of BC/DR, but first, we should look at what frames the difference between backup and BC/DR. BC/DR normally has two facets:

Business Continuity Planning This planning process is company-wide and culture-changing.

Industry and Regional Regulations These are regulations that force compliance from an operational point of view, as well as from a technical perspective.

Real Business Continuity Planning

Throughout this book, when we have referred to the terms disaster recovery and business continuity, we have alluded to the fact that they are not just technology solutions but have much to do with people and process. To prove the point, DRI International (`www.drii.org`) has been certifying professionals for over 20 years, first as Certified Disaster Recovery Planners (CDRP) and now as Certified Business Continuity Planners (CBCP).

MCSE and CBCP

If you are certified in technologies such as the Microsoft Certified Systems Engineer (MCSE), you might be interested to know that the CBCP is a different kind of certification. Sure, there are classes to attend and tests to take, but they also do background checks, contact former customers, and so forth. At the time that I received my CBCP, there were nearly one million Microsoft certified professionals (MCPs) and under 5,000 CBCPs.

Here are the 10 official professional practices for a CBCP, along with a summary of each practice, taken from the DRI website (`https://www.drii.org/professionalprac/index.php`). You can refer to the site for their formal definitions.

1. Program Initiation and Management Unlike backup, which is often just an assumed part of IT, BC/DR programs often require some level of executive sponsorship or endorsement before doing anything. You will be enlisting a lot of non-IT personnel and looking closely at a range of business processes, so getting as many of the relevant players identified as early as possible will help you later.

2. Risk Evaluation and Control We discussed this in Chapters 2 and 3, when we looked at what could go wrong, including people issues, facility issues, and technology issues. Part of the evaluation will consist of understanding the potential losses from each kind of crisis. In some cases, a risk evaluation will uncover some opportunities for easy-to-do enhancements that negate the risk, such as using some of the protection and availability technologies covered in Chapters 4–9.

3. Business Impact Analysis As we discussed in Chapter 2, you will need to turn technology issues into financial terms, so that all of the decision makers (technical and business) can make an informed decision as to the severity of the risks and the viability of solutions. Here is where you will use the formulas as well the RTO/RPO and SLA from Chapter 2.

4. Business Continuity Strategies Use your findings from the risk evaluation and the business impact analysis to form your initial strategies and tactics for reducing risk in ways that are financially justifiable. Here, you will be matching your RPO/RTO goals with the financial impact, so that you can determine which solution components have the right TCO/ROI.

5. Emergency Response and Operations Do you know what to do during the crisis itself? Develop and enact a plan defining what steps the organization will need to take during the site-level emergency until the appropriate authorities arrive.

6. Business Continuity Plans Based on the quantified business impacts and reasonable risks, develop and implement your actual business continuity plan that recognizes the specific needs of your business units and your technical capabilities. This is often the only phase (out of the 10 listed) that many IT folks think about when discussing DR or BC.

7. Awareness and Training Programs BC/DR plans don't work if the IT staff and a few executives are the only ones who know about them. You have to educate people and change the company culture. Some changes are small, such as perhaps holding an annual one-hour training session on what to do during a disaster, or training "floor captains" and asking them to train their peers. Other changes related to how people think about securing their data may require more work and perhaps additional technology controls. The point is to be sure that BC/DR really is a company thing and not an IT thing.

8. Business Continuity Plan Exercise, Audit, and Maintenance The best BC/DR tests are those that fail—meaning that, if your BC/DR test passes all your expectations, you probably weren't thorough enough. The failures will teach you where you need to revisit your plans and perhaps implement additional measures. The key here is to routinely test your plan.

In addition, you need to consider how often your plan should be reassessed. If some of your key business processes change, if your company falls under different or new regulations than it did before, or if you haven't assessed your plan in a year, revisit your plan.

9. Crisis Communications Can you imagine your customers first hearing about some crisis because one of your coworkers happened to tell an outsider that the crisis was really bad, the company lost all its data, and it is doubtful that the company will recover?

Not just for crises, but in general, your company likely already has (or should have) designated spokespeople who will speak to external agencies, media, and other stakeholders. Those folks should also be part of your BC/DR plan, and it should be a high-priority item during your initial BC/DR recovery steps that they be kept up-to-date.

10. Coordination with External Agencies Depending on the size or industry of your organization, you may need to align your crisis-handling and recovery plans with local, regional, or national agencies. And even if you don't officially need to be aligned, some of these agencies (such as Federal Emergency Management Agency [FEMA]) may have local programs to help you think about your BC/DR plans in new ways and be better prepared. Your recovery plan may also have mandates based on the industry you are in. We will talk about some of the more common regulations later in this chapter.

CBCP Practices 2 and 3 deal with the quantitative metrics of the business impact due to a technology problem. This is done early in the process so that you can assess your risk and understand the scope of your business continuity planning task. We covered this in Chapter 2, including BIA, SLA, RPO, RTO, and other metrics.

CBCP Practice 4 is about what can you do in advance (which falls under the term *risk mitigation*) and what will you plan to do when something does happen. All of the high-availability technologies that we covered in Chapters 5–9 fall into this category, where you have deployed a technology proactively in order to mitigate the risk of a systems failure. Similarly, Chapter 4 showed us better ways to back up so that we can reliably recover if we need to.

CBCP Practice 6 is about creating what most of us think of as the business continuity plan. But, as you can see from the list, the plan will include much more than just technology. Technology has to be part of it, because most of the other processes and planned steps will assume that the company has an IT infrastructure that is running and that has data.

To state what may be obvious by now, CBCP Practices 1, 5, 7, 8, 9, and 10 have little or nothing to do with technology. But this book does, so we will spend the rest of our time talking about the technology aspects of disaster recovery and business continuity.

DISASTER UN-PREPAREDNESS

One of the scarier challenges of disaster preparedness is the different assessments and assumptions between a company's business executives and its IT leadership. Often, they hold very different opinions as to how prepared the company is.

An EMC/RoperASW survey of 274 executives at major US corporations and other large organizations found that, while just 14 percent of business leaders feel that their important business information is very vulnerable to being lost in the event of a disaster, 52 percent of information technology executives in the same organizations state that their data is very vulnerable.

The danger is that if the senior executives incorrectly assume that they are already protected enough (whatever "enough" means to them), then IT will have challenges in acquiring budget and prioritization to get what is needed.

According to Carl Greiner, senior vice president of META Group:

> *Even with everything that has transpired over the past two years, there's still a perception that protecting data is an IT problem, not necessarily a business priority. Resuming normal business operations after three days would cost a company millions and millions of dollars and/or immeasurable damage in terms of customer satisfaction and reputation. These results would suggest that business leaders need to open their eyes, ears and most likely their wallets to address some vulnerability in their organizations.*
>
> `www.ContinuityCentral.com/news0405.htm`

Framing a preparedness conversation with terms such as compliance regulations can often reset the business owners' viewpoint, so that both sides can have a mutual assessment of your preparedness.

Regulatory Compliance

BC/DR may be a mandated thing, but not as often as you might think. For the last several years, regulatory compliance has continued to gain attention in IT environments. There are several regulations out there that apply to different industries, as well as to different geographies. But what has always surprised me is that so many of the regulations mandate a result without specifying a method. This has resulted in an entire industry of consultants who each push his or her own favorite technologies and best practices in an attempt to comply with their interpretation of the regulation.

Regulations That Everyone Points to but Nobody Knows

When you say the phrase *regulatory compliance* to someone in IT, most folks will raise an eyebrow or sigh dramatically and list mandates such as:

- Continuity of operations (CO-OP) for the US federal government
- Health Insurance Portability and Accountability Act (HIPAA)
- Joint Commission on the Accreditation of Healthcare Organizations (JCAHO)
- Gramm-Leach-Bliley (GLB) for US financial institutions
- US Securities & Exchange Commission (SEC) and US Treasury
- Sarbanes-Oxley (SOX) for publicly traded companies in the United States

For the most part, what you should remember about these regulations is that they are not typically about technology, and certainly not about data protection or high availability or disaster recovery. They are about the organization as a whole, but there may be data dependencies, which is why IT folks often shudder when the regulations are mentioned.

In the next few sections, we will look at some of the components of the various regulations that are most commonly applied to data protection, high availability, or BC/DR technology initiatives.

A few disclaimers:

- Deploying a technology will rarely make you compliant to an entire regulation. It will enable you to check a box related to a tactical objective, which is part of a subparagraph, which is under a section, which is part of a regulation.
- The clippings of the regulations that follow are believed to be current as of this writing, but the regulations are periodically reviewed and updated.
- Your satisfactory compliance with the parts of the regulations related to data protection is based on your auditors' assessment, as well as the judgment of your executive leadership who are ultimately responsible for a lack of compliance. One of the goals of this chapter is to help you understand where data protection fits within the broader regulations. There are some expensive consultants out there who would be happy to engage with you, so that they can apply their interpretation or experience to the regulations and your business.

Before we look at the industry-specific regulations that many of us may have heard of before (and some that you may not have), let's start by looking at one law that can affect your data protection strategy as much as any industry-specific regulation.

PLAN FOR YOUR TAPES TO FAIL

In 2007, Symantec's Michael Parker, global product marketing manager for Backup Exec, said that "85 percent of systems are not backed up. And even companies that do attempt to back up their systems can be in for a rude awakening as 17 percent to 40 percent of tape restores fail."

Source: `www.internetnews.com/storage/article.php/3672326/`

The E-SIGN Law

In 2000, President Clinton signed the Electronic Signatures in Global and National Commerce Act, known as E-SIGN (`www.gpo.gov/fdsys/pkg/PLAW-106publ229`). The federal law gives electronic signatures, contracts, and records the same validity as their handwritten and hard-copy counterparts.

> *Soon, vast warehouses of paper will be replaced by servers the size of VCRs. Online contracts will now have the same legal force as equivalent paper contracts. Signing one's name online will soon become a common way to hire a lawyer, sign a mortgage, open a brokerage account, or sign an insurance contract.*
>
> *President Bill Clinton at the signing of E-SIGN Law, June 2000*

In retrospect, 10 years later, there are still many warehouses full of paper contracts and other important documents, likely to the relief of many offsite storage companies. The timeframe may be up to debate, but as the amount of key information continues to radically expand, many legal documents are now created, signed, and stored without ever being printed on paper. To whatever degree your organization protects valuable contracts and other signed documents, electronic documentation should also be guarded.

Where this becomes even more interesting is if your company (or your client) uses a courier service or some other means of storing your paper documents offsite. Are you protecting your electronic data at least as well? Ironically, data cartridges are much smaller than boxes of paper and folders, so the actual amount of required physical storage is comparably much smaller.

In recognition of this, companies that have traditionally stored paper documents are beginning to offer data vaulting services; the data is replicated directly to the repository instead of shuttling tapes.

CONSIDER THIS

According to a 2004 study by McGladrey and Pullen (www.mcgladrey.com), every year, 1 out of 500 datacenters will experience a severe disaster. That same study reveals that 43 percent of companies that experience a significant disaster never reopen.

CO-OP, THE GOVERNMENT'S CONTINUOUS OPERATIONS MANDATE

What the private sector calls business continuity, the US public sector (government) calls continuity of operations (CO-OP). CO-OP is not a new directive. The mandate for the government to continue to provide core services no matter what has occurred dates all the way back to the 1780s. But we can focus on a few defining documents and the subsections that relate to technology.

The recent wave of CO-OP started with Federal Preparedness Circular (FPC) 65 in July 1999, which was titled Federal Executive Branch Continuity of Operations (CO-OP). The focus at that time was to ensure that the executive branch of government continued to offer key services. It had a clear overall goal but left most of the implementation details to each department within the executive branch.

It was updated with FPC 67 in April 2001, with a directive on creating alternative facilities that could resume delivering key services within 12 hours of a crisis but was geographically remote from the primary center of operations. This spawned a wave of investigation into secondary IT and service facilities soon after. The challenge was that the directives still expected each department to assure its own resilience.

Three years later, FPC 65 was updated with two significant changes. More specifics were added around how the goals were to be met, and the Federal Emergency Management Agency (FEMA) was placed into an oversight role above the other agencies for purposes of assuring CO-OP compliance. This was in part in recognition that, after 3 years, many departments had not yet delivered a CO-OP plan on their own.

Three more years went by, and in the wake of disasters like Hurricane Katrina, where many were disappointed with FEMA's ability to react quickly and resume service, more mandates came in the form of DHS Homeland Security Presidential Directive 20: National Continuity Policy (HSPD-20). The entire policy is at `www.fema.gov/txt/library/fpc65_0604.txt`, but the most relevant sections as they relate to data protection and availability are as follows:

4. *Continuity requirements shall be incorporated into daily operations of all executive departments and agencies. As a result of the asymmetric threat environment, adequate warning of potential emergencies that could pose a significant risk to the homeland might not be available, and therefore all continuity planning shall be based on the assumption that no such warning will be received. Emphasis will be placed upon geographic dispersion of leadership, staff, and infrastructure in order to increase survivability and maintain uninterrupted Government Functions. Risk management principles shall be applied to ensure that appropriate operational readiness decisions are based on the probability of an attack or other incident and its consequences.*

The key in HSPD-20 section 4 is the emphasis on geographic dispersion of infrastructure in order to increase survivability and maintain uninterrupted functions. This clarified some of the earlier mandates and specifically called out the need for IT in secondary facilities that were near ready to go.

11. *Continuity requirements for the Executive Office of the President (EOP) and executive departments and agencies shall include the following:*

    C. *Vital resources, facilities, and records must be safeguarded, and official access to them must be provided;*

    D. *Provision must be made for the acquisition of the resources necessary for continuity operations on an emergency basis;*

Here in HSPD-20 section 11, we can see mandates that relate directly to backup (c), as well as securing additional IT resources for failover or rapid restoration (d).

16. *The Secretary of Homeland Security shall:*

    F. *Develop and promulgate continuity planning guidance to State, local, territorial, and tribal governments, and private sector critical infrastructure owners and operators;*

    G. *Make available continuity planning and exercise funding, in the form of grants as provided by law, to State, local, territorial, and tribal governments, and private sector critical infrastructure owners and operators;*

The keys point in HSPD-20 section 16 is to note that the mandates at the federal government level can also be applied to state and local governments. This means a few things. The federal government cannot mandate implementation at a state or local level, except where a failure at the state level would impact the federal government's ability to deliver its service (f). More interestingly, it is actually in the state's and local's governments' best interest to adopt a similar method of resilience. If so, they are assured interoperability and perhaps co-funding (g).

In February 2008, FEMA released two Federal Compliance Directives (FCDs) that provided additional guidance to supplement HSPD-20, on how the agencies should achieve their CO-OP mandates. FCD 1 includes 16 annexes (appendices) that cover different implementation areas. FCD 1 Annex I covers protection of vital records and can be applied directly to data protection methodology, such as the backup mechanisms that we discussed in Chapter 4. Other annexes in FCD 1 discuss regular testing, and the mitigating smaller crises proactively (such as the high-availability technologies that we discussed in Chapters 5–9.

`www.fema.gov/txt/about/offices/FCD1.txt`

APPLYING THESE REGULATIONS TO YOUR CIRCUMSTANCES

If you are looking for items in these regulations that will specifically mandate things like "must use clustering" or "should use disk-based backup prior to or instead of tape," you won't find them as such.

Perhaps this is because the regulations recognize that even within a certain industry segment, companies will vary dramatically in size and criticality of data.

Or perhaps it is because the government understands that technology advances so quickly that it is impractical.

Or perhaps it is because the government does not want to specifically endorse one particular vendor or technology model, which might imply favoritism.

Or perhaps it is because the regulations were often written by executives who were not aware of the specific technologies that are available.

So you may not find pragmatic and definitive guidance in the regulation that specifically applies to your company on *how* to fulfill the mandates, but you will find out *what* the goal should be. The remainder of this section includes several other regulations and commentary of how you might interpret their mandates.

The key to success is to understand what is mandated, and more specifically what is not mandated. Then, with an understanding of intent for the regulation, consider how to apply it to the data protection and availability technologies that you may already be considering (as covered in the earlier chapters).

DoD 5015.2-STD for Federal Agencies and Contractors

DoD 5015.2-STD started as a records retention regulation by the US Department of Defense (DOD) for the US military in 2002, to be in effect by June 2004. The current version of the regulation can be found at `http://jitc.fhu.disa.mil/recmgt/standards.html`.

When first recommended by the DoD in 2002, the US National Archives and Records Administration (NARA) quickly adopted it as the standard for data retention across the agencies within the federal government. These policies were originally defined for what the DoD refers to as Records Management Applications (RMAs). But the policies have since become applicable to almost all forms of electronic data within the same infrastructure. In January 2003, NARA Bulletin 2003–03 was published and included:

> This bulletin advises agencies that the National Archives and Records Administration (NARA) endorses the Department of Defense Electronic Records Management Software Application Design Criteria Standard for use by all Federal agencies.
>
> C2.2.9. <u>System Management Requirements.</u> The following functions are typically provided by the operating system or by a database management system. These functions are also considered requirements to ensure the integrity and protection of organizational records. They shall be implemented as part of the overall records management system even though they may be performed externally to an RMA.
>
>> C2.2.9.1. <u>Backup of Stored Records.</u> The RMA system shall provide the capability to automatically create backup or redundant copies of the records and their metadata.
>>
>> C2.2.9.2. <u>Storage of Backup Copies.</u> The method used to back up RMA database files shall provide copies of the records and their metadata that can be stored off-line and at separate location(s) to safeguard against loss due to system failure, operator error, natural disaster, or willful destruction (see 36 CFR 1234.30).
>
> C2.2.9.3. <u>Recovery/Rollback Capability.</u> Following any system failure, the backup and recovery procedures provided by the system shall:
>
>> C2.2.9.3.1. Ensure data integrity by providing the capability to compile updates (records, metadata, and any other information required to access the records) to RMAs.

C2.2.9.3.2. Ensure these updates are reflected in RMA files, and ensuring that any partial updates to RMA files are separately identified. Also, any user whose updates are incompletely recovered, shall, upon next use of the application, be notified that a recovery has been attempted. RMAs shall also provide the option to continue processing using all in-progress data not reflected in RMA files.

C2.2.9.4. Rebuild Capability. The system shall provide the capability to rebuild from any backup copy, using the backup copy and all subsequent system audit trails.

The 5015.2-STD now reaches beyond the original DoD organizations themselves. It is also mandatory for DoD contractors, when the contractors are engaged on any DoD collaboration. It is recommended to state agencies for the purposes of interoperability as well.

This is one of the most specific regulations that relates to data protection, and yet, notice that the technology or method is not clearly defined—just the desired outcome. We could look at the variety of data protection mechanisms discussed in Chapters 3 and 4 for alternatives that would support this. Where compliance gets blurry is when we apply a replication and availability mechanism such as what we saw in the application chapters (5, 7, or 8) that provides not only the protection via replication, but also the rebuild capability via a manual or automated failover event.

US Food and Drug Administration: 21 CFR 11

The Food and Drug Administration (FDA) regulation 21 CFR 11 is another good example of a rule that is centered on records retention, this time applied to drug manufacturers, medical device companies, and similar organizations that are creating items used in human life sciences. It was originally published in 1997 and revised in 2009. The entire regulation can be found on the `www.fda.gov/` website under its CFR (Code of Regulations) as:

CFR Title 21 regarding Food and Drugs

Part 11 on Electronic Records and Electronic Signatures

Subpart B—Electronic Records

The entire text can be found at

`www.accessdata.fda.gov/scripts/cdrh/cfdocs/cfCFR/CFRSearch.cfm?CFRPart=11`

but here is the relevant text for a data protection discussion:

11.3 Definitions

(4) Closed system means an environment in which system access is controlled by persons who are responsible for the content of electronic records that are on the system.

(6) Electronic record means any combination of text, graphics, data, audio, pictorial, or other information representation in digital form that is created, modified, maintained, archived, retrieved, or distributed by a computer system.

(9) Open system means an environment in which system access is not controlled by persons who are responsible for the content of electronic records that are on the system.

11.10 Controls for closed systems.

Such procedures and controls shall include the following:

(a) Validation of systems to ensure accuracy, reliability, consistent intended performance, and the ability to discern invalid or altered records.

(b) The ability to generate accurate and complete copies of records in both human readable and electronic form suitable for inspection, review, and copying by the agency. Persons should contact the agency if there are any questions regarding the ability of the agency to perform such review and copying of the electronic records.

(c) Protection of records to enable their accurate and ready retrieval throughout the records retention period.

11.30 Controls for open systems.

Such procedures and controls shall include those identified in § 11.10, as appropriate, and additional measures.

The relevant text basically mandates the reliability of backups and restores for the specified retention time, which varies but is almost always at least 10 years due to the need for long-term understanding of how a drug or device affects a range of patients over time.

Health Insurance Portability and Accountability Act (HIPAA)

HIPAA certainly does deal with technology, but its data protection and availability mandates are relatively slim. The major areas of regulation are in Title II and focus on simplifying administration of healthcare paperwork and finances. More specifically, a primary goal of HIPAA is to enable data to easily move from health providers to insurers and other relevant parties. It is because of all the data sharing that most Americans have noticed more authorizations and privacy paperwork when visiting a healthcare professional.

Within Title II are five core rule sections:

2.1 Privacy

2.2 Transactions and Code Sets

2.3 Security

2.4 Unique Identifiers

2.5 Enforcement

The 2.3 Security Section deals with administrative, physical, and technical controls. Rule 164.308 sets the security standards that are related to data protection and availability. The final ruling for 164.308 was published in 2003 and went into effect on April 21, 2005. The complete text of 164.308 can be found at

`http://edocket.access.gpo.gov/cfr_2007/octqtr/pdf/45cfr164.308.pdf`

The relevant sections for data protection and recovery are:

164.308 (a)(7) Contingency plan.

Establish (and implement as needed) policies and procedures for responding to an emergency or other occurrence (for example, fire, vandalism, system failure, and natural disaster) that damages systems that contain electronic protected health information.

(A) Data backup plan (Required).

Establish and implement procedures to create and maintain retrievable exact copies of electronic protected health information.

(B) Disaster recovery plan (Required).

Establish (and implement as needed) procedures to restore any loss of data.

(C) Emergency mode operation plan (Required).

Establish (and implement as needed) procedures to enable continuation of critical business processes for protection of the security of electronic protected health information while operating in emergency mode.

(D) Testing and revision procedures (Addressable).

Implement procedures for periodic testing and revision of contingency plans.

(E) Applications and data criticality analysis (Addressable).

Assess the relative criticality of specific applications and data in support of other contingency plan components.

164.308 (a)(8) Evaluation

Perform a periodic technical and nontechnical evaluation, based initially upon the standards implemented under this rule and subsequently, in response to environmental or operational changes affecting the security of electronic protected health information that establishes the extent to which an entity's security policies and procedures meet the requirements of this subpart.

164.310 (a)(2)(i) Contingency operations.

Establish (and implement as needed) procedures that allow facility access in support of restoration of lost data under the disaster recovery plan and emergency mode operations plan in the event of an emergency.

Notice that each of the five implementation details (A, B, C, D, E) are annotated as either Required or Addressable. Required means that it must be implemented. Addressable entries should be assessed as to whether the specification is a reasonable and appropriate safeguard for the particular environment and whether it would contribute to protecting the information. Based on the assessment, you can either:

- Implement it.
- Document why it is not reasonable and appropriate to implement it, and then implement an alternative measure, if reasonable and appropriate.

The helpful part of the HIPAA 164.308 security rule is that backups, disaster recovery planning, and even regular testing are all mandated. The less than helpful part of this specification is the disaster recovery mandate (164.308.a.7.B), which specifies no data loss but doesn't say how to accomplish it. In fact, the HIPAA technical specifications are intentionally technology neutral.

This can sound like flexibility if you already have something that you believe satisfies the mandate. It can sound like an opportunity if you are a salesperson trying to sell a data protection product. In fact, go to your favorite search engine and search for the terms *HIPAA* and *backup*. You will likely find pages of products that you have never heard of and, in many cases, would never trust with your data.

This flexibility can also sound less than defensible, because your assessment of data loss and a viable recovery plan may be different than the auditor. In fact, your same plan may have been considered compliant to the standard just three years ago but not considered satisfactory today, because the potential technology choices are better than they were. Almost every single technology discussed in this book didn't exist in 2005 when the HIPAA security rule went into effect.

The key to navigate this is to understand what is in the regulation versus what your auditor or consultant is describing. Beyond that, what you will be measured against is often what is considered either mainstream best practice or a higher standard based on new technologies that are now available. In that, books like this one can help you get there.

The Joint Commission, formerly JCAHO

While HIPAA has seen the majority of awareness due to its visible impact on interoperability and standardization, it was not the first healthcare industry regulation in regard to data protection or continuity. The Joint Commission, a healthcare-industry nonprofit organization that used to be called the Joint Commission on Accreditation of Healthcare Organizations, has had standards for healthcare providers for many years, including standards for IT.

The Safely Implementing Health Information and Converging Technologies standards include guidance for Data Integrity and Continuity of Information.

Source: `http://www.jointcommission.org/NewsRoom/PressKits/Prevent+Technology-Related+Errors/app_standards.htm`

Standard IM.2.20 (formerly IM. 02.01.03)

Information security, including data integrity, is maintained.

Rationale

Policies and procedures address security procedures that allow only authorized staff to gain access to data and information. These policies range from access to the paper chart to the various security levels and distribution of passwords in an electronic system. The basic premise of the policies is to provide the security and protection for sensitive patient, staff, and other information, while facilitating access to data by those who have a legitimate need. The capture, storage, and retrieval processes for data and information are designed to provide for timely access without compromising the data and information's security and integrity.

Elements of Performance

1. The hospital has a written policy(ies) for addressing information security, including data integrity that is based on and consistent with law or regulation.
2. The hospital's policy, including changes to the policy, has been communicated to staff.
3. The hospital implements the policy.

4. The hospital monitors compliance with the policy.
5. The hospital improves information security, including data integrity, by monitoring information and developments in technology.
6. The hospital develops and implements controls to safeguard data and information, including the clinical record, against loss, destruction, and tampering.
7. Controls to safeguard data and information include the following:
    - Policies indicating when the removal of records is permitted
    - Protection against unauthorized intrusion, corruption, or damage
    - Minimization of the risk of falsification of data and information
    - Guidelines for preventing the loss and destruction of records
    - Guidelines for destroying copies of records
    - Protection of records in a manner that minimizes the possibility of damage from fire and water
8. Policies and procedures, including plans for implementation, for electronic information systems address the following: data integrity, authentication, nonrepudiation, encryption (as warranted), and audit-ability, as appropriate to the system and types of information, for example, patient information and billing information.

There are a few notable aspects of the JCAHO IM.2.20 regulation that are helpful for a data protection discussion. Notice that Element 5 dictates that the hospital should improve its processes by monitoring developments in IT. So, it recognizes that the minimum standard and potential solutions will evolve over time. This is extremely helpful when you have an auditor who is not as well versed at progressive IT methods as your department may be. This formalizes that you may be more progressive than the mainstream. However, it can also be a detriment, if your auditor is technology progressive and your environment is not, since the auditor may determine that you have failed to monitor the changing capabilities in IT. Of course, if you are reading this book, then that probably does not apply.

Elements 6 and 7 of IM.2.20 can be satisfied, in part, by a reliable backup and recovery solution. However, in the bigger picture of not allowing any data loss or destruction, nightly tape backup does not satisfy the mandate. Data created in the morning cannot be lost in the afternoon, so you will need a data protection mechanism that runs more often than nightly, as we discussed in Chapters 3 and 4, as well as the replication solutions for files (Chapter 5), email (Chapter 7), and databases (Chapter 8).

Another Joint Commission standard also applies to our focus:

Standard IM.2.30 (formerly IM. 01.01.03)
Continuity of information is maintained.

Rationale

The purpose of the business continuity/disaster recovery plan is to identify the most critical information needs for patient care, treatment, and services and business processes, and the impact on the hospital if these information systems were severely interrupted. The plan identifies alternative means for processing data, providing for recovery of data, and returning to normal operations as soon as possible.

Elements of Performance

1. The hospital has a business continuity/disaster recovery plan for its information systems.
2. For electronic systems, the business continuity/disaster recovery plan includes the following:
   - Plans for scheduled and unscheduled interruptions, which includes end-user training with the downtime procedures
   - Contingency plans for operational interruptions (hardware, software, or other systems failure)

IM.2.30 is a straightforward mandate for a business continuity or disaster recovery plan for the IT assets, such that the key services continue to operate.

SEC, NYSE, AND NASD

The Securities & Exchange Commission (SEC) oversees the New York Stock Exchange (NYSE) and the National Association of Securities Dealers (NASD), among other financial institutions. Originally, the primary rules that member companies, including almost any publicly traded corporation, had to comply with were related to records retention, based on long-standing mandates:

- SEC Rule 17a-3 is the primary rule related to records required to be made by all broker-dealers.
- SEC Rule 17a-4 establishes the time periods and the manner in which such records must be preserved and made accessible.

These rules and NYSE rules relating to record maintenance, such as NYSE Rule 440 (Books and Records) apply to all members and member organizations, even including those acting just as brokers on the trading floor who may never conduct business directly with public customers.

But in 2004, partially in response to lessons learned from 9/11, the SEC approved mandates for business continuity plans by the NYSE (Rule 446) and the NASD (Rules 3510 and 3520), which were very similar. NYSE Rule 446 (`www.sec.gov/rules/sro/34-48502.htm`) is as follows:

(a) Members and member organizations must develop and maintain a written business continuity and contingency plan establishing procedures relating to an emergency or significant business disruption. Such procedures must be reasonably designed to enable members and member organizations to meet their existing obligations to customers. In addition, such procedures must address their existing relationships with other broker-dealers, and counter-parties. Members and member organizations must make such plan available to the Exchange upon request.

(b) Members and member organizations must conduct, at a minimum, a yearly review of their business continuity and contingency plan to determine whether any modifications are necessary in light of changes to the member's or member organization's operations, structure, business or location. In the event of a material change to a member's or member organization's operations, structure, business or location, the member or member organization must promptly update its business continuity and contingency plan.

Sections (a) and (b) essentially require every US publicly traded company to have a written business continuity plan. Note that the plan is not just for the benefit of the company itself, but orchestrated in such a way for the business to meet its obligations with its customer base. The plan must be presentable to the SEC upon request. Something in (b) that is not in most of the

other industry mandates is a requirement to regularly review the plan and make changes based on the current situation within the company's business.

(c) The elements that comprise a business continuity and contingency plan shall be tailored to the size and needs of a member or member organization [so as to enable the member or member organization to continue its business in the event of a future significant business disruption]. Each plan, however, must, at a minimum, address, if applicable:

1) books and records back-up and recovery (hard copy and electronic);
2) identification of all mission critical systems and back-up for such systems;
3) financial and operational risk assessments;
4) alternate communications between customers and the firm;
5) alternate communications between the firm and its employees;
6) alternate physical location of employees;
7) critical business constituent, bank and counter-party impact;
8) regulatory reporting;
9) communications with regulators; and
10) how the member or member organization will assure customers prompt access to their funds and securities in the event the member or member organization determines it is unable to continue its business.

To the extent that any of the above items is not applicable, the member's or member organization's business continuity and contingency plan must specify the item(s) and state the rationale for not including each such item(s) in its plan. If a member or member organization relies on another entity for any of the above-listed categories or any mission critical system, the member's or member organization's business continuity and contingency plan must address this relationship.

Section (c) provides fairly specific guidance on what must be in the business continuity plan. These are not specific to a particular industry and are what most good business continuity plans ought to have as a minimum basis. However, the clarifying paragraph after the list recognizes that the size of the organization may warrant adaptation of the required components, and so a provision is made to document what you believe are exceptions to the rule, based on something in your environment.

The rest of the SEC publication for the NYSE Rule 446, as well as commentary and the change revisions before adoption, can be found at `www.sec.gov/rules/sro/34-48502.htm`, but the remaining sections are relatively straightforward:

(d) Each member or member organization must disclose to its customers how its business continuity and contingency plan addresses the possibility of a future significant business disruption and how the member or member organization plans to respond to events of varying scope. At a minimum, such disclosure must be made in writing to customers at account opening, posted on the Internet website of the member or member organization (if applicable) and mailed to customers upon request.

(e) The term "mission critical system," for purposes of this Rule, means any system that is necessary, depending on the nature of a member's or member organization's business, to

ensure prompt and accurate processing of securities transactions, including order taking, entry, execution, comparison, allocation, clearance and settlement of securities transactions, the maintenance of customer accounts, access to customer accounts and the delivery of funds and securities.

(f) The term "financial and operational risk assessments," for purposes of this Rule, means a set of written procedures that allow members and member organizations to identify changes in their operational, financial, and credit risk exposure.

(g) Members and member organizations must designate a senior officer, as defined in Rule 351(e), to approve the Plan, who shall also be responsible for the required annual review, as well as an Emergency Contact Person(s). Such individuals must be identified to the Exchange (by name, title, mailing address, e-mail address, telephone number, and facsimile number). Prompt notification must be given to the Exchange of any change in such designations.

Under the new rules, every NYSE and NASD member company must create, publish, and test a business continuity plan that ensures that they can meet their current obligations to their customer base, regardless of the type of crisis that might unfold. The new rules cover everything from tactical backup and recovery, similar to what we discussed in Chapters 3 and 4, as well as risk mitigation (high availability) mechanisms and BC/DR plans.

Most notable, perhaps because of the SEC's function in oversight, the business continuity plan must be discloseable to the general public customers.

SEC and US Treasury Guidance (Post-9/11)

After the terrorist attacks of 9/11, the SEC not only approved new business continuity mandates for the member companies but also looked at what needed to be done to better fortify the US financial system. To that end, the SEC, along with the US Federal Reserve and the US Treasury, released the "Interagency Paper on Sound Practices to Strengthen the Resilience of the U.S. Financial System" in April 2003.

- Federal Reserve System, Docket No. R-1128
- Department of the Treasury, Office of the Comptroller of the Currency, Docket No. 03-05
- Securities and Exchange Commission, Release No. 34-47638; File No. S7-32-02

You can read the entire document at `www.sec.gov/news/studies/34-47638.htm`, but it can be summarized from its objectives summary:

> Three business continuity objectives have special importance for all financial firms and the U.S. financial system as a whole:
>
> - Rapid recovery and timely resumption of critical operations following a wide-scale disruption;
> - Rapid recovery and timely resumption of critical operations following the loss or inaccessibility of staff in at least one major operating location; and
> - A high level of confidence, through ongoing use or robust testing, that critical internal and external continuity arrangements are effective and compatible.
>
> *Source: Interagency Paper on Sound Practices to Strengthen the Resilience of the U.S. Financial System, SEC.GOV, April 2004.*

The interagency paper identified four sound practices for the core clearing and settlement organizations that play significant roles in the financial markets.

1. **Identify clearing and settlement activities in support of critical financial markets.** In much the same idea as the business impact analysis that we discussed in Chapter 2, and from the CBCP practices at the beginning of this chapter, these core financial institutions need to understand their internal processes that are responsible for settling trades within the general market.

2. **Determine appropriate recovery and resumption objectives or clearing and settlement activities in support of critical markets.** Because these organizations are most responsible for the movement of money throughout the US financial system, it is imperative that they and the contributing financial institutions have sound practices for ensuring their swift resumption of service after a crisis, so that the rest of the financial infrastructure that depends on these core organizations can also begin to resume service.

3. **Maintain sufficient geographically dispersed resources to meet recovery and resumption objectives.** One of the lessons learned in 9/11 was that some of the companies that had their primary datacenter impacted by the tragic events of the day could not resume operations in their secondary facility because it was perhaps in another of the affected buildings, or elsewhere in Manhattan or across the river in New Jersey. The secondary site needs to be far enough away that a crisis surrounding the primary site will not affect the secondary site. In addition, the secondary site should not be dependent on the staff from the primary site, so that their unavailability does not impact the secondary site from coming online.

4. **Routinely use or test recovery and resumption arrangements.** We will discuss this more later in the chapter, but this step cannot be overemphasized. A plan that is never tested does not count as a plan—it is just a theory.

The interagency paper goes on to emphasize that without the resilience of key financial institutions, the rest of the market cannot re-engage. Imagine if all the small banks and financial services companies came back online, but the large organizations that facilitated the trading among them were not accessible. The money would not move. Literally, those core clearing companies create the pipes through which the US markets' money flows.

Therefore, it is incumbent on those core clearinghouses to have resiliency in their infrastructure and secondary sites that ensure those organizations' resumption of service. Similarly, with those core organizations now online, the next tier of financial services companies must also have resilience and business continuity plans, so that they too can resume service. From there, the rest of the financial ecosystem can resume operation.

With that in mind, the interagency paper does make some additional technology recommendations:

> *The business continuity planning process should take into consideration improvements in technology and business processes supporting back-up arrangements and the need to ensure greater resilience in the event of a wide-scale disruption.*
>
> *Core clearing and settlement organizations that use synchronous back-up facilities or whose back-up sites depend primarily on the same labor pool as the primary site should address the risk that a wide-scale disruption could impact either or both of the sites and their labor pool. Such organizations should establish even more distant back-up arrangements that can recover and resume critical operations within the business day on which the disruption occurs.*
>
> *Plans should provide for back-up facilities that are well outside of the current synchronous range that can meet within-the-business-day recovery targets.*

Let's break that last piece of guidance apart:

... well outside of the current synchronous range ... In Chapter 3, we discussed that storage mirroring can only be synchronous for a limited distance before the latency between the two arrays starts to degrade the performance of the server and its applications. So, if the data must be further apart than what synchronous storage mirroring can handle, then the data must be asynchronously replicated—either at a storage array, server host, or application level.

... can meet within-the-business-day recovery targets ... Also in Chapter 3, we discussed that tape cannot usually meet same-day recovery goals, which means that disk-based protection is a must.

Put together, we see that the only way to achieve the recommendation of the SEC and Treasury is to use an asynchronous disk-based protection model, which includes many of the technologies that we discussed so far:

System Center Data Protection Manager (Chapter 4)

Distributed File System Replication (Chapter 5)

Exchange database availability groups (Chapter 7)

SQL database mirroring (Chapter 8)

Gramm-Leach-Bliley for Financial Institutions

The Gramm-Leach-Bliley Act (GLB) of 1999 includes provisions designed to protect the privacy of individuals, in regard to their interactions with financial institutions. Almost all financial organizations that deal with nonpublic personal information are required to comply with GLB. Those organizations must provide reasonable administrative, technical, and physical safeguards to protect their customers' information from unauthorized disclosure, alteration, or deletion. The regulations also require organizations to take reasonable steps to engage and utilize only services providers that are capable of safeguarding the protected customer information.

In short, while GLB is about many other things, one of them is how the data of a financial institution should be maintained or protected. Some of the specific mandates include:

- Preserve the records exclusively in a nonrewritable, nonerasable format.
- Ensure the security and confidentiality of customer information.
- Protect against any anticipated threats or hazards to the security or integrity of such information.
- Protect against unauthorized access to or use of such information that could result in substantial harm or inconvenience to any customer.
- Access to data is date- and time-stamped by user, providing a clear audit trail.

Sarbanes-Oxley (SOX)

Perhaps no regulation has caused as much consternation as Sarbanes-Oxley (SOX), enacted primarily to ensure ethical behavior of public companies. There is surprisingly little guidance on data protection and retention. In fact, here are some of the words that you will *not* find in the regulation:

- Backup
- Disaster

- Recovery
- Continuity
- Contingency

You can read the complete regulation at

`www.gpo.gov/fdsys/pkg/PLAW-107publ204/content-detail.html`

My point is not that data protection does not apply, but that you have to understand the context of the business problem that SOX is addressing to see where your IT capabilities need to be applied. SOX Title I deals with accounting oversight, which in IT can translate as retention and availability requirements.

Section 103: Auditing, Quality Control, and Independence Standards and Rules Section 103 deals with creating, providing, and retaining audit reports, since SOX is all about ensuring sound business practices. Those auditable materials become very important data objects, whose servers should be highly available and whose data must be kept for seven years. Can you imagine the accounting department telling your CFO that they couldn't prepare for the SOX audit because one of the servers was offline? The auditor needs to be able to get the data on demand—so a reliable recovery mechanism for the seven-year retention window is also necessary. You wouldn't want to have to tell the CFO that the reason the audit failed was because you couldn't produce the audit reports from four years ago. Remember, it is the company's executive team that is civilly and criminally liable.

FEATURE NEEDS TITLE

Even in large enterprise data centers, nearly one quarter of respondents report that 20% or more of their tape-based recoveries fail.

Enterprise Storage Group, "The Evolution of Enterprise Data Protection," January 2004

Section 104: Inspections of Registered Public Accounting Firms Section 104 allows for inspections, including impromptu inspections by the SEC. Again, this translates to not only a retention requirement, but a fast and reliable restoration mechanism. If the data is held only on backup tape or other media, are you confident in the restore mechanisms? If the data is held on servers, are the servers available when needed? The auditor's mood can change when their first experience with IT is a bad one.

Section 105: Investigations and Disciplinary Proceedings; Reporting of Sanctions Section 105 regards the documents prepared by the company's board as confidential and privileged. But if you have to retain them for seven years, are they secure? Are your tapes encrypted? Is your offsite facility secure? Is your service provider trustworthy?

SOX Title VIII and XI deal with aspects of fraud, with Sections 802 and 1102 specifically addressing altered documents. Again, this speaks to being able to reliably produce the original documents from a preserved backup, in a timely way, to ensure that nothing has been altered.

There may be a few other nuances, but this hopefully gets you started. More importantly, this may get your compliance team and accounting team started.

TRANSLATING REGULATIONS INTO IT IMPLEMENTATIONS

Here is a suggestion.

Take the 2 or 3 pages of this book that are related to SOX or your regulation from earlier to your company's next compliance prep/status meeting (please feel free to buy each one of them a full copy of this book).

Help them understand how you are attempting to translate their compliance requirements into IT implementations, such as retention periods, or highly available servers for the auditors, or a published business continuity plan including test schedule.

This is similar to what was suggested in Chapter 2 when we discussed determining service level agreements, assessing business impact, and meeting recovery objectives in partnership with the business owners.

In this case, if your teams can collectively work out a two-column list, where the left side is the text from the regulation and the right side is what IT needs to do to satisfy it, then you have bought yourself a seat at the table. It makes you a partner in the discussion, instead of a victim of the regulation or a perceived obstacle to corporate compliance. The change in thinking may also change you from Systems Administrator to Director of IT.

The Real Reason to Do Disaster Recovery

Because it is the right thing to do.

I bet that when you read the last section, you breezed over it (and that is okay), mostly because not every regulation applied to you. All of those regulations collectively add up to several parental-sounding "I told you to" edicts. I have three children and none of them regularly and unquestionably obey me because I told them to do something once. And if the regulations were the only reasons to do disaster recovery planning, you might not regularly and unquestioningly follow them either. It might even be cheaper for your company to face the noncompliance fines than to spend the money on consultants to become compliant.

The real reason to do disaster recovery is that, statistically speaking, a crisis will impact your business. Your choice is to either be part of the solution or exacerbate the problem. Everyone who deals with disaster recovery has their favorite statistics. Here are a few of mine:

> *43% of U.S. companies experiencing disasters never re-open, and 29% close within 2 years.*
>
> *US Department of Labor*

> *A company denied access to mission-critical data for more than 48 hours will likely be out of business within one year.*
>
> *DRPlanning.org*

> *Two out of five enterprises that experience a disaster will go out of business within five years of the event.*
>
> *www.dataquest.com/press_gartner/quickstats/busContinuity.html, Gartner*

> *93% of companies that lost their data center for 10 days or more due to a disaster filed for bankruptcy within one year of the disaster, and 50% filed for bankruptcy immediately.*
>
> *US National Archives & Records Administration*

Get Your Data Out of the Building

There are all kinds of terms for getting your data out of the building, including:

- Vaulting
- Offsite or multisite replication
- Disaster recovery (DR)
- Business continuity (BC)
- Continuity of operations (CO-OP)

There are differences between each of them, but they all equate to survivability of your data. Where they differ is in the expectations of what you do with the data during a crisis. In fact, we can lump them all together, shake them around a bit, and come out with two focus areas:

Data Survivability The data will survive a site-wide crisis at the production location, because it is being actively transmitted and stored at an alternate location that is geographically separate, so the original crisis will not impact it.

Resumption of Services After determining that the primary site, servers, and services are not recoverable, the alternate copies of data are brought online, so that IT services can resume serving the business.

For our purposes, *disaster recovery* (DR) is about *data survivability*, while *business continuity* (BC) is about *resumption of services.*

Notice that we haven't mentioned how the data will survive or services will be resumed. BC and DR are not technology mandates—they are business objectives. In fact, successful BC/DR initiatives are usually much more about people and processes than they are about technologies. But without the data, the people don't have anything to apply their processes to. Without the data, nothing else will matter.

Real World Scenario

DISCLAIMER TO REFINE THE BC/DR DISCUSSION

In almost any circumstance that qualifies for a large-scale usage of business continuity or disaster recovery processes, a site-wide crisis has occurred. And the reality is that any crisis that can impact an entire facility will put life and property in harm's way.

Said another way, the most important thing is life safety. Are your people OK?

Only after that question is satisfactorily understood should we look at whether the business is OK. To do that, your people have to apply the processes that you have predetermined for them. And those processes are usually related to ensuring access to your property (assets) and your data, so that your business can eventually resume.

This is a technology book, so I will spend some time later putting the technology aspects into the bigger picture of BC/DR planning. But in the interest of not sounding heartless, the people are the most important thing, the data is next most important, and that is the focus for this chapter.

Disaster recovery ensures that the data survives so that it can eventually be used to bring the business back up. Business continuity is the resumption of service by utilizing the data that survived. So, we can think of BC as a superset of DR. And any way that you slice it, the first thing is getting your data out of the building.

Here are a few anecdotes to frame the conversation:

August 2005, New Orleans A company headquarters in New Orleans had a well-defined disaster preparedness plan. A secondary site had all of its data and was ready to start coming online, but the secondary site did not come online because none of the IT staff traveled to the secondary location. They were tending to their own flooded homes.

September 2001, New York City A services company had one of its main IT data centers in World Trade Center Tower One. However, due to the amount of data and the high value of the data, business continuity and high availability technologies were fully deployed to ensure a seamless transition to a secondary data center. The secondary datacenter was in Tower Two.

April 1992, Chicago A company had its primary offices in the financial district of Chicago, but a flood started with a leak in tunnels under Lake Michigan; eventually buildings were closed and power was cut off to a large part of the financial district. Stock trading, as well as all other business, halted.

Don't Cry "I Wasn't Ready Yet"

I have three children and somewhere along the way, someone in each of their classes has taught them the game of Slaps. Slaps works by one person putting their hands out, palms up. The other player, my kid, then holds their hands, palms down, hovering over the first players.' The game is played as the experienced person on the bottom tries to quickly slap my kid's hands, while my kid tries to pull back really quickly. If the top player flinches three times, they have to hold still for a free, and usually stinging, slap. If the bottom player misses three times, the roles reverse. But the player on the bottom doesn't miss much. Much more often, the kid on top screams out *"I wasn't ready."*

So, they set up again; my kid is still trying to figure things out, gets slapped, and again shouts "I wasn't ready." They start watching the left hand of the bottom player, and get slapped by the right. They watch the last hand that hit them, and the other one gets them. And all of the time, they are (hopefully) giggling but emphatically saying, "Wait, I am still not ready."

The same experience is true with many IT managers who are just starting down the road of BC/DR planning. They start working on an impressive three-ring binder, with lots of plans and worksheets to fill out. Maybe they go to a CBCP class for a few weeks. Perhaps they solicit bids for a consultant to come in. Later, they start interviewing the business owners, assessing business risk and all of the other things that a good BC/DR plan should do.

And then the crisis happens.

The people aren't trained. The data didn't survive. There is nothing left to do but close the doors for the last time. And all that the former IT manager can say to their now ex-boss, who told them to start preparing, is that they were working on the plan.

Have you ever heard the term *planning paralysis*? It refers to times when you are so busy planning and analyzing that you forget to act. Certainly, BC/DR needs a plan, but in the bigger picture, the most important thing is to get your data out of the building. Do that first. Then, you can start working on the impressive three-ring binder.

65% of small- and medium-sized firms do not have a disaster recovery plan.

www.dataquest.com/press_gartner/quickstats/busContinuity.html, Gartner

Tactical DR vs. Strategic Disaster Preparedness

Look back at the last several chapters of the book. You have lots of options to get the data out of the building:

- Storage (Chapter 3) can be mirrored from one onsite array to an offsite array, or from one Windows host onsite to another Windows host offsite using asynchronous replication software.
- DFS replication (Chapter 5) was built for remote replication of files. But instead of going from a branch office to the datacenter, turn it around. Send the data from your datacenter to someplace else.
- Exchange 2007 SCR and Exchange 2010 DAG (Chapter 7) both provide for a node to be off-premise.
- SQL database mirroring or log shipping (Chapter 8) enable long-distance replication of databases.
- Data Protection Manager (Chapter 4) can replicate from an on-premise DPM server to an off-premise DPM server.

You have options. Most of these assume that you have more than one site, and we will talk about how to achieve this when you do not. But the most important thing that you can do is to ensure that the data survives.

This may sound like Ready, Fire, Aim. But, the reality is that whether you do your analyses first or later, one of your absolutely understood tasks that you will end up deciding to do is to ensure that your data survives, so start there. If you aren't ready for any of those other options yet, then reach out to a data vaulting company (which we will talk about later in this chapter, in the "*Data Vaulting Providers*" section). The reason that data survivability is so important is because without it, almost nothing else in your eventual plan will work. So, you may as well start there.

- If, in six months when your plan is complete, you decide that you want to accomplish your offsite data protection with a different means, at least you can do it with a pragmatic understanding of how at least one good options works.
- If, in six months when your plan is complete, you decide that your current vaulting technology is working fine, that is one less thing to implement while you are implementing the rest of your new BC/DR plan.

But most importantly, if three months from now (and your plan is not yet complete) a crisis occurs, at least you can roll up your sleeves and work as quickly as you can to get your infrastructure patched together for the most critical processes—because your data survived.

In most cases, you will want to do more than have your data survive. You will want to utilize it—perhaps from the remote site (BC) or as part of repairing your primary site (DR). Let's take a closer look at these two related solutions.

BC = DR + HA

The formula really is that simple.

- If we define *disaster recovery* (DR) as simply the survivability of the data across a distance after a site-level event,

- And we consider *high availability* (HA) to be the methods by which an application service or data continues to be available,
- Then, *business continuity* (BC) really is about the resumption or assurance of IT services from a remote location.

The key to this definition is that the resumption of service in BC happens at the remote location. Because DR is simply about the survivability of the data, the assumption is that that the data will be moved someplace else before the recovery process starts. This is why DR used to be synonymous with having tapes taken offsite by a courier service. The expectation was that upon declaring a disaster, those tapes would be hastily returned to you so that you could set up an alternate facility and start restoring your data back into your new makeshift infrastructure.

That model started to change when companies like SunGard and Comdisco began offering warm sites. They would courier your tapes for you (like Iron Mountain), but they would also maintain similar hardware on request within their large warehouse facilities that included rows of empty cubicles, some with empty computers or phones. When you suffered a disaster, SunGard or Comdisco would begin to restore your data for you into similar computers, so that you and your labor pool could go to one of their facilities and start doing business within a few days.

Today, it is much more common for companies to have completely self-contained business continuity solutions, where the data is protected offsite and a variety of methods are used to quickly resume services and business operations. Let's look at a few methods for this.

Multiple Datacenters

Having multiple datacenters within your company may be assumed to be the easiest scenario in order to provide business continuity (or disaster recovery). In this case, you own all the assets.

- You own the datacenters in the multiple facilities, so you can configure the servers you need for both hot (automatic) failover, as well as warm (manual) standby, or cold (build when you need them) provisioning.
- You own the computers at the desks, so it is not a great challenge to provide additional desk space for users from a failed site to come to another site and resume work.
- In many cases, if Site 1 were to fail and its users were unavailable, it is the users in Site 2 who need the data anyway. So having the data already at Site 2 is ideal.

With that being said, there are still some things to consider.

Application Resiliency Across Sites

Many of the technologies that we discussed in the earlier chapters were designed with the multiple datacenter, self-maintained application resiliency scenario. Let's use File Services as the first example of how this works.

File Services Using DFS-R and DFS-N from Chapter 5, you can transparently configure a DFS namespace across your company. For any given file share within the namespace, two physical instances of that file share can be hosted on servers that are in the separate datacenters. Users within each datacenter will each access their local copy for best performance, but all the users are able to access the other copy if theirs fails.

This is really HA that just contributes to a bigger BC solution. So, when everything else is working fine but a single file server within Site 1 fails, the users at Site 1 will simply (and transparently) access the copy of the data on the Site 2 file server instead. As long as the WAN can sustain the additional bandwidth of the additional users requests, the HA comes easy. If you have a complete crisis of Site 1, the users (or a subset of them) would physically go to Site 2 or remotely connect to the corporate network. After a site failure and failover, the experience may be different, depending on where the user is located:

- For users who are typically remote anyway, such as a field-based sales force, there is no difference in their experience, but instead of dialing in and using the data from a Site 1 server, they get the copy from Site 2, likely with no perceived difference.
- For users who office in Site 1, they might travel to Site 2, or use a rented facility, or begin dialing in.

If your applications or services natively run on peer-level servers in between sites, then HA and BC are relatively easy and intrinsically related. This is true not only for file services, but also for the other application services that we discussed in earlier chapters:

Exchange Exchange 2007 provided cluster continuous replication (CCR) for resiliency within a site, and Exchange 2007 SP1 added standby continuous replication (SCR) specifically for multisite resiliency. As discussed in Chapter 7, a CCR cluster would run from Site 1, while the SCR node would run from Site 2. If a single node failed within the CCR pair, the other node within the pair would continue operation almost seamlessly. If the clustered pair were to fail (or a complete crisis occurred at Site 1), then the SCR node could be activated from Site 2. Exchange 2010 blends and refines CCR and SCR functionality into database availability groups (DAGs), where multiple nodes might be at Site 1 and other node(s) at Site 2.

SQL Server Database mirroring or failover clustering of SQL Server may be ideal for high availability within Site 1, and can be paired with SQL log shipping to provide additional copies of the data at Site 2.

SharePoint It is worth mentioning that the resiliency mechanisms within a SharePoint farm are made up of only a few resilient components. The web front end (WFE) servers can use network load balancing, as discussed in the beginning of Chapter 6. The SharePoint content databases are SQL Server databases and can therefore use database mirroring. But there are no farm-centric resilience technologies built into SharePoint—not yet, anyway.

Better Backups That Are Always Offsite

In Chapter 4, we looked at improving backups by protecting to disk before protecting to tape, referred to as disk-to-disk-to-tape (D2D2T). By doing this across datacenters, you can protect your data from the production servers to a disk-based backup server onsite at Site 1, to a disk-based backup server that is offsite at Site 2, to tape-based media at Site 2. We can call this D2D2D2T.

Not every backup solution can offer this. In Chapter 4, we discussed one example of a next-generation backup product that does this: System Center Data Protection Manager. There are a few great benefits of D2D2D2T:

The offsite backup server has your DR data. Unlike having to use a remote replication technology like those covered in Chapter 3 (disk mirroring or software replication), this is part of your backup scenario. Your backup solution has all your data at a secondary site. If the primary site has a failure, the backup server at the secondary site is ready to restore it wherever.

DR happens across all applications in the same way. Without having to configure and maintain application-specific offsite nodes, all the data is protected to a backup platform onsite and then transparently replicated to a secondary site with no additional maintenance.

Your tapes are already offsite. By doing your tape-based backups from the alternate site—meaning that the data from Site 1 is protected to disk at Site 1, then disk at Site 2, and finally to tape from Site 2—the tapes can be taken out of the tape drive (or left in a changer) but are already considered offsite tapes, because they are in a different geography than the production servers in Site 1. This meets the offsite retention and preservation requirements of any of the regulations discussed earlier, as well as common best practices.

What Is the Downside?

This may sound great, but there is a downside of maintaining redundancy between datacenters in the operational costs of the redundant hardware, as well as the personnel costs to manage the secondary site's assets and connection. This solution essentially means more servers to manage and maintain, more resources to power and cool, more space that is consumed, more bandwidth that has to be allocated. And depending on what kinds of application or storage replication that you choose, there may be some additional complexity added to your overall infrastructure.

As the data is replicated from the primary datacenter to the secondary, bandwidth is impacted. If each datacenter does not have its own connection to the Internet, the same connection that will be used for data replication will also be used for Internet and intranet traffic. As you deploy data replication between datacenters, you may see complaints, as the link might now be slower to access resources across the corporate WAN, as well as the Internet, because of the additional data streams. Of course, the incremental data doesn't have to impact the wire—as long as you pay more for additional bandwidth capacity. Similarly, there will be incremental costs for power, cooling, and space—as well as the management labor to maintain those machines, including software costs not only for the OS and primary applications, but also the management software necessary to monitor the health of the redundant systems (see Chapter 11) and maintain them (Chapter 10).

Branch Offices' BCDR

Depending on your business model, much of your data may not be in your datacenters at all. It may be in your branches. And if it is, your real data protection (and disaster recovery) challenge is about protecting all the distributed data out there. Typically, the data in branch offices falls into one of three categories:

- Desktop and laptop data
- File server data located in the branch
- Database application data in a branch-office server

Desktop and Laptop Data

The easiest way to protect this data, assuming that you have a file server within the branch, is to use My Documents redirection. MyDocs redirection is a method where a directory on the client machine is actually a directory on the server. While, as a user, I might think that my data is on `C:\MyDocs`, it is really on `\\FS1\data\jbuff`. This is transparent, so that when I am on the network, as well as when I am traveling, I always go to `C:\MyDocs`. But because the data is transparently synchronized, the data is protected from laptop to file server. To take that one additional step, the copy on the file server can be protected from the branch office to the corporate datacenter. More on that is covered in the next section (as well as in Chapter 5).

Branch Office File Servers

As always, the mantra of this chapter is "Get your data out of the building." There is no exception for branch offices. In this case, the data should go to either the corporate headquarters or a peer-level office, depending on the kinds of data and the geographical boundaries. It might seem easy enough to replicate it from one branch office in New York City to a nearby branch in Hoboken, New Jersey (across the river). You would be protected against theft or fire within a single office, but any weather pattern or other regional event will likely impact both offices. Even across the street is better than only having your data in one place, but if you think about a branch as needing the same kinds of data preservation methods as a datacenter, it should be more apparent where the secondary sites might need to be.

Providing disaster recovery and centralized backup of a branch office server can be achieved in two ways:

- Chapter 4 showed us disk-to-disk-to-tape solutions like Data Protection Manager, where the data can be replicated from the branch office server to a DPM server, and then protected to tape—without having tape drives in the branch offices. Or if you want to be able to recover points in time within the branch, install DPM locally on the branch office file server for local restores, and then replicate from the branch server with DPM to a headquarters server with DPM.
- Chapter 5 showed us file server–to–file server replication via Distributed File System Replication (DFS-R). This alone gives us disaster recovery of the data. By leveraging DFS-N as a namespace, we get business continuity also. And by using DPM or another backup solution at corporate, we can back up the centralized copy, instead of the iterations at each branch.

Databases

While there are cases of Exchange or other applications running in the branches, those cases are rarer than applications that are built on top of Microsoft SQL Server. But the answer is actually the same for both SQL and Exchange. You have choices similar to what was discussed for file servers, meaning its built-in replication solution or a backup solution that provides D2D2T.

SQL Server can use database mirroring, log shipping, or database replication to provide a copy of the database at the headquarters location. Exchange could use SCR (in 2007) or DAG (2010) in the same way. However, using the application to do the replication adds an appreciable amount of complexity in the bigger picture. Imagine that you had 200 branch offices and each one was running a SQL database and an Exchange server. Can you imagine having a farm of Exchange and SQL servers in the central datacenter that were simply doing data replication? The larger the number of branches, the less likely this is for most environments. Instead, this is where either an asynchronous replication solution (Chapter 3) or a disk-to-disk backup like DPM (Chapter 4) starts to be really advantageous, because the amount of data traversing the intranet is similar to how much data those built-in mirroring solutions do, but without the application servers at the headquarters location. Instead, a simple replication target (Chapter 3) or a D2D2T backup server is a common and consolidated receiver.

WHAT IS THE DOWNSIDE?

There isn't one. Providing BC/DR of your branch offices by adding some incremental infrastructure at your headquarters is likely one of the most cost-justifiable implementations in this entire book. In so doing, you get:

- Reduced downtime for remote employees
- Centralized backup that removes the need (and cost) for tape management in the field
- Distributed data becomes centralized for compliance and retention purposes
- Loss of a branch does not mean loss of a branch's unique data

Branch Offices for DR

You can blend the last two scenarios of multiple data centers and branch offices' BC/DR to consider how you can use a branch office as the disaster recovery site for your datacenter itself. The idea here is that if you do not have multiple datacenters but you do have branches, then you do still have a second site (other than your primary datacenter) that is under your control. Perhaps it does not have all of the niceties of a datacenter, but if you can increase the bandwidth to that site and provide a physically secure area for the servers that will receive the corporate data, this can be a good choice.

A big requirement here is physical security. In most organizations, the branch offices have less physical security than corporate datacenters. However, in this scenario, that branch office will now be containing servers that hold redundant copies of the corporate data—so encryption of the disk storage, physical cages, and other access control of the servers themselves, and even additional power conditioning and supply, are important details.

However, note that unlike the previous two examples, this is likely not a BC/DR scenario, just DR. The reason is that, while the data will survive (DR), your branch location is likely not able to sustain the additional bandwidth required to resume business operations remotely nor have your headquarters' staff all report to the branch office location to resume work. But as a DR scenario, the methods that were already discussed apply for file services, Exchange, SQL replication, as well as D2D2T backup solutions.

NOTE Notice that as we go down the list of choices, the amount of infrastructure that you maintain goes down, but so do your recovery scenarios. We start going from a full-fledged and potentially automatic failover scenario, through business continuity capabilities, and disaster recovery options, and down to just plain data survivability.

Hosted Providers

Now, let's presume that you have only one datacenter and no branches (or no branches that meet the physical security requirements). Or, perhaps you are a midsized organization with only one facility. You still have options. One of them is to utilize a hosting provider in your local area. This may be your Internet service provider (ISP) or perhaps your local Microsoft partner or reseller, particularly if you are a small business.

Some ISPs in your local area have rack space to rent. The normal scenario is that you would put a web server in the rack and pay for space, along with a potential surcharge for bandwidth. But if you want to maintain your own DR server and just do not have a secondary site, this is an option. Things to consider for this scenario are:

- Physical security to your server

- Surcharges for bandwidth—this will get expensive
- Port firewalling to the degree that you cannot get your data replication software (asynchronous host-based from Chapter 3 or D2D2D from Chapter 4)

Again, this is a DR-only scenario, with the expectation that you would pick up the server and move it to your production facility or makeshift facility to start resumption of service. Having your users remotely connect to this machine, while still at the ISP, is likely not practical. You may also find that this only works well for true small business environments.

Service Providers

This scenario no longer requires you to maintain the redundant receiving hardware. Instead, you simply engage in a service contract, whereby a software agent runs on at least one machine in your environment and sends the data over the Internet to a data vaulting facility that is managed by the service provider. There are three variations of this offering that are worth exploring, with 2010 starting to see an upshift in the number of providers, as well as the number of adopters.

Local Channel Resellers

One good choice for small business owners is to have their data protected by the local reseller or systems integrator that normally provides them with technical services. The idea here is to eliminate the need for managing backups within the small business (and also gain a data survivability or disaster recovery capability) by letting the reseller do it at their facility. The additional benefit for the small business is that if a crisis were to occur, even if they had their data somewhere else, the reseller/integrator is likely who they would call to order additional hardware and start the recovery process. Instead, in this arrangement, the reseller already has their clients' data. So, when a small business client suffers a crisis, the partner can immediately begin preparing restoration gear.

This scenario is ideal for the small business that is dependent on a local partner for their technical expertise and does not have the IT knowledge to recover themselves—as long as the partner is considered trustworthy and viable for the long term. In addition, small business customers choosing this scenario should investigate what the resiliency capabilities are of the partner. If the partner's primary facility (which has all of the customers' data and backups) were to fail, does the partner have a secondary site to continue offering their protection service?

Using a local channel partner can be a great solution for DR, especially for the small business that will be calling the partner at the first sign of trouble. But there is also a drawback to the arrangement—in the word *local*. If a regional event like a flood were to occur, a local partner may be impacted by the same crisis as you are. Even if your data is protected outside the regional boundaries, your company may find that the staff from the local partner are unavailable to help (because they are helping get their own company or homes fixed first).

Data Vaulting Providers

Alternatively, instead of going to a general-purpose local reseller, there are a few reputable companies that provide data vaulting as a service, meaning that the data goes from your facility to their data repository via the Internet. While there are certainly some start-up and burgeoning players in the market, particularly for individual users and small businesses, one company that should be considered for medium and large companies is Iron Mountain. Yes, these are the same folks who pick up your tapes or securely shred your documents. While Iron Mountain certainly has a long reputation for picking up tapes and paper records for offsite storage, they have a division (Iron

Mountain Digital) that eliminates the courier service and replicates your data directly to their repository. In this scenario, you put an agent on either your production servers directly or on your DPM backup server, and then replicate the data to their offsite datacenter via the Internet. This kind of service is also called *backing up to the cloud*, or *backup software as a service* (SaaS).

Data vaulting companies have an entire business model built on delivering a resilient infrastructure that reliably backs up your data to their facility. In choosing a data vaulting provider, the big differentiators will be the cost of the service compared with your assessment of their long-term viability and trustworthiness. A few vaulting providers may have additional service offerings, such as outsourced backups, instead of simply a recovery to the most recent point in time after a disaster. As an example, unlike most providers that need to not only protect your data over the Internet but also restore all your data over the Internet, Iron Mountain has the ability to deliver a small data appliance to your location that has your data on it—for a local and fast restore. This is due to the fleet of vehicles that already drive throughout your locale.

A recommended vaulting solution is the partnership between Microsoft Data Protection Manager and Iron Mountain, in a service called CloudRecovery (`www.microsoft.com/DPM/cloud`). In this way, you take advantage of the backup capabilities discussed in Chapter 4 on premises, and get an off-premises solution through a trusted partner.

Hybrid On-Premise and Vault/Cloud Providers

In the previous Channel Reseller and Backup as a Service models, no on-premise backups were performed. You were able to completely forget the task of backup; however, you also lost the ability to restore data quickly from a local repository.

One hybrid approach is to look for backup software vendors who have partnerships or extensions with cloud or service providers. In some cases, the backup software vendors are attempting to establish a service themselves; such is the case with Symantec, as well as EMC Legato with its Mozy acquisition. In other cases, the solution is a partnership such as Microsoft Data Protection Manager with Iron Mountain (also discussed earlier).

The solution assumes a reliable backup solution on premise that supports a Disk-to-Disk-to-Cloud (D2D2C) solution, as described in Chapter 3. The data is replicated from the production server's disk to an on-premise backup server disk, and then replicated from the backup server to the cloud repository.

BC/DR Solution Alternatives

There are at least two fundamental ways to look at the technologies that can be used for a enabling a remote data protection and availability solution:

- Application- or workload-specific features
- Whole server or site solutions

Application- or Workload-Specific Features

As we've discussed in the application and storage chapters, many of the core workloads discussed in this book have a long-distance replication and resiliency feature set.

Storage mirroring (Chapter 3) between two arrays, when done asynchronously, will provide a second and resilient instance of the storage at the remote location. This is asynchronously mirrored so that the production server at the primary site is not hindered in performance due to the long-distance array mirroring. However, resilient storage alone is not sufficient, so a second Windows server connected to the redundant storage is also necessary for resumption of service. This is a common scenario for geographically split clusters (Chapter 6).

Also, as discussed previously, File Services (Chapter 5), Exchange SCR and DAG (Chapter 7), and SQL Server (Chapter 8) all provide for long-distance replication (DR) with resumption of service (BC) from a secondary site.

These solutions are desirable for scenarios where you are not actually suffering a site-wide crisis from the primary location but instead have simply lost one or more production servers, such as a server failure or a part of the datacenter floor, while the remainder of the production environment continues to function.

These solutions may be less desirable for site-wide crises only because each platform has different failover and resumption activity. Exchange SCR fails over one way, while SQL mirroring fails over with a different method, and DFS does something else. During a real site-wide crisis, there will be many other details to manage—so having to ensure that a File Services specialist, an Exchange operator, and a database administrator are all on hand (in case their components do not fail over as planned) may add to the complexity. This is not to say that you want everything to happen automatically. In fact, when failing over an entire site, you explicitly do not want it to happen automatically. You want to make an informed and executive-sponsored decision to fail over. But after that decision, anything that you can do to automate the execution (scripts or stored procedures) will make the actual failover more achievable (especially when considering that your primary site's experts may not be available during the resumption activities). Certainly, for each piece that does reliably fail over, the availability is near immediate and can help the business resume quickly. You will need to choose between utilizing each workload's resiliency features or a whole-server/site scenario.

Application-Agnostic Replication and Failover

In Chapter 3, we discussed how some host-based replication software is application-agnostic, meaning that it replicates file-based data at a block or byte level. These technologies can often replicate the partial-file changes within an Exchange `.edb` file with the same mechanism as a SQL Server `.mdf` database file, or a really big Notepad `.txt` file for that matter.

These kinds of technologies can provide a single UI and model for replicating the data from multiple workloads such as SQL Server or Exchange, and then initiating failover at the secondary site either manually or automatically. However, in reality, you will still have to depend on all the various application resumption mechanisms. For the application to come online, it must be preinstalled on the redundant servers in the same manner as it was installed on the original production servers. And because the application was not used during the replication, the resumption of service will behave much like a server coming online after a hard power outage. The databases and logs will have to be compared for application consistency and rolled back or forward, as appropriate and based on the recovery mechanisms of each application.

While the single UI and replication mechanism may appear attractive, the reality is that by allowing the applications (Exchange, SQL Server, Windows File Services) to handle the replication and resumption of service, you get a more efficient replication and a more reliable resumption of service.

Real World Scenario

DISCLAIMER ON APPLICATION-AGNOSTIC REPLICATION AND FAILOVER

I must confess to having previously sold a product from this application-agnostic replication category for about nine years. In looking at the data protection landscape as it was in the early 1990s and as described in Chapters 1 and 3, asynchronous host-based replication enabled some recovery scenarios that were otherwise nonviable to most IT environments. It was a great approach to solving data protection and availability.

But by 2005, SQL Server database mirroring (with failover) was starting to become more popular, as well as Windows 2003 R2 DFS replication and namespaces. With the public disclosure of what would be Exchange 2007 CCR, as well as the imminent release of Data Protection Manager, it was clear to me that host-based replication approaches would need to adapt to address new data protection or availability challenges—or risk becoming extinct. Third-party replication and failover was being usurped by the original vendor of those applications and operating systems—Microsoft. So, I joined Microsoft.

Today, those software technologies are not extinct. In fact, as is common in a partner ecosystem, the agile vendors are adapting to address different and broader IT challenges in data protection, availability, and movement, now that their original markets of Exchange, SQL Server, Windows File Services, and centralized backup are often addressed by native Microsoft technologies.

Using Virtualization to Achieve Business Continuity

We have discussed using the native replication and availability features of the various workloads to provide resumption of services from a secondary site, and their advantages over using a preconfigured host-based replication solution. But there is another option, whereby the original servers from the production facility are replicated as whole objects and re-seated at the secondary site during a crisis.

In times past, this might have been done by having physical duplicates of the production servers at the secondary site and then using either host-based or storage-array based mirroring to replicate the data underneath them between sites, as discussed in Chapter 3. This was often referred to as maintaining a warm site with servers predeployed or staged at a disaster recovery location.

Challenges with Traditional Disaster Recovery Staging

There were two traditional methods for staging a redundant site for disaster recovery purposes:

Offsite Tape Couriers For large companies that have either a regulatory requirement or a common business practice of retaining key documents at an offsite location, it was common to utilize courier services to shuttle copies of tapes to a storage location that was considered agile and able to start performing restores as soon as the primary site declared a disaster. If the servers were already onsite, you might call this a warm site. If the servers were prenegotiated to be expeditiously shipped upon request, this was a cold site. Either way, the presumption was that new physical servers would be hastily restored from offsite tapes (or data vaulting).

Replicated Datacenter Other companies chose to maintain the secondary datacenter that we discussed earlier, and in so doing maintained a great deal of redundant hardware. The idea was a good one, especially when leveraging the built-in replication and resiliency features of the workloads. But as described earlier, a downside of this approach was purchasing, operating, and maintaining that additional equipment, particularly when the equipment would be underutilized but still require space, power, cooling, and management.

Disaster Recovery Staging, Virtually

But, after reading Chapter 9, we know that there is a better way to address underutilized servers and eliminate many of the space, power, cooling, and management costs associated with server infrastructure: virtualization. The key to success therefore becomes how to get your data and server configurations from your physical production environment into a virtualized disaster recovery site.

To accomplish this goal, using technologies that we have already discussed, we will utilize Microsoft Windows Server 2008 R2 with Hyper-V R2 as a virtualization hypervisor, along with multiple Microsoft management tools from System Center (SC), including:

- System Center Data Protection Manager (DPM) from Chapter 4
- System Center Virtual Machine Manager (VMM) from Chapter 10
- System Center Operations Manager from Chapter 11

Protecting the Whole Production Server

Fundamentally, three types of information should be protected per physical server for disaster preparedness, as shown in Figure 12.1:

- The operating systems and applications of the physical production server farm—for use at the disaster recovery location

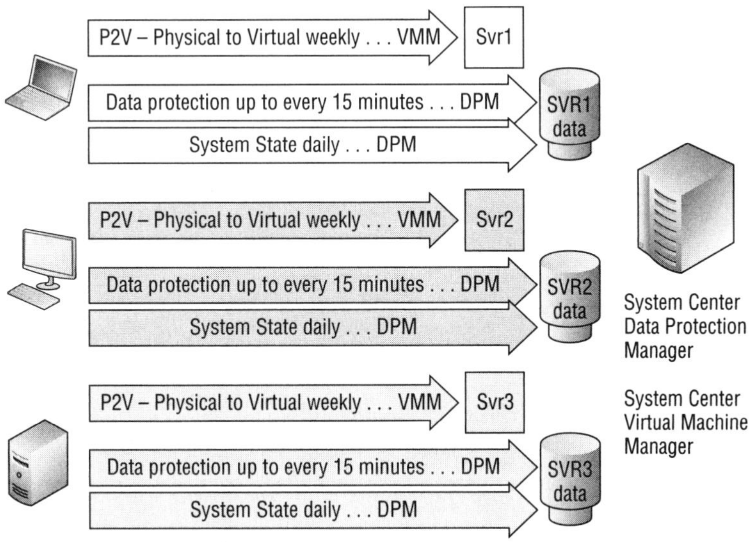

FIGURE 12.1
Disaster recovery staging, via DPM and VMM
Source: Microsoft

- The operating systems and applications of the physical production server farm—for the purposes of recovering the original physical servers after the crisis has been resolved
- The data

Using VMM to Protect the Operating System and Applications

VMM provides a utility for migrating physical production servers into virtual environments. The Physical-to-Virtual (P2V) utility is usually run once per physical production server; the result is the encapsulation of the physical hard drives as a series of VHD files for a virtual machine. Typically, this is done as part of migrating a server resource into a new virtualization infrastructure, as we did in Task 23, "Physical-to-Virtual Migration," in Chapter 10.

In most cases, you can execute the P2V utility safely without interrupting the production server. Then, as part of a migration scenario, you would power down the physical server and then bring the virtualized copy online. In our case, as part of staging a disaster recovery site, you can run this same process routinely to capture a physical operating system and application set to a VHD, which you can then replicate from the production facility to the disaster recovery site. Instead of being used for migration purposes, these VHDs will be left dormant until needed due to a crisis at the primary site.

Because VMM is scriptable with Windows PowerShell, you can automate this process weekly or perhaps execute it ad hoc after server maintenance or configuration changes. This dramatically reduces the amount of redundant server hardware at the disaster recovery site. Instead of racks of underutilized physical servers, companies can deploy a few dedicated virtualization hosts—while retaining complete and autonomous instances of the entire production physical server farm.

> **If Your Production Servers Are Already Virtualized**
>
> If your production servers are already virtualized, you do not need to P2V them. Instead, simply back up the virtual machines from a host-based backup. This serves the same purpose because the virtual machine is now portable between the backup systems and contains the VHDs and virtual machine configuration necessary to bring the virtual server online someplace else.

Using DPM to Protect the Data

As discussed in Chapter 4, Data Protection Manager can protect the data as often as every 15 minutes, as a disk-to-disk solution, as well as to tape for long-term retention. DPM can also replicate from one DPM server to another.

In this case, you can use a primary DPM server at the production facility to protect the data for normal backup and recovery tasks, as well as the virtual machines. These would likely be done in two separate protection groups (policies) on the primary DPM server at the production site:

DPM Protection Group 1: Data

- Providing 30 days of disk-based protection, with up to 15-minute synchronizations
- Protecting the various Exchange storage groups, SQL databases, and file shares of the production servers

If your production servers are physical, you will want to protect the virtual machines that were just P2V'd. If your production servers are already virtualized, then protect them too:

DPM Protection Group 2: The VMs

- Providing 5 days of disk-based protection, running nightly at 11 p.m.
- Protecting the Hyper-V virtual machines that were P2V'd from the production servers

This provides for a typical window of data recovery of the production data as discussed in Chapter 4. In addition, a copy of the VMs from the P2V utility is stored on the DPM server, along with a few potential recent iterations to roll back to, if necessary, but only for a few days. At the secondary location, a second DPM server would also have two protection group policies defined:

DPM-DR Protection Group 1: Data

- Providing 14 days of disk-based protection, synchronizing every few hours
- Providing 7 years of tape-based protection, using a weekly, monthly, annual tape rotation scheme
- Protecting the primary DPM server's copy of the Exchange storage groups, SQL databases, and file shares of the production servers

DPM-DR Protection Group 2: The VMs

- Providing 14 days of disk-based protection, synchronizing nightly at 3 a.m.
- Protecting the primary DPM server's copy of the VMs

This provides the data with another layer of protection, as well as tape-based backup. In this case, because the tape backups are occurring at the secondary location, they already qualify as offsite backups without having to transport the tapes between locations. Additionally, the VMs are also replicated to the secondary site using the block-level synchronization method of DPM. Now the VMs are almost ready to be brought online, if necessary.

Guest and Host-Based Protection of the Same Data

If your production servers are already virtualized, and you follow the protection groups described here, you may end up protecting the actual data twice (depending on how your VMs are configured). This is okay because it enables different kinds of recovery scenarios:

- For whole-server recovery, the host-based backup has everything ready to go.
- For partial data recovery or to recover the data to a previous point in time, the guest-based backup has all the data in its native state.

Admittedly, this does consume additional storage space. But the additional recovery capabilities, and the value of the data, almost always far outweigh the component costs. So, cost should not be the reason to not do this (see Chapter 2).

In addition, DPM can protect the system state of the production servers. In the more common scenario where you don't lose the entire production facility but just a single server, you can use the system state to restore an individual server configuration back to similar hardware, if needed.

Planning for Long-Term Server Restoration

In the event of a true site calamity, where the entire production server farm is critically affected, you may be operating within the virtualized environment for a while. Your initial disaster recovery execution may include a plan whereby all your production physical servers are replicated but the virtualization host environment can't sustain all of them running simultaneously. It's perfectly reasonable, based on your business impact analysis (Chapter 2), to predetermine that only a percentage of production servers can be brought online immediately after averting a crisis. Based on your future outlook, you may then plan to expedite additional virtualization hosts to bring the remaining virtualized servers online.

At some point, however, you'll need to enact your long-term server-restoration plan:

- Some companies, after confirming that the virtualized servers are performing adequately, may use the crisis as a forcing function toward an all-virtual infrastructure and remain in production from the virtualized machines. If that is the case, additional Hyper-V hosts, likely with resiliency such as Live Migration, should be considered for the new production virtualization infrastructure.
- Other companies wish to rebuild their physical production server farm. Currently, the VMM P2V utility does not provide a virtual-to-physical (V2P) mechanism, meaning that the virtualized server cannot be used to reconstruct the original physical server. But because DPM can protect the physical servers' system state along with the production data, the system state can be used to reconstitute the production-server farm. Protecting system state with DPM 2010 was discussed in Chapter 4 and would likely be a third protection group policy.

DPM Protection Group 3: The VMs

- Providing 17 days of disk-based protection, running weekly on Sundays
- Protecting the system state of the production servers

Here, we see the system state is only captured once per week. The 17-day retention policy ensures that you have at least two previous weekly iterations of the system state to restore back to. The additional days are the margin between a Sunday backup and the software updates that happen the following Tuesday, so that the oldest iteration isn't discarded until after the patches are successfully applied.

Restoring Your Infrastructure within Hyper-V

Assuming that you've been routinely capturing your physical server configurations using VMM P2V, as well as continually protecting your data with DPM, let's now look at the recovery procedure after a disaster. The highest priorities of a disaster recovery plan include ensuring the safety of personnel and enacting the larger disaster recovery plan as defined by your executive leadership. That being understood, most disaster recovery efforts succeed or fail based on your ability to access your corporate information. Said another way, without your data, the rest of your plan may not work.

Using VMM to Bring Servers Online

The first task is to bring the virtualized production servers online. Depending on your needs for rapid recovery, you may choose to have pre-restored the VMs on a Hyper-V host on a regular and automatically scripted basis. When you do this, the virtual machine configuration is set up within the new host, so that all you have to do is bring it online. To do that, VMM provides a PowerShell cmdlet (`Start-VM`):

```
Start-VM -VM Dallas_EX27  -RunAsynchronously
```

Bringing 20 VMs online can literally be done as a 20-line batch file. Alternatively, by using the smart-placement technology in VMM 2008, you can be more selective or judicious about which virtualization hosts bring up which virtualized guests. In addition, you may not have enough processing power at the secondary site to bring all the VMs online immediately. Instead, you may choose to only bring up the most critical servers first, and then expedite additional Hyper-V hosts to bring the rest online within a business day or two. In that case, the immediate recovery script to bring up the most important four servers could be as simple as this:

```
Start-VM -VM Dallas_EX27  -RunAsynchronously

Start-VM -VM Dallas_FS3   -RunAsynchronously

Start-VM -VM Dallas_SQL25 -RunAsynchronously

Start-VM -VM Dallas_SQL28 -RunAsynchronously
```

Using DPM to Restore Data

After the VMs are brought online, most will have a recent `C:` partition, with its operating system and applications in their first VHD, but be either missing the data areas completely or have an older set of data from when the last P2V was taken (depending on the storage configuration of the production servers). You can use VMM to add storage to each VM, if necessary—as if a production server had lost one or more hard drives and new one(s) were installed.

Similar to VMM, DPM can be controlled using PowerShell. The cmdlet isn't as universal because the options vary based on the data type being restored. However, because these scripts are defined before a disaster occurs, you're encouraged to explore the Microsoft TechNet center on DPM PowerShell scripting. Look at the `Recover-RecoverableItem` and `New-RecoveryOption` cmdlets at

`http://technet.microsoft.com/en-us/library/bb842063.aspx`

With the VMs online and the data restored, your company can now begin to resume IT operations.

Making the Process Even Better

With the basics understood, you can do several things to optimize this recovery process:

Create a script per server, instead of per VMM or DPM phase. Consider creating individual scripts that include all the VMM and DPM PowerShell commands per virtual machine. This provides a few benefits, including these:

- You can choose to stagger the server booting process so that critical servers can be completely brought online first while less essential servers are deferred, if necessary.
- If the entire production site has not failed entirely but only one or more physical servers have been critically affected, you can choose to selectively bring just those virtualized servers online.

Here is an example script that brings a production SQL Server and its three primary databases online, including both the VMM and DPM logic:

```
Get-VMMServer localhost
Start-VM -VM Dallas_SQL25

sleep 60

Connect-DPMServer DPM
$PS = SQL25.contoso.com

$ds = SQL25\ACCOUNTING\PAYROLL
$rp = Get-RecoveryPoint -Datasource $ds
$rop = New-RecoveryOption  -TargetServer $PS -SQL -RecoveryLocation original
   -OverwriteType overwrite  -RecoveryType Restore
Recover-RecoverableItem -RecoverableItem $rp -RecoveryOption $rop

$ds = SQL25\ACCOUNTING\RECEIVABLES
$rp = Get-RecoveryPoint -Datasource $ds
$rop = New-RecoveryOption  -TargetServer $PS -SQL -RecoveryLocation original
   -OverwriteType overwrite  -RecoveryType Restore
Recover-RecoverableItem -RecoverableItem $rp -RecoveryOption $rop

$ds = SQL25\ACCOUNTING\HUMAN_RESOURCES
$rp = Get-RecoveryPoint -Datasource $ds
$rop = New-RecoveryOption  -TargetServer $PS -SQL -RecoveryLocation original
   -OverwriteType overwrite  -RecoveryType Restore
Recover-RecoverableItem -RecoverableItem $rp -RecoveryOption $rop
```

Use SC Operations Manager to monitor the production environment and provide intelligent information about the scope of the disaster. You can embed the VMM/DPM recovery scripts seen earlier as tasks within Operations Manager. Then, the recovery tasks can be invoked by the same operator who has determined the scale of the crisis. By first defining rigorous diagnostic criteria, you may choose to automate the entire disaster recovery process, to be invoked when the appropriate conditions are met in Operations Manager. You should do this with care, however, to avoid a false positive where the disaster recovery environment is enabled when a site crisis hasn't actually occurred.

Automate the network resolution for remote clients. For remote users outside the primary production facility, consider using either a dynamic/round-robin DNS configuration or an Internet gateway, so that remote clients can be transparently switched from accessing the primary production facility and the disaster recovery site.

Collectively, you can use virtualization along with data protection to address your disaster recovery goals with products and technologies that you're already familiar with—and thus deliver capabilities that may otherwise be cost-prohibitive.

Additional Notes on Virtualized BC/DR Sites

Here are a few last details to consider when leveraging a virtualized disaster recovery site:

If your production servers are already virtualized, it is even easier. If your production servers are already virtualized, the process is even easier. You do not need to P2V the production servers, since they are already virtualized. Instead, simply back up the virtual machines from a host-based backup. This serves the same purpose because the virtual machine is now portable between the backup systems and contains the VHDs and virtual machine configuration necessary to bring the virtual server online someplace else. You will still want to replicate them from the primary DPM server to the secondary DPM server for DR staging.

You could do BC/DR without virtualization, but why? There are many folks who probably believe that every server should be virtualized, almost always. And from a cost-benefit and operational efficiency perspective, I am usually one of them. There are exceptions, usually deriving from hardware requirements of certain production workloads or supportability issues since not all workloads are supported by the vendor if running in a virtualized environment. But changing the production server infrastructure can be a daunting task that you may not have tackled yet (or believe is necessary).

That's okay, but even if your production server farm is still predominantly physical servers, your disaster recovery site does not have to be. Without virtualization, your disaster recovery site will likely be either:

- A small subset of your production server farm, based on which production workloads can cost-justify the additional hardware at the redundant site
- Very expensive to purchase and then maintain, in hardware and software, operational, and labor and management costs

HOW WILL YOU GET THE DATA BACK?

We have covered a range of data protection and availability technologies in this chapter, and this book, so restoring the data back to the original facility has too many variables to provide an all-encompassing answer. But here are some factors for you to consider:

Plan in advance how the data will be restored to the original facility. Surprisingly, while most BC/DR plans include how business will be resumed from the secondary site soon or immediately after the crisis, many do not include a well-thought-out mechanism for the eventual restoration of the primary facility. This is ironic because you are dealing with another site-to-site move of your critical IT infrastructure, so plan for it in advance, if for no other reason than in the horrible event that some of your IT resources are not available after the crisis.

Be aware how the data mover that you used to stage your secondary data can be used in reverse. This will vary based on the technology. In the case of the built-in application resiliency features, such as Windows DFS, Exchange DAG, or SQL database mirroring, this is easy. Any node can send or receive, so instead of replicating from the primary facility to the secondary facility, you will configure the opposite. And on a per-server basis, if your users have resumed work from the primary facility, you can switch each workload or even individual server from the secondary site to the primary site with a right-click and then another click or two. If you are using D2D host-based replication or backup software, you may need to create additional policies or settings so that the secondary data is essentially protected back to the production facility.

Planning for BC/DR to Get Better Backups and Availability

One of my favorite aspects of working with clients who are moving ahead with BC/DR technology plans is that they already have an understanding of what is necessary to achieve reliable backups, with adequate recovery points and highly available production systems:

Your BC/DR BIA and RA will yield RMs that you already wanted. In Chapter 2, we discussed quantifying the cost of not having reliable backups or systems availability. Earlier in this chapter, we discussed the formal CBCP Professional Practices when developing a business continuity strategy. If you do these, then when you do your business impact analysis (BIA) to calculate the cost of downtime along with the risk assessment (RA) for how likely each of the wide range of calamities might be, you will find tactical opportunities to improve your current infrastructure. You will quickly see that adding some risk mitigation (RM) technologies, such as clustering, replication/mirroring, and disk-based backups, will significantly reduce your most likely sources of outages. In short, by deploying the resiliency techniques discussed in Chapters 3–9, along with better management methods from Chapters 10 and 11, you are both addressing tactical operational improvement as well as strategic disaster preparedness.

Easy DR usually results in D2D2D2T. We have said it before in passing, but to be clear: if you back up your data from your disaster recovery site instead of your production site, your disaster recovery site is giving you offsite backups without courier services. In fact, some companies have been able to pay for their offsite replication mechanisms (bandwidth, additional servers, or software) simply by eliminating their courier services budget. From an accounting perspective, there is often a benefit in spending even the same amount of money in depreciating hardware and software over an operational line item like couriers. This can help pay for a part of your DR plan, just by doing your tape backups in a smarter way.

You will get operational uptime from your BC/DR resources, because not all disasters are big. Not all disasters impact an entire facility. Perhaps a small part of the IT room floods; everything else is running fine, but you have lost a percentage of your production resources. Then, failover that percentage to the secondary site while the remainder of your environment runs normally. Perhaps just one really important server fails? Ideally, that server is resilient within the same site, but if you can only justify two servers, then you may have deployed the second instance at the DR site. And for DFS, Exchange DAG, or SQL with mirrored databases, that is completely fine. Transparently utilize the offsite copy while you rebuild the onsite copy, and when it is repaired, fail back. Statistically speaking, you are obviously much more likely to lose a server, or even part of a computer room, than the entire facility. So, plan to use your BC/DR resources for the little disasters, as well as the big ones.

Summary

To finish this chapter (and the book), let's look at BC/DR as it is now and where it is heading.

Where BC/DR is today

Disaster recovery (DR) technologies ensure your data survives. Business continuity (BC) technologies leverage the surviving data so that your company can remain operational, even after a crisis.

Consultants get paid quite a bit to help companies comply with regulations. But the reality is that hardly any of the regulations have specific guidance on how to protect your data. In fact, only some of them even address that you should. Most of the regulations cover broader issues related to the organization as a whole, and that is why you should do BC or DR, because your organization needs it—not because a regulation may or may not mandate it.

Remember, no one cares as much about your business surviving as you do. Consultants may be sincere in wanting to partner with you, but at the end of the day, they have other customers too. You, as part of your collective organization, have only one company, so do not outsource or delegate its survival.

Virtualization does have many operational benefits, but it can also be a key to success in your BC/DR infrastructure.

Where BC/DR is heading

The evolving mechanisms of BC/DR are a result of the evolution in data protection (DP) and high availability (HA) technologies — as well as changing regulations and mandates. As our summary, let's close the book with the same view as we started it: with a look at the changing landscape of data protection and availability.

In 1990, there were two mainstream IT solutions at opposite extremes: disk-based mirroring for data resiliency and nightly tape-based backup.

In 1995, asynchronous replication started offering some middle ground for many IT environments to gain better data protection than nightly tape, at a cost far less than array-based storage mirroring.

In 2005, we started seeing disk-to-disk backups becoming standard as a precursor to tape for higher reliability and granular restore, while applications such as SQL Server started mirroring its own databases and providing built-in replication and availability instead of relying on third parties.

In 2007, we saw failover clustering get easier and accessible with Windows Server 2008, while Exchange 2007 also added built-in replication and availability.

In 2010, we now have:

- Exchange 2010 with database availability groups that provide onsite and offsite replication and service resiliency

- SQL Server 2008 R2, which continues to improve a wide range of built-in replication, mirroring, and failover mechanisms
- Windows Server 2008 R2 with not only resiliency in DFS for File Services, but also Live Migration for Hyper-V R2 for a highly available virtualization platform
- System Center Data Protection Manager 2010 with unified protection of Windows servers and clients, to disk, tape, and clouds

The core platforms are continuing to mature and offer data availability and data protection that used to be addressed only by third-party solutions. Sometimes, those capabilities are delivered as features, such as DAG. In other cases, the capabilities are delivered by extending the solution across products, such as enabling SQL to utilize failover clustering within Windows. And in some cases, the capabilities are delivered through new Microsoft products that are designed exclusively for Windows, such as DPM.

But as interconnecting bandwidth becomes increasingly affordable, the technology aspects of business continuity and disaster recovery become simply a distance-based extension of the evolving technologies around high availability and data protection.

As promised, here is one last piece of advice:

Get your data out of the building.

Appendix

Links and Resources

Here are some resources that I used in writing this book.

Microsoft Software

Almost every exercise in the book was done using evaluation software that is publicly downloadable from a Microsoft website. You may have other sources available for your materials, but this provided a consistent way to ensure that you could follow along and do the same activities.

Product Evaluation Software Some software was downloaded directly from the individual product websites, such as `www.microsoft.com/DPM` for System Center Data Protection Manager (DPM) from Chapter 4.

TechNet Evaluation Software Some software was downloaded from Microsoft TechNet (`http://technet.microsoft.com/EvalCenter`), which provides a centralized repository of EXE and ISO installation media for most mainstream Microsoft products.

TestDrive VHDs In some cases, I downloaded entire virtual machines that already included not only Windows Server, but also a common application server, such as SQL Server or Microsoft Exchange. TestDrive VHDs contain time-bombed versions of the OS and applications so that folks like you and me can learn more about the solution without wrestling with installing the base OS, prerequisites, and applications. TestDrive VHDs can also be found at the TechNet evaluation center: `http://technet.microsoft.com/EvalCenter`.

In most cases, the exercises were done using virtual machines that were primarily hosted on one or two Windows Server 2008 R2 hosts running Hyper-V, as well as one host running Virtual Server 2005 R2 for running some older VHDs. The storage for the virtual machines was provided by the iSCSI Software Target on a Windows Storage Server 2008 platform.

Topical Resources

Here are some of the resource links that are related to technologies discussed in the book.

Almost every product at Microsoft has a great TechCenter, as a primary landing place for all IT Implementer technical knowledge, to which the product groups, documentation teams, and other subject matter experts contribute.

Chapter 4: Data Protection Manager

Admittedly, I did not require much in the way of external resources for DPM, since this is one of the products that I manage during my day job. Here are some good resources on DPM:

The main website for DPM, with customer-facing whitepapers, webcasts and related material, is `www.microsoft.com/DPM`.

The TechCenter for DPM, with the official product documentation, as well as support articles and deployment tips, is `technet.microsoft.com/DPM`.

Resources for Microsoft Partner can be found at `http://partner.microsoft.com/DPM`.

There are two Microsoft blogs on DPM that are good places for up-to-date support and deployment guidance, as well as announcements about the product or upcoming webcasts:

Product Team's Blog: `blogs.technet.com/DPM`

Product Manager's Blog (mine): `blog.JasonBuffington.com`

DPM and I are on Twitter at `@SCDPM` and `@JBUFF`, respectively.

In addition, here are a few external resources that are great for DPM 2010 and DPM 2007 SP1:

David Allen, a Microsoft MVP, writes a blog and has some great insight into running DPM in multiple enterprises. He even built a better Management Pack for DPM 2007 than the one that ships for it. David blogs at `www.SCDPMonline.com` and tweets as `@AquilaWeb`.

Mike Resseler, in the System Center Users Group in Belgium, also has some great DPM resources and is one of the most active bloggers and tweeters for DPM that I know. Mike blogs at `http://scug.be/blogs/mike/` and `http://scug.be/blogs/scdpm` and tweets as `@MikeResseler`.

Chapters 4, 5, and 6: Windows Server

Windows Server includes several technologies described in Chapters 4–6, among them:

- Volume Shadow Copy Services (VSS), covered in Chapter 4
- Windows Server Backup (WSB), also covered in Chapter 4
- Distributed File System (DFS), covered in Chapter 5
- Failover Clustering (WFC), covered in Chapter 6

The Windows Server TechCenter (`http://technet.microsoft.com/windowsserver`) provided a great resource to officially confirm ideas discussed about Windows Server 2008 and 2008 R2. In addition, the Windows Server blog and website have great resources available:

`www.microsoft.com/WindowsServer`

`blogs.technet.com/WindowsServer`

Volume Shadow Copy Services

Here are some good resources related to VSS. Both refer to VSS in Windows Server 2003 but are great resources to understanding VSS overall:

How Volume Shadow Copy Service Works: `http://technet.microsoft.com/en-us/library/cc785914(WS.10).aspx`

TechNet Magazine article on VSS: `http://technet.microsoft.com/en-us/magazine/2006.01.rapidrecovery.aspx`

File Services

Three great blogs provide the very best information on Windows File Services and storage solutions, one by the File Services product team and the other two from program managers within the team:

File Services Team: `blogs.technet.com/FileCab`
Jose Barreto: `blogs.technet.com/josebda`
Adi Oltean: `blogs.msdn.com/adioltean`

Distributed File System

While originally published for Windows Server 2003 R2, some of the best resources for DFS, DFS-R, and DFS-N are in the Distributed File System Technology Center at `www.microsoft.com/windowsserver2003/technologies/storage/dfs/`.

Beyond that, the Windows Server TechCenter has good articles on DFS deployment, as well as what changed from 2003 R2 to 2008, and from 2008 to 2008 R2. Searching the Internet for the names of either of the two DFS program managers who reviewed Chapter 5 will also provide some great resources: Mahesh Unnikrishnan and Drew McDaniel.

Windows Failover Clustering

The first place to look regarding Failover Clustering is the Windows Server website (`www.microsoft.com/WindowsServer`). From the top navigation bar, click Product Information ➢ Technologies ➢ Failover Clustering for a wealth of information. The Clustering Team within Microsoft also writes a great blog at `blogs.msdn.com/clustering/`.

In addition, I am a member of the Elden Rocks Fan Club, meaning that whenever you have the opportunity to watch a webcast or attend a session from Elden Christensen, you will learn great stuff about clustering Windows Server. I do not have a particular URL or event from Elden to list here, but plugging his name into your favorite search engine will give you a variety of clustering-related topics, some of which I have attended during webcasts or live events.

Chapter 7: Exchange

The two best folks that I know for Exchange availability and storage solutions are Scott Schnoll and Ross Smith IV. Most of my more recent Exchange knowledge comes from watching their webcasts and conference sessions. Both of them contribute to the Exchange Team's blog EHLO at `http://msExchangeTeam.com`. Scott also blogs at `http://blogs.technet.com/scottschnoll`.

Scott was kind enough to mercilessly review Chapter 7. The technical editor for this book was Paul Robichaux, who is also an Exchange MVP. Searching the Internet for either of their names will yield some great information on Microsoft Exchange. Paul blogs at `www.robichaux.net/blog`.

Information on how to back up Exchange can be found at `www.microsoft.com/DPM/exchange`.

Chapter 8: SQL Server

SQL Server was perhaps one of my favorite chapters to research, because of the wealth of online resources, whitepapers, and videos. I have watched quite a few webcasts and event breakout sessions over time on SQL Server availability. Here are three good SQL websites:

- The primary SQL Server website for most of the technologies discussed in Chapter 8 is `www.microsoft.com/SQLserver`.

- Microsoft recently refreshed their SQL Books Online (product documentation) within the SQL Server TechCenter, and provides some additional depth on mechanisms from Chapter 8 at `http://technet.microsoft.com/SQLserver`.
- Information on how to back up SQL Server can be found at `www.microsoft.com/DPM/sql`.

Chapter 9: Virtualization

Very few technologies at Microsoft have seen as much new material and in-depth guidance as its wide range of virtualization technologies:

Website: `microsoft.com/virtualization`

Blog: `blogs.technet.com/virtualization`

Twitter: `@Virtualization` and `@MS_Virt`

In regard to Hyper-V itself, as well as the LiveMigration and Cluster Shared Volumes (CSV) scenarios, the best resources start at the Windows Server website (`www.microsoft.com/WindowsServer`). From the top navigation bar, click Product Information ➢ Technologies ➢ Virtualization With Hyper-V for a wealth of information.

My favorite guru on Hyper-V virtualization is Jeff Woolsey. Search the Internet for Hyper-V resources by him and you will come away virtually smarter. A great book on Hyper-V is *Windows Server 2008 Hyper-V: Insiders Guide to Hyper-V* (Sybex, 2009). I wrote the DPM chapter of the first edition (ISBN 978-0470440964) and read a good bit of the rest. The second edition covering Hyper-V in Windows Server 2008 R2 (ISBN 978-0470627006) is being released about the same time as this book.

Information on how to back up Hyper-V can be found at `www.microsoft.com/DPM/virtualization`.

Chapters 10 and 11: System Center

I was grateful to have three friends of mine contribute material for these two management chapters. Here are some great resources to help you with System Center:

Website: `www.microsoft.com/SystemCenter`

Blog: `blogs.technet.com/SystemCenter`

Twitter: `@System_Center` and `@MSmanageability`

Because System Center is a family of products, here are some direct links to the products covered in Chapters 10 and 11:

System Center Configuration Manager I learn the most about Configuration Manager by attending sessions by and searching the Internet for resources from Jeff Wettlaufer (Twitter: `@JeffWettlaufer`), Bill Anderson or Wally Mead (who was so gracious to write a large part of Chapter 10). Here are some additional Configuration Manager resources:

Website: `www.microsoft.com/SCCM`

Support Blog: `blogs.technet.com/ConfigurationMgr`

System Center Operations Manager I learn the most about Operations Manager by listening to Sacha Dawes, who was nice enough to write a good bit of Chapter 11. Here are some additional Operations Manager resources:

Website: `www.microsoft.com/systemcenter/OpsMgr`

Support Blog: `blogs.technet.com/OperationsMgr`

System Center Virtual Machine Manager There are some great resources that provide information across the portfolio of Microsoft's virtualization technologies. I've learned the most about Microsoft's virtualization management technologies from Edwin Yuen (Twitter: `@EdwinYuen`), who was kind enough to write the VMM components of Chapter 10.

Website: `www.microsoft.com/SCVMM`

Support Blog: `blogs.technet.com/SCVMM`

System Center Essentials Some great resources can be found by searching the Internet for SCE information from Eamon O'Reilly or Dustin Jones.

Website: `www.microsoft.com/SCE`

Blog: `blogs.technet.com/SystemCenterEssentials`

Twitter: `@SCEssentials`

Chapter 12: BC and DR

Here are the regulations referenced in Chapter 12:

E-SIGN

`www.gpo.gov/fdsys/pkg/PLAW-106publ229`

DoD 5015.2 STD for Federal Agencies

`http://jitc.fhu.disa.mil/recmgt/standards.html`

Federal Continuity of Operations (CO-OP)

`www.fema.gov/txt/library/fpc65_0604.txt`

`www.fema.gov/pdf/about/offices/fcd1.pdf`

US Food and Drug Administration

`www.accessdata.fda.gov/scripts/cdrh/cfdocs/cfCFR/CFRSearch.cfm?CFRPart=11`

Health Insurance Portability and Accountability (HIPAA)

`edocket.access.gpo.gov/cfr_2007/octqtr/pdf/45cfr164.308.pdf`

Joint Commission

`www.jointcommission.org/NewsRoom/PressKits/Prevent+Technology-Related+Errors/app_standards.htm`

Securities Exchange Commission (SEC)

www.sec.gov/rules/sro/34-48502.htm

www.sec.gov/news/studies/34-47638.htm

Sarbanes-Oxley (SOX)

www.gpo.gov/fdsys/pkg/PLAW-107publ204/content-detail.html

Other topics discussed in Chapter 12 included what the official practices of a Certified Business Continuity Planner (CBCP) might entail, as well as additional disaster recovery capabilities:

Disaster Recovery Institute

www.DRII.org

https://www.drii.org/professionalprac/prof_prac_details.php

CloudRecovery by Iron Mountain

www.microsoft.com/DPM/cloud

The Author

To complete the list of links, here are mine:

MY LINKS

ME	URL RESOURCES AND TAGS
My Professional Blog	http://JasonBuffington.com
My Gaming Blog	www.XboxDad.com
Twitter	@JBUFF
Xbox Live	DarkJediHunter
Linked-In	www.linkedin.com/in/JasonBuffington
This book's website	www.DataProtectionBible.com

Index

G

H

M

N

S

W

X

Z